W9-ARG-334

When Cultures Collide

Collide

Managing successfully across cultures

Richard D Lewis

NICHOLAS BREALEY
PUBLISHING
LONDON

To

Jane, Caroline, Richard and David, multicultural all...

First published by
Nicholas Brealey Publishing Limited in 1996

36 John Street
London
WC1N 2T, UK
Tel: +44 (0)171 430 0224
Fax: +44 (0)171 404 8311

17470 Sonoma Highway
Sonoma
California 95476, USA
Tel: (707) 939 7570
Fax: (707) 938 3515

http://www.nbrealey-books.com

Reprinted 1996 (twice), 1997 (twice), 1998

The rights of Richard D Lewis to be identified as the author of this work have been asserted in accordance with the Copyright, Designs and Patents Act 1988.

ISBN 1-85788-086-2

Library of Congress Cataloging-in-Publication Data

Lewis, Richard D
    When cultures collide: managing successfully across cultures / Richard D. Lewis.
        p.   cm.
    Includes bibliographical references (p.   ) and index.
    ISBN 1-85788-086-2 (hardcover)
    1. International business enterprises—Management—Social aspects.
2. Management—Social aspects. 3. Intercultural communication. I. Title
    HD62.4.L49 1996
    658'.049–dc20   95-47015
                                                     CIP

British Library Cataloguing in Publication Data
A catalogue record for this book is available from the British Library.

Contents

Preface: Us and Them   *1*

Part One: Getting to Grips with Cultural Diversity   **7**
  1   Different Languages, Different Worlds   *8*
  2   Cultural Conditioning   *25*

Part Two: Managing Across Cultures   **35**
  3   Categorising Cultures   *36*
  4   The Use of Time   *52*
  5   Status, Leadership and Organisation   *65*
  6   Horizons and Team Building   *85*
  7   Bridging the Communication Gap   *94*
  8   Meetings of the Minds   *115*
  9   Manners and Mannerisms   *142*

Part Three: Getting to Know Each Other   **164**
  10 United States of America   *165*
  11 Britain   *172*
  12 Australia, New Zealand and South Africa   *179*

  13 Finland   *189*
  14 France   *202*
  15 Germany   *209*
  16 Italy   *219*
  17 Portugal   *223*
  18 Russia   *229*
  19 Spain   *239*
  20 Sweden   *243*

  21 Arab Countries   *251*

22   Japan   257
23   China   273
24   India and South-East Asia   285

Epilogue: Achieving Empathy   307

Bibliography   317
Glossary   321
Index   325

Preface

US AND THEM

I was once in charge of an English language summer course in North Wales for adult students from three countries – Italy, Japan and Finland. Intensive instruction was relieved by entertainment in the evenings and by day excursions to places of scenic or historical interest.

We had scheduled a trip up Mount Snowdon on a particular Wednesday, but on the Tuesday evening it rained heavily. Around 10 o'clock that night, during the after-dinner dancing, a dozen or so Finns approached me and suggested that we cancel the excursion, as it would be no fun climbing the muddy slopes of Snowdon in heavy rain. I, of course, agreed and announced the cancellation. Immediately I was surrounded by protesting Italians disputing the decision. Why cancel the trip – they had been looking forward to it (escape from lessons), they had paid for it in their all-inclusive fee, a little rain would not hurt anyone and what was the matter with the Finns anyway – weren't they supposed to be tough people?

A little embarrassed, I consulted the Japanese contingent. They were very, very nice. If the Italians wanted to go, they would go, too. If, on the other hand, we cancelled the trip they would be quite happy to stay in and take more lessons. The Italians jeered at the Finns, the Finns mumbled and scowled, and eventually, in order not to lose face, agreed they would go. The excursion was declared on.

It rained torrentially all night and also while I took a quick breakfast. The bus was scheduled to leave at half past eight, and at twenty-five past, taking my umbrella in the downpour, I ran to the vehicle. Inside were 18 scowling Finns, 12 smiling Japanese, and no Italians. We left on time and had a terrible day. The rain never let up, we lunched in cloud at the summit and returned covered in mud at 5 o'clock, in time to see the Italians taking tea and chocolate biscuits. They had sensibly stayed in bed. When the Finns asked them why, they said because it was raining...

Getting to grips with cultural diversity

Cultural diversity is not something that is going to go away tomorrow, enabling us to plan our strategies on the assumption of mutual understanding. It is in itself a phenomenon with its own riches, the exploration of which could yield incalculable benefits for us, both in terms of wider vision and more profitable policies and activity. People of different cultures share basic concepts but view them from different angles and perspectives, leading them to behave in a manner which we may consider irrational or even in direct contradiction of what we hold sacred. We should nevertheless be optimistic about cultural diversity. The behaviour of people of different cultures is not something willy-nilly. There exist clear trends, sequences and traditions. Reactions of Americans, Europeans and Asians alike can be forecasted, usually justified and in the majority of cases managed. Even in countries where political and economic change is currently rapid or sweeping (Russia, China, Hungary, Poland, Korea, Malaysia, etc.) deeply rooted attitudes and beliefs will resist a sudden transformation of values when pressured by reformists, governments or multinational conglomerates. Post-*perestroika* Russians exhibit individual and group behavioural traits strikingly similar to those recorded in Tsarist times – these had certainly persisted, in subdued form, in the Soviet era.

By focusing on the cultural roots of national behaviour, both in society and business, we can foresee and calculate with a surprising degree of accuracy how others will react to our plans for them, and we can make certain assumptions as to how they will approach us. A working knowledge of the basic traits of other cultures (as well as our own) will minimise unpleasant surprises (culture shock), give us insights in advance, and enable us to interact successfully with nationalities with whom we previously had difficulty. This book aims to facilitate the acquisition of such insights.

Cultural differences in international business

International business, especially where joint ventures or prolonged negotiations are involved, is fraught with difficulties. Apart from practical and technical problems (to which solutions are often readily found), national psychology and characteristics frequently interfere at the executive level, where decisions tend to be more complex than the practical accords reached between accountants, engineers and other technicians. Corporate cultures vary widely inside one country (compare Apple and IBM in the US, or Sony and Mitsubishi in Japan); national business styles are markedly more diverse. In a Japanese–US joint venture, where the Americans are interested mainly in profit and the Japanese in market share, which direction is to be taken? When a capitalistic company from the west sets up business in a socialist country, the areas for conflict are even more obvious. But how similar will be the business ethics or cultural background of Sweden and Greece, both European?

National characteristics

Determining **national** characteristics is treading a minefield of inaccurate assessment and surprising exception. There exist excitable Finns, wooden Italians, cautious Americans and charismatic Japanese. There is, however, such a thing as a national norm. For instance, Italians are in general more loquacious than Finns. Yet talkative Finns and silent Italians will overlap. The individuals who overlap are actually **deviates** in terms of that particular characteristic.

In this book, with the object of making meaningful comparisons between different cultures, I have made certain generalisations regarding the national characteristics of one people or another. Such generalisations carry with them the risk of stereotyping as one talks about the typical Italian, German, American, etc. It is evident that Americans differ greatly from each other and that no two Italians are alike. However, my experience during 30 years of living abroad and rubbing shoulders with individuals of many nationalities has led me to the conviction that the inhabitants of any country possess certain core beliefs and assumptions of reality which will manifest themselves in their behaviour.

Culture, in the sense that it represents one's outlook and world view, is not, however, a strictly national phenomenon. In some countries **regional** characteristics can prevail to the extent that they relegate the 'national type' to second position. Basques and Andalucians have little in common apart from a Spanish passport; Milanese businesspeople often feel more at home with French and Austrians than with Sicilians. In the USA – nation of many subcultures – differences in race and language have led to the creation of three major divisions: Black, Hispanic, English-speaking whites.

In certain cases **cities** have developed such a strong cultural identity that it transcends the traits of the region. Thus Londoners are not just southern English, Parisians not simply northern French, Berliners are more than just east Germans. The inhabitants of Marseille have created their own city culture, the citizens of Liverpool have an accent and lifestyle completely different from the northerners surrounding them. Hong Kong, even after integration, is likely to be a special enclave in southern China.

Cultural groups can cross or span frontiers of nations or regions; they may also align themselves in ways other than geographical. Muslims and Christians are cultural groups; so are engineers and accountants. Graduates of the universities of Oxford, Cambridge, Harvard and Yale would claim separate cultural identities. **Corporate** culture affects the lives of many of us to a greater or lesser degree. It is particularly strong in Japan. In other countries, such as Italy, Spain and China, **family** culture is considered more important. The smallest cultural unit is the personal one – the **individual**. Individualistic views are shown great respect in countries such as Britain, France, Australia and the USA.

Perhaps the greatest cultural divide is not national, religious, corporate or professional, but that based on **gender**. It is quite possible that an Italian woman has a world outlook more similar to that of a German woman than to that of a male Italian.

What the book is about

In Part One we explore the vital question of how the mind is **conditioned**, culturally, at an early age. Once one realises the almost irreversible nature of this childhood training, creating in each of us a set of values so different from those extolled in other parts of the world, the possibilities for complex or hampered interaction in later life become clear. This book attempts to show that there is no good or bad, logical or illogical, in cultural values, just as one cannot argue about taste. The British, American, Chinese each see themselves as rational and normal. Cross-cultural training makes one see others as normal too, when viewed from a different perspective. We also discuss the fascinating subject of the inter-relationship between **language and thought**.

In Part Two we classify the world's cultures in three rough categories:

✦ **Linear-actives** – those who plan, schedule, organise, pursue action chains, do one thing at a time. Germans and Swiss are in this group.

✦ **Multi-actives** – those lively, loquacious peoples who do many things at once, planning their priorities not according to a time schedule, but according to the relative thrill or importance that each appointment brings with it. Italians, Latin Americans and Arabs are members of this group.

✦ **Reactives** – those cultures that prioritise courtesy and respect, listening quietly and calmly to their interlocutors and reacting carefully to the other side's proposals. Chinese, Japanese and Finns are in this group.

We go on to demonstrate how each group **gathers information** in a different way – the linear-actives relying mostly on data, the multi-actives on face-to-face encounters and dialogues, the reactives on a combination of both styles.

Further chapters in Part Two show how the values taught to us in early life give us an entrenched approach to the use of **space and time** and how we accord **status**, respond to different types of **leadership**, and organise our society and business to fit in with these attitudes.

Language is an important part of our functional activity and we indicate, often in diagrammatic form, the varying **communication patterns** used in meetings and during negotiations. **Listening habits** are also important to communication, and a discussion of these leads us on to aspects of sales, marketing and advertising.

Body language is said to convey anything up to 80 per cent of our message, and a chapter on this is followed by a comprehensive survey of **manners** in business and society around the world.

There are then separate chapters devoted to a particular country or area, explaining why people's behaviour there follows certain paths and giving practical advice on how to minimise friction with each group.

Part Three anticipates the changing perspectives of management and strategy at the turn of the twenty-first century and shows that widely diverging 'horizons' and credos can be managed – collapsed together – especially in the creation of **international teams**. The very **language of management** itself becomes a vital inspirational tool for the leaders of tomorrow. Empathy, tact, understanding, subtlety, positive reaction – these are the resources of the multicultural executive.

Acknowledgements

No new work on cross culture escapes the influence of Edward and Mildred Hall and Geert Hofstede, and I would like to acknowledge their pioneering of certain concepts which figure prominently in this book. I am equally indebted to the perceptive writings of Desmond Morris on body language, to Glen Fisher for his comprehensive analysis of the international negotiation scene, and to David Rearwin and John Paul Fieg for their authoritative views on Asian countries. Yale Richmond, Margaret Nydell and Joy Hendry have written impeccably penetrating insights into the cultures of Russia, the Arab world and Japan respectively, and I have leant leavily on their experience in the relevant chapters of *When Cultures Collide*.

Part One

Getting to grips with cultural diversity

1

DIFFERENT LANGUAGES, DIFFERENT WORLDS

For a German and a Finn, the truth is the truth. In Japan and Britain it is all right if it doesn't rock the boat. In China there is no absolute truth. In Italy it is negotiable.

COMPARISONS OF NATIONAL CULTURES OFTEN BEGIN BY HIGHLIGHTING differences in social behaviour. Japanese do not like shaking hands, bow when greeting each other and do not blow their nose in public. Brazilians form unruly bus queues, prefer brown shoes to black and arrive two hours late at cocktail parties. Greeks stare you in the eye, nod their head when they mean 'no', and occasionally smash plates against walls in restaurants. French people wipe their plate clean with a piece of bread, throw pastry into their coffee and offer handshakes to strangers in bistros. Brits tip their soup plate away from them, eat peas with their fork upside down and play golf in the rain.

Appearance and reality

These various manners and mannerisms cause us great amusement. We smile at foreign eccentricity, congratulating ourselves on our normality. And yet we are aware that these idiosyncrasies are largely superficial. If we stay in France a while we are sooner or later happy to dunk our croissant and make a mess; we discover the unhurried delight of turning up outrageously late in Brazil; we throw vodka glasses over our shoulder with abandon in St Petersburg. Such adaptation of our behaviour leaves no scar on our psyche. We join strangers in their little ways partly to conform and partly for fun. Our appearance is not our reality. We can become French or Greek for an evening, a party or a dinner, we can sit on *tatami* with Japanese and eat legs of lamb with one hand among Arabs. But what goes on in our head remains a private, well-protected constant. We may put on a show for others, but all the while we follow our own silent programme.

Concepts and notions

Part of the superficial public behaviour we have cited above is cultural in origin, and yet we can adopt these manners without prejudice to our own core beliefs. Actions are not difficult to emulate, even different varieties of speech can be imitated to some extent. Thought is a different matter. We cannot see it, we cannot hear it, it may be revealed to us with reluctance, simulation or cunning. Cross-cultural problems arise not so much on account of our unfamiliarity with a bow, a Gallic shrug or chopsticks. Our society has trained us to adopt certain concepts and values. We know that many of these **concepts** are shared by other cultures. We can teach a Spaniard nothing about honour, the Japanese are masters of courtesy, Swedes, English and Germans are all convinced of their own honesty. It is remarkable, given the size of the world, its long history and immeasurable variety, how many common concepts are rooted so firmly in a similar manner in wildly different societies. Honour, duty, love, justice, gratitude and revenge are basic tenets of the German, Chinese, Arab and Polynesian alike. A Tasmanian knows his or her duty as clearly as a Greenlander does. What we often overlook is the fact that everyone has different **notions** of these concepts which appeal to so many cultures. Chinese duty is not American duty. Romantic love is seen differently in France and Finland. The English notion of revenge bears little similarity to the Sicilian.

Extreme differences

We readily accept that cultural diversity is vast and formidable. If we take an extreme example, the barriers against communication or mutual comprehension between an Eskimo and an African Bushman might prove insurmountable. Given their different backgrounds, what could they talk about? They would be completely unaware of the structure or politics of each other's society; it is hardly likely that they could imagine the opposite extremity of climate; their religion, taboos, values, aspirations, disappointments and life style would be in stark contrast. Subjects of conversation (if they had some mode of communication) would be minimal, approaching zero. Weather, sex and food, you say? Those are certainly basic issues. Yet if they met in a temperate climate (say England in spring) the Eskimo would find it hot, the Bushman cold. Their notions of sexual attractiveness would differ so strikingly that it is hardly likely that they would want to indulge in wife swapping. A tasty snack? Here, try this bit of blubber – ugh! Give me snake *flambé* any time.

The wildly differing notions of time, space, life after death, nature and reality held by isolated societies will have little impact on international business (although they may contribute usefully to our morals or philosophy). The Navahos with their nuclear concept of speech, the Zulus with their 39 greens, the Eskimos with their 42 types of snow, the Aborigines with their dreamtime, the Lapps with their eight seasons, all provide us with cultural gems, striking insights, unique thought and speech processes which intrigue and fascinate those of us who have time to study them. We are thrilled by these phenomena, take joy in their appreciation. We see, learn and sometimes understand. Deceived we are not. They are differences which we perceive, acknowledge and accept. We know, more or less, where we stand with these people. They live in another world and we know we live in ours.

Closer to home

In our world, there are others who are more like us. They have modern civilisations, political parties, factories, cars and stocks and shares. We meet them regularly and their clothes resemble ours. We appear to have similar concepts and values. They seem to talk 'our language'. Yet for some reason, French and Germans don't always get on. In Belgium half of society dislikes the other. Chinese and Japanese are wary of each other, to say the least; neighbourly Swedes and Norwegians snipe at each other, and the mutual exasperation that British and American cousins experience is only too well documented.

Truth

The concepts are shining and clear: our notions of them are different. Both Germans and British people conducting a business meeting wish for a successful outcome. The German notion is that truth, absolute honest truth, even if somewhat unpalatable, will achieve this. The British, by contrast, give priority to not rocking the boat. But *die Wahrheit ist die Wahrheit* say the Germans. Not so, the Chinese would add – these is no absolute truth. Two conflicting views may both be correct. Most Orientals and many Italians would agree with the Chinese.

In Germany, Sweden and Finland, where people are generally concerned about what the neighbours think, the drive towards conformity imposes checks and constraints on a person's ability to refashion veracity. Brits and Americans, with that wonderfully idiomatic, nuance-rich tool of expression (the English language) at their disposal, are economical with the truth. The French, Italians and other Latins are not famous for their candour, which might interfere with the smooth social intercourse they are so fond of. In Japan, where no one must face exposure, be confronted or lose face, truth is a dangerous concept. In Asia, Africa and South America, strict adherence to the truth would destroy the harmony of relationship between individuals, companies and entire segments of society. Only in Australia is a spade called a spade continent wide, and even there truth often occasions dismay and leads to fist-fights.

Contracts and ethics

As the globalisation of business brings executives more frequently together, there is a growing realisation that if we examine concepts and values, we can take almost nothing for granted. The word 'contract' translates easily from language to language, but notionally it has many interpretations. To a Swiss, German, Scandinavian, American or British person it is something that has been signed in order to be adhered to. Signatures give it a sense of finality. But a Japanese regards a contract as a starting document to be rewritten and modified as circumstances require. A South American sees it as an ideal which is unlikely to be achieved, but which is signed to avoid argument.

Members of most cultures see themselves as ethical, but ethics can be turned upside down. The American calls the Japanese unethical if the latter breaks the contract. The Japanese says it is unethical for the American to apply the terms of the contract if things have changed. Italians have very flexible views on what is ethical and what is not, which sometimes causes Northern Europeans to question their honesty. When Italians bend rules or 'get round' some laws or regulations, they consider they are less ideal bound than, say, the Swiss, and actually closer to reality. They do not consider themselves corrupt, or immoral, nor do they admit to illegality. There are many grey areas where 'short cuts' are, in Italian eyes, the only intelligent course of action. In a country where excessive bureaucracy can hold up 'business' for months, currying favour with an official is a matter of common sense.

Common sense

The very term 'common sense' has to be watched carefully, for it is not as common as it seems. The English dictionary defines it as judgement gained from experience rather than study; the American lexicon gives it as judgement which is sound but unsophisticated. Academics are uncomfortable with common sense, which tends to preempt their research by coming to the same conclusion months earlier. But we must not think that this rough-and-ready wisdom will unite our mix of nationalities. Common sense, although basic and unsophisticated, cannot be neutral. It is derived from experience, but experience is culture bound. It is common sense in Germany or Sweden to form an orderly bus queue. In Naples or Rio it is common sense to get on the bus before anyone else. It would seem common sense for the Japanese to have discarded the Chinese writing system which does not suit their language and which takes ten years for Japanese children to learn. But they have not done so. Japan is a rather regimented society, yet the police let a man urinate against a public wall if he really has to and will drive him home in his car if he is too drunk to drive himself. When asked why they are so lenient in such matters, they reply it is common sense.

Gossip

Gossip has negative connotations in the Nordic countries and hardly a good name in the Anglo-Saxon world. Yet gossip proves far more important to us than we would at first admit. It is a vital source of information in business circles in many countries. In cultures like Spain, Italy, Brazil and Japan, gossip quickly updates and bypasses facts and statistics, provides political background to commercial decisions, and facilitates invaluable debate between people who do not meet officially. The Italian *chiacchiera* or Spanish *paseo* may be largely limited to women and youngsters, but the cafés of Madrid and Lisbon overflow with businessmen, Japanese executives make momentous decisions every evening from 6–10pm in the bars of the Ginza, and the whole of Central and South America 'networks' merrily until one or two in the morning.

The corridors of power in Brussels, where European business and political legislation are inevitably intertwined, reverberate with gossip. European countries which do not have access to this hot-house exchange of information will be severely disadvantaged.

Another positive aspect of gossip is that it appears to be good for us – that is to say, in line with our natural evolution. Professor Robin Dunbar of University College London points out that humans live in much larger groups than other primates and that language may have evolved as a form of social glue holding us together. While some animals obviously communicate well in small groups, it is hardly likely that they can gossip about third parties. This ability enables us to form social or working groups of approximately 150 members. This number holds true for ancient 'clans', military fighting units (a company) and even modern firms. Once a commercial enterprise swells well beyond that it has to be organised into divisions or it becomes less manageable. Intense interest in what other people are doing, finding out from our 'group' the latest news about third parties, enables us to network on a large scale and calculate our positions and reactions accordingly. So the Latins, Greeks and Arabs have got it right after all!

Silence

Silence can be interpreted in different ways. A silent reaction to a business proposal would seem negative to American, German, French, Southern European and Arab executives. In countries as dissimilar as the USA, Peru and Kuwait, conversation is a two-way process, where one partner takes up when the other one leaves off. The intervening silence is two or three seconds in Britain or Germany, less than that in Greece or Kuwait and hardly noticeable in France, Italy and America. However, the 'listening cultures' of East Asia find nothing wrong with silence as a response. 'Those who know do not speak; those who speak do not know', says an old Chinese proverb. Japanese and one European nation (Finland) do not quarrel with this assertion. In both these countries silence is not equated with failure to communicate, but is an integral part of social interaction. What is **not** said is regarded as important and lulls in conversation are considered restful, friendly and appropriate. Silence means that you listen and learn; talking a lot merely expresses your cleverness, perhaps egoism and arrogance. Silence protects your individualism and privacy; it also shows respect for the individualism of others. In Finland and Japan it is considered impolite or inappropriate to force one's opinions on others – it is more appropriate to nod in agreement, smile quietly, avoid opinionated argument or discord.

Powerful mental blocks

As international trade and scientific and political exchange intensify, there is a growing effort on the part of academics, multinational organisations and even nations and governments to improve communication and dialogue. It is becoming increasingly apparent that in pursuit of this goal it is desirable not only to learn foreign languages on a much wider scale, but to show a sympathetic understanding of other peoples' customs, societies and culture. Many binational and international bodies have been created to further this aim, and the personnel and training departments of many large companies have invested substantial sums of money in cross-cultural and internationalisation programmes and briefings for those staff members who will represent them abroad.

The question I would like to raise is whether or not cross-cultural training and a willingness to adapt will achieve anything at the end of the day, in view of the interlocking nature of our own language and thought. I am not necessarily suggesting that cross-cultural training might eventually be seen to be in vain – I believe the contrary to be true – but I would like to play devil's advocate for a while and consider how powerful mental blocks may hinder our ability to change our attitudes or adopt new approaches.

In infancy we are conditioned by various factors and influences – not least by the behaviour and guidance of our parents, teachers and society. But they and we are subjected at every turn to that dominating and pervasive 'conditioner' – our common language.

Many linguists adhere to the Benjamin Whorf theory or hypothesis, which states that the language we speak largely determines our way of thinking, as distinct from merely expressing it. In other words, Germans or Japanese behave in a certain manner because the way they think is governed by the language they think in. A Spaniard and a Briton see the world in different ways because one is thinking in Spanish and the other in English. People in the British Isles act and live in a certain way because their thoughts are channelled along Anglo-Saxon grooves which are different from neo-Latin, Japanese or Chinese grooves.

The Briton, the German and the Eskimo may share a common experience, but it appears to each as a kaleidoscopic flux of impressions which has to be organised by the mind. The mind does this largely by means of language. Thus the three individuals end up seeing three different things. What is 'fair play' to the Briton may be something else to the German, who needs to translate the concept into different words, and it may mean nothing at all in a society where there are no organised games.

English and Zulu

If you think 'fair play' is rather abstract, let us go to another instance where a very basic concept is seen in a completely different way by two people of diverse origins. My example involves an Englishman and a Zulu. While the cultural chasm is clear, it is the linguistic factor which dominates this instance.

As you may know, Zulu tongues have 39 words for 'green', while English has only one. (If we wish to modify the shade we have to bring in another word, e.g. bottle green, leaf green). I was interested in how the Zulus could build up 39 one-word concepts for green, and discussed this at length with a former Zulu Chief who had taken a doctorate in philology at Oxford. He began by explaining why Zulus needed 39 words for green. In the days before automotive transport and national highways, the Zulu people would often make long treks across their savannah grasslands. There were no signposts or maps and lengthy journeys had to be described by those who had travelled the route before. The language adapted itself to the requirements of its speakers. English copes with concepts such as contract deadlines and stock futures (Zulu doesn't), but our tongue is seen as poverty stricken and inadequately descriptive by Africans and Amerindians whose languages abound in finely wrought, beautifully logical descriptions of nature, causation, repetition, duration and result.

'But give me some examples of different green-words,' I persisted.

My friend picked up a leaf. 'What colour is this?' he asked.

'Green,' I replied.

The sun was shining. He waited until a cloud intervened. 'What colour is the leaf now?' he asked.

'Green,' I answered, already sensing my inadequacy.

'It isn't the same green, is it?'

'No, it isn't.'

'We have a different word in Zulu.' He dipped the leaf in water and held it out again. 'Has the colour changed?'

'Yes.'

'In Zulu we have a word for "green shining wet".'

The sun came out again and I needed another word (leaf-green-wet-but-with-sunshine-on-it!)

My friend retreated 20 metres and showed me the leaf. 'Has the colour changed again?'

'Yes,' I screamed.

'We have another word,' he said with a smile.

He went on to indicate how different Zulu greens would deal with tree leaves, bush leaves, leaves vibrating in the wind, river greens, pool greens, tree trunk greens, crocodile greens... he got to 39 without even raising a sweat.

Language strait-jacket

It was evident that my Zulu friend and I saw the world through different eyes. And yet it was not a question of eyes. However 'international', multicultural or all-embracing I wished to be, there was no way I could perceive or feel about nature the way he did, **because I didn't have the language to do it with**. It was not just a matter of familiarising myself with the cultural habits, preferences and taboos of his tribe or even adopting his religion and philosophies. I could only experience reality as fully as he did by learning his language and escaping (in terms of descriptive ability) from the strait-jacket of my own.

Just as seeing with two eyes gives us stereoscopic vision, and a sense of depth, thinking in two different languages gives us added dimensions of reality. Finn–Swedes are a case in point. A striking thought is that while French (a language very similar to English) would give a Briton maybe an extra 10 per cent of the observable universe, a 'primitive' language wildly different from our own, with its other logic and set of assumptions, might show us things we have never dreamed of!

It is not difficult for us to comprehend (once we are awake to the language strait-jacket phenomenon) that the Japanese, for example, with their reverse word order will organise their thoughts and priorities in a different manner from that of Europeans. But if we think more closely about the European scene, we discover that English, French and Spanish speakers use language and think in quite different ways, and may seem at times to be on a common wavelength when in fact they didn't really know what the other has said or what they actually meant when they said it.

Translation inadequate

The Greeks, who were the first people to enquire in depth into logic and reason, assumed that language was a universal, untampered-with element of reason. They believed it was a phenomenon shared by all mankind and, in the case of educated people, would provide a standard yardstick for comparison of ideas, experience and reality. They also assumed that ideas could be translated freely into any language. This is only true up to a point. Swedish translates readily into English and vice versa, but with Finnish and English the task is far more complicated.

Even those of us who have learned languages at school have noticed the difficulty our teachers have in translating such words as *panache*, *esprit de corps*, *Gemütlichkeit* and *Zeitgeist* into English. Interpreters at the United Nations are faced daily with similar problems, even with languages which are closely related. In one recorded case, the English speaker said 'I assume', the French interpreter translated as 'I deduce', and this was rendered by the Russian as 'I consider' – by which time the idea of assumption had been lost!

Different worlds

If this can happen working with three close relatives of the Indo-European group, we see that two languages as different as English and Navaho literally operate in two different worlds. I think it is important for businesspeople to consider carefully the implication of the words 'in two different worlds'. All observers are not led by the same physical evidence to the same picture of the universe, unless their linguistic backgrounds are similar, or can in some way be calibrated. English, French, German, Russian and other Indo-European languages can be roughly calibrated (although not always satisfactorily), but where does this leave us with Chinese, Indonesian, Finnish or Japanese? If the structure of a person's language influences the manner in which they understand reality and behave with respect to it, then we could have four individuals who will see the universe through Sino-Tibetan, Polynesian, Altaic and Japanese eyes respectively and then comport themselves accordingly.

Internalised thought

There is a good deal of scientific support for the hypothesis that higher levels of thinking depend on language. Language can be regarded as internalised thought. Most of us conduct an interior monologue, often accompanied by visual imagery. The more educated and literate the individual, the more complex and sophisticated this monologue becomes. It was not until the Middle Ages that people learned to read without reading aloud. Today, talking to or reasoning with oneself is accepted as quite common and there is no doubt that most of this goes on 'in words', whether expressed aloud or not.

We can assume that German, Italian and Malaysian businesspeople do the same thing in their own language. When each speaks, we merely glimpse the tip of a huge iceberg of verbal activity which never breaks the surface of audibility. If you make this reasonable assumption, then you can presume that whatever is said to you will be a brief projection of that inner world of the other person's thoughts. What is said may be grammatically accurate or erroneous in the extreme, but it will be coloured by the foreigner's view of reality, this itself influenced by the rigidity of his or her own language structure.

This line of reasoning tends to become somewhat involved – and clearly thought may also influence one's choice of expression – but to clarify the point, one can take a few practical examples.

The German language is a tightly disciplined, no-nonsense entity with long, compound words often expressing complex concepts. We might

therefore expect the internal monologue of a German person to be serious
rather than casual, concentrating on weighty issues, and resulting in
verbalisation which will be anything but flippant.

Mobile American

Contrast this with the interior monologue of an American counterpart.
The nature of American English is interwoven with the character and history of the youthful United States. American speech or thought is mobile
and opportunistic; it shifts quickly for advantage or compromise and excels
in casual and humorous shafts. The German will take Americans seriously
when they do not intend to be taken as such. A further complication is the
deep slide that American English has taken into clichés and 'tough' talk.
Such expressions as 'gotta deal', 'gotta be jokin', 'no way', 'full of shit',
'over the top', 'you can't do this to me' and 'give away the store' fail to indicate properly what the American is really thinking, but are verbal escape
routes to simplified analyses or solutions not necessarily in their favour.

Britons are guilty of other clichés indicative of near-stultifying vagueness of thought, well designed to convey very little or nothing at all to their
foreign interlocutors. Such expressions, occasionally derived from sport,
include 'fair play', 'sticky wicket', 'a good innings', 'good show', 'bad news',
'not on' and 'a bit thick'.

Clinical French

The French thought monologue is quite different. They have dissected
their universe better than most of us and they try to think about it clearly.
They know where they are going and what it is that they want. Their clinical vocabulary is conducive to quick thinking, its lack of vagueness leads to
a cutting directness, and their ruthless pursuit of logic will often irritate
Anglo-Saxons or Japanese, who tend to 'feel their way' towards a solution.

The Spanish speaker's monologue is earthy, emotional and generous.
The wealth of Spanish vocabulary and the wide range of endearments and
diminutives (shared with Italian and Portuguese and often untranslatable
into English or Finnish) enable the Spaniard to communicate in a warm,
human manner indicative of an expansive character and lack of cunning.
Exporters should not, however, read this as a sign that the Spanish speaker can necessarily be taken advantage of.

Foggy Japanese

The Japanese have the most difficult task of all in making the transition from their internal monologue to actual verbal utterance. In their thoughts they agonise over striking a balance between gaining advantage and correctness of behaviour. Their thought (we can also regard this as internalised speech) has to be polite in the extreme in view of the fact that they are to address others. But the speech mechanisms involved in such politeness often lead to incredible vagueness of expression, so that whatever message they seek to convey may well get lost in a fog of impeccable behaviour. On top of that, their formidable battery of honorific expressions – so useful in communication between Japanese – are rendered useless in the face of impossibility of translation, so that their conversation with their foreign counterpart emerges as terribly platitudinous, even if grammatically correct.

Humour across frontiers

It has been said that humour crosses national boundaries with difficulty, especially when heading east. If we analyse this assertion for a moment, several implications emerge. First, it is self-evident that the victim of a humorous attack is hardly likely to see the funny side of it. French anecdotes depicting the Belgians as a collection of slow-witted yokels fail to gain appreciation in Brussels. Dutch people resent similar treatment at the hands of the Belgians.

Secondly, failure to appreciate the funny side of a 'foreign' anecdote does not necessarily depend on one's being the victim. Serious-minded, factual Germans do not split their sides on hearing American jokes about Texas, which usually depend on gross exaggeration. The story about the Mexican driving just as fast as he could for 24 hours to get out of Texas, but finding he had not managed it, thrills the American imagination but sounds far fetched to the German, who would usually reply, 'He should have used a German car.' This response would be considered very funny in Germany and fairly good in England and Scandinavia.

Apart from the Koreans (who seem to like everybody's jokes), few Orientals are amused by American or (most) European jokes. The Confucian and Buddhist preoccupation with truth, sincerity, kindliness and politeness automatically eliminates humour techniques such as sarcasm, satire, exaggeration and parody, and finds little merit in crazy humour or jokes about religion, sex and underprivileged minorities. Sick or black humour is definitely out.

So what is left, you might ask? Eastern humour, such as we understand it, is couched in subtlety, gentle, indirect reproach or reprimand, occasionally victimising listeners in a sly but non-aggressive manner which yet leaves them room for response and stops short of depriving them of their dignity. Even the rougher, occasionally bawdy Koreans take great care to protect the listener's 'wholeness' or standing. Chinese are noted for their aphorisms and proverbs, and they and Indians find great sources of humour in parables, which we in the west find only moderately funny, although they do combine wisdom, moralising and a sense of perspective. We can understand the point of most Confucian aphorisms and Indian or Malaysian tales, while we rarely understand Japanese jokes. But then, neither do the Chinese.

Is there such a thing as a 'national style' of humour? Before answering this question directly, one must accept the fact that there **is** such a thing as international humour – that is to say, some types of humour and some jokes gain international acceptance. In particular, this is true of slapstick, age-old in its use and laughed at by Europeans, Americans, Africans and Orientals alike. It is very much in evidence, for instance, on Japanese television. There seems to be a general love of witnessing violence, which may compensate, in the international arena, for not always being allowed to practise it. There are also 'international' jokes repeated across many borders, such as the one about who must jump first out of the aeroplane, elephant jokes, restaurant jokes and hilarious stories about golfers.

Even in the area of international jokes, however, the national 'rinse' begins to show. Take, for example, the old joke about the journalists who organised a competition to write an article about elephants. The titles were as follows:

English	Hunting elephants in British East Africa
French	The love life of elephants in French Equatorial Africa
German	The origin and development of the Indian elephant in the years 1200–1950 (600 pages)
American	How to breed bigger and better elephants
Russian	How we sent an elephant to the moon

Swede	Elephants and the welfare state
Dane	Elephant-meat smørrebrød
Spaniard	Techniques of elephant fighting
Indian	The elephant as a means of transportation before the railway era
Finn	What the elephants think about Finland

This joke, which probably originated at a conference of journalists, pokes fun at various national *faiblesses* – French lust, German seriousness, American bragging, British colonialism, etc. The punchline is the laugh about Finns' preoccupation with what others think about them. In Helsinki, however, they developed an alternative punchline where a Norwegian was added, the title being: 'Norway and Norway's mountains'.

Finns, Swedes and Danes find this alternative absolutely side-splitting. The Norwegians (who consider themselves a humorous people) do not find this ending funny at all. In fact, **they do not understand it**. Do you?

Humour in business

As world trade becomes increasingly globalised, businesspeople meet their foreign partners more frequently and consequently feel that they know them better. It is only natural that when one develops a closer relationship with a stranger there is a tendency to avoid overseriousness and to begin to converse in a more relaxed manner. Swapping anecdotes is a good way of melting the ice in many situations and gaining the confidence of one's listener. A funny incident involving some personal discomfort or embarrassment is a good start; a sly attack on a 'common enemy' may soon follow.

Humour during business meetings is not infrequent in most European countries, although it is less common among Latins than with Northern peoples, where it is a valuable tool for breaking the ice. Perhaps among the Spaniards, Portuguese and Italians, there is little ice to break. Their own racy, gossipy, confiding, conversation style constitutes in itself, however, a valid humorous element.

It is in the Anglo-Saxon countries that humour is used systematically. Relaxed in Canada and New Zealand, it can be barbed and provocative in Australia. In the USA particularly, sarcasm, kidding and feigned indignation are regarded as factors which move the meeting along and get more done in less time. Time is, after all, money. It is perhaps in the UK that humour is most intertwined in business talks. The British hate heavy or drawn-out meetings and will resort to various forms of humour and distracting tactics to keep it all nice and lively.

However, two nationalities in particular avoid jokes and other forms of humour during the actual business sessions. Germans find it out of place during negotiations. Business is serious and should be treated as such, without irrelevant stories or distractions. If you do not concentrate on the issue, you are not showing respect to your interlocutor. Kidding is, in their eyes, not honest and creates confusion in business discussion. They want to know about price, quality and delivery dates, with some precision, please.

After the meetings are over, Germans are quite willing to relax and joke with their partners in bars, restaurants and at home. Humour and anecdotes are more than welcome in these circumstances. Relaxation, like business discussion and many other activities in Germany, is fairly strictly compartmentalised.

Japanese also fail to see any benefit in introducing humour into business meetings. They will laugh if they are aware that you have told a joke (it is unlikely they will have understood it) but that is out of sheer politeness. They are normally nervous about understanding your straight talk in the first place, so that any clever nuances or tongue-in-cheek utterances will leave them floundering. They take anything you say quite literally. Americans using expressions like 'You are killing me' or 'Say that once again and I'll walk away from this deal' cause great consternation among their Japanese partners. One US executive who said a certain clause would blow the deal out of the water was asked, 'What water?' An Englishman was asked by the waiter at the end of a business dinner if the ten men present required ice-cream for dessert. As the table was laden with beer, the Englishman replied humorously that everyone was having beer for dessert. Two minutes later the waiter appeared with ten beers.

While the introduction of humour in international business talks may bring considerable gain in terms of breaking the ice, speeding up the issues, escaping from deadlock, putting your partners at ease and winning their confidence in you as a human being, the downside risks are often just as great. What is funny for the French may be anathema to an Arab; your very best story may be utterly incomprehensible to a Chinese; your most innocent anecdote may seriously offend a Turk. Cultural and religious differences may make it impossible for some people to laugh at the same thing. Who can say with certainty that anything is funny? If all values are relative and culture based, then these include humour, tolerance, even truth itself. And remember that laughter, more often than not, symbolises embarrassment, nervousness or possibly scorn.

Making allowances

International businesspeople cannot escape the bottom line – a good American expression – of the considerations made above. The picture of the universe shifts from tongue to tongue, and the way of doing business shifts accordingly. There is no one metaphysical pool of human thought – or of behaviour. Different languages provide different 'segments of experience' and there is little we can do about it, except to learn more languages. We cannot learn all of them, but at least the awareness of the problem and any allowances we can make for a foreign friend's *Weltanschauung* will help us to establish whatever degree of communication our different mentalities permit.

2

CULTURAL CONDITIONING

We think our minds are free, but, like captured American pilots in Vietnam and North Korea, we have been thoroughly brainwashed. Collective programming in our culture, begun in the cradle and reinforced in kindergarten, school and workplace, convinces us that we are normal, others eccentric.

What is culture?

HOFSTEDE DEFINED CULTURE AS 'THE COLLECTIVE PROGRAMMING OF THE mind which distinguishes the members of one category of people from another'. The key expression in this definition is **collective programming**. Although not as sinister as 'brainwashing' – with connotations of political coercion – it nevertheless describes a process to which each one of us has been subjected immediately after birth (some people would say even before birth, but that is a little deep for me!) Certainly when parents, returning from hospital, carry a baby over the threshold, the first decision has to be made – where to sleep. A Japanese child is invariably put in the same room as the parents, near the mother, for the first couple of years. British and American children are often put in a separate room – right away or after a few weeks or months. The inferences for the child's dependence/interdependence and problem-solving abilities are obvious. To follow up one theory, Japanese children – used to doing everything jointly with their parents 24 hours a day for the first year, then acting thereafter in strict unison with 50 clones in kindergarten – develop an addiction to group activity and 'group think' which leads to (and is reinforced by) close cooperation and joint pursuits in school, university, clubs and ultimately their company.

Parents and teachers obviously give children the best advice they can. It fits them out for successful interaction in their own culture and society, where good and bad, right and wrong, normal and abnormal are clearly defined. Unfortunately (at least in one sense) American and European children are being given a completely different set of instructions, although equally valid in their own environment.

As we grow up, these taught-and-learned 'national' concepts become our core beliefs, which we find almost impossible to discard. We regard others' beliefs and habits (Russian, Chinese, Hungarian...) as strange or eccentric, mainly because they are unlike our own. There is no doubt about it, Japanese are not like Americans!

On the other hand, we have a sneaking feeling (and we frequently hear it expressed) that 'deep down all people are alike'. There is also truth in this, for there are such things as universal human characteristics. They are not too numerous, for our national collective programming 'distorts' some of our basic instincts (Scots thrift v American free spending). Figure 1 shows how national collective programming is 'grafted onto' inherited traits. In the top section we add individual characteristics. Some people, by dint of personal originality, extra powers of perception, stubbornness or even genius, stand apart from their colleagues and deviate sharply from the national track. Such people often become famous for their 'idiosyncrasies' and a few have actually changed the course of their nation's destiny (King Henry VIII, Kemal Atatürk, Emperor Meiji of Japan).

In general, however, our national or regional culture imposes itself on our behaviour rather than the other way round, and we become a solid German, a good Swede, a real American or a true Brit, as the case may be. Interacting with our compatriots, we generally find that the closer we stick to the rules of our society, the more popular we become.

Culture shock

Our precious values and unshakeable core beliefs take a battering when we venture abroad. 'Support the underdog!' cry Guy Fawkes-loving English.

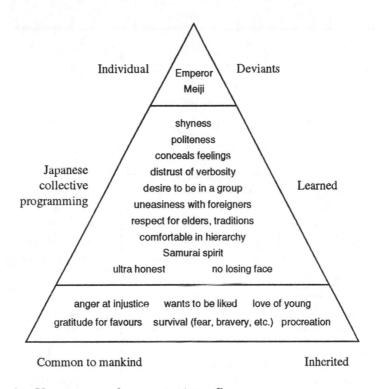

Individual · Emperor Meiji · Deviants

Japanese collective programming

shyness
politeness
conceals feelings
distrust of verbosity
desire to be in a group
uneasiness with foreigners
respect for elders, traditions
comfortable in hierarchy
Samurai spirit
ultra honest · no losing face

Learned

anger at injustice · wants to be liked · love of young
gratitude for favours · survival (fear, bravery, etc.) · procreation

Common to mankind · Inherited

Figure 1   Human mental programming – Japan

The Australians – famous historical underdogs themselves – echo this to the full. Germans and Japanese, although temporary underdogs themselves after the Second World War, tend to support the **more powerful** of two adversaries, seeing the underdog as necessarily the less efficient. The Japanese government, through MITI (Ministry of Trade and Industry), issues directives to the larger banks to lend money to those industries which are currently thriving and have the potential for further growth, while discouraging loans to enterprises which have become old-fashioned or have little hope for future success. This attitude is in marked contrast to that so long prevalent in Britain, where ancient factories were kept alive and industrial underdogs such as textiles and coal-mining were supported long after they were economically viable.

Figure 2 shows the different paths which our core beliefs take according to the culture we try to impose them on. Others are not aware of our values simply by looking at us. They may draw certain conclusions from the manner in which we dress, but these days most businesspeople dress in a similar way. It is only when we **say** or **do** something that they can gain

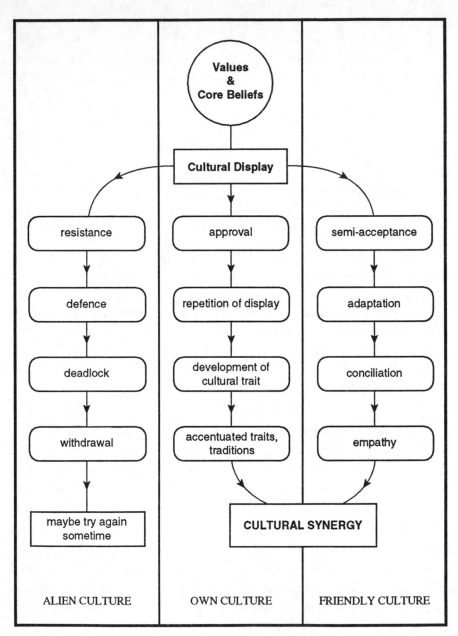

Figure 2   Paths for core beliefs

deeper insight into what makes us tick. This utterance or action may be described as a **cultural display** or **event**, since, by its execution, we reveal our cultural attitudes. In Figure 2, the cultural display might be that an Italian (probably Roman) turns up half an hour late for a scheduled meeting. In her own cultural environment this will make no waves, for most of the others will be late too. Her behaviour is approved and eventually it becomes a cultural tradition. Were she to turn up 30 minutes late in an alien culture (say Germany) she would deliver a culture shock of no mean proportions. Germans do not like to be kept waiting for three minutes, let alone thirty. Immediate resistance and protest leads to Italian defence (traffic jam, daughter was ill) and eventually a defence of the Italian way of life ('Why are you Germans so time dominated – you are like clocks!') Such confrontation leads to deadlock and probable withdrawal from a project.

In a friendly culture (shall we say the French), the criticism will be couched in cynicism, but will be less final or damning. (*'Mon vieux, tu m'as volé une demie heure, tu sais!'*) The Italian, sensitive to Latin objections, next time comes only 20 minutes late. The Frenchman, no great believer in punctuality himself, eventually settles for 15 minutes. The Italian concurs. This is Latin understanding.

Who is normal, anyway?

Most English people think they are normal and that all others (whom they call 'foreigners') are abnormal – that is to say, they might be all right, but they really cannot act and think like the English, because, after all, they are foreign. You only have to look at them, you'll know what that means…

Chauvinism

Americans think America is the biggest and the best, the newest and the richest, and all others are a bit slow, old fashioned, rather poor and somewhat on the small side. They can't call the British foreigners, so they call them 'limeys'.

Spaniards think they are the bravest because they kill bulls, the French think they are intellectually superior to everybody else, the Japanese are quite **sure** they are superior to others, including the French. The Germans admit that they are not as big as the Americans, as agile as the Japanese, as historical as the French, as smooth as the British, but what really counts in life? Efficiency, punctuality, *Gründlichkeit*, method, consistency and organisation. Who can match Germans on these counts?

There are few countries in Europe or the world where people do not believe, at the bottom of their heart, that they are the best, or the most intelligent, or at least normal. Perhaps in Europe the Italians and the Finns are the most innocent in this regard, often being willing to criticise themselves before others, yet both still consider themselves normal.

I am reminded of the old story of the 80-year old couple sitting by the fireside looking back on their lives. The wife says to the husband: 'John, everybody is strange except you and me. And even you are strange sometimes.'

Normal and abnormal

If each culture considers itself normal, then the corollary is that it considers everybody else abnormal. By this token Finns consider Italians over-emotional because they wave their arms while talking. The individualistic Spaniards consider the Swiss stuffy and excessively law-abiding. Lively Italians find Norwegians gloomy. French-influenced Vietnamese find Japanese impassive. Argentinians are considered conceited by all other South Americans. Germans think Australians are undisciplined. Japanese see straight-talking Americans as rude.

We can achieve a good understanding of our foreign counterparts only if we realise that our 'cultural spectacles' are colouring our view of them. In fact, both calm and excitable Italians use many gestures during conversation. Finns see them as overdemonstrative, Spaniards see them as normal. Conversely, Finns would not agree with Italians about Norwegians being excessively gloomy. Germans view the law-abiding Swiss as correct. The stereotypes described above derive largely from the 'abnormality' of the viewer, e.g. the ultra-politeness of the Japanese, the social shyness of the Finn, the Spanish tendency towards lawlessness.

What is the route to better understanding? To begin with, we need to examine the special features of our own culture. Finnish taciturnity scores good points in Britain and Japan, but will forever be considered very odd indeed in Portugal, Greece, the Middle East and Latin America. The

Japanese will have to learn one day that when they say 'yes' the rest of world does not know that they mean 'no'.

Our second task, once we realise that we too are a trifle strange, is to understand the subjective nature of our ethnic values. While Scots see stubbornness largely as a positive trait, flexible Italians may see mainly intransigence, the diplomatic English possibly lack of artfulness or dexterity. We also make assumptions on the basis of our subjective view and, even worse, assumptions of other people's assumptions. The Italian who assumes that French people feel intellectually superior also judges that French assume Italians are suitable mainly for manual labour when emigrating to France. The Finn who judges Swedes are snobs also assumes that Swedes assume Finns are rough and rustic. There may be a grain of truth in many of these judgements and assumptions of assumptions, but the danger involved in making them is only too obvious!

Legal and illegal

Our perception of reality (what a word!) may be assisted if we can wear someone else's shoes for a moment – if we can see how they view some matter in a way very different from our own. Figure 3 illustrates differing viewpoints of Finns and Spaniards on legality and illegality.

Both nationalities agree that trafficking in drugs is bad and that laws against drunken driving are socially beneficial and justified. When it comes to restrictive immigration laws, the Finns' subjective view is that the fragile, delicately balanced national economy must be protected, while semiconsciously their instinct is to protect the purity of their race. Spaniards, born in a country where no one dares trace their ancestry further back than 1500, have a reflex distaste for prohibitive immigration policies which hinder the free movement of Spaniards seeking better wages abroad. Such policies or laws they see as negative, or simply bad. A Finn consistently making expensive telephone calls for which she need not pay will ultimately fall victim to her own inherent sense of independence, not least because she is building up a debt to her friend in Finnish Telecom. The Spaniard, on the other hand, would phone Easter Island nightly (if he could get away with it) with great relish and unashamed glee.

It is by considering such matters that we realise that all that is legal is not necessarily good and everything illegal not necessarily bad. Finns,

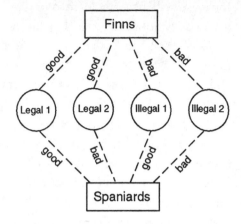

Legal 1 = restrictive drink-driving laws

Legal 2 = restrictive immigration laws

Illegal 1 = consistently making use of
a friend at the telephone exchange to
make free international calls

Illegal 2 = drug traffic

Figure 3

Swedes, Swiss and Germans do not make this discovery very easily. Americans, Belgians, Danes, Hungarians, Slovenes, Croats, Chinese, Koreans and Australians can accept it without losing too much sleep. Latins, Arabs, Polynesians, Africans and Russians see it clearly from the beginning. A Sicilian friend of mine has not paid for a telephone call since 1948. His father owns a vineyard.

Recently I tested mature Finnish executives on cross-cultural seminars with the following exercise:

NATIONAL CHARACTERISTICS

heavy   humorous   excitable   honest   risk taking   snobbish
serious   diplomatic   talkative   slow   opportunistic   weak willed
humourless   laid back   sly   emotional   reliable   true
money minded   collective   wise   take things literally   open   shy
good manners   unreliable   direct   joking   sociable   hard working
conservative   individualistic   loud   no manners   caring   extrovert
efficient   punctual   flexible   reserved   quick   polite
time dominated   vague   boring   polished   strong willed
old fashioned

*Study the characteristics above and select eight for each of the following
nationalities: German, British, Italian, Finnish, Swedish, American*

Attributing 8 of the 48 available characteristics to 6 different nationalities, Finns invariably select the following qualities to describe themselves:

honest, slow, reliable, true, shy, direct, reserved, punctual

Six of these characteristics are clearly positive; even 'shy' and 'slow' do do not have negative connotations in Finnish ears.

Germans could be considered punctual, Swedes honest, Britons true and reliable, Americans direct, but the seminarists had a natural tendency to paint a positive picture of the Finnish character. Swedes, Germans and Britons, when tested in a similar manner, do the same, selecting euphemistic adjectives to describe their own culture.

In another exercise, Finnish seminarists were asked to perform role plays in which Finnish, Russian, American and Polynesian characters were involved. The executives played the Finnish and Russian roles well, but invariably exaggerated the traits of Americans and Polynesians, magnifying and distorting the brashness and blustering nature of the former and the innocence, clamour and chatter of the latter. This illustrated the Finnish tendency to resort to stereotype categorising when actual familiarity is lacking. (Russian characteristics, on the other hand, are well observed by Finns).

Stereotyping is dangerous, but it is also a fair guide at the national level. A particular Dane may resemble a certain Portuguese, but a Danish choir or football team is easily distinguishable from its Portuguese equivalent. Generalising on national traits breaks down with individuals but stands firm with large numbers.

Cultural spectacles continue to blur the vision of any nationals when they look at their foreign interlocutors. Figure 4 illustrates the barriers to communication which Japanese reticence erects when faced with Latin exuberance, and Figure 5 shows the relative ease with which two Latin peoples can communicate with each other by virtue of wearing similar spectacles.

It is worth pointing out that French and Italian people do not like each other particularly, but they are both good communicators and there are no substantial barriers in the way of rapid and mutually intelligible discourse.

If a Japanese or anyone else takes off their national spectacles, the world is initially blurred and out of focus. Many other pairs of spectacles will have to be tried on before 20/20 vision is achieved. This is the process of **developing intercultural sensitivity**.

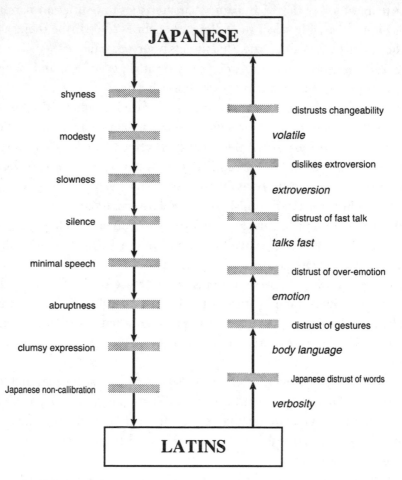

Figure 4   *Barriers to communication*

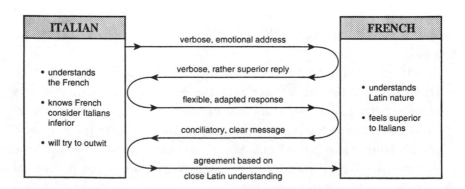

Figure 5   *Interaction among Latins*

Part Two

Managing Across Cultures

3

CATEGORISING CULTURES

The several hundred national and regional cultures of the world can be roughly classified into three groups: task-oriented, highly organised planners (linear-active); people-oriented, loquacious interrelators (multi-active); introvert, respect-oriented listeners (reactive). Italians see Germans as stiff and time-dominated; Germans see Italians gesticulating in chaos; the Japanese observes and quietly learns from both.

Linear-active and multi-active cultures

SVEN SVENSSON IS A SWEDISH BUSINESSMAN, LIVING IN LISBON. A FEW weeks ago he was invited by a Portuguese acquaintance, Antonio, to play tennis at 10am. Sven turned up at the tennis court on time, already in tennis gear and ready to play.

Antonio arrived half an hour late, in the company of a friend, Carlos, from whom he was buying some land. They had been discussing the purchase that morning and had prolonged the discussion, so Antonio had brought Carlos along in order to finalise the details during the journey. They continued the business while Antonio changed into his tennis clothes, with Sven listening to all they said. At 10.45 they went on court and Antonio continued the discussion with Carlos, while hitting practice balls with Sven.

At this point another acquaintance of Antonio's, Pedro, arrived in order to confirm a sailing date with Antonio for the weekend. Antonio asked

Sven to excuse him for a moment and walked off court to talk to Pedro. After chatting to Pedro for five minutes, Antonio resumed his conversation with the waiting Carlos and eventually turned back to the waiting Sven to begin playing tennis at 11. When Sven remarked that the court had only been booked from 10 to 11am, Antonio reassured him that he had phoned in advance to rebook it until 12 noon. No problem.

It will come as no surprise to you to hear that Sven was very unhappy about the course of events. Why? He and Antonio live in two different worlds or, to put it more exactly, use two different time systems. Sven, as a good Swede, belongs to a culture which uses linear-active time – that is to say, he does one thing at a time in the sequence he has written down in his diary. His diary that day said 8am get up, 9am breakfast, 9.15 change into tennis clothes, 9.30 drive to tennis court, 10–11am play tennis, 11–11.30 beer and shower, 12.15 lunch, 2pm go to the office, and so on.

Antonio, who had seemed to synchronise with him for tennis from 10 to 11, had disorganised Sven's day. Portuguese like Antonio follow a multi-active time system, that is, they do many things at once, often in an unplanned order.

Multi-active cultures are very flexible. If Pedro interrupted Carlos's conversation which was already in the process of interrupting Sven's tennis, this was quite normal and acceptable in Portugal. It is not acceptable in Sweden, neither is it in Germany or Britain.

Linear-active people, like Swedes, Swiss, Dutch and Germans, do one thing at a time, concentrate hard on that thing and do it within a scheduled timescale. These people think that in this way they are more efficient and get more done.

Multi-active people **think they get more done their way**. Let us look again at Sven and Antonio. If Sven had not been disorganised by Antonio, he would undoubtedly have played tennis, eaten at the right time and done some business. But Antonio had had breakfast, bought some land, played tennis and fixed up his sailing, all by lunchtime. He had even managed to rearrange the tennis booking. Sven could never live like this, but Antonio does, all the time.

Multi-active people are not very interested in schedules or punctuality. They pretend to observe them, especially if a linear-active partner insists. They consider reality to be more important than manmade appointments. Reality for Antonio that morning was that his talk with Carlos about land was unfinished. Multi-active people do not like to leave conversations unfinished. For them completing a human transaction is the best way they can invest their time. So he took Carlos to the tennis and finished buying the land while hitting balls. Pedro further delayed the tennis, but Antonio would not abandon the match with Sven. That was another human transaction he wished to complete. So they played till 12 or 12.30 if necessary. But what about Sven's lunch at 12.15? Not important, says Antonio. It's only 12.15 because that's what Sven wrote in his diary.

A friend of mine, a BBC producer, often used to visit Europe to visit BBC agents. He never failed to get through his appointments in Denmark and Germany, but always had trouble in Greece. The Greek agent was a popular man in Athens and had to see so many people each day that he invariably ran over time. So my friend usually missed his appointment or waited three or four hours for the agent to turn up. Finally, after several trips, the producer adapted to the multi-active culture. He simply went to the Greek's secretary in late morning and asked for the agent's schedule for the day. As the Greek conducted most of his meetings in hotel rooms or bars, the BBC producer would wait in the hotel lobby and catch him rushing from one appointment to the next. The multi-active Greek, happy to see him, would not hesitate to spend half an hour with him and thus make himself late for his next appointment.

When people from a linear-active culture work together with people from a multi-active culture, irritation results on both sides. Unless one party adapts to the other – and they rarely do – constant crises will occur. Why don't the Mexicans arrive on time? ask the Germans. Why don't they work to deadlines? Why don't they follow a plan? The Mexicans on the other hand ask: Why keep to the plan when circumstances have changed? Why keep to a deadline if we rush production and lose quality? Why try to sell this amount to that customer if we know they aren't ready to buy yet?

Recently I visited a wonderful aviary in South Africa where exotic birds of all kinds were kept in a series of 100 large cages, to which the visiting public had direct access. There was plenty of room for the birds to fly around and it was quite exciting for us to be in the cage with them. One proceeded, at one's leisure, from cage to cage, making sure one closed doors carefully.

Two small groups of tourists – one consisting of four Germans and the other of three French people – were visiting the aviary at the same time as us. The Germans had made their calculations, obviously having decided to devote 100 minutes to the visit; consequently they spent one minute in each cage. One German read the captions, one took photographs, one videoed and one opened and closed doors. I followed happily in their wake.

The three French people began their tour a few minutes later than the Germans, but soon caught them up as they galloped through the cages containing smaller birds. As the French were also filming, they rather spoilt cage 10 for the Germans, as they made a lot of noise and generally got in the way. The Germans were relieved when the French rushed on ahead towards more exciting cages.

The steady German progress continued through cages 11–15. Cage 16 contained the owls (most interesting). There we found our French friends again, who had occupied the cage for five minutes. They filmed the owls from every angle while the Germans waited their turn. When the French eventually rushed out, the Germans were five minutes behind schedule.

Later on, the French stayed so long with the eagles in cage 62 that the Germans had to bypass them and come back to do the eagles later. They were furious at this forced departure from their linear progression, and eventually finished their visit half an hour 'late'. By then the French had departed, having seen all they were interested in.

A study of attitudes to time in a Swiss–Italian venture showed that each side learned something from the other. After initial quarrelling, both parties cooperated for a few months. The Italians finally admitted that adherence at least in theory to schedules, production deadlines and budgets enabled them to clarify their goals and check on performances and efficiency. The Swiss, on the other hand, found that the more flexible Italian attitude allowed them to modify the timetable in reaction to unexpected developments in the market, to spot deficiencies in the planning which had not been evident earlier, and to make vital last-minute improvements in 'extra time'.

Germans, like Swiss, are very high on the linear-active scale, since they attach great importance to analysing a project, compartmentalising it, tackling each problem one at a time in a linear fashion, concentrating on each segment and thereby achieving a near perfect result. They are uneasy with people who do not work in this manner, such as Arabs and those from many Mediterranean cultures.

Americans are also very linear-active, but there are some differences in attitude. As Americans live very much in the present and the future, they sometimes push Germans into action before the latter want to act. Germans are very conscious of their history and their past and will often wish to explain a lot of background to American partners to put present actions in context. This often irritates Americans who want 'to get on with it'.

Figure 6 gives a suggested ranking on the linear/multi-active scale, showing not unsurprising regional variations. German and other European influences in Chile have caused Chileans to be less multi-active than, for instance, Brazilians or Argentinians. The differences in behaviour between northern and southern Italians are well documented. Australians, with a large number of southern European immigrants, are becoming less linear-active and more extrovert than most northern peoples.

Figure 7 lists the most common traits of linear-active, multi-active and reactive cultures.

LINEAR-ACTIVE–MULTI-ACTIVE SCALE

1. Germans, Swiss
2. Americans (WASP)*
3. Scandinavians, Austrians
4. British, Canadians, New Zealanders
5. Australians, South Africans
6. Japanese
7. Dutch, Belgians
8. American subcultures (e.g. Jewish, Italian, Polish)
9. French, Belgians (Walloons)
10. Czechs, Slovenians, Croats, Hungarians
11. Northern Italians (Milan, Turin, Genoa)
12. Chileans
13. Russians, other Slavs
14. Portuguese
15. Polynesians
16. Spanish, Southern Italians, Mediterranean peoples
17. Indians, Pakistanis etc.
18. Latin Americans, Arabs, Africans

* White Anglo-Saxon Protestant

Figure 6

LINEAR-ACTIVE	MULTI-ACTIVE	REACTIVE
introvert	extrovert	introvert
patient	impatient	patient
quiet	talkative	silent
minds own business	inquisitive	respectful
likes privacy	gregarious	good listener
plans ahead methodically	plans grand outline only	looks at general principles
does one thing at a time	does several things at once	reacts
works fixed hours	works any hours	flexible hours
punctual	unpunctual	punctual
dominated by timetables and schedules	timetable unpredictable	reacts to partner's timetable
compartmentalises projects	lets one project influence another	sees whole picture
sticks to plans	changes plans	makes slight changes
sticks to facts	juggles facts	statements are promises
gets information from statistics, reference books, database	gets first-hand (oral) information	uses both
job-oriented	people-oriented	people-oriented
unemotional	emotional	quietly caring
works within department	gets round all departments	all departments
follows correct procedures	pulls strings	inscrutable, calm
accepts favours reluctantly	seeks favours	protects face of other
delegates to competent colleagues	delegates to relations	delegates to reliable people
completes action chains	completes human transactions	reacts to partner
likes fixed agendas	interrelates everything	thoughtful
brief on telephone	talks for hours	summarises well
uses memoranda	rarely writes memos	plans slowly
respects officialdom	seeks out (top) key person	ultra honest
dislikes losing face	has ready excuses	must not lose face
confronts with logic	confronts emotionally	avoids confrontation
limited body language	unrestricted body language	subtle body language
rarely interrupts	interrupts frequently	doesn't interrupt
separates social/ professional	interweaves social/ professional	connects social and professional

Figure 7

Reactive cultures (listeners)

Japan belongs to the group of reactive or listening cultures, the members of which rarely initiate action or discussion, preferring first to listen to and establish the other's position, then react to it and formulate their own.

Reactive cultures are to be found in Japan, China, Taiwan, Singapore, Korea, Turkey and Finland. Several other East Asian countries, although occasionally multi-active and excitable, have certain reactive characteristics. In Europe, only Finns are strongly reactive, but Britons, Turks and Swedes fall easily into 'listening mode' on occasion.

Reactive cultures listen before they leap. They are the world's best listeners in as much as they concentrate on what the speaker is saying, do not let their minds wander (difficult for Latins) and rarely, if ever, interrupt a speaker while the discourse/speech/presentation is going on. When it is finished, they do not reply immediately. A decent period of silence after the speaker has stopped shows respect for the weight of the remarks, which must be considered unhurriedly and with due deference.

Even when representatives of a reactive culture begin their reply, they are unlikely to voice any strong opinion immediately. A more probable tactic is to ask further questions on what has been said in order to clarify the speaker's intent and aspirations. Japanese, particularly, go over each point many times in detail to make sure there are no misunderstandings. Finns, although blunt and direct in the end, shy away from confrontation as long as they can, trying to formulate an approach which suits the other party. Chinese take their time to assemble a variety of strategies which would avoid discord with the initial proposal.

Reactive cultures are introvert, distrust a surfeit of words, and consequently are adept at non-verbal communication. This is achieved by subtle body language, worlds apart from the excitable gestures of Latins and Africans. Linear-active people find reactive tactics hard to fathom, since they do not slot into the linear system (question/reply, cause/effect). Multi-active people, used to extrovert behaviour, find them inscrutable – giving little or no feedback. The Finns are the best example of this, reacting even less than the Japanese, who at least pretend to be pleased.

In reactive cultures the preferred mode of communication is monologue — pause — reflection — monologue. If possible, one lets the other side deliver their monologue first. In linear-active or multi-active cultures, the communication mode is a **dialogue**. One interrupts the other's 'monologue' by frequent comments, even questions, which signify polite interest in what is being said. As soon as the opponent stops speaking, one takes up one's turn immediately, since the westerner has an extremely weak tolerance of silence.

People belonging to reactive cultures not only tolerate silences well, but regard them as a very meaningful, almost refined, part of discourse. The opinions of the other party are not to be taken lightly, or dismissed with a snappy or flippant retort. Clever, well-formulated arguments require – deserve – lengthy silent consideration. The American, having delivered a sales pitch in Helsinki, leans forward and says, 'Well, Pekka, what do you think?' If you ask Finns what they think, they begin to **think**. Finns, like Orientals, think in silence. Another American, asked the same question, might well jump to his feet and exclaim, 'I'll tell you what I think!', allowing no pause to punctuate the proceedings or interfere with western 'momentum'. Oriental momentum takes much longer to achieve. One can compare reactions to handling the gears of a car, where multi-active people go immediately into first gear, enabling them to put their foot down to accelerate (the discussion) and to pass quickly through second and third gears as the argument intensifies. Reactive cultures prefer to avoid crashing through the gear box. Too many revs might cause damage to the engine (discussion). The big wheel turns more slowly at first and the foot is put down gently. But when momentum is finally achieved it is likely to be maintained and, moreover, tends to be in the right direction.

The reactive 'reply-monologue' will accordingly be context centred and will presume a considerable amount of knowledge on the part of the listener (who, after all, probably spoke first). Because the listener is presumed to be knowledgeable, Japanese, Chinese or Finns will often be satisfied with expressing their thoughts in **half-utterances**, indicating that the listener can fill in the rest. It is a kind of compliment one pays one's interlocutor. At such times multi-active, dialogue-oriented people are more receptive than linear-oriented people, who thrive on clearly-expressed linear argument.

Reactive cultures not only rely on utterances and semi-statements to further the conversation, but they indulge in other oriental habits which confuse the westerner. They are, for instance, 'roundabout', using impersonal verbs ('one is leaving') or the passive voice ('one of the machines seems to have been tampered with'), either to deflect blame or with the general aim of politeness.

As reactive cultures tend to use names less frequently than westerners, the impersonal, vague nature of the discussion is further accentuated. Lack of eye contact, so typical of the east, does not help the situation. The Japanese, evading the Spaniard's earnest stare, makes the latter feel that they are being boring or saying something distasteful. Oriental inscrutability (often appearing on a Finn's face as a sullen expression) adds to the feeling that the discussion is leading nowhere. A Finn or a Japanese, embarrassed by another's stare, seeks eye contact only at the beginning of the discussion or when they wish their opponent to take up their 'turn' in the conversation.

Japanese 'opposing' delegations are often quite happy to sit in a line on one side of the table and contemplate a neutral spot on the wall facing them as they converse sporadically or muse in joint silence. The occasional sidelong glance will be used to seek confirmation of a point made. Then it's back to studying the wall again.

Small talk does not come easily to reactive cultures. While Japanese and Chinese trot out well-tried formalisms to indicate courtesy, they tend to regard questions such as 'Well, how goes it?' as direct questions and may take the opportunity to voice a complaint. On other occasions their over-long pauses or slow reactions cause westerners to think they are slow witted or have nothing to say. Turks, in discussion with Germans in Berlin, complained that they never got chance to present their views fully, while the Germans, for their part, thought the Turks had nothing to say. A high-ranking delegation from the Bank of Finland told me recently that, for the same reason, they found it hard to get a word in at international meetings. 'How can we make an impact?' they asked. Japanese suffer more than any other people in this type of gathering.

The westerner should always bear in mind that the actual content of the response delivered by a person from a reactive culture represents only a small part of the significance surrounding the event. Context-centred utterances inevitably attach more importance not to **what** is said, but **how** it is said, **who** said it and what is **behind** what is said. Also, what is **not** said may be the main thrust of the reply.

Self-disparagement is another favourite tactic of reactive cultures. It eliminates the possibility of offending through self-esteem; it may draw the opponent into praising the oriental's conduct or decisions. The westerner must beware of presuming that self-disparagement is connected with a weak position.

Finally, reactive cultures excel in subtle, non-verbal communication which compensates for the absence of frequent interjections. Finns, Japanese and Chinese alike are noted for their sighs, almost inaudible groans and agreeable grunts. A sudden intake of breath in Finland indicates agreement, not shock, as it would in the case of a Latin. The 'oh', 'ha' or 'e' of the Japanese is a far surer indication of concurrence than the fixed smile they often assume.

To summarise, the programme for reactive cultures is sequential in the following manner:

+ listen carefully
+ establish understanding of the other's intent
+ allow a period of silence in order to evaluate
+ query further
+ react in a constructive manner
+ maintain a certain amount of inscrutability
+ imitate the other's strengths or products
+ improve on them
+ refine
+ perfect if possible

Reactive people have large reserves of energy. They are economical in movement and effort and do not waste time reinventing the wheel. Although they always give the impression of having power in reserve, they are seldom aggressive and rarely aspire to leadership (in the case of Japan, this is somewhat surprising in view of her economic might). France, Britain and the USA, on the other hand, have not hesitated to seize world leadership in periods of economic or military dominance.

Data-oriented, dialogue-oriented and listening cultures

Interaction between different peoples involves not only methods of communication, but also the process of gathering information. This brings us to the question of dialogue-oriented and data-oriented cultures. A data-oriented culture is one where one does research to produce lots of information which is then acted on. Swedes, Germans, Americans, Swiss and

1.   Japan   **Strongly**
2.   China   **reactive**
3.   Taiwan
4.   Singapore, Hong Kong*
5.   Finland*
6.   Korea
7.   Turkey+
8.   Vietnam, Cambodia, Laos+
9.   Malaysia, Indonesia+
10.   Pacific Islands (Fiji, Tonga, etc.)+

----

11.   Sweden*
12.   Britain*   **Occasionally**

----

* Linear-active tendencies when reacting
+ Multi-active tendencies when reacting

Figure 8   Reactive cultures (listeners)

Northern Europeans in general love to gather solid information and move steadily forward from this database. The communications and information revolution is a dream come true for data-oriented cultures. It provides them quickly and efficiently with what dialogue-oriented cultures already know.

Which are the dialogue-oriented cultures? Examples are the Italians and other Latins, Arabs and Indians. These people see events and business possibilities 'in context' because they already possess an enormous amount of information through their own personal information network. Arabs or Portuguese will be well informed about the facts surrounding a deal since they will already have queried, discussed and gossiped in their circle of friends, business acquaintances and extensive family connections. The Japanese (basically a listener) may be even better informed, since the very nature of Japan's web society involves them in an incredibly intricate information network operational during schooldays, college, university, Judo and Karate clubs, student societies, developed intelligence systems and family and political connections.

People from dialogue-oriented cultures like the French or Spanish tend to get impatient when Americans or Swiss feed them with facts and figures which are accurate but, in their opinion, only a part of the big human picture. A Frenchman would consider that an American sales forecast in France is of little meaning if he (the Frenchman) does not have time to develop the correct relationship with the customer on whom the success of the business depends.

It is quite normal in dialogue-oriented cultures for managers to take customers and colleagues with them when they leave a job. They have developed their relationships.

There is a strong correlation between dialogue-oriented and multi-active people. Antonio does ten things at once and is therefore in continuous contact with humans. He obtains from these people an enormous amount of information – far more than Americans or Germans will gather by spending a large part of their day in a private office, door closed, looking at the screen of their personal computer.

Multi-active people are knee deep in information. They know so much that the very brevity of an agenda makes it useless to them. At meetings they tend to ignore agendas or speak out of turn. How can you forecast a conversation? Discussion of one item could make another meaningless. How can you deal with feedback in advance? How can an agenda solve deadlock? Dialogue-oriented people wish to use their personal relations to solve the problem from the human angle. Once this is mentally achieved, then appointments, schedules, agendas, even meetings become superfluous.

If these remarks seem to indicate that dialogue-oriented people, relying on only word of mouth, suffer from serious disadvantages and drawbacks, it should be emphasised that it is very difficult to pass over from one system to the other. It is hard to imagine a Neapolitan company organising its business along American lines with five-year rolling forecasts, quarterly reporting, six-monthly audits and twice-yearly performance appraisals. It is equally hard to imagine Germans introducing a new product in a strange country without first doing a market survey.

It is noticeable that most of the successful economies, with the striking exception of Japan, are in data-oriented cultures using processed information. Japan, although dialogue-oriented, also uses a large amount of printed information. Moreover, productivity also depends on other significant factors, particularly climate, so that information systems, while important, are not the whole story of efficiency and its logic.

One might summarise by saying that a compromise between data-oriented and dialogue-oriented systems would probably lead to good results, but that there are no **clear** examples of this having happened consistently in modern international business communities.

Figure 9 gives a suggested ranking for dialogue-oriented and data-oriented cultures. Figures 10–12 illustrate the relatively few sources of information that data-oriented cultures draw on. The more developed the society, the more we tend to turn to print and database to obtain our facts. The information revolution has accentuated this trend and Germany, along with the USA, Britain and Scandinavia, is well to the fore. Yet printed information and databases are almost necessarily out of date (as anyone who has purchased mailing lists has found out to their cost). Last night's whispers in a Madrid bar or café are hot off the press – Pedro was in Oslo last week and talked Olav off his feet till two in the morning. Few data-oriented people will dig for information and then spread it in this way, although Germans do not fare badly once they get out of their cloistered offices. Northerners' lack of gregariousness again proves a hindrance. By upbringing they are taught **not to pry** – inquisitiveness gains no points in their society – gossip is even worse. What their database cannot tell them they try to find out through official channels – embassies, chambers of commerce, circulated information sheets, perhaps hints provided by friendly companies with experience in the country in question. In business, especially when negotiating, information is power. Sweden, Norway, Australia, New Zealand and several other data-oriented cultures will have to expand and intensify their intelligence-gathering networks in the future if they are to compete with information-hot France, Japan, Italy, Korea, Taiwan and Singapore. It may well be that the EU itself will develop into a **hot-house exchange** of business information to compete with the Japanese network.

Listening cultures

Listening cultures, reactive in nature, combine deference to database and print information (Japan, Finland, Singapore and Taiwan are high tech) with a natural tendency to listen well and enter into sympathetic dialogue. Japanese and Chinese will entertain the prospect of very lengthy discourse

Dialogue

1.   Latin Americans
2.   Italians, Spanish, Portuguese, French
      Mediterranean peoples
3.   Arabs. Africans
4.   Indians, Pakistanis
5.   Chileans
6.   Hungarians, Romanians
7.   Slavs
8.   American subcultures
9.   Benelux
10.   British, Australians
11.   Scandinavians
12.   North Americans (US WASPS* and Canadians),
      New Zealanders, South Africans
13.   Germans, Swiss

Data

* White Anglo-Saxon Protestant

Figure 9   Dialogue-oriented, data-oriented cultures

in order to attain ultimate harmony. In this respect, they are as people oriented as the Latins. The Finns, inevitably more brief, nevertheless base their dialogue on careful consideration of the wishes of the other party. They rarely employ 'steamrollering' tactics frequently observable in American, German and French debate. Monologues are unknown in Finland, unless practised by the other party.

Listening cultures believe they have the right attitude to information gathering. They do not precipitate improvident action, they allow ideas to mature, they are ultimately accommodating in their decisions. The success of Japan and the four Asian tigers – South Korea, Taiwan, Hong Kong and Singapore – as well as Finland's prosperity despite few economic strengths, all bear witness to the resilience of the listening cultures.

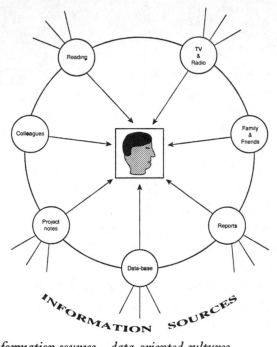

Figure 10   Information sources – data-oriented cultures

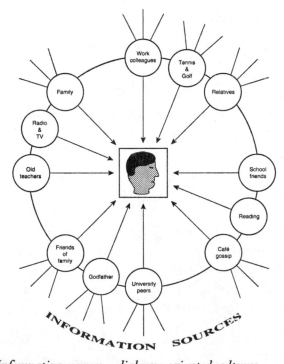

Figure 11   Information sources – dialogue-oriented cultures

WEB SOCIETY

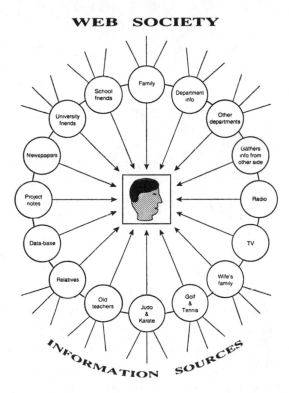

Figure 12   Information sources – listening culture (Japan)

4

THE USE OF TIME

THE WORLD VIEWS HELD BY DIFFERENT CULTURES VARY WIDELY, AS DO A multiplicity of concepts which constitute and represent a kaleidoscopic outlook on the nature of reality. Some of these concepts – fatalism, work ethic, reincarnation, *sisu*, Confucianism, *Weltschmerz*, *dusha*, etc. – are readily identifiable within specific groups, societies or nations. Other concepts – central and vital to human experience – are essentially universal, but subject to strikingly different notions of their nature and essence. Such concepts are those of space and time.

Time, particularly, is seen in a different light by eastern and western cultures and even within these groupings assumes quite dissimilar aspects from country to country. In the western hemisphere, the USA and Mexico employ time in such a diametrically opposing manner that it causes intense friction between the two peoples. In western Europe the Swiss attitude to time bears little relation to that of neighbouring Italy. Thais do not evaluate the passing of time in the same way that the Japanese do. In Britain the future stretches out in front of you. In Madagascar it flows into the back of your head from behind.

Linear time

Let us begin with the American concept of time, for theirs is the most expensive, as anyone who has had to do with American doctors, dentists or lawyers will tell you.

For an American, time is truly money. In a profit-oriented society, time is a precious, even scarce, commodity. It flows fast, like a mountain river in spring, and if you want to benefit from its passing, you have to move fast with it. Americans are people of action; they cannot bear to be idle. Past time is over, but the present you can seize, parcel and package and make it work for you in the immediate future.

Time looks like this:

Figure 13

This is what you have to do with it:

Past	Present	Future	
over	today's tasks A B C D E	plans for January	worries for February	etc.

Figure 14

In America you have to make money, otherwise you are nobody. If you have 40 years of earning capacity and you want to make $4 million, that means $100,000 per annum. If you can achieve this in 250 working days that comes to $400 a day or $50 an hour.

Figure 15 suggests that you can make $400 a day if you work 8 hours, performing one task per hour in a planned, time-efficient sequence. In this orientation Americans can say that their time costs $50 an hour. The concept of time **costing** money is one thing. Another idea is that of **wasting** time. If, as in Figure 16, appointments D and E fail to show up, Americans might say that they have wasted 2 hours – or lost $100. Thus:

'Time is money!'

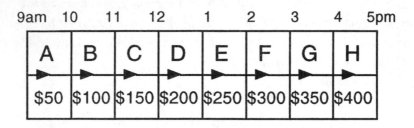

8 hours of his time <u>cost</u> $400

Figure 15

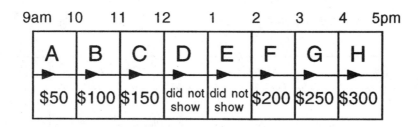

he wasted 2 hours or lost $100!

Figure 16

This seems logical enough, until one begins to apply the idea to other cultures. Has the Portuguese fisherman, who failed to hook a fish for two hours, wasted his time? Has the Sicilian priest, failing to make a convert on Thursday, lost ground? Have the German composer, the French poet, the Spanish painter, devoid of ideas last week, skipped opportunities which can be qualified in monetary terms?

The Americans are not the only ones who sanctify timekeeping, for it is a religion in Switzerland and Germany, too. These countries, along with Britain, the Anglo-Saxon world in general, the Netherlands, Austria and Scandinavia, have a linear vision of time and action which the above figures have illustrated. They suspect, like the Americans, that time passing without decisions being made or actions being performed is streaking away unutilized in a linear present and future.

Anglo-Saxon, Germanic and Scandinavian peoples are essentially linear-active, time-dominated and monochronic. They prefer to do one thing at a time, concentrate on it and do it within a scheduled timescale. They think that in this way they get more things done – and efficiently. Furthermore, being imbued with the Protestant work ethic, they equate working time with success. (The harder you work – more hours, that is – the more successful you will be, the more money you will make). This idea might sound reasonable in American ears, would carry less weight in class-conscious Britain, and would be viewed as entirely unrealistic in southern European countries where authority, privilege and birthright negate the theory at every turn. In a society such as existed in the Soviet Union one could postulate that those who achieved substantial remuneration by working little (or not at all) were the most successful of all.

Multi-actives

Southern Europeans are multi-active, rather than linear-active. The more things they can do or handle at the same time, the happier and the more fulfilled they feel. They organize their time (and lives) in an entirely different way from Americans, Germans and Swiss. Multi-active peoples are not very interested in schedules or punctuality. They pretend to observe them, especially if a linear-active partner insists, but they consider reality to be more important than appointments. In their ordering of things, priority is given to the relative thrill or significance of each meeting. Spaniards, Italians, Arabs ignore the passing of time if it means that conversations would be left unfinished. For them, completing a **human transaction** is the best way they can invest their time. Germans and Swiss love clock-regulated time, for it appears to them as a remarkably efficient, impartial and very precise way of organising life – especially in business. For an Italian, on the other hand, time considerations will usually be subjected to human feelings. 'Why are you so angry because I came at 9.30?', he asks his German colleague. 'Because it says 9am in my diary', says the German. 'Then why don't you write 9.30 and then we'll both be happy?' is a logical Italian response. The business we have to do and our close relations are so important that it is irrelevant at what time we meet. The **meeting** is what counts. Germans and Swiss cannot swallow this, as it offends their sense of order, of tidiness, of pre-arrangement.

A Spaniard would take the side of the Italian. There is a reason for the Spaniard's lax adherence to punctuality. The German believes in a simple truth – scientific truth. The Spaniard, in contrast, is always conscious of the double truth – that of immediate reality as well as that of the poetic whole.

The German thinks they see eye to eye, as in Figure 17:

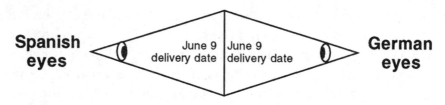

Figure 17

In fact the Spaniard, with the consciousness of double truth, sees it as in Figure 18:

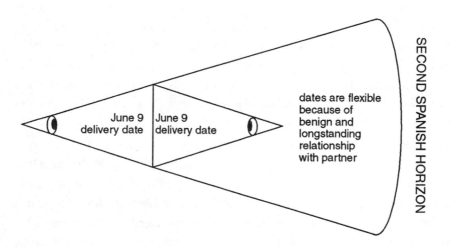

Figure 18

As far as meetings are concerned, it is better not to turn up strictly on time for Spanish appointments. **In Spain, punctuality messes up schedules**, as in Figure 19.

Few northern Europeans or North Americans can reconcile themselves to the multi-active use of time. Germans and Swiss, unless they reach an understanding of the underlying psychology, will be driven to distraction. Germans see compartmentalisation of programmes, schedules, procedures

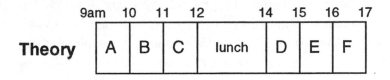

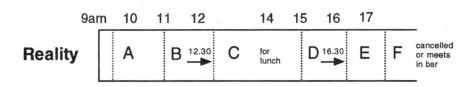

Figure 19

and production as the surest route to efficiency. The Swiss, even more time and regulation dominated, have made **precision** a national symbol. This applies to their watch industry, their optical instruments, their pharmaceutical products, their banking. Planes, buses and trains leave on the dot. Accordingly, everything can be exactly calculated and predicted.

In countries inhabited by linear-active people, time is clock and calendar related, segmented in an abstract manner for our convenience, measurement and disposal. In multi-active cultures like the Arab and Latin spheres, time is event or personality related, a subjective commodity which can be manipulated, moulded, stretched or dispensed with, irrespective of what the clock says. 'I have to rush.' says the American, 'my time is up'. The Spaniard or Arab, scornful of this submissive attitude to schedules, would only use this expression if death were imminent.

Cyclic time

Both the linear-active Northerner and the multi-active Latin think that they **manage** time in the best way possible. In some Eastern cultures, however, the **adaptation** of humans to time is seen as a viable alternative. In these cultures time is viewed neither as linear nor event–personality related, but as **cyclic**. Each day the sun rises and sets, the seasons follow one another, the heavenly bodies revolve around us, people grow old and die, but their children reconstitute the process. We know this cycle has gone on for one hundred thousand years and more. Cyclical time is not a scarce commodity. There would seem to be an unlimited supply of it just around the next bend. As they say in the East, when God made time, he made plenty of it.

As many Asians are keenly aware of the cyclical nature of time, business decisions are arrived at in a different way from in the West. Westerners often expect an Asian to make a quick decision or treat a current deal on its present merits, irrespective of what has happened in the past. Asians cannot do this. The past formulates the contextual background to the present decision, about which in any case, as Asians, they must think long term – their hands are tied in many ways. Americans see time passing without decisions being made or actions performed as 'wasted'. Asians do not see time as racing away unutilised in a linear future, but coming round again in a circle, where the same opportunities, risks, dangers will re-present themselves when people are so many days, weeks or months wiser. How often do we (in the West) say 'If I had known then what I know now, I would never have done what I did'?

Figure 20 compares the speed of Western **action chains** with Asian reflection. The American goes home satisfied with all tasks completed. The German and the Swiss probably do the same; the French or Italian might leave some 'mopping up' for the following day. John Paul Fieg, describing the Thai attitude to time, saw it as a pool which they could gradually walk around. This metaphor applies to most Asians, who, instead of tackling problems immediately in sequential fashion, circle round them for a few days (weeks etc.) before committing themselves. After a suitable period of reflection, A,D and F may indeed seem worthy of pursuing. B,C and E may be quietly dropped. Contemplation of the whole scene has indicated, however, that task G (not envisaged at all earlier on) might be the most significant of all.

In a Buddhist culture – Thailand is a good example, although Buddhist influence pervades large areas of Asia – not only time but life itself goes round in a circle. Whatever we plan in our diary, however we organise our particular world, generation follows generation, governments and rulers will succeed each other, crops will be harvested, monsoons, earthquakes and other catastrophes will recur, taxes will be paid, the sun and moon will rise and set, stocks and shares will rise and fall. Even the Americans will not change such events, certainly not by rushing things.

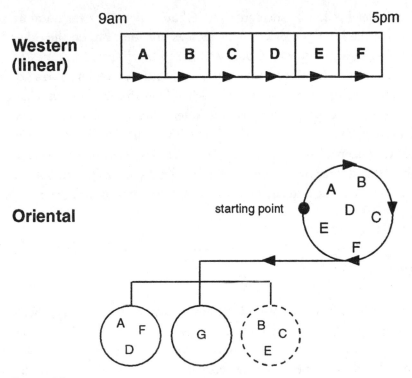

Figure 20

Chinese

Chinese, like most Asians, 'walk round the pool' in order to make well-considered decisions, but they also have a keen sense of the value of time. This can be noticed especially in their attitude towards taking up other people's time, for which they frequently apologize. It is customary, at the end of a meeting in China, to thank the participants for contributing their valuable time. Punctuality on arrival is also considered important – more so than in many Asian countries. Indeed, when meetings are scheduled between two people, it is not unusual for a Chinese to arrive 15–30 minutes early 'in order to finish the business before the time appointed for its discussion', so not stealing any of the other person's time! It is also considered polite in China to announce, 10 or 15 minutes after a meeting has begun, that one will soon have to be going. Again, the worthy aim involved is to economise on their use of your time. The Chinese will not go, of course, until the transaction has been completed, but the point has been made.

This is indeed a double standard. The Chinese penchant for humility demands that the interlocutor's time be seen as precious, but on the other hand Chinese expect a liberal amount of time to be allocated to repeated consideration of the details of a transaction and to the careful nurturing of personal relationships surrounding the deal. They frequently complain that Americans, in China to do business, often have to catch their plane back to the US 'in the middle of the discussion'. The American sees the facts as having been adequately discussed; the Chinese feels that he has not yet attained that degree of closeness – that satisfying sense of common trust and intent – that is for him the bedrock of the deal and of other transactions in the future.

Japanese

The Japanese have a keen sense of the **unfolding** of time – this is well described by Joy Hendry in her book *Wrapping Culture*. People familiar with Japan are well aware of the contrast between the breakneck pace maintained by the Japanese factory worker on the one hand, and the unhurried contemplation to be observed in Japanese gardens or the agonisingly slow tempo of a Noh play on the other. What Hendry emphasises, however, is the meticulous, resolute manner in which the Japanese **segment** time. This segmentation does not follow the American or German pattern, where tasks are assigned in a logical sequence aiming at maximum efficiency and speed in implementation. The Japanese are more concerned, not with how long something takes to happen, but with how time is divided up in the interests of properness, courtesy and tradition.

There are various phases and layers, for instance, in most Japanese social gatherings, e.g. retirement parties, weddings, parent–teacher association meetings. On such occasions in Sicily or Andalucia, people would arrive at different times, the event would gradually attain momentum and most satisfaction would be derived from spontaneous, often exuberant behaviour or speech-making which would follow no strict pattern or ritual. There would be no distinct phases for passing from one activity to the next, whether eating, drinking, toasting, playing music, dancing or gossiping.

In Japan, by contrast, there would be quite **marked beginnings and endings**. At Japanese weddings, for example, guests are often required to proceed from room to room, as the ceremony and celebrations unfold, usually according to a strict schedule. The total time involved is not so important; it is the significance of passing from one phase of activity to another which puts a particular Japanese stamp on the event.

In a conformist and carefully regulated society, Japanese like to know at all times where they stand and where they are at: this applies both to social and business situations. The mandatory, two-minute exchange of business cards between executives meeting each other for the first time is one of the clearest examples of a time activity segment being used to mark the beginning of a relationship. Hendry points out that this 'marking' applies to a wide variety of events in Japanese society, in many cases where 'phases' would have little significance in the West. An example she gives is the start and finish of all types of classes in Japan, where activity cannot take place without being preceded by a formal request on the part of the students for the teacher to begin and a ritualistic expression of appreciation at the end.

Other events which require not only clearly defined beginnings and endings, but also unambiguous phase-switching signals, are the tea ceremony, New Year routines, annual cleaning of the house, cherry blossom viewing, spring 'offensives' (strikes), wrapping up of agricultural cycles, midsummer festivities, gift-giving routines, get-togethers of school and university colleagues, company picnics, *sake*-drinking sessions, approaching Shinto shrines or Buddhist temples, even the peripheral rituals surrounding judo, karate and kendo sessions. None of the above activities can be entered into by a Japanese in the casual, direct manner which a westerner might adopt. The American or northern European has a natural tendency to make a quick approach to the heart of things. The Japanese, in direct contrast, must experience an 'unfolding' or 'unwrapping' of the significant phases of the event. It has to do with Asian indirectness, but in Japan it also involves love of compartmentalisation of procedure, of tradition, of the beauty of ritual. Hendry suggests that this 'unwrapping' is a consequence of the Japanese having wrapped things up in the first place – social wrapping, the wrapping of the body, of space, of people. The fact that the Japanese imposed both the Chinese and Gregorian calendars on their earlier system means that the Japanese year itself is a veritable series of layers of openings and closings.

To summarize, when dealing with Japanese, one can assume that they will be generous in their allocation of time to you or your particular transaction. In return, you are advised to try to do the 'right thing at the right time'. In Japan, form and symbols are more important than content.

Back to the future

In the linear-active, industrialised western cultures time is seen as a road along which we proceed. Life is sometimes referred to as a 'journey' – one also talks about the 'end of the road'. We imagine ourselves as having travelled along that part of the road which is behind us (the past) and we see the untrodden path of the future stretching out in front of us.

Linear-oriented people do not regard the future as entirely unknowable, for they have already nudged it along certain channels by meticulous planning. American executives, with their quarterly forecast, will tell you how much money they are going to make in the next three months. The Swiss stationmaster will assure you, without any hesitation, that the train from Zurich to Luzern will leave at 9.03 tomorrow morning and arrive at exactly 10.05. He is probably right, too. Watches, calendars and computers are devices which not only encourage punctuality, but get us into the habit of working towards targets and deadlines. In a sense, we are 'making the future happen'. We cannot know everything (it would be disastrous for horse racing and detective stories), but we eliminate future unknowns to the best of our ability. Our personal programming tells us that over the next year we are going to get up at certain times, work so many hours, take holidays for designated periods, play tennis on Saturday mornings and pay our taxes on the 28th of each month.

Observers of cyclic time are less disciplined in their planning of the future, since they believe that it cannot be managed and that humans make life easier for themselves by 'harmonizing' with the laws and cyclic events of nature. Yet in such cultures a general form of planning is still possible, for the seasons and other features of nature (except earthquakes, hurricanes, etc.) are fairly regular and well understood. Cyclic time is not seen as a straight road leading from our feet to the horizon, but as a curved one which in one year's time will lead us through 'scenery' and conditions very similar to what we experience at the present moment.

Cultures observing both linear and cyclic concepts of time see the past as something we have put behind us and the future as something which lies before us. In Madagascar, the opposite is the case (see Figure 21). The Malagasy imagine the future as flowing into the back of their head, or passing them from behind, then becoming the past as it stretches out in front of them. The past is **in front of** their eyes because it is visible, known and influential. They can look at it, enjoy it, learn from it, even 'play' with it.

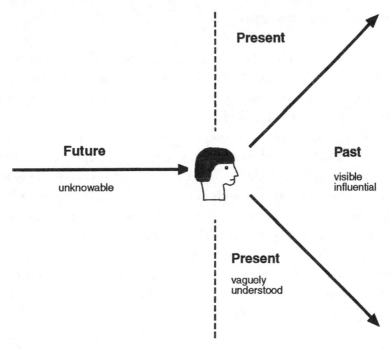

Figure 21   Malagasy concept of time

The Malagasy people spend an inordinate amount of time consulting their ancestors, exhuming their bones, partying with them.

By contrast the Malagasy consider the future unknowable. It is behind their head where they do not have eyes. Their plans for this unknown area will be far from meticulous, for what can they be based on? Buses in Madagascar leave, not according to a predetermined timetable, but when the bus is full. The situation triggers the event. The Malagasy sees this as common sense: the 'best' time for the bus departure is when it fills, for not only does this make economic sense, but it was also the time that most passengers chose to leave. Consequently in Madagascar stocks are not replenished until shelves are empty, filling stations order petrol only when they run dry, and hordes of would-be passengers at the airport find that, in spite of OK tickets, in reality everybody is waitlisted. The actual assignation of seats takes place between the opening of the check-in desk and the (eventual) departure of the plane.

Validity of time concepts

The Malagasy, the Thai, the Japanese, the Spaniard and many others will continue to use time in ways which will conflict with linear-oriented cultures in social and business spheres. The conflict is sharpest in the fields of economics, commerce and industry.

The objective view of time and its sequential effects is, however, favourable to historicity and to everything connected with industrialised organisation. Just as we conceive of our objectified time as extending in the future in the same way that it extends in the past, we mirror our records of the past in our estimates, budgets and schedules. We build up a commercial structure based on time *pro rata* values: time wages, rent, credit, interest, depreciation charges and insurance premiums. In general we are confident (in North America and northern Europe) that we have approached the optimum management of time. Many cultures (including powerful economies of the future, such as China, Japan and South-East Asia) will only allow the linear-oriented concept of time to dictate their behaviour to a limited extent. Industrial organisation demands a certain degree of synchronisation of schedules and targets, but the underlying philosophies concerning the best and most efficient use of time – and the manner in which it should be spent – may remain radically different.

5

STATUS, LEADERSHIP AND ORGANISATION

Cultural roots of organisation

THE BEHAVIOUR OF THE MEMBERS OF ANY CULTURAL GROUP IS dependent, almost entirely, on the history of the people in that society. It is often said that we fail to learn the lessons of history – and indeed we have seen mistakes repeated over hundreds of years by successive generations – but in the very long run (and we may be talking in millennia) a people will adhere collectively to the set of norms, reactions and activities which their experience and development have shown to be most beneficial for them. Their history may have consisted of good and bad years (or centuries), migrations, invasions, conquests, religious disputes or crusades, tempest, floods, droughts, sub-zero temperatures, disease and pestilence. They may have experienced brutality, oppression or near-genocide. Yet, if they survive, their culture, to some extent, has proved successful.

Besides being a creation of historical influence and climatic environment, the mentality of a culture – the inner workings and genius of the mindset – are also dictated by the nature and characteristics of the language of the group. The restricted liberties of thought that any particular tongue allows will have a pervasive influence on considerations of vision, charisma, emotion, poetic feeling, discipline and hierarchy.

Societal training

Historical experience, geographic and geo-linguistic position, physiology and appearance, instinct for survival – all combine to produce a core of beliefs and values which will sustain and satisfy the aspirations and needs of a given society. Based on these influences and beliefs, societal cultural conditioning of the members of the group is established and consolidated (for as many generations as the revered values continue to assure survival and success). Infants and youth are trained by their parents, teachers, peers and elders. The characteristics of the group gradually emerge and diverge from those of other groups. Basic needs of food, shelter and escaping from predators are dealt with first. Social, economic and military challenges will ensue. Traumatic historical developments may divert the traditional thrust of the programming. Japan's *samurai* traditions, discredited in 1945–6, gave way to growing enthusiasm for success in industry and commerce.

At all events, in victory or defeat, in prosperity or recession, a society needs to be organised, adapted or reorganised according to external pressures and its own objectives. Cultural groups organise themselves in strikingly different ways and think about such matters as authority, power, cooperation, aims, results and satisfaction in a variety of manners.

Individual and collective leadership

The term 'organisation' automatically implies leadership – people in authority who write the rules for the system. There are many historical examples of leadership having been vested in the person of one man or woman – Alexander the Great, Tamerlane, Louis XIV, Napoleon, Queen Elizabeth I, Joan of Arc are clear examples. Others, equally renowned and powerful but less despotic (Washington, Bismarck, Churchill) ruled and acted with the acquiescence of their fellow statesmen. Parliamentary rule, introduced by the British in the early part of the seventeenth century, initiated a new type of collective leadership at government level, although this had existed at regional, local and tribal levels for many centuries. Minoan collective rule – one of the earliest examples we know about – inspired a similar type of leadership both in the Greek city-states and later in Rome. In another hemisphere, Mayan and North American Indians held similar traditions.

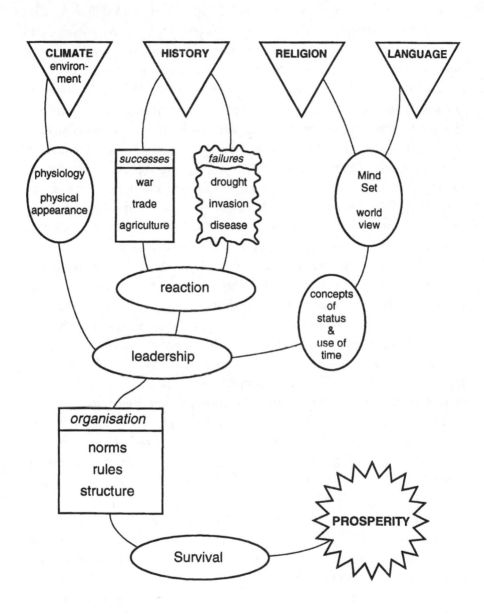

Figure 22   Factors leading to the organisation of society

In the business world, a series of individuals have also demonstrated outstanding abilities and success in leadership – Ford, Rockefeller, Agnelli, Berlusconi, Barnevik, Gyllenhammer, Iacocca, Geneen, Matsushita and Morita are some of them. It is now common for leadership and authority also to be vested in boards of directors or management committees.

The way in which a cultural group goes about structuring its commercial and industrial enterprises or other types of organisations usually reflects to a considerable degree the manner in which it itself is organised. The basic questions to be answered are how authority is organised; and what authority is based on. Western and eastern answers to these questions vary enormously, but in the West alone there are striking differences in attitude. There is, for instance, precious little similarity in the organisational patterns of French and Swedish companies, while Germans and Australians have almost diametrically opposing views as to the basis of authority.

Organisations are usually created by leaders, whether the leadership is despotic, individual or collective. Leadership functions in two modes – one of **networking** and one of **task orientation**. In network mode the concerns, in order of appearance, are the status of the leader(s), the chain of command, the management style, the motivation of the employees and the language of management used to achieve this. In task-orientation mode, the leadership must tackle issues, formulate strategies, create some form of work ethic, decide on efficiency, task distribution and use of time.

Managers in linear-active cultures will demonstrate and look for technical competence, place facts before sentiment, logic before emotion; they will be deal oriented, focusing their own attention and that of their staff on immediate achievement and results. They are orderly, stick to agendas and inspire with their careful planning.

Multi-active managers are much more extrovert, rely on their eloquence and ability to persuade, use human force as an inspirational factor. They often complete human transactions emotionally, assigning the time this may take – developing the contact to the limit.

Leaders in reactive cultures are equally people oriented, but dominate with knowledge, patience and quiet control. They display modesty and courtesy, despite their accepted seniority. They excel in creating a harmonious atmosphere for teamwork. Subtle body language obviates the need for an abundance of words. They know their company well (having spent years going round the various departments): this gives them balance – the ability to react to a web of pressures. They are paternalistic.

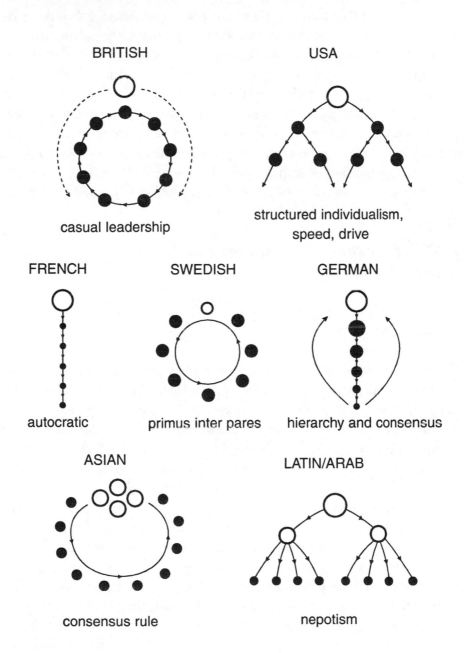

Figure 23   Leadership styles

Because of the diverse values and core beliefs of different societies, concepts of leadership and organisation are inevitably culture bound. Authority might be based on achievement, wealth, education, charisma or birthright. Corporations may be structured in a vertical, horizontal or matrix fashion and may be moulded according to religious, philosophical or governmental considerations and requirements. No two cultures view the essence of authority, hierarchy or optimum structure in an identical light. International exposure and experience will suggest a series of norms, rationalisations and patterns; these will invariably be eroded, even in the short run, by unswerving local beliefs about human values and interaction.

Different concepts of status, leadership and organisation

GERMANY

Germans believe in a world governed by *Ordnung*, where everything and everyone has a place in a grand design calculated to produce maximum efficiency. It is difficult for the impulsive Spaniard, the improvising Portuguese or the soulful Russian to conceive of German *Ordnung* in all its tidiness and symmetry. It is essentially a German concept which goes further in its theoretical perfection than even the pragmatic and orderly intent of Americans, British, Dutch and Scandinavians.

Germans, just as they believe in simple, scientific truth, believe that true *Ordnung* is achievable, provided that sufficient rules, regulations and procedures are firmly in place. In the business world, established, well-tried procedures have emerged from the long experience of Germany's older companies and conglomerates, guided by the maturity of tested senior executives. In Germany, more than anywhere else, there is no substitute for experience. Seniors pass on their knowledge to people immediately below them. There is a clear chain of command in each department and information and instructions are passed down from the top. Status of managers is based partly on achievement, but this is seen as interwoven with the length of service and ascribed wisdom of the individual, as well as formal qualifications and depth of education.

Hierarchy and consensus

German management is, however, not exclusively autocratic. While the vertical structure in each department is clear, considerable value is placed on consensus. German striving for perfection of systems carries with it the implication that the manager who vigorously applies and monitors these processes is showing faith in a framework which has proved successful for all. Few junior employees would question the rules. As there is adequate protection in German law for dissenting staff, most Germans feel comfortable in a rather tight framework which would irritate Americans and British. Germans welcome close instruction: they know where they stand and what they are expected to do. They enjoy being told twice, or three or four times.

German managers, issuing orders, can motivate by showing solidarity with their staff in following procedures. They work long hours, obey the rules themselves and, although they generally expect immediate obedience, they insist on fair play.

In task-orientation mode, German basic values dominate strategies. The use of time resembles the American: meetings begin on the dot, appointments are strictly observed, late arrivals must be signalled by telephone calls in advance, time is linear and should not be wasted. The work ethic is taken for granted and although staff working hours are not overlong and holidays are frequent, the German obsession with completing action chains means that projects are usually completed within the assigned period. Each department is responsible for its own tasks and there is far less horizontal communication between equals across the divisions of a German company than there is in US and British firms. Secrecy is respected in Germany both in business and private. Few German companies publish their figures for public consumption or even for the benefit of their own employees.

Working with Germans

Latins and some Anglo-Saxons frequently experience some difficulty in working or dealing with Germans on account of the relatively rigid framework of procedures within which many German companies operate.

Cooperating successfully with Germans means respecting their primary values. First, status must be established according to **their** standards.

Efficiency and results will win the day in due course, but a foreign national must have adequate formal qualifications to make an initial impression. The German manager with a university degree is promoted on an average every four years and those possessing doctorates have a career path to top management. Punctuality and orderliness are basic. Get there first, avoid sloppiness or untidiness in appearance, behaviour and thought. Procedures should always be written down, for Germans read them, and so should you. While familiarising yourself thoroughly with the rules and processes of the organisation, any instructions you yourself issue should be firm and unambiguous. If you want something written in black ink, not blue, then you should make this clear. Germans want content, detail and clarity – they hate misunderstandings.

It is advisable to strive for consensus at all times, although no one is going to chop and change. Consensus is obtained by clarification and justification, not by persuasion or truly open discussion. Consensus taking creates solidarity, which makes everyone feel comfortable. Each participant in the discussion makes a contribution, but does not query a superior too energetically and certainly does not question their judgement.

Hierarchical constraints necessitate your knowing the exact pecking order in the chain of command; you should also know **your** rung. Superiors generally address subordinates in a low voice, contrary to what many non-Germans believe. German directness enables you to point out when something is being done in an incorrect manner or when mistakes are being made. If the criticism is clearly constructive or designed to help, it will usually be accepted readily. If you are too subtle in your criticism, it may not register at all.

Subordinates in difficulties should be supervised, helped, advised, instructed, monitored. If no help is asked for, or probably not required, then tasks should not be interrupted. Quiet single-mindedness is admired in Germany, so don't try to do six things at once. Don't leave anything unfinished. If you are working hard, **show** it; a casual approach will be misunderstood.

Finally, communication is vertical, not horizontal. Don't go **across** the company to chat with people at your level in other departments. Most of your business ideas should be communicated to either your immediate superior or immediate subordinate. You do **not** have the ear of the chairman, however benignly he may smile at you – unless you are vice-chairman.

FRANCE

French management style is more autocratic than German, although this is not always evident at first glance. German companies are highly structured with clearly visible hierarchies, but these are normally readily accepted and welcomed by the staff. In France the boss often seems to have a more roving role, using '*tu*' to subordinates and often patting them on the back. Such behaviour is, however, quite deceptive, as is the frequent donning of overalls by Japanese company presidents when they visit the factory floor.

Oratorical style

The French chief executive's status is attributed on grounds of family, age, education and professional qualifications, with the emphasis on oratorical ability and mastery of the French language. Preferably he was 'finished' at the *Ecole normale supérieure* – an élitist establishment way ahead in prestige of any French university. French managers can well be described as élitist themselves – all-round *cadres* who are familiar with all or most of the aspects of their business or company, able to deal with production, organisational procedures, meetings, marketing, personnel matters and accounting systems as the occasion requires. They have less specialisation than US or British managers, but generally have wider horizons and an impressive grasp of the many issues facing their company.

The French leader

French history has spawned great leaders who have often enjoyed (frequently with little justification) the confidence of the nation. Napoleon and Pétain are remembered for their heroics rather than for their disasters; Louis XIV, Joan of Arc, Charles de Gaulle, André Malraux were charismatic figures who excited the French penchant for *panache* and smashed the mediocrity and mundanity that surrounded them. Ultimate success in French culture is less important than the collective soaring of the national pulse – the thrill of the chase or crusade. French failures are always glorious ones (check with Napoleon Bonaparte).

While mistakes by German executives are not easily forgiven and American managers are summarily fired if they lose money, there is a high tolerance in French companies of blunders on the part of management. As management is highly personalised, it falls on the manager to make many decisions on a daily basis and it is expected that a good proportion of them will be incorrect. The humanistic leanings of French and other Latin-based cultures encourage the view that human error must be anticipated and allowed for. *Cadres* assume responsibility for their decisions, which they made individually, but it is unlikely that they will be expected to resign if these backfire. If they are of the right age and experience and possess impeccable professional qualifications, replacing them would not only be futile, but would point a dagger at the heart of the system. For the French, attainment of immediate objectives is secondary to the ascribed reputation of the organisation and its sociopolitical goals. The highly organic nature of a French enterprise implies interdependence, mutual tolerance and teamwork among its members as well as demonstrated faith in the (carefully) appointed leader. French managers, who 'relish the art of commanding', are encouraged to excel in their work by the very intensity of expectation on the part of their subordinates.

Role in society

Such expectation produces a paternalistic attitude among French managers not unlike that demonstrated by Japanese, Malaysian and other Asian executives. In the case of the French, emotion is a factor and managers or department heads will concern themselves with the personal and private problems of their staff. In addition to their commercial role in the company, French managers see themselves as valued leaders in society. Indeed, *cadres* see themselves as contributing to the well-being of the state itself. Among the largest economies of the world, only Japan exercises more governmental control over business than the French. French protectionism dates back to the seventeenth century, when increased trade and exports were seen as a natural consequence of French military successes. Modern French companies such as Rhône Poulenc, Aérospatiale, Dassault, Elf Aquitaine, Framatome, Renault and Peugeot are seen as symbols of French grandeur and are 'looked after' by the state. A similar situation exists in Japan and to some extent Sweden.

The prestige and exalted position enjoyed by the French manager is not without its drawbacks both for the enterprise and for the national economy. By concentrating authority around the chief executive, opinions of experienced middle managers and technical staff (often close to customers and markets) do not always carry the weight that they would in Anglo-Saxon or Scandinavian companies. It is true that French managers debate issues at length with their staff, often examining all aspects in great detail. The decision, however, is usually made alone and not always on the basis of the evidence. If the chief executive's views are known in advance, it is not easy to reverse them. Furthermore, senior managers are less interested in the bottom line than in the perpetuation of their power and influence in the company and in society. Again, their contacts and relationships at highest levels may transcend the implications of any particular transaction. A Swedish executive I interviewed who had worked for a French company was appalled by the secrecy of motivation maintained by French senior executives. Information was not allowed to filter down below certain levels. In Sweden authority is delegated downwards as much as possible. In high context France, managers expect that their staff will know what to do – the logic will be evident.

BRITAIN

The feudal as well as imperial origins of status and leadership in England are still evident in some aspects of British management. A century has passed since Britain occupied a preeminent position in industry and commerce, but there still lingers in the national consciousness the proud recollection of once having ruled 15 million square miles of territory on five continents. The best young men were sent abroad on overseas postings to gain experience and to be groomed for leadership. It was the English, Scots and Irish who provided the main thrust of society in the USA – the power which was to assume the mantle of economic hegemony.

The class system persists in the UK and status is still derived, in some degree, from pedigree, title and family name. There is little doubt that the system is on its way to becoming a meritocracy – the emergence of a very large middle class and the efforts of the left and centrist politicians will eventually align British egalitarianism with that of the US and Northern Europe – but it is worth noting that many characteristics of British management hark back to earlier days.

British managers could be described as diplomatic, tactful, laid back, casual, reasonable, helpful, willing to compromise and seeking to be fair. They also consider themselves to be inventive and, on occasion, lateral thinkers. They see themselves as conducting business with grace, style, humour, wit, eloquence and self-possession. They have the English fondness for debate and regard meetings as occasions to seek agreement rather than to issue instructions.

Toughness and insularity

There is a veneer to British management style which hardly exists in such countries as Canada, Australia, Germany, Finland and the USA. Under the casual refinement and sophistication of approach exists a hard streak of pragmatism and mercenary intent. When the occasion warrants it, British managers can be as resilient and ruthless as their tough American cousins, but less explicitly and with disarming poise. Subordinates appreciate their willingness to debate and tendency to compromise, but also anticipate a certain amount of deviousness and dissimulation. Codes of behaviour within a British company equip staff to absorb and cope with a rather obscure management style. Other problems arise when British senior executives deal with European, American and Eastern businesspeople. In spite of their penchant for friendliness, hospitality and desire to be fair, British managers' adherence to tradition endows them with an insular obstinacy resulting in a failure to comprehend differing values in others.

Linguistic arrogance

At international meetings British delegates frequently distinguish themselves by their poise, charm and eloquence, but often leave the scene having learned little or nothing from their more successful trading partners. As such conferences are usually held in English, they easily win the war of words; this unfortunately increases their linguistic arrogance. One huge German insurance firm bought a sizeable British firm lock, stock and barrel. The top and middle executives of the German company were nearly all fluent in English, but advised the managers of the British company to acquire a modicum of German to use in social situations. This was issued in the form of a directive. Two years later none of the senior staff of the British firm had taken a single German lesson.

I recently gave a series of cross-cultural seminars to executives of an English car group which had been taken over by a German auto industry giant. The Germans attending the seminars, although occasionally struggling with terminology, listened eagerly to the remarks about British psychology and cultural habits. The British participants, with one or two notable exceptions, paid only casual attention to the description of German characteristics, took hardly any notes, were unduly flippant about Germany's role in Europe and thought the population and GDP of the two countries were roughly equal! Only one of the British spoke German and that at a very modest level.

Calm approach to tasks

As far as task orientation is concerned, British managers perform better. They are not sticklers for punctuality, but time wasting is not endemic in British companies and staff take pride in completing tasks thoroughly, although in their own time frame. British managers like to leave at five or six, as do their subordinates, but work is often taken home. As for strategies, managers generally achieve a balance between short- and long-term planning. Interim failures are not unduly frowned on and there are few pressures to make a quick buck. Teamwork is encouraged and often achieved, although it is understood that individual competition may be fierce. It is not unusual for managers to have 'direct lines' to staff members, especially those whom they favour or consider intelligent and progressive. Chains of command are observed less than in German and French companies. The organisation subscribes in general to the Protestant work ethic, but this must be observed against a background of smooth, unhurried functions and traditional self-confidence. The contrast with the immediacy and driving force of American management is quite striking when one considers the commonality of language and heritage as well as the Anglo-Celtic roots of US business.

AMERICA

The Puritan work ethic and the right to dissent dominated the mentality of the early American settlers. It was an Anglo-Saxon-Celtic, Northern European culture, but the very nature and hugeness of the terrain, along with the advent of independence, soon led to the 'frontier spirit' which has characterized the US mindset since the end of the eighteenth century.

The vast lands of America were an entrepreneur's dream. Unlimited expanses of wilderness signified unlimited wealth which could be exploited, if one moved quickly enough, without taking it away from others. Only Siberia has offered a similar challenge in modern times.

The nature of the challenge soon produced American values: speed was of the essence; you acted individually and in your own interest; the wilderness forced you to be self-reliant, tough, risk taking; you did not easily cede what you had claimed and owned; you needed to be aggressive against foreign neighbours; anyone with talent and initiative could get ahead; if you suffered a setback, it was not ultimate failure, there was always more land or opportunity; bonds broken with the past meant that future orientation was all important; you were optimistic about change, for the past had brought little reward; throwing off the yoke of the King of England led to a distrust of supreme authority.

American managers symbolise the vitality and audacity of the land of free enterprise. In most cases they retain the frontier spirit: they are assertive, aggressive, goal and action oriented, confident, vigorous, optimistic, ready for change, achievers used to hard work, instant mobility and making decisions. They are capable of teamwork and corporate spirit, but they value individual freedom above the welfare of the company and their first interest is furthering their own career.

Dollar status

In view of their rebellious beginnings, Americans are reluctant to accord social status to anyone for reasons other than visible achievement. In a land with no traditions of (indeed aversion to) aristocracy, money was seen as the yardstick of progress and very few Americans distance themselves from the pursuit of wealth. Intellectuality and refinement as qualities of leadership are prized less in the USA than in Europe. Leadership means getting things done, improving the standard of living, finding short cuts to prosperity, making money for oneself, one's firm and its shareholders.

With status accorded almost exclusively on grounds of achievement and vitality, age and seniority assume less importance. American managers are often young, female or both. Chief executives are given responsibility and authority and then expected to act. They seldom fail to do so. How long they retain power depends on the results they achieve.

Motivation of American managers and their staff does not have the labyrinthine connotations that it does in European and Oriental companies, for it is usually monetary. Bonuses, performance payments, profit-sharing schemes and stock options are common. New staff, however, are often motivated by the very challenge of getting ahead. Problem-solving, the thrill of competition and the chance to demonstrate resolute action satisfy the aspirations of many young Americans. Unlike Europeans and Orientals, however, they need constant feedback, encouragement and praise from the senior executive.

Strict procedures

In terms of organisation, the rampant individualism in American society is strictly controlled in business life through strict procedures and paperwork. American executives are allowed to make individual decisions, especially when travelling abroad, but usually within the framework of corporate restrictions. Young Americans' need for continual appraisal means that they are constantly supervised. In German companies staff are regularly monitored, but German seniors do not hover. In the USA senior executives pop in and out of offices, sharing information and inspiration with their subordinates ('Say, Jack, I've just had a terrific idea'). Memos, directives, suggestions in writing are ubiquitous. Shareholder pressure makes quarterly reporting and rolling forecasts imperative. The focus is on the bottom line.

Americans can be quickly hired and just as rapidly fired (often without compensation). Being sacked carries no stigma, ('It just didn't work out, we have to let you go'). For the talented, other jobs and companies beckon. There is precious little sentimentality in American business. The deal comes before personal feeling. If the figures are right you can deal with the Devil. If there is no profit, a transaction with a friend is hardly worthwhile. Business is based on punctuality, solid figures, proven techniques, pragmatic reasoning and technical competence. Time is money and Americans show impatience during meetings if Europeans get bogged down in details or when Orientals demur in showing their hand.

Europeans, by contrast, are often miffed by American informality and what they consider to be an oversimplistic approach towards exclusively material goals. Eastern cultures are wary of the litigious nature of American business. Two-thirds of the lawyers on earth are American – a formidable deterrent for members of those societies who settle disputes out of court and believe in long-term harmony with their business partners.

SWEDEN

The Swedish concept of leadership and management differs considerably from other European models and is dealt with in some detail in Chapter 20. Like Swedish society itself, enterprises are essentially 'democratic', although a large percentage of Swedish capital is in private hands. Managers of thousands of middle-sized and even large firms have attained managerial success through subtle self-effacement, but the big multinationals have also thrown up some famous executives who might well claim to be among the most far-seeing business leaders in the world: Carstedt, Gyllenhammar, Wennergren, Barnevik, Carlzon, Wallenberg, Svedberg.

Modern Swedish egalitarianism has age-old cultural roots. Although some historical Swedish monarchs such as Gustav av Vasa and Charles the Great were dominating, compelling figures, the Swedish royals, like those of Denmark and Norway, have espoused democratic principles for many centuries, no doubt mindful of the old Viking *lagom* tradition when warriors passed round the drinking horn (or huge bowl) in a circle where each man had to decide what amount to drink. Not too little to arouse scorn; not too much to deprive others of the liquid.

LATINS

The business cultures of Italy, Spain and Portugal are described in later chapters. In Latin Europe, as well as in South America, the management pattern generally follows that of France, where authority is centred around the chief executive. In middle-sized companies, the CEO is very often the owner of the enterprise and even in very large firms a family name or connections may dominate the structure. More than in France, sons, nephews, cousins and close family friends will figure prominently in key positions. Ubiquitous nepotism means that business partners are often confronted with younger people who seem to have considerable influence on decision making. Delegations may often consist of the company owner, flanked by his brother, son, cousin or even grandson. Women are generally, although not always, excluded from negotiating sessions.

Status is based on age, reputation and often wealth. The management style is autocratic, particularly in Portugal, Spain and South America, where family money is often on the line. There is a growing meritocracy in Brazil, Chile and in the big northern Italian industrial firms, but Latin employees in general indicate willing and trusting subservience to their 'establishments'.

Task orientation is dictated from above, strategies and success depend largely on social and ministerial connections and mutually beneficial cooperation between dominant families. Knowing the right people oils the wheels of commerce in Latin countries, just as it does in Arab and oriental cultures. It helps anywhere, but assumes greater importance in those societies which prioritise the nurturing of human relationships over pragmatic, rapid implementation of transactions based on mere notions of opportunity, technical feasibility and profit.

THE EAST

Cultural values dominate the structure, organisation and behaviour of eastern enterprises more than is the case in the West, in as much as deeply-rooted religious and philosophical beliefs impose near-irresistible codes of conduct. In the Chinese sphere of influence (People's Republic of China, Taiwan, Hong Kong, Singapore) as well as in Japan and Korea, Confucian principles hold sway. Thailand is Buddhist, Indonesia and Malaysia strongly Moslem. Although national differences account for variations in the concepts of status, leadership and organisation, there is a clearly discernible 'eastern model' which is compatible with general Asian values.

This model, whether applied to corporations or departments of civil service or government, strongly resembles family structure. Confucianism, which took final shape in China in the twelfth century, designated family as the prototype of all social organisation. We are members of a group, not individuals. Stability of society is based on unequal relationships between people, as in a family. The hierarchies are father–son, older brother–younger brother, male–female, ruler–subject, senior friend–junior friend. Loyalty to the ruler, filial piety to one's father, right living, would lead to a harmonious social order based on strict ethical rules and headed up in a unified state, governed by men of education and superior ethical wisdom. Virtuous behaviour, protection of the weak, moderation, calmness and thrift were also prescribed.

Confucianism entered Japan with the first great wave of Chinese influence between the sixth and ninth centuries AD. For some time it was over-shadowed by Buddhism, but the emergence of the centralized Tokugawa system in the seventeenth century made it more relevant than it had been before. Both Japan and Korea had become thoroughly Confucian by the early nineteenth century in spite of their feudal political systems. In the twentieth century Japanese have wholeheartedly accepted modern science, universalistic principles of ethics, as well as democratic ideals, but they are still permeated, as are the Koreans, with Confucian ethical values. While focusing on progress and growth, strong Confucian traits still lurk beneath the surface, such as the belief in the moral basis of government, the emphasis on interpersonal relationships and loyalties, the faith in education and hard work. Few Japanese and Koreans consider themselves Confucianists today, but in a sense almost all of them are.

Confucianism in business

What do these cultural influences mean in terms of status and leadership? The Chinese ideal was rule by men of superior education and morality rather than by those merely of superior birth. Japanese and Korean business leaders today flaunt qualifications, university and professorial connections more than family name or wealth. Many of the traditional Japanese companies are classic models of Confucian theory, where paternalistic attitudes to employees and their dependants, top-down obligations, bottom-up loyalty, obedience and blind faith are observed to a greater degree than in China itself. Prosperity makes it easier to put Confucianism into practice: in this regard Japan has enjoyed certain advantages over other countries. The sacred nature of the group and the benevolence attributed to its leaders, however, permeate Asian concepts of organisation from Rangoon to Tokyo.

Buddhist and Islamic variations

In Buddhist Thailand and Islamic Malaysia and Indonesia, slight variations in the concept of leadership do little to challenge the idea of benign authority. Thais see a strict hierarchy with the King at its apex, but there is social mobility in Thailand, where several monarchs had humble origins. The patronage system requires complete obedience, but flexibility is assured by the Thai principle that leaders must be sensitive to the problems of their subordinates and that blame must always be passed upwards. Bosses treat their inferiors in an informal manner and give them time off when domestic pressures weigh heavily. Subordinates like the hierarchy.

Buddhism decrees that the man at the top earned his place by meritorious performance in a previous life. In Malaysia and Indonesia status is **inherited**, not earned, but leaders are expected to be paternal, religious, sincere and above all gentle. The Malay seeks a definite role in the hierarchy and neither Malaysians nor Indonesians strive for self-betterment. Promotion must be initiated **from above**; better conformity and obedience than struggling for change. Age and seniority will bring progress.

Life in a group

Although Confucianism, Buddhism and Islam differ greatly in many respects, their adherents see eye to eye in terms of the family nature of the group, the non-competitive according of status, the smooth dispersal of power, the automatic chain of command and the collective nature of decision making. There are variations on this theme, such as the preponderance of influence among certain families in Korea, governmental intervention in China, the tight rein on the media in Singapore and fierce competition and individualism among the entrepreneurs of Hong Kong. Typical Asians, however, acknowledge that they live in a high context culture within a vital circle of associations from which withdrawal would be unthinkable. Their behaviour, both social and professional, is contextualised at all times, whether in the fulfilment of obligations and duties to the group (families, community, company, school friends) or taking refuge in its support and solidarity. They do not see this as a trade-off of autonomy for security, but rather as a fundamental, correct way of living and interacting in a highly developed social context.

In a hierarchical, family-type company, networking is relatively effortless. Motivation is the enhancement of the reputation and prestige of the group, which will result in greater protection and support for its members. Managers guide subordinates to achieve these goals and work longer hours as a shining example. As far as task orientation is concerned, immediate objectives are not as clearly expressed as they would be in, for example, an American company. Long-term considerations take priority and the slow development of personal relationships, both internally and with customers, often blur real aims and intent. Asian staff seem to understand perfectly the long-term objectives without having to have them spelled out explicitly. In Japan, particularly, staff seem to benefit from a form of corporate telepathy – a consequence of the homogeneous nature of the people.

What is work?

The work ethic is taken for granted in Japan, Korea and the Chinese areas, but this is not the case throughout Asia. Malaysians and Indonesians see 'work' as only one of many activities which contribute to the progress and welfare of the group. Time spent (during working hours) at lunch, on the beach or playing sport may be beneficial in deepening relationships between colleagues or clients. Time may be needed to draw on the advice of a valued mentor or to see to some pressing family matter which was distracting an employee from properly performing their duties. Gossip in the office is a form of networking and interaction. Work and play are mixed both in and out of the office in Thailand, where either activity must produce fun (*sanuke*) or it is not worth pursuing. Thais, like Russians, tend to work in fits and starts, depending partly on the proximity of authority and partly on their mood. Koreans – all hustle and bustle when compared to the methodic Japanese – like to be seen to be busy all day long and of all Asians most resemble the Americans in their competitive vigour.

Asian management, when organising activity, attaches tremendous importance to form, symbolism and gesture. The showing of respect, in speech and actions, is mandatory. There must be no loss of face either for oneself or one's opponent and as far as business partners are concerned, red carpet treatment, including lavish entertaining and gift giving, is imperative. Ultimate victory in business deals is the objective, but one must have the patience to achieve this in the right time frame and in the correct manner. This attitude is more deeply rooted among the Chinese and Japanese than in Korea, where wheeling and dealing is frequently indulged in.

Is the Asian, 'family model' efficient? The economic success of Japan and the rates of growth in China, Korea, Malaysia and Taiwan, among others, would indicate that it is. Whatever the reality may be, it would not be easy for westerners to convert to Asiatic systems. Individualism, democratic ideals, material goals, compulsive consumerism, penchant for speed, environmental concerns and a growing obsession with the quality of life (a strange concept in Asia) are powerful, irreversible factors to be reckoned with in North America and Northern Europe. The globalisation process and the increasing determination of the multinational and transnational giants to standardise procedures will result in some convergence of aims, concepts and organisational structure, but divergence in values and world view will sustain organisational diversity well into the twenty-first century.

6

HORIZONS AND TEAM BUILDING

Life within horizons

OUR GENES, OUR PARENTAL AND EDUCATIONAL TRAINING, OUR SOCIETAL rules, our very language, enable us to see so far. Any human being can see as far as their horizon, and that is the limit. We can broaden our horizon to some degree by living in other countries, learning foreign languages, reading books on philosophy, psychology, alien cultures and a variety of other subjects. Unless we make such efforts, our horizon remains a British horizon, an American horizon, a Japanese horizon or one of many other world views. In other words, each culture enjoys a certain segment of experience, which is no more than a fraction of the total possible available experience. Benjamin Whorf believed that such segments of experience were limited by the vocabulary and concepts inherent in one's language. By learning more languages, especially those with excitingly different concepts, one could widen one's vision and gain deeper insight into the nature of reality. Many graduates in Romance studies feel enriched by being able to see the world through Spanish eyes or using French rationality. Scholars of Chinese or Japanese often develop two personalities when immersing themselves in one of these two languages.

Multicultural people strive towards 'totality of experience' (impossible to achieve in a lifetime) not only by learning foreign tongues, but by cultivating empathy with the views of others, standing in their shoes in their

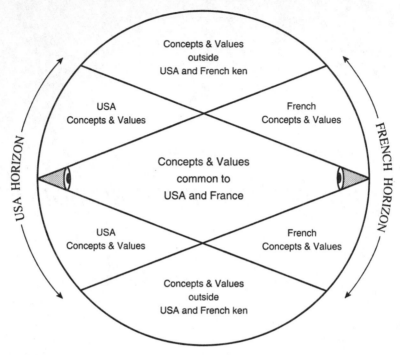

Figure 24

geographical, historical and philosophical location, seeing themselves from that location. But for the moment we live within our limited horizons. Figures 24 and 25 show how Americans and French people look at the world from different standpoints, see some things in a similar light (science, profit, consumerism) while other concepts are visible only to one nationality. A third area, containing a variety of beliefs and philosophies, lies outside the ken of either Americans or French.

Figure 26 shows how two nationalities speaking different languages miss out on several linguistically based concepts. Figure 27 indicates how two cultures united by the same language (England and the USA) are developing different horizons in the twentieth century, where concepts such as subtlety and understatement are invisible to many Americans and 'tough talk', clichés or a certain variety of hype meaningless to most English. In the case of Brits and Yanks, however, the overlapping areas of common experience still dominate the thinking. This is far from being the case with the Americans and Japanese or even neighbours like the Poles and Germans.

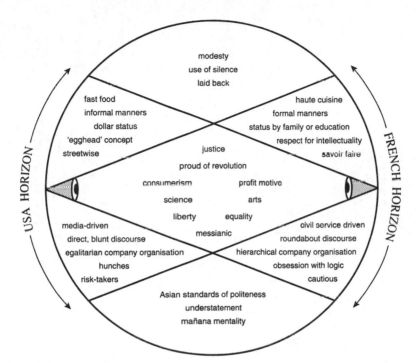

Figure 25

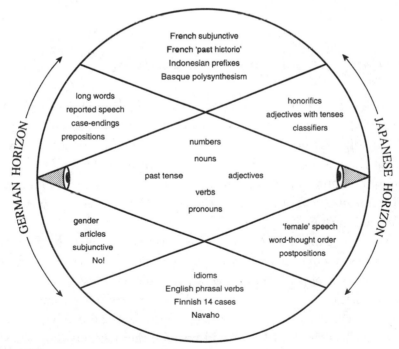

Figure 26

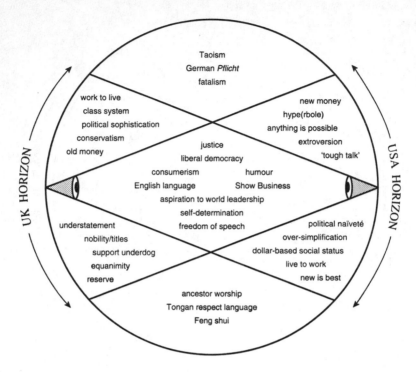

Taoism
German *Pflicht*
fatalism

work to live
class system
political sophistication
conservatism
old money

justice
liberal democracy
consumerism
English language
aspiration to world leadership
self-determination
freedom of speech

new money
hype(rbole)
anything is possible
extroversion
'tough talk'

humour
Show Business

understatement
nobility/titles
support underdog
equanimity
reserve

political naïveté
over-simplification
dollar-based social status
live to work
new is best

ancestor worship
Tongan respect language
Feng shui

UK HORIZON

USA HORIZON

Figure 27

Managing the horizons – teambuilding

As business is increasingly internationalised and globalised, the problem of coordinating individuals or groups who hold quite different world views is constantly highlighted. Teambuilding has long been a subject of study on management courses, even when members were generally from one country or culture; now international teams are with us for good. No multinational company can afford to ignore their special character or neglect their training and nurture.

Many joint ventures get off to a flying start, as the injection of new capital and the synergy emanating from the merging of two layers of experience produce a euphoric honeymoon between the partners. When business is smooth, national 'idiosyncrasies' rarely assume significant importance. Should, however, money or customers be lost, local cultures will quickly retire to their entrenched beliefs and criticise the methods and values of others.

The education factor

We live in an era of improved education and training, but education systems vary considerably from country to country, both as to content and objectives. The French all-round senior manager, carefully groomed in wideranging skills in the *hautes écoles*, views the vocationally trained manager from a German *Volkswirtschaftshochschule* as a highly competent technician. Practical Japanese engineers wonder why their French counterparts evince no inclination to change tyres or fix malfunctioning TV sets. The German *Diplom-Kaufmann* may wonder why his British opposite number seems to have no official qualifications in commerce. Action-oriented American managers, many of whom climbed from the bottom rung of the corporate ladder to the very top through sheer ability, energy and aggressive ambition, may set no store by diplomas of any kind.

Even if all the members of a team have had a 'good' university education, there is no guarantee that this will facilitate international understanding. While universities have revolutionised their teaching of science, mathematics, engineering and medicine over the past two or three decades, there has been little new introduced in the study of social sciences. Only those graduates in foreign languages, literature, philosophy or history are in some ways equipped to interact in a more meaningful way with foreign nationals, and few of these graduates end up in international business.

Language and culture

How can we set about achieving a relatively harmonious and integrated international team? To begin with, one should face the fact that to understand what makes foreign colleagues tick, there is no substitute for learning their language, reading books produced by the culture and familiarising oneself with the country's basic history. This means a sizeable investment not so much in financial terms as in time. To achieve modest fluency in a European language, 250–500 hours of direct teaching will be required, preferably over a three-month period. This should include an intensive course of two to three weeks of full-time (minimum 40 hours) tuition. Japanese, Chinese, Arabic and Russian (to name four other major languages) will require almost double the time. By contrast, study of the country's basic history and main cultural traits could be comfortably dealt with in two or three weeks and done simultaneously with the language training.

Companies which discount the importance of such training do so at their peril. A malfunctioning joint venture with a foreign partner can result in catastrophic financial loss. One large, traditional British company (turnover several hundred million pounds) branched out in three European countries five years ago without giving sufficient attention to cultural diversity. The initial investment was around £10 million. Probably language and cultural training as outlined above for 20 key executives would have cost in the region of £200,000. In 1994 in one European branch alone the British company incurred losses of £100 million. Yet the subsidiary in question was showing a profit at the time of its acquisition!

What had happened? The British parent – vastly successful in the UK – had moved quickly to mushroom the size and scope of the branch operation, applying strategies and policies which had many years of proven success in the UK. Most of the new products and the general monolithic approach found little favour in the local culture. The problems were spotlighted by the local managers who offered polite, guarded criticism and advice. The British, although reasonable, bulldozed on in the firm belief that their name, impressive home record and lengthy experience would carry the day. The locals, in retaliation for the snub, clammed up. The much-heralded synergy was lost.

Executives operating in an international framework must be given a training which will at least exempt them from the charge of complete ignorance of the culture of their colleagues. This implies language training, but also cognisance of some very basic facts about the country concerned, such as politics, history and geography, as well as elementary business behaviour.

Horizons, common ground, divergence

Members of an international team, once they are familiar with the national profile, should be advised as to the cultural traits of their partners. What do the French, German, Japanese see on their horizon? What is essentially (and perhaps irrevocably) different? What overlaps? There are areas of agreement between any two nationalities. Latins are generally considered difficult partners for the British yet Britons can find common ground with French, Spaniards and Italians, although that ground differs in each case.

UK / France	UK / Spain	UK / Italy
sense of superiority	love theatre, plots	flexible
messianic	support underdog	reasonable
long term	vague, 'muddle through'	exports to survive
conservative	humorous	diplomatic, tactful
interest in arts and science	distrust the French	love of art
ex-imperial	dignified	sociable, good at small talk
linguistic arrogance	individualists	uses first names
	poor linguists	compromisers
	out of European mainstream	

It is valuable to focus on common ground; divergences of approach merit no less attention. One's first step towards adaptation must at the very least be to avoid irritants. An Italian, however, well-disposed towards a Brit, finds little subtlety of humour in being reminded that the best-known Italian product is spaghetti. The English may weary of incessant French ramblings at meetings, but they risk hostility if they attempt to quash it as irrelevant. Spaniards, touchy about personal style, do not take kindly to British references to their unpunctuality or overt body language. Japanese and most Orientals should be treated with as much respect and deference as Anglo-Saxons can muster: a good performance will in any case only slightly mitigate their opinion of us as somewhat unsophisticated types. Disruption of harmony and protocol by Anglo-Saxon informality and wise-cracking does not mean that British and Americans are the only miscreants. Latins and Germans alike take liberties in judging Brits as slow-moving, old-fashioned amateurs with no linguistic skills, while Americans are often categorised as dollar-mad salespeople lacking dress sense, tact, finesse and any values other than material.

Building on strengths

Common sense, good breeding and a modicum of unhurried thought are all useful resources for avoiding behaviour which might prove irritable to our partners. If we accept that certain things are not going to disappear (American drive, German seriousness, French sense of superiority, Japanese opacity, Spanish tardiness, Italian deviousness, Norwegian obstinacy, Swiss secrecy, Russian sentiment, Arab passion) we may come to the realisation that these very traits can make a positive contribution to our team effort. For example, American enthusiasm harnessed by thorough German planning and supervision could be very effective. Spaniards are slow starters, but can be good finishers, often displaying stamina and verve in the hours leading up to midnight. Italians are generally good deal-makers, finding ways of 'making the business' when others may be too entrenched or even deadlocked. They are valuable, too, in handling other Latins. Managers in experienced multinationals like IBM, Unilever and ABB are skilled at using 'horses for courses'. Unilever recently needed a man to supervise their marketing operations in South America. A Brazilian or an Argentinian might have been resented in some of the smaller countries and certainly in each other's. They chose an Indian, who was given language and cross-cultural training. A keenly perceptive executive, not only did his nationality place him above inter-regional rivalry, but his Indian characteristics of people orientation, subtle negotiating skills and warmth made him someone Latin-Americans would easily relate to.

Teambuilding exercises

There is a wide variety of teambuilding exercises; multinational corporations have tried all of them. At business schools, budding MBAs work together on hundreds of case studies. Promising managers and key staff from different countries are assembled to go camping together, climb mountains, raft down rivers and cross deserts. A basic principle of most teambuilding exercises is that all members shall face some kind of difficulty together, help each other out according to individual ability and with the resources that are at hand. The environmental constraints of a tent, raft, yacht or classroom necessitate working closely together and avoiding needless friction. When the teams are international, interesting things occur. Individuals strive to put their personal skills at the service of the team – sometimes practical, sometimes inspirational, sometimes intuitive. Leaders emerge: different people take charge of provisioning, planning, direction taking, financing, logistics, social affairs, even cooking. A language of communication evolves, as do problem-solving routines. Even on a language course this spirit of cooperation emerges. Latins recognise long literary or scientific words in English easily, but have difficulty with pronunciation; Dutch and Scandinavians pronounce beautifully, but are short on Latin-based vocabulary. Swedes help Finns with unfamiliar prepositions. Germans struggle with English word order. Everyone learns from everyone else.

Back to cultural cooperation: working with someone at close quarters for a protracted period of time enables you not only to observe foreign patterns of behaviour but to perceive some of the reasoning behind them. You also have the opportunity to explain your own actions and concepts (perhaps eccentric for others) as you go along. The talkative Italian, possibly irritating at first, may prove to be the social adhesive holding the group together. The disconcertingly withdrawn, opaque Japanese, sitting quietly in the corner, may later remind the group of things they have forgotten. The hustling American gets everyone to the restaurant on time, the superior Frenchman gets you the right wine, the fussy German has a minibus and umbrellas waiting for you in the rain.

7

BRIDGING THE
COMMUNICATION GAP

Whatever the culture, there's a tongue in our head. Some use it, some hold it, some bite it. For the French it is a rapier, thrusting in attack; the English, using it defensively, mumble a vague, confusing reply; for Italians and Spaniards it is an instrument of eloquence; Finns and East Asians throw you with constructive silence. Silence is a form of speech, so don't interrupt it!

Use of language

ONE OF THE FACTORS LEADING TO POOR COMMUNICATION IS OFTEN overlooked: the nationals of each country use their language and speech in a different way. Language is a tool of communication, delivering a message – but it is much more than that, it has strengths and weaknesses which project national character and even philosophy.

How do the French use their language? Like a rapier. French is a quick, exact, logical language and the French fence with it, cutting, thrusting and parrying, using it for advantage, expecting counter thrusts, retorts, repartee and indeed the odd *touché* against them. French is a good tool for arguing and proving one's point. It is fair play for the French to manipulate their language, often at great speed, to bewilder and eventually corner their opponent, leaving the latter breathless and without reply.

The English use their language differently – to its best advantage, certainly, but they are not quick to attack with it. They will lean heavily on understatement and reservation; they will concede points to their opponent early on to take the steam out of the argument, but their tone implies that even so, right is on their side. They know how to be vague in order to maintain politeness or avoid confrontation, and they are adept at waffling when they wish to procrastinate or cloud an issue. (It is impossible to waffle in French, as each word has a precise meaning.) The English will use a quiet tone to score points, always attempting to remain low key. Scots or the Northern English may emphasise their accent in order to come across as genuine, sincere or warm-hearted, while the Southern English may use certain accents to indicate an influential background, a particular school, or good breeding.

Spaniards and Italians regard their languages as instruments of eloquence and they will go up and down the scale at will, pulling out every stop if need be, to achieve greater expressiveness. To convey their ideas fully they will ransack an extensive vocabulary, use their hands, arms and facial expressions and make maximum use of pitch and tone. They are not necessarily being dramatic or overemotional. They want you to know how they feel. They will appeal, directly and strongly, to your good sense, warm heart or generosity if they want something from you, and often you have to decide there and then whether to say yes or no.

Germans, like the French, rely to a large extent on logic, but tend to amass more evidence and labour their points more than either the British or the French. The French, having delivered their thrust, are quite prepared to be parried and then have their defence pierced by a superior counter thrust. Germans are not; they come in with heavier armour and have usually thought through the counter arguments. Often the best way to deal with a German is to find common ground and emphasise solidarity and reliability in cooperation. The splendid German language is heavy, cumbersome, logical, disciplined and has such momentum that it is invincible in any head-on collision with another language. But that momentum can be deflected by a sensitive negotiator and all parties can benefit.

Scandinavians are something else. In the long dark nights they have thought about matters well in advance and they list all the 'pros and cons' before giving you their conclusion, which they will justify. They will not abandon their decision easily for they believe they have proved their case, but on the other hand they do not ask for too much. Swedes wield their language in a democratic manner with only a modicum of personal deference and with great egalitarian informality. They cut out the niceties and get down to brass tacks. Finns are friendlier and more reticent, but with the same modern equal-footing approach. The Finnish language is much more eloquent and flowery than Swedish, Danish or Norwegian, but the bottom line is still drily factual, succinct and well thought out. You can use any kind of humour with a Finn, linguistic or otherwise. A Dane will go along with you for a while, especially if the joke is at the expense of the Swedes. Swedes will accept your humour if it doesn't affect their profit margin. Never tell jokes about Norway to Norwegians. They don't understand them.

American speech is quick, mobile and opportunistic, reflecting the speed and agility of the young USA. The wisecrack is basic to their discourse. American humour excels in quips, barbed retorts and repartee – short, sharp, smart-alec shafts, typical of the dog-eat-dog society of early America, where the old hands had all the clichés and the answers, and newly arrived immigrants had to learn to defend themselves quickly. Exaggeration and hyperbole are at the bottom of most American expressions, contrasting sharply with the understated nature of the British. In the early days of pioneering, when immigrants speaking many varieties of halting English were thrown together in simple, often primitive surroundings, plainness and unsophistication of language were at a premium. The well-worn cliché was more understandable than originality or elegance of expression. The American language has never recovered from the exigencies of this period. The ordinary man's speech tends to be 'tough talk', rather reminiscent of cowboy parlance or Chicago gangland speech of the 1920s. The nation's obsession with show business and the pervasive influence of Hollywood have accentuated and, to some extent, perpetuated this trend. To make a start is to get the show on the road, to take a risk in a business venture is to fly by the seat of your pants, lawyers are shysters, accountants are bean counters, and, if you have no choice, it's the only game in town.

The Japanese use language in a completely different way from the rest of us. What is actually said has no meaning or significance whatsoever. Japanese use their language as a tool of communication, but the words and sentences themselves give no indication of what they are saying. What they want and how they feel are indicated by the way they address their conversation partner. Smiles, pauses, sighs, grunts, nods and eye movements convey everything. The Japanese leave their fellow Japanese knowing perfectly well what has been agreed, no matter what was said. Foreigners leave the Japanese with a completely different idea. Usually they think that everything has gone swimmingly, as the Japanese would never offend them by saying anything negative or unpleasant.

In English, French and a good number of languages, people often aspire to elegantly polite discourse in order to show respect to their interlocutor. This process is carried on to a much greater degree in Japanese, where standards of politeness are much higher than in the USA or Europe. On all ceremonial occasions, and these may include formal business meetings, a whole sequence of expressions is used which bears little or no relation to the actual sentiments of the individuals present. The language is instead aimed at conveying the long-term relationships which are envisaged and the depth of expectation that each participant has.

When these Japanese thoughts are translated, other nationalities tend to look at the content rather than the mood. Consequently, all they hear is platitudes or, even more suspicious, flattery. There is no doubt that most Japanese businessmen in England and the US are often successful at conveying the idea that they are very agreeable people to deal with. Later, toughness in negotiating appears and seems to contradict the early pleasantries. When at each meeting hosted by the Japanese they go through the ritual of thanking the visitors for giving up their valuable time and for suffering the prevailing weather conditions, Anglo-Saxons in particular feel uncomfortable about the sincerity of their hosts. The Japanese, however, are simply being courteous and caring.

The phenomenon of the different effects caused by national tongues has been noticed throughout the centuries. Charles V of Spain said he thought German could be spoken to soldiers, English to horses, Italian to women and Spanish to God. Vincenzo Spinelli remarked that while Italian is sung, Spanish is declaimed, French is danced and only Portuguese is really spoken.

The whole question of people using different speech styles and wielding their language in the national manner inevitably leads to misunderstanding not only of expression, but intent. Japanese or English may distrust Italians because they wave their hands about, or Spaniards because they sound emotional or prone to exaggeration. The French may appear offensive because of their directness or frequent use of cynicism. No one may really know what Japanese or Finns were thinking or what they actually said, if they said anything at all. Germans may take the English too literally and completely miss nuances of humour, understatement or irony. Northern peoples may simply consider that Latins speak too fast to be relied on. Languages are indeed spoken at different speeds. Hawaiian and some Polynesian languages barely cover 100 syllables per minute, while English has been measured at 200, German at 250, Japanese at 310 and French at 350 syllables per minute.

The communication gap

We have, therefore, a variety of cultures using speech not only according to the strictures imposed by grammar vocabulary and syntax, but in a manner designed to achieve the maximum impact. These different speech styles, whether used in translation or not, do nothing to improve communication in the international forum.

The communication gap assumes three forms: linguistic, practical and cultural. It is with the first of these that we are concerned in this chapter. Practical problems are usually the easiest to solve, as expatriate executives soon learn how to conduct themselves in this country or that. They tip generously in French restaurants, but not at all in China. They use first names in Finland, take flowers to Swedish homes, draw up their rolling forecast for the Americans, and talk business on the golf course in the UK and Japan. (More information on manners and mannerisms is given in Chapter 9).

Of more lasting difficulty for expatriate executives are behavioural differences of cultural or linguistic origin. To be successful, on a long-term basis – to gain the edge over competitors – they must achieve proficiency in both these areas.

Not many people are clever linguists and all over the world thousands of misunderstandings are caused every day through simple mistakes. Here are some examples:

Germany
+ Next week I shall become a new car (*get*)
+ Thank you for your kidneys (*kindness*)
+ What is your death line? (*deadline*)

Japan
+ I have split up my boyfriend
+ My father is a doctor, my mother is a typewriter
+ I work hardly 10 hours a day (*hard*)

Portugal

✦ What will you do when you retire? I will breed with my horses.

✦ Butchers have been fined for selling monkey meat (*donkey*)

Sweden

✦ Are you hopeful of any change? No, I am hopeless.

Finland

✦ We are sitting in the glass room (*classroom*)

✦ He took two trucks every night (*drugs = pills*)

✦ He took a fast watch (*quick look*)

✦ How old is your son? Half past seven.

Communication patterns during meetings

We attempt to surmount the linguistic hurdle by learning the language of
our partner well or by using an interpreter. The former method is preferable as we get more fully involved in the negotiation and are able to express
ourselves better in terms of intent, mood and emotion. When the issues are
non-controversial and the agenda is smooth, few obstacles arise. When
misunderstanding arises, our language abandons its neutrality and swings
back into culture-bound mode.

Italians, who believe in full explicitness, will become more explicit, wax-
ing even more eloquent than before (see Figure 28). Finns, by contrast, will
strive to rephrase their statement of intent in even fewer words, as in their
culture this is the route to succinctness and clarity (see Figure 29).

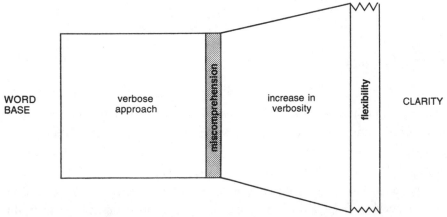

Figure 28   Italy

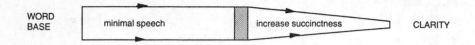

Figure 29   Finland

Germans tend to push resolutely forward in a constant, believing-in-oneself style (Figure 30). The French use a variety of tactics, including imaginative appeal, but invariably adhering to strict principles of logic throughout their discourse (Figure 31).

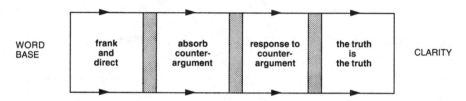

Figure 30   Germany

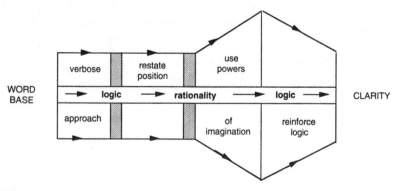

Figure 31   France

English people, like Germans, go steadily forward, but often introduce humour or understatement as negotiating tactics to soften their style (Figure 32). South Americans and Swedes go in for long discussions although in an entirely different manner (Figure 33 and 34).

Spaniards use lengthy discourse to get to know their interlocutor well and to develop friendship and loyalty as a basis on which they can build their transaction (Figure 35).

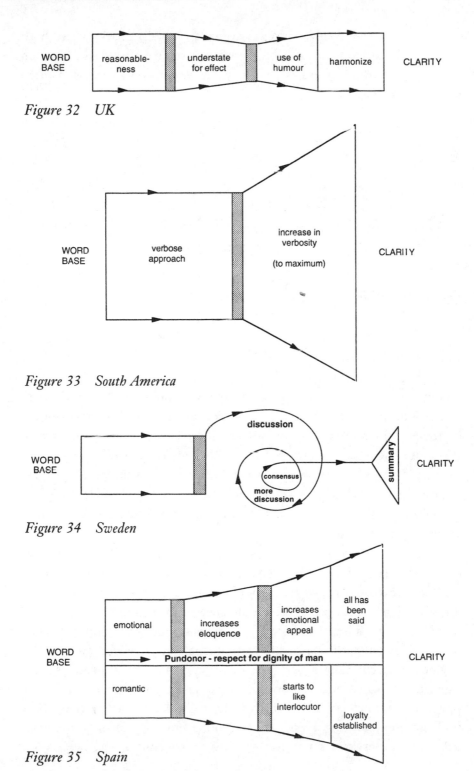

Figure 32   UK

Figure 33   South America

Figure 34   Sweden

Figure 35   Spain

Americans regard negotiation as a give-and-take scenario where both sides should put all their cards on the table at the beginning and waste no time beating around the bush. Their style is confrontational and often aggressive (Figure 36).

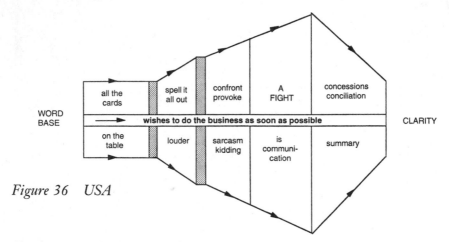

Figure 36   USA

Listening habits

Communication is a two-way process, involving not only the communicative skill of the presenter but, just as important, the listening habits of the customer. Different cultures do not use speech the same way, neither do they listen the same way. There are good listeners (Germans, Swedes) and there are bad ones (French, Spaniards). Others, such as the Americans, listen carefully or indifferently, depending on the nature of address. Figures 37–45 give some indication of the main concerns of several nationalities when they are obliged to listen.

At a recent conference on cross-cultural diversity, a fellow consultant presented a paper in which he gave an account of a problem experienced by Rolls-Royce in their aircraft engine division. A new engine had been introduced and sold with considerable success to their customers around the world. After a certain period the engines started seizing up in a selection of countries, although they worked perfectly well in others. The engine was technically sound, the operating and service manuals were explicit, and highly qualified engineers had taken great pains to make full presentations in all countries which had bought the engine. In view of the problem, these top engineers were sent out again to go through the manuals with the servicing technicians to ensure that things were being done

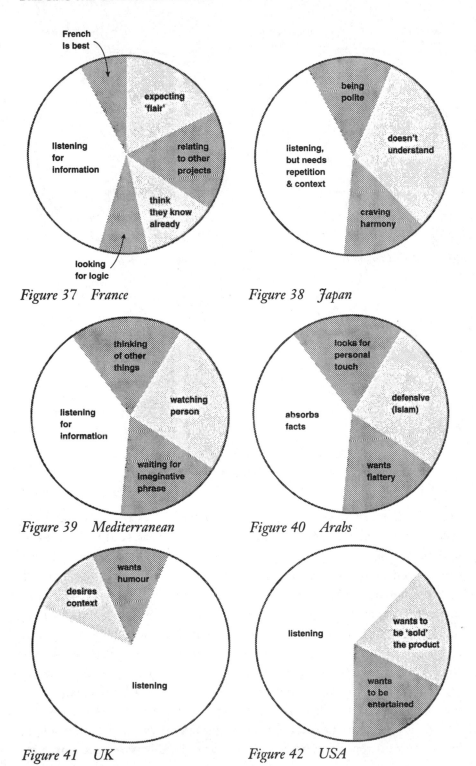

Figure 37   France

Figure 38   Japan

Figure 39   Mediterranean

Figure 40   Arabs

Figure 41   UK

Figure 42   USA

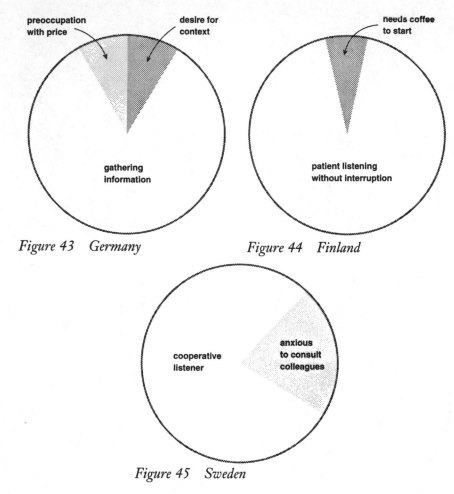

Figure 43   Germany   Figure 44   Finland

Figure 45   Sweden

properly. The British company, conscientious in the extreme, engaged the
above-mentioned consultant to interview the engineers. It turned out to be
basically a language problem. The well-spoken, highly educated and very
experienced engineers explained the manuals in the same professional
manner that they employed with British technicians. This met with full
understanding in the USA and some other countries where English listening comprehension was high. In other countries, such as Germany, the
technicians asked questions when necessary to make sure they had understood correctly. In the instances where the engines were giving problems
the technicians belonged to cultures where the level of English, although
high, was insufficient to absorb instructions delivered in an idiomatic style.
Also their cultures inhibited them from revealing their lack of understanding – to ask for repetition of the presentation would have seemed impolite.

Figure 46 summarises the principal expectations of audiences belonging to different cultures.

US	UK	GERMANY
• humour • joking • modernity • gimmicks • slogans • catch phrases • hard sell	• humour • a story • 'nice' product • reasonable price • quality • traditional rather than modern	• solidity of company • solidity of product • technical info • context • beginning – middle – end • lots of print • no jokes • good price • quality • delivery date
attention span: 30 mins	attention span: 30–45 mins	attention span: 1 hour+
FRANCE	JAPAN	SWEDEN
• formality • innovative product • 'sexy' appeal • imagination • logical presentation • reference to France • style, appearance • personal touch • may interrupt	• good price • USP • synergy with co. image • harmony • politeness • respect for their co. • good name of your co. • quiet presentation • well-dressed presenter • formality • diagrams	• modernity • quality • design • technical information • delivery dates
attention span: 30 mins	attention span: 1 hour	attention span: 45 mins
MED/ARAB	FINLAND	AUSTRALIA
• personal touch • rhetoric • eloquence • liveliness • loudness • may interrupt • want 'extra' talk afterwards	• modernity • quality • technical information • modest presentation • design	• matey opening • informality throughout • humour • persuasive style • no padding • little contexting • innovative product • essential technical info • personal touch • may interrupt • imagination conclusion
attention span: short	attention span: 45 mins	attention span: 30 mins

Figure 46   Audience expectations during presentations

Advertising

The same characteristics which influence the receptivity of an audience naturally have an effect on the way they plan their own advertising and promotion. Information-hungry Germans will issue lengthy brochures for foreign consumption, just as if they were providing information for

Germans. Newspaper or magazine advertisements will be print oriented as opposed to the more pictorial approach of people such as the Spaniards. The German will also tend towards serious, factual persuasion, rather than using catchphrases or slogans common in American advertising. Once when I was at London Heathrow airport in the company of a friend of mine, we contemplated a huge billboard advertisement:

First Bite at the Big Apple

Fly UNITED AIRLINES

My German friend was somewhat puzzled. Big Apple? I explained that that was a fairly common 'nickname' for New York. 'Oh yes,' he said, 'first visit to New York – I see. But why United?' The ad carried little conviction with me, a Brit – no logic in it. For a German it was utter nonsense.

An advertisement for Lufthansa which appeared frequently in a variety of international news magazines with a mainly Anglo-Saxon readership repeats 'serious' concepts such as responsibility (four times), quality (five times), compromise (three times), perfection (three times). Also noticeable is the mention of accurate information – DM 1.1 billion (not 1 billion) – 11,000 technicians (not 10,000). By contrast, an Air France ad shows light French touch and *panache*. It shows a tray laid with cheese and wine and the words 'Flavour of France'. Let's fly Air France and have a bit of fromage *en route*. What a splendid idea. American characteristics take over in this ad for Delta:

DELTA SERVICE
Each year we fly more people than the largest airlines
of Great Britain, Germany and France...COMBINED.
Come Experience Travel That's Anything But Ordinary.

The biggest, therefore, the best. Size justifies the airline to its American mind. A Lucky Goldstar ad, in a different vein, refers to the impressive size of the company in question, but indicates that Korean success has its origins in the age-old traditions of the country's art and taste.

Finnish companies such as Nokia and Valio make frequent use of blue and white in their ads – the colour of the national flag – conveying to the Nordic reader, at least, a sense of Finnish cleanliness and reliability. Swedes tend to use blue and yellow with the same aim.

Firms planning print or television advertising in foreign countries clearly have need for guidance from local advertising agencies to indicate native preferences, pitfalls and taboos. There are some advertising agencies which claim to cater for requirements in any country, but they are few and far between.

The language of management

Different languages are used in different ways and with a variety of effects. Hyperbolic American and understated British English clearly inform and inspire staff with separate allure and driving force. Managers of all nationalities know how to speak to best effect to their compatriots, yet they are in fact only vaguely aware of their dependence on the in-built linguistic characteristics which make their job easier.

German

Germans belong to a data-oriented, low context culture and like receiving detailed information and instruction to guide them in the performance of tasks at which they wish to excel. In business situations German is not used in a humorous way, neither do its rigid case-endings and strict word order allow the speaker to think aloud very easily. With few homonyms (in contrast, for example, to Chinese) and a transparent word-building system, the language is especially conducive to the issuing of clear orders. The almost invariable use of the *Sie* form in business fits in well with the expectation of obedience and reinforces the hierarchical nature of the communication.

As far as motivating subordinates is concerned, German would seem to be less flexible than, for instance, bubbly American English. The constrictive effect of case-endings makes it difficult for German speakers to chop and change in the middle of a sentence. They embark on a course, plotted partly by gender, partly by morphology, in a straitjacket of Teutonic word order. The verb coming at the end obliges the hearer to listen carefully in order to extract the full meaning. The length and complexity of German sentences reflect the German tendency to distrust simple utterances.

Information-hungry Germans are among the best listeners in the world; their language fits the bill.

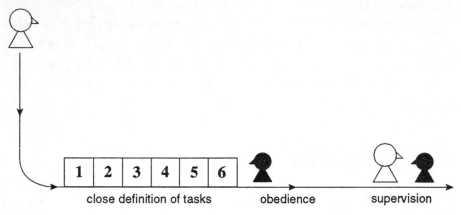

Figure 47   German

American English

In the USA the manager, if not always a hero, is viewed in a positive and sympathetic light, as one of the figures responsible for the nation's speedy development and commercial services. It is a young, vigorous, ebullient nation and its language reflects the national energy and enthusiasm. Americans exaggerate in order to simplify – low-key Britons feel they go 'over the top', but the dynamic cliché wears well in the US.

The frequent tendency to hyperbolise, exaggerating chances of success, overstating aims or targets etc., allows American managers to 'pump up' their subordinates – to drive them on to longer hours and speedier results. American salespeople do not resist this approach, for they are used to the 'hard sell' themselves. Tough talk, quips, wisecracks, barbed repartee – all available in good supply in American English – help them on their way.

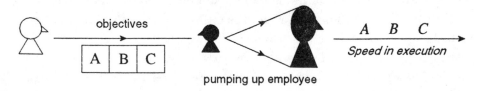

Figure 48   American English

The ubiquitous use of 'get' facilitates clear, direct orders. You get up early, you get going, you get there first, you get the client and you get the order, got it? The many neologisms in American English, used liberally by managers, permit them to appear up to date, aphoristic, humorous and democratic.

British English

In Britain the language has quite different qualities and, as a management tool, is much more subtle. British staff members who would be put off by American exaggeration and tough talk fall for a more understated, laid-back version of English which reflects their own characteristics. Managers manipulate subordinates with friendly small talk, humour, reserved statements of objectives and a very casual approach to getting down to work. You don't arrive on the dot and work round the clock. The variety of types of humour available in the UK enables managers to be humorous, to praise, change direction, chide, insinuate and criticise at will. They may even level criticism at themselves. Irony is a powerful weapon either way.

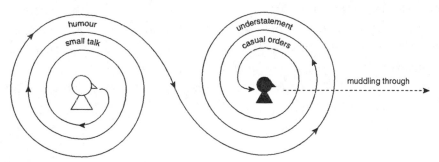

Figure 49   British English

Both British and American English are excellent media for brainstorming, due to the richness of vocabulary, double meanings, nuances and word-coining facilities. American managers and staff often used coined-yesterday business terminologies which neither fully understands, but which unite them in wonder at the spanking newness of the expression. British, in contrast, shy away from neologisms, often preferring woolly, old-fashioned phrases which frequently lead to sluggish thinking. 'Muddling through' is the result – the British are famous for it.

Foreigners follow with difficulty, for in fact they are listening to messages in a code. American or German criticism is blunt and direct; British critique is incidental and oblique. Managers, when praising, may seem to condemn. When persuading, they will strive to appear laid back. When closing a project, they will do so in a casual manner. When being tough they will feign great consideration, even kindness.

Japanese

There is a certain similarity in the language of management in Britain and Japan, although the basic and ever-present indirectness of the Japanese style makes the British, by comparison, seem clinical thinkers! Nevertheless, they have something in common – an aversion to 'rocking the boat'. British managers' understated criticisms, their humorous shafts in attack, their apparent reasonableness of expression at all times, are gambits to preserve harmony in their team. In Japan the drive towards harmony is so strong that it takes priority over clarity, even over truth.

Japanese managers do not issue orders: they only hint at what has to be done. The language is custom designed for this. The structure, which normally stacks up a line of subordinate clauses before the main one, invariably lists the justifications for the directive before it reaches the listener.

'Complete September's final report by 5.30 pm' comes out in Japanese as: 'It's 10th October today, isn't it? Our controller hasn't asked to see September's report yet. I wonder if he'll pop round tomorrow. You never know with him...' The actual order is never given – there is no need, the staff are already scrambling to their books.

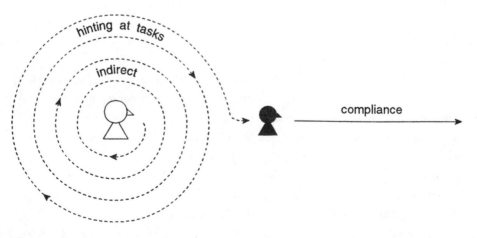

Figure 50   Japanese

Japanese has built-in mechanisms creating a strong impact on the listener. The general mandatory politeness creates a climate where staff appear to be quietly consulted in the most courteous manner. This very courtesy encourages their support and compliance. In fact they have no choice, as the hierarchy of communication is already settled by the status of the manager based on the quality and date of his university degree. The use of honorifics, moreover, reinforces the hierarchical situation. The different set of expressions (again mandatory) used in formulating the subordinates' responses to the manager's remarks closes the circle of suggestion, absorption, compliance.

Other features of the Japanese language which serve managers in instructing and motivating staff are the passive voice, used for extra politeness; the impersonal verb, which avoids casting direct blame; and the use of silence on certain issues, which indicates clearly to the subordinate what the manager's opinion is. Reported speech is not popular in Japan, for Japanese people subscribe to the myth that all one-to-one conversations are delivered in confidence and should not be repeated to others, and indeed the language does not possess a reported speech mechanism.

French

French managers inhabit quite a different world. They are clinically direct in their approach and see no advantage in ambiguity or ambivalence. The

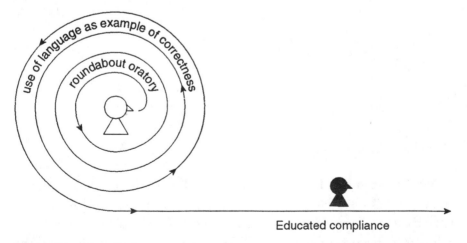

Educated compliance

Figure 51   French

French language is a crisp, incisive tongue, a kind of verbal dance or gymnastics of the mouth, which presses home its points with an undisguised, logical urgency. It is rational, precise, ruthless in its clarity.

The French education system, from childhood, places a premium on articulateness and eloquence of expression. Unlike Japanese, Finnish or British children, French children are rarely discouraged from being talkative. In the French culture loquacity is equated with intelligence and silence does not have a particularly golden sheen. *Lycée*, university and *École normale supérieure* education reinforces the emphasis on good speaking, purity of grammar and mastery of the French idiom. The French language, unquestionably, is the chief weapon wielded by managers in directing, motivating and dominating their staff. Less articulate French people will show no resentment. Masterful use of language and logic implies, in their understanding, masterful management.

Other languages

In the Gulf States a good manager is a good Moslem. The language used will make frequent references to Allah and align itself with the precepts and style of the Koran. A didactic management style is the result. The inherent rhetorical qualities of the Arabic language (see Figure 52) lend themselves to reinforcing the speaker's sincerity. A raised voice is a sign not of anger, but of genuine feeling and exhortation.

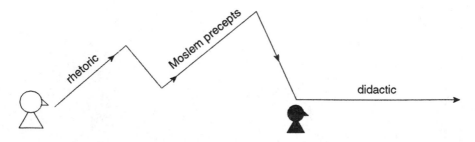

Figure 52   Arabic

Nigel Holden sees Russian, where social distance is encoded in highly subtle ways, as resembling Japanese as a flexible management language in network mode. Soviet managers were involved little in such areas as leadership or motivation of employees. The management style utilised threats and coercion to produce results demanded by socialist 'planning'. How

coercion

compliance

fudging
results

Figure 53   Russian

Russian will develop as a language of management in the future will depend on modes of address using names and titles and the development of formal and informal mechanisms which do not remind subordinates of coercion and control.

Swedish as a language of management leans heavily on the *Du* form and dry, courteous expressions which clearly stratify managers at the same level as their colleagues or, at the very worst, as *primi inter pares*. I recently heard a TV journalist in his mid-twenties address the prime minister as *Du*.

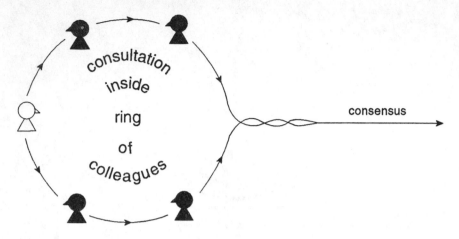

Figure 54   Swedish

To take a very different example, Spanish is directed towards staff at a much more vertical angle. Spanish managers are usually happy to use the *tu* form to subordinates, but the declaimed nature of their delivery, with typical Spanish fire and emphasis, makes their pronouncements and opinions virtually irreversible. Spanish, with its wealth of dimunitive endings, its rich vocabulary and multiple choice options on most nouns, is extremely suitable for expressing emotion, endearments, nuances and intimacies. Spanish managers' discourse leans on emotive content. They woo, persuade, cajole. They want you to know how they feel. The language exudes warmth, excitement, sensuousness, ardour, ecstasy and sympathy.

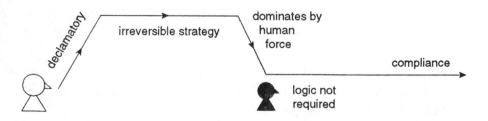

Figure 55   Spanish

8

MEETINGS OF THE MINDS

Meetings can be interesting, boring, long, short, or unnecessary. Decisions, which are best made on the golf course, over dinner, in the sauna, or in the corridor, rarely materialise at meetings called to make them. Protracted meetings are successful only if transport, seating, room temperature, lunch, coffee breaks, dinner, theatre outings, nightcaps and cable television facilities are properly organised.

Beginnings

THERE ARE MORE MEETINGS THAN THERE USED TO BE. JET TRAVEL enables businesspeople to go to a meeting in another continent and often leave for home the same day. It may well be that video-conferencing will reduce business travel in the future, but this facility, too, is a type of meeting.

For the moment, however, consider how people conduct meetings, face-to-face, in different countries. Meetings are not begun in the same way as we move from culture to culture. Some are opened punctually, briskly and in a 'business-like' fashion. Others start with chit-chat and some meetings have difficulty getting going at all. Figure 56 gives some examples of unalike starts in a selection of countries.

Germans, Scandinavians and Americans like to get on with it. They see no point in delay. Americans are well-known for their business breakfasts (a barbaric custom in Spanish eyes). In England, France, Italy and Spain it

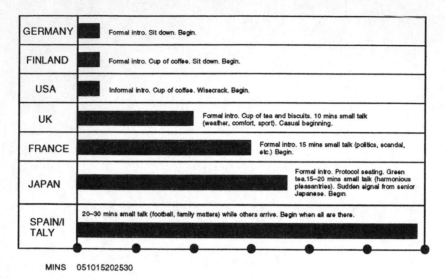

GERMANY	Formal intro. Sit down. Begin.
FINLAND	Formal intro. Cup of coffee. Sit down. Begin.
USA	Informal intro. Cup of coffee. Wisecrack. Begin.
UK	Formal intro. Cup of tea and biscuits. 10 mins small talk (weather, comfort, sport). Casual beginning.
FRANCE	Formal intro. 15 mins small talk (politics, scandal, etc.) Begin.
JAPAN	Formal intro. Protocol seating. Green tea.15–20 mins small talk (harmonious pleasantries). Sudden signal from senior Japanese. Begin.
SPAIN/I TALY	20–30 mins small talk (football, family matters) while others arrive. Begin when all are there.

MINS   051015202530

Figure 56   Opening a meeting

would be considered rude to broach the issues immediately. It is seen as much more civilised to ease into the subject after exchanging pleasantries which can last from 10 minutes to half an hour. The English, particularly, are almost shame-faced at indicating when one should start (Well, Charlie, I suppose we ought to have a look at this bunch of paperwork...). In Japan, where platitudes are mandatory, there is almost a fixed period which has to elapse before the senior person present says: '*Jitsu wa ne...*' (The fact of the matter is...) at which point everybody puts their head down and starts. Japanese meetings are conducted in phases:

✦ platitudinous preamble
✦ outline of subjects to be discussed (language used formal)
✦ airing of views (less formal in tone)
✦ replies of each party to other's views (more formal and non-confrontational)
✦ summary by both sides (formal)

Negotiation

Many meetings between people of different cultures are held to conduct negotiations, and the approach of each side is affected by cultural factors.

Germans will ask you all the difficult questions from the start. You must convince them of your efficiency, quality of goods and promptness of service. These are features Germans consider among their own strong cards and they expect the same from you, at the lowest possible price. They will give you little business at first, but much more later when they have tested you. French tend to give business much faster, but may also withdraw it more quickly. Spaniards often seem not to appreciate the preparations you have made to facilitate a deal. They don't study all the details, but they study you. They will only do business with you if they like you and think you are 'honourable'.

The Japanese are similar in this respect. They must like you and trust you, otherwise no deal. Like the Germans, they will ask many questions about price, delivery and quality, but the Japanese will ask them all ten times. You have to be patient. Japanese are not interested in profits immediately, only in the market share and reputation of the company.

Finns and Swedes expect modernity, efficiency and new ideas. They like to think of themselves as being up to date and sophisticated. They will expect your company to have the latest office computers and streamlined factories. The American business approach is to get down quickly to a discussion of investment, budgets and profits. They hurry you along and make you sign the five-year plan.

Businesspeople from small nations with a long tradition of trading, such as the Netherlands and Portugal, are usually friendly and adaptable, but prove to be excellent negotiators. Brazilians never believe your first price to be the real one, and expect you to bend it later, so you must take this into your calculations.

In short, one gets down to business in different ways, according to the customs of the host country. Concepts of time, space and protocol all play their part. It is only when the meeting gets underway, however, that deeper chasms of cultural difference begin to yawn.

Established principles

Business schools, management gurus, trade consultants and industrial psychologists have focused, for most of the twentieth century, on the goal of reducing the process of negotiation to a fine art, if not a science. Papers have been written, seminars have been held, manuals have been devised and published. The Americans in particular, by dint of their obvious successes in the development of business techniques, not to mention their decades-long supremacy in world trade, have held a dominant position in the expounding and dissemination of the principles of negotiation.

One could be forgiven for assuming that relatively unchanging, universally accepted principles of negotiation would by now have been established – that an international consensus would have been reached on how negotiators should conduct themselves in meetings, how the phases of negotiation should proceed and how hierarchies of goals and objectives should be dealt with. One might assume that negotiators with their common concepts (learned from manuals) of ploys, bargaining strategies, use of data, fallback positions, closing techniques, restriction gambits, mix of factual, intuitive and psychological approaches, are interchangeable players in a (serious) game where internationally recognised rules of tactics, points won and gained, positions achieved would lead to a civilised agreement on the division of the spoils. This 'game plan' and its successful prosecution are not unusual or infrequent in domestic negotiation between nationals of one culture. But the moment international and intercultural factors enter into the equation, things change completely. Nationals of different cultures negotiate in completely different ways. In view of the common information obtainable by all participants and, to some extent, a fair amount of common commercial training and theory, why should this be so?

The problems

These derive from two sources: the professionalism of the negotiating team; and cross-cultural bias.

As far as professionalism is concerned, what is often forgotten is that negotiating teams rarely consist of professional or trained negotiators. While this does not apply so much to government negotiation, it is often readily observable at company level. A small company, when establishing contact with a foreign partner, very often is represented by its managing director and an assistant. A medium-sized firm will probably involve its export director, finance director and necessary technical support. Even large companies rely on the performance of the MD supported by, perhaps, highly specialised technical staff and finance people who have no experience whatsoever in negotiating. Engineers, accountants or managers used to directing their own nationals are usually completely lacking in foreign experience. When confronted with a different mindset, they are not equipped to capture the logic, intent and ethical stance of the other side. Often, when discussing the basic situation executives may be wasting time talking past each other. This leads us to cross-cultural bias.

Cross-cultural bias

When we find ourselves seated opposite well-dressed individuals politely listening to our remarks, their pens poised over notepads similar to the one before us, their briefcases and calculators bearing the familiar brand names, we tend to assume that they see what we see, hear what we say and understand what our intent and motives are. In all likelihood they start with the same innocent assumptions, for they, too, have not yet penetrated our cosmopolitan veneer. But the two sets of minds are working in different ways, in different languages regulated by differing norms and certainly envisaging different goals.

Humanity has a common development up to a certain point and in this respect the negotiators opposite us know what we feel, desire and suspect. Like us, they love their young, feel anger at injustice, fear powers which seek to destroy them, want to be liked and are grateful for favours and kindness. The average Chinese, German, Japanese or American will rarely deviate from this inherited pattern. That can be the extent of our trust, both in a social and business environment. After that we enter a different area — that of learned national culture. Now deviations of attitude and view are certain and we must be on our guard during the meeting to avoid irritants or outright offence, establish mutually understood facts and know when to 'agree to disagree', simply because the other culture cannot accept or even see our point of view.

National character and negotiation

Even before the meeting begins, the divergences of outlook are exerting decisive influence on the negotiation to come. If we take three cultural groups as an example – American, Japanese and Latin-American – the hierarchy of negotiating objectives are likely to be as in Figure 57.

US	JAPAN	LATIN AMERICA
1. Current deal	1. Harmonious relationships and 'direction taking'	1. National 'honour'
2. Short-term profit and rapid growth	2. Securing market share	2. Personal prestige of chief negotiator
	3. Long-term profit	3. Long-term relationship
3. Consistent profit		
4. Relationships with partner	4. Current deal	4. Current deal

Figure 57   Negotiating objectives

Americans are deal-oriented, as they see it as a present opportunity which must be seized. American prosperity was built on opportunities quickly taken and the immediate profit is seen as the paramount reality. Today, shareholders' expectation of dividends creates rolling forecasts which put pressure on US executives to deal now in order to fulfil their quarterly figures. For the Japanese, the current project or proposal is a trivial item in comparison with the momentous decision they have to make about whether or not to enter into a lasting business relationship with the foreigners. Can they harmonise the objectives and action style of the other company with the well-established operational principles of their own *kaisha*? Is this the right direction for their company to be heading in? Can they see the way forward to a steadily increasing market share? The Latin Americans, particularly if they are from a country such as Mexico or Argentina (where memories of US exploitation or interference are a background to discussion), are anxious to establish notions of equality of standing and respect for their team's national characteristics before getting down to the business of making money. Like the Japanese, they seek a long-term relationship, although they will inject into this a greater personal input than their group-thinking eastern counterparts.

This 'master programming' supplied by our culture not only prioritises our concerns in different ways, but makes it difficult for us to 'see' the priorities or intention pattern of others.

Stereotyping is one of the 'flaws' in our master programme, often leading us to false assumptions. Here are three examples:

✦ French refusal to compromise indicates obstinacy.
(Reality: French people see no reason to compromise if their logic stands undefeated.)

✦ Japanese negotiators can't make decisions.
(Reality: the decision was already made before the meeting, by consensus. The Japanese see meetings as an occasion for presenting decisions, not changing them.)

✦ The Mexican senior negotiators are too 'personal' in conducting negotiations.
(Reality: their 'personal' position reflects their position of authority within the power structure back home.)

The social setting

French, Spaniards, most Latin-Americans and Japanese regard a negotiation as a social ceremony to which are attached important considerations of venue, participants, hospitality and protocol, timescale, courtesy of discussion and the ultimate significance of the session. Americans, Australians, Britons and Scandinavians have a much more pragmatic view and are less impacted by the social aspects of business meetings. The Germans and Swiss are somewhere in between.

US executives, although outwardly smiling and friendly, generally tend to get the session over with as quickly as possible, with entertaining and protocol kept at a minimum. Mutual profit is the object of the exercise and Americans send technically competent people to drive the deal through. They persuade with facts and figures and expect some give and take, horse-trading when necessary. They will be argumentative to the point of rudeness in deadlock and regard confrontation and in-fighting as conducive to progress. No social egos are on the line – if they win, they win; if they lose, what the hell, too bad.

Senior Mexican negotiators cannot lose to Americans, least of all to technicians. Their social position is on the line and they did not enter into this negotiation to swap marbles with engineers and accountants. Their

Spanish heritage causes them to view the meeting as a social occasion where everybody is to show great respect for the dignity of the others, discuss grand outlines as opposed to petty details, speak at length in an unhurried, eloquent manner, and show sincerity of intent while maintaining a modicum of discretion to retain some privacy of view.

Japanese view the session as an occasion to ratify ceremonially decisions which have previously been reached by consensus. They are uncomfortable both with Mexican rhetoric and American argumentativeness, although they are closer to the Latins in their acceptance of protocol, lavish entertainment and preservation of dignity. As befits a social occasion, the Japanese will be led by a senior executive who sets standards of courtesy and deference. He may have no technical competence, but represents the weighty consensus which backs his authority.

The French view the setting of the negotiation both as a social occasion and a forum for their own cleverness. Their sense of history primes them for the traditional French role of international mediator. Their leader will be their best speaker, usually highly-educated and self-assured. It will require a skilful American, Briton or Japanese to best him or her in debate. The leader will be unimpressed by American aggressive ploys and Cartesian logic will reduce 'muddling-through' Englishmen and belly-talking Japanese to temporary incoherence. This is not a session for give and take, but for presenting well-formulated solutions. Lavish French hospitality will compensate for sitting through lengthy speeches.

Scandinavians, while relatively at home with Americans and Anglo-Saxons and familiar enough with German bluntness and protocol, have little feel for the social nuances displayed by Latins and Japanese. In their straight-forward egalitarian cultures a business meeting is for business to be conducted without regard to social status. Who the other negotiators are, their class, their connections, who they are related to – all these things are irrelevant to Finns and Swedes. Although more polite than Americans, Scandinavians have difficulty in settling down to a role in meetings where social competence dominates technical know-how.

Values & self-image

We see, therefore, how diverse cultures view the negotiating process in a different light, with dissimilar expectations about its conduct and outcome.

Once the talks begin, the values, phobias and rituals of the particular cultural groups soon make themselves evident. For the Americans, time is money and they wish to compress as much action and decision making as possible into the hours available. They rely on statistical data and personal drive to achieve this. The Dutch, Finns and Swiss, although somewhat less headlong, will be similarly concerned with the time/efficiency equation. The Germans will place emphasis on thoroughness, punctuality and meeting deadlines, making sure they always complete their action chains. For this they require full information and context and, unlike Latins, will leave nothing 'in the air'.

The French give pride of place to logic and rational argument. The aesthetics of the discussion are important to them and this will be reflected in their dress sense, choice of venue, imaginative debating style and preoccupation with proper form. The Japanese have their own aesthetic norms, also requiring proper form, which in their case is bound up with a complex set of obligations (vertical, horizontal and circular!). In discussion they value creation of harmony and quiet 'groupthink' above all else. The British also give priority to quiet reasonable, diplomatic discussion. Their preoccupation with 'fair play' often comes to the fore and they like to see this as a yardstick for decision making. Latins place emphasis on personal relationships, 'honourable' confidences and the development of trust between the parties. This is a slow process and they require an unhurried tempo to enable them to get to know their counterparts. This is well understood by the Japanese, but conflicts with the American desire for quick progress.

Self-image is part and parcel of value perception and negotiators see themselves in a light which may never reach their foreign counterpart, although their playing of the role may irritate. English people often assume a condescending, abitrarial role which is a carry-over from the days when they settled disputes among the subjects of Her Majesty's Empire. They may still see themselves as judges of situations which can be controlled with calm firmness and funny stories. The French have an equally strong sense of history and consider themselves the principal propagators of western European culture. This encourages them to take a central role in most discussions and they tend to 'hold the floor' longer than their counterparts would wish.

Latin Americans see themselves as exploited by the US and they display heightened defensive sensitivity which may often delay progress. They consider themselves culturally superior to North Americans and resent the latters' position of power and dominance.

The Japanese, on the other hand, are comfortable with American power – as victors in the Second World War they earned the number one spot. Inequality is basic in both Japanese and Chinese philosophies and the former are quite satisfied with the number two spot for the time being. The Japanese see themselves as far-sighted negotiators and courteous conversationalists. They have no aspirations to dominate discussion any more than they have towards moral world or even Asian leadership. They are privately convinced, however, of their uniqueness of which one facet is intellectual superiority. Unlike the French, they base this belief not on intellectual verbal prowess, but on the power of strong intuition.

Decision making

Negotiations lead to decisions. How these are made, how long they take to be made and how final they are once made are all factors which will depend on the cultural group involved.

Americans love making decisions as these usually lead to action and they are primarily action oriented. The French love talking about decisions which may or may not be made in the future. If their reasoned arguments do not produce what in their eyes is a logical solution, then they will delay decisions for days or weeks if necessary.

Japanese hate making decisions and prefer to let decisions be made for them by gradually building up a weighty consensus. In their case, a decision may take months. This exasperates Americans and many northern Europeans, but the Japanese insist that big decisions take time. They see American negotiators as technicians making a series of small decisions to expedite one (perhaps relatively unimportant) deal. Once the Japanese have made their decisions, however, they expect their American partner to move like lightning towards implementation. This leads to further exasperation.

What westerners fail to understand is that Japanese, during the long, painstaking process of building a consensus, are simultaneously making preparations for the implementation of the business. The famous *ringi-sho* system of Japanese decision making is one of the most democratic procedures of an otherwise autocratic structure. In many western countries action is usually initiated at the top. In Japan younger or lower-ranking people often propose ideas which are developed by middle management and ultimately shown to the president. There is a long, slow process during which many meetings are held to digest the new idea and at length a draft will be made to be passed round for all to see. Each person is invited to attach his or her seal of approval so that unanimity of agreement is already assumed before the president confirms it. He will not do this lightly since he, not middle management, will have to resign if there is a catastrophe. To ask a Japanese negotiator during a meeting to take 'another direction' is quite unacceptable. No hunches or sudden change-abouts here. Drastic swings of intent would force the Japanese team to go right back to the drawing board.

Mediterranean and Latin-American teams look to their leader to make decisions and do not question his personal authority. His decision making, however, will not be as impromptu or arbitrary as it seems. Latins, like Japanese, tend to bring a cemented-in position to the negotiating table, which is that of the power structure back home. This contrasts strongly with the Anglo-Saxon and Scandinavian willingness to modify stances continuously during the talk if new openings are perceived.

French negotiators seldom reach a decision on the first day. Many a British negotiator has asked (in vain) French colleagues at 4 pm, 'Well, can we summarise what we have agreed so far?' French dislike such interim summaries, since every item on the agenda may be affected by later discussion. Only at the end can everything fit into the Grand Design. Short-term decisions are seen as of little consequence.

Ethics

Once a decision has been made, the question then arises as to how final or binding it is. Anglo-Saxons and Germans see a decision, once it has been entered into the minutes of a meeting, as an oral contract which will shortly be formalised in a written, legal document. Ethically, one sticks to one's decisions. Agenda items which have been agreed on are not to be resurrected or rediscussed once a tick has been put against them.

Neither Japanese nor southern Europeans see anything wrong, ethically, in going back on items previously agreed. Chop and change (anathema to Anglo-Saxons) holds no terrors for many cultures. The Japanese consider it would be unethical to insist on a decision which had been rendered invalid or irrelevant by rapidly changing circumstances. How ethical is a share swop agreement if the market crashes the next day? New tax laws, currency devaluations, drastic political changes can make previous accords meaningless.

The French show lack of respect for adherence to agenda points or early mini-decisions. This is due not so much to their concern about changing circumstances as to the possibility (even likelihood) that, as the discussions progress, Latin imagination will spawn clever new ideas, uncover new avenues of approach, improve and embellish accords which later may seem naïve or rudimentary. For them a negotiation is often a brainstorming exercise. Brainwaves must be accommodated! Italians, Spanish, Portuguese and South Americans all share this attitude.

Contracts

Different ethical approaches or standards reveal themselves in the way diverse cultures view written contracts. Americans, British, Germans, Swiss and Finns are among those who regard a written agreement as something which, if not holy, is certainly final. For the Japanese, on the other hand, the contract which they were uncomfortable in signing anyway is, in their eyes, a statement of intent. They will adhere to it as best they can, but will not feel bound by it if market conditions suddenly change, anything in it contradicts common sense, or they feel 'cheated' or legally trapped by it. If the small print turns out to be rather nasty, they will ignore or contravene it without qualms of conscience. Many problems arise between Japanese and US firms on account of this attitude. The Americans love detailed written agreements covering themselves against all contingencies with legal redress. They have 300,000 lawyers to back them up. The Japanese, who have only 10,000 registered lawyers, regard contingencies to be *force majeure* and consider that contracts should be sensibly reworked and mofidied at another meeting or negotiation.

The French tend to be precise in the drawing up of contracts, but other Latins require more flexibility in adhering to them. An Italian or Argentinian sees the contract as an ideal scheme in the best of worlds, which sets out the prices, delivery dates, standards of quality and expected gain, or a fine project which has been discussed. But we do not live in the best of worlds and the outcome we can realistically expect will fall some-what short of the actual terms agreed. Delivery of payment may be late, there may be heated exchanges of letters or faxes, but things will not be so bad that further deals with the partner are completely out of the question. A customer who pays six months late is better than one who does not pay at all. A foreign market, however volatile, may still be a better alternative to a stagnating or dead-end domestic one.

Propriety

If Anglo-Saxons and Scandinavians have a problem with the ethics of volatility, they have an even greater one with those of propriety. Which culture or authority can deliver the verdict on acceptable standards of behaviour or appropriate conduct of business? If it is recognised that Italian flexibility poses problems for law-abiding Swiss or time-dominated Germans, what are the sanctioned limits of such flexibility?

Italian flexibility in business often leads Anglo-Saxons to think they are 'dishonest'. They frequently bend rules, break or 'get round' some laws and put a very flexible interpretation on certain agreements, controls and regulations. There are many grey areas where short cuts are, in Italian eyes, a matter of common sense. In a country where excessive bureaucracy can hold 'business' up for months, smoothing the palm of an official or even being related to a minister is not a sin. It is done in most countries, but in Italy they talk about it.

When does lavish entertaining or regular gift giving constitute elegant bribery or agreeable corruption? French, Portuguese or Arab hosts will interlard the negotiation sessions with feasting far superior to that offered by the Scandinavian canteen or British pub lunch. Expense-account-culture Japanese would consider themselves inhospitable if they had not taken their visiting negotiators on the restaurant night-club circuit and showered them with the usual expensive gifts.

Few Anglo-Saxons or Scandinavians would openly condone making a covert payment to an opposing negotiator, but in practice this is not an uncommon occurrence when competition is fierce. I once heard an American define an honest Brazilian negotiator as one who, when bought, would stay bought. More recently the leader of the negotiating team of a large Swedish concern tacitly admitted having greased the palm of a certain South American gentleman without securing the contract. When the Swede quietly referred to the payment made, the beneficiary explained: 'Ah, but that was to get you a place in the last round!'

Judgements on such procedures are inevitably cultural. Recipients of under-the-table payments may see them as no more unethical than using one's influence with a minister (who happens to be one's uncle), accepting a trip around the world (via Tahiti or Hawaii) to attend a 'conference', or wielding brute force (financial or political) to extract a favourable deal from a weaker opponent. All such manœuvres can be viewed (depending on one's mindset) as normal strategies in the hard world of business. One just has to build these factors into the deal or relationship.

Compromise

It is not uncommon for negotiations to enter a difficult stage where the teams get bogged down or even find themselves in deadlock. When such situations occur between nationals of one culture (for a variety of reasons), there is usually a well-tried mechanism which constitutes an escape route whereby momentum can be regained without loss of face for either side. Deadlocks can be broken by, for instance, changing negotiators or venue, adjourning the session, or 'repackaging' the deal. Arab teams will take a recess for prayer and come back with a more conciliatory stance; Japanese delegations will bring in senior executives 'to see what the problem is'; Swedish opponents will go out drinking together; Finns will retire to the sauna.

These mechanisms are not always available in international negotiations. The nature of the deadlock, moreover, may be misconstrued by both parties as, for instance, when French insist on adhering to their logic which the Japanese have misunderstood or completely failed to follow. The mechanism used by Anglo-Saxons is usually that of compromise. The British, with their supposedly innate sense of fair play, see themselves as the champions of compromise. The Scandinavians are very British in this respect, while the American willingness to compromise is seen in their give-and-take tactics, deriving from the bartering traditions in US history.

Other cultures, however, do not see compromise in the same favourable light and remain unconvinced of its shining merit. In French eyes 'give and take' is Anglo-speak for 'wheel and deal', which they see as an inelegant, crude tactic for chiselling away at the legitimate edifice of reason they have so painstakingly constructed. 'Yes, let's all be reasonable,' they say, 'but what is irrational in what we have already said?'

For the Japanese, compromise during a negotiation is a departure from a company-backed consensus, and woe betide the Japanese negotiators who concede points without authority. Adjournment is the least they must ask for. Many a senior Tokyo-based executive has been got out of bed in the middle of the night by trans-Pacific telephone calls asking for directives. Delays are, of course, inevitable.

Among the Latins, attitudes towards compromise vary. The Italians, although they respect logic almost as much as the French, know that our world is indeed irrational and pride themselves on their flexibility. They are closely followed by the Portuguese who, in their long history of trading with the English, have acquired close familiarity with Anglo-Saxon habits. The Spaniards' obsession with dignity makes it hard for them to climb down without good reason. South Americans see compromise as a threat to their *pundonor* (dignity) and several nations, including Argentina, Mexico and Panama, display obstinacy in conceding anything to 'insensitive, arrogant Americans'.

Compromise may be defined as finding a middle course and, to this end, both the Japanese and Chinese make good use of 'go-betweens'. This is less acceptable to westerners who prefer more direct contact (even confrontation) to seek clarity. Confrontation is anathema to orientals and most Latins and disliked by Brits and Swedes. Only Germans ('the truth is the truth'), Finns and Americans might rank directness, bluntness and honesty above subtle diplomacy in business discussions. Arabs also like to use 'go-betweens'. The repeated offer of King Hussein of Jordan to mediate in the dispute between Saddam Hussein and George Bush unfortunately fell on deaf ears, even though, as a thoroughly westernised Arab (with British and American wives to boot) he was the ideal middleman for that particular cross-cultural situation.

The problem remains that intelligent, meaningful compromise is only possible when one is able to see how the other side prioritises their goals and views the related concepts of dignity, conciliation and reasonableness. These are culturally affected concepts, therefore emotion bound and prickly. However, an understanding of them, and a suitable step or reaction to accommodate them, form the unfailing means of unblocking the impasse. Such moves are less difficult to make than one might believe. They do, however, require knowledge and understanding of the traditions, cultural characteristics and way of thinking of the other side. What is suitable or inappropriate in their eyes? What is logical and illogical?

Logic

French debating logic is Cartesian in its essence, which means that all pre-suppositions and traditional opinions must be cast aside from the outset, as they are possibly untrustworthy. Discussion must be based on one or two indubitable truths on which one can build through mechanical and deductive processes to clarify further truths and knowledge. Descartes decreed that all problems should be divided into as many parts as possible and the review should be so complete that nothing could be omitted or forgotten. Given these instructions and doctrine, it is hardly surprising that French negotiators appear complacently confident and long-winded. They have a hypothesis to build and are not in a hurry.

Opponents may indeed doubt some of the French 'indubitable truths' and ask who is qualified to establish the initial premises. Descartes has an answer to this: rational intellect is not rare, it can be found in anyone who has been given help in clear thinking (French education) and is free from prejudice. What is more, conclusions reached through Cartesian logic 'compel assent by their own natural clarity'. There, in essence, is the basis for French self-assurance and unwillingness to compromise.

Fellow French people would certainly meet thrust with counter-thrust, attempt to defeat the other side's logic. Many cultures feel little inclined to do this. The Japanese – easy meat to corner with logic – have no stomach for arguing or public demonstrations of cleverness. During the perorations of the other side, their internal telepathy system has been hard at work – their reactions and conclusions are ventral and visceral, emotional and intuitive. They, like some other Orientals, acquire convictions without always knowing why – as occasionally do the 'muddling-through' British.

Anglo-Saxons, particularly Americans, show a preference for Hegelian precepts. According to Hegel, people who first present diametrically opposed points of view ultimately agree to accept a new and broader view that does justice to the substance of each. The thesis and antithesis come together to form a synthesis (compromise). Everything must have an opposite – were it not so, nothing could come into existence. The essence of this cause-and-effect doctrine is activity and movement, on which Americans thrive. An American negotiator is always happy to be the catalyst, ever willing to make the first move to initiate action.

Chinese logic is different again – their background is Confucian philosophy. They consider the French search for truth less important than the search for virtue. To do what is right is better than to do what is logical. They also may show disdain for western insistence that something is black or white, that opposite courses of action must be right or wrong. Chinese consider both courses may be right if they are both virtuous. Confucianism decrees moderation in all things (including opinion and argument); therefore, behaviour towards others must be virtuous. Politeness must be observed and others must be protected from loss of face. Taoist teaching encourages Chinese to show generosity of spirit in their utterances. The strong are supposed to protect the weak, so the Chinese negotiator will expect you not to take advantage of your superior knowledge or financial strength! Another dimension of Chinese thinking is *feng shui* (wind-and-water superstition) which means that the seating arrangements, the position of the furniture, alignment of doors and even the placing of mirrors will have significance for Chinese negotiators. Each individual is also supposed to possess the qualities of the animal of the year he or she was born. For example, the horse means stamina, the snake wisdom, the rat bravery and cleverness – so negotiators, beware!

Language

Negotiators, unless they are using interpreters, need a common language. As English is now the language of diplomacy as well as international trade, they think they have one. English can, however, be a communication link or a semi-invisible barrier. When Americans use in discussion words like 'democratic', 'fair', 'reasonable', 'obvious', 'evidence', 'common sense', 'equitable', 'makes business sense', they often fail to realise that Japanese understand quite different things under these headings and that most Latins will instinctively distrust each word listed above. 'Democracy' has a different meaning in every country; American 'evidence' is statistical, in many cultures it is emotional; in Russia the phrase 'makes business sense' has virtually no meaning. Language is a poor communication tool unless each word or phrase is seen in its original cultural context. This is naturally true also of other languages. Words such as *Weltschmerz* (German), *sisu* (Finnish), *saudades* (Portuguese) mean little to other cultures even when translated, while no westerner could possibly appreciate the spider's web of duties and obligations implied by the Japanese words *giri* and *on*.

The non-verbal dimension

While verbal discussion might occupy 80–90 per cent of the time devoted to a negotiation, psychologists tell us that the 'message' conveyed by our actual words may be 20 per cent or even less. Our understanding, tolerance, sense of comfort and our very mood is more likely to be strongly influenced by other factors (Fisher calls it 'cross-cultural noise').

The **venue** itself may have positive or negative implications. Are we 'home' or 'away'? Are we seated comfortably? (French negotiators are said to arrange lower seats for their opponents!) American businesspeople are used to sitting in a confrontational style, facing their interlocutors across the table and maintaining challenging eye contact, while Japanese by contrast like to sit side by side and stare at a common point (often a blank wall or the floor), punctuating their remarks with occasional sideways glances.

Hierarchy of seating is also important, but of more significance in the early stages of discussion are the negotiators' physical and social attitudes. Each culture has its own concept of the **'space bubble'** – the personal space the individual requires to be able to think, talk and gesture in comfort.

Related to the 'distance of comfort' is the question of **touching**. The Spaniard's grip on your upper arm shows confidence in you, an African may continue to hold your hand when talking to you, but touching of any kind is anathema to Japanese, who regard it as unhygienic; it is little loved by Finns, Swedes, Germans, British and many Orientals.

American informality

Americans are ambivalent in this respect, normally occupying a space bubble equal in size to that demanded by most Anglo-Saxons, but only too frequently indulging in pumping hands, slapping backs and playful punches, which score no points whatsoever with Japanese, Germans and French. Americans in particular, in their eagerness to downplay status and social hierarchy, have created consistent protocolar havoc in business meetings around the world. The last thing the Japanese wants, on first meeting, is to be manhandled (even in a friendly manner); German senior executives have no wish whatsoever to be addressed by their first names; French negotiators abhor people who take their jackets off and loosen their ties during the first encounter. Other American habits such as chewing gum, slouching in their chairs, showing the soles of their shoes as they cross their legs, constitute 'cultural noise' of the first order. Japanese and Finns, on the other hand, can give rise to unease in their counterparts with 'absence of noise' (in their eyes, constructive silence).

Dress, formal and informal, correct and innappropriate, can also give negotiators false impressions of the seriousness or casualness of the other side. **Gestures** (of the Latin variety), can denote overemotion or unreliability to northerners. Impassive faces and absence of body language can cause Latins to suspect cunning or slyness in Japanese, and the lack of feedback from the politely listening Finn can disorient them.

Silence

Listening habits can clearly play an important part in the negotiating process. Finns and Japanese consider they make an important contribution to the discussion with their culture-oriented silence! 'Those who know do not speak; those who speak do not know' is a second-century Chinese proverb which the Finns, like the Japanese, do not quarrel with. In Finland, as in Japan, silence is not equated with failure to communicate, but is an integral part of social interaction. In both countries what is not said is regarded as important and lulls in conversation are considered restful, friendly and appropriate. Silence means that you listen and learn; talking a lot merely expresses your cleverness, perhaps egoism and arrogance. Silence protects your individualism and privacy; it also shows respect for the individualism of others. In Finland and Japan it is considered impolite or inappropriate to force one's opinions on others – it is more appropriate to nod in agreement, smile quietly, avoid opinionated argument or discord.

The American habit of 'thinking aloud', the French stage performance, the Italian baring of the soul in intimate chatter, the rhetoric of the Arabs – all these are communicative gambits designed to gain the confidence of the listener, to share ideas which can then be discussed and modified. The Finn and the Japanese listen with a kind of horror, for in their countries a statement is a sort of commitment to stand by, not to change, twist or contradict in the very next breath.

Body language

Facial expressions and loudness of voice or manner are also cultural factors which may disturb interlocutors. Members of a Spanish delegation may argue fiercely with each other while opponents are present, causing Japanese to think 'they are fighting'. Orientals are bemused when the same 'quarrelling Spaniards' pat each other like lifelong friends a few moments later. Smiles, while signifying good progress when on the faces of British, Scandinavians or Germans, might mean embarrassment or anger when adopted by Japanese and often appear insincere in the features of the constantly beaming American. Finns and Japanese often look doleful when perfectly happy, whereas gloom on an Arab face indicates true despondency. The frequent bowing of the Japanese is seen as ingratiating by Americans, while the hearty nose-blowing of westerners in public is abhorred by Japanese, who invariably leave the room to do this.

Man is the only animal that speaks, laughs and weeps. Other species we can observe obviously have their own means of communication, but, except for the dolphins, we stop short of saying that they possess speech. Animals growl, bark, grunt and squeal, imparting messages not only to each other, but also to more articulate humans. Inevitably these sounds are accompanied by the appropriate body language – a threatening crouch, hair standing on end, a showing of teeth, imminent flight, submissive posture or cowering, etc. Body language, with its accompanying odours, is probably the principal mode of communication among animals.

Speech as auxiliary to body language

Anthropologists tell us that before humans possessed speech – and possibly in the early days of its acquisition and development – they probably depended as much on body language as do the beasts today. They assume that speech developed to make body language more explicit and that as the former became more sophisticated, gestures became less necessary. The ability to deliver an icy 'I'll break your neck' made club-waving superfluous and 'Would you mind passing me a little more of that delicious cold lamb?' has almost eliminated snatching, at the table or round the camp fire.

The theory that speech – first used minimally as an auxiliary to the basic messages of body language – developed into the main form of communication, gradually reducing body language to the auxiliary role, is a neat one.

Surprisingly, it is not that simple. In spite of the incredible sophistication, subtlety and flexibility of speech, it seems that some humans still rely basically on body language to convey (especially where intense feelings are concerned) what they really mean. Such people are the Italians, South Americans and most Latins, as well as many Africans and people from the Middle East. Others, such as Japanese, Chinese, Finns and Scandinavians, have virtually eliminated overt body language from their communication.

The space bubble

People from reactive and linear-active cultures are generally uncomfortable when confronted by the theatrical, excitable gestures and behaviour of the multi-actives. The feeling of discomfort generally begins at the outset when the 'space bubble' is invaded. Orientals, Nordics, Anglo-Saxon and Germanic people mostly regard space within 1.2 metres of the self as inviolable territory for strangers, with a smaller bubble of 0.5 metres in radius for close friends and relatives. Mexicans (and many of their cousins) happily close within half a metre of strangers for business discussions.

When a Mexican positions himself 0.5 metres away from an Englishman, he is ready to talk business. The Englishman sees him in English personal space and backs off to 1.2 metres. In doing so, he relegates the Mexican to the South American 'public zone' (1.2 metres) and the latter thinks the Englishman finds his physical presence distasteful or does not want to talk business. For a Mexican to talk business over a yawning chasm of 1.2 metres is like an English person shouting out confidential figures to someone at the other end of the room.

Different types of body language

Multi-actives – French, Mediterranean people, Arabs, Africans, South and Central Americans – possess a whole variety of gestures and facial expressions, largely unused and often misconstrued or disliked by reactive, linear-active and data-oriented cultures.

Finns and Japanese do not seem to have any body language – an assumption which administers cultural shock to first-time visitors in Finland and Japan. I say do not seem, because in fact Finns and Japanese do use body language which is well understood by fellow nationals in each country. Finns and Japanese have to be good 'body watchers', as the verbal messages in their countries are kept at a minimum. In the Finnish and Japanese cultures, upbringing and training discourage gesticulations, exaggerated facial expressions and uninhibited manifestations of glee, sorrow, love, hate, hope, disappointment or triumph. In both societies the control and disciplined management of such emotions leads to the creation of a much more restrained type of body language which is so subtle that it goes unnoticed by the foreign eye. Finns and Japanese are able to detect nonverbal messages in each other's culture, as their own nationals behave in a similar manner. As Finns and Japanese are accustomed to looking for minimal signs, the blatantly demonstrative body language of Italians, Arabs and South Americans produces strong culture shock for them. It is as if someone used to listening to the subtle melodies of Chopin or Mozart were suddenly thrown into a modern disco. The danger is, of course, that over-reaction sets in – a judgmental reaction which causes Japanese to consider Americans and Germans as charging bulls and Finns to see French as too 'clever', Italians as over-emotional and even Danes as a bit slick.

The body language of multi-active people often incorporates the following features.

Eyes

Eyes are among the more expressive parts of the body. In multi-active cultures, where power distance between people is greater, speakers will maintain close eye contact all the time they deliver their message. This is particularly noticeable in Spain, Greece and Arab countries. Such close eye contact (Finns and Japanese would call it 'staring') implies dominance and reinforces one's position and message. In Japan this is considered improper and rude. Japanese avoid eye contact 90 per cent of the time, looking at a speaker's neck while listening and at their own feet or knees when they speak themselves.

In great power-distance societies, it is easy for us to detect what the 'pecking order' is by observing people's eye behaviour. Lower ranking people tend to look at superiors, who ignore them unless they are in direct conversation with them. When anyone cracks a joke or says something controversial, all the subordinates' eyes will switch immediately to the chief personage to assess his reaction. This is less evident in northern countries where head-and-eye switching would be much more restrained, sometimes avoided.

Mediterranean people use their eyes in many different ways for effect. These include glaring (to show anger), glistening eyes (to show sincerity), winking (very common in Spain and France to imply conspiracy) and the eyelash flutter (used by women to reinforce persuasion). Eyebrows are also raised and lowered much more frequently than in northern societies, again to show surprise, disapproval, aggression, fearlessness etc.

Weeping is another form of body language little used by monochronic cultures for communication and almost unknown in Finland, Korea and Japan. Weeping is seen frequently in Latin and Arabian societies, even occasionally used in moments of drama in the UK (Winston Churchill was a memorable public weeper). Biologists tell us that weeping is good for us, not only to relieve tension, but tears apparently release excess chemicals from the body and even contain benign bacteria which protect the eye from infections. The Latins know more than we do!

Nose and ears

French and Hispanic people indulge in the nose twitch, snort or sniff, to express alertness, disapproval or disdain respectively. Portuguese tug their ear lobes to indicate tasty food, though this gesture has sexual connotations in Italy. In Spain the same action means someone is not paying for their drinks and in Malta it signifies an informer. It is best to recognise these signs, but not embark on the risky venture of attempting to imitate them.

Mouth

It is said that the mouth is one of the busiest parts of the human body, except in Finland where it is hardly used (except for eating and drinking). This is, of course, not strictly true, but most societies convey a variety of expressive moods by the way they cast their lips. De Gaulle, Fernandel, Saddam Hussein, Marilyn Monroe and James Stewart made the mouth work overtime to reinforce their message or appeal. The tight-lipped Finn shrinks away from such communicative indulgences as the mouth shrug (French), the pout (Italian), the broad, trust-inviting smile of the American, or even the fixed polite smile of the Oriental. Kissing one's fingertips to indicate praise (Latin) or blowing at one's finger-tip (Saudi Arabian) to request silence are gestures alien to the Nordic and Asian cultures.

Shoulders

Non-demonstrative people living in another culture for a prolonged period can progress to an understanding of demonstrative gestures. Multi-active peoples have very mobile shoulders, normally kept still in northern societies. The Gallic shoulder shrug is well known from our observations of Maurice Chevalier, Jean Gabin and Yves Montand. Latins keep their shoulders back and down when tranquil and observant, push them up and forward when alarmed, anxious or hostile.

Arms

Arms are used little by Nordics during conversation. In Italy, Spain and South America they are an indispensable element in one's communicative weaponry. Frequent gesticulating with the arms is one of the features which northerners find hardest to tolerate or imitate. It is inherently associated in the northern mind with insincerity, overdramatisation, therefore unreliability. As far as touching is concerned, however, the arm is the most neutral of body zones and even Englishmen will take guests by the elbow to guide them through doorways or indulge in the occasional arm pat to deserving subordinates or approaching friends.

Hands

The hands are among the most expressive parts of the body. Kant called them 'the visible parts of the brain'. Italians watching Finnish hands may be forgiven for thinking that Finns have sluggish brains. It is undeniable that northern peoples use their hands less expressively than Latins or Arabs, who recognize them as a brilliant piece of biological engineering. There are so many signals given by the use of the hands that we cannot consider them all here. Among the most common are 'thumbs up', used in many cultures but so ubiquitous in Brazil they drive you mad with it, hands clasped behind back to emphasize a superior standing (see Prince Philip and various other Royals and company presidents). The akimbo posture (hands on hips) denotes rejection or defiance, especially in Mediterranean cultures.

Legs

As we move even further down the body, less evident but equally significant factors come into play. Northerners participate in leg-language like
everybody else. As no speech is required, it inflicts no strain on them. In
general the 'legs together' position signifies basically defensiveness, against
a background of formality, politeness or subordination. Most people have
their legs together when applying for a job. It indicates correctness of attitude. This position is quite common for Anglo-Saxons at first meetings,
but changes to 'legs crossed' as discussions become more informal. Formal
negotiators such as Germans or Japanese can go through several meetings
maintaining the 'leg together' position. There are at least half a dozen different ways of crossing your legs, the most formal being crossing ankles
only, the average being crossing the knees, and the most relaxed and informal being the ankle-on-knee cross so common in North America.

When it comes to walking, the English and Nordics walk in a fairly
neutral manner, avoiding the Latin bounce, the American swagger and the
German march. It is more of a brisk plod, especially brisk in winter when
the Spanish dawdle would lead to possible frostbite.

Feet

It is said that the feet are the most honest part of the body: although we are
self-conscious about our speech or eye and hand movements, we actually
forget what our feet are doing most of the time. The honest Nordics,
therefore, send out as many signals with their feet as the Latins do. Foot
messages include tapping on the floor (boredom), flapping up and down
(want to escape), heel lifting (desperate to escape), multi-kicking from a
knees-crossed position (desire to kick the other speaker). Nordic reticence
sometimes reduces the kicking action to wiggling of the toes up and down
inside shoes, but the desire is the same. Foot stamping in anger is common
in Italy and other Latin countries, but virtually unused north of Paris.

Body language in business

Some forms of sales training involve a close study of body language, especially in those societies where it is demonstrative. Italian salespeople, for
instance, are told to pay great attention to the way their 'customers' sit

during a meeting. If they are leaning forward on the edge of their chair they are interested in the discussion or proposal. If they sit right back, they are bored, or confident to wait for things to turn their way. Buttoned jackets, and arms or legs tightly crossed, betray defensiveness and withdrawal. A salesperson should not try to close his sale in such a situation. Neither should a proposal be made to someone who is tapping with feet or fingers – they should be asked to speak. Italian salespeople are taught to sit as close as they can to their customers when attempting to close the deal. Latin people tend to buy more from a person sitting close to them than from a distance.

Solutions

Cross-cultural factors will continue to influence international negotiation and there is no general panacea of strategies which ensure quick understanding. The only possible solutions lie in a close analysis of the likely problems. These will vary in the case of each negotiation, therefore the combination of strategies required to facilitate the discussions will be specific on each occasion. Before the first meeting is entered into, the following questions should be answered:

1. What is the intended purpose of the meeting? (Preliminary, factfinding, actual negotiation, social?)
2. Which is the best venue?
3. Who will attend? (Level, number, technicians?)
4. How long will it last? (Hours, days, weeks?)
5. Are the physical arrangements suitable? (Room size, seating, temperature, equipment, transport, accommodation for visitors?)
6. What entertainment arrangements are appropriate? (Meals, excursions, theatre?)
7. How much protocol does the other side expect? (Formality, dress, agendas?)
8. Which debating style are they likely to adopt? (Deductive, inductive, free-wheeling, aggressive, courteous?)
9. Who on their side is the decision maker? (One person, several, or only consensus?)

10. How much flexibility can be expected during negotiation? (Give and take, moderation, fixed positions?)
11. How sensitive is the other side? (National, personal?)
12. How much posturing and body language can be expected? (Facial expressions, impassivity, gestures, emotion?)
13. What are the likely priorities of the other side? (Profit, long-term relationship, victory, harmony?)
14. How wide is the cultural gap between the two sides? (Logic, religion, political, emotional?)
15. How acceptable are their ethics to us? (Observance of contracts, timescale?)
16. Will there be a language problem? (Common language, interpreters?)
17. What mechanisms exist for breaking deadlock or smoothing over difficulties?
18. To what extent may such factors as humour, sarcasm, wit, wise-cracking and impatience be allowed to spice the proceedings?

Good answers to the questions in the above 'checklist' will help to clear the decks for a meeting which will have a reasonable chance of a smooth passage. It is to be hoped that the other side has made an attempt to clarify the same issues. French people often hold a preliminary meeting to do just this – to establish the framework and background for discussion. This is very sensible, although some regard the French as being nitpicking in this respect.

9

MANNERS (AND MANNERISMS)

"Manners maketh man". Cross-culturally speaking, they can unmaketh him as well. In a really free world we should be able to wipe our plates with bread like the French, hawk and spit like the Mongolians, belch like the Fijians, drink ourselves legless like the Finns, voice unpopular opinions like the Germans, turn up late like the Spaniards, snub people like the English and eat with our left hand in Saudi Arabia. In theory, there is no such thing as international etiquette, but certain mannerisms are acceptable only at home!

IN OUR OWN CULTURE WE ARE PROVIDED WITH A CODE FOR BEHAVIOUR. There is right and wrong, proper and improper, respectable and disreputable. The code, taught by parents and teachers and confirmed by peers and contemporaries, covers not only basic values and beliefs, but correctness of comportment and attitudes in varying circumstances. The rules may or may not be enshrined in law, but in one's own society they may not be broken without censure or with impunity. Unless we are eccentric, we conform. At home we know how to behave at table, at cocktail parties, in restaurants, at meetings and at a variety of social occasions. We are also fully cognisant of the particular taboos which our own culture imposes.

Comfortable code

The well-brought-up citizen not only feels comfortable with the code, but in the main actually welcomes it. It is a familiar regulatory mechanism which stops people making fools of themselves or being considered outsiders. All societies have outsiders, of course, but most of us prefer to be insiders. Generally speaking, it is less hassle. A problem arises, however, when we go abroad. As a representative of our country, we would like to show what good manners we have. Unfortunately, what are good manners in one country can be eccentricity or downright bad manners in another, as anyone who blows their nose in a beautiful white handkerchief in front of a Japanese will soon find out. International travellers face a dilemma. Should they maintain their impeccable behaviour from back home and risk inevitable *faux pas*, or should they imitate the people they visit and risk ridicule?

Unfortunately, there is no such thing as international etiquette. When someone begins to formulate an international code for correct behaviour, they instinctively look to their own norms as being the logical, acceptable, inoffensive ones. So we are back where we started.

Sincerity helps

Sincerity takes us a long way. Europeans, Asians and Americans meet regularly on business and at conferences and manage to avoid giving offence, by and large, by being their honest selves. The Americans are genial and sincere, the French gallant and sincere, the British reasonable and sincere, Germans and Russians unsmiling but sincere, Finns clumsy but sincere, the Japanese smiling and sincere (although unfortunately Europeans and Americans think their smiles are insincere). The odd dinner or business meeting we carry off well in the euphoria generated by the host's generosity and the guest's appreciative attentiveness. At such initial gatherings *faux pas* are ignored, even considered charming. The question of correct comportment in a foreign environment only becomes pressing when the exposure is lengthened. A protracted host–guest relationship or, even more, an ongoing business relationship, places greater strain on the tolerance and patience thresholds of both parties as time goes by. The American habit of sprawling in chairs at business conferences may seem friendly and disarming to the British, but would place Germans in a constant state of unease either in their own offices or the American's. Mexican unpunctuality, forgiven once, becomes unacceptable if endemic. Latin loquacity, engaging at first for Finns and Swedes, soon drives them up the wall. There is a limit to the number of cups of green tea a European can accept in a day.

Learning the ropes

Once the honeymoon of first acquaintance is over, international travellers/businesspeople seek a behaviour pattern which will serve them adequately wherever they find themselves. Some things come easily – handshaking or bowing, ladies first or ladies last, chocolates or flowers for the hostess. Other features give a little more trouble – the use of chopsticks, the texture of local small talk, the concept of time in a particular country. The deeper we delve, the harder it gets. What are the important social norms? What are the core beliefs? The real sensitivities? Above all, what is strictly taboo?

They don't always tell you. Everyone knows that it is inadvisable to send the firm's best-known drinker to represent you in Saudi Arabia and that Arabs do not eat pork, but is one aware that it is bad manners to point one's foot at an Arab in conversation or ask about the health of any of his womenfolk? Did you know that sending yellow flowers to a woman signifies, in some European countries, that she has been unfaithful to her husband?

Let us take a look at the areas where major *gaffes* may cause offence and minor ones some embarrassment – dining table etiquette, cocktail parties, restaurant behaviour, meetings, social norms and finally taboos.

Table manners

An old Malagasy proverb says: 'Men are like the lip of a cooking-pot, which forms just one circle.' By this one might understand that the basic human need for food serves as a uniting factor, at least temporarily. This is more than likely, though what people do around that cooking pot can differ to a startling degree. To begin with, eating is actually more important to some of us than to others. We often hear it said that Americans eat to live and that the French live to eat. This may be an oversimplification, but it is a fact that many Americans have a Coke and burger in the office, the English a sandwich or pub lunch, and Scandinavians are in and out of the company canteen in 30 minutes flat. In contrast, the French attach social importance to the midday meal, which may last from one to two hours. Spaniards, Portuguese and Greeks rarely rush it either.

Eating hours

People also eat at very different times. Nordics, who begin work early, have very little breakfast, but are starving by noon. Finns have lunch at 11.30, while 12.30–1 is a European norm. Spaniards rarely get the meal on the table before 2 and used to carry on until 4 or 5pm, although their membership of the EuropeanUnion is causing the younger executives at least to get back to the office by 3 and cut out the siesta. An even greater variety of eating times is apparent for the evening meal. Finns are starving again around four and they, along with the Japanese 'salarymen' and the British working classes, precede the rest of us to the table around 5.30 pm. Canada and New Zealand, too, take an early 'supper'. The Australians hang on a bit longer, the Americans and most northern and central Europeans sit down around 7.30, while the Spaniards and Portuguese, still digesting lunch, do not want to see food again till 9 or 10pm, often leaving it much later than that. A dinner invitation in Spain or Portugal for 8 or 8.30 means that the main course is likely to be served between 10 and 11. Chinese and other Asians start the evening meal at 8–9pm, although Indonesians have an aversion to dining early.

When invited to dinner at someone's home, most nationalities turn up at the appointed time – it is quite a different matter for cocktail parties. Unpunctuality, is, however, no disgrace in Spain, when an invitation for 9pm means 9.30 in any case.

Protocol

Seating arrangements, when round a table, are often casual and left to the last minute in many countries, although Asians invariably seat the most important guest facing the door. In Europe, the French and Germans are more careful about placing people, bearing in mind their various interests and status. It is the Swedes, however, who behave most formally at table. Swedish hospitality notwithstanding, dinner in Stockholm can be quite an ordeal. The chief guest escorts the hostess to the table and sits on her left, unlike most countries, which prefer the right. Schnapps are served at the beginning and the guest of honour must initiate the toasting. The first toast will be to the hostess and a short speech is required. One raises one's glass, proclaims the toastee's name, looks into his or her eyes, utters the magic word '*skål*', knocks back a fair amount of the firewater, holds one's glass up again for another two-second eye contact, then places the glass firmly on the table. As the dinner proceeds each person round the table must *skål* and be *skål*ed in this way. If anyone is forgotten by anyone else, it might not be forgiven easily. The biggest scandal, of course, is if you *skål* the hostess if more than eight people are present at the table. A Swedish couple from the small town of Gävle told me that some years earlier an important French visitor had done this to his hostess and that the people of Gävle had talked about little else since. Swedes are great after-dinner speakers and at large dinners (50 guests or more) lengthy toasts and speeches can take up to two hours. Guests are expected to speak in English, French or German if they can't manage Swedish. You can be either humorous or pompous – both styles seem to go down well.

Bon appétit

In most countries the signal to start eating is given by the host or hostess. In France it is '*bon appétit*', in Germany '*guten Appetit*', in Italy '*buon appetito*' and so on. Anglo-Saxons have no equivalent for this formula and often mutter 'right' or say nothing. This is very disconcerting for French people who invariably come out with 'good appetite'. One Frenchman, on being told one says nothing, waved his spoon hesitatingly over his soup for a moment, then grunted '*Eh bien, alors – bonne nuit*' before tucking in. The Japanese formula is '*itadakimasu*' (I am receiving), although they will probably have preceded this by saying something nice about the appearance of the food. Japanese attach as much importance to the aesthetic arrangement or layout of the food as its actual taste, so in Japan you should not attack a dish without complimenting your hostess on her artistry.

How many courses

Anglo-Saxons are used to eating three courses – starters, main dish and dessert. In other societies, the number of dishes may be far more numerous. The French, for instance, serve many side dishes such as lettuce, *haricot verts*, endives, asparagus and artichoke separately, whereas the British tend to put as much as they can on one plate. In Asia one can lose count of the number of dishes, although in China they will be placed on the table five or six at a time. The Japanese, when seeking to impress, can serve a very large number of dishes one after the other, each containing a small, easily digestible amount. Once hosted by a Japanese college principal, I counted 19 consecutive courses, all paper-thin slices of fish or meat (17 fish to 2 meat) and arranged concentrically overlapping to cover the whole plate. My mother, who was 92 at the time, was worried that the very multiplicity of cuts would be too much for her ageing stomach, but the principal, who was 90 himself, assured her she would be able to digest the lot without any problem. This proved to be true, until they served up the twentieth dish (strawberries) which promptly sent off both nonagenarians to the rest room to be sick.

Customs

According to the customs of the country, meals may be taken sitting or at table, on the floor or on the ground. In Japan it is common to sit on *tatami* matting, in Arabian countries on carpets, linoleum or polished surfaces, in Tonga, Fiji and most of Polynesia on grass or firm soil. When not at table, Europeans and Americans have to decide how to arrange their legs, not being able in general to squat for long in the eastern manner. In Japanese and Arabian households shoes are generally removed and left in the hall. Chopsticks are used in several Asian countries, particularly Japan and China, and Caucasians are advised to acquire enough aptitude with them at least to get morsels into the mouth. Clumsiness is normally overlooked, although goodness knows what they really think of us. We get our own back when some of them use knives and forks. In Arab countries one usually eats with the hand – the right one – as the left is reserved for 'dirty' tasks, whatever those may be. It is not easy to eat a huge leg of lamb oozing gravy with one hand. You need to roll up the right sleeve before you start – the gravy will run down your forearm in any case. Most homes have an adjoining washroom to which you repair periodically to wash the gravy off. The choicest cuts are handed to you by the host – it is bad manners to take a piece yourself or to decline the piece he offers you, too big though it may be. Rice will be squeezed into balls by the host (by hand) and given to you directly. You may squeeze further balls of rice yourself but do not touch the lamb on the serving plate. Don't touch any food with your left hand unless you have informed the host at the beginning of the meal that you are left-handed, in which case remember that your right hand is the dirty one. In Malagasy families the leg of lamb is exclusively the father's portion.

Starters

Starters vary in different countries. Japanese *sashimi* (raw fish) is arguably among the most delicious (and expensive), raw or smoked fish also being popular in Scandinavian countries. French *hors d'oeuvre* often consist of *crudités*. Italians favour *antipasta* (often Parma ham). Americans shrimp cocktails and (recently) potato skins, Greeks *tsatsiki* and *taramasalata* and Turks yoghurt. Spaniards like to have a *tapas* session before dinner. Americans whet their appetite with pre-dinner *guacamole* and cheese dips. In virtually all countries, however, soups are a great stand-by and often a particular soup is closely associated with the national cuisine. In Spain, it is *gazpacho*, in France *soupe à l'oignon* and *bouillabaisse*, in Austro-Hungary *goulasch*, in Russia *bortsch*, in China shark's fin or bird's nest, in Nordic countries pea, in Italy *minestrone*, in Germany oxtail and in the United States clam chowder. All of these soups, whether hot or cold, are normally ordered as starters. In Japan *misoshiro* soup is eaten at or near the end of the meal, as is the *sopa alentejana* in the Portuguese province of Alentejo. In the latter case, the peasants used to fill up on soup, as main courses were often inadequate in this once poverty-stricken region.

Soups are normally eaten with metal soup spoons; in China they are ceramic and a special shape. In Japan and Korea one lifts the soup bowl to the mouth and drinks the contents accompanied by legitimate slurping. In these countries rice is also slurped up from close quarters with chopsticks. It is a noisy process, but perfectly good manners. Most Europeans tip their soup dish towards themselves when spooning out the last dregs – in England it is considered good manners to tilt the soup plate away from oneself in the closing stages.

Main courses

Main courses around the world are too numerous and varied to describe here. Strange though many foods may seem, most dishes are edible and even tasty when one has familiarised oneself with them. *Sashimi*, which puts a lot of Anglo-Saxons off at first tasting, is one of the world's great dishes, priceless for its subtlety and delicate flavour. One can hardly say the same of Korean *kimshi*, some Vietnamese fish and eel dishes and various offerings in the small villages along the Yangtse. Fijian *kava* tastes (and looks) like mud to the uninitiated and I would not recommend the

Pyongyang *sake* with a snake in the bottle even to people who owe me money. Finnish *kalakukko* and *mämmi* take a little negotiating, but are good in the end, although *calamares en su tinta* (squid in its own ink) has few supporters outside the Hispanic world.

International travellers should eat as much as they can, to avoid offending their hosts. Americans and particularly English are well placed to get their revenge if they want to by offering their own cooking to visitors on Anglo-Saxon shores. In general, although one offers one's best and tries to follow the good manners of the host country. It is as well to know that an Australian country breakfast may consist of a huge beefsteak with two fried eggs on top and that in Madagascar you should not hand an egg directly to another person, but place it on the floor first. In Tonga and Hawaii you bury meat for a while before you eat it, in Japan you can eat whalemeat and live lobsters (they watch you eat them) and in Finland I have enjoyed succulent steaks of bear, beaver, elk and reindeer. Portuguese mix pork and clams and cook cod in 53 different ways. Malagasy slaughter zebu cattle on sacrificial occasions and put a little blood on guests' heads to integrate them into the festivities.

Unusual table manners are not limited to Third World or out-of-the-way countries. The English take the use of a knife and fork for granted, but Americans do not keep a knife in their hand while eating. First they cut the meat with their knife in the right hand and fork in the left. Then they put the knife down by the side of the plate, transfer the fork from left hand to right, slightly dip the left shoulder and start eating in what to the British looks like a lopsided manner. The British habit of eating vegetables (even peas) with the fork upside down is scorned by the Americans and Europeans. The French – great eaters – use bread as an extra utensil, pushing anything else around with it and eventually employing a chunk to wipe the plate clean and save the dish washers extra effort. It might not look very civilized around Cadogan Square, but what are the French to think of a society which eats its cheese after dessert?

Japanese, westernised in many things, do not usually eat dessert. Neither are they very fond of cheese or lamb, so remember that when you invite them home. In Japan the main things to remember are to say how nice everything looks, keep eating a little of each dish at a time without finishing any off, and lifting up your glass when someone offers to fill it. You in turn should fill up their glass, and any others you can reach. When you have drunk enough *sake*, turn your *sake* cup upside down. In China you should never take the last morsel from a serving plate and never at any time during the meal say you are hungry.

In the Finnish countryside they serve new potatoes with their skins on at the table and you are supposed to peel them before eating. Finns can do this with a knife and fork without touching the hot potatoes, which burn the fingers of the uninitiated. In England we are told not to put our elbows on the dining table and to sit with our hands in our lap when we have finished. Mexicans are told to put both hands on the table during and after the meal; it is taboo to hide them under the table. In Fiji and some other countries it is polite (even mandatory) to belch or burp after completing your meal, to show appreciation. Don't do it in the wrong country. (Swedish hostesses would faint.) In China you know when the meal is ended, for the host stands up and thanks you for coming.

In the United States many Britons have been shocked when on their first helping of the main course, the host asks them, 'Did you get enough?' The use of the past definite (instead of the present perfect, 'Have you had enough?') implies to the Brit that there is no more to be had. In fact the American is offering more, so you may legitimately reply, 'I sure didn't!'

Cocktail parties

There are no fixed rules for cocktail parties, which in themselves are often interesting exercises in cross-cultural behaviour. No one is quite sure what is the best time to arrive, the best time to leave and how long the party should last. Then there is the question of what one drinks, how much one eats and what one talks about. Having a few friends at home for drinks in one's own country is a relatively simple affair. Larger parties with a multinational guest list require considerably more thought.

My wife and I spent five years on the Tokyo cocktail circuit – a very lively one – where attendances averaged well over 50 and involved a minimum of a dozen different nationalities, often more. They were usually held in the homes of business executives; embassies entertained on a somewhat larger scale on National Days and other occasions.

We counted among our circle of friends in Tokyo acquaintances from 20-odd countries as well as a liberal sprinkling of Japanese. Under such circumstances there is no such thing as a cocktail party of short duration. How does one schedule an event where the Japanese will turn up 10 minutes early, the Germans and the Swiss on time, the Americans and British a bit late, the French after them and the Brazilians an hour after the party was due to end? One could put something like 6.30–8.30 on the invitation card, but nobody took any notice of it. Few parties ended before 11 or 12 unless one ran out of liquor.

Another basic problem was how many people to invite. Even among the British and American communities, with which we were chiefly involved, it was likely that there would be half a dozen cocktail parties held every night. Consequently one counted on an acceptance rate of one in three and invited 150. If you were unlucky enough to hit a day when for some reason there were few parties, you might get landed with 100 guests or more – this happened to us on more than one occasion. The problem was further complicated by the fact that Japanese tend not to answer the RSVP – but they usually turn up. Furthermore most Japanese executives do not bring their wives, although some do! One just had to play the averages.

Small talk

Some nationalities thrive in the cocktail party atmosphere and others do not. Russians, for instance, like drinking sitting down, especially as they devote a considerable amount of time to it. Chinese, too – used to mammoth dinners seated at banquet tables – are less at ease shuffling round from group to group of noisy strangers. Americans, with their mobile nature and easy social manners, excel in such a kaleidoscopic ambience. Australians and Canadians, used to formulating strategies for meeting new arrivals, have no difficulty in integrating themselves with circle after circle and conversation always comes easily to them. The British and the French – past masters at small talk – are also practised cocktailers. Yet the very issue of small talk poses a substantial problem for some other nationalities. Germans simply do not believe in it, Finns and Japanese are frightened to death by it, Swedes usually dry up after about 10 minutes. Russians and Germans – more than willing to have long, soul-searching conversations with close friends – see no point in trotting out trivialities and platitudes for two hours to a complete stranger. Swedes – fluent in English and happy to talk about their job and technical matters – find little to say in addition and often admit they become boring after the first half-hour. Finns, unused to chatter, actually buy booklets on small talk (one recently published in Helsinki was a great success).

The Japanese – masters of polite trivia among themselves – are never quite sure what to talk about with foreigners. At Japanese business meetings, there is the obligatory 15-minute session of platitudes and harmonising, after which one can get down to business. At cocktail parties they run up against a void.

Not so the South Americans. Although relatively deficient in foreign language skills, they maintain an incessant patter which often saves the day for Japanese or Scandinavian partners. Mexicans, Peruvians, Argentinians never run out of steam. I once attended an all Latin-American cocktail party in Caracas which began at 7 and finished at 1am. There were 300 people present, very little to eat, nobody stopped talking except to draw breath for six hours flat; I do not remember a single word that was said.

Personal space

At cocktail parties it is sometimes difficult to maintain the integrity of one's 'space bubble', especially when there are a few Latins around. A common sight in Tokyo was a Brazilian or Colombian businessman towering over a diminutive Japanese, gripping his upper arm to show confidence, while the Japanese would back-pedal, striving to keep his glass and himself on an even keel. The Latin in his eagerness pushes ever forward into personal space; in 20 minutes they traverse the length of the room, the Japanese ending up with his back against a wall. The South American notices nothing of the other's discomfort; the latter politely asks the whereabouts of the toilet and flees, drink in hand.

What to drink

For a big party it is necessary to stock a large variety of drinks, although drinking habits are now far more standard than they used to be. This is largely due to the ascendancy of whisky and gin and tonic as international beverages. The French, for instance, who formerly drank Scotch only after dinner, now regard it as an apéritif and import huge quantities of it. English frequently drink it with soda, Americans often on the rocks, Scots neat and Japanese with water ('*mizuwari*'). Gin and tonic sells well on hot evenings and is a favourite with ladies of most nationalities, as is Campari soda or Campari and orange. Germans like white wine, Spaniards and Portuguese red, Russians vodka, Scandinavians anything with a label on it.

When Americans ask for a martini they mean 99 per cent dry gin with just a drop of vermouth in it, often with an olive or cocktail onion for good looks. With the olive it is called a Martini, with an onion a Gibson. When Americans ask for whisky, they mean Bourbon; if they want whisky they say Scotch. When you've worked this out, they ask for whisky sour, so you don't know what to put in it. When you think you're well stocked they will request things like Manhattans, Screwdrivers and White Ladies and see if you know the difference between Tom and John Collins. The British get their revenge at American parties by ringing the changes on Pimms No. 1 Cup, Pimms No. 2 Cup and Pimms No. 3 Cup.

Embassies

Embassy cocktail parties can be long and boring affairs where most of the diplomats talk to each other for hours and leave businesspeople and other lesser mortals to fend for themselves. On these occasions it is advisable to arrive and leave early, as the food usually runs out after the first hour. Japanese embassies provide the best food, the Germans and Americans at least serve enough. Paradoxically the embassies most oriented towards businesspeople were the Soviet, Chinese and Eastern bloc countries, as their attachés were actually the people who developed commercial outlets for command economies.

Leaving

There is no foolproof way of calling an end to cocktail festivities. American businesspeople can get so involved in discussing deals over drinks that they sometimes forget they are at a party, never mind the time. Latins can talk for ever. British, Germans, Dutch, Swiss and Japanese are relatively disciplined cocktail party leavers, but the same cannot be said for Danes, Scots, Slavs and Irish. In Asia it is the duty of a host to end a party, in Europe and the USA it usually depends on the guest. An old English gentleman I knew used to go to the front door at midnight, open it and stand quietly by it. After 10 minutes or so everybody used to get the idea and leave. A Swedish party-giver told me recently that there was only one way to make Finns and Russians leave. Simply announce there was plenty of food left, but nothing more to drink.

Restaurants

Restaurant entertaining plays an important part in the life of the international businessperson. It is not unusual for travelling executives to find themselves being hosted four or five times a week when on a foreign trip. They will be required to reciprocate when their partners or associates return the visit. The choice between entertaining at home or at a restaurant depends on varying circumstances. American, British, Canadian, Australian and New Zealand hostesses are quick to open their homes to foreign visitors. Spaniards, Portuguese and other Latins are less inclined to do so, until firm personal relationships have been established. Dining out is still rather good value for money in Madrid, Lisbon, Athens and Istanbul, whereas astronomical prices in Oslo, Stockholm and Helsinki make Nordics think twice about indulging in this once popular and time-honoured practice.

A deductible expense

Restaurants tend to be packed in the evenings in cities renowned for their gastronomic excellence – Brussels, Paris, Lyon, San Francisco, New York, New Orleans, Vienna, Florence, Bologna and some other big Italian cities are good examples – while nowhere is dining out more popular than in Japan, where restaurant bills are fully deductible items for tax purposes and where companies or fiscal authorities rarely question the validity of entertaining expenses which do not exceed 4 per cent of the firm's turnover. With companies like Mitsubishi, Mitsui and Hitachi footing the bill, that entails substantial activity in eating and drinking! Japanese and other Orientals, furthermore, consider that the relative smallness of their homes in comparison to, say, those of their American or European counterparts, prohibits them from being able to entertain at home in the style the occasion calls for.

Ethnic cuisines

When being entertained by a foreign colleague in a restaurant, one need not be so fully attuned to the table manners of the country, since often the establishment will be chosen on account of its ethnic cuisine, which could be from anywhere. Although Parisians tend to invite you to French restaurants, Germans, Dutch or Swiss executives like to offer you a choice of cooking, while the London executive would have some difficulty in finding an 'English' restaurant once Simpson's and Wheeler's have been used. Americans, too, prefer European or Asiatic cuisine; Japanese executives usually offer you the western or Japanese alternatives.

It is as well to remember that some national cuisines are best represented outside their country of origin. This is certainly true of Russian food, for which Russian restaurants in Paris, Helsinki and Stockholm set standards nearly impossible to reach at establishments within the former Soviet Union. The best Hungarian meals I have ever eaten have been in Vienna, while nothing I ate during my month-long odyssey down the Yangtse even vaguely approached the excellence of Chinese dishes available in London or Hong Kong. London and England in general have unbelievably good Indian restaurants, while the 80-odd Japanese eating places in the British capital serve an expensive but delicious fare which can be bettered only with difficulty in Japan itself. With 50,000 Japanese permanent residents in London, it is not so surprising that such standards have been reached.

Most astonishing of all, Tokyo arguably possesses the best French restaurants in the world! The bounding strength of the yen, plus the traditional Japanese admiration for various aspects of western excellence, has motivated several rich Japanese entrepreneurs (in some cases well-known companies) to set up top French restaurants in Tokyo such as Maxim's and Tour d'Argent, housed in sumptuous premises and staffed by the very best chefs and *maîtres d'hôtel* that Japanese money can buy. These establishments – frequented nightly by expense-account senior executives – have achieved levels of cuisine, service and ambience which could be said to equal or surpass those of competitors anywhere. The variety of dishes on offer cover most of the regional specialities of France. The quality of Kobe beef and Japanese seafood ensure that no ingredients are lacking. Wine is flown in from France – wine lists can include 200–300 of the best vintages from Bourgogne and Bordeaux – and it is not unusual for 'good' bottles to cost $3000–$5000 a time. One shudders when envisaging what the total bill might be when half a dozen Japanese executives who know their wines (and they really do) have a good evening out.

Major league and minor league

Somewhat removed from this fast-lane living are middle managers anxious to impress their foreign customers on a night out on the limited budget that their enterprise permits. It is often a good idea to ask the guests which ethnic type of meal they prefer. There are, surprisingly, a very small number of cuisines which can be said to be truly famous internationally. These are French, Italian, Chinese and Indian. Such restaurants can be found in good numbers in almost every city in the world. Most businesspeople automatically opt for one of these styles. There is a growing 'second division league' of ethnic cuisines which are gradually establishing their reputation on an international basis. These include Greek, Mexican, Russian, Spanish, Korean, Indonesian, Thai and now Japanese restaurants, which are bobbing up more frequently in large cities, although they do not rival the 'big four' in general distribution. Other types of cooking such as Portuguese, German, Hungarian, Scandinavian, Vietnamese and Lebanese can be very tasty, especially when a native *gourmand* can guide you as to what to select. One rarely talks about Anglo-Saxon cuisine (American, British, Australian, New Zealand, Canadian), unless one is addicted to pig-meat for breakfast. Dutch, Finnish, Baltic, African, South American and Central and Eastern European restaurants are rarely found in other countries, although Argentinian steakhouses are beginning to gain international acceptance.

Varying ambiences

Given such a variety of eating houses, dining out offers a multiplicity of experiences. In general one adapts to the ambience. Restaurants in Spain, South America, China, Hong Kong and Indonesia are usually convivial and noisy. In England, the USA and Japan the atmosphere is more conducive to quiet socialising or business discussion, while in Sweden and Finland guests are asked to leave if they are too boisterous or unduly inebriated. Moderate intoxication is readily permitted in restaurants in Germany, Austria, Denmark and Greece, while in Japan it is considered good form for the boss to drink more than his subordinates, then perhaps leave early.

In Russia and Bavaria it is not uncommon for strangers to join you at table, particularly where the restaurant is rather large or has certain beer-hall characteristics. In Munich people occasionally bring their dogs and ask if they may sit them under the table.

Lunch or dinner in France assumes much more importance than in some other countries and the choice of dishes, and especially wine, will be attended with considerable fuss and ceremony. Wine has in the last decade become much more popular with Anglo-Saxons and Scandinavians and it is as well that you possess a reasonable knowledge of wines from at least France, Spain and Italy if you are a regular host. It is a far cry from the days when Swedes, Norwegians and Finns were not allowed to drink in restaurants unless they ordered another dish with each glass. In the Katarina restaurant in Stockholm, they used to have the *specialrätten* (the special dish) which one ordered with each additional cognac. It was cheap (to ease the strain on the diner's pocket) and was in fact pea soup. One ordered this time and time again with the accompanying brandy, the waiter ceremoniously placing the soup plate in front of the customer. One sniffed momentarily at the soup, waved one's spoon once over it, then let the waiter remove it. You didn't actually eat nine soups, but they would be on the bill.

Japanese modesty

When taking Japanese out to a restaurant one should exercise care that they are not allowed to choose freely from the menu. The reason for this is that the senior Japanese in the group will choose the cheapest thing listed and his colleagues will have to follow suit. In Japan it is good manners, when given the choice of dish, to show that you are not being extravagant with your host's money. This is certainly very meritorious behaviour on the part of the Japanese, but it may not be what you want. Very probably, for business reasons, you wish them to have a costly meal and wind up in your debt. The correct course of action is not to let them choose, but to recommend strongly the most expensive dish on the menu. The *châteaubriand* is what I am having, Mr Suzuki, it's the best dish in this restaurant and I insist you accompany me. He (and his subordinates) will be delighted to concur. It is not a cheap way of doing business, but it will almost certainly get you orders. Suzuki would have no hesitation in treating you with equal generosity in Japan.

Paying the bill

When it comes to paying the bill, it is usual to pay on one's home ground, as the foreign guests will already be in the hole after paying for their air tickets. Junior managers often agree to 'go Dutch' if they meet frequently. On no circumstances should one propose this arrangement with Asians. In most Asian countries, especially in Japan and China, the question of who pays the bill is quite clear before the evening commences. It is permissible for you to invite them out in their own country, though normally only after they have entertained you at least once. Guests are given the seat facing the door and from this position you should never try to pay. When you have seen the amount on the bill in many Japanese restaurants, it is unlikely you will be eager to pay in any case.

Tipping

Tipping can be such a minefield of error and embarrassment that it is better to ask foreign nationals on their ground what is the accepted custom. Suffice it to say that tips are awaited more anxiously by some waiters than others. The safest situation is when service is included in the bill, although it is not unusual for Latin waiters to expect an additional sum in recognition of smart attention. There is no danger of having to pay for extra quick service in Eastern Europe. Elsewhere, alacrity of service varies enormously according to the establishment, but is noticeably efficient in Portugal, Turkey, Australia, the USA and Switzerland. In most Asian countries the standard of service is excellent, whether you tip or not. In Japan and China tipping is not expected. In France waiters are capable of throwing the tip on the floor if they consider it insufficient.

Home in safety

Once the bill is paid, the waiter rewarded and the appropriate belching (if required) executed, then one is free to leave. In Asia the host generally will include your transport home as part of the evening's obligations. This is not so common in the West, but care should be taken to ensure safe delivery of the guest in such cities as Naples, St Petersburg, Rio, Los Angeles and New York, not to mention spots such as Bogotá and Antananarivo, where not even locals venture out on the street after dark.

Manners in society

In addition to the accepted practices for wining and dining, most cultures have an intricate set of rules governing general social behaviour. These directives are referred to as 'good manners' and are designed to help avoid the embarrassing pitfalls which lie in wait for the uninitiated.

Fortunately, manners are not what they used to be. In England they reached their peak of stringency in the days of Queen Victoria, when gentlemen wore hats just so they could take them off when meeting ladies on the street and inexperienced diners almost starved to death at table for fear of exhibiting inadequate etiquette. Alice Thomas Ellis recently reviewed a terrifying Victorian volume, *Manners and Tone of Good Society, or Solecisms to be Avoided* (circa 1899), which devoted 22 pages to the etiquette of leaving cards and went on to detail suitable instructions for morning calls, introductions, titles, periods of mourning and five o'clock teas.

At the turn of the century, similar behaviour was being advocated in Paris, Budapest, Vienna, St Petersburg and other fashionable metropoles. Good manners, invented by the upper classes theoretically in the interests of smooth social intercourse, in fact developed into a repressive code which put people in their place. Happily, Americans resent being sorted out in this way and shortly afterwards invented bad manners, which saved us all a lot of trouble. In this they were capably supported by the Canadians, with their disarmingly casual social graces, and particularly by the Australians, who, as we all know, don't give a XXXX about etiquette and generally behave as they please.

If some of England's colonies scrapped the tenets of correct behaviour held by the mother country, others imitated them well into the twentieth century. This was particularly true of India, where formality of posture and flowery speech habits even today retain Victorian overtones. Also New Zealanders and many South Africans appear very polite to present-day English people, who, since the Second World War, have largely adopted easy-going American social attitudes.

The Anglo-Saxons, along with the Scandinavians, are probably the most informal societies in the late twentieth century. The Japanese lead the world in standards of politeness, while Asians in general display consistent courtesy to foreigners and to each other. In Europe social ease fluctuates from Spanish warmth and Italian flexibility to Swiss pedantry and German righteousness; the French are probably the most formal of the Europeans.

The problem with observing the manners of others is not so much the degree of formality or informality to adopt (this can be quickly regulated) but to know what the manners are in certain regions. In Japan, for instance, the correct thing to do for a bereaved neighbour is to send them money in a sealed envelope. This custom makes some westerners uncomfortable, but nevertheless has considerable merit. If the family is rich they send the money back, if they are poor they keep it for funeral expenses. What more practical way to help them in their misfortune? To complicate the situation, bereaved Japanese often send you and your wife gifts in appreciation of your gesture.

Gift giving

Gift giving, particularly in Japan and China, is in itself a difficult area to negotiate. In brief, westerners cannot avoid indulging in this practice in the long run without running the risk of Orientals considering them churlish or stingy. Gift giving will almost invariably be initiated by the Asian; when reciprocating, be careful not to outgift a Japanese or a Chinese. It is a game you are not going to win anyway; extravagance on your part will only result in escalating expense on theirs. More important is the thought behind the gift. Something ethnic and tasteful from your own country is the safest (prints, ceramics, lace, illustrated books and so on). In general one should not open gifts in front of Asians and Arabs when an exchange of presents is taking place. The danger of someone losing face is too great.

When in Rome do as the Romans do

In Rome, imitating people's behaviour entails little hardship, as foreign visitors are more often than not quite willing to indulge in the wining, dining and other aspects of *la dolce vita* available in the Italian capital. In some countries and environments, however, one has to use one's judgement as to how far one is expected to 'go native'. Taking one's shoes off in Japanese homes comes easily, but what degree of politeness should one exhibit? For instance, Japanese apologise regularly for personal defects, minor transgressions, even for wrongs they have not done and can be embarrassingly self-deprecating in front of westerners. How much should Americans or Europeans run themselves down or accept Japanese apologies? Paradoxically, Japanese wives, in flower arranging or *origami* classes, speak disparagingly about their husbands, as this is regarded as a sign of modesty and good manners. Should the British wife follow suit? In Japan, Korea and some other countries men walk in front of women and precede them up and down stairs. British, French and Nordic males find this hard to do, though Australians manage it.

Male visitors to Australia are soon disconcerted by being called 'bastards'. An Englishman is a 'Pommie bastard', a Frenchman a 'Froggy bastard' and so on. One realises eventually that this form of address is a sign of affection among Australian males and that if an Englishman is not soon called a Pommie bastard, then the Aussies don't like him. Americans (Yanks) are called septic tanks.

In Russia it is polite to make a short speech with every toast, but it is better not to smash your vodka glass to the floor unless it is evident that your host expects you to. It's the same with plates in Greece – check it out. In Thailand a pale face is a sign of beauty in a woman (don't ask if she is unwell); in Asia one generally wraps up presents in red paper; white, on the other hand, is an unlucky colour associated with death. In Russia people don't answer other people's telephones – they just let them ring. And so it goes on – one just lives and learns how other people behave.

Strange or far out

Some traditions are so unusual that it is not advisable to imitate them. Cattle stealing is a proof of manhood in some African areas and it may be the only route to secure a worthwhile wife. In other, drought-stricken regions it is customary to take soap with you on long journeys, in case opportunities arise for running water. Polynesians bite the head of a newly deceased relative to make sure he has really passed away; it is better to stand respectfully at one side, if you are present.

Chinese decide on how to construct buildings and arrange furniture according to their *feng shui* beliefs, which will mean little to you. Few customs, however, are stranger or more impressive than the Malagasy *famadihana*, which means 'the turning of the bones'. In Madagascar when a relative has been dead and buried for a decent period of time, he or she is exhumed on some suitable anniversary or auspicious occasion, the bones are wrapped in a shroud and lovingly paraded at a family ceremony where a hundred or more people may be present. The bones are examined, fondled, shown to others and even talked to. In Madagascar the dead are considered more important and more influential than the living and the occasion often sees their reinstallation in a costly family tomb which offers considerably more comforts and amenities than the average Malagasy home. A fascinating sideline to this ceremony (to which foreigners are occasionally invited) is the question of taxation. The government taxes the *famadihana* severely, so that not infrequently three or four other families will surreptitiously whisk their own ancestral bones in and out of the tomb, rewarding the 'host' family by sharing the tax levy. This must be the world's quaintest tax fiddle!

Taboos

Taboos exist in every country and we do well to observe them as they are often deep rooted in the history and beliefs of the region. Madagascar again leads the field with a bewildering list of forbidden practices:

+ A woman may not wash her brother's clothes.
+ Pregnant women may not eat brains or sit in doorways.
+ Eggs may not be passed directly to others.
+ Children may not say their father's name or refer to any part of his body.

Closer to Europe, Russians also have an impressive list:

+ Coats should not be worn indoors.
+ It is bad form to stand with your hands in your pockets.
+ You should not sit with your legs apart.
+ No whistling in the street.
+ No lunches on park lawns.
+ No public displays of affection.
+ It is poor form to ask people where the toilet is, and never from the opposite sex.

On the other hand, it is perfectly acceptable to wander round hotel corridors at all hours of the evening or night wearing only pajamas.

In Malaysia it is taboo to point with one's index finger, although one may point with one's thumb. In Indonesia the head is regarded as a sacred, inviolable part of the body and should not be touched by another. You must suppress the desire to pat young children on the head. It is also taboo in Indonesia to have your head in a higher position than that of a senior person. This point of deference is easily engineered while sitting (a low chair or a crouch) but harder to achieve when meeting someone on the street. It is common to see Indonesians bobbing up and down on bent knees as they pass senior citizens or people of authority.

In Korea well-brought-up young people do not smoke or drink in front of elders. In Taiwan it is unthinkable to write messages in red ink. In England, Scandinavia, Japan and China it is bad form to blow your own trumpet, although others seem to see nothing wrong with it.

In Arab countries it is taboo to drink alcohol, eat pork or to ask about the health of a man's womenfolk. You will make an Arab uncomfortable by pointing your feet at him in conversation and you will insult him if you display the sole of your shoe or hold up your hand in front of his face. Do not openly admire his possessions, as he may feel obliged to give them to you. A harmless remark like 'I like that camel' may put you in an embarrassing situation in the Gulf.

Part Three

Getting to Know Each Other

We are normal, they are abnormal. Why do they have to be so devious, unpunctual, unsmiling, unreliable, undisciplined, cunning, lazy, corrupt, two-faced, aloof, distant, inscrutable? Why can't they be more like us? But appearance is not reality. Let's see why they are so pig-headed, etc.

10

UNITED STATES OF AMERICA

The United States of America has the world's biggest economy – four times greater than anyone else's (with the exception of Japan) and ten times bigger than that of Russia. America is first in volume of trade, first in industry, first in food output and first in aid to others. They spend, too, being the top consumers of energy, oil, oil seeds, grain, rubber, copper, lead, zinc, aluminium, tin, coffee and cocoa. They have the four busiest airports in the world and fly three times more passenger miles than anyone else. They have the world's longest road network and longest rail network. They own more cars, telephones, refrigerators, television sets, video cassettes, dishwashers and microwave ovens than any other people. They are the top tourist spenders and also gross the biggest tourist receipts (twice as much as popular France, in second place). The USA leads the rest of us as water users, polluters and consumers of newsprint. They also have the highest rates of divorce and murder.

Breakneck pace

The pace of American life is different from that of other countries. In the eighteenth and nineteenth centuries vast tracts of open, unclaimed land to the west beckoned with some urgency to poorer settlers and new arrivals. For decades it was first come, first served – you staked your claim, cleared the land, tilled, planted and defended it. They were days of land grab and gold rush. There was no time to lose as immigrants poured in, out west there were no ruling classes or aristocrats, royal claims or decrees, no constraining ideologies or regulations – only practicality, if it worked, you did it before anyone else did.

One might have assumed that with the majority of goals attained and the visible advent of the affluent society, this frenzied tempo of life would have slackened. It has not. Modern Americans continue at the headlong pace of their nineteenth-century forbears. Work equates with success, time is money. They have to get there first. The chief difference is that in the nineteenth century, everybody knew where 'there' was. Today's Americans, unrelentingly driven by the traditional national habit of pressing forward, conquering the environment, effecting change and reaching their destination, are no longer sure what that destination is.

The rest of the world looks on in awe, for none of us are in the same grip of this achievement fever. It can be argued that Germans and Japanese share the same work tempo as Americans, but the Germans, with their long holidays, social welfare and impressive culture, value quality of life much more. The Japanese, with no more leisure than the Americans, nevertheless achieve what they do at a much more relaxed pace and have created a calm, relatively crime-free society where moral and spiritual values take priority over materialistic goals. The four 'Asian tigers' – Singapore, Hong Kong, Korea and Taiwan, breakneck export powerhouses all – most closely resemble the USA in unrelenting effort, although their eastern philosophies incline them to view success as collectivist as opposed to the American view that the individual must triumph. In America you start at the very bottom, give it all you've got, pull yourself up by your own boot straps, guts it out and get to the very top. It's rags to riches, in a land where everybody is equal. It's a daunting task, but fortunately Americans are unfailing optimists (see human mental programming) and future-oriented.

Americans are not afraid of challenge or competition, although the strain is beginning to tell. Up to the 1970s the economic and political development of the United States had been an undoubted success story. Other nations had had their ups and downs, peaks and valleys, successes and reverses. Only in America had progress been invariably forward, up and one-way. Then came Vietnam, mounting trade balance deficits and the slowing of the economy. Even so, no one in their right mind writes off the Americans. Their industrial, commercial, financial and military assets are of a muscular nature not yet approached by their rivals for twenty-first-century dominance. A greater problem for the American people is not so much the maintenance of their material strengths as the attainment of inner harmony.

How should wise Asians, or Europeans with their variety of ideals, handle this time-keeping, media-driven, dollar-minded phenomenon? Hitch one's star to their wagon and make a fast buck? Or tough it out with them?

How to deal with the Americans

American businesspeople have the reputation of being the toughest in the world, but they are, in many respects, the easiest to deal with. That is because their business philosophy is uncomplicated. Their aim is to make as much money as they can as quickly as they can, using hard work, speed, opportunism, power (also of money itself) as the means towards this end. Their business decisions are usually not affected by sentiment and the dollar, if not God, is considered at least almighty. This single-minded pursuit of profit results in their often being described as ruthless.

Northern Europeans are well placed to deal with Americans successfully. Their reputation as straightforward managers is well-received by the open, frank Americans, who often get seriously irritated by what they see as the 'devious' manners of Latins and Orientals.

At meetings, Americans show the following tendencies:

+ They are individualistic, they like to go it alone without checking with head office. Anything goes unless it has been restricted.
+ They introduce informality immediately: take their jacket off, use first names, discuss personal details, e.g. family.
+ They give the impression of being naïve by not speaking anything but English and by showing immediate trust through ultra-friendliness.
+ They use humour whenever they can, even though their partner fails to understand it or regards it as out of place.
+ They put their cards on the table right from the start, then proceed on an offer and counter-offer basis. They often have difficulty when the other side doesn't reveal what they want.
+ They take risks, but make a definite (financial) plan which must be adhered to.
+ They consider most proposals on an investment/return or investment/timescale basis.

✦ Time is always money. 'Let's get to the point.'

✦ They try to extract an oral agreement at the first meeting. 'Have we got a deal?' They want to shake hands on it. The other party often feels the matter is far too complex to agree on the spot.

✦ They want 'yes' in principle and will work out details later. But they can be very tough in the details and check on everything in spite of apparent trust. Germans, French and others prefer to settle details first.

✦ They don't like lulls or silence during negotiations. They are used to making up their minds fast (quick on the draw).

✦ They are opportunistic – quick to take chances. The history of the USA presented many golden opportunities to those who grabbed fastest.

✦ Opportunism and risk taking often result in Americans going for the biggest possible slice of the business ('piece of the action'), 100 per cent if possible.

✦ They often lack patience, and will say irritating or provoking things ('Look at our generous offer') to get things moving.

✦ They are persistent. There is always a solution. They will explore all options when deadlocked.

✦ They are consistent. When they say 'You gotta deal' they rarely change their mind.

✦ They put everything in words. But when they use words like 'fair', 'democratic', 'honest', 'good deal', 'value', 'assume', they think the other party understands the same as they do. This is because US subcultures, e.g. Czechs, Germans, Poles, do understand.

✦ They are blunt, they will disagree and say so. This causes embarrassment to Japanese, Arabs, Italians and other Latins.

✦ They often reveal brute force as argument, e.g. their financial strength or unassailable position. They will use majority vote unhesitatingly if they have it and will not spend (waste) much time striving for consensus. They are happy to fire anyone standing in the way of the deal.

✦ They assume all negotiators are technically competent and expect to win on their own technical knowledge. They forget the other side may see it as a matter of the status of the chief negotiator. How can a Mexican company president lose to an American engineer?

✦ They regard negotiating as problem solving through give and take based on respective strengths. They do not appreciate that the other side may have only one position.

✦ Uncle Sam is best. But successful negotiating must enter the cultural

world of the other party. Many Americans see the USA as the most suc-
cessful economic and democratic power, therefore assume that
American norms are the correct ones.
✦ This leads to lack of interest in or knowledge of the foreign culture.
   Americans often know little of such matters as saving face, correct dress,
   use of business cards, social niceties and formalities important to Arabs,
   Greeks, Spaniards etc.
✦ In the USA, the dollar is almighty and will win most arguments.
   Americans don't always realise that Mexicans, Arabs, Japanese and oth-
   ers will rarely, if ever, sacrifice status, protocol, or national honour for
   financial gain.

Calm, pragmatic northerners can live with most of these characteristics.
They, too, are used to informality, first names, humour, persistence, bluntness, technical competence, give-and-take bargaining and general consistency in sticking to what has been agreed. They also wish to conclude the
deal without unnecessary time wasting or labrynthine procedures. Yet care
must be exercised. Americans are fast talking and if the language is English,
there may be certain traps. With Americans one always has to read the 'fine
print', for their apparent openness and trust in the other party are usually
underpinned by tight legal control in their contract, and they will not hesitate to sue you later if you do not comply with every clause you have put
your name to. American law is also quite different from many other legal
systems.

   You should always attempt to appear straightforward, honest, but quite
tough in your dealings with Americans, who will respect resilience, open
disagreement, alertness and strong cards. You don't have to 'beat about the
bush' as you would have to with the Japanese or Italians. 'Yes, but what
happens if...?' is a good question with Americans.

   If you appear tough often enough, Americans will argue, provoke, certainly push brute strength, but it is all part of their game. They, too, want
the deal. They will use far more words than you are comfortable with, but
your relative quietness will cause them discomfiture and eventually gain
you points. You will only irritate Latins with reticence, but Americans will
respect it. The answer to the oft-repeated 'Have we gotta a deal?' should
be 'Maybe'. Don't be rushed. They, too, are taking risks, but more likely
than not, they can afford to lose more than you can. They are looking at
this particular deal more than the long-term relationship. They have quar-

terly forecasts to satisfy. They want profit now, as opposed to the Japanese, who want your market. Realisation of such American aims helps you in dealing with them. Their friendliness means nothing, although it is pleasant while it lasts. They will forget your name the day after the deal is made.

You have a lot of cards up your sleeve. You know a lot more about Americans and their country than they know about you and yours. Many Americans think Finland is in Canada and confuse Lapps with Eskimos. You can enter their cultural world without difficulty – you have seen hundreds of American films, read many US books and journals. You speak their language and therefore have insight into their thought processes. They will find many Europeans disarming, but also deep. British people deal with Americans by occasionally using Americanisms in their speech, then retreating into British vagueness or semi-incoherence when they wish to confuse. Americans are tough, cunning, but also naïve. You should blow hot and cold with them, appearing half the time to be on the American wavelength and the other half of the time your own person. Americans find this disconcerting; they want to follow the script, or 'scenario' as they often call it.

This is never more apparent than when the Americans are buying – they want to hear your sales pitch. Soft sell is not necessary in the US. Any American walking into a car showroom expects the salesperson to attack him from the word go. He wishes to be told every good point about the car, the true and the peripheral, the fine discount and the personal concession, he then wants to hit back hard with his own demands, finally after much tough talk arriving at the 'deal' neither of them trusts, but both want and fully accept. You can improve on this dialogue by showing all your toughness, but slipping in a quiet injection of 'niceness', even humility.

A certain amount of modesty scores points with Americans. If you are too modest with Latins, you run the risk of their believing you ('They have a lot to be modest about'), but the Americans, as native English speakers, will hear the linguistic nuances and respect your reserve. They, for their part, are incapable of being modest in speech, as American English is irrevocably tough, clever and tending towards the exaggerated and sensational. Learn how to translate your natural modesty into suitable British English:

US	British
Jack'll blow his top	Our chairman might tend to disagree
You're talking bullshit	I'm not quite with you on that one
You gotta be kidding	Hm, that's an interesting idea (disagreement)
That's a beautiful scenario	We might find a way of making that work
I tell you, I can walk away from this deal	We'll have to do our homework
You're going to get hurt	I'm not sure this is advantageous for you
Bean-counters drive me mad	Accountants can be frustrating
It's the only game in town	I have no other choice
We had sticker-shocked the consumers right off their feet	We had overpriced the product
Go for broke	Stake everything on one venture
He'll do his best to make it fly	He'll do all he can to ensure success
If they ever come back from the grave	If they are ever a force in business again
When you scramble, you scramble like a son-of-a-bitch	Speed of action is advisable

Finally, when dealing with Americans, it is advisable to have on your team someone who knows their country well. This applies when dealing with any nationality, but at least many Europeans have spent years in the USA and such 'experts' are readily available. Northern Europeans, with their language abilities and wide knowledge of the Anglo-Saxon world, are today quite close culturally to the British, but often assume that Americans are similar, because they speak the same tongue. But Americans live in a different hemisphere and a different world. They do things their way and people who have lived in the USA know the short cuts in doing business with them.

11

BRITAIN

ONE EVENING, SWEDISH CUSTOMS OFFICIALS AT ARLANDA AIRPORT WERE puzzled by the behaviour of an elderly gentleman who, long after his cotravellers had passed through the immigration channels, paced up and down with a bewildered look on his face. Finally, one of the Swedes went up to him and asked why he had not come through passport control.

'I don't know where my channel is,' replied the old gentleman. 'There it says "Swedes" and there it says "Foreigners". But I am neither a Swede nor a foreigner, I'm an Englishman.'

The Swedes, like others in Europe as well as Americans and Asians, are well informed as to what Englishmen are like. For decades the British film industry, enriched by the talents of such actors as Alec Guinness, Peter O'Toole, John Gielgud, Ralph Richardson, Alastair Sim, George Cole and Charles Laughton, have put him on the screen for the world to see. The BBC, in such admirable programmes as *Upstairs Downstairs*, *The Duchess of Duke Street* and *Yes, Minister*, has reinforced the image.

The Englishman dresses in tweeds or a three-piece pin-striped suit and a Burberry mackintosh on rainy days. He wears a bowler hat, carries a tightly furled, black umbrella with a cane handle, has a pink newspaper tucked under his left armpit. He goes to church on Sunday mornings and eats roast beef with Yorkshire pudding for Sunday lunch. He is a man of principle, insists on fair play for underdogs, does things in a proper manner and shows more affection for horses, cats and dogs than for children, foxes and grouse. He probably went to Eton and Oxford (Cambridge?) and frequents Ascot, Wimbledon, Twickenham, Lord's and Wentworth. He believes in the Monarchy, the Empire and the Conservative Party. When not in his Club (no ladies allowed) he sits in the local (pub) with gardeners and game wardens, with whom he sips warm beer called 'real ale'. Often he has tea with the vicar, with whom he discusses the Church of England, farming, poaching, the village fête and his years with the Guards.

Englishmen are fond of cricket, croquet, rugby, sheepdog trials, detective stories and queuing. When queues are slow, one does not complain, as English people must never make a scene, not even if they have a double-barrelled name. The same applies to poor service in restaurants, railway stations and that place where you get your passport.

The antidote to such frustrating situations is the stiff upper lip. When queuing or sitting in a train one does not enter into conversation with others – that is the reason for carrying a newspaper everywhere. When a train was derailed in a tunnel in the London Underground a few years ago, an elderly City gentleman walked half a mile down the line to the next station, where he proclaimed: 'It's horrible down there in the dark. People are talking to each other!'

This powerful stereotype of the British character has been etched on other nations' minds by several generations of British films. Huge populations abroad, including the Japanese, Indians, South-East Asians and Africans, still subscribe to it and send their children to Britain to be educated along the same lines.

The majority of British people bear little resemblence to the stereotype. Not only is the image one of an upper class personage of a former era, but it does not take into account regional differences, which in the UK are extremely marked. If you draw a latitudinal line through the city of Oxford, it is questionable if you will find anyone north of it who behaves in the manner of the stereotype. In the first place, nearly 10 million Britons are Celts (Scots, Welsh, Irish, Cornish and Manx). These people are essentially romantic, poetic and emotional. They, like millions of midland and northern English people in the 'wilds' beyond Oxford, are extremely critical of the archetypal Englishman existing in foreign minds. There is a type of English person who roughly corresponds to the projected image, but he is southern, upper class and almost extinct! Even in the south, we are talking about a tiny, although often highly visible (and audible) fraction of society. Foreigners, often laughing at the eccentric English stereotype, are unaware that 50-odd million Britons laugh at him too. Northern, midland and Celtic Britons feel much more affinity with some Europeans (Norwegians,

Danes, Swedes, Finns, Dutch, Belgians, Germans, Swiss) than they do with
the braying figure in tweeds. Britons are supposed to be poor at learning
languages – this is a myth. Scots, Welsh, Irish and most people north of
Watford learn foreign languages well and often with a good accent.

What are real English people like? The 'world image' bears some
resemblance to the reality, but not much. The class system is still in evidence in Britain – an unfortunate anachronism which North America and
most of Europe have dispensed with – but in fact most British people could
be called middle class. They do not have a strong political party to represent them, although both Conservatives and Labour eagerly pretend to do
so. The absence of a moderate centrist party contributes, sadly, to the continuing polarisation of British society.

Polarised or not, how do British people behave? Whatever the status, a
pattern can be observed. Yes, we are a nation of queuers and probably the
only time British people complain vociferously is when someone jumps the
queue. But the stiff upper lip can move – British people today hold nothing sacred. While royalty is respected, the Royal Family is often ridiculed,
both in the press and on TV. If the British can laugh at themselves, so can
the monarchs – what could be more democratic than that?

Humour is a saving factor in British life – some say it is a product of a
fickle climate – and many English people feel that as long as there is
humour, there can never be utter despair. It is no accident that the BBC –
the most humorous television service in the world – is highly popular in
most countries fortunate enough to be able to receive it.

It is true that British people love detective stories. Agatha Christie is the
world's most translated novelist and the British easily lead the world in
library book loans. Sherlock Holmes is one of the most famous and popular Englishmen of all time. The fact is, the British have a strong conspira-
torial streak – they love plotting. The most beloved characters in the extensive British theatrical literature are villains. Guy Fawkes, who was hanged
after failing to blow up Parliament, became an instant hero and the nation
still celebrates his anniversary every 5 November. The biggest heroes of
British naval history were Francis Drake and John Hawkins – both pirates.
Apparently polished and sophisticated in diplomacy, the British are masters
of intelligence gathering and political blackmail.

And yet British people regard themselves as honest, reasonable, caring
and considerate. Their originality often borders on the eccentric, but it is
true that throughout history, they have been lateral thinkers with great

powers of invention. Often academic and woolly, they can excel in science and technology. Portrayed as a nation of amateurs who 'muddle through' crises, they have shown their visceral strength in the worst adversity.

Their insularity is incurable. Each evening on television British weather forecasters routinely end their message with the prognosis of the next day's temperature: 'The high will be 22 degrees Celsius – that is 72 degrees Fahrenheit.' That after two decades of metric systems!

Don't ask the British to change their double-decker buses or red post boxes, or to drive on the right. Even when they venture abroad, they take their cocoon of insularity with them. It used to be 5 o'clock tea in long dress in the heat of the African jungle; now it's fish and chips and bacon and eggs eagerly provided by Spanish hoteliers on the Costa del Sol.

Fixed habits, fixed ideas, slow to change, unprofessional. How do these characteristics apply to the British way of doing business? How should these eccentrics be handled?

How to handle the British

The British feel at home with other English-speaking nationalities, with whom they have little difficulty in establishing an easy-going but effective relationship. They also feel comfortable with Nordics, Dutch and (when they get to know them) Japanese. They think that they strike the golden mean between excessive formality (French, German tendencies) and premature familiarity (American, Australian traits).

Britons, of course, belong to different classes, and foreign people should always bear this in mind. When dealing with the wealthier, more class-conscious southern English, one should stress one's civilised, educated side; when dealing with the more hard-headed northern English, Scots or Welsh, one should lay more emphasis on sincerity and straight, uncomplicated dealing.

At business meetings, the British are rather formal at first, using first names only after two or three encounters. After that they become very informal (jackets off, sleeves rolled up) and first names will be used and maintained from then on.

British people like to show themselves as family oriented (though less than the Latins) and it is normal for you to discuss children, holidays, reminiscences during and between meetings.

Humour is important in business sessions in the UK and it is advisable for you to arrive well stocked with jokes and anecdotes. People who are good at this should use their talent to the full. British people expect you to match story with story and an atmosphere conducive to doing business will result.

A word of warning: British executives can use humour (especially irony or sarcasm) as a weapon in ridiculing an opponent or showing disagreement or even contempt. Sarcasm is rarely used against Nordics, however, since their modesty and restraint hardly ever deserve it. The British can use humour cruelly against some Latins and overdemonstrative people.

One can learn a lot about the British by observing how they use humour against themselves or their own colleagues. The following uses are common:

+ self-deprecation
+ to break up tension in a situation which is developing intransigence
+ to speed up discussion when excessive formality is slowing it down
+ to direct criticism towards a superior without getting fired
+ to introduce a new, possibly wild idea to unimaginative colleagues (the 'trial balloon')
+ to introduce the unexpected in over-rigid negotiation
+ to laugh at overelaborate or 'mysterious' management priorities and perspective in solemn corporate planning

In short, humour is regarded as one of the most effective weapons in the British manager's arsenal and some people can gain the confidence of the British by showing that they can be a match for them in this area. (A Swiss, Austrian, Turk or German has difficulty in doing this.)

British executives try to show during meetings that they are guided by reasonableness, compromise and common sense. One may find, however, that the British, even in the absence of disagreement, will rarely make a final decision at the first meeting. They do not like to be hurried. Americans like to make on-the-spot decisions when they can, using instinct. The British, more tradition bound, prefer using instinct to logic, but exercise more caution. With them one should suggest, 'Could we have a final decision at our next meeting?'

British rarely disagree openly with proposals from the other side. They agree whenever possible, but qualify their agreement ('Hm, that's a very interesting idea'). Other nationals are more open in this respect. They must watch for hidden signs of disagreement, e.g.:

+ 'Well, we quite like that, however...'
+ vagueness in reply
+ understatement showing, in fact, opposition ('That might be a bit tricky')
+ humour

Some nationalities understand the use of understatement and humour well, but can be irritated by British vagueness. They use it to stall, confuse opponents, or delay the business. Ask them for a decision and they are likely to reply, 'Let me tell you a story'. You listen to the story with interest, for it will probably be a good one. When it ends you will say 'Fine, but what about a decision?' 'I already told you,' the Briton will say. You would do well to show you understand the relevance of the story, or tell one back.

Using charm, vagueness, humour, understatement and apparent reasonableness, British negotiators can be smiling but quite tough for lengthy periods. They always have a fallback position which they disguise as long as possible. You should attempt to discover this position by being equally reasonable, smiling, modest and tenacious. In the end you may find it is similar to your own fallback in most circumstances. The area for bargaining may be somewhat greater with the British (remember they have hundreds of years of experience with India, the Middle and Far East).

Representatives of a British company will make normal use of their firm's reputation, size and wealth in their negotiating hand, and you can do likewise in dealing with them. What they do not reveal so readily is the strength of their behind-the-scenes connections. The 'old school tie', or the 'old boy network', is very much a reality in British executive life and should not be underestimated. It is particularly active in the City, the Ministries and in legal circles, and nationals from a small country should always bear in mind that they may be dealing with greater influences than are apparent on the surface.

The British are generally interested in long-term relationships rather than quick deals. This is a factor you can reckon with and use to your advantage, even though sometimes you may wish to conclude arrangements rather faster.

A lot of business is done in some countries on the telephone. The

British are also capable of discussing terms at length, but nearly always ask you to put it in writing immediately afterwards. They keep thick files.

Finally, there is the question of British insularity. Brits generally have a feeling that 'foreigners' intend to outsmart them.

12

AUSTRALIA, NEW ZEALAND AND SOUTH AFRICA

A SURVEY OF THE WORLD'S CULTURES WOULD BE INCOMPLETE (DARE I SAY top heavy?) if it did not include some consideration of the cultural forces at work and the fascinating geographical, historical and racial influences observable among the English-speaking countries of the southern hemisphere.

There are a large number of islands and communities in the south Pacific where English is dominant, or a *lingua franca*, or it coexists with melodious Polynesian tongues. Space constrains us to focus on only three of these peoples – Australians, inhabitants of the largest island in the world; New Zealanders, tyrannised by their remoteness; and vibrant South Africans, durable, multicultural, energetically building a new nation in the southern Atlantic.

What cultural traits do these peoples have in common? Is there such a thing as 'down under' solidarity or mentality? Do these English-speaking peoples relate comfortably to each other, taking advantage of similarities in linguistic and literary heritage? Do they respect, envy or dislike each other?

Australians

There is no better clue to the 200-year development of Australian society and culture than the Australian language itself. Australia is the largest English-speaking country in the southern hemisphere. Australian – the sixth largest variety of English (after American, British, Filipino, Indian and Canadian) – is a fascinating, young, vibrant, irreverent, humorous, inventive language.

Newcomers to Australia – who now arrive by jumbo jet, not convict ship – get a distinct impression of southern hemisphere Cockney when they first hear the local pronunciation. The similarity is in fact far from accidental. In the decades leading up to the discovery of Australia, the Industrial Revolution caused tens of thousands of destitute farm workers from Kent, East Anglia and Essex to come tumbling into the East End of London in search of work. They linked together with the dockland people – street traders, hawkers and artisans who had been driven out of the City and West End by the upper and middle classes. This hybrid East End population, crowded together in eighteenth-century slums and cross-fertilising their rural and urban traditions, developed a racy, witty, vulgar type of street English which became known as 'Cockney'.

It was not unnatural that these needy, lowly but fast-living city dwellers provided a sizeable number of candidates for the vessels bound for the penal colonies in Australia. They were joined aboard by town-bred petty criminals from the overcrowded cities of Yorkshire and Lancashire, especially Liverpool which had a large out-of-work Irish population.

Let stalk Strine!

It is an interesting linguistic phenomenon that the Australian language, like Black English 200 years earlier, had its first origins at sea. The officers and crew of the slave ships on the long voyage to America had had to communicate with their charges in Pidgin – a mixture of basic English and several African languages – which gave an unalterable direction to Black English. On the much longer voyage to Australia the melting pot of Cockney, Irish and Northern English dialects led to an on-board fusion of accents, grammar and syntax which formed the basis of penal colony speech as the convicts stepped ashore in New South Wales and Queensland. In this hurly-burly of dialects, Cockney emerged as the clear winner (there were more Cockneys), and the resultant speech variant was larded with dozens of old English dialect forms (*cobber, dust-up, tucker*), with Irish lilt, euphemism and volubility, and with a definite slant towards convict slang (*swag, flog, nick, pinch*). Swear words and vulgar expressions were abundant, as might be expected under the circumstances, but picturesque Cockney rhyming slang also found its way into the mixture and remains one of the fascinating features of Australian English (*trouble 'n strife* = wife; *Bugs bunny* = money; *eau de cologne* = phone).

As the language developed, 'outback' speech was quickly added to the already rich mixture. The language of the outback (or the Bush) had two main elements – Aborigine and frontier inventions. The influence of the former was limited, although picturesque in the extreme. From the Aborigines came such words as *boomerang, kangaroo, wombat, koala, jumbuck, dingo* and *budgerigar*. Frontier words and expressions were more numerous and showed the hardy humour of the explorers: *digger* (= Australian), *amber* (= beer), *banana bender* (= Queenslander), *roo* (= kangaroo), *heart starter* (= first drink of the day), *neck oil* (= beer), *grizzle* (= complain) and *across the ditch* (= New Zealand) are some examples.

The modern Aussie is a townie through and through. Australia is the least densely populated country on earth; it is also among the most highly urbanised. It was in the cities where the Cockneys and the Irish ('both in love with talk') thrived, and it was here that the Australian language gained momentum and vitality. Unused English words were resuscitated (*creek, paddock*), more fossilisms from dialects were prised out – *fair dinkum* (= genuine), *clobber* (= clothes) – and scores of words were truncated with glee – *arvo* (= afternoon), *beaut* (= beautiful), *garbo* (= garbageman), *barby* (= barbecue), *Oz* (= Australia).

Twentieth-century Australian is still undergoing change. There are the pressures of Americanisms, such as *freeway* and *elevator*, and of foreign words brought in by new Australians (*ciao, pizza, kebab*). Some features of Cockney have disappeared (no glottal stops, no dropped *h*s, less rhyming slang), while the 'rising inflection' has become an Australian invention in recent years ('What's your friend's name?' Reply: 'John Bennett?')

Australia is a relatively classless society and so is the language. There are hardly any regional variations, no class pressures on one's way of speaking, and people switch from broad to cultivated Australian at will. There is a tendency, however, for men and women to use different forms, and schoolchildren do influence each other to speak 'broad'. But although Australian speech is in the main uniform, boring it is not. The language of Crocodile Dundee is human, humorous, inventive, original and bursting with vitality. Few languages can come up with similes and metaphors to match – *uglier than a robber's dog, blind Freddie could have seen it, he had kangaroos in his top paddock* (he's crazy).

Most Australians refer to each other as 'mate', even at the first meeting. Women are called 'love'. 'Fair go' is also central to the Australian outlook, based on common sense, equality and a healthy disregard for authority and ideology. This is why Australians always sympathise with the 'battler' and underdog. They don't like the exercise of power and privilege over the weak. The two deadly sins are *scabbing* and *dobbing* – informing against one's mates.

Communicating with Australians

There is no manual for correct behaviour in Australia, as the country lacks a clearly defined social and conversational map. Most Australians see this as a strength, a licence to be either erudite or rude in any situation. This keeps conversation lively, no one knowing what twist or turn it is likely to take. Will it end up a torrent of abuse, or warm bonhomie and sensitive human exchange, or none of these?

While not entirely true, egalitarianism is a cherished myth and the foreigner must always be very careful not to threaten this notion when talking to an Australian from any background. This egalitarianism is based on the idea of a classless society in which everyone is treated equally – regardless of wealth, education or background.

Working from this 'fair go' premise conversation will be easier, but still fraught with traps. In many countries accent and education will tell you a lot about a person. Not in Australia! The political map has also become very blurred. The longest surviving political party is the Australian Labour Party (ALP) which grew out of the trade union movement. Traditionally, the ALP and its supporters have been pro worker, social welfare and a genuine 'fair go' for the underdog. It was also, until the early 1970s, very isolationist and anti-Asian. Many Labour supporters are very upwardly mobile middle-class professionals living in the most prestigious suburbs of the major cities. They share their political party with single parents and day labourers.

Although the basic fabric of Australian society is complex yet appears deceptively simple, there are certain subjects that are in general 'safe' or 'dangerous'. All sport is generally safe and most Australians respond well to a sporting analogy. They love criticising themselves, but take very poorly to being criticised. This makes it very difficult for you as the newcomer because you will often find yourself in the middle of torrid condemnation of Australia or Australians, but should you agree too enthusiastically or even mildly, you run the risk of being dubbed a 'whinger' (complainer). This could lead to your own country being very negatively compared to Australia. If you persist, you could be told in a variety of ways to 'go back where you came from'.

But Australians also do not like or trust people who constantly or too enthusiastically praise them. They suspect that they are being set up to be either humiliated or deceived. Too much praise raises expectation and puts the high achiever under unsufferable pressure – and Australians hate being pressured. When the Australian cricket team won the coveted Ashes from their arch-rival England, the Captain's first response to being congratulated was not of joy but almost of regret. 'Now everyone will expect us to play as well next time. It has put a pressure on the whole team,' he lamented to a long-faced Australian interviewer.

This tortured form of modesty is greatly respected by most Australians and if it is not observed by the successful they will rapidly fall victim to the 'tall poppy syndrome'. One version of this is: any Australian who achieves success will be brought down to size through a variety of abusive techniques. This leaves them either totally humiliated and regretting their achievements, or packing their bags and heading for those parts of the world where success is allowed to be overtly enjoyed.

Equally, never take yourself or your national symbols too seriously, or a similar fate will befall you. It is a source of great pride to Australians that the Prime Minister is frequently booed at public appearances and that quite a few Australians do not know the words of the national anthem.

Perhaps the greatest strength of the Australian personality, although it is under threat, is their monumental cynicism. Australians are totally cynical of people in power or with too much wealth, respecting the little person, 'the battler', rather than the winner.

If you keep this in mind and don't oversell yourself or undersell your Australian hosts, success, friendship and good times will be yours down under.

Australians in their hemisphere

The world's biggest island is also the smallest continent. Geographical location and climatic conditions play a large part in shaping national character. Australia is the flattest and driest of the continents – when travelling around it one is impressed by the awesome, mind-numbing, parched flatness. The love of outdoor activities, the ubiquitous beach culture, the fashion for a suntan has led to a national health problem (skin cancer) of major proportions. The heat produces a tendency towards apathy and procrastination in many areas, expressed in a general *laisser faire* attitude – 'no worries' or 'she'll be all right in the end'. The darker side of Australian life is not to be discounted – they consume more alcohol and painkillers per capita than any other English-speaking country. Their racial policy has been largely unsuccessful and the aborigines are in dire straits as a result.

Yet Australians remain very positive human beings. Few can match their friendliness and even fewer their spontaneous generosity. Half a million New Zealanders enjoy the benefits of Australian unemployment benefit, but resentment is minimal. Aussies see New Zealanders as astute, sometimes tight-fisted individuals, more British than themselves but still possessing a lot of synergy with Australians in terms of sheep, farming and outdoor activities (sailing, cricket, rugby). There is a sense of solidarity, particularly with regard to French nuclear testing in the Pacific.

The disadvantages of Australia's geographical remoteness have now been mitigated by the exponential increase in the capabilities of telecommunications. People in Perth, once the most isolated city in the world (1500 miles from Adelaide and 3000 miles from Singapore), can now communicate orally, aurally and visually with any business partner in a matter of seconds. This technology will continue to improve, making inexpensive locations such as Perth, Darwin and Adelaide far more attractive propositions for multinationals to locate their Asia-Pacific headquarters in than crowded Tokyo, Hong Kong, Manila or Singapore. Over 100 large companies currently run their regional businesses out of Australia. With the entry of Britain into the EC, Australia lost its automatic access to traditional markets and was forced to face the reality of its location on the edge of Asia. Asian immigrants, with no sentimental attachments to British institutions, have accentuated this realisation. Australian schoolchildren now learn Japanese, not French, as their first foreign language. The fact that Japanese people are not particularly fond of lamb or mutton may put at risk the future of the smallest continent's 60 million sheep!

New Zealanders

New Zealanders are more conservative, placid and reserved than Australians. They are more British, not only in their calmness of manner, but in their racial composition. They see Australians as cosmopolitan and somewhat excitable.

The original settlers who in the 1840s founded the then colony of New Zealand were all English speaking – predominantly a middle-class and working population drawn principally from rural areas of England and Scotland. They were literate and, at least during the early settling-in period in the mid-nineteenth century, much of their educational thinking and all of their reading matter came from Britain. As New Zealand's 'foreign' immigrants have always been small minorities, the English spoken in New Zealand has never been distorted (or invigorated) by waves of non-English speakers similar to those which posed a challenge to the English of the USA. New Zealand speech, although affected to some extent by linguistic interchange with Australian, has retained much old rural vocabulary from British dialects and remains, apart from some give-away front vowels ('*pin*' for pen and '*fush*' for fish), resolutely southern English.

The islands of New Zealand are similar in size to the British Isles and not entirely dissimilar in climate. New Zealanders tend to identify more strongly with their insular forebears and regard both Australians and Americans as a different, continental breed. Their stereotype of Australians is as loud mouthed, brash and arrogant, who often interrupt others' speech or talk in tandem, which is frowned on in New Zealand. New Zealanders see themselves as more laid back, certainly more cultured and much more likely to treat women sensitively. Australians often regard New Zealanders as Victorian, outdated, poor country cousins – but New Zealand produces efficient, innovative managers who often do well in Australia, being more adventurous than their Ozzie counterparts. Deregulation has gone much further in New Zealand than in Australia, where business is often seen as a closed shop. Australians are more price oriented than New Zealanders, who are more inclined to value quality.

New Zealanders emigrate in rather large numbers to Australia on account of the scarcity of work in their own country. The things they like about Australia (often referred to as 'The West Island') are the wide-open outback and winter warmth, the cosmopolitan cities and shopping opportunities, the classless society and friendly, helpful attitude of the people.

Australians show a lot of down-under solidarity with New Zealanders, especially in moments of adversity; although on occasions when this bond is broken, the latter feel that they are not the ones who break it.

Many New Zealanders visit Europe and the 'Old Country' once or twice in their life, but are more and more oriented towards the Pacific and spend most of their holidays in Australia or the Islands. They have good relations with Pacific Islanders (Tonga, Fiji, Cook Island) and believe that their Maori policy has been fairly successful. Many Maoris do not share this opinion, feeling they were ruthlessly exploited in the past and that present atonement falls far short of what is morally required. The Maori attitude to white New Zealanders is 'They are guests in our country.' An interesting cultural sideline is that the whites tend to behave like Maoris when living it up, for instance on certain sporting occasions and when singing and dancing. Most whites possess a fair knowledge of the Maori language (without being able to speak it) and sing Maori songs, as well as doing the *haka* with great gusto at ceremonies. This rather engaging symbiotic relationship is noticeably absent in the case of Australians and Aborigines.

South Africans

At the time of writing, the system of government in South Africa is in transition. Apartheid has gone, hopefully for ever. New South Africa emerges into the world limelight as one of the most multicultural nations on earth. It is not a melting pot of immigrants like the USA or Australia, but a society where several communities and races – British, Afrikaans, Malay, Indian, Zulu, Xhosa and other black tribes – will remain as separate and integral forces forging a new union which has aspirations to provide leadership to a depressed and seemingly disintegrating continent.

South Africa possesses the multicultural strengths of a Switzerland, a Singapore, and much more. The rich combination of British, French and Dutch experience, the artistry and ardent aspirations of the blacks, the diligence and tenacity of the Indians and Malays, are ingredients for a dynamic, inspired and unique future. Yet the colourful variety of the country's cultures itself poses a number of problems.

Apart from the friction among the black tribes, the history of warfare between the British and Afrikaans settlers is too recent not to have left a residue of resentment between the two communities. Each group has inherited characteristics from their forebears. English-speaking South Africans are somewhat reserved in nature, proud of their cultural heritage and set great store by good manners, elegant, expressive speech and avoidance of unnecessary conflict. In this respect they differ strongly from the Afrikaners who, like their Dutch ancestors, are blunt (often tactless) and have the American tendency to 'tell it like it is'.

Although British and Afrikaners differ sharply in their style of communication, a white South African lifestyle is discernible. Pragmatism is paramount, but South Africans resent deeply the implication that they are insensitive to the plight of less fortunate human beings. A visitor to South Africa cannot avoid being aware of the eager hospitality and thoughtful kindness of the whites living there. Power corrupts and the years of racial suppression and injustice cannot be pardoned, but there is in fact far less colour consciousness in the country than in many other parts of the world. South Africans have been brought up in a multicoloured society – it is a natural state.

White South Africans are entrepreneurial and decisive in business. At meetings they come well prepared and usually have a few cards up their sleeves. They are familiar with many African cultures and customs, and accept that bribery and accommodation are part of life on their continent if one is to achieve anything. They are, however, flexible in such matters and do not apply the same judgements when dealing with the West. At discussion time they will often sit back to listen and learn, but are not averse to assuming dominance and taking control of a meeting when they perceive an opportunity. In spite of the latitudinal distance, they focus much more on Europe than towards east or west. Africa, the continent they hope to lead, has close connections with Britain and France.

One hears many pessimistic predictions about the deterioration of South African society, in the manner which has been observed in other African states. South African whites recognise that their country can survive only if the blacks play an integral role in the development of the new South Africa. The pool of managerial talent is worryingly shallow: education of the blacks is vital but will take many years. Yet the potential contribution of the black and coloured populations is even greater than that of the 6 million educated, talented, highly organised and relatively wealthy whites.

The Indians, who number about 1 million, are concentrated in Natal and are very industrious and almost completely middle class (traders, professionals, businesspeople, etc.). The coloured population (about 3.5 million) is mostly in the Western and Northern Cape and derives from mixed breeding between white, black, Malay and Bushmen. Occupationally they tend to be farm workers in rural areas, but in urban districts they are either middle class or highly skilled workers and artisans. Sixty per cent of the coloured population speak Afrikaans. Both the coloured and Indian groups are conservative; the great majority voted for the National Party in the 1994 election.

Black South Africans really hold the key to the nation's future. They have many qualities, not least of which are patience, tolerance and a delightful sense of humour. While they are not as well educated as the whites, they are very well educated in comparison with the rest of Africa. They earn better incomes than other Africans and in the 50 per cent which is already urbanised there is a substantial and rapidly growing middle class. Their access to government posts, and the international contact this will bring, will quickly add to their experience and sophistication. Nelson Mandela himself is a shining example of a black South African politician.

South Africa's GDP is already four times that of the combined GDP of the ten other countries of southern Africa. The emergence of a dynamic, stable, prosperous South Africa would be a triumph not only for its people, but for viable multiculturalism itself, following a road which many countries will find themselves on in the twenty-first century.

13

FINLAND

ONCE UPON A TIME, LONG LONG AGO, THERE WAS A FAR-OFF LAND CLOSE to the Arctic circle – a chilly, bleak patchwork of forests and lakes where bears, wolves, elks and lynxes roamed freely and where Christmases were always white. A strange tribe from faraway arrived in this land where no other people had chosen to live and set about the task of making themselves comfortable there. They cut wood to construct dwellings, they planted crops on open land and they fished the lakes and rivers.

They were an unusual people, of an independent nature, devoted to hard work, yet modest in their aspirations and jealous of their honest reputation. They were clean in their habits, physically fit and enjoyed the outdoor life. They spoke very little, for loquaciousness and especially boasting were taboo. Solitude was the safest and they loved the great space that the new land offered.

Like other peoples, they had jealous neighbours and they had to fight many battles to defend their territory. They did not always win and they were subjugated for long periods. Notwithstanding their suffering and humiliation, they never gave up and in the end they made their land secure and have lived happily there up to the present day.

If this sounds like a fairy tale, it is perhaps because it possesses the elements of one, but we are talking about a modern nation which really exists. This nation, clinging to the old values in the fairy tale, fought a modern giant (state) of 200 million people to hold on to what we today call a democracy. The honest tribe continues to pay off all its debts, protect its environment and vanquish crime, injustice and poverty. The quiet people solve modern problems such as treatment of its minorities, resettlement of refugees (400,000 Karelians) and the struggle against pollution without any fuss.

The tribe is still not very well known in the lands to the south and they are notoriously poor at blowing their own trumpet. Their Altaic language does not calibrate with the majority of the world's tongues, their basic shyness and dislike of exhibitionism lend thickness to an intervening curtain of cultural complexity, voluntary withdrawal and geographical remoteness. They feel a sense of separateness from other peoples.

Yet this tribe is warm-hearted, wishing to be loved and anxious to join the rest of us. They are energetic, essentially inventive and have much to offer others.

The unprecedentedly high degree of national self-consciousness in Finland indicates that the Finns are aware of being a very special people, yet it falls to the outsider to evaluate and quantify just how special they are. Certain peculiarly Finnish characteristics, e.g. contempt for verbosity or an inner, burning desire to rid oneself of debt, seem natural to Finns but rare indeed to the student of comparative culture.

Hero nation

The Finnish character, too, remains mysterious to outsiders. Here we have an outstanding example of a hero nation, one with a virtually unblemished record in its internal and international dealings. To list the Finnish virtues is not difficult. After a long and what must have been arduous migration, the Finns settled the Baltic shores some 2000–3000 years ago. A first testimony to their fortitude is that they have proved to be the only people capable of creating a successful society on territory lying in its entirety above 60°N latitude. (Iceland has also done this on a smaller scale, though most Icelanders went there because they had to, as their blood-stained history indicates.) For hundreds of years the Finns were subjected to foreign domination, yet neither once-mighty Sweden nor monolithic Russia was able to eliminate Finnish customs, language or culture and historical references from both great powers constantly mention Finnish bravery, reliability and diligence.

When the opportunity came to achieve independence, the Finns took it, swiftly and efficiently. They recognised their historical moment and they were fortunate with their leadership at the time. Bloodshed was kept at a minimum, reprisals were few. As quickly as they could, the Finns set about establishing a modern state based on equality and freedoms. Nationalist fervour was high, but arrogant chauvinism has been noticeably absent in Finnish history. Their treatment of the Swedish-speaking minority (now 6 per cent) was scrupulously fair. Swedish is retained along with Finnish as a national language and Finn–Swedes (who feel Finnish, not Swedish) have their own political party, newspapers and equal rights.

For 20 years (1919–39) Finland's progress was steady, at times spectacular. Many athletic triumphs followed – particularly at the 1936 Olympics – women were given the vote and genuine democracy blossomed. Sibelius, Kajanus, Saarinen, Järnefelt, Gallen-Kallela and Alvar Aalto assured the country's representation at the highest artistic levels; intelligent management of the Finnish forest and other resources led to a quickly rising standard of living.

The Second World War was a cruel shock and a severe setback to the young nation, but even defeat was a victory, since independence was maintained and the subsequent fate of 10 East European countries has served to emphasise Finland's good fortune earned by her determination to fight to the end for what she believed in.

After the war, the saga continued. Finland's achievement in resettling 400,000 refugees from Karelia in the space of a few months went largely unrecognised by the world at large. The war-battered country immediately set about the task of paying off unjust war reparations to the Soviet Union – settled in full by the appointed date. The 1950s and 1960s were difficult economically, with Finland starting off as the poor relation in the Nordic family. National diligence eventually triumphed: first Finland surpassed Sweden in cross-frontier investment and eventually enjoyed a boom for the ten years beginning in 1978. A clean, crime-free and poverty-less society entered the ranks of the world's 10 most prosperous countries in the early 1980s. And without ruining the environment.

Pessimism and paradox

Finns sweep their nation's achievements under the carpet in periodic fits of pessimism and self-debasement. Foreigners are cleverer than we are, they say. We are rustic, gullible and easily deceived. We can't learn languages (a myth) and we are rude and clumsy. It is hard for the British and French to imagine a nation which has triumphed over so much adversity fall prey to an inferiority complex! There are a string of such contradictions. Finns are warm-hearted people, but they have a desire for solitude. They are hard-working and intelligent, but they despair openly of emerging from a recession. They love freedom, but they curtail their own liberty with early closing of shops, limited access to alcohol, prohibiting baths after 10 pm and taxing themselves to death. They worship athletics and fitness, but used to eat a diet which gave the highest incidence of heart disease in western Europe. They admire coolness and calm judgement, but drink far too much. They are eager to internationalise but pretend they can't learn languages. They want to communicate, but wallow in introversion. They make fine companions, but love to brood alone by a lake shore. They are tolerant, but secretly despise peoples who are melodramatic or seemingly overemotional. They are essentially independent, but often hesitate to speak their mind in the international arena. They are genuinely democratic, but often let the 'tyranny of the majority' rule. They are fiercely individualistic, but are afraid of 'what the neighbours might say'. They are western in outlook but, like the Orientals, cannot 'lose face'. They are resourceful but often portray themselves as hapless. They are capable of acting alone, but frequently take refuge in group collusion. They desire to be liked but make no attempt to charm. They love their country, but seldom speak well of it.

The Finns, probably on account of exceptional historical and geographical circumstance, have a higher degree of national self-consciousness than most peoples. It is a characteristic they share with the Japanese, Chinese and the French, although the Finns are less chauvinistic.

They are acutely aware of the specialness of their own culture and they are very interested in it. They are also interested in cultural relativism, that is to say, the ways in which they differ from others. They discuss this subject at length and tend to develop complexes which are not always corresponding to reality. The question of 'the Finnish difference' once had its primary involvement in the arts, literature and assertion of political independence. Today it raises its head in the development and conduct of international business.

Finnish qualities

What are the generally accepted qualities of Finnish managers and to what extent are they advantaged or disadvantaged by these characteristics?

Intially, the image of the Finnish businessperson emerges from the general *Suomi-kuva* (Finnish image) which is perpetuated by the Finns themselves and accepted, hook, line and sinker, by foreigners who have little knowledge of Finland. In the Suomi-kuva the true Finn is fair-haired and blue-eyed (in both senses) and is slow, honest, reliable and easily deceived by other peoples. They are a strong, silent type with a rural background and thrive in an environment consisting of forests, lakes, snow, fishing through the ice and minimal conversation with neighbours who live 5 kilometres away. Other pursuits are running, skiing and (now and then) drinking hard liquor. They live in a democracy with a written constitution, are fiercely independent, a true friend, a good soldier, a bad enemy. They have no head for languages and are uneasy with foreigners, but give them strong coffee and take them to the sauna. They are Lutheran, work hard when the money is right and always pay their debts.

The image of the Finnish manager cannot be completely separated from this myth (with its basis of truth). Foreigners expect Finnish businesspeople to behave like Finns. The myth therefore has to be enlarged, to become credible. Finnish executives did not want to learn foreign languages, but disciplined themselves to do so. They prefer to keep quiet, but now and again they speak – and what they say they really mean (it might even be final). They pay their debts, but get their 90 days' credit. They make contracts with the Middle East and southern peoples, but watch their backs and take precautions. They deal with the West, but with Eastern Europe too and this includes the Russians, whom they understand like no other Europeans do. They know Finland cannot compete with the larger countries, but they sniff out niche industries, where Finnish original thinking can score points. Finnish managers insist on up-to-date technology, state-of-the-art factories and offices, and thorough training for all personnel. Profits are speedily reinvested in fine offices, training centres, sports facilities and anything else which will increase productivity.

Finnish strengths

Cold climates inevitably engender cool, sturdy, resilient peoples with an inordinate capacity for self-reliance and instinct for survival. The Arctic survivor must have stamina, guts, self-dependence and powers of invention. In managerial terms, these qualities translate into persistence, courage, individuality and original thinking. Unlike their Scandinavian neighbours, the Finns originate from the East, though they are not Slavic. The uniqueness of their language and their outpost mentality encourage an independent outlook and lateral thinking, which enhances not only Finnish literature, music and fine arts, but extends to brilliance of industrial design and penetrative insight into various branches of technology. It is not by accident that Finland has, in recent times, figured among the foremost innovators in glass, textiles, furniture, imaginative shipbuilding and electronic technology.

Finnish managers, establishing a branch abroad, do not arrive with the heavy feet of the German or the sweeping, complacent logic of the French. They may be regarded as a bit dull, or even gullible, but they are adaptable, ready to learn and compromise.

Their lack of a strong national business culture enables them to consider membership of trade 'clubs' readily and Finland's successful experience within EFTA will undoubtedly be followed by a fruitful association with the European Union. As a bridge between East and West, Finland could blossom into a key EU member, particularly if East European nations such as Hungary, Poland and the Soviet Union gain entry.

Finnish business history is short, but it is replete with a succession of self-made men and rugged individuals who created the companies which are household names in the country today. Such men are less in evidence as business-by-consensus comes into vogue, but their tradition lives on in Finnish respect for the strong leader who plunges onwards. Most Finnish managers make decisions without constant reference to HQ and this agility and mobile management is seen as a David-like advantage when dealing with foreign corporations of Goliathan proportions.

Finns respect, even cherish, the rights of the underdog, so woe betide the Finnish boss who tries to bully or unduly coerce subordinates! This informality of corporate climate facilitates interchange of ideas and development of mutual respect within Finnish companies. The parallel distaste for foreign-imposed bureaucracy has led to Finnish business being seen as a meritocracy and certainly the high level of education of Finnish executives gives them an edge over many foreign counterparts.

From Sweden and, it must be said, from other western countries, Finns absorbed Lutheranism, the Protestant work ethic, a strong sense of social justice, respect for education and social stability (including the establishment of a strong position for women). The solidarity of this background, added to the typical Scandinavian absence of violence in peacetime, facilitated the development of Finnish industry in the twentieth century, culminating in the boom years of 1980–88 and the resultant high standard of living enjoyed today.

Finnish weaknesses

Historical and geographical conditions have also bequeathed weaknesses on the Finns with regard to their bent for business and trade. First, they have been until recent times a rural, agricultural society and their commercial history is young. The Swedes internationalised in 1870, Finland only in 1970. Finnish managers are still living out their first generation in international management, therefore making the mistakes that others have learnt by. Domination by Sweden and Russia has led to a general Finnish belief that they are somewhat backward and even the unquestioned successes of the last decade have not totally eradicated occasional lapses in self-confidence. One sometimes observes a reversal of attitude ('to hell with the foreigners – Finns are best') and this, too, hampers entry into the international arena.

There are obvious weaknesses in the field of communication – Finns speak little, often delay in replying to correspondence, and avoid showdowns with other peoples because of shyness or feeling that they lack *savoir faire*. Clashes between Finnish industry and the Finnish media in the 1970s and 1980s caused many business circles to avoid contact with press and television. This reluctance to communicate has also extended to the foreign media (a pity, because in some countries, eg. the US or Britain, the media can be very helpful in the public relations sphere). Finnish managers, with their reputation as straightforward players, would often be most favourably received by the foreign press.

Europe can manage without Finnish industry, but the converse is not the case. The niche strategy of Finnish companies has proved itself a valuable option for a country severely limited by the smallness of its home market. In the future, Finnish industry cannot afford to neglect any viable overseas markets and there is an urgent requirement to get on trading terms with Europeans, Americans, Arabs, Japanese and other Eastern nations. This also means getting on talking terms, which for the Finn has traditionally been seen as difficult. In Finland, silence is not equated with failure to communicate, but is an integral part of social interaction.

In the Anglo-Saxon world and in Latin and Middle Eastern countries, talking has another function. In Britain the well-known habit of discussing the weather with neighbours or even strangers shows not only the British preoccupation with their fickle climate, but also their desire to show solidarity with and friendliness towards other people. This sociable discourse is even more evident in the USA, Canada and Australia, where speech is a vital tool for getting to know people and establishing a quick relationship.

Their view of language appropriacy isolates Finland and Japan in international discourse. In both countries one hears the same whispers ('foreigners talk so fast – we are slow by comparison – we can't learn languages – our pronunciation is terrible – it's because our own language is so difficult – foreigners are more experienced than we are – they are cleverer and often deceive us – they don't mean what they say – we can't rely on them – we are the truest people'). Having lived many years in both countries, I have great respect for and sympathy with the admirable reserve and obvious sincerity of Finns and Japanese. But the fact is that Pekka Virtanen and Ichiro Tanaka will have to enter the verbal fray. Japan has already set up factories and offices throughout the world and is currently grappling with the cultural and communicative problems of working side-by-side with foreign nationals or actually managing them. Finland, admittedly on a smaller scale, is in the process of doing the same.

Speech-and-thought icebergs

As we all know, most of an iceberg is below the surface. We can also draw the concept of a person's speech-and-thought ratio in the form of an iceberg. In the case of the British and German icebergs the 'section of thought' presented to others in speech is roughly equal. The French iceberg shows more ice visible, corresponding to more speech on the part of the French. South American icebergs break the surface of audibility to a much greater degree. The Finnish iceberg shows a more introspective nature is involved, indicating minimum thought revealed. Japanese tell you even less.

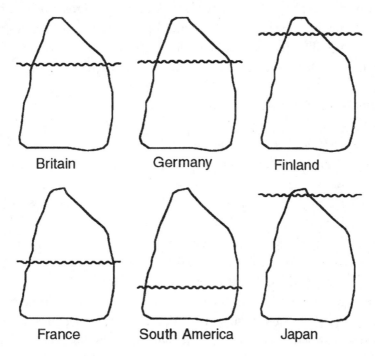

Britain   Germany   Finland

France   South America   Japan

Figure 58   Speech-and-thought icebergs

Culture shock

We often hear the term 'culture shock' which many people experience when transferring from one culture to another. Finns first hitting Cairo or Naples will suffer their own version of culture shock. Culture shock is caused by the lack of culture-specific cues, or indications, which tell you how to behave in that society. One of the problems for foreigners new to Finland is that Finnish shyness and silence provide few cultural cues. This causes foreigners to follow their own course and when Finns fail to react openly, newcomers begin to question their role or identity.

To give an example, an Englishman always feels he is a quiet, solid individual when in France, Spain and Italy. He is the typical reserved Englishman, listening to the Latins babbling on. Suddenly, in Finland he is the talkative one. What should he do? Maintain an out-of-character loquaciousness and behave like a Neapolitan, or imitate his Finn and silently watch the sun set over Lake Näsijärvi?

If a northern European questions his image among Finns, imagine how Italians and Spaniards feel as they talk and talk and wave around their arms. 'I feel constantly like an actor on the stage,' said one Italian executive, 'and I have to play the lead role for five acts, night after night.'

Leadership roles

In the business area, this obviously causes problems for foreign managers who have to decide which role or profile of leadership they should adopt among Finnish colleagues. There is clearly room for foreign managers in Finland, in order to bring in fresh ideas and see things from new angles. And yet should they adopt a high or low profile?

Should the French, with their great powers of imagination, attempt to fire and inspire the Finns with their exuberance and enthusiasm, or will they always be regarded as theatrical and overemotional with a lot of wild ideas? Should Germans, with their firm concepts of orderliness and '*Gründlichkeit*', try to install solid systems and a greater sense of respect, or will they just be regarded as Teutonic, heavy, inflexible, or even old-fashioned or outdated? Should the Swede emphasise polished management skills within a workers' council framework, or has the more individualistic Finnish approach already bypassed Swedish methods?

Again we must take into account the factor that Finns appear different to various nationalities. The Italians find them wooden, the Spaniards excessively law-abiding. The ultra-polite Japanese see Finns as a bit rude (without knowing it). Danes see them as big drinkers (the women too!) and Swedes often consider them slightly dangerous. The British, with their sense of history, see them as David against Goliath, but otherwise fairly normal, although on the quiet side.

The good, the bad and the ugly

Given these different viewpoints, the life of foreign managers in Finland is probably what they make it. If they look for the good, the bad and the ugly they will probably find all three.

You might say the bad is the tight-lipped, so-called winter behaviour, which causes Finns to hurry by wordlessly on the street (temperature −20°C) and gulp down their Koskenkorva to thaw out their irritability. Some see Finland as a land full of martyrs, making life difficult for themselves in an already inhospitable corner of Europe which they are reluctant to join. In 1952 there was no alcohol without food, you couldn't have a bath after 11 pm if you lived in an apartment block, you were not permitted to enter good restaurants unless you wore formal attire and the shops usually closed about 10 minutes before your working hours allowed you to get to them. Many of these things have changed, but one still has the worries of prices and taxes being so high that one can hardly breathe. Why do Finns have to build houses of such good quality that you can't pay the rent? In Finland the standard of living is so high that most people can't reach it.

But then there is the good. Finnish leadership practices are sound. Finnish managers, like Finnish army officers, usually lead from the front and they generally strike the right balance between authoritarianism and consultative style.

Although the ice breaks slowly, foreign managers will find that the informal business climate gives them freedom of action. They will not be encumbered by too many manuals, systems or hierarchical paths. Finns leave work early, but they start early and one can have achieved a fine day's work by the time most Britons are heading for lunch. Finnish employees are honest, reliable, punctual and generally loyal and their *sisu* qualities are well documented. Bureaucracy is kept at a minimum.

How to approach Finns

Your best starting point is to get it crystal clear in your mind that a Finn is a formidable person. The slow, reticent and apparently backward behaviour often referred to by Swedes, Germans and French among others is no more than a deceptive veneer covering a very modern individual. The more one has to do with Finns, the more one realises that they are, in effect, perfectionists. They defer politely to your cleverness or smoothness but, in fact, they usually upstage you.

The upstaging is done discreetly, but effectively. Your modest Finnish partners, so complimentary of your own attributes, turn out to be highly qualified technocrats with very solid assets. Their office, car and clothes may well be of better quality than yours, their house almost certainly will be. They have *ne plus ultra* standards of cleanliness, honesty, stamina, workmanship, reliability, hygiene, safety and education. In Finland you can drink tap water, doctors know how to cure you if you are ill, buses, trains and aeroplanes leave on time, there are no hurricanes. Newspapers are printed on good quality paper and the ink doesn't come off on your hands; Finnish money may sometimes devalue, but the banknotes have a nice feel to them. Finnish milk and coffee are the best in the world. Food is wholesome, society is solid. The Germans, Dutch, Swiss and other peoples also say how solid they are, but the Finns possess a squat, flat-footed solidity which always makes you feel you know where you are with them.

Finns look for solidity in others. Refer to your own culture's achievements, but always in a modest tone. Low profile works wonders with Finns. Never boast. When you have said your piece, don't expect any feedback. They are thinking about what you have said. They don't think and talk at the same time. Enjoy the silence – not many people give you this luxury. Consider silence as a positive sign, then you can relax. Go to the sauna and have a drink. When working with Finns you should try to set clear goals, define objectives and appeal to the inner resources of individuals to achieve the task under their own steam and to be fully accountable for it. Finns like to demonstrate their stamina in a lone task – they excel in such lonely pursuits as long-distance running, skiing, and rally driving.

Finnish businesspeople wish to have both their responsibility and authority well defined. They don't want one without the other. Self-discipline is taken for granted. Finns do not like being closely supervised; they prefer to come to you with the end result. You should listen well to Finns, for when they eventually have something to say, it is often worth listening to. You have to watch for subtle body language, as they have no other. You may not oversell to them, but charisma is OK. You can be humorous on any occasion, you can talk about the cultural values of others, but don't praise the Swedes too much. Finnish newspapers are among the best and most objective in the world, so they are probably better informed on most matters than you are. Show lively interest in Finnish culture – it is rewarding in any case. Make it clear that you know that Finland and Finnish products are high tech.

If you are managing Finns, remember that they are high on self-respect and inner harmony, as opposed to craving the support of teamwork. They like the idea of profit centres and accountability. They will sometimes be slow in making up their mind but, once it is made up, you are unlikely to succeed in changing it.

Finally, remember they are very dry (this quality, too, brings its delights). The great Finnish composer Jean Sibelius, who occasionally used to go on three- or four-day drinking sprees with other intellectuals, was once phoned by his long-suffering wife asking him for a forecast of when he might come back home. 'My dear, I am a composer. I am involved in the business of composing music, not delivering forecasts,' was the reply.

14

FRANCE

IN BOTH POLITICS AND BUSINESS THE FRENCH LIKE TO BE INDEPENDENT (at times maverick) and can appear frustrating to Americans, Japanese and Europeans alike.

French people live in a world of their own, the centre of which is France. They are immersed in their own history and tend to believe that France has set the norms for such things as democracy, justice, government and legal systems, military strategy, philosophy, science, agriculture, viniculture, *haute cuisine* and *savoir vivre* in general. Other nations vary from these norms and have a lot to learn before they get things right.

The French know virtually nothing about many other countries, as their education system teaches little of the history or geography of small nations or those which belonged to empires other than their own. Their general attitude towards foreigners is pleasant enough, neither positive nor negative. They will do business with you if you have a good product, or if you buy, but their initial posture will be somewhat condescending. You may not speak French, you appear to be Anglophiles. That is not a good start in their eyes.

You are not seen as an equal. You may be better or worse, but you are different. The French, like the Japanese, believe they are unique, and do not really expect you will ever be able to conform completely with their standards. What approach should one adopt when dealing with the French? Should one 'gallicise' oneself to some degree, becoming more talkative, imaginative and intense? Or should one maintain stolid, honest manners at the risk of seeming wooden or failing to communicate?

In order to get the best of one's dealings with the French, one has to study their psychology and tactics when they enter commercial transactions. They approach negotiation in a very French manner, which includes the following characteristics:

✦ They arrive at a meeting formally dressed, regarding it as a formal occasion.
✦ Surnames and formal introductions are used, seating will be hierarchical.
✦ Politeness and formal style will be maintained throughout the negotiation if the French 'manage' it.
✦ Logic will dominate their own argument and they will be quick to pounce on anything illogical said by the opposition.
✦ Their use of logic will lead to extensive analysis of all matters under discussion. Therefore the meeting will be long and wordy.
✦ They do not present their demands at the beginning, but lead up to them with a carefully constructed rationale.
✦ They reveal their hand only late in the negotiations (this causes people such as Americans to see this as cunning).
✦ French try to find out what all the other side's aims and demands are at the beginning. Americans usually oblige by putting all their cards on the table.
✦ French are suspicious of early friendliness in the discussion and dislike first names, taking off jackets, or disclosure of personal or family details.
✦ They pride themselves on quickness of mind, but dislike being rushed into decisions. For them negotiation is not a quick procedure.
✦ They rarely make important decisions inside the meeting. Often the chief decision maker is outside the meeting.
✦ They will prolong discussion, as they regard it as an intellectual exercise during which they are familiarising themselves with the other party and perhaps discovering their weaknesses.
✦ Their objectives are long term; they try to establish firm personal relationships.
✦ They will not make concessions in negotiations unless their logic has been defeated. This often makes them look stubborn in the eyes of the 'give-and-take' Americans and 'muddle-through' British.
✦ During deadlock they remain intransigent but without rudeness, simply restating their position.

✦ They try to be precise at all times. The French language facilitates this.

✦ They can be somewhat touchy if due respect is not shown or if protocol is not observed, but they are less sensitive to questions of 'honour' than the Spanish or South Americans and less worried about losing face than the Orientals.

✦ They are perceptive and opportunistic, but in the end always cautious.

✦ They believe they are intellectually superior to any other nationality.

✦ They often depart from the agenda and talk at length on a number of issues in random order.

✦ British and Americans often complain that 'we talked for hours but no decisions were arrived at or action taken'. (The French are actually clarifying their own thoughts through extensive discussion and have not yet decided on their course of action.)

✦ They will link the negotiation to other transactions they may be conducting.

✦ Personal views will influence their dealings on behalf of the company.

✦ Other members of their negotiating team are often close friends, colleagues from university or even relations.

✦ Communication style is extrovert, personal, often emotional, but adhering to logic.

✦ They arrive at the negotiation well informed in advance, but seeing things through French 'spectacles' often blinds them to international implications. Sometimes they are hampered by lack of language skills.

When dealing with the French, one should behave much more formally than usual, using only surnames and showing almost exaggerated politeness to French senior executives.

One should stick to logic at all times, avoiding American-style hunches or British-style 'feel for situations'. If one contradicts anything one said even months earlier, a French person will pounce on the contradiction.

One should be willing to appear 'more human' than usual, as the French are after all Latins, in spite of their logic and exactness. They like a good talk and observe few time limits for this. If you don't talk enough, they will call you monosyllabic afterwards.

If you want to gain points, you can score by criticizing the English – a favourite French pastime. You need not be unfair to anyone, you just show that you are not entirely in the Anglo-Saxon camp. French do not mind if you have a go at their other neighbours – the Italians and the Spaniards.

Do not criticise Napoleon – he has a kind of lasting identity with the French soul. You can say what you want about De Gaulle, Mitterand or any current French prime minister. They probably won't know who your prime minister is, so they can't crucify him.

The French are often criticised by people of other nationalities and it is not difficult to see why. Essentially argumentative and opinionated, they frequently find themselves out on a limb at international meetings, isolated in their intransigence when all the others have settled for compromise. This naturally leaves them open to charges of arrogance. And yet one must have some sympathy for them. They are clear-sighted, perceptive thinkers who feel that they have a better historical perspective that most of us. They would rather be right than popular. Are they usually right? Like all others, they are fallible in their judgement and subject to bias, but they have great experience in politics, warfare, domestic and overseas organisation and administration and the humanities. Like the Germans, they cannot be accused of taking things lightly. Their long and significant involvement in European and world affairs gives the French the conviction that their voice should be heard loud and clear in international forums. Their political, military, economic strengths may no longer predominate as they once did, but French people perceive no diminishment or fading in their moral and didactic authority. Like the Americans, British and Russians, they have a strong messianic streak. They would not be human if they did not resent the rise of the British after the fall of Napoleon, the decline of the French language as a world tongue, the incursions of the Japanese on the European economic scene, and, most of all, the pernicious Americanisation of large parts of the world, including once-French-dominated Europe and even French culture itself.

Though often seen as selfish defenders of their own territory, it is not inconceivable that with their old-fashioned doggedness and resistance to precipitated globalisation, they might one day emerge as the champions of age-long values and philosophies which Europe subconsciously cherishes. The maverick of Europe may well turn out to be its moral bedrock. At all events, the French merit a closer examination of their apparent obstinacies and negative features.

French as others see them

Appearance	Reality
French people are obstinate, always hold a different opinion from everybody else.	They stick to what they believe is right unless they are proved wrong.
They think they are cleverer than anyone else.	True: the length and magnificence of their historical achievements leave them convinced that their mission is to civilise Europe.
They don't like to speak foreign languages, especially English.	French was once the internationally accepted language of diplomacy and spoken widely in four continents. It is a clinical, precise language; many foreigners also find it beautiful. French people feel sadness at its decline *vis-à-vis* English. England was the traditional enemy. American English often sounds vulgar, anti-intellectual to them.
They know little about and are not interested in other countries and cultures.	History lessons in their education system tend to concentrate on French history. They are not very international in their knowledge, but they do know a lot about Asia and Africa and possess extensive scholarship in the study of ancient cultures.
They are overemotional.	Like all Latins they raise their voice and gesticulate when excited, but they rarely abandon rationality and are not blind to others' virtues.

Appearance	Reality
They are inquisitive, ask personal questions and cannot mind their own business.	French is such an exact language that it is difficult not to be direct when using it. They are often personal, as they are interested in you personally, but they have an innate politeness often unseen by foreigners.
They talk too much at meetings.	A logical argument takes longer to build up than an intuitive one. Cartesian theory requires building blocks. French people also like to consider every aspect of a question before making decisions.
They can't keep to an agenda.	As they inter-relate all the points, they feel they must go back and forth to balance their decisions.
They are finicky.	They generally have a clear idea of what they want and take pains to get things right.
They make grandiose plans.	True, they think big and hate the mediocre. But having established *les grandes lignes*, they are later quite analytical about details.
They make poor team members.	They are very individualistic and not lacking in self-confidence. This, allied to (generally) a good education, encourages them to go it alone. This is counteracted within France itself by a high degree of centralisation.

Appearance	Reality
They can't relax	Relaxing does not come easily to people who are quick, imaginative and culture rich.
They are too quick to attack others.	French people like a tidy universe. They feel compunction to redress what they perceive as injustice, stupidity or laxity. They do not hesitate to intervene.
They prefer ideas to facts and won't make decisions in a normal, straightforward manner.	Statistics can prove anything. Facts are not always what they seem. What is wrong with exploring ideas?
They are cynical.	If you have the British on one side of you, the Germans on the other and the Americans on your TV screen, you have to be.
They are irrevocably chauvinistic	Malraux pointed out that nations usually act nationalistically and are unimpressed by specious internationalisation. Social justice is best obtained in a nation that knows its own ground.
French people are selfish, care little for others	Not true. As Malraux said further, France is never completely effective when fighting for herself. When the French fight for mankind, they are wonderful.
They are messianic.	True. Malraux's brief when being appointed Minister of Culture was the expansion and *rayonnement* of French culture. It is good for us.

15

GERMANY

BASIC CHARACTERISTICS OF GERMAN BUSINESS CULTURE ARE A MONO·
chronic attitude towards the use of time, e.g. a desire to complete one
action chain before embarking on another; a strong belief that they are
honest, straightforward negotiators; and a tendency to be blunt and
disagree openly rather than going for politeness or diplomacy.

German companies are traditional, slow-moving entities, encumbered
by manuals, systems and hierarchical paths regarded by many Europeans
and Americans as over-rigid and outmoded. Hierarchy is mandatory, often
resulting in exaggerated deference for one's immediate superior and CEO.

The German boss is an extremely private person, normally sitting isolated in a large office behind a closed door. American and Scandinavian
senior executives prefer an open door policy and like to wander round the
corridors and chat to colleagues. This horizontal communication contrasts
with the German vertical system, where instructions are passed down to
immediate inferiors only and kept rigidly within one's own department.

In many countries there exists departmental rivalry, but when dealing
with the Germans one should remember that they can be especially touchy
in this area. Always try to find the right person for each message. Tread on
a German executive's toes and he or she will remember it for a long time.

Germans have great respect for possessions and property. Solid buildings, furniture, cars and good clothing are important for them and they will
try to impress you with all these things. You should acknowledge the
grandeur of German possessions and be unafraid in displaying your own
solidity, facilities, etc. Germans wish to believe you are as solid as they are.

When advertising your company's products to Germans, you should put as much as possible in print. Germans are unimpressed by flashy television advertising, clever slogans or artistic illustration. Their newspapers are full of heavy, factual ads giving the maximum amount of information in the space available. Brochures aimed at the German market should be lengthy, factual, serious and should make claims which can later be fully justified. No matter how long or boring your brochure is, the Germans will read it. They will also expect your product to conform exactly to the description you have given.

Germans have their own particular style of conducting meetings and negotiations, and you may find that procedures with big German companies are much more formalised than in your country. It is generally advisable to adopt a rather more formal approach with Germans at meetings and to note the following German characteristics, to which one must react appropriately:

✦ Germans will arrive at the meeting well-dressed and with a disciplined appearance. You must match this.
✦ They will observe hierarchical seating and order of speaking.
✦ They will arrive well informed as to the business and expect you to be also.
✦ They will present logical, often weighty arguments to support their case.
✦ They often have thought over your possible counter-arguments and have their second line of attack ready.
✦ They do not concede their case or arguments easily, but tend to look for common ground. This is often your best approach to make progress. Head-on collision with a sizeable German company seldom leads to results.
✦ They believe they are more efficient (*gründlich*) than others and do not change position easily.
✦ They compartmentalise their arguments, each member speaking about his or her speciality. They expect your side to do the same.
✦ They do not interfere with a colleague's remarks and generally show good teamwork throughout. They do, however, argue with each other in private between sessions. As they are not poker-faced (like Japanese) or simulating (like French) it is often possible to detect difference of opinion among them by their facial expressions or body language.

+ Like Japanese, they like to go over details time and time again. They wish to avoid misunderstanding later. You must be patient.
+ They don't like being rushed.
+ They are willing to make decisions within meetings (unlike the Japanese or French), but they are always cautious.
+ They generally stick to what they have agreed orally.
+ If you are selling to them they will question you aggressively on what are German strong points, e.g. quality of goods, delivery dates, and competitive price. Be ready.
+ They expect, in the end, to get the very best (lowest) price. They may only give you a little 'trial' business even at that. Take it – it will lead to much more business later if they are satisfied.
+ They will look earnestly for deficiencies in your products or services and will criticise you openly (even energetically) if you fail to match up to all your claims. Be prepared to apologise if you have failed in some respect. They like receiving apologies, it makes them feel better. Also you will have to compensate.
+ They can be very sensitive to criticism themselves, therefore you must go to great lengths to avoid embarrassing them, even unwittingly.
+ Use surnames only and show respect for their titles. There are many Doktors in Germany.
+ Do not introduce humour or jokes during business meetings. They are not Americans, they don't like kidding. Business is serious. Tell them funny stories afterwards over a beer. You will find many of their stories unfunny or heavy. Do your best to laugh.
+ They will write up their notes carefully and come back well prepared the next day. It is advisable for you to do the same.
+ Germans generally have good language abilities (especially English and French) but often suffer from lack of knowledge of foreign cultures (they may know a lot less about your country than you think they know). They like to use German whenever they can.
+ They are generally convinced that they are the most honest, reliable and sincere people in the world, also in their business negotiations. Show them that in this respect you are their equal.

Germans are indeed very sincere people and assume that others are too. They are often disappointed, as other people who prefer a casual or flippant approach to life do not always give serious answers to serious questions. Germans tend to search long and deep for the true meaning of life and like to spend their time profitably, whether it is to enrich their coffers or their soul.

In their seriousness, they try hard to be dutiful, untroublesome citizens. In a crowded country pressures to conform in public are very strong and Germans do not wish to be seen as mavericks or unorthodox. They have no desire (like many British, French or American people) to be eccentric. Germans try not to make mistakes and generally succeed. If you make a mistake they will tell you about it. They are not being rude – it is their unstoppable drive towards order and conformity. Germans like to be fair and often lean over backwards to show how fair they are.

Germans often appear intense and humourless to Anglo-Saxons, who long for periodic levity in conversation. Germans do not have the British and American addiction to funny stories and wisecracks. They long for deep friendships and have heart-felt discussions of life's problems and enigmas. Anglo-Saxons do not always see the way towards making quick friendships with them, but when they succeed in entering into the somewhat complicated structure of a German friendship, they find rich rewards. A German is generally a loyal and true friend of incredible durability. Outwardly often glum and cautious, they are inwardly desperate for affection and popularity. They want to be cherished just as the rest of us do. When they find that English, American or French individuals – on the surface easy-going and witty – can also be as steadfast as a German, they are delighted and receptive. A German friendship is indeed a very worthwhile investment.

Germans as seen by others

Appearance

Germans are time dominated,
punctuality is an obsession.

Germans are slow at making
decisions, as they discuss
things too long.

Germans give you very lengthy
explanations, going right
back to the beginning of
every matter.

Delays in delivering things are
common in Germany. This
contradicts their love of
promptness.

Germans are not good at providing quarterly financial
reports according to the
American system.

Americans and Australians find
the pace of German
business life too slow.

You always have to knock on
the door before entering a
German's office.

Reality

Time is central to German culture. It is one of the principal
ways of organising life.

Germans have a consensus deci-
sion-making process, whch
requires extensive back-
ground research and often
lateral clearances.

Germans, when explaining
something, like to lay a
proper foundation. For them
events in the present are a
result of the past. Historical
context is important.

Germans plan well into the
future. They are not preoccupied with immediate
results or deliveries.

Germans prefer annual reports.
Three months is too short a
time frame to be meaning-
ful. Writing quarterly reports
disrupts normal work.

Germans like to complete
action chains and wish to be
thorough (*gründlich*) rather
than speedy.

Yes, it is good manners.

Appearance	Reality
Germans are too private. They do not interact well with foreigners and are not mobile. They don't lend things easily.	Germany is not a melting-pot society like the USA or Australia, where people have developed strategies for interacting with strangers. Privacy is important in order to complete action chains without interruption. They don't borrow things easily.
Germans are too formal, using only surnames with office colleagues even after 20 years.	Formality and use of surnames are signs of respect.
Germans are stiff, distant and do not smile much.	In Germany, smiling is for friends. They are more reserved when being introduced to people than, for instance, Americans or Australians. Smiles are not always sincere!
Germans don't like people standing too close to them or touching them.	In Germany, the 'distance of comfort' is approximately 1.2 metres. It is a non-tactile culture.
Germans don't like you entering their office. They get upset if you move a chair or item of furniture.	Privacy is important for concentration on work. Offices (and homes) should be kept in good order. Why move things? The layout has been carefully planned.
There is too much secrecy in German organisations. Information does not flow freely.	Knowledge is power. Also compartmentalisation of German companies hinders lateral information flow. Power flows from the top down.

Appearance

Germans admire military and economic power more than other kinds.

Germans display power and Influence through material possessions – fine offices, homes, cars, clothes. They are less modest about those than, say, the British.

Germans are noisy people.

Germans have too many rules and regulations and do not take human needs into consideration sufficiently.

Germans are too law-abiding, conform too much and are always worried about what others will think.

Decentralisation and compartmentalisation represent serious handicaps in German business.

Germans in conversation and when developing ideas make things too complex

Reality

Not true. They admire intellectual power most. Many heads of German firms have doctorates.

Germans like to display symbols of power and success, but handle them with much more grace and reserve than, for instance, Americans.

True only of German tourists abroad. In meetings, the most powerful person usually speaks in a soft voice.

Germans believe good procedures and processes solve most problems and give order paramount importance to create general well-being.

German sense of order requires conformity. Signs and directions are there to be obeyed. Eccentrics or law-breakers do not gain sympathy as they might do in the UK, France or Australia.

These are structural features in German society. Germany was unified late and dislikes too much central power. The *Länder* are still important. Unlike the French, they prefer dispersion of power.

Life is complicated. Germans think Americans and others oversimplify.

Appearance

German possessions, especially furniture, buildings, cars, TV sets, are heavy and lack grace.

Germans have a mania for keeping things in spotless order. They are always washing cars, windows, floors, and constantly servicing equipment.

German neighbours or colleagues criticise you if you do anything wrong, make mistakes or too much noise, transgress any regulation. It is none of their business what I do!

Germans are class-conscious, much more so than in the US or Australia. A class system still exists, especially in top levels of business.

The Germans persist in using 'Sie' when most Anglo-Saxons would start using first names (equivalent of 'Du')

Germans take work too seriously. They have no fun at work. They don't tell jokes during business meetings. They are boring.

Reality

Germans like solidarity in all things. Cars are made to last 10–15 years. Doors, houses, chairs, and tables should be solid – also characters!

Germans do not believe in waste. If you keep things in good order they will last longer. German goods are of high quality and deserve proper upkeep.

In Germany, proper observation of the rules is everybody's business. If every citizen is conscientious, then not so many police will be needed!

This is true to some extent. But top level Germans are very well mannered. They also work very hard and place value on education.

Germans are not casual about friendships. They do not wish to become immediately familiar with strangers.

Germans think business is a serious matter. Why tell funny stories during business meetings? You can tell them afterwards. Why waste time? Being serious is being honest, not boring.

Appearance

Germans are stubborn and lack flexibility. They don't compromise enough.

Germans disagree with people openly and have no tact at business meetings. They are often *too* frank and lack delicacy. They upset people.

Germans make poor conversation partners at cocktail parties. They can't make 'small talk'.

German head offices often fail to react to local conditions abroad and persist in doing things the 'German way'.

Germans are not adaptable. They are unable to effect changes quickly within their organisation to meet changing circumstances.

Germans spend an inordinate amount of time every day shaking hands with colleagues.

Reality

Germans stick to what they believe in. If you want to change their mind, you must show them they are wrong.

Frankness is honesty. 'Diplomacy' can often mean deviousness or not saying what you think. The truth is always the truth. Why pretend?

Germans do not see the point in 'small talk'. They say what there is to say. They discuss business and serious issues very well. They do not wish to open their private lives or opinions to strangers at parties.

There is some truth in this, but German expatriate managers are often successful in convincing HQ of the need for flexibility.

Germans do not like making 'lightning' decisions. They believe an organisation will be successful if procedures are first perfected and then kept in place. Changes in management are less frequent than in the USA.

Shaking hands shows respect for one's colleagues and is the normal way for a German to say 'hello'.

Appearance	Reality
German managers rarely compliment their workers on the job.	Germans are perfectionists, therefore they expect a job to be well done. Why constantly compliment someone who is simply doing their duty? But German managers are very fair to their employees and help them with difficulties.
German advertising is heavy, boring and not visual enough.	Germans like lots of information, therefore they wish an advert to describe the product in detail. They are not impressed by clever slogans, catchphrases or hype. They do not appreciate striking illustrations which often have little to do with the product.
German conventions are long, serious and boring.	Germans regard conventions as occasions where business is done. If one takes the trouble to get a large number of people together it is an ideal opportunity to exchange ideas. They see entertainment as an unnecessary distraction.

16

ITALY

THE ITALIANS ARE CHARMING, INTELLIGENT PEOPLE TO WHOM EUROPE owes a great cultural debt. They are excellent communicators and combine ultra-keen perception with ever-present flexibility. Their continuous exuberance and loquacious persuasiveness often produce an adverse reaction with reserved Britons, factual Germans and taciturn Scandinavians. Yet such northerners have everything to gain by adapting to Italians' outgoing nature, meeting them halfway in their idea for dialogue. There is plenty of business to be done with the Italians, who export vigorously in order to survive. The following remarks attempt to give the northerner a few clues on how some concessions towards extroversion can reap rewards.

Italians like to share details of families, holidays, hopes, aspirations, disappointments, preferences. Show photographs of children, etc. Reveal some of your political or religious opinions – this is normal in Italy, you need not be an island unto yourself. Discuss beliefs and values. Do not be afraid to appear talkative. No matter how hard you try the Italian will always consider you reserved (and talk 10 times as much as you).

One characteristic of Italians is that they are relatively non-chauvinistic and do not automatically believe that Italian must be best. This national modesty is rarely seen outside Finland and Italy. Capitalise on this trait by discussing Italy in a frank manner.

Italians, unlike Spaniards, Germans or French, are not particularly sensitive or touchy. They accept criticism and are very flexible. You may speak much more freely with them than with most Europeans, but do not exaggerate directness or bluntness. They are flexible, but also delicate.

Remember that the communication style is eloquent, wordy, demonstrative and apparently emotional. This is normal for them, over-dramatic for you. Do not be led into the belief that waving arms and talking with the hands denotes instability or unreliability. They think you, by contrast, are rather wooden and distant. Make them feel comfortable by showing more facial expression and body language.

Italians have a different concept of time from that of northerners and Americans. They do not arrive for appointments on time. Punctuality in Milan means they are 20 minutes late, in Rome half an hour and in the South 45 minutes. You will not be able to change this, except in a fixed-hours factory or office environment. You must therefore adapt. Be prepared to wait 15–45 minutes before your Italian counterpart appears or lets you into his office. Take a good book or magazine. Alternatively you can deliberately show up half an hour late, but in fact few northerners are able to do this. There is also a variance in the concept of space. Italians are used to being crowded and working in close proximity to each other. This creates an atmosphere of teamwork approximating to that of the Japanese. A Briton, American or German needs more space or 'elbow room' to work effectively and this shows itself in such matters as office layout and use of space both in factories and in administrative areas. Be prepared to 'rub shoulders' with Italians.

The 'distance of comfort' is greater for northerners than Italians. The English like to keep a minimum of 1.2 metres between themselves and their interlocutor. Italians are quite comfortable at 80 centimetres. If you retreat from such a position, they will think you are avoiding them or that you find their physical presence distasteful. Make them feel more welcome by 'standing your ground'.

Italians may touch your arm or shoulder or perhaps hug you if they are feeling friendly. After some months' acquaintance, they may kiss you on both cheeks when greeting you or departing. They are showing affection and you must find some way of reciprocating. At least smile occasionally, your face will not break (in a southern climate).

Italian flexibility in business often leads you to think they are 'dishonest'. They frequently bend rules, break or 'get round' some laws and put a very flexible interpretation on certain agreements, controls and regulations. Remember that this is the way they do business and you may well be able to benefit from this 'flexibility'. They will regard your rather rigid, law-abiding approach as somewhat old-fashioned, short-sighted or even blind. In this respect they probably are closer to reality than you are and less ideal bound. They do not consider their approach to be in any way corrupt, immoral or misleading. They will happily take you into their 'consipiracy'. They will share the 'benefits' with you, if you accept. If you stick to the letter of the law, they will go on without you. We are not talking about clear illegalities. There are many grey areas where short cuts are, in Italian eyes, a matter of common sense.

Italians are less private persons than linear-active people and they will borrow your property (or time) with freedom. Eventually they will repay or return your property (calculator, car, report, etc.) so do not be unduly stuffy about it. Remember you can borrow from them whenever you like.

Italians often 'borrow' your money in the sense that they pay late. This is another area where change of habit is very difficult to bring about. The best you can do is try to arrange satisfactory payment schedules in advance and/or take the probability of delayed payments strongly into consideration. Remember the Italians will allow you similar latitude (if they can afford it).

At meetings, Italians do not follow agendas as strictly as do northerners. They will jump ahead to later points or will rediscuss points you think have already been settled. They will talk loudly, excitedly and at length. Often several people will speak at once, and you may find two or three more micro-meetings going on simultaneously. They do not like silences of more than 5 seconds. If you are not running the meeting, there is nothing you can do except sit back and enjoy. If you are in the chair, you have to create some kind of order, but you can only do this by establishing firm rules in advance. One German I know used yellow, red and green cards to discipline people at South American meetings. This humorous but firm approach achieved the desired result.

Italian wordiness v northern succinctness is a constant pain in internal company communication, as both sides wish to achieve clarity, one through many words and the other through short messages and memos. A compromise must be reached. Northerners must teach themselves to be more explicit and explanatory, but also encourage their Italian colleagues to be more concise, economical with words and ideas, and whenever practical to put them in writing. The invention of the fax has been a valuable weapon for Scandinavians and other concise peoples.

Italians are much more polite, on the surface, than northerners, so you will often appear overfrank, blunt and even rude, although you do not intend this. Try to adopt a certain Italian smoothness or delicacy and use flattery more than you normally would. They like it. Open doors for women and stand up and sit down at the right times. You probably do this anyway, but notice how the Italians do it with charm and style. When leaving a room an Italian often says '*Con permesso*'. Try a few tricks like that. If you still feel a bit awkward, console yourself by remembering that to a Japanese an Italian looks clumsy, emotional and often rude.

You will often find it difficult to rid yourself of the impression that the Italians are an unruly, disorganised bunch. They do not seem to plan methodically like you do. Do not forget they are the fifth industrial nation in the world and have outperformed even the Germans and Americans in such areas as domestic appliances and some categories of cars. On top of that they have an enormous hidden or 'black' economy, the extent of which is unknown. Therefore they must be doing something right. Your task should be to discover where they act in a superior manner to you and whether you can learn to do the same. Their efficiency is not as 'obvious' as yours, but it may have something to do with their gregariousness, flexibility, working hours, people orientation, teamwork, quickness and opportunism. Try to get into their shoes.

Italian negotiators are friendly, talkative, and ultimately flexible. They are less direct than northerners and often seem to proceed in a roundabout manner. Italians will discuss things from a personal or semi-emotional angle ('Look at the good relations between our presidents'), while northerners try to concentrate on the benefit for their company and stick to the facts of the particular deal. Northerners should approach negotiation with Italians with adequate time for the exercise and a large store of patience. They must be prepared to discuss at length and maintain calm. An Italian may get overheated on some point, but changes a moment later into the friendliest of negotiators. Italians may quarrel among themselves at the table, but are solid colleagues minutes later. Their starting price may be high, but they are prepared for a lot of negotiating down. The Scandinavian or Briton selling to them must show a first price which allows some room for a reduction later. They will expect it. They must come away from the deal showing they have won or gained something. Each member of their team must be granted something. Northerners will be at their best if they regard the negotiation as a kind of interesting game which must be played with many Italian rules, but which leads to a serious and beneficial result (for both).

17

PORTUGAL

If the Portuguese people were not very different from the Spaniards, Portugal would not exist. Looking at a map of the Iberian peninsula, we have the impression that the roughly pentagonal mass – so clearly separated from the rest of Europe by the Pyrenees and so narrowly cut off from Africa by the Straits of Gibraltar – seems geologically formed for unity: the intermediary between two seas and two continents.

A Portuguese friend of mine likes to play a trick on his Spanish acquaintances. He hints at the patchy quality of Spanish education and challenges them to draw the outline of Spain. Stung by his insinuations, they invariably put pen to paper and draw the following shape:

My friend plays with them a bit, suggesting that the outline is not quite perfect, whereupon the hapless Spaniards tweak a line or curve here and there, or do the whole outline again with greater care. My friend then does it for them, thus:

Subconsciously most Spaniards think of the Iberian Peninsula as theirs; subconsciously most Portuguese see the Spaniards as potential invaders. There is a parallel situation in the way English, Welsh and Scots feel about each other, although in their case the political union is a fact.

The matter was settled with Spain in 1297 when Portugal won its independence under King Afonso Henriques. For 60 years (1580–1640) the Spaniards reestablished dominion, but since then the divorce has been made final. Geographically, in fact, the division makes sense, just as the separation of Norway and Sweden does. Each party wants its own side of the mountain and the lifestyle has adapted to the environment. Norway and Portugal were forest-clad and coastal, inclining their populations towards seafaring and fishing occupations; in the case of Portugal the fishermen, sailors, foresters and fruit-growers were too unlike the migratory shepherds on the Castilian plateau to share any lasting future with them. Spain has often been seen as a collection of separate provinces. With the advent of Portuguese independence, it counted one less.

Portugal is an Atlantic country, Spain is principally Mediterranean. The Portuguese, with their backs to Spain, face the ocean and the western hemisphere. Cut off from Europe by Spanish land, they had easy sea routes to the British Isles, the African coast, Madeira, the Canaries, the Azores and ultimately the Americas.

Landlocked countries are, in a sense, unlucky. At the mercy of sudden, unexpected attacks by neighbours, their policies are necessarily suspicious, cautious and (when feeling strong) vindictive. They have little freedom of movement, as they are blocked by foreign territory. Those Mediterranean countries without an Atlantic seaboard are to some degree landlocked, as their access to greater seas has historically been barred by Spain, Britain (Gibraltar) and the Moors. Black Sea neighbours Russia, Romania and Bulgaria are unable to proceed even to the Mediterranean without Turkish permission. In the same manner the states bordering on the Baltic had their exit to the Atlantic barred by Viking sea power. Portugal belongs to the luckier maritime countries. If you have stood by Vasco de Gama's statue on the sea shore of his home town of Sines and looked out over the beckoning blue ocean on a fine sunny day, you are left in little doubt as to why the Portuguese sailed forth and sought lands beyond the horizon. The ocean is exhilarating and those people who are substantially exposed to it – Vikings, Britons, French, Spaniards, Polynesians, Dutch and Portuguese – have proceeded literally to the ends of the earth and carved out their own destiny in times when such exploits were still feasible.

Adjoining foreign-held land threatens – it creates an obsession with national security (e.g. Russia). Oceans, on the other hand, are natural defences, providing early warning against foreign aggression and a battle-ground where it may be halted before it reaches your shores. Oceans, moreover, are bridges for easy access to other countries, to bilateral trade and exchange of new ideas without the neighbours getting involved as intermediaries. The Atlantic provided West-facing Portugal with an unhindered link with England, its natural ally against Spain and (later) Napoleon's France. It opened up a country which would otherwise have been claustrophobic, with no contact with fellow Europeans except through the Spanish filter.

Most importantly, the Atlantic gave newly independent Portugal the attractive opportunity for overseas exploration at the very time when large parts of the world were ripe for colonisation. Science, although still in its infancy, was providing an invaluable aid to ocean-going vessels. England, France, Spain and Holland were all gearing up to expand by means of ambitious colonisation. The 500-mile strip of Atlantic sea-coast destined the Portuguese to join these maritime powers and enabled this tiny country to acquire an enormous empire, rivalling in size and resources those of France, Spain and Britain.

In business, although the organisation of firms is based on vertical hierarchy with authority concentrated in the person at the top, Portuguese managers avoid direct conflicts with staff members whenever possible by adopting a benign manner of address and considering the personal problems of subordinates.

The same friendly attitude is observed in their relationship with clients. The Portuguese begin the relationship with the open assumption that trust exists between the two parties. Their manner is so cheerful and communicative that they have no difficulty in establishing this ambience, even in the initial stages of discussion. In Portugal clients are seen as friends, otherwise it is unlikely they will remain clients.

In countries where bureaucracy is heavy – and in Portugal it has this unfortunate characteristic – there is a tendency for the conduct of business to rely largely on good personal relations and mutual confidence of individuals, otherwise there will be no short cuts. In Portugal, as in Italy, the ability to generate close relations, to secure good introductions, to create long-term goodwill, is not only an essential prerequisite to doing business, but is the criterion of efficiency itself! Portuguese executives, who have this gift, make excellent ice-breakers at international gatherings where some of the delegates exhibit initial stiffness.

The Portuguese possess great oratorical skills, but they also like things in writing. This is not only a product of Portuguese bureaucracy (they borrowed heavily from the Napoleonic model) but they consider that well-expressed documents help to avoid uncertainty and ambiguity. There the contrast with Spaniards is startling. Portuguese generally write their language carefully and well; this characteristic serves them admirably in the bureaucratic procedures often required in large multinational companies.

The Portuguese are more formal than the Spaniards who nowadays use the *tu* form all over the place. 'You' in Portugal can be *O Senhor* (*A Senhora*), *tu* or *Você* and these forms can be combined with either first or second names or with titles such as *Professor* or *Engenheiro*. The permutations are many. When in doubt, it is advisable to err on the side of formality. Do not hesitate to address as *Doutor* anyone who appears well-qualified or more intelligent than you are.

Negotiating with the Portuguese

The Portuguese are among the best negotiators in the world. When they negotiated the terms of their entry into the Common Market at the same time as the Spaniards, they obtained considerably better conditions than their fellow Iberians.

Their imperial past and inclination to distance themselves from the Spaniards have made them far more international in outlook than most people give them credit for. Their language abilities are excellent – among the Latins they are easily the best speakers of English, and enrolments on English, French and German courses are staggering. The famous Cambridge School of Languages in Lisbon regularly enrols more than 10,000 students per annum.

Portuguese are easily able to negotiate in English. The following are the chief characteristics of the Portuguese negotiator:

+ They negotiate individually or in small teams. Team members know each other well, and may be related.
+ They will achieve the best agreement for the company, but individual preferences, family and social position will be a background to the decisions.
+ They regard the negotiation result as a credit or debit to personal prowess.
+ Their multi-active nature leads them to link the negotiation to other transactions or business in which they are currently involved. They do not compartmentalise the negotiation.
+ They use surnames and titles, but are friendly, even charming, from the outset.
+ They believe they are smarter than the other side, but try to give the impression they are dumber.
+ They know what they want from the outset, but have an open mind as to the route they will take to achieve it.
+ They are suspicious by nature, but disguise this suspicion.
+ They are quick, perceptive and opportunistic.
+ They exercise maximum flexibility.
+ They often say they understand, when in fact they plan to understand.
+ They make decisions individually or by consensus, according to circumstances.

+ They begin with a high price to leave room for manoeuvre later, but are quick to modify if they sense tension.
+ They state what they really want as late as they can in the negotiation.
+ They argue in a roundabout manner as opposed to French logical build-up or American up-front demands.
+ They will often change course dramatically during a negotiation and make a platform out of something they didn't come to the table with.
+ They will often throw an extremely imaginative (wild) proposal on the table to confuse the opponent or gain time.
+ They rarely turn down any business offered during negotiation, scooping up whatever peripheral or accessorial transactions are available.
+ Generous by nature, they entertain lavishly in between meetings, often choosing the entertainment themselves.
+ They expect to pay and be paid promptly.
+ National honour is not a major factor. They are not touchy about race, religion or colour.
+ Their communicative style is personal, eloquent, emotional, but more restrained than Italian or Spanish (Atlantic influence).
+ They come to the negotiation well informed about all aspects of the transaction.
+ They are experienced on a global scale. Centuries of trading with India, Africa and the Far East have taught the Portuguese to be flexible, devious, realistic and 'good losers'.
+ A lack of technology and resources often puts Portuguese in a disadvantageous position which they must compensate for with clever negotiation, resulting in a sophisticated approach.

18

RUSSIA

THE DISINTEGRATION OF THE SOVIET UNION HAS ELIMINATED THE gigantic, multicultural phenomenon constituted by the bewildering assortment of countries, races, republics, territories, autonomous regions, philosophies, religions and credos that conglomerated to form the world's vastest political union. The cultural kaleidoscope had been so rich that the mind could only boggle while contemplating it. Its collapse, however, serves to make us focus on something more simple yet unquestionably fecund *per se* – the culture of Russia itself.

It is only too easy to lump Soviet ideology and the Russian character together, since during 70 years of strife and evolution one lived with the other. Stalin – a Georgian – was no Russian, Mikoyan was Armenian, but Lenin, Trotski, Kerensky – the early Bolshevik thinkers – were all Great Russians, as were Kruschev, Andropov, Molotov, Bulganin, Gorbachev and Yeltsin. Yet Soviet Russians were no more than one regimented stream of Russian society – a frequently unpopular, vindictive and short-sighted breed at that, although their total grasp of power and utter ruthlessness enabled them to remain untoppled for seven decades.

That same society, however, in the same period of time produced Pasternak, Solzhenitsyn, Sakharov, as well as thousands of courageous individuals who supported them. A culture that bred Chekhov, Tschaikowski, Rachmaninov, Dostoievski, Tolstoy, Peter the Great and Alexander Nevski simply does not vanish into thin air during a brief period of political oppression and drudgery. Its individuality was obliged in a sense to go underground, to mark time in order to survive, but the Russian soul is as immortal as anyone else's. Its resurrection and development in the twenty-first century is of great import to us all.

Some of the less attractive features of Russian behaviour in the Soviet period – exaggerated collectivism, apathy, suspicion of foreigners, pessimism, petty corruption, lack of continued endeavour, inward withdrawal – were in fact not products of the Bolshevik regime. Russia was Communist for 70 years, it had been Russian Orthodox for 1000 years. The basic traits of the Russian character were visible hundreds of years before Lenin or Karl Marx were born. Both Tsarist and Soviet rule were facilitated by the collective, submissive, self-sacrificial, enduring tendencies of the sentimental, romantic, essentially vulnerable subjects under their sway. Post-Soviet Russian society is undergoing cataclysmic evolution and change and it remains to be seen how some eventual form of democracy and the freeing of entrepreneurial spirit will affect the impact that Russians make on the rest of us.

The Russian character has been determined to some extent by unrelenting autocratic rule and governance over many centuries, but the two chief factors in the formation of Russian values and core beliefs were over and above any governmental control. These prevailing determinants were the incalculable vastness of the Russian land and the unvarying harshness of its climate. Figure 59 shows how the boundless, often indefensible steppes bred a deep sense of vulnerability and remoteness which caused groups to band together for survival and develop hostility to outsiders.

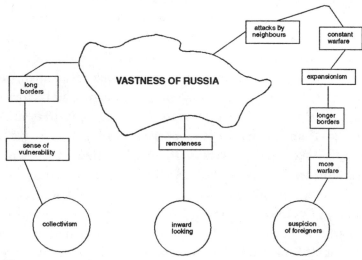

Figure 59

Figure 60 indicates how the influence of climate (a potent factor in all cultures) was especially harsh on Russian peasants, who traditionally are forced virtually to hibernate for long periods, then struggle frantically to till, sow and harvest in the little time left. Anyone who has passed through Irkutsk or Novosibirsk in the depth of winter can appreciate the numbing effect of temperatures ranging from minus 20–40 degrees Celsius, while the high winter suicide rate in slightly warmer countries such as Sweden and Finland suggests that Russians are not the only ones to wallow in bleakness for a considerable portion of their days.

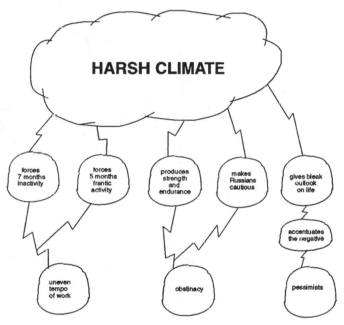

Figure 60

The long-suffering Russian peasants, ill favoured by cruel geography and denied (by immense distances and difficult terrain) chances of adequate communication among themselves, were easy meat for those with ambitions to rule. Small, uneducated groups, lacking in resources and cut off from potential allies, are easy to manipulate. The Orthodox Church, the Tsars, the Soviets, all exploited these hundreds of thousands of pathetic clusters of backward rustics. Open to various forms of indoctrination, the peasants were bullied, deceived, cruelly taxed and, whenever necessary, called to arms. In the sixteenth century military service could be 25 years; in 1861 when serfdom was 'abolished' it was reduced to 16 years! Russians have lived with secret police not just in KGB times, but since the days of Ivan the Terrible, in the sixteenth century. Figure 61 shows how oppressive, cynical governance over many centuries developed further characteristics – pervasive suspicion, secrecy, apparent passivity, readiness to practise petty corruption, disrespect for edicts – as added ingredients to the traditional Russian pessimism and stoicism in adversity.

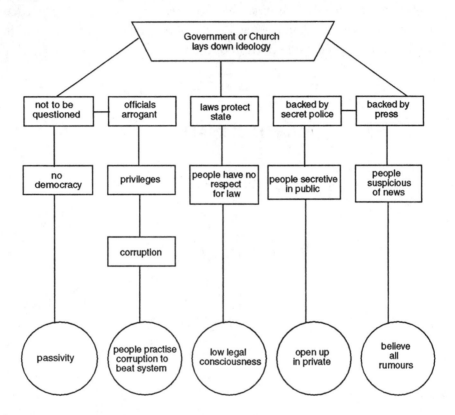

Figure 61

If all this sounds rather negative, there is good news to come. Although resorting to expediency for survival, Russians are essentially warm, emotional, caring people, eagerly responding to kindness and love, once they perceive that they are not being 'taken in' one more time. Finns – victims of Russian expansionism on more than one occasion – readily acknowledge the warmth and innate friendliness of the individual Russian. Even Americans, once they give themselves time to reflect, find a surprising amount of common ground. Rough Russian hospitality is reminiscent of the cosy ambience of the Wild West (or perhaps the deep South) and the Russians, like the Americans, tried to tame a continent. Both peoples distrust aristocrats and are uncomfortable, even today, with the smooth talking of some Europeans. Bluntness wins friends both in Wichita and Sverdlovsk. Both nations, like the French, think big and consider they have an important role to play – a 'mission' in world affairs.

Figure 62 – our familiar 'horizon' comparison – shows that while Russians and Americans are destined by history and location to see the world in a very different manner, there is sufficient commonality of thinking to provide a basis for fruitful cooperation. Their common dislikes are as important in this respect as some of their mutual ambitions.

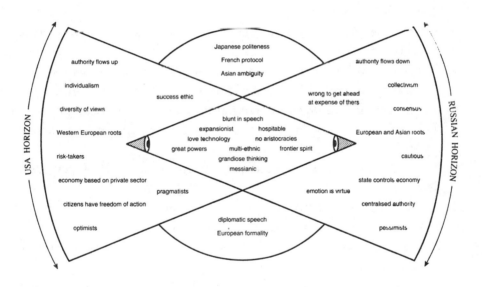

Figure 62   US/Russian horizons

As far as their attitudes to the world in general are concerned, how do Russians see the rest of us and – importantly – how do they deal? While it is clear that they are a society in transition, certain features of their business culture inevitably reflect the style of the command economy which organised their approach to meetings over a period of several decades. Russian negotiating characteristics, therefore, not only exhibit traditional peasant traits of caution, tenacity and reticence, but indicate a depth of experience born of thorough training and cunning organisation. They may be listed as follows.

Russian negotiating characteristics

✦ Russian negotiating teams are often composed of veterans or experts, consequently they are very experienced.

✦ They negotiate as they play chess, i.e. they plan several moves ahead. Opponents should think of the consequences of each move before making it.

✦ Russians often represent not themselves, but part of their government at some level.

✦ Sudden changes or new ideas cause discomfort, as they have to seek consensus from higher up.

✦ Negotiations often relate the subject under discussion to other issues in which they are involved. This may not be clear to the other side.

✦ Russians regard willingness to compromise as a sign of weakness.

✦ Their preferred tactic in case of deadlock is to display patience and 'sit it out'.

✦ They will only abandon this tactic if the other side shows great firmness.

✦ The general tendency is to push forward vigorously as the other side seems to retreat, to pull back when meeting stiff resistance.

✦ Delivery style is often theatrical and emotional, intended to convey clearly their intent and requests.

✦ Like Americans, they can use 'tough talk' if they think they are in a stronger position.

✦ They maintain discipline in the meeting and speak with one voice. When Americans or Italians speak with several voices, the Russians become confused about who has real authority.

✦ Russians often present an initial draft outlining all their objectives. This is only their starting position and far from what they expect to achieve.

✦ They will, however, concede points only in return for concessions made by the other side.

✦ They often make minor concessions and ask for major ones in return.

✦ They may build into their initial draft several 'throw-aways' – things of little importance which they can concede freely, without damaging their own position.

+ They usually ask the other side to speak first, so they may reflect on the position given.

+ They are sensitive and status conscious and must be treated as equals and not 'talked down to'.

+ Their approach to an agreement is conceptual and all-embracing, as opposed to American or German step-by-step settlement.

+ Acceptance of their conceptual approach often leads to difficulties in working out details later and eventual implementation.

+ They are suspicious of anything which is conceded easily. In the Soviet Union days, everything was complex.

+ Personal relationships between the negotiating teams can often achieve miracles in cases of apparent official deadlock.

+ Contracts are not so binding in the Russian mind as in the western. Like Orientals, Russians see a contract as binding only if it continues to be mutually beneficial.

A study of the above leads one to the conclusion that Russian negotiators are not easy people to deal with. There is no reason to believe that the development of entrepreneurism in Russia, giving added opportunities and greater breadth of vision to those who travel in the West, will make Russians any less effective round the negotiating table. Westerners may hold strong cards and may be able to dictate conditions for some length of time, but the ultimate mutual goal of win–win negotiations will only be achieved through adaptation to current Russian mentality and world attitudes. The following hints might be of help.

Hints for dealing with the Russians

+ If you have strong cards, do not overplay them. Russians are proud people and must not be humiliated.

+ They are not as interested in money as you are, therefore they are more prepared to walk away from a deal than you.

+ You may base your decisions on facts which are cold to you, emotive to them.

+ They are people rather than deal oriented. Try to make them like you.

✦ If you succeed, they will conspire with you 'to beat the system'. They dislike stringent regulations more than you do. They are very Italian in this respect.

✦ Indicate your own distrust of blind authority or excessive bureaucracy as often as you can.

✦ Do them a favour early on, but indicate it is not out of weakness. The favour should be person directed, rather than relating to the business being discussed.

✦ You need not be unduly impacted by their theatrical and emotional displays, but you should show sympathy with the human aspects involved.

✦ When you show your own firmness, let some glimmer of kindness shine through.

✦ They will generally behave collectively, so do not single out any one individual for special attention. Envy of another's success is also a Russian characteristic.

✦ Drink with them between meetings if you are able to. It is one of the easiest ways to build bridges.

✦ They prefer to drink sitting down with time to make frequent toasts and short speeches.

✦ They like praise, especially related to Russian advances on technology, but also about their considerable artistic achievements.

✦ They are sensitive about war talk, considering most Russian wars as defensive ones against aggressive neighbours. They have not been given your version of history.

✦ Their attitude towards America is one of suspicion, tinged with outright admiration.

✦ They love children more than most of us; exchange of photographs of your children is an excellent manner to build bridges.

✦ They respect old people and scorn Americans' treatment of the elderly. In the cruel Russian environment, family love was often the only enduring form of riches. Display your own family closeness, if appropriate.

✦ Indicate your human side – emotions, hopes, aspirations etc. They are much more interested in your personal goals than in your commercial objectives.

✦ During your business discussions, their priorities will be personal relationships, form and appearance, opportunity for financial gain – in that order.

✦ They often appear excitable, but are skilled at keeping their temper.

✦ The eastern and western elements in their make-up often make them appear schizophrenic. Do not let this faze you – the other face will always reappear in due course.

✦ They have, in their history, never experienced democracy, therefore do not expect them to be automatically egalitarian, fair, even-handed and open to straight debate.

✦ In this respect, it is advisable to show them clearly how you think about such matters and how you are basically motivated by these factors.

✦ Terms such as 'democratic', 'fair play', 'profit', 'turnover', 'cash flow', 'public relations', 'goodwill' have little meaning for them in any language, therefore use such words cautiously.

✦ They like to say they understand when in fact they don't, and also have the tendency to say things they think you want to hear (an Oriental trait), so do not take what is said and heard for granted.

✦ Anything you introduce as an official directive or regulation they will distrust. Something you indicate as a personal recommendation, they will embrace.

✦ Excessive profits are looked on as illegitimate. Don't be greedy, either for yourself or for them.

✦ Russians are basically conservative and do not accept change easily. Introduce new ideas slowly and keep them low key at first.

✦ Russians often push you and understand being pushed, but they rebel if they feel the pressure is intolerable. Try to gauge how far you can go with them.

✦ It remains to be seen to what extent they will become risk takers in a free market environment.

✦ Dissidence in general is not popular with them, as security has historically been found in group, conformist behaviour. Do not try to separate a Russian from his or her 'group', whatever that may be.

✦ Right and wrong, in most Russians' eyes, is decided by the feelings of the majority, not by law.

✦ Russians are essentially nostalgic – the present does not dominate their thinking as it might with many Americans and Australians, for instance.

✦ They love conversation. Do not hesitate to unburden yourself in front of them. Like Germans, they are fond of soul searching.

✦ They achieve what they do in their own country largely through an intricate network of personal relationships. Favour is repaid by favour. They expect no help from officials.

✦ Like Germans, they enter meetings unsmiling. Like Germans, they can be quickly melted with a show of understanding and sincerity.
✦ When they touch another person during conversation, it is a sign of confidence.

Russians' values are essentially human, their heroes universally authentic, their manifestations and symbols richly artistic and aesthetic. To succeed with Russians, one must maintain these qualities in clear focus as opposed to paying too much attention to the enigmatic and often paradoxical aspects of their behaviour and current attitudes.

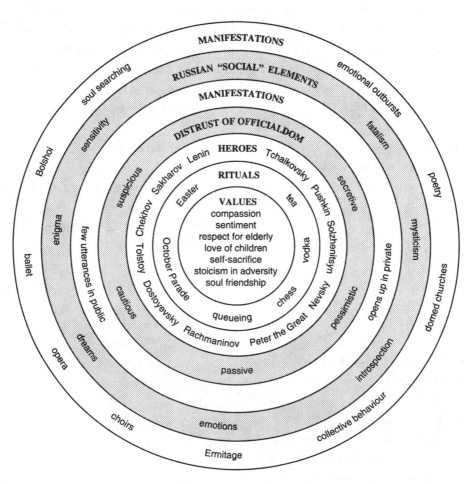

19

SPAIN

THERE IS ONLY ONE ENGLAND OR FRANCE, BUT THERE ARE SEVERAL Spains. Spain was plural to the Romans and its multiple aspects are still evident in its clear-cut regions. Castilians are in the majority and continue to dominate, but you would do well to check on a Spaniard's origins when beginning to do business with him or her. Galicians are practical and melancholy, sharing some common ground with some northerners. Aragonese stubbornness finds an echo in Finnish *sisu*. Basques have a talent for industry and commerce and, along with Finns, Hungarians and Estonians, stand apart from Indo-European ancestry. Northerners share the cult of efficiency with Catalans, who face France rather than Spain. On the other hand, they have little in common with two other regions – Asturias, where the people are extremely haughty, and Andalucia, where every one is an orator and timetables are for cats and dogs.

So much for the regions – let us now take a close look at Castile and its people. Castilians are basically Latins and indeed for many centuries they were the guardians of the Roman heritage, preserving its linguistic and literary monuments as well as its traditions of conquest and Empire. Latin characteristics evident in Castile are verbosity and eloquence (the Castilian word '*hablar*' – to speak – comes from '*fabulare*' meaning to invent, to romance, to revel in the joys of conversation). Northerners will hardly feel comfortable confronted by such wordiness, nor with the Spaniard's favourite role of the supreme romantic. Proud of their history and purity of descent, Castilians are at heart crusaders, mystics, impractical individualists who were supreme as *conquistadores* but signally unable to organise their empire. British and Americans may admire Castilian individualism, since it is a trait cherished by them, but individualism in Spain has resulted in refractoriness to authority and organisation, even scorn for government. In the southern part of the country the hot climate reinforces a tendency towards apathy and inertia where laws and regulations are concerned.

The pauper in Spain is considered as noble as the wealthy. Beggars are treated gently, respect is shown to the poor and needy, and an innate aristrocracy is noticed in the very humblest. Personal dignity must be clung to whatever else may be lost. Time, money, even prudence, are of secondary importance.

If pragmatic northerners find this hard to swallow, they will experience even more perplexity with Castilian fatalism. 'Why organise our fate so much?' says the Castilian – all that happens now has happened before and will certainly happen again. While full of boundless energy in the thrill of action or great moments of vision, Spaniards have little taste for the routine, banal tasks of consolidation and coordination. Tomorrow is another day; if it is our destiny to succeed, we shall. Northerners who have little time for fatalism and consider themselves masters of their own fate have little sympathy for this attitude. We may insist that facts are stubborn things, but the Spaniard asserts things are not what they seem. There is a double truth, that of the immediate detail and that of the poetic whole. The second is more important for the Castilian, since it supplies a faith or vision to live by. One must realise the futility of material ambition.

Consideration of these Spanish concepts and credos makes it fairly clear that the Spaniard and the northerner have quite different perceptions of reality. Dialogue between the two is never going to be easy. A grandiloquent, circumlocutory orator and supreme romanticist addresses a passive listener and taciturn pragmatist. There will probably be a language barrier. Yet dialogue there must be, in the world of business.

There are some bridges between Spanish and northern cultures. Castile is a barren land with extremes of cold and heat. The severity of climate and landscape has accustomed Castilians to austerity – a phenomenon not unknown to northerners – and hard times in many countries have encouraged frugality. Although Spain is a land of rich and poor, the egalitarian Britons, Scandinavians or Americans can detect in the Spaniards' protection of the underdog that country's version of true democracy.

People wishing to do business with Spaniards must first accept that they will never act like northerners and that their scale of values is quite remote from the modern age.

Like other people, they buy and sell and are friendly, but they look at you in an old-fashioned way and they are more interested in you than your goods. I once acted as interpreter for three German salesmen presenting their new product to the board of a Madrid company. The Germans had a slick presentation lasting 30 minutes with slides, graphs, diagrams and video. The six Spanish managers facing them hardly watched the presentation at all. They were watching the salesmen. Were these the type of people they wanted to do business with? Did they like them? Were they really human? All Germans give perfect presentations, so why watch it? After the session was over the breathless Germans waited for the response. The Spaniards took them for lunch, which lasted till 4 o'clock. After that everybody took a siesta.

You must work hard at making a Spaniard like you. If you succeed in this, the business will follow automatically. You must show you have a heart and that you do not take everything seriously. Northerners have big hearts, but they are often experts at hiding them. You need to talk to Spaniards with a twinkle in your eye. Their 'distance of comfort' is much closer than that of most Europeans and they like both physical and eye contact. They are more robust than French, Italian or Portuguese people – they are the roughest of the Latins. '*Macho*' is a Spanish word and the essential masculinity of the northern businessman stands him in good stead in a Spaniard's company. Northern businesswomen will also be comfortable with male Spaniards, as their relative aggressiveness will score points.

Spaniards are very human. When conversing with them it is best to shed some of your cool tendencies, forget the dictates of time, admit that some roguery actually exists in your country, confess to a few private sins or misdemeanours, ask them some rather personal questions, stay up drinking with them till 3 in the morning and in general let your hair down.

When relaxing in the company of Spaniards, keep one consideration in the forefront of your mind: they are touchy and sensitive. You may laugh at the French and Germans as much as you like, you can even criticise certain Spanish customs such as siestas or the bull fight, but do not in any circumstances say anything that might be interpreted to impinge on their personal dignity or honour. For many Spaniards '*pundonor*' (point of honour) is the most important word in the language. They may be poor, but they are noble. They may have been in jail, but they are honest. They may be unpunctual, but they are true. They may owe you money, but they are sure to pay you when they can. They may have failed, but they cannot be humiliated. Like a Japanese or a Chinese, they cannot be made to lose face.

This deference to a Spaniard's dignity, the careful nurturing of their personal, human prowess, the respect shown for their station, personality and soul, is the key to their cooperation, alliance and affection. They will reciprocate in full – if you command a Castilian's loyalty he will be your best friend. He will buy your company's product and send you Christmas cards for 25 years. He will lie and occasionally die for you. He is an honourable man.

20

SWEDEN

IN THE WORLD AT LARGE, AND ESPECIALLY IN THE ENGLISH-SPEAKING world, the Swedes seem to be universally popular. Their clean-cut profile as honest, caring, well-informed, efficient plodders, producing quality goods delivered on time, sits well with their frequently well-groomed appearance, good sense of dress and (forgive the stereotyping) blond hair and blue eyes. Their English, grammatically proficient, is clean and crisp, like that of Scots who went to Oxford. In society set pieces, at least, they have impeccable manners and say all the right things for the first 15 minutes.

It is somewhat surprising, therefore, to discover that they are unpopular, often ridiculed and occasionally despised inside the Nordic area. The fact that none of the Swedes' neighbours – Denmark, Norway, Finland – have any undue reputation for aggressivity makes the antipathy all the more unexpected. What is wrong with the Swedes?

This is a question which the Swedes themselves have been trying to answer over the last few decades. Statistically speaking, there is very little wrong with Sweden. Superb medical care has produced the oldest population in the world (18.1 per cent of the population is over 65) and only the Japanese have higher life expectancy (Japan 79, Sweden 78). Infant mortality is the fourth lowest in the world. With a population of 8.6 million occupying an area of 450,000 square kilometres, Sweden's population density is comfortably placed at 19 per square kilometre. Although only the 54th largest country in the world, Sweden is ranked 18th in GDP and a meritorious 5th in GDP per head at $25.487 per annum.

This affluence is reflected in the standard of living – Swedes are first in the world in telephone ownership, fifth in dishwashers, sixth in microwaves, seventh in fridges and videocassette recorders, and tenth in cars. With 99 per cent literacy, Swedes had the second highest percentage of the population in the labour force in 1990–1 (after Zimbabwe!) at 69.3 per cent. Foreign debt is low, foreign aid very high – ninth in the world in bilateral help (fourth as bilateral donors as a percentage of GNP). Sweden occupies a significant position in industrial output (world 14th) and is 15th in world trading. These are excellent figures for a country with a population of under 9 million, considering that Sweden is no 'sweat shop'.

With a slow-growing population (Sweden already has the world's smallest households at 2.2 people per dwelling) and ample land, mineral and energy resources, Sweden would seem to have few material problems. According to the the UN Human Development Index, again Sweden is well to the fore. The HDI, which combines such factors as GDP per head, life expectancy, adult literacy, years of schooling, purchasing power, etc., places Sweden fifth behind only Japan, Canada, Norway and Switzerland in terms of human development standards.

The only significant negative statistics for Sweden are: heart attacks – highest in the world at 37.3 per cent of deaths; murders – Sweden stands 18th; drug offences – second place. Swedish brides are second oldest in the world at 27.6 years and the country has the seventh highest cost of living, but these last two factors may also be viewed as positive.

Sweden is obviously a country that functions well, as the enviable statistics quoted above clearly demonstrate. Why the friction between the Swedes and their neighbours? In the first place, they **are** neighbours: neighbourly love is not a human characteristic. Norway, Denmark and Finland are less impressed than others by the splendour of the Swedish welfare state, as they have similar creations of their own (and there is a growing doubt in all four countries that the system will really work in the very long run). Their cynicism *vis-à-vis* Sweden seems to derive from various historical factors:

✦ Denmark was for a long period a major player in the area.
✦ Swedes often laid siege to Copenhagen.
✦ Swedes ruled Finland for 600 years.
✦ Sweden and Norway shared an uncomfortable union until 1905.
✦ Norway, Denmark and Finland were battered in the Second World War. Sweden was not.

Swedish industry enjoyed a period of prosperity in the the years 1945–60 when Norway and Denmark got off to a much slower post-war start and Finland was badly handicapped by having to pay huge (and unfair) war reparations to the Russians (1945–52). The big Swedish multinationals – Volvo, Saab, Electrolux, SKF, Axel Johnson and so on – boomed during these years, when Swedish steel was reputedly the best in the world. Others' prosperity often gives rise to neighbours' envy, especially when accompanied by a certain complacency. In the Nordic zone, Sweden was seen as big, export-minded, financially strong, well-fed and irritatingly smug.

There is little doubt that the Swedes are much less self-satisfied today than they were in the 1950s and 1960s, but in a recent survey I conducted among 100 Swedish business people, an all-Swedish compilation of their values resulted in the following:

> Conscientiousness, honesty, loyalty, tolerance, equality,
> love of peace, love of nature, cleanliness, kindness, modesty.

It is not without significance that the respondents chose 10 positive values and no negative ones. Laine-Sveiby comments that Swedes fail to see themselves as others see them; in this respect they differ from the more worldly Danes and also from the Finns, who are extremely interested in cultural relativism and constantly worry about what others think of them. Swedes, on the other hand, worry very much about what other Swedes think!

Decision making

Swedish management is decentralized and democratic – the organigram of the typical Swedish company has a decidedly horizontal look about it. Power distance is small and the manager is generally accessible to staff and available for discussion. There will be fewer echelons in a Swedish firm than there would be for instance in France or Germany. There is actually a Swedish law (MBL) which stipulates that all important decisions must be discussed with all staff members before being implemented! The rationale is that better informed employees are more motivated and consequently perform better. This collectivist form of decision making bears an interesting comparison with the Japanese system. In both countries it is seen as important that all colleagues have ample opportunity to discuss projects thoroughly, since the right to debate and express one's opinion is paid for by strict adherence to the company policy once it has been settled. In Sweden, as in Japan, decisions may be considerably delayed, but, once made, are unanimous; everyone in the company will subsequently be pulling the same way. This contrasts sharply with, for instance, the situation in many US companies where individual convictions often lead to internal discord and infighting.

A major difference, however, between the Swedish and Japanese models is that power distance between managers and employees is in reality much greater in Japan. In both systems, prolonged discussion and evaluation leads to good communication of information and generates a feeling of confidence and trust between employees.

The Swedish model is not without its critics. Moran mentions the following as Swedish weaknesses in the implementation of business:

+ avoidance of conflict or taking sides
+ fear of confrontation
+ reliance on the team for initiatives
+ avoidance of competition with others in the company

While employee participation in decision making is clearly desirable in modern firms, the speed at which business is conducted today (enhanced by the facilities afforded by information technology) often requires quick and clear decisions. Probably decision making is faster in the USA than anywhere else; it is slowest in Japan and some other Asian countries. Most European countries lie somewhere in between these two extremes. Sweden is dangerously near Japan. One uses the word 'dangerously' in the sense that while it is an accepted Oriental concept that big decisions take months, it is by no means the case in Europe and the USA. French, British and Finnish managers have experienced frustration, when working with or in Swedish companies, with the constant consultation going on at all levels, the endless meetings, habitual deferment of decisions, obsession with people orientation, ultra-cautiousness, woolly personnel policies, unclear 'guidelines' from managers.

The Swedish manager

Swedish managers are skilled at handling human resources, using charisma, a gentle but persuasive communication style and clever psychological approaches. They are good because they have to be! Their lot is not a simple one. As in Japan, it is not easy to rid oneself of an incompetent, even lazy or less than fully honest employee in Sweden. As it is also unseemly to get rich, managers lack both a carrot and a stick. They cannot fire and they cannot motivate very much with money (bonuses and use of a company car drive up the tax). Consequently they take great pains to get the best out of those they command. Unfortunately they don't command them very much either. They don't issue orders – they are better described as guidelines and are often not more than suggestions. They don't implement even these directives, but delegate authority downwards to have them carried out. If the employee is incompetent or idle, there is a lot of mopping up to do. To be fair to Swedes, one must point out that most Swedish staff members are extremely conscientious, cooperative and loyal. The problem arises (as it often does in Japan) when the task assigned is too big for the capabilities of the individual.

One Swedish professor remarked that in order to exercise power in Sweden one has to create an image of not being powerful. Swedish managers walk a tightrope between undue personal intervention and woolly, ineffective control. They try to establish their line through careful planning and procedures. It is said that detailed planning helps Swedish managers to sleep better!

The feminine society

Geert Hofstede, in his well-known study of business cultures, concludes that of all those covered in the survey, Sweden is the most feminine. In masculine cultures the dominant values are success, money, rewards, objects and possessions. In feminine ones interpersonal aspects, quality of life, physical environment, rendering service, nurturance are considered more important – in short, the creation of a caring society. In the case of today's Sweden, people (including Swedes) are beginning to ask themselves if it is too caring. The welfare system – arguably the best in the world – is very expensive to maintain. Taxes are so high they hurt, and the country is ageing fast. Every year there are fewer breadwinners for more dependants. In a non-competitive world, Swedes might go on selling quality products at high prices to support their living standards, but competition in the twenty-first century will be ferocious. Asians and Americans do not take six weeks holidays plus all kinds of long weekends and rush out of the office at four in summer. The Swedish manager is constantly confronted by requests to take leave for pregnancies, sick children, sabbaticals, right to study, home guard, trade union work, etc.

Capital and industry had been left largely in private hands in Sweden, but the taxation system sees to it that nobody gets rich legally. Those who threaten to do so (Ingmar Bergman, Björn Borg), are forced to go and live abroad to avoid paying tax which might reach more than 100 per cent of income. Monte Carlo has a better climate, too!

One suspects that there is more wrong with the Swedish system than with the Swedes themselves. They are kind, intelligent, steadfast people who want to do well, although it will not be easy for them to eradicate their work-to-rule mentality when things get tougher. An over-regulated society, irrespective of its politics, can engender very boring members, all spontaneity taxed out of them.

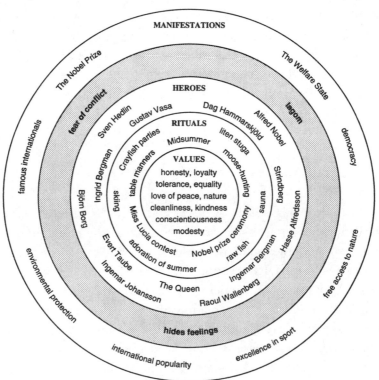

When dealing with Swedes, remember:

+ They believe they are honest and always tell the truth.
+ They don't like to contradict their own colleagues.
+ Authority is delegated down in Swedish companies so you may not be hearing what their boss really thinks.
+ Price may be inflexible, as Swedes believe their starting prices are fair.
+ They may appear inflexible in other respects, as they believe strongly in their group consensus decision.
+ Like Japanese, they find it hard to make changes individually, as it would go against the consensus.
+ They are good listeners and will be sympathetic to your point of view.
+ If they wish to accommodate you, they will need time to arrange it.
+ They are not as profit minded as you are.
+ In spite of their 'caring' nature, they are more deal than people oriented.
+ They are pragmatic as far as technical quality is concerned.
+ Their strong points when selling are quality, design, and prompt delivery.
+ When buying, they also look for quality and are not overly price conscious.
+ They entertain well and generously when this is part of their programme.
+ Like Americans and Finns, they attach little importance to the food at a 'working' lunch and carry on discussing details while eating. French and Spanish people cannot stand this.
+ They can discuss technical details *ad infinitum*, but run out of small talk after 10–15 minutes. Their jokes and anecdotes, however, are first class!
+ They are formal in toasting and expect speeches to be made during and after dinner.
+ They are extremely informal in address, using only the '*Du*' form.
+ Silence in Sweden is not necessarily negative. They are reflective and rather introvert.
+ They are not a 'touching' culture, so don't get too close.
+ They use very little body language and facial expression during business meetings, although they smile much more than Germans and Finns.
+ They remain calm and courteous during discussions and don't quite know how to deal with rudeness or Latin exuberance.
+ They show no particular respect for rank, and address important personages as equals. French, German, South American and Asian people

do not always react well to this very egalitarian manner.
+ They are never overbearing. They do not use brute force, even if they
  have the upper-hand.
+ Your best approach is to defer to their wish for long, all-round consultation and demonstrate clearly your own patience and understanding,
  allied to firmness and integrity.

21

ARAB COUNTRIES

WESTERNERS AND ARABS HAVE VERY DIFFERENT VIEWS ABOUT WHAT IS right and wrong, good and evil, logical and illogical, acceptable and unacceptable. They live in two different worlds, each organised in its own manner. Unless one gains a deeper understanding of how these two mindsets differ, one group will end up with an unfavourable impression of the other. It is worthwhile, therefore, to list the main cultural divergences, which go a long way towards explaining why each side sees certain events in a completely different light. The following is only a summary:

+ The West sees Arab society as one which is in decline, propped up temporarily by oil revenues. The Arabs, by contrast, are very conscious that their civilisation once led the world and believe they are capable of doing so again (in a moral sense).
+ The West generally separates Church and State. Most Islamic countries do not and religion strongly influences social behaviour, politics and even business.
+ In the West, the individual is the basic social unit; with the Arabs it is the family.
+ In the West, status is gained by achievement; in the Arab world by class.
+ Westerners like to deal in cold facts; Arabs will not let facts destroy their honour.
+ Westerners want to be fair, but just. Arabs want to be just, but flexible.
+ The West believes in organisations and institutions; Arabs believe in persons (guided by God).

✦ Westerners in principle wish to modernise. Arabs strive to find a way of adopting modern modes of behaviour without disrupting the traditions they value.

✦ Most western countries have succeeded in creating equality for men and women. Arabs believe the two sexes have vastly different personalities.

✦ Western societies differ greatly in their world view. Arabs, by contrast, largely subscribe to the same tenets of morality.

✦ Arabs move around less than westerners, therefore they are more conservative.

✦ Westerners must appear to behave rationally. For Arabs, it is important to impress others with their integrity.

✦ Westerners respect the strong. In Arab societies piety is one of the most admirable qualities: the weak must be respected and protected. This characteristic has been implanted by the Arabs into Spanish cultural attitudes.

✦ In the West, friends are good company. In the Arab world a friend is a person who cannot refuse your request. Neither can you refuse theirs.

✦ When introducing themselves, westerners usually restrict the amount of information they give. Arabs tend talk a lot about their family and connections.

✦ Westerners like to use official channels to further their business interests. Arabs use personal relationships.

✦ Arabs expect regular praise when they have done good work, whereas westerners are content if they keep their job. Conversely, Arabs are more hurt by criticism than westerners.

✦ When negotiating, westerners try to find logical conclusions, whereas Arabs use personalised arguments, appeals and persistent persuasion.

✦ Arabs stand or sit much closer to their interlocutor than does a westerner. It is normal to breathe on them and touch them frequently.

✦ Arabs are less 'private' than westerners. Visiting and long conversations are frequent.

✦ Men and women mingle freely in western societies, in most Arab countries they do not. Moslem sexuality is a territorial one. Women trespassing into public places (male spaces) are expected to wear a veil to make themselves invisible. They are rarely seen by westerners indoors.

✦ Hospitality is more effusive in the Arab world than in the West. They have the tradition of 'open house' even to strangers. A Bedouin will supposedly kill his last camel to feed his guest.

✦ Westerners, especially Swiss, Swedes and other northerners, tend to turn up on time to dinner and other appointments. Arabs are much more relaxed in their timing. Social occasions or business meetings need not have fixed beginnings or endings.
✦ Unlike westerners, Arabs prefer arranged marriages. On the whole, they are very stable, involving mutual respect.
✦ Pork is taboo to Arabs, unlike in the West.

British, Americans and Northern Europeans will realise that they and Arabs are at the two extremes of the monochronic–polychronic scale, therefore communication will not take place in a natural manner. The exigencies of the Moslem religion complicate the interchange of ideas even further. Yet Arabs are used to dealing with foreigners and readily forgive them for not behaving like Arabs. You will even be forgiven for behaving like an infidel, as long as you make certain modifications. The most important thing is to avoid saying or doing anything which they consider insulting or derogatory. This includes the use of alcohol, improper dress, over-familiarity with the few women they allow you to meet, and challenging the basic concepts of Islam.

Foreign women are accepted without veils provided they dress conservatively. They may go shopping and travel alone, but should avoid all-male cafés (which is most of them). Women may not drive in Saudi Arabia.

Arabs are looking for sincerity in your dealings with them and expect to be shown the same respect they show you. If you come across as sincere and true, there is no problem. The natural northern tendency to look down on multi-active behaviour (talkativeness, invasion of privacy, poor time keeping, demonstrative body language) must be firmly suppressed, as the Arabs are not going to change their personality.

It is virtually impossible for multi-active people, especially Arabs, to act like Nordics or Americans. The only solution for good communication therefore is for the linear-active northerner to make some concessions in the direction of extroversion. Many find this difficult, even painful, but the rewards for doing so can be considerable. To begin with, one must stand much closer to an Arab when talking to him than one would with a Briton or a German. If you keep your distance, the Arab will think you find his physical presence distasteful or that you are a particularly cold individual. Arabs speak volubly and earnestly to someone they like, so you must attempt to do the same. They are very dependent on eye contact, so take your sunglasses off when talking to them and look them right in the eye (normally not difficult). Northerners may be uncomfortable with flattery or professions of friendship, but Arabs love these utterances, therefore you should not hesitate to praise their country, their arts, their dress and food (but not their women!).

When talking business with them, you must always do this against an intensely personal background. You want to do the business, but above all you want to do it with him, in whom you must always show close personal interest. If the Arab boasts about his connections and 'network' he is showing you the value of personal relationships, and if his uncle is influential in a government department (or is the Minister) he will expect you to take delight in the possibility of that influence being helpful in the furthering of your business. Do not appear detached and reluctant to accept favours. Your Arab friend will ask favours of you in due course.

Because the family structure is of paramount importance in Arab life, you should pay close attention to all family members he introduces you to. You should enquire regularly about the health (and happiness) of his brothers, uncles, cousins and sons. This would be very unusual in the north, but is a sure (and easy) way to gain your Arab friend's affection and loyalty. When visiting his country it is appropriate to take gifts for all these relatives. Do not expect Arabs to open gifts in front of you.

At mealtimes, eat only with your right hand, take only the food that is offered to you and, while you must praise the food, do not pay too much attention to those who have cooked it. Do not ask to meet the cooks (wives, mothers or sisters) who have laboured so long over the preparation of your meal. Your hosts will offer you the best morsels to eat, which you must accept. They will force too much on you – you will have to overeat a little in order not to upset them. You are not expected to talk much at mealtimes, so in that sense a meal can be a welcome break.

Returning to the subject of words, this is clearly a difficult area for northerners interacting with Arabs. Your shyness, succinctness and reflective silences will gain you no points with Arabs. Your verbal modesty – so much appreciated by Japanese – will be highly disconcerting to them. If you are quiet, they will simply think something is wrong and will fuss around you with all kinds of queries until they find out what it is. Not only do you have to speak **more** when you are with Arabs, but you have to step up the **volume** as well. Loudness of voice, rising pitch and tone, even shouting, all denote sincerity in Arab discourse. You may find this very hard to do. Do your best. Remember the Gulf War took place partly because Bush spoke softly and Saddam did not believe he meant what he said (about declaring war etc.). In Arab society it is quite normal to use speech in a rhetorical, almost aggressive manner to make a point clearly. They are great admirers of eloquence and if you can aspire to eloquence in their presence they will take it as a sign of education, refinement and sincerity, no matter how verbose it may sound in your own ears.

Oaths are quite common in Arabic, so that even if you slip in one of your less vehement ones when you get excited, it would not sound offensive to Arabs, who bring Allah into their arguments in almost every conversation. Arabs do not like discussing unpleasant matters such as illness, misfortune, accidents or death. Do not introduce any. They are even reluctant to tell you bad news about business, so bear this in mind when everything looks rosy. Connected with this habit is the Arab tendency to use euphemisms. Someone who is sick is described as 'tired', teachers magically become 'professors' and slums are referred to as 'low-cost dwellings'.

Arabs have great respect for the written word, especially if it has a religious connotation. Do not wrap up anything in an Arabic-language newspaper – it might have Allah's name on it. If you handle a copy of the Koran, you should show it even more respect than a Japanese business card.

Then there is the ordeal of a business meeting in an Arab country, which for a northerner can be particularly onerous. We have referred earlier to the Arab concept of 'open house' where visitors may gain access at all times. In the twentieth century the concept or tradition has been extended to include 'open office'. This may sound friendly enough, but things can become chaotic if you have the first appointment. Northerners expect to be guaranteed some kind of privacy while they discuss their business matters. In England or Germany, secretaries do not allow bosses to be disturbed by new arrivals during the course of a meeting. It can happen in Portugal, Spain, South America or Sicily, but even there newcomers are often asked to wait. In Arab countries they are shown straight into the office, according to the age-old tradition. Northerners, who normally expect the privilege of speaking without interruption, soon become nonplussed as anything up to half a dozen Arab visitors join the seance.

Not only are northerners unused to hearing several people speak at the same time, but they stand little chance of making their sober tones heard in the general hubbub. Arabs shout and speak loudly for dramatic effect or out of pure joy at seeing friends. They also seem to have the knack of absorbing three or four conversations at once. Even more problematic is how to proceed with the proposals which the northerner has travelled 3000 kilometres to present. Making an appointment for the next day is of no help, since the number of interruptions is unlikely to be less. Recently I asked the Commercial Counsellor at one of the embassies in Abu Dhabi, how one solves this dilemma. He answered as follows: You have to manoeuvre your chair so that you are sitting right next to the man you are doing business with. On the other side of his desk is not close enough – you have to be no more than a foot away and nearer to him than anybody else. When you have secured this position, you then shout down his right or left ear, depending on which side you are on. You continue to pound his ear with your propositions until he agrees with them. He is unlikely to give any trouble as he is suffering from numerous distractions from various angles, and acquiescence is usually the easiest way out. Enterprising multi-actives, such as Italians, often push documents to sign in front of him in these circumstances. You may be unable to do this, but modesty will get you nowhere.

In conclusion, although the cultural gulf between Arabs and northerners yawns wide, there is a fair chance of making a favourable impression. An Arab will admire education and expertise and welcomes representatives of small countries who show less arrogance than Americans, French and British. A Nordic or Dutch person will never be completely comfortable with Arab loquacity, subjectivity, unpunctuality and fatalism, but they can make progress in their relations with Arabs by showing keen personal interest in them, praising and flattering rather than criticising, memorising the basic tenets of their religion, dressing smartly, receiving and extending favours without qualms, showing great respect for old people and traditions and being very flexible and relaxed at all times.

22

JAPAN

THE JAPANESE ARE CULTURALLY VERY DIFFERENT, THEIR UNIQUENESS
probably deriving in the main from three principal factors: their history of
isolation; the crowded conditions imposed by their geography; and the
Japanese language itself.

Isolation

Although Japan for many centuries had a close cultural connection with
China, the period of autocratic Tokugawa rule beginning in 1603 led to
almost complete isolation from the rest of the world until the advent of
Commander Perry of the USA in 1853. For 250 years Japan, cut off from
foreign stimulus, developed a distinct society and culture which has no
equal in terms of group cooperation. The main organisational features
developed in this closed period remain characteristic of Japanese society
today in spite of the evident changes occurring in the twentieth century.
Packed together in large numbers in big cities they developed complex
social skills which led to the phenomenon known as the 'web society'.

Web society

A web society is one where there is great interdependence between all
members of a group and an abundance of moral and social obligations,

both vertically and horizontally. It all begins at birth. Whereas western babies are soon separated from their mothers and put in a room of their own, Japanese children are kept close to their parents' side day and night, for two or three years. Western children quickly develop an intitiative of their own and gain early experience in problem solving. Japanese children, by contrast, are encouraged to be completely dependent on human beings close to them and develop a sense of interdependence which stays with them throughout life. They can demand favours from people in their group and these have to be granted. Their first 'group' is the family, but later it becomes high school, then university, then the company. Age and seniority have their priorities, but also their obligations. The Japanese language has separate words for elder brother and younger brother etc., since the duties of one to the other are different and must be sharply defined. Protection can be demanded from those who have 'gone before'. Section leaders will unashamedly demand promotion for mediocre employees in their section, simply because they are under their wing and have remained loyal. It is almost impossible for a general manager to resist these demands.

The 'web society' structure brings advantage to the Japanese businessperson in terms of what many westerners today call 'networking'. Japanese, although great respecters of privacy, are very gregarious in business situations. Consequently the 'spider's web' of which they are part provides them with a unrivalled high context information network.

The Japanese language

Japanese behaviour is also strongly affected by the nature of the language. According to the Benjamin Whorf theory, the language we speak largely determines our way of thinking. The Japanese themselves use language in a completely different way from the rest of us. Japanese is often described as a vague or ambiguous language. For instance, the verbs are impersonal, so often you do not know who is being referred to. This vagueness is frequently used on purpose by Japanese conversants who wish to absolve anyone of possible blame and demonstrate politeness. The well-known honorific terms in Japanese enhance this politeness, while often adding to the vagueness. Long indirect clauses usually precede the main statement. Everything must be placed in context in Japan, therefore, blunt language is too brief and out of place. No Japanese boss would say 'Tidy up the office.'

They are obliged to say to their subordinates, 'As we have some important visitors coming at 12 o'clock and since we wish them to get the best impression of our company, perhaps we could improve the orderliness around here.' Another way in which the language reflects the society is that there is no reported speech mechanism in Japanese. Japanese people do not like to report other people's statements, as failure to be accurate could result in embarrassment or injustice. My secretary in Japan always refused to describe the contents of telephone calls made in my absence and invariably asked me to ring back the caller to get the message.

Japanese business climate and practices

The Japanese are therefore conditioned by exceptional historical and geographical constraints as well as by their thought processes in a language very different from any other. How does this affect foreign businesspeople dealing with them? Let us consider a few well-known eastern phenomena.

At the beginning there is the first meeting. Japanese, unlike westerners, do not like meeting newcomers. In their own web society Japanese executives know exactly the manner they should use to address superior, inferior or equal. Americans who stride across the room and pump their hand are a source of great embarrassment to them. First, unless they have been properly introduced, they are unable to define their stance. Secondly, it is likely that westerners will initiate a person-to-person exchange of views, which poses an even greater danger to the Japanese. They represent their group, therefore cannot pronounce on any matters there and then without consultation. The exchange of visiting cards is a familiar ceremony in Japan, although the information gained from these will be insufficient without prior knowledge.

Westerners are individuals, but the Japanese represent a company, which is part of a group, which in turn represents Japan. In these circumstances, how can they deal face to face, alone? Westerners show their priorities on introducing themselves – 'My name is Bill Robinson, Export Manager, Threadwell Textiles Inc.' The Japanese replies, 'Mitsubishi's General Affairs Section, Assistant Manager, Yamamoto I am' (putting things in the correct order).

Westerners often complain that on six visits to a company they will be met by 18 different people in groups of 3 and will have to say the same thing six times. This is time-consuming, but necessary for the Japanese, as all the members of the group have to become acquainted with them.

After this ordeal, Westerners often press for a quick decision. They will not get one. If they impose a time limit, the Japanese will back out quietly.

Losing face

As we all know, orientals do not like to lose face. I had a striking example of this during my first week in Japan when a colleague and I were negotiating for the lease of a building. After some trouble we had secured an appointment with the president of the company which owned the building and he – a 70-year-old man – spoke for half an hour (through an interpreter), explaining the merits and high reputation of the building, terminating his remarks with the price for the rental. It seemed a little on the high side to me; my colleague, who had been brought up in an Arab country, promptly offered him half. The elderly President and the interpreter immediately rose to their feet, smiled and bowed simultaneously and left the room. We never saw them again.

Japanese politeness

The Japanese do in fact negotiate, but not in the Arab manner. Face must not be lost and politeness must be maintained at all times. The Japanese go to incredible lengths to be polite. I was once having dinner at the home of a very elegant Japanese lady in the seaside resort of Atami. The dinner party consisted of about 16 people – Japanese, British and American. In the middle of the main course the phone rang and our hostess went to answer it. She spoke Japanese, which most of us understood, and we listened idly to what she said. Someone was obviously asking her about property prices in Atami, for she indicated what she had paid for her villa, how prices increased as you went up the slope and how they decreased if you went too far up or too far to the left hand side. She discussed inflation and the advantages of investing in property, as well as the general state of the property market in Japan and in Atami in particular. She was a knowledgeable woman and the call took 10 minutes. Finally, with a lot of bowing on the phone she concluded the conversation and hurried back to the table with her apologies to the guests. 'Who was that?' asked one of her friends. 'Wrong number,' she replied.

Japanese politeness can take many strange forms. Their reluctance to say 'no' is well-known. If you say to Japanese 'I want you to lend me a hundred dollars,' they will say 'yes', without actually offering the money. What they mean is, 'Yes, you want me to lend you a hundred dollars.' If they do not wish to enter into a deal with a foreign partner, they will not come out with a negative reply. However, you will not be able to get in touch with your contact in that company thereafter. He or she will always be ill, on holiday or attending a funeral.

A German sales executive spoke to me recently about the behaviour of a Japanese company president into whose office he had penetrated after months of trying. He had been told he had only 10 minutes to deliver his presentation and he did this in good English. The Japanese closed his eyes after the first minute and kept them closed for the rest of the time. The German asked me if this was impolite or had the company president actually fallen asleep? I had to reassure him that this was the Japanese way of indicating that he was listening intently to what was being said.

Another incident illustrating Japanese politeness occurred once during a course I taught in a British university. Three of us had invited Mr Suzuki out to dinner and we arranged to meet him at eight o'clock in the Common Room Bar. Knowing he was rather formal, we had all put suits on. Entering the bar, we saw him at a distance in a casual shirt and slacks. We quickly exited before he saw us and went back to our rooms to change into casual attire. We rushed back to the bar, where Mr Suzuki stood awaiting us in his best blue suit (he had caught a glimpse of us).

Japanese negotiating characteristics

✦ The first person you contact in a Japanese company (or who contacted you) will be present throughout the negotiating period.

✦ Japanese normally negotiate in teams, each member of which has a different speciality.

✦ The members of the team may change or be increased, as the Japanese wish as many members of their company as possible to get to know you.

+ They usually outnumber opposing teams.

+ There will be a senior staff member present who will dictate tactics, but he is rarely the one who does the talking. Each member will ask questions within the field of his or her competence, using the best linguist as the interpreter.

+ Their questions constitute an information-gathering process. They are not about to make a decision on hearing your answers.

+ Their decisions will eventually be made by consensus, therefore no person will display any individuality. They use the name of their company or 'we' – never 'I'.

+ However strong the team, they will have to refer back to head office. Therefore no decision will be made at the first meeting and probably not at the second.

+ New faces almost invariably appear at the second meeting, as someone in head office will have requested a 'second opinion'.

+ The second meeting tends to go over the same ground as the first, but the questions will be in more depth.

+ The Japanese negotiators bring their company's position to the table with little authority to change it. Therefore there is little flexibility.

+ Flexibility is more evident between meetings, when they have checked with head office.

+ Japanese are willing to go over the same information many times to avoid later misunderstandings and achieve clarity, although the ambiguities of their own speech style often leave westerners far from clear on their intentions.

+ They are cautious, skilled in stalling tactics, won't be rushed. They need time to reach their consensus.

+ Their decisions are long term, e.g. Do we want these people as partners in the future? Do we trust them? Is this the right direction for the company to be heading? Big decisions take time. They see American negotiators as technicians making a series of small decisions speedily to expedite one (perhaps relatively unimportant) 'deal'.

+ Once the Japanese company has made its decision, the negotiating team then expects quick action and many criticise the partner if there is a delay.

+ Japanese negotiators are invariably polite, understanding of others' problems and good listeners.

- They will break off negotiations if the other side is too blunt, impatient or fails to observe protocol.
- They must never lose face. If insufficient respect is shown or if they are cornered by ruthless logic, there will be no deal.
- If great respect and very reasonable demands are shown, they are capable of modifying their own demands greatly.
- They go to great lengths to preserve harmony throughout the negotiations. They strive to bring the two 'respectable' companies closer together. They are happy to socialise in between meetings.
- They never say 'no', never refute entirely another's argument, never break off negotiations as long as harmony prevails. This leaves them room for renegotiation some time in the future if circumstances change.
- They will cancel a meeting if they think the conditions on which it was set up have changed.
- They will show exaggerated respect to your senior negotiator and expect you to do the same to theirs.
- They will sometimes bring to the meeting a very senior person (e.g. former minister) who is only a consultant to the company, but commands (your) respect and deference.
- They will use a middleman or go-between if they can find one. After all, if both sides trust him, then there must be harmony.
- Negotiating style will be non-individualistic, impersonal and unemotional, but emotion is important (it is just under the surface). Logic and intellectual argument alone cannot sway Japanese. They must like you and trust you wholeheartedly, otherwise no deal!

The company is sacred

We all know that in Japan the company is sacred. Once employees are accepted, they show complete loyalty to the company and there is no clear dividing line between life and job. Their loyalty is rewarded by lifetime employment and regular promotion. They steadily climb the ladder in a vertical society and are completely satisfied with their status on every rung. Their fidelity and long hours will guarantee them promotion to important positions, whether they are intelligent or effective or not. This often leads to problems in companies which are anxious to make good profits.

Japanese success

Why have Japanese companies been so successful in the last few decades?
This is a question often asked by westerners to which there is no single
answer. Hard work, good education, unpaid overtime and short holidays all
play their part. But if there is one key to Japanese success it is their ability
to conduct a company's internal affairs in a spirit of harmony and cooperation. Americans and Europeans seem to have more energy as individuals,
but often are pulling in different directions within a company. There is certainly submarine infighting in Japanese companies, but once unanimity of
agreement has been reached (and the president insists on it) then everyone
pulls the same way. Japanese will discuss and discuss until everybody
agrees. They will not permit what they call the tyranny of the majority.
Endless discussion often results in slow decisions, but the Japanese think
the gain in solidarity is worth it. Results seem to show that they are right.

Tension

All this is not without its tension, since Japanese executives frequently have
to submit, even if their ideas are good ones. One evening in Tokyo I was
watching a boxing match on television for the Featherweight
Championship of the World. Sitting next to me was a Japanese business
friend of mine, Okada, who was eagerly supporting the Japanese boxer
involved. It was a close fight and after 14 rounds both men were still on
their feet. At this point Okada rushed out of the room. I watched the deciding 15th round, which was thrilling in the extreme, alone. A few minutes
after the fight had finished, Okada came in again and asked me who had
won. I told him. I also asked him why he had to dash out just before the
last round. 'I couldn't stand the tension,' he replied. This incident serves to
illustrate how two individuals sharing the same experience may react in different and surprising ways. Anyone observing Okada and myself during the
fight would have said I was the more excited of the two. I, for my part, was
quite unaware of the degree of his inner tension.

Complexes

A lot has been said about the Japanese having an inferiority complex and their readiness to imitate foreign models is usually quoted as an example of this. The Japanese seldom refute the accusation of being imitators and indeed Japanese company presidents have occasionally apologised to foreign firms who have shown them a new product for having copied and improved it and quickly put it on the market at half the price. The Japanese approach is strictly pragmatic. Why waste money on research and development if it has already been done? Their own contribution is improvement and higher productivity. A discussion on the Japanese inferiority complex can quickly lead to the opposite conclusion – that they have a superiority complex. This is reflected in their racist attitude to blacks and Indians and in periodic arrogance regarding their economic might. They are fully aware that they are second in the world in GNP, first in shipbuilding, first in longevity and probably first in their ability to save. Perhaps their feelings of superiority and inferiority might best be described as national self-consciousness. The pendulum seems to swing between frantic efforts to catch up with the West in technology and equally energetic assertations of national independence and true Japanese values.

Japanese translators

Their attitude to foreigners, even educated people and high-ranking businesspeople, is clear. You are always an outsider. Your efforts to speak Japanese will be smiled on, but seldom taken seriously. As many senior Japanese do not speak English, Japanese translators are often used. They can be unbelievably bad and seldom give real translations when Americans or Europeans wish to be blunt. Often the message, lost in an endless labyrinth of polite vagueness, will not get across at all. The translator in Japan has an unhappy lot. Usually they will be abused by westerners for not translating properly and criticised by their own superiors for being unclear. They are not really trusted anyway, as they speak two languages.

The language curtain

Japan exists behind a language curtain and is unfortunately unaware of her intellectual isolation. While millions of Japanese attempt to learn English, results are generally poor and consequently Japan's voice in the world is not heard to the extent which her economic might justifies. Few Japanese politicians have understood this problem, although business leaders are beginning to realise more and more the disadvantage they are at. One great barrier is the Chinese script, unfortunately adopted by the Japanese early in their history. This makes it extremely difficult for foreigners to learn Japanese and Japanese schoolchildren lose valuable time mastering two or three thousand complex characters, when they could be learning English.

Why don't the Japanese simply switch to the Roman alphabet? First, they would cut themselves off from their literature and calligraphic art. More important still, Japanese people are bound up emotionally with the visual aspect of the written characters. They have a kind of magic quality. A European text written in Roman characters can only be linear or factual. A complex Chinese character, with perhaps 10 or 15 strokes, conveys not only the meaning but has an aesthetic value. Visual aspects are important for the Japanese, as can be seen in their pretty ways of arranging food. Where westerners often imagine things in words, Japanese can imagine them visually. This is difficult to explain to anyone who has not studied written Japanese, but let me try to give you a practical example, which in fact has nothing to do with writing. You probably know that in most Japanese shops the attendants will calculate your purchases not on a calculator but on an abacus. They can do this extremely quickly and rarely make mistakes. What is astonishing is that when they do not have an abacus nearby they go through the motions on their open palm, look at it and tell you the amount. This always used to surprise me and once, out of interest, I challenged my local shopkeeper as to the accuracy of his calculation. He actually stared at his hand again and then looked at me and insisted he was correct. He even showed me his hand! The physical memory is in his fingers which have flicked the imaginary beads, just as it is in the fingers of an English typist who can imagine linear Romanic script by pretending to type certain words.

Japanese as seen by others

Appearance	Reality
They are aloof.	Extreme shyness makes it difficult for them to initiate conversation.
They are short on words.	True. Japanese distrust words. Also they may have poor command of the language you speak.
They deafen you with silence.	Silence shows respect for the speaker.
They often look glum.	In Japan, happiness hides behind a straight face.
When they smile, they don't look sincere.	Japanese often smile to make you feel comfortable. You should be thankful – if they don't like you a smile is still better than a scowl!
They say 'yes' when they mean 'no'.	They don't like to offend you by showing open disagreement or refusal.
We can never tell what they really thinking.	By generally keeping a straight face, Japanese are rather impassive. They are not trying to deceive you.
They never look you right in the eye.	Japanese are taught that it is rude to stare.
They sit up straight all the time and don't seem to relax in meetings.	Japanese don't like to slouch. Maintaining correct posture is polite.
They go to sleep during meetings.	Not often. When they close their eyes it means they are concentrating on what you are saying.
They delay in making decisions, don't answer letters and faxes when we press them.	They don't like to be rushed. They must complete their consensus.

Appearance	Reality
They never make decisions during meetings.	Japanese regard meetings as information-gathering sessions or occasions to state their position. They make decisions outside meetings, seeking the consensus of their colleagues.
They lack individualism and all behave the same way.	They prefer teamwork and group decisions to individualism. Homogeneity makes them act alike.
They talk Japanese during meetings so we can't understand them.	It is their language! Also they may find it difficult to concentrate for long periods in a foreign language.
They are often ambiguous. We are never quite sure what they mean.	Japanese is an ambiguous, vague language which carries over into the English translation. Also their language level may be low.
They delay in making an order for six months, then they expect you to deliver tomorrow!	Japanese companies tend to proceed with implementation while they await an order. That way they are never caught flat-footed.
Sometimes they don't seem interested in immediate profit. This is annoying to westerners.	Japanese shareholders do not press for dividends. They believe more in increasing market share, improving share price and eventually making capital gains. They think long term.
They often talk and act like 12-year olds.	General McArthur made the mistake of saying and believing this. The low language level gives this impression.

Appearance

They are tough negotiators, often refusing to change their position.

They don't like foreigners, believing they are a superior race.

They don't mix easily with other nationalities.

They are noisy in groups and behave badly when abroad.

They try to bribe westerners with gifts.

They do not always respect contracts, often asking for renegotiation after several months.

Reality

Tough negotiators are good ones! Japanese meet force with intransigence. But when treated with respect, they are often willing to modify their position considerably.

It is true that Japanese people consider themselves unique, but they have often been willing to learn from others. In Japan they treat foreigners very well. Their hospitality is unsurpassed.

Those Japanese who have had little contact with foreigners are often afraid to mix with them, as they feel they won't know how to behave.

In Japan there are very strict rules on social behaviour. When abroad the relaxation of these rules tends to make them let their hair down and be boisterous. Also they tolerate alcohol badly.

Not true. Gift giving is a tradition in Japan and applies also to foreign guests. You can reciprocate.

They respect oral contracts and the spirit in which they were made. They wish to renegotiate if market or other conditions have changed.

Hints on doing business with the Japanese

What advice should one give to a foreign businessperson who goes to
Japan? First, restrict your body language. Do not wave your arms, do not
touch people unnecessarily and above all do not put your arm round their
shoulders as you pass through doorways. Do not report conversations you
have had with Japanese to third parties unless it is clear that you may do so.
Do not mention business for the first 15 minutes of any conversation
unless the Japanese says '*Jitsu wa ne...*' which means 'the fact of the matter
is...' Never address any Japanese businessman by his first name and never,
never talk about the war. (Germans, on the other hand, like talking about
the war.)

If you are dealing with a group of Japanese (and they usually come to
see you in groups), address your remarks to the senior man and bow to him
as low as he bows to you. You may talk about golf or ski jumping as much
as you like, but do not tell jokes unless they are at your own expense and
can easily be understood.

It is not a good idea to ask to see a Japanese home, since even important businesspeople often live in tiny apartments – a fact which causes them
some embarrassment. They are quite happy to go to your home, however,
since you are likely to have more space. Do not shake hands with them
more than necessary as they regard this practice as unhygienic. On the
other hand, you should always present your visiting card immediately at
the first meeting.

It is essential to remember that a Japanese likes doing business in a harmonious atmosphere, therefore you should do nothing which reduces harmony. The Japanese rarely criticise each other or even third parties and
never say 'no' directly. Excessive frankness is therefore usually out of place.

When dealing with a Japanese company which may superficially resemble your own, do not assume similarities that are not there. Japan has **mod-
ernised, not westernised**, and true similarities are mainly only technical.
Don't assume that they mean the same as you do when they use words like
'leadership' or 'motivation'. They have something quite different in mind.
Also 'machine' means sewing machine, 'green car' means first class railway
carriage and 'Arbeit' means part-time work.

If there seem to be a lot of 'don'ts' with regard to your behaviour when
dealing with the Japanese, there is also a list of 'dos'. Above all you should
be modest and reserved. Bow if you can manage it and begin your conver-

sation by asking about their families. It is quite correct to enthuse over the Japanese economic miracle, as well as their reputation for honesty and lavish hospitality. Another positive subject is the long unbroken history of Japan and its achievements in the arts.

It is also quite correct for you to apologise for your rudeness when you last met. Japanese always do this whether they were rude or not. What it means is that you speak in a disparaging manner about your unpunctuality or poor hospitality or any other personal defect you can think of. For instance, Japanese apologise regularly for having had a cold, having taken you to see a poor film, having given you a ride in their noisy car or having beaten your country at karate.

Finally, if you want to do business with the Japanese you must also try to look the part. Remember that normally all Japanese executives dress conservatively in blue or grey with a white shirt and dark tie. A Japanese businessman looks at you in a manner not unlike that of the Spaniard. He must like you and he must trust you, otherwise no deal. He likes people who are clean, well-dressed, not too hairy, not too young, modest and of quiet voice and above all, polite. You must also convince him that you are respectable. For a Japanese, respectability comprises a certain age and several of the qualities just mentioned above, but also a proven record in business, an absence of any doubtful partners or deals and evidence of unquestioned solvency. Many Japanese businesspeople will ask you openly at the first meeting who are your board of directors, what is the capital of the company, who your chief customers are and if you have a chairman's report to show them.

How to win friends and influence people from Japan

+ Treat them quietly.
+ Be ultra-polite at all times. This involves often standing up when you would normally sit down, perhaps bowing when you would shake hands and apologising several times for rudenesses you have not committed.
+ Entertain generously with splendid meals which you apologise for afterwards.
+ Never say 'no' or 'impossible' or 'we can't'.
+ If you disagree, just be silent.
+ Never corner them or make them lose face.
+ Open business discussions only after 20 minutes.

✦ Flatter them a lot. They like it.
✦ Give them your business card at th first meeting and show great
  respect for theirs. Put it on the tabl in front of you and look at it
  regularly during conversation.
✦ Show great respect for their compar
✦ Emphasise the size, age, wealth and reputation of your own company.
✦ Don't tell jokes during business meetings. You may afterwards, they
  won't understand them anyway.
✦ Remember that anything you say they take literally. Flippant remarks
  such as 'This is killing me' or 'you must be kidding' would be misconstrued.
✦ Be less direct in your utterances that you would be with others.
  Remember the Japanese do not admire bluntness and strive at meetings
  to achieve 'harmony' on which they can build long-term relations.
✦ What you say matters little to them. It's how you say it that counts. You
  must never hurt their feelings. Remember this and the business will
  probably come automatically. Show great respect for their 'leader'
  and/or anyone over 50 who is present.
✦ Learn some Japanese and show you have an interest in their culture.
  Don't overdo it – they don't like foreigners who speak fast Japanese.
✦ When speaking English (if this is your common language) speak slowly
  and distinctly. They smile and nod constantly but understand only 30
  per cent of the time.
✦ Be prepared to say everything five times at a succession of meetings and
  anything vital at least ten times.
✦ They prefer oral agreements to written ones, so don't push documents
  at them until they are ready.
✦ If they make an oral agreement, they will stick to it. They do not necessarily want to shake hands on it. A nod or slight bow is much better.
✦ Try not to extract decisions from them at meetings. Remember they
  have to check with head office Tokyo.
✦ Things are often agreed between meetings, so be prepared to talk business during socialising.
✦ Imitate or adapt to their pace, manners and demeanour as much as possible, satisfy all their requirements and desires if you can. Meet them
  halfway in concessions and style, but remain yourself, as they probably
  respect your country's historical record, and way of life.
✦ Find common ground when you can. They love sharing.

23

CHINA

CHINA IS NOT ONLY THE WORLD'S MOST POPULATED COUNTRY, IT ALSO boasts the planet's oldest civilisation – an agriculture-based society formed on the Yellow River 5000 years ago. During this long period – practically all of recorded human history – China, essentially an isolated country, cut off from other peoples by a vast ocean to the east, jungles to the south, towering mountain ranges to the west and freezing steppes to the north, has never formed a lasting, friendly relationship with a distant country. For two millennia the Chinese Empire was its own universe, sucking in Korea, Vietnam and other neighbours, while exacting tributes from others, including Japan. Its unbroken culture spread itself over many centuries throughout East Asia, where its influence is manifest in music, dance, paintings, religion, philosophy, architecture, theatre, societal structure and administration and, above all, language and literature.

Westerners who see China as a Third World, relatively backward nation in terms of crude technology, sparse infrastructure, appalling hygiene, rampant pollution, outdated politics and inadequate communication fall into the trap of misjudging, underestimating and misunderstanding the power and impact of the Chinese people on their neighbours and, in another sense, the world at large. China sees herself as *Chung-Kuo* – the middle kingdom, the centre of the universe and venue of the world's oldest lifestyle. A visitor from the Tang Dynasty (China's golden age) would see its legacy intact in the streets and fields of China today. The Chinese, a billion strong, see no diminishment of their moral authority – exercised with such power for thousands of years – and their sense of cultural superiority is greater than even that of the Japanese, whom they civilised. Foreigners in the eyes of Chinese are inferior, corrupt, decadent, disloyal and volatile, frequently hegemonistic, barbaric and, in essence, 'devils'.

Once you are fully aware how Chinese view you, you will find it easier to deal with them. They did not make these assumptions lightly. In the 'Opium Wars' between 1839 and 1860 Britain forced Bengal opium on the Chinese, annexed Hong Kong and claimed enclaves in several Chinese ports, including Shanghai. France, Germany and Russia soon followed the British, while the Japanese, imitating the West as usual, smashed China in the war of 1894–5 and annexed Taiwan. This proved merely a prelude to a full-scale invasion of the mainland, followed by civil war after the Japanese withdrawal, culminating in victory for Mao's forces in 1949. The foreign 'devils' had to abandon their profitable ghettoes in Shanghai and other cities, leaving only Hong Kong in alien hands.

That xenophobia might be an understandable reaction to the events cited above can be readily perceived. Whether the Chinese actually possess cultural superiority over the rest of us is another matter. They believe they do. The numerous and magnificent spiritual and artistic achievements and accomplishments of Chinese civilisation do not go unrivalled in other parts of the world. While the brevity of the European occupation of the Americas might disqualify them from serious competition, the clear thinking and spiritual values of the Ancient Greeks must put them in contention; the organising abilities and breadth of conquest of the Roman Empire matched the Chinese; above all the Italian Renaissance threw up artistic giants who might be considered to have equalled (or even surpassed) Chinese aesthetic masterpieces, whether in the field of music, painting, opera, dance or architecture. Leonardo, Michelangelo, Titian, Raphael, Verdi, Rossini and Dante are a hard act to beat.

The Chinese would not deny this. They are capable of expressing admiration for European artistic creation, *dans son genre*, just as they appreciate the efficiency of American, British and French political systems and technological progress. Where they feel superior is in the area of moral and spiritual values. In as much as most nations feel that their norms are the correct ones – that their behaviour alone is truly exemplary – this is not surprising in itself. The Chinese, however, like the Russians and the Muslims, combine their sense of moral righteousness with fierce criticism of western societies. The large European nations of former imperial glory – Britain, France, Spain and Portugal – they see in decline, decay and spiritual disintegration. They see the American culture as having begun to decline before it reached its peak. The Japanese, once earnest students of Chinese philosophies and precepts, have succumbed to materialism and consumerism. Russia was never admired.

What are these superior Chinese values? They are not slow to tell you. They list them as follows:

modesty
tolerance
filial piety, courtesy, thrift
patience, respect for elderly
sincerity, loyalty, family closeness, tradition
trustworthiness, stoicism, tenacity, self-sacrifice, kindness
moderation, patriotism, asceticism, diligence, harmony towards all
resistance to corruption, learning, respect for hierarchy
generosity, adaptability, conscientiousness
sense of duty, pride (no losing face)
being undemanding, friendships
gratitude for favours
impartiality, purity
gentleness
wisdom

A westerner, ploughing through this list of self-ascribed values, might wonder about modesty and impartiality, but, in the main, the Chinese do go about their daily lives, especially at the individual level, exhibiting many of those characteristics. Whatever they might think of us, we can hardly fail to see them as hard-working, conscientious, patient, undemanding and thrifty. They seem generally to be in harmony with each other (good team members) and towards us they are usually courteous and compliant.

To understand why individual Chinese go about their affairs in an orderly, respectful fashion, we would do well to examine some of the basic tenets of their beliefs and philosophies. The most important influence is that of Confucianism.

Stability of society in China, according to Confucian views, is based on unequal relationships between people. This is almost diametrically opposed to British, American and Scandinavian ideas, but it is hardly questioned in China. The five relationships basic to ethical behaviour are:

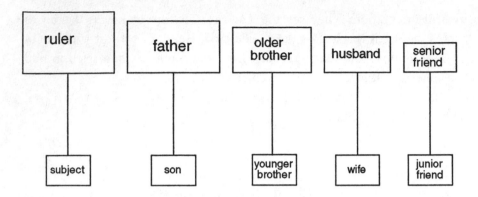

Figure 65

The Chinese believe that non-observation of these relationships is responsible for disorder, crime and lack of societal responsibility in many western countries, where only the husband–wife relationship (now threatened by frequent divorce) is generally adhered to, apart from occasional respect granted to a ruler here and there.

Unequal relationships do not simply imply unlimited advantages for the superiors. While their authority must not be questioned, their obligations are also mandatory. They must protect and exhibit kindness to those who show them obedience and allegiance. The basic teaching of Confucius can be summarised as:

✦ The observance of the unequal relationships.
✦ The family is the prototype of all social organisation. We are members of a group, not individuals.
✦ One must behave in a virtuous manner towards others. Everbody's 'face' must be maintained.
✦ Education and hard work must be prized.
✦ One should be moderate in all things. Save, stay calm, avoid extremes, shun indulgence.

Confucianism exercises a strong influence on the daily lives and business cultures in China, Japan, Korea, Taiwan, Singapore, Hong Kong, and, to a lesser extent, other East Asian countries. Westerners wishing to deal with these Asians should take this into account and adapt accordingly.

The Chinese are also influenced by several other factors which do not feature in the western mindset. These are, among others:

✦ **Taoism** – insistence on healthy lifestyle, adequate vegetarianism, generosity of spirit.
✦ **Buddhism** – harmony through meditation.
✦ **Ancestor worship** – past figures strongly influencing present action.
✦ **Feng shui** – 'wind and water' superstition, affecting decisions on building and arrangement of furniture, mirrors and doors.
✦ **Herbal medicine and acupuncture** – frequently used and believed in.
✦ **Animal years** – giving an individual the qualities of the animal.

What might seem old-fashioned superstition to Europeans is present-day reality to the Chinese. If you were born in the year of the Horse, they will conclude you have stamina and they will not try to outlast you. If you are a Rat they will exercise great care in dealing with you, as you are smart, brave and clever. They may consider that you will be unlucky, as your office has two doors in a straight line, but their natural courtesy will make them refrain from telling you. They will agree in a compliant manner to most of your business proposals, especially if you show great keenness in making them. They wish to avoid a discordant note. They will let you wait half an hour at the bus stop rather than disappoint you with the news that the bus had left just before you arrived.

Collectivism is very strong in China. It originated in the early agrarian economies and is enhanced in the teachings of Confucius; it is not a product of Communism, although the Communist regime found it useful. A Chinese belongs to four basic groups in each of which he or she is, to some degree, a prisoner – the work unit (*danwei*), family, school and community. Their obligations to each group, from which they may not distance themselves, mean that they have virtually no social or geographic mobility. No westerner labours under such constraints, therefore finds it hard to understand to what extent a Chinese's hands may be tied when it comes to making a decision requiring sudden change or independence of action. Lack of mobility also gives the Chinese an added problem as to the question of losing face.

An American who lands in disgrace in New York can begin again next week in California. The Chinese who loses face may well have to guts it out for the next 40 years in the same community, workplace or academic environment. Neither do they just have one face to maintain. Their different social obligations (laid down by Confucius) force them to be many things to many people (see Figure 66).

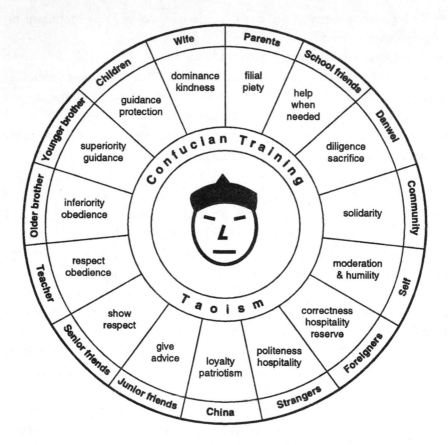

Figure 66   *Keeping one's face...is hard work!*

Traditionally the Chinese have been locked into the 'extended' family system where links between children and parents, uncles and aunts, cousins, grandchildren, husband's and wife's families and a host of distant relations both in China and overseas are much closer than anything we experience in the West. The 'networking' advantages of such a system are obvious, although the acute interdependence involved can cause considerable stress. Additional responsibilities towards school friends, teachers and neighbours increase the strain. Under the Communist regime it was, however, the individual's involvement with the '*danwei*' or work unit that pinned them down to the greatest degree. The relationship went much deeper than simply paying wages for a job done – the *danwei* solves disputes, administers government regulations, sees to housing, medical care, day care and kindergarten, arranges recreation, picnics and holiday homes, and makes funeral arrangements.

Americans, British and northern European people, unused to paternalistic companies or 'work units' and jealous of individual rights and privacy, abhor this type of group interference. Yet western insistence on individualism at all costs is blamed by the Chinese for their problems of crime, addiction and family breakdown. China is not alone among Asian nations in evolving an alternative philosophy – that of 'group rights', where the extended family is seen as more important than the individual. According to Confucius the individual owes as much to society as the other way round and, if these duties are scrupulously carried out, the resulting social cohesion, mutual protection of face and continuing harmony will lead to economic success.

This leads us to the question of human rights. Virtually all European countries see these as a prerequisite to other areas of development, while in the USA they are the bedrock of the constitution itself. There is nothing Americans hold more dear. China, in company with some other Asians, have a different set of priorities. 'Starving people are not in a position to exercise human rights' is the argument.

The West may well argue that after 5000 years of civilisation China should already be further along the road towards individual prosperity than she is today. Chinese answer that their late development is partly due to nineteenth-century western colonialism (look how Japan has prospered) and that with one billion persons speaking umpteen different dialects, group prosperity and cohesion are safer goals. Each nation shies away from the problems of its past history and takes steps to avoid their repetition. Russia, Poland and Finland fear invasion, Japan humiliation and nuclear bombs, Korea and the Baltic States foreign occupation, Mexico exploitation, Germany inflation and conflagration, America slump, China anarchy and foreign devils.

Chinese core beliefs and their consequences in business

Chinese people cannot adhere to their strong Confucian beliefs and other age-old traditions without their business culture being affected. Some of the consequences are listed below:

✦ Power distance is large. 4000 years of centralisation result in a tradition of obedience.

+ Inequalities are expected and desired.
+ Less powerful people should be dependent on the powerful who must protect them and take care of their careers and welfare.
+ Parents, teachers, bosses, must all be obeyed.
+ Age brings seniority.
+ There is a wide salary range between the top and bottom of the organisation.
+ The ideal boss is a benevolent autocrat.
+ Privileges for managers are expected and popular.
+ Subordinates expect to be told what to do.
+ Individualism is taboo.
+ Relationships are more important than tasks.
+ Confrontation is avoided, harmony and consensus are ultimate goals.
+ The search for virtue is more important than the search for truth. A and B can both be right if both are virtuous.
+ Long-term orientation and goals.

Chinese behaviour at meetings and negotiations

+ Chinese prefer meetings to be formal, although dress is usually comfortable.
+ Seating will be according to hierarchy. Business cards are exchanged.
+ The senior man must be shown great respect and attention at all times, even though he takes little part.
+ The deputy or vicechairman is often the decision maker.
+ The real decisions will be made outside the meeting, which is principally for information gathering
+ The pace will be slow and repetitious. The time frame is too long for westerners who may see the slow-down techniques as bargaining ploys.
+ Politeness is observed at all times. Confrontation and loss of face (for both sides) must be avoided.
+ Chinese rarely say 'no' – only hint at difficulties.
+ A collective spirit prevails, nobody says 'I', only 'we'.
+ In a collectivist culture, accountability for decisions is avoided. Authority is not passed downwards from the leaders.
+ Decisions have a long-term orientation. Negotiations in China are important social occasions during which one fosters relationships and

Accountability

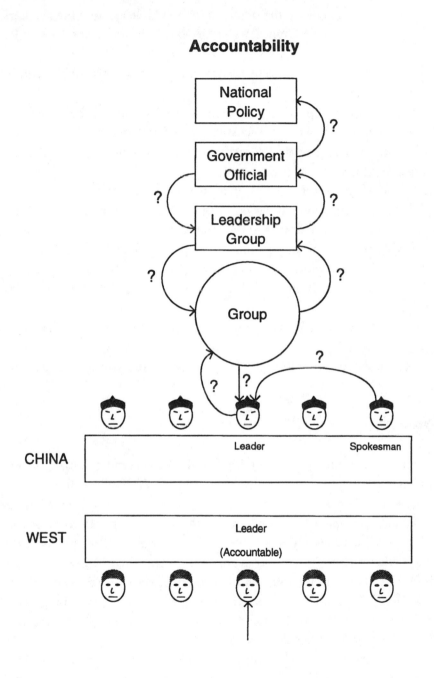

Figure 67   Accountability

decides if the people on the other side of the table are suitable partners in the long run. The Chinese, who have been doing business for 4000 years, certainly are.

✦ They consider you technically competent, otherwise **inexperienced** in business relations.

✦ They negotiate step by step in an unhurried manner. They prefer to open proceedings with a discussion of general principles of mutual interest. That is probably enough for the first day. They dislike US eagerness to sign a contract.

✦ Deal-oriented Americans and many Europeans agree to perform specific tasks over an agreed period of time. Chinese, looking beyond the deal, prioritise mutual trust in the long term.

✦ They are thrifty, cautious, patient. You will have to match their patience and stamina, otherwise deals and opportunities will be lost.

✦ They combine flexibility with firmness and expect both these qualities in you.

✦ Once they have decided who, what, when and how is best, they are very trustworthy.

✦ They know the size of their market and use this in their pricing strategy.

Etiquette

Chinese are basically very welcoming people who extend generous hospitality and courtesy both to Asians and 'barbarians'. Sit-down dinners are the norm, usually lasting about two hours and ended by the host standing up. On these occasions you should try all the delicacies put in front of you by your host, without actually leaving any dish empty. Protocol is easygoing. Chinese slurp and make all sorts of noises when eating, they also indulge in smoking at the table and have been known to spit on the floor. You are unlikely to disgrace yourself unless you are particularly inept with chopsticks, handle food with your fingers – or insist on paying the bill before your host has the chance to do so.

As far as meetings are concerned it is often necessary to make appointments one or two weeks in advance with officials, only a day or so with entrepreneurs and acquaintances. You should turn up on time. Individual Chinese often arrive 15 minutes early and say they can finish the business before the meeting was scheduled to begin, so as not to waste your time.

You need not take punctuality to these lengths but you should not be late.

When saying farewell, Chinese mention their imminent departure early on in the meeting, as opposed to westerners who delay it till just before leaving. A Chinese prolongs the farewell on the street, perhaps accompanying you part of your way.

Guanxi and gift giving

Guanxi means the linking of two people in a relationship of mutual dependence. It involves reciprocal gifts and favours. While this is a charming custom, it can also be fraught with danger as the recipient of an usually expensive gift will almost certainly be asked shortly for a huge personal favour. It may well compromise a business situation and cause embarrassment to those who are closely restricted by their companies in the area of discounts, arbitrary pricing, etc.

Humility

Courtesy in China also involves excessive humility and self-disparagement. All good Asians are self-effacing, but Chinese take it to ridiculous lengths. You may try to fit into the picture by being a good listener, using deference and understatement in your replies, never mentioning your impressive business or academic qualifications, and trying to get in the back row when someone takes a photograph.

The twenty-first century, the People's Republic of China and you

Asians are destined to be world leaders in industrial, economic and trade growth in the next century. China with her mammoth population and land area will be the dominant force in the region. Japan will also be a major player, but China has 10 times Japan's population and 25 times its land area. Breathtaking development and growth in China are only a question of time – the West would be wise to start establishing meaningful and durable links and relationships **now** while the Chinese currency is weak and investment is cheap.

The return on investment, provided it is long term, may well be staggering. One should foresee the biggest economic development in world history. What happened in Japan between 1954 and 1990 is bound to happen in China, but on an unimaginably greater scale. Forecasts indicate that average production per head in China will rise from $350 at the beginning of 1992 to $12,000 in 2050. A country with a GDP of $10,000 billion a year will be the world's biggest market and possibly leading exporter. Americans, Europeans and other Asians will compete ferociously to sell into that market.

How can one go about establishing one's position and image in Chinese eyes? Policy and direction taking must be long term, otherwise one wastes one's time on relatively unimportant ventures. Westerners should bear in mind the following factors:

✦ You are dealing with people who place values and principles above money and expediency.

✦ The Chinese will not stray from their reverence of Confucian views on order, family and consensus. Show unqualified respect for these.

✦ The Chinese see their language not only as a cultural tool which has historically influenced Japan, Korea, Indo-China and other areas, but as a repository for transmitting cultural values. The undisputed link between language and culture gives them a strong motive to increase the currency of the Chinese language, at least on a regional basis. You would do well to have one or two individuals in your company or organisation develop reasonable fluency in Chinese.

✦ Britain in particular has long experience in China and many connections in East Asia. Chinese also react favourably to Nordic calmness, German technology and French *savoir faire*. Europeans should study Buddhist and Confucian behaviour and show compassion for Chinese difficulties. It will pay off.

✦ Final golden rules – be extremely deferential at all times, combine courtesy with firmness, show humility and respect for age and rank, don't overdo the logic, prepare your meetings in detail, don't speak in a loud voice or rush them, know your Chinese history, always keep your calm and remember that patience and allowing adequate time for reflection are the keys to making progress, however slow it may seem.

24

INDIA AND SOUTH-EAST ASIA

CHINA AND JAPAN ARE THE GIANTS OF ASIA, DOMINATING THEIR neighbours in one case by sheer size of population and land area and in the other through economic/financial muscle and technology. There are, however, other major players, for Asia is massive. The Indian subcontinent is the home of over 1 billion people. Indonesia, already the world's fourth most populated nation, hovers around 200 million. Seoul, Tokyo, Bombay, Jakarta, Shanghai, Beijing, Karachi, Tientsin, Delhi and Bangkok each have in excess of 5 million inhabitants.

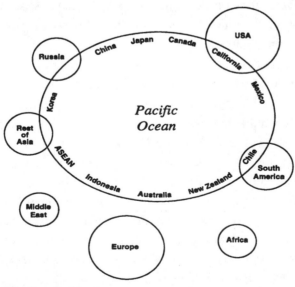

Figure 68   The Pacific Rim

Apart from the question of size and numbers, Asians are making their mark through sheer performance. During the period 1980–91 the country with the fastest economic growth (the average annual percentage increase in real GDP) was South Korea at 10 per cent for the decade. China was second at 9.4 per cent while Thailand was 6th, Taiwan 7th, Singapore 9th, Indonesia 16th and Malaysia 17th. The top European country was Luxemburg at 4.2 per cent! If we look at the four Asian Tigers (the 'small' ones – Singapore, Hong Kong, Taiwan and South Korea) even the total production figures are impressive. Korea is probably the star (the world's 15th biggest economy in 1993), and Taiwan, Singapore and Hong Kong are all in the top 30 in terms of GDP per head.

After 1970 it was a popular prediction among economists/futurologists that if the nineteenth century had belonged to the British and the twentieth century to the Americans, the twenty-first century would be that of the Japanese. This is now less evident than it was. While Japan's economy is still twice that of Germany and closing in on the USA, the current rate of growth of China and other East Asian countries, as well as the continued technological and productive resilience of California (itself eighth in the world in GDP), suggest that an important centre of gravity in the twenty-first century will lie somewhere in the middle of the Pacific Ocean. The Pacific Rim, as we now like to call it, is lined not only by China, Japan, the ASEAN countries and Siberian Russia on one side, but by high-ranking economic powerhouses on the other – USA, Canada, Australia, Mexico, not to mention Chile, New Zealand and half a dozen other countries with potential for growth and trade.

After 1948 political developments resulting in cold wars on various fronts seriously interfered with world trade. Deep and lasting ideological divisions prohibited commercial relations between countries and areas which normally would have been natural partners by virtue of propinquity. In Europe there was no free trade between East and West. Hungary, Poland, Czechoslovakia, East Germany and possibly Romania probably felt they were facing the wrong way. Communist Soviet Union could not be an interesting Pacific partner for Japan or the North Americans and the Soviet–Chinese split after the death of Stalin reduced Soviet–Chinese trade to a minimum. India's quarrel with China over Tibet meant that the world's two most populous nations, while close neighbours, exchanged few goods or services.

The demise of Communism in most areas and the improvement of relations between China and other major powers have opened the way for regional economics and trade to follow more normal geographic paths. It would seem likely that in the twenty-first century all of Europe will be internally tariff free and will develop into a 500 million-strong market of some clout. As such it would challenge Japan and even the USA as a major economic bloc and its proximity to Africa would give it some advantages. These considerations all point to the Pacific countries getting their act together, as indeed Europe is (sometimes frantically) trying to do. The USA, now earnestly trying to mind its fences with Central and South America, has every advantage in looking out over the Pacific for new partners in long-term alliances (trade, development, investment). They will not wish to surrender their industrial, financial and political hegemony easily. Collaboration, rather than outright competition, with their neighbours in the western Pacific would seem to be the safest way to prolong dominance. Europeans have fewer bones of contention with the Chinese countries, Korea and Indonesia than have Russia, Japan, and the USA, therefore they can be expected to compete energetically in certain Asian areas. In this regard, both the Europeans and the Americans will have to develop a much fuller understanding of Oriental psychology and values if they are to be successful. Which brings us back to the Asians – what is the key to winning their hearts (or at the very least to doing business of mutual benefit)?

What Asians have in common

Although regional rivalries in Asia are intense, the peoples inhabiting that vast continent do indeed possess certain behavioural features which, although modified in each state, distinguish them sharply from Americans and most Europeans. No country in the area has completely escaped the influences of Confucianism and Buddhism – two creeds which automatically bestow a certain lifestyle on their followers. Even in those Asian countries which are officially Muslim – Indonesia and Malaysia – behavioural patterns resemble East Asian *mores* far more than those of Islamic co-believers in the Middle East.

Westerners doing business with Asians will encounter many difficulties and suffer from numerous misunderstandings. While eastern 'idiosyncrasies' are many, one might do well to focus on four central aspects of Oriental psychology, in order to get to grips with the correct procedures for reducing friction and bafflement. These features might be grouped under four main headings.

+ **Courtesy** – this includes the high Asian standards of politeness in social and business environments; respect for seniority and elderly people; humility and gentleness.
+ **Patience** – including the eastern concept of time and time management.
+ **Harmony** – including indirectness, consensus and face.
+ **Pragmatism** – Asian style.

Courtesy

Oriental courtesy is not confined to Japan. It took one linguist 64 pages to describe in detail the elaborate system of pronouns which exists in the Thai language to enable a person in any situation to show just the right amount of respect, deference and intimacy. Confucian teaching emphasises the respect due to age, seniority and rank. In Islamic Malaysia and Indonesia this deference is observable to an equal degree. Both these countries exhibit a great degree of gentleness to friends and strangers. While humility of expression is carried to great lengths in China and Japan, no eastern country tolerates egocentric speech; many Europeans and especially Americans fall into the trap of sounding too full of themselves, often boastful in eastern ears and, worst of all, indulging in the hard sell. Even the British, with their considerable sense of diplomacy, often fail to appear reasonably polite to Asians when joking with them. Clive James points out that to the Japanese the English sense of humour often seems to consist of asking them to share their (British) delight at a mortal insult.

Patience

It is fatal for any westerner to try to 'hustle' Orientals, yet that is what happens most of the time. Decision making in eastern countries is a slow process – painfully so for western go-getters. Americans and northern Europeans particularly prefer linear thinking leading up to quick decisions. Orientals do not think in linear fashion. Figure 69 shows the circular route to eastern decision making.

Asians do not like deadlines. They enter into the spirit of an agreement which may stipulate that goods are to be delivered at a certain time, but the

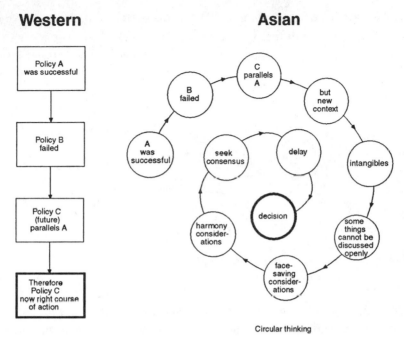

Figure 69   *Circular thinking*

actual date is of no importance in their eyes, since they consider that having given their word to do their best, they will not indulge in unnecessary delay.

Westerners often establish contact with Asian partners and show eagerness to contract a lot of business in a short time. They are usually disappointed. Besides taking their time about deciding whether or not to do business at all, Asians are reluctant to give large contracts to partners whom they have known for a short time. In their eyes, the further back a relationship goes in time, the more business it will guarantee in the future.

Asians are also concerned about the personalisation of business. Americans see persons as instruments to be used deal per deal (they can be discarded when the business is concluded). Their view is shown in Figure 70.

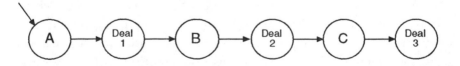

Figure 70   *Personalisation of business (West)*

Northern Europeans tend to follow this pattern, but multi-active Latins and Arabs have a different approach. They seek close contact with a key person (A) from whom they hope to spawn a series of deals (see Figure 71).

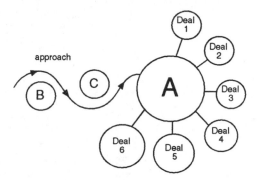

Figure 71   Personalisation of business (Latin and Arab)

In Asia, business must be personalised to a similar degree, but in a different manner. One focuses not just on one key figure, but more likely on at least three. The first one, Mr C, is a contact man, possibly roving, who has enough communicative ability to initiate relations with new partners. The second man, Mr B, will be the head or assistant head of the department which handles your product or service. If he is satisfied that the transaction is feasible, there will soon appear a third figure, Mr A, who is unlikely to be a specialist in your field, but will be 50 years of age or more and carry a visiting card of considerable importance. Thereafter your business will be conducted with the ABC team where C will be present at all meetings, B when details or technical matters are to be discussed and A when sizeable contracts are signed or ratified. On their home ground C will take you out to dinner regularly, B and (less frequently) A will honour you with their presence from time to time.

Linear-active peoples, and Americans in particular, see time as linear – a straight line showing the route from the past to the future. Straight lines are easily divided into segments which, for linear-active cultures, facilitates planning. Americans thus see time passing without decisions being made or actions performed as 'wasted'. Asians do not see time as streaking away unutilised in a linear future, but coming round again in a circle, where the same opportunities, risks and dangers will represent themselves when they are so many days, weeks or months wiser. How often do we in the West say, 'If I had known then what I know now, I would never have done what I did?'

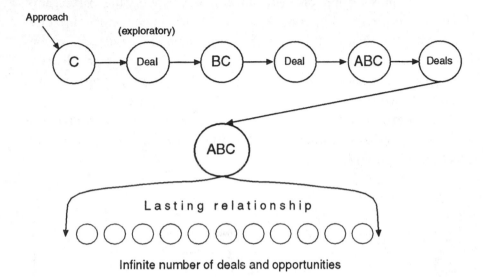

Figure 72   Unfolding of business in Asia

This does not mean that Asians do not engage themselves in planning. The Japanese in particular are meticulous planners, but their scheduling is un-American. US businesspeople, under steady pressure from shareholders to achieve the profits forecast in the quarterly report, set ambitious yet realistic one-off goals for the next three or six months. The Japanese, and other Asians, consider past records and achievements carefully, using previous goals, attainments and precedents as a guide to future objectives. Past, present and future merge, blurring or synchronising demarcation lines. The past and future are seen as equally important, while present-day technology and opportunities are utilised to ensure the continuity of the culture.

Harmony

Different cultures assess the success of a business meeting in a variety of ways. For an American the meeting was successful if the deal was done and the contract signed. A French person is satisfied if a thorough discussion has covered the basic issues in a logical debate where he or she has been allowed to speak for most of the time. Italians, Spaniards and Russians are happy if they have found a soul-mate on the other side. Asians look above all to the preservation of all-round harmony among the participants. Harmony is preserved by courtesy and deference, low tone of voice, indirect statements which obviate possible confrontation as well as by various pleasantries and platitudes which enhance the 'face' of the other side. Such exemplary behaviour will, in their eyes, produce eventual consensus and viable transactions.

Americans and northern Europeans, while not wishing to be discourteous or abrupt, have a natural inclination to make a one-stage game plan. It looks like Figure 73.

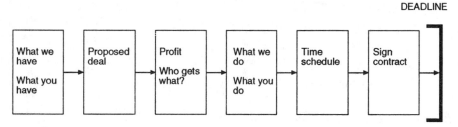

Figure 73

The Asian game plan (Figure 74) is **at least** two-stage. Stage One establishes harmony and, as much as possible, a closer familiarity with the nature of the other side. Stage Two is the planning – it will be open-ended in terms of time and opportunities.

South Americans, Portuguese and Mediterranean peoples will feel comfortable with this concept and the pace at which it proceeds. Other Westerners see time and money as more important than delicate relationships and may wish to eliminate various stages of the 'courtship'. Americans and Scandinavians obviously feel that harmony and goodwill can also be engendered by swift and direct fulfilment of agreed commitments and friendly pragmatic discussions.

Asian pragmatism

Which leads us to the Asians as pragmatists. While their business cultures are based on respect, harmony, often philosophical ideals, they can be as coldly pragmatic as anyone else. Like others, they will use all the cards they hold in their hand, or up their sleeve. The former may include distribution channels, wide connections, cheap labour, sheer hard work; the latter may

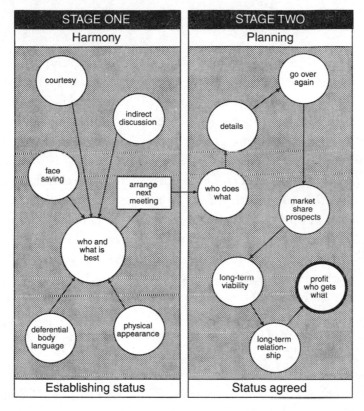

Figure 74

be their influence with officials, hidden backers, antiwestern regulations and inscrutability extending to opaqueness.

Their patience will enable them to 'sit out' difficult situations or deadlocks where French or German equanimity shatters and American forbearance disintegrates. It is not unusual for Asians to introduce major proposals after westerners have reconfirmed their flights back home. American reluctance to reschedule is seen a weakness in their ability to negotiate.

Without dwelling unduly on the aspects of Asian pragmatism, it is useful to point out that Asians will often refrain from making apparently reasonable concessions until they are forced to. This has been evident, over a number of years, in the matter of Japan lifting import restrictions on US goods. Finally, and not entirely unconnected with this, one must remember that Asian correctness and courtesy, hospitality and lavish entertaining, apparent compliance and reasonable, humble discussion style all are pragmatic strategies to secure, whenever possible, irreversible advantage.

Differences among Asians

Seen through western eyes, many Asians look alike, and react to our more headlong personalities in a uniform manner. To us they appear quiet, patient and polite, collectivist, principled, hard-working, uninventive, inscrutable and lacking in charisma. Many westerners, unless they have lived in Asia, cannot distinguish between Chinese, Koreans or Japanese until they open their mouth, and often not even then.

Yet Asia is the world's biggest continent and cultural differentials are numerous. Although the influence of Confucian and Buddhist thought has a unifying effect on Asian behaviour in the same way that Catholicism and Protestantism conventionalise the conduct of certain European groups, Orientals interpret eastern philosophies in a variety of ways.

In the first place, Asians are not very fond of each other. The reasons for this are mainly historical. Japan, on account of her war record, has blotted her copybook in many Asian nations and her exemplary post-war behaviour has so far failed to normalise attitudes. Koreans, invaded by both China and Japan, bear continued resentment, although they trade heavily with the latter. Military confrontations have dominated relations between the two Koreas as well as China and Taiwan, and even Malaysia and Indonesia were in an official state of *Konfrontasi* (confrontation) for two decades. The political problems existing between China and India are well documented and the traditional hostility between Russians and Chinese has inhibited the development of closer relations between these giant neighbours. Cambodians fear aggressive Vietnamese, Viets fear giant China, Thailand has had her problems with all neighbouring states. Last, but not least, an uneasy, ambivalent relationship exists between China and Japan – that of the wise old master who has received some sharp lessons from his most brilliant pupil.

Koreans

The westerner doing business in Asia will not fail to observe diversity and dissimilarity in regional/national deportment. The Koreans, although attaching greater importance to the preservation of 'face' (*kibun*) than anyone else, are the roughest of the Asians. A few weeks before these lines were written, an incident occurred in a Seoul cinema which illustrated this characteristic. The cinema concerned was showing a Western horror film, which seems to have offended rival cinema owners. The latter arranged for a couple of dozen snakes to be released down the aisles in the middle of the performance, providing an extra dimension that the cinema goers had not bargained for. This type of rough retaliation is not infrequent in Korea. Perhaps for this reason they often appear the most westernised. They trade humour with westerners (an unusual trait in Asia) and they are quicker to decide and initiate than either the Japanese or Chinese, who regard them as inconstant. They show greater readiness to sign western contracts than many other Asians, but evince less adherence to them if they find new partners. They are proud of their ability to work harder than the Japanese and of being able to outperform them in certain industries. Like the Japanese, they keep upgrading their technologies and farm out lower-tech industries to Indonesia and less advanced countries.

Malaysia and Indonesia

If the Koreans are the roughest Asians, the oriental Muslims are the most gentle. In both Malaysia and Indonesia standards of deference are sky high and these are reflected both in comportment and language. In Islamic Asia the work ethic is not implanted to the same degree as it is among the Chinese, Koreans and Japanese. Success is definitely not equated with hard work, although a more subtle form of diligence discernible in the nurturing of deep (and sometimes useful) relations with colleagues and family is highly prized. Malaysians and to some extent Indonesians are intrinsically not interested in the mechanics of commerce and in these nations westerners may find that they are dealing chiefly with overseas Chinese in business transactions. Islamic taboos such as the use of pork and alcohol are in observance in Muslim Asia, although less so in Indonesia than Malaysia. The veiling of women has been discarded in the former country, where females enjoy voting, social and employment advantages.

Thais

In Thailand the work ethic is less admired than in Confucian-inspired areas – Buddhist fatalism and acceptance of one's *karma* renders it somewhat superfluous, if not tedious. Commerce in Thailand is often in Chinese hands, although Thais, like Russians, can work with unbelievable energy in short bursts. For them work must, however, also incorporate

some fun, otherwise it will be shunned. Thais are the most pro-American
of all Asians and about 10,000 Thais study annually in the USA. The USA
is also Thailand's biggest export market and the Americans probably feel
that their $1 billion investment (in loans and grants) in that country has
been justified in view of the continued pro-US stance.

Filipinos

Pro-American feeling is decidedly more ambivalent in Korea and the
Philippines – two countries where large US military bases have given rise
to local frictions. The Koreans remain jealous of American closeness to the
Japanese, who, in their eyes, made too much money out of the Korean war.
The Philippines, as the second largest English-speaking country in the
world, is unlikely to abandon its special relationship with the USA,
although successive post-Marcos regimes may well manoeuvre for more
support in difficult times. The Filipinos, with their vestiges of Spanish
influence and their vulnerability to the absorption of certain Anglo-Saxon
values due to their extensive use of the English language, are somewhat
enigmatic both to westerners and other Asians.

Indians

Indians have a special and unique culture which varies considerably from
East Asian cultures. Their communicative style is more verbose than the
Chinese, Japanese or Korean and they are as dialogue oriented as most
Latins. Essentially multi-active, they have created a society where privacy
is rarely indulged in and even more rarely sought. They make little attempt
to conceal their feelings – joy, disappointment and grief are expressed
without inhibition.

Their values revolve around a strong family orientation as well as loyalty to a 'group' which often has to do with their profession. Examples are
the diamond trade community or textile merchants. The honour of both
family and group is strongly defended and arranged marriages are common
within the trade. Further values are material success and creativity. It is
important to do well in business and this automatically brings increased
status. Creativity is admired, especially in adversity: improved technology
often prospers in India during periods when the country is closed to outside influence and benefits. Under such circumstances Indians often shine

with a DIY mentality. A keenness to find solutions pervades Indian business – a very positive attitude to experimentation. Honesty is not a major issue as a value, being seen as essentially relative. Stealing crops is seen to be as honourable as growing them and highwaymen are recognised as a social group! They have their own honour.

Philosophical considerations surrounding values are largely positive. The objective in doing business is success, but one has to play the game well with flashes of brilliance rather than confining oneself to the narrow goal of victory. Fatalism is widespread and gives one a comforting fallback option. If you succeed, you are well off; if you fail, it is destiny that was unkind. These attitudes encourage Indians to be risk takers. The experience gained in many ventures (for failure is no stigma) results in many Indians developing considerable commercial skill. Indians living overseas rival the Chinese in their ability to capture and conduct local business.

Indians accept a hierarchical system with its obligations and duties. The boss must be humanistic and initiate promotion for his subordinates. In family businesses the elder son rarely decides what he wants to be – he is born to carry on the trade of the father. The father is expected to groom him for the job. First a good education will be provided. The son must study hard – then the next step will be indicated.

A strong work ethic is visible in Indian commerce, especially when people are working in their own or family business. Indians do not work by the clock. There is an easy acceptance of foreigners in business dealings. Indians do not fear foreigners – many invasions have brought familiarity. They are, however, suspicious of the iniquity that the foreigners may bring with them (perhaps a certain fear of division and subsequent loss of national identity).

As far as negotiating style is concerned, Indians have few superiors. Although highly collectivist in their local group, they develop individuality and brilliance when dealing on their own with outsiders. They are clever at buying and selling. The following points indicate just one pattern of negotiation which they employ with great skill when selling (each successive step may take place after days or weeks of negotiation).

- ✦ I don't want to sell at all.
- ✦ This business is the jewel in the crown of all the businesses that my family controls.
- ✦ We don't need the money.

+ I am not intending to sell, but if I ever did sell, I would sell to you.
+ If I should sell, I have no idea whatsoever how we should evaluate such a successful business.
+ If one should try to estimate a price, it would be by analogy with similar deals that were done in the past.
+ A selling X to B was such a deal.
+ A only sold X to B because he needed the money.
+ Perhaps I would like to sell to you, but I shall never be able to carry my family with me.
+ I have heard your proposed price and I have stormed out of the room.
+ I have to tell you in all honesty that we have received a very serious bid from a third party. It is higher than yours.
+ I do not expect you to pay more than they are willing to, but I expect you to match their offer.
+ I am willing to give the deal to you and not them, because I promised to sell to you.
+ I know that this price is not based on the usual multiple of profit, but how do you decide the worth of a business which has 70 per cent of the market share?

There are many other ploys that Indians use. Basically Indians, like most Chinese, are disappointed if you do not engage in bargaining with them. Determination of price must come last, after all the benefits of the purchase or deal have been elaborated. Indians use all their communicative skills to get to the price indirectly.

Where East meets West – Singapore and Hong Kong

Of the four Asian Tigers the most impressive performances are those recorded by Hong Kong and Singapore. Their combined area, even with considerable land reclamation, barely equates with that of Los Angeles. Although densely inhabited, the combined population only just exceeds that of London. Yet not only do Hong Kong and Singapore rank 33rd and 47th respectively in the world's economies, but they are 23rd and 24th in GDP per head – well ahead of Taiwan, ranked 31, and South Korea, 39.

East is east and west is west and never the twain shall meet, goes the old adage. But in some places they do meet, every day, on a large scale – and impressive economic activity is generated as a result. Hong Kong,

Singapore and possibly Kuala Lumpur rank among the most culturally fascinating cities in the world, where the received wisdom of western business is tested against the behavioural norms and intricate social lifestyles and values of Asia.

Singapore, and to some extent Hong Kong (until 1997), are 'city-states' which, perhaps because of their compact nature, have been extremely successful in becoming vibrant hubs of commerce. This is in fact nothing new. Athens, Rome, Carthage and Alexandria were great centres of political power in ancient times; in the Middle Ages, many centuries before Italy and Germany came into being as countries, European trade was dominated by the seaports of Genoa, Venice and Hanseatic cities such as Hamburg, Lübeck, Rotterdam, Bergen and Riga. Trade was the lifeblood of these towns, also characterised by their internationalism and bustling energy. In the modern world, Hong Kong and Singapore have far exceeded other examples of this type. The seven largest ports in the world are Rotterdam, Singapore, Kobe, Shanghai, Nagoya, Yokohama and Hong Kong, in that order. Only Singapore and Hong Kong are self-governing; only they have achieved their economic miracles by their own efforts; only they derive their success from the dynamic fusion of eastern and western knowhow, techniques and social *mores*.

Singapore

Perhaps Singapore never intended to become a tiger. Its name, Singapura, is Sanskrit meaning 'Lion City', but even that description was euphemistic for a port which was notorious as a dreaded pirate haunt and remained a jungled backwater from 1400 to 1800. But better times were soon to come. Singapore is not a tale of two cities, but rather a tale of two men, both remarkable individuals and visionaries to whom the city owes its present prosperity. If you have stayed at Raffles Hotel, you may be aware that it was named after Thomas Raffles, son of an undistinguished sea captain. He joined the East India Company at the age of 14 and in his mid-twenties was posted to Penang where he took the trouble to learn Malay, an initiative which contrasted strongly with the linguistic lethargy of better-educated colonial officials. His common sense and ability to communicate with all manner of people stood him in good stead. He held many important posts as an administrator – at one time he was Governor of Java – but his most significant achievement was the founding of Singapore. A great believer in free trade, he was anxious to establish a British trading post on the China trade route. He selected the site at the mouth of the Singapore river and used his communication skills and personal charm to persuade the local Sultan to grant permission for his base. This was achieved on 6 February 1819 and Raffles set sail for England the next day! He did not return until 1822, by which time it had developed into a booming port with 10,000 inhabitants.

Raffles, who is still greatly honoured in Singapore, was the right man in the right place at the right time. Without any inhibiting social pretensions, he was unusually multicultural for an Englishman and a great humanist to boot. A friend of William Wilberforce, he fought against slavery and piracy and worked unselfishly to bring prosperity (through free trade) to a region which had been hampered by previous Dutch monopolies in the area. Besides Singapore, he founded two other things: London Zoo and The Raffles Institution. It was at this college that the second of the two great men of Singapore was educated – the first Prime Minister, Lee Kuan Yew.

While Raffles fathered the original colony, Lee can truly be described as the father of modern Singapore. His parents were Straits-born Chinese of Hakka origin. After studying at the Raffles Institution, he went to Cambridge where he got a First (with distinction) in law. He set up a law firm in Singapore but became increasingly involved in politics and became Prime Minister in 1959. His tenure lasted 31 years. It was characterised by benevolent dictatorship based on efficiency, honesty, intolerance and an unswerving sense of mission. At the time of its breakaway from the Malaysian Federation, Singapore was considered by many critics to be a non-viable economy on account of its bulging population and complete lack of natural resources. Lee proved them all wrong. He perceived that the teeming inhabitants of Singapore, like those of the Japanese islands, were the country's greatest asset. Unlike the homogeneous Japanese, however, Singaporeans had to be welded into a team. Although all imbued with a desire to create wealth (here they resemble the people of Hong Kong), Singaporeans were of extremely diverse origin – Chinese, Malay, Indian, European and Eurasian. In the space of 25 years, moreover, they had been British subjects, Japanese subjects, Malaysians and Singaporeans. Lee took it on himself to create a sense of national identity, to build a nation, to run it as it should be run. As *The Economist* said, 'Lee ran Singapore like a well-run nursery.' He felt he knew what was best for the country and, showing great political adroitness, he allowed no one to defy him. In his three decades in power he created a powerful economy: Singaporeans who might have wished to oppose or obstruct him were crushed by the sheer weight of the city-state's achievements. In one of his speeches he declaimed, 'The greatest satisfaction in life comes from achievement. To achieve is to be happy... Achievement generates inner or spiritual strength, a strength which grows out of an inner discipline.'

Discipline there certainly was. Chewing gum, littering and (for some time) long haircuts were taboo. Fines were heavy, including ones for failing to flush the toilet. Singaporeans were imbued with Lee's Confucian values – filial respect, duty, moderation and the work ethic were mandatory. Censorship of the media, including television, was strict. Welfare, job stability, good education, cheap housing and affluence were thrust on Lee's citizens. The people of Singapore were going to be happy, whether they liked it or not.

It is only natural that a dictator with such long tenure and puritanical policies should have been heavily criticised. But where would Singapore have been today without him? Ruling even a homogeneous nation is never easy. Lee created a proud sense of nationhood, almost after the Swiss model, among diverse cultural groups who frequently in history have hated and killed each other. It is true that his attempts at state-directed genetic engineering (ostensibly to produce more intelligent offspring) were impractical and unlikely to succeed, but little else he tried failed. The city-state truly bears his own image.

Hong Kong

Hong Kong was acquired by the British government by way of a 99-year lease from China expiring in 1997. The seventh biggest port in the world, its historic function was to serve as an *entrepôt* for trade between China and western countries. In this role it developed successfully up to the Second World War, but when, in 1950–1, the United Nations placed an embargo on trade with China and North Korea during the Korean War, Hong Kong could no longer survive on trade alone. The colony was forced to change from a trading to an industrial economy; rapid developments were effected in garment and textile industries, electronics, shipbuilding, steel rolling, cement manufacture, aluminium extrusion, and a variety of light products from toys and wigs to plastic flowers.

From the very beginning Hong Kong had a clear *raison d'être* – to make money. It certainly succeeded. In the absence of any significant natural resources, Hong Kong's wealth, like that of Singapore, Japan and Korea, is created by its one asset – industrious people. In this case 99 per cent of them are Chinese, about half of whom immigrated from the neighbouring Chinese provinces of Kwangtung and Fukien. The other half are native Hong Kongers. The dominant Chinese dialect in Hong Kong is Cantonese – quite different from Mandarin.

The major non-Chinese elements in the population are from Britain and the Commonwealth, the USA, Portugal and Japan. As in the case of Singapore, the combination of western commercial knowhow and eastern diligence has produced several decades of impressive productivity and prosperity.

The seemingly unending boom has been facilitated by several factors. Although China covets its 'South Gate', the colony has functioned as an excellent point of contact with the West, even at the most critical periods of the Cold War. Trade between Hong Kong and China has flourished. In 1994 China exported $72 billion worth of goods. Of these 45 per cent went to or through Hong Kong which, in turn, sent 30 per cent of its exports to China.

Hong Kong is valuable to China as a conduit for trade, investment and technology transfer. Its existence enables China to trade extensively with two other Tigers – Taiwan and South Korea – without having to compromise her political stance. Western confidence in the ability to continue trading strongly in the area after 1997 is reflected in the rising value of real estate, the frenetic construction in both Hong Kong and Shenzen and the increasing number of foreign companies actually entering Hong Kong. There are more than 500 American trading companies doing business with China from Hong Kong and Kowloon.

Hong Kong is many things that Singapore is not, and vice versa. Both Tigers take gold medals for industriousness, tenacity, risk taking and efficiency. Both have made their fortunes by shrewdly combining strengths from East and West. Both populations are predominantly Chinese, who have demonstrated their infinite potential and talent, given the right conditions for development. After that the comparison becomes more of a striking contrast.

Hong Kong has expensive housing, high salaries and job mobility, little red tape, no inhibitions and people who live from deal to deal. Singapore, in contrast, has cheap housing, moderate salaries and job stability, strict regulations, decorum and long-term planning. Opinions vary, among both westerners and Orientals, about which is the better place to live and work. Singapore impresses with its discipline, racial tolerance and successful multiculturalism. Westerners frown on the direct control exercised by parliament over 600 companies, but admire the overall efficiency and honesty of conduct. Hong Kong dazzles you with sheer, unbridled energy, single-mindedness and pluralism. It is interesting to note that, although Hong Kong is 99 percent Chinese, Singapore has generally enjoyed better relations with China than the colony has. China finds pluralism hard to understand; Singapore speaks with one voice – a more traditional oriental practice. Moreover, the voice is in Mandarin, better accepted in Beijing than singsong Cantonese!

There is naturally a questionmark against Hong Kong's future. The reincorporation of a 99-year-old British colony into a motherland possessing 5000 years of unbroken heritage is truly a collision of cultures, in spite of racial commonalities. Communication styles and listening patterns are far apart (see Figures 75 and 76).

People's Republic of China

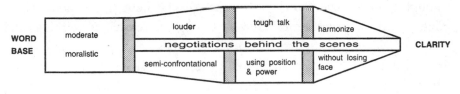

Hong Kong

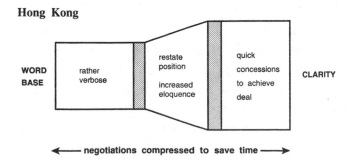

Figure 68   Communication patterns

People's Republic of China   **Hong Kong**

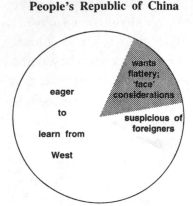

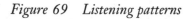

Figure 69   Listening patterns

Hong Kong, with entrepreneurism in its blood, sense of urgency, driving always in the fast lane, stands in close comparison to the bustling USA. It remains to be seen what the cultural collision with the bureaucratic motherland will produce.

Japanese

Enough has been said about the Chinese and Japanese in this book. One might finish, in discussing differences among the Asians, in pointing out that the Japanese are often seen by other orientals as being 'more different' or more out on a limb, than anyone else. Certainly the Japanese do not hesitate to emphasise and value their own uniqueness – probably enhanced by their 250 years of international isolation. This Japanese specificity or particularity does not help them in their own dealings with foreigners. Whereas in most Asian countries it is quite normal to use English textbooks at universities, in Japan nearly all foreign books are translated. Korean, Thai and Chinese business people from Hong Kong and Taiwan send their children to overseas universities for protracted periods, so they can familiarise themselves with the western mind. Japanese, it is true, are sent abroad at a later stage (often after entering a company's service) but on their return to Japan their foreign experience is often unutilised or even resented.

The massive commercial cross-ownership and intricate bilateral trade between Japan and the USA make disengagement from each other so difficult and costly as to be almost impossible. The fact remains that on the psychological and cultural planes the Americans and Japanese still fail to understand and appreciate each other's behaviour. As a consequence of their growing involvement with Europe, the Japanese are in the process of realising that they share a good number of national traits with certain European peoples. These include British conservatism and reserve, German thoroughness, Danish and Swedish proclivity to consensus and teamwork, and Finnish shyness and use of silence. Japan, the most insular of Asian countries, will tend in the European sphere to lean more and more towards calm, stable, manufacture-minded, monarchistic, insular Britain, already chosen as her main base inside the potentially rich European Union.

Epilogue

ACHIEVING EMPATHY

Changing perspectives in international management strategy

THE POLITICAL CHANGES IN EUROPE AND OTHER PARTS OF THE WORLD IN the last few years have been quite startling in their suddenness and dimensions. The rapid *volte face* in Czechoslovakia, Romania and for former East Germany, the increasing self-confidence visible in Hungary and Poland, the incredible rapprochement between the USA and Russia, the regaining of independence in the Baltic republics, are all signs of a global transformation in ideological alignments and longstanding alliances.

But these political and military developments are only symptoms of much more deeply rooted changes, over which politicians, governments and international organisations have little or no control. Forces are at work beyond anything we have previously had to deal with. The Industrial Revolution had a tremendous impact on society, but it never quite ran away with us. One invention led to another and the capitalist system organised the finance, labour and production techniques to deal with it. The Information Technology Revolution has left us all floundering. Too much information is available, at too great a speed, from too many sources.

Modern business has faster access to more information than ever before, but by the time it has been sifted and analysed, codified, processed and entered into the system, by the time managers and board members have decided on its impact and implementation, it is often already obsolete.

Furthermore, information management systems are frequently wrong. Information coming from news broadcasts, TV, the press, even news agencies, are more often than not biased or at least flavoured by the source. People at the top of management don't really know where they are going, don't get the information on time, face contradictions such as simultaneous centralisation and decentralisation, teamwork versus initiative, consensus versus speed of decision, etc.

Besides the irreversible changes being brought about by the information explosion and computer dictatorship, other tides which sweep us helplessly along are the incredible advances in medicine, the greenhouse effect and the changes in climate, the unstoppable march of science, the killing off of hundreds of species, the drive for ecological awareness, the collapse of communism and the rising strength of Islam. Add to these factors the reunification and burgeoning power of Germany, the prospect of a Pacific Basin economic club for the twenty-first century, the elimination of most small, middle and even big companies by the multinational giants, a few jokers in the pack like the export powerhouses of Korea, Taiwan and Singapore – and it is no wonder that planning a global strategy is beyond the abilities of the great majority of managers and business leaders today.

Moreover, leading management consultants tell us that the bigger the company, the more difficult the internal and external communication, the more cumbersome the decision making, the more chaotic the organisation. Nevertheless, the vaster the conglomerate, the bigger its domestic market, the greater seems its need to expand, export and establish itself abroad. The latter part of the twentieth century has seen takeovers, mergers and acquisitions on a hitherto unimaginable scale and the trend is for even large national companies to merge or become insignificant. Large banks have begun to group themselves in twos and threes. Sanwa and Dai-Ichi Kangyo became the two largest banks in the world through amalgamation.

Ford bought Jaguar, Toyota and Nissan manufacture heavily in Britain, Deutsche Bank has a large stake in Mercedes, IVECO is a merger of the Fiat, Magirus-Deutz and Unic truck companies, AT&T tried to work with Olivetti, even Finland's Kone, Nokia and Huhtumäki have become international conglomerates.

How well are companies prepared for global integration? If the solution is cultural synergy, do we know how to achieve it? What is the route to take?

The interdependence of nations also becomes clearer every day. Leaders are at the centre of an on-going dialogue to achieve mutual security, lessening of tension and confrontation, control of nuclear threat and all-round raising of living standards.

At the business level, global interdependence is emerging fast. The European Union is trying to create a market equal in size to that of the USA. Japan depends on the Middle East for oil and on the USA to buy its products. Russia needs American and Argentinian grain. Countries such as Italy, Britain and Korea, with few natural resources, depend on manufacturing and exports for survival. Small nations such as Finland, Denmark and Singapore develop niche industries with high quality products to assure they maintain the high standard of living they have already achieved. Countries not belonging to one of the large economic blocs hunt desperately around to find one. Geographically isolated countries such as New Zealand and Australia have an ever-increasing problem.

In terms of regional cooperation, there can be no better example than the collaboration and goodwill evident in the Nordic area, where Scandinavian Swedes, Danes, Norwegians and Icelanders enjoy relatively untroubled relations and mutual benefits with Altaic Finns. These peoples often look askance at each other, but there is little doubt that the over-riding factor in arrangements between Scandinavians and Finns is common sense. The rest of Europe would do well to study its merits!

Europeans form a large, fascinating, talented, original family. Unfortunately, like real families, they have their ups and downs, moods, disputes, loves and hates. Yet although impetuous and quarrelsome, this family can be quite brilliant. The calm, disciplined Nordics have demonstrated what regional cohesion can do. British, Dutch and Germans are equally tranquil and organised, neither are they incapable of cooperation. The French have vision, the Italians and Spaniards flair and, once harnessed, great energy. Romania, Poland and the Ukraine have huge agricultural potential. Czechs and Hungarians are knowledgeable, inventive and strikingly capable.

There can be no accurate assessment of the ultimate size, composition or political nature of the European Union. Its realisation in terms of economic, monetary, political, military and cultural integration will, of necessity, be slow, frustrating and painful. One tends to forget that the USA, homogeneous and powerful as it is now, took nearly 150 years to emerge as a unified, purposeful power – and they all speak the same language!

But cohesive or not, Europe is there – and it has several cards to play. First, it is big. European Russia cannot be excluded indefinitely from the Union: this presupposes a market of 750 million people. It is also a sizeable workforce. Europeans are educated: 17 of the world's 23 most literate countries are in Europe. The USA and Japan have the world's two biggest economies, but Europe claims 6 out of the top 10. As far as GDP per head and purchasing power are concerned, European countries have 14 places in the top 20. National debt is very low (6 places in the top 40, 5 of these being ex-communist countries).

The USA and Japan, currently undisputed leaders in production and finance, take Europe very seriously. Both countries have invested heavily in the continent and created strong bases inside the Single Market. London is the home of the world's most sophisticated financial institutions. Rotterdam is the biggest port. German and Swiss machinery and precision instruments are second to none.

However, if we are considering a management model for the twenty-first century, we cannot ignore Japanese systems. The Japanese people do not cast themselves in the role of teachers or mentors, but in an age when our own analysts advocate teamwork before individualism, collaboration and amalgamation before competition, we are seeing a shift from western to eastern culture. It could just be that the Asian model fits the era. The current success of Japan, Korea, Taiwan, Singapore, Hong Kong and China would suggest this. Indonesians, Malaysians and Thais follow in their wake. It is interesting to note that the Japanese (certainly orderly, normative, disciplined people) accept and believe that a disorderly, fast-changing scenario lies ahead of us which will have to be managed.

All is not negative. The world labours under threat of warfare, political dissension, inequality of wealth, uncertainty of the future, lack of morality, complexity of change; but on the plus side we have growing opportunities for social justice, world peace and growth for all. Many new technologies are widely available, easier mobilisation of labour is developing, and some elements of the new generation show moral strength, desire for peace and ecological awareness.

How do we translate good ideas into action? Study of good models shows us that teamwork and people training make an enormous difference, e.g. a pleasant working environment is ubiquitous in Scandinavia. Managers must have multinational skills. They will have to work shoulder to shoulder with many nationalities in the global village of the twenty-first century. They must understand them, speak to them, cooperate with them, handle them, not lose out to them, yet like and praise them. These are our cultural challenges.

The multicultural executive

In this book we have discussed the phenomenon of **cultural myopia** – how ethnocentrism blinds us to the salient features of our own cultural make-up, while making us see other cultures as deviations from the correct. For some powerful societies, confident of their historical success or brilliance (USA, France), it is a short leap from cultural myopia to **cultural imperialism**. At the height of their power, Americans, British, French and Spanish conquerors did not hesitate to set up policies and regulations which were congruent with their own cultural values and not with those of their 'subjects'. Economic imperialism in our present era has hardly lessened this tendency, further complicated by the desire of multinational companies to impose strong (global) corporate cultures.

We have stated earlier that we shall never fully understand the 'others', particularly if the separating factors of language, geography and ideology have been distant. The best we can hope for is to acquire an orientation that enables us to set off in a certain direction to lessen the communication gap between ourselves and our partner. All of us are wrapped up in prejudice – subject to a **natural dynamic of bias**. We cannot proceed to an evaluation or judgement of another without starting with an acute sharpening of our own self-awareness.

A behavioural spectrum

All of us have our place on a complicated spectrum of comportment with dizzying extremes of rudeness and courtesy, violence and gentleness, humility and conceit, and dozens of other behavioural dimensions. We perceive and judge others from the point in the spectrum where we stand rooted. We have a relative, not complete, view. If Swedes look at others through blue-and-yellow spectacles, they will fail to see them or their manners as they really are. They will suspect that all Italians are neurotic poseurs and see the individualistic Americans as lacking in respect for the beloved Swedish consensus. Americans will sees Japanese with 'shifty' eyes, while the same Japanese considers Spaniards rude because they constantly 'stare'. The route to self-understanding is to question many of those values which were pumped into you when you were young. Is it always wise for a Finn or a Brit to keep a stiff upper lip? What is wrong with a little Italian feeling? Would not Germans and Japanese – deadly serious at meetings – improve a little if they joked like the Americans? Can't the French, obsessed by logic, feel the power of Japanese intuition or the American hunch? What is special about Spanish honour? Why is silence necessarily golden? If one can't ask a friend (or relation) to do one a business favour, what are friends and relations for?

Once one realises that many of one's cherished values or core beliefs were drummed into us by a biased community which possibly represents only a very small percentage of international opinion, presenting a very limited or blinkered world view, one is more likely to accept the opinions and manners of others as being at least equally valid, if not occasionally superior.

Eliminating one's own barriers

If one is able to see oneself or one's culture from the outside and think more objectively as a consequence, one has a good chance of clearing away certain cultural barriers which would have impeded access to others' thoughts or personalities. Finns must shed their excessive shyness, their bumbling modesty and their distrust of fast talkers. The Japanese must discard their ultra-politeness if the end result is only a fog of incomprehension. The French must rid themselves of their sense of intellectual superiority, and the Germans must realise that their cult of efficiency is not the only one around and may indeed have counter-productive overtones. Americans must occasionally see themselves as an insensitive, dollar-minded pragmatists who erect barriers of misunderstanding, often through well-meant bluntness or excessive informality. As people are shocked when they see themselves on video playing golf or tennis ('God, do I look like that?'), they may see from intercultural training that they are equally gauche or unacceptable in others' eyes.

Empathy

Better self-evaluation and elimination of one's principal cultural idiosyncrasies leads one to the final step towards achieving harmony – that of developing empathy with the other side. **Sympathy** is based on cultural similarities – Swede to Dane, Italian to Spaniard. **Empathy** is based on accepting differences and building on these in a positive manner. The Japanese may come to accept that American directness is, after all, honest. The American may perceive that exaggerated Japanese courtesy is, after all, better than hostility. If the Italian wants to talk 90 per cent of the time with a Finn, who is anyway content to be silent (in Finland silence is fun), then are they not both happy and doing what they do best? Contrasting debating styles can accommodate each other if common goals are clearly seen.

Weapons for empathy are:

+ tact
+ humour
+ sensitivity
+ flexibility
+ compromise
+ politeness
+ calm
+ warmth
+ patience
+ preparedness for discussion
+ will to clarify objectives
+ observation of other side's protocol
+ care to avoid irritants
+ careful listening
+ respect of confidentiality
+ inspiration of trust
+ above all, constantly trying to see things from the other's (cultural) point of view

This is the profile of the international negotiator. Small side effects, such as eye-contact, posture, personal space and etiquette are all important, but the over-riding factor is the ability to decipher what is basic human nature (which can be trusted by all) and which learned cultural habits will cause variation in human behaviour and therefore must be recognised, accepted and adapted to.

The very act of adaptation, however, is fraught with difficulties. Quiet, introverted Swedes and Finns are reluctant to emerge from their shell of reticence to indulge in an evening's soul-baring with loquacious Italians. They feel that too much unwonted exuberance will lead to loss of identity. Yet it is easier for the introvert to build bridges towards the extrovert than it is the other way round, for the Nordic thought pattern remains opaque to Mediterranean people.

Culture is designed for success and survival – if we are alive, healthy and solvent, we have compelling reasons to believe in our particular formula. Temporary setbacks or, in certain cases, shocking failures, can undermine this confidence. The humiliating defeat of Japan in 1946 led to many Japanese, especially the youth, imitating various aspects of American culture. But certain features of Japanese behaviour could not be subject to adaptation. In Japan, men do not report to women, whatever system of administration the Americans installed.

How much should we try to change others, if we truly believe that our culture is superior? A safe answer is that we should not, thereby escaping the charge of cultural imperialism. But moral conflicts can arise. If we live in a culture where wife beating is the norm, do we advise, accept or adapt?

It is important that we examine closely the nature of conflicts. Besides the clearly moral type mentioned above, other real conflicts arise from deeply rooted philosophical, religious or even political convictions. Thus Islamic beliefs with regard to alcohol, pork and the status of women, or Chinese attitudes to basic inequalities in humans, will continue to clash with what we perceive as more tolerant and humanitarian western attitudes. Such core beliefs are so well buttressed in their respective societies that we are well advised not to persist in challenging them, as changes can only come from within. In fact it is not often that we try.

Another type of clash is **pseudo-conflict,** that is to say that we feel irritated, bemused or even offended by some aspect of another's behaviour and proceed to condemn it (strongly or mildly) without really attempting to see it in perspective. We see *mañana* mentality, Swiss pedantry and the assumed Asian smile as essentially negative, instead of trying to put these qualities into an understandable framework of cultural behaviour. Pseudo-conflict equates with misunderstanding, or over-fondness for the stereotype.

We cannot exist without stereotyping – it gives us points of reference in determining our behaviour towards strangers. The mind tends to simplify complex feelings and attitudes, including our own. For intercultural understanding we must learn to manage stereotypes, that is, to maximise and appreciate the positive values we perceive, minimise and laugh off (if we can) what we see as conflicting or negative. It is possible to do more accurate stereotyping, e.g. Swedes are often cold and formal, but they conceal, under the diffident exterior, a kind of desperation to prove their warmth and loyalty. Germans often shock with blunt, direct criticism, but in fact they believe they do it in your interest – they are improving your behaviour! We tend towards excessive stereotyping when we are under **stress.** Stress also reinforces our own cultural characteristics, so a vicious circle develops. Stressful conflict during meetings causes Americans to speak louder, South Americans to gesticulate, Japanese to clam up, Germans to bridle in righteousness and French to restate their position with icy logic. Without stress, Americans are friendly and generous, South Americans affectionate, Japanese courteous, Germans fair and French exuding charm.

Self-criticism, avoidance of irritants and stress, more accurate assessment of the individual, tact, tolerance, adaptation without sacrificing one's integrity, substantial study of our partner's culture, history and language – all these are resources to be drawn on when cultures collide.

We may enrich our own existence by absorbing certain features of other cultures – change them by our own efforts we will not. History has so far allowed cultures that have not been militarily over-run to prosper, survive, languish or atrophy at their own sedate rate of persistence or decline. It remains to be seen if the new forces represented by galloping information technology, rapid globalisation of business and ferociously competing giant countries and economies will result in the devastation of minor or weakened cultures which show inability to adapt to the truly dynamic changes foreseeable in the twenty-first century.

Bibliography

Axtell, Roger E. ed. (1985) *Do's and Taboos Around the World*, compiled by the Parker Pen Company.

Barzini, Luigi (1964) *The Italians*, London: Hamish Hamilton.

Berry, Michael (1992) *Know Theyself and the Other Fellow Too: Strategies for Effective Cross-Cultural Communication*, Institute for European Studies.

Bradnock, Robert and Roma eds (1995) *India Handbook*, with Sri Lanka, Bhutan and The Maldives, Bath: Trade & Travel Publications.

Condon, John C (1985) *Communicating with the Mexicans*, Yarmouth, ME: Intercultural Press.

Dahl, Øyvind, *Malagasy and Other Time Concepts and Some Consequences for Communication*, Centre for Intercultural Communication.

Fieg, John Paul (1989) *A Common Core: Thais and Americans*, Yarmouth, ME: Intercultural Press.

Fisher, Glen (1980) *International Negotiation: A Cross-Cultural Perspective*, Yarmouth, ME: Intercultural Press.

Furnham, Adrian and Bochner, Stephen (1986) *Culture Shock: Psychological Reactions to Unfamiliar Environments*, Methuen.

Gochenour, Theodore (1990) *Considering Filipinos*, Yarmouth, ME: Intercultural Press.

Hall, Edward T. and Reed Hall, Mildred (1983) *Hidden Differences, Studies in International Communication: How to Communicate with the Germans*, Hamburg: Stern Magazine/Gruner & Jahr.

Hall, Edward T. and Reed Hall, Mildred (1990) *Understanding Cultural Differences: Germans, French and Americans*, Yarmouth, ME: Intercultural Press.

Hampden-Turner, Charles and Trompenaars, Fons (1993) *The Seven Cultures of Capitalism: Value Systems for Creating Wealth in the United States, Britain, Japan, Germany, France, Sweden and The Netherlands*,

New York: Doubleday.

Harris, Philip R and Moran, Robert T (1979) *Managing Cultural Differences: High-Performance Strategies for Today's Global Manager*, Houston: Gulf.

Hendry, Joy (1993) *Wrapping Culture: Politeness, Presentation, and Power in Japan and Other Societies*, Oxford: Clarendon Press.

Hofstede, Geert (1980) *Culture's Consequences: International Differences in Work-Related Values*, Newbury Park, CA: Sage.

Hofstede, Geert (1991) *Cultures and Organizations: Software of the Mind, Intercultural Cooperation and its Importance for Survival*, Maidenhead: McGraw-Hill.

Holden, Nigel J. (1992) *Management, Language and Eurocommunication, 1992 and Beyond*, Institute for European Studies.

Hu, Wenzhong and Grove, Cornelius, L. (1991) *Encountering the Chinese: A Guide for Americans*, Yarmouth, ME: Intercultural Press.

James, Clive (1991) *Brrm! Brrm! or The Man from Japan or Perfume at Anchorage*, London: Pan.

Kawasaki, Ichiro (1969) *Japan Unmasked*, Rutland, Vermont/Tokyo: Charles E. Tuttle.

Kulke, Hermann and Rothermund, Dietmar (1986) *A History of India*, Croom Helm Australia.

Kusy, Frank (1987) *Cadogan Guides – India: Kathmandu Valley–Nepal*, Old Saybrook, CT: Globe Pequot Press.

Lanier, Alison R. (1990) *The Rising Sun on Main Street: Working with the Japanese*, Morrisville, PA: International Information Associates.

Lehtonen, Jaakko (1990) *Kultur, Språk och Kommunikation*, University of Jyväskylä Press.

Lewis, Richard D. (1993) *Finland, Cultural Lone Wolf*, Otava.

Mole, John (1995) *Mind Your Manners: Managing Business Cultures in Europe*, London: Nicholas Brealey.

Morris, Desmond (1985) *Bodywatching, A Field Guide on the Human Species*, London: Jonathan Cape.

Nurmi, Raimo (1986) *A Cross Cultural Note on Australian and Finnish Values*, Deakin University.

Nurmi, Raimo (1989) *Management in Finland*, Turku Commercial High School.

Nydell, Margaret K. (1987) *Understanding Arabs: A Guide for Westerners*, Yarmouth, ME: Intercultural Press.

Peers, Allison E. (1948) *Spain: A Companion to Spanish Studies*, London: Methuen.

Phillips-Martinsson, Jean (1991) *Swedes as Others See Them: Facts, Myths or a Communication Complex?* Lund: Studentlitteratur.

Rearwin, David (1991) *The Asia Business Book*, Yarmouth, ME: Intercultural Press.

Reischauer, Edwin O. (1977) *The Japanese*, Cambridge, MA: Belknap Press.

Richmond, Yale (1992) *From Nyet to Da: Understanding the Russians*, Yarmouth, ME: Intercultural Press.

Sapir, Edward (1966) *Culture, Language and Personality, Selected Essays*, Berkeley and Los Angeles: University of California Press.

Sinclair, Kevin with Wong Po-yee, Iris (1991) *Culture Shock! China*, London: Kuperard.

Stewart, Edward C. and Bennett, Milton J. (1991) *American Cultural Patterns: A Cross-Cultural Perspective*, Yarmouth, ME: Intercultural Press.

Storti, Craig (1989) *The Art of Crossing Cultures*, Yarmouth, ME: Intercultural Press.

Tan, Terry (1992) *Culture Shock! Britain*, London: Kuperard.

Trend, J.B. (1957) *Nations of the Modern World: Portugal*, London: Ernest Benn.

Trompenaars, Fons (1993) *Riding the Waves of Culture: Understanding Cultural Diversity in Business*, London: Nicholas Brealey.

Wanning, Esther (1991) *Culture Shock! USA*, London: Kuperard.

Whorf, Benjamin Lee (1956) *Language, Thought and Reality*, Cambridge, MA: Massachusetts Institute of Technology Press.

Glossary

atavistic (atavism)   reappearance in a person of a characteristic which has not been seen for generations

Buddhism   a religion of east and central Asia growing out of the teachings of Buddha, that one must become free of human desires in order to escape from suffering

cadres   an inner group of highly trained and active people in a particular group (company, army, etc.) (French)

Cartesian   relating to René Descartes, French philosopher and mathematician

chauvinism   very great and often unthinking admiration for one's country; proud and unreasonable belief that one's country is better than all others

collective programming   the way a particular group of people or nationalities is trained from a very early age to internalise the behaviour and attitudes of the group

communication gap   lack of understanding of people of other cultures, because of differences in language, cultural attitudes, etc.

compartmentalize projects   concentrate single-mindedly on a project, not allowing it to be influenced by other goals or activities

complete action chains   finish one task completely before commencing another one

complete human transactions   finish all one's business with a particular individual before going on to another task

Confucianism   a Chinese way of thought which teaches that one should be loyal to one's family, friends and rulers, and treat others as one would like to be treated, developed from the ideas of Confucius

context centred   depending on a situation

core beliefs   basic concepts of a national group which have been learned and internalised from an early age

cross-culture	comparison of beliefs, attitudes etc. of different cultural groups or nationalities
cultural display, event	something we do or say which reveals our core beliefs (cultural attitudes) to people of other cultures
cultural imperialism	attempt to impose the tenets of one's culture on others
cultural myopia	inability to see another culture's points of view
'cultural spectacles'	the way our own core beliefs influence how we view other cultures
culture	the customs, beliefs, art and all the other products of human thought made by a particular group of people at a particular time
culture shock	the feeling of shock or of being disorientated which someone has when they experience a different and unfamiliar culture
cyclic time	recurring events
danwei	work unit (Chinese)
data-oriented (culture)	a culture whose people gather information mainly through print and database sources
deviants	people who are different in moral or social standards from what is considered normal
dialogue-oriented (culture)	a culture whose people gather information through direct contact with other people
double truth	two ways of looking at things: the immediate reality and the poetic whole
dusha	the Russian soul (Russian)
école normale superiéure	prestigious tertiary level institute of learning in France specialising in various areas of pedagogy, leading to a career in higher education of research (French)
empathy	the ability to imagine oneself in the position of another person and so to share and understand that person's feelings
extrovert	a person who likes to spend time in activities with other people rather than being quiet and alone
faux pas	social mistake in words or behaviour (French)
feng shui	wind-and-water superstition (Chinese)
force majeure	an event beyond one's control (French)
gaffe	an unintentional social mistake (French)
GDP	gross domestic product
giri	duty (Japanese)
guanxi	the linking of two people in a relationship of mutual dependence (Chinese)
hara kiri	ritual suicide using a sword to cut open one's stomach, formerly practised by Japanese Samurai to avoid dishonour

hautes écoles	tertiary level education in France in specialised areas, such as commerce, engineering etc. (French)
high context (culture)	networking, dialogue-oriented culture
honorific expression	indicating respect for the person being addressed, especially in Oriental languages
horizon (cultural)	one's world view (limited)
human mental programming	the practice of instilling one's beliefs in the young under one's responsibility (or any 'captive' audience)
inscrutable	decribes people whose meaning or way of thinking is not at all clear, mysterious
introvert	concerning oneself with one's own thoughts rather than sharing activities with others
Islam	the Muslim religion started by Mohammed
itadakimasu	literally: I am receiving (Japanese) – similar to *bon appétit*
kaisha	company, firm (Japanese)
karma	the force produced by a person's actions in life which will influence him or her later or in future lives
kibun	saving face (Korean)
lagom	spirit of moderation in all things (Swedish)
language mould	the way our language channels or moulds our thoughts
language of management	how certain management styles are facilitated by the nature of the language of the manager and the group being managed
linear time	a concept of time as a 'line' of sequential events with the past behind us and the future in front
linear-active (culture)	a culture whose people are task-oriented, highly organised planners, preferring to do one thing at a time in the sequence shown in their diary
listening (culture)	a culture whose people listen well, never interrupt and show great deference to others' opinions; they do not precipitate improvident action, allowing ideas to mature
low context (culture)	data-oriented culture, few oral contacts
meritocracy	a social system which gives the highest positions to those with the most ability
messianic	belief that one has an important mission
monochronic (culture)	a culture dominated by precision and propriety, preferring to concentrate on doing one thing at a time
mores	the moral customs of a particular group
'muddling through'	achieving one's goal without proper planning
multi-active (culture)	a culture whose people tend to do many things at once, often in an unplanned order, usually people oriented, extrovert.

networking	the establishing of professional connections with the aim of sharing information, advice or support
notions	the perception by a cultural group of certain basic concepts
on	obligation (Japanese)
Ordnung	order (German)
polychronic	someone who likes to do many things at once, often without precise planning
power distance	a measure of the interpersonal power of influence between superior and subordinate as perceived by the latter, often determined by the national culture
pundonor	honour, dignity (Spanish)
reactive (culture)	a culture whose people rarely initiate action or discussion, preferring first to listen to and establish the other's position, then react to it and formulate their own
ringi-sho	decision making through consensus (Japanese)
saudades	nostalgia, sentimentality (Portuguese)
sisu	perseverance, stamina (Finnish)
skål	cheers! to your health! (Swedish)
space bubble	the personal space which an individual dislikes being encroached on
stereotyping	fixing a set of ideas about what a particular type of person or nationality is like, which is (wrongly) believed to be true in all cases
task orientation	giving instructions or directives to colleagues or subordinates
tatami	straw floor mat, the number of which is often used to denote the size of a room in Japan
tenets	principles, beliefs
USP	unique selling point
values	standards or principles, ideas about the importance of certain qualities, especially those accepted by a particular group
Volkswirtschafts- hochschule	tertiary level education in Germany in the area of economics and commerce (German)
web society	an interdependent society excelling in networking
Weltanschauung	world view (German)
Weltschmerz	'world pain', i.e. depressed state (German)

Index

ABB, 92
advertising, 5, 105–7
  in Germany, 210
Aerospatiale, 74
America
  concepts of leadership, 77–9
  concepts of organisation, 77–9
  concepts of status, 77–9
American English, language of management, 108–9
Americans, dealing with, 167–71
Apple, 3
Arab countries, 251
  cultural divergences, 251–3
Arabic, language of management, 112
Arabs
  business meeting, 255
  family structure, 254
  mealtimes, 254
  oaths, 255
  talking business with, 254
Asians
  courtesy, 288
  differences among, 294
  harmony, 291–2
  patience, 288–91
  pragmatism, 292–3
  what they have in common, 287–8
AT&T, 308
Australians, 179–80

communicating with, 182–3
geographical location and climatic conditions, 183–4
language, 180–2

barriers, eliminating, 312
BBC, 38
behaviour
  Chinese ethical, 275–6
  cocktail parties, 150–1
  codes of, 142–3
  customs, 147
  eating hours, 145
  how many courses, 146–7
  main courses, 148–50
  protocol, 145–6
  signal to start eating, 146
  sincerity, 143
  starters, 148
  table manners, 144
behavioural spectrum, 311–2
body language, 5, 6
  different types of, 135–40
  eyes, 136
  feet, 139
  hands, 138
  in business, 139–40
  legs, 139
  mouth, 137
  multi-actives, 135

body language (cont.)
  negotiation, 134
  nose and ears, 137
  shoulders, 138
brainwashing, 25
Britain, 172–5
  concepts of leadership, 75–7
  concepts of organisation, 75–7
  concepts of status, 75–7
British English, language of manage-
    ment, 109–10
British
  how to handle, 175–8
  linguistic arrogance, 76
  management style, 76
  managers, 75
  task orientation, 77
Buddhism, 20, 81
  concept of leadership, 82
  culture, 58
building on strengths, 91
business
  climate and practices, Japanese,
    259–60
  Confucianism in, 82
  globalisation of, 11
  humour in, 22–4
  meetings with Arabs, 255
  talking with Arabs, 255
  travel, 115
  with Japanese, 270–2

changing perspectives of management,
    5
chauvinism, 29–30
China, 273–9
  and the twenty–first century, 283–4
Chinese
  behaviour at meetings, 280–2
  core beliefs, 279–80
  dealing with, 284

ethical behaviour, 275–6
etiquette, 282–3
extended family, 278
gift giving, 283
humility, 283
time, 59–60
values, 275
cocktail parties, 8
  embassies, 153
  leaving, 153
  personal space, 152
  rules for, 150–1
  small talk, 151
  what to drink, 152
collective
  leadership, 66–70
  programming, 25–6
common sense, 12
communication
  gap, 98–9
  listening, 102–5
  patterns, 99–102
compromise, in negotiation, 128–9
Confucianism, 20, 21, 81, 82, 275, 276
  in business, 82
contracts, ethics in, 11, 126–7
corporate culture, 4
cross–cultural
  bias, 119
  problems, 9
  programmes, 14
  seminars, 32, 76
  training, 4, 14
cultural
  attitudes, 29
  differences, international business, 2
  display, 29
  divergences, Arab countries, 251–3
  diversity, 2, 9
  event, 29
  group, 66, 68

cultural (cont.)
  roots of organisation, 65
culture, definition, 25
culture shock, 2, 26–9
  Finland, 197–8
cultures,
  Buddhist, 58
  data–oriented, 45–8
  dialogue–oriented, 45–8
  linear–active, 36–41, 62
  linear–oriented, 64
  listening, 48–9
  multi–active, 36–41
  reactive, 42–45
customs, codes of behaviour, 147
cyclic time, 57–9, 62

Dassault, 74
data–oriented cultures, 45–8
dealing with
  Americans, 167–71
  British, 175–8
  Chinese, 284
  Russians, 235–8
  Swedes, 249–50
decision making, 124–5
  Sweden, 245–7
despotic leadership, 68
Deutsche Bank, 308
dialogue–oriented cultures, 45–8
different
  languages, 8
  worlds, 8, 17–18
Dunbar, Professor Robin, 13

East, the
  concepts of leadership, 81–4
  concepts of organisation, 81–4
  concepts of status, 81–4
eating hours, 145
Elf Aquitaine, 74

eliminating barriers, 312
embassies, cocktail parties, 153
empathy, 313–5
  weapons for, 313–5
ethics
  contracts, 11, 126–7
  negotiation, 125–6
  propriety, 127–8
etiquette, Chinese, 282–3

family culture, 4
Fiat, 308
Fieg, John Paul, 6, 58
Filipinos, 296
Finland, 189–90
  culture shock, 197–8
  leadership roles, 198
Finnish
  character, 190–1
  pessimism and paradox, 191–2
  qualities, 193
  strengths, 194–5
  weakness, 195–7
Finns
  how to approach, 199–201
  managing, 200
Ford, 308
Framatome, 74
France, 202–5
  concepts of leadership, 73–5
  concepts of organisation 73–5
  concepts of status, 73–5
French
  as others see them, 206–8
  characteristics, 203–4
  language of management, 111–12
  leaders, 73
  management style, 73
  manager's role in society, 74
  oratorical style, 73

gender, cultural divide, 4
German
  characteristics, 210–11
  language of management, 107–9
  management, 71
Germans
  as seen by others, 213–18
  working with, 71–2
Germany, 209–12
  advertising in, 210
  concepts of leadership, 70–2
  concepts of organisation, 70–2
  concepts of status, 70–2
gift giving, and the Chinese, 283
global interdependence, 309
globalisation of business, 11
gossip, 12
groups
  cultural, 66, 68
  life in, 83
  societal training, 66

Hendry, Joy, 6, 60, 61
Hofstede, Geert, 6, 247
Hong Kong, 298–9, 301–4
Huhtumäki, 308
humility, of Chinese, 283
humour
  across frontiers, 20–2
  in business, 22–4

IBM, 3, 92
illegalities, 31–4
immigration laws, 31
India and South–east Asia, 285–7
Indians, 296–7
  negotiating style, 297–8
individual leadership, 66–70
Indonesia, 295
integrated international team, setting
  up, 89–90

internalised thought, 18
international
  negotiation management, changing
  perspectives in, 307–11
  negotiation scene, 6
  negotiation, solutions, 140–1
  negotiator, profile of, 313–4
  teams, 5
internationalisation programmes, 14
Islamic concept of leadership, 82
Italian
  company communication, 221
  flexibility in business, 220
  negotiators, 222
Italians
  and money, 221
  at meetings, 221
  communication style, 220
  concept of time, 220
Italy, 219–22
IVECO, 308

Jaguar, 308
Japan
  company sacredness, 263
  isolation, 257
  web society, 257
Japanese, 304–5
  as seen by others, 267
  business climate and practices, 259–60
  complexes, 265
  doing business with, 270–2
  language, 258–0
  language barriers, 266
  language, management of, 110–11
  losing face, 260
  negotiating characteristics, 261–3
  politeness, 260–1
  time, 60–61
  translators, 265
  success, 264

Kone, 308
Koreans, 294–5

language
  Japanese, 258–9
  Japanese barriers, 266
  negotiations, 131
  of management, 5
  strait–jacket, 16–17
  use of, 94–98
languages, different, 8
Latins
  concepts of leadership 80–1
  concepts of organisation 80–1
  concepts of status, 80–81
leaders
  French, 73
  reactive cultures, 68
  status of, 68
leadership, 5
  collective, 66–70
  despotic, 68
  individual, 66–70
  networking, 68
  roles, Finland, 198
  task orientation, 68
leadership, concepts of
  America, 77–9
  Britain, 75–7
  Buddhist, 82
  East, the, 81–4
  France, 73–5
  Germany, 70–2
  Islamic countries, 82
  Latins, 80–81
  Sweden, 80
Lee Kuan Yew, 300–1
legalities, 31–34
life in a group, 83
linear time, 52–5, 62
linear–active cultures, 5, 36–41, 62

  managers in, 68
linear–oriented cultures, 64
linguistic arrogance, British, 76
listening
  cultures, 48–9
  habits, 5, 102–5
logic, 130–1

Magirus–Deutz, 308
Malaysia, 295
management
  British style, 76
  changing perspectives of, 5
  concept of, Sweden, 80
  French, 73
  German, 71
  international, 307–11
  Latin sytle, 80
  Swedish, 245–7
management, language of, 5, 107
  American English, 108–9
  Arabic, 112
  British English, 109–10
  French, 111–12
  German, 107–9
  Japanese, 110–11
  Russian, 113
  Spanish, 114
  Swedish, 113
managers
  British, 75
  linear–active cultures, 68
  multi–active, 68
  Swedish, 247
manners, 5
  gift giving, 160
  in society, 159–62
  marketing, 5
  meetings, 115–16
  mental blocks, 14–15
  Mercedes, 208

Minoan collective rule, 66
Mitsubishi, 3
multi–active
  cultures, 36–41
  managers, 68
  people, 37, 47, 253
multi–actives, 5
  and time, 55–57
  body language, 135
multicultural executives, 311

national
  characteristics and negotiation,
  119–21
  characteristics, 3,
  collective programming, 26
  cultures, 8
negotiating
  characteristics, Japanese, 261–3
  characteristics, Russian, 234–5
  with Indians, 297–8
  with the Portuguese, 227–8
negotiation, 116
  body language, 134
  and Chinese behaviour, 280–2
  compromise, 128–9
  decision making, 124–5
  ethics, 125–6
  language, 131
  logic, 130–1
  and national character, 119–21
  non–verbal dimension, 132–3
  and professionalism, 118–9
  and silence, 133
  social setting, 121–2
  values & self–image, 122–4
networking, 68
New Zealanders, 185–6
Nissan, 308
Nokia, 308

Olivetti, 308
oratorical skills, Portuguese, 226
oratorical style, French, 73
organisation, cultural roots of, 65
organisation, concepts of
  America, 77–9
  Britain, 75–7
  East, the, 81–4
  France 73–5
  Germany, 70–2
  Latins, 80–1
  Sweden, 80

perspectives, changing, in international
  management, 307–11
Peugeot, 74
politeness, Japanese, 260–1
Portugal, 223–7
  organisation of firms, 226
Portuguese
  negotiating with, 227–8
  oratorical skills, 226
principles of negotiation, 117–8
programmes, cross–cultural, 14
  internationalisation, 14
programming, collective, 25
propriety, ethics, 127–8
protocol, 145–6

Raffles, Thomas, 299–300
reactive cultures, 5, 41, 42–5
  leaders in, 68
Renault, 74
restaurants, 154–8
  ethnic cuisine, 154–5
  home in safety, 158
  Japanese modesty, 157
  major and minor league, 156
  paying the bill, 157–8
  tipping, 158
  varying ambiences, 156–7

Rhône Poulenc, 74
Russia, 229–34
Russians
  dealing with, 235–8
  language of management, 113
  negotiating characteristics, 234–5

sales, 5
seminars, cross–cultural, 76
setting up an integrated international team, 89–90
silence, 13–14
  and negotiation, 133
sincerity, 143
Singapore, 298–9, 299–300
social setting, negotiation, 121–2
societal training, 66
society, manners in, 159–62
Sony, 3
South Africans, 186–8
space and time, 5
space bubble, 132, 135
Spain, 239–242
Spanish, language of management, 114
status, concepts of
  America, 77–9
  Britain, 75–7
  East, the, 81–4
  France, 73–5
  Germany, 70–2
  Latins, 80–1
  Sweden, 80
strengths, building on, 91
Sweden 243–5
  concepts of leadership, 80
  concepts of management, 80
  concepts of status, 80
  decision making, 245–7
  femine society, the, 247–8
Swedes, dealing with, 249–50

Swedish
  language of management, 113
  management, 245–7
  managers, 247

table manners, 144
taboos, 162–3
task orientation, 68
  British, 77
teambuilding, 88
  exercises, 92–3
Thais, 295–6
thought, internalised, 18
time
  Chinese, 59–60
  concepts, validity of, 64
  cyclic, 57–9, 62
  Japanese, 60–1
  linear, 52–5, 62
  multi-actives, 55–7
Toyota, 308
training, societal, 66
translators, Japanese, 265

Unic truck companies, 308
Unilever, 92
USA, pace of life, 165–7
use of language, 94–8

values, Chinese, 275
values & self–image, negotiation, 122–4
videoconferencing, 115

Whorf, Benjamin, 15, 85
work, nature of, 84
worlds, different, 8, 17–18

RICHARD LEWIS
C O M M U N I C A T I O N S

THE SLEEP OF REASON

The Sleep of REASON

Fantasy and reality
from the Victorian age
to the First World War

DEREK JARRETT

1817

Harper & Row, Publishers, New York
Cambridge, Philadelphia, San Francisco
London, Mexico City, São Paulo, Singapore, Sydney

93-598

CONTENTS

Introduction   1

1   Paradise lost   8

2   Aspects of Antichrist   22

3   The harrowing of hell   39

4   Other gods before me   56

5   The coming of the Lord   72

6   The uses of fantasy   92

7   Watchers upon the high towers   112

8   The triumph of fiction   128

9   All truth is change   143

10 The power of evil   161

11 The waste land   177

    Postscript   199

    Notes   202

    Index   221

INTRODUCTION

In 1936, A FEW MONTHS BEFORE THE CENTENARY OF Queen Victoria's accession, Sir Charles Ensor in *The Oxford History of England* gave his verdict on her reign. 'No one will ever understand Victorian England,' he wrote, 'who does not appreciate that among highly civilized, in contradistinction to more primitive, countries it was one of the most religious the world has known... hell and heaven seemed as certain as tomorrow's sunrise and the Last Judgement as real as the week's balance sheet.' It was a slightly condescending observation and it seemed to suggest that by confusing dream and reality, fact and fantasy, the Victorians had slipped back into the credulous superstitions of a primitive society instead of advancing towards the rationalism of a highly civilized one. For all their energy and in spite of their enormous achievements they had been in some sense asleep, lost in dreams of eternal bliss and nightmares of endless torment. By contrast Ensor's own enlightened generation was of course awake, living in the real world rather than in an imagined one and knowing that sunrise was more certain than hell and heaven. His readers could only conclude that in the course of ninety-nine painful years the human mind had come of age and put away childish things. Fantasy had been banished and reality reigned.

Many years earlier, as the eighteenth century's supposed Age of Reason drew to its close, the Spanish painter Francisco Goya had portrayed *El sueño de la razon*, the sleep of reason, in which the dreamer was surrounded by dark creatures of the night. 'Imagination deserted by reason begets impossible monsters,' he had explained. 'United with reason she is the mother of all the arts and the source of their wonders.' Was it a premonition of what was to come? Were the Victorians and their American contemporaries doomed to sleep the sleep of reason and beget impossible monsters? Certainly not in their own view. On

1

the contrary, they knew it was the sceptics who slept. On one side of the Atlantic Henry Francis Lyte looked forward confidently to the moment when 'Heaven's morning breaks and earth's vain shadows flee', while on the other Henry Wadsworth Longfellow declared that life was real precisely because the grave was not its goal. 'Tell me not in mournful numbers, Life is but an empty dream,' he cried, 'For the soul is dead that slumbers, And things are not what they seem.' The sleep of the soul, the sleep that was death to all true wisdom, was the same as the sleep of reason because reason came from God and was God. The dark creatures of the night were the vain and shadowy imaginings of the atheists, empty materialistic dreams which mistook appearance for reality and conjured up unreal nightmares without meaning and without purpose. For all his civilized condescension Ensor had achieved only an understatement. The English-speaking world of the nineteenth century did not put immortality on the same plane of reality as mortality but on a far higher one. All that was open to doubt was whether tomorrow's sunrise was as certain as hell and heaven, whether the week's balance sheet was as real as the Last Judgement.

There was nothing new about this. The Victorians were not an eccentric and aberrant generation which had strayed from the paths of rational thought under the influence of some self-injected dose of piety. Centuries ago Christianity had inherited from the ancient world the idea that reality was invisible and beyond man's ken. Lyte's phrase about earth's vain shadows was in direct line of descent from Plato's picture of the human race as men chained at the mouth of a cave and able only to peer into its depths at shadows cast by the real world which lay unseen behind them. This view of things extended even to the insubstantial world of fantasy to which Ensor wanted to consign heaven and hell. Since the source of all human imagining was the unseen world of ultimate reality it followed that all fantasies other than those of the insane could spring only from that world. Samuel Taylor Coleridge's famous definition of imagination as 'a repetition in the finite mind of the eternal act of creation in the infinite' was made only a few years after the appearance of Goya's drawing, while his subsequent remark that poetic genius had good sense as its body and the imagination as its soul was an echo of Goya's insistence on the need for imagination to be united with reason. The notion that outward appearances might be more real than ideas in the mind of God was not only an unthinkable thought:

2

it was also an unimaginable fantasy.

Yet in the course of a century or so the unthinkable came to be thought, the unimaginable imagined. For the first time in human history the invisible was no longer the necessary framework within which truths about the visible world could be discerned. Fantasy and reality changed places. It was clearly one of history's great turning points and well worth our study. But how should we study it? Some see it as a chapter in the history of religion, which at best is rather like investigating truancy by looking at the children who still go to school. At worst it is more like charting a voyage into outer space by examining the launching pad. Others would have us call it a chapter in the history of ideas, which usually means fitting allegedly significant thinkers and their allegedly significant thoughts into a kind of intellectual ladder up which the human race is supposed to have climbed. Unfortunately most such ladders tell us more about the retrospective thought of those who assemble them than about the creative thought of those who are said to be their rungs. In any case the change with which we are concerned was not a series of disjointed debates taking place at some rarefied philosophical level. It was a continuous and collective and often very painful human experience. Most of those who took part in it moved not from thought to thought but from fantasy to fantasy. They modulated the imagination into a new key rather than coaxing the intellect into a new philosophy. Although thinking has sometimes been regarded as the most respectable activity of the human mind imagining has always been far more prevalent and far more potent.

Can there be such a thing as the history of the human imagination? Some have tried to write it along Freudian lines, exposing and dissecting the fantasies of the dead in the way the psycho-analyst exposes and dissects those of his patients. This approach has its uses for the biographer, who deals only with the fantasies of an individual, but it has seldom been effective in the hands of the historian and it certainly seems unsuited to an investigation which must take account of millions of people on both sides of the Atlantic from the accession of Queen Victoria to the First World War. More promising is Jungian psycho-analysis with its notion of the collective unconscious and its emphasis on myths and universal archetypes. Jung's impact on literary critics has certainly been greater than that of Freud. And since the psycho-analyst and the literary critic are both in the business of assessing fantasies the historian of fantasy should perhaps look to their

3

disciplines. For the truth of the matter is that if hell and heaven and the Last Judgement were myths, mere products of the human imagination as Ensor seemed to suggest, then they did not simply vanish at reason's touch in the way dreams die when the dreamer awakes. Their place was taken by other myths, less pious but just as powerful. The prescribed fantasies of religion were replaced by secret fantasies confessed on the psycho-analyst's couch or more respectable ones engendered by popular fiction. The fact that thousands of people refused to believe that God was real is one side of the coin: the fact that almost as many refused to believe that Sherlock Holmes was fictitious is the other.

Once we have the courage or the impertinence to put God and Sherlock Holmes on the same plane things begin to fall into place. Holmes established his claim to be an archetype pretty convincingly in 1894, when he came back to life after he had been sent to his death over the Reichenbach Falls. Arthur Conan Doyle was forced to realize then that the great detective had an existence outside that of his creator. There are also literary critics who give the text or structure of a piece of fiction a reality which transcends the consciousness of its author and may even make a study of his or her intentions irrelevant. Others view creativity in a way which looks back beyond Coleridge to his mediaeval predecessors. When Coleridge spoke of imagination he distinguished it from fancy, an inferior faculty which could only juggle with images conveyed to it by the senses. 'Fancy has no other counters to play with,' he wrote, 'but fixities and definites'. Mediaeval thinkers put it the other way round, contrasting 'Imaginatio', a humble faculty of copying and imitation, with 'Phantasia', something truly creative. But Phantasia could not conceive anything God had not imagined, any more than Coleridge's finite imagination could outdo the eternal act of creation it was repeating. In both cases the lower faculty is merely mechanical while the higher one mirrors something outside itself. The layman or the Freudian may think of fantasy as something which begins and ends within one mind but the critic and the Jungian give it a wider meaning.

In *The Sign of Four*, his second public appearance, Holmes looked out on the 'dreary, dismal, unprofitable world' and exclaimed that 'no qualities save those which are commonplace have any function upon earth.' Shortly afterwards he advised Watson to read Winwood Reade's *The Martyrdom of Man*, which he said was one of the most remarkable books ever written. It ended with a vision of a world

4

drained of meaning and reduced to the commonplace because it had lost its faith. 'A season of mental anguish is at hand,' Reade wrote, 'and through this we must pass in order that our posterity may rise. The soul must be sacrificed; the hope in immortality must die. A sweet and charming illusion must be taken from the human race, as youth and beauty vanish never to return.' Did he really think that a world without the hope of life after death would be one from which youth and beauty had vanished for ever? Did he look to a future in which the finality of the grave would cast its shadow even over the years of hope and vigour? Perhaps not; but the fact that he felt it necessary to indulge in such rhetoric showed how important the sweet and charming illusion was. Goya had suggested that imagination could not survive without reason but Reade knew that for most of his readers reason could not survive without the conventional images of Christianity. If heaven and hell were unreal then reality itself could have no meaning. And no one understood this better than Holmes, perhaps because he had come to remedy the situation and trade old myths for new. It was certainly ironic that one of the few people to appreciate the significance of Reade's epitaph on fantasy should himself have been a fantasy.

The Martyrdom of Man appeared in 1872, rather more than halfway through Queen Victoria's reign. A few months before its publication a powerfully built young man wearing a shooting-coat and a wide-awake hat dived into the Thames from the parapet of London Bridge and rescued a man who had fallen overboard from the Woolwich steamer. 'Here is the sort of Christianity which all of us, little and great, learned and unlearned, can read as we run,' enthused the *Daily Telegraph* in a leading article, 'the gallant fellow going through the air like an angel in a shooting-coat and wide-awake'. It later transpired that the young man was a swimming instructor who owned the Wellington Baths in Leeds. The man he had rescued was his brother, also a swimming instructor, and the incident had been a publicity stunt. The *Daily Telegraph* was much mocked yet its talk of angels was of more than passing significance. Angels and archangels and all the company of heaven were part of the illusion which Reade saw as being under threat but they also had a status of their own which might enable them to outlive it. It was possible to reject conventional Christianity and still believe in 'guardian angels', just as half a century later even the irreligious talked of the Angels of Mons who were said to have come to the aid of British soldiers in Flanders. Powerfully

built young angels in shooting-coats were especially desirable: if the imagination could not accept the fantastic as real it could at least turn the real into the fantastic.

No newspaper hailed Holmes as an angel in a deer-stalker and he was never called upon to investigate the mysterious affair at Mons. Yet there was a basic human need which linked the great detective with the enterprising swimming instructor and also linked Winwood Reade's traumatic vision with the traumatic realities of the First World War. It was the need to believe in heroism and self-sacrifice, in man's readiness to fight the good fight. Even Reade's farewell to conventional fantasies was couched in the form of a challenge, a summons to sacrifice: one generation must pass bravely through a season of mental anguish in order that its children and its children's children might rise to higher things. Holmes was 'an expert singlestick player, boxer and swordsman' and if he worshipped a god at all it was the god of battle. On the eve of the First World War, when Watson felt that 'God's curse hung heavy over a degenerate world', Holmes assured him that the English would turn from that world and purge themselves in battle: 'There's an east wind coming, such a wind as never blew on England yet. It will be cold and bitter, Watson, and a good many of us may wither before its blast. But it's God's wind none the less, and a cleaner, better, stronger land will lie in the sunshine when the storm has cleared.'

The relationship here between fantasy and reality was more complex and also more surprising than in the case of the Last Judgement and the week's balance sheet. The fantasy was that in 1914, before the appalling realities of war had made themselves apparent, a detective told his friend that the coming conflict had been sent by God to make England cleaner and better and stronger. The reality was that Sir Arthur Conan Doyle passed this message to the British and American reading public not on the eve of the war but three years into it, when millions of his countrymen had already been driven like cattle to be killed or maimed and when the same thing was about to happen to the young men of the United States. However unpleasant the fantasy may seem the reality is a great deal worse. Yet Doyle was only doing what he thought to be his duty, as were thousands of others who preached the need for more slaughter. Reality had become so obscene that it needed fantasy to make it bearable. And all the professional myth-makers of society, from the pundits of popular fiction to the potentates of church and state, hastened to clothe the senseless killing

in garments of pride. What was the God of the Christians to do? The truth was that if by some miracle he could have made the rulers of the warring nations follow Christ's precepts the values of civilized society might have been saved. The myth was that if he had done so the world would have been cursed and degenerate, dishonoured and disgraced. It was a harsh and terrible myth which defaced and distorted the image of God to suit the needs of men. The image of God never fully recovered. The First World War succeeded in doing what all the sneers and disbelief of the nineteenth-century sceptics had failed to do. It was not the war to end wars but it was perhaps the illusion to end illusions.

1 PARADISE LOST

THE VICTORIAN MIND INHERITED THE FEARS AND uncertainties of a revolutionary age. Lord Melbourne, British Prime Minister at the time of Queen Victoria's accession in 1837, had been thirteen when the fall of the French monarchy in 1792 had ushered in a quarter of a century of bloodshed and devastation. Martin Van Buren, the American President, had been ten. Future ages would see worse things but to Melbourne and Van Buren and their generation it seemed they had lived through the world's greatest cataclysm, 'the day when heaven was falling, the hour when earth's foundations fled'. In the real world they had had some success in shoring up earth's foundations but in the world of the imagination heaven's intentions still gave rise to anxiety. In retrospect the Victorians may seem to have been walking serenely in the paths of righteousness but in 1837 there was more concern about God's absence than delight in his presence. Certainly few of the young queen's subjects and even fewer of their American contemporaries thought in terms of a new dawn of godliness and piety.

To many it seemed that darkness was already closing in, a darkness which foreshadowed the end of the Christian era. Paradise had perhaps already been lost. The world of their forefathers, a simple innocent world close to God, was slipping away. The revolutionary upheavals of the 1790s had brought war and violence and terror, shaking to its foundations the optimistic and rational view of mankind which had inspired them. It was a time of strange irrational fears, fears which coloured the early Victorian imagination and helped to shape its concepts of fantasy and reality. Men and women were not as yet worried by the thought that God might not exist but some of them were very worried indeed by the thought that he might have turned his face from them, perhaps for ever. A clergyman in Birmingham

8

warned his congregation that 'the spirit of infidelity and atheism manifested during the French Revolution' was still at work, separating
man from God and helping Antichrist to take over the earth. 'Beloved
brethren, perilous times are come,' he concluded.

The young Gladstone, twenty-seven years old and Member of Parliament for Newark, used the same adjective: Victoria had been left
a perilous legacy, he noted in his diary on the day of her accession.
Her predecessor, King William iv, had died muttering anxiously, 'The
church! The church!' A few months later, standing in St Peter's in
Rome, Gladstone lamented the rift between the Roman Catholic and
Protestant churches. Unless God himself did something about it the
state of Christendom could only get worse: it was 'in every human
sense hopeless'. The Church of England was particularly under threat
because some of its most eminent clerics seemed to be tending towards
Catholicism just when popular fear of Rome was at its height. Sydney
Smith, man of letters and Canon of St Paul's Cathedral, declared
that it was the new queen's duty to avoid anti-Catholic prejudice
and not to 'mistake fanaticism for religion.' Tennyson, who was also
twenty-seven when the Victorian age began, had already written
'Morte d'Arthur', in which he had seen his dead friend Arthur Hallam
in the guise of an undying king miraculously healed. Now, in the
first winter of the new queen's reign, he felt the need to put the poem
into a contemporary setting where men mourned the decay of faith
and the passing of the old forms of worship. In the countryside people
could remember going to the water's edge on Easter morning to watch
'the angels who were at the resurrection' playing in the sun; but such
bright visions were now fading into the hard light of day. Wordsworth
was not the only one to feel that 'there hath pass'd away a glory
from the earth'.

Wordsworth's lost paradise was the world of his own childhood.
Others, especially poets and artists, idealized the childhood of their
nation or their race, evoking images of ancient times when men and
women had supposedly lived close to the glory and the magic of nature
and had not yet been corrupted by the gross and greedy ways of
an increasingly materialistic age. Architects made their contribution
to the current nostalgia, disguising factories and railway stations as
castles or cathedrals. Aspiring politicians wove fantasies about the
past in order to attack the present. And through it all, in art and
in literature and in society's view of itself, the same theme kept recurring: a world that had once known God naturally and instinctively

9

had somehow lost touch with him. John Keble, whose verse best seller *The Christian Year* had evoked the former world with enormous success, was unsparing in his attacks on the present one. He had already preached an uncompromising sermon accusing the British of 'direct disavowal of the sovereignty of God' and now he and his supporters were suggesting that the country was farther from God than it had been in the Catholic Middle Ages. The group of young churchmen he gathered round him in Oxford soon came near to splitting the Church of England apart as debate over the lost paradise moved from nostalgia to theological confrontation. The Victorian age opened not in pious confidence but in anxious uncertainty.

As well as the threatened divisions within the Church there was the widening gulf between scientific research and revealed religion. Charles Lyell's *Principles of Geology*, which came out at the same time as Keble's sermon, paid careful respect to the Christian view of creation. 'In whatever direction we pursue our researches, whether in time or space,' Lyell wrote, 'we discover everywhere the clear proofs of a Creative Intelligence, and of His foresight, wisdom and power.' Such homage did not save the book from being attacked by the orthodox because it questioned the chronology laid down by the Book of Genesis. Parson Holmes, the irascible clergyman in Tennyson's 'Morte d'Arthur', singled out 'geology and schism' as twin evils which were separating mankind from God and sapping the foundations of faith. How was God to be regained, how would he once again manifest himself? Tennyson dreamed of a world reassured by miracle, of a mighty wind blowing King Arthur's ship to shore while the waiting crowds cried out in ecstasy: 'Arthur is come again: he cannot die'. The once and future king, stepping effortlessly from the days of chivalry into the nineteenth century 'like a modern gentleman of stateliest port', would re-establish man's communion with God and restore the glory that had passed away.

Parson Holmes did not share the dream and real-life parsons were even less ready to countenance it. They had a different picture of God's coming, one which rested on biblical authority and was to influence the Victorian mind even more powerfully than the fashionable nostalgia for the days of chivalry. The Book of Revelation had predicted long ago that mankind's drift into unbelief would result in the seven vials of God's wrath being poured out upon the earth while the Four Horsemen of the Apocalypse – Death, Famine, War and Pestilence – rode out to ravage mankind. God would not return

10

as a kindly mediaeval monarch in latter-day disguise but on the wings of the storm, ushering in his reign by delivering a faithless generation over to Antichrist. Interpretation of this prophecy had never been easy and the exact sequence of events which it foretold was still a matter for argument; but by the time Queen Victoria came to her throne most commentators were agreed that the French Revolution had marked the pouring out of the first vial. The Rev. Edward Bishop Elliott, fellow of Trinity College Cambridge, proved the point in a massive work in four volumes which went through three triumphant editions in as many years. There was but a short time left, he warned, before the end of all things.

It seemed that across the Channel in Europe three of the four horsemen were already saddled. The French Revolution had plunged the continent into twenty years of war and it had also led to civil strife and appalling barbarity not only in France but in other countries as well. The fiendish atrocities and obscenities committed in Spain had led Goya to produce the series of drawings for which 'The Sleep of Reason' had been intended as a frontispiece. To some Christians it seemed it was the angels who slept while monsters continued to walk the earth. Many parts of Europe were still subject to the sort of superstitious tyranny which was later summed up by Gladstone as 'the negation of God erected into a system of government'. There was widespread starvation and by the 1830s there was cholera as well. 'The sword, famine and *the Pestilence* are represented in the Holy Scriptures as peculiar judgements on the sins, and particularly the national sins, of men,' wrote the Rev. William Marsh, 'We have, then, nothing to dread as men but a continuance in sin and unbelief; and we have nothing to dread as Britons but a perseverance in those national crimes which would be visited with national judgements.' Even Parson Holmes, when he had finished berating the geologists and the schismatics, had to admit that the real danger came from outside: if there was little faith left at home there was none at all abroad.

Englishmen in their complacency had always known this. Whilst Europe had been divided between the superstition of the Roman Catholics and the fanaticism of the extreme Protestants, the Church of England prided itself on holding the balance between authority and enthusiasm, between the stability given by an established church and the right of individuals to interpret the scriptures for themselves. Revolution had resulted from kingly and priestly tyranny and European states and European churches had fallen like ninepins before the

11

onslaught of atheism and rationalism. Only the British and their American cousins had stood firm. An impartial observer might think this had something to do with the oceans which had prevented the revolutionary armies from getting to the English-speaking peoples but the English-speaking peoples themselves did not doubt that it was because of their superior piety and good sense. The European nations had moved from superstition to blasphemy and back within a generation and it was hardly surprising that God had turned his face from them.

By 1841 Marsh was beginning to fear that the British had neglected his warning and were risking divine retribution. Soon God's patience would be at an end and the whole world with it. The Chartists, agitators for working-class rights and parliamentary reform, had just set up a church in Birmingham and Marsh warned his Birmingham congregation that this blasphemy signified the coming of Antichrist. 'What is Chartism but opposition to all human government?' he thundered in a sermon later published as *Antichrist detected*, 'What is Socialism but opposition to all moral and religious control, or Infidelity under its most dangerous form?' Both were insidious manifestations of Antichrist, 'approaching their victims in the garb of philanthropy while leaving unrestrained all the sinful passions of man'. The holocaust threatened in the Book of Revelation could not be long delayed.

Rumour had it that London rather than Birmingham would be the first to be punished. Early in 1842 word went round that the city was to be engulfed by an earthquake on 16 March and a week before the appointed day the credulous were reporting that St Paul's Cathedral had already sunk five feet. Printed notices were circulated, stamped with the royal arms, announcing that the event had been officially postponed for a week. They served only to amuse the few rather than to reassure the many. Streams of people fled before the approaching catastrophe and hotels in Brighton reported that 'numbers of families of the middle and upper classes have arrived to avoid its consequences'. On the day itself 'frantic cries, incessant appeals to Heaven for deliverance, heart-rending supplications for assistance' were heard from the poorer quarters while 'large bodies of respectable inhabitants' went up to Hampstead and Highgate in order to watch 'the demolition of the leviathan city'. Unfortunately, recorded *The Times*, 'the darkness of the day and the thickness of the atmosphere prevented it being seen.' When the weather improved it became clear that the earth had not opened up, the city had not after all been consumed by the fires of hell.

It was sad that a sense of the absence of God should find expression in prophecies of punishment, in visions not of heaven but of hell. Not since the Middle Ages had there been such an obsession with the Devil and his works. Earthquakes, even those which did not happen, were seen not simply as natural disasters but as hell's incursions. Even the geologists, impious questioners of the Book of Genesis, agreed that the earth beneath their feet was the abode of fire as well as the abode of the dead. Londoners had this underlined for them by Dr John Cumming, an eloquent prophet of apocalypse who drew audiences of many thousands to his lectures on the approaching end of the world:

The fire, which I told you geologists have admitted and which the Scripture confirms, to be a large ocean of restless and liquid lava, that rolls and heaves in the innermost recesses of the earth, of which our volcanoes are but the safety-valves and our earthquakes as the reverberations of its ceaseless waves lashing its desolate and dreary shores, shall burst forth at a thousand orifices; the gases that compose our atmosphere shall ignite and the earth shall melt; Christ's people shall be taken up into the air a certain distance while the wicked shall be left on earth, the living punished on it, the dead buried beneath it.

In many ways the picture was a conventional one. The Christian imagination had for centuries placed a lake of fire at the centre of the infernal regions and Milton in *Paradise Lost* had depicted its flames as giving out 'no light, but rather darkness visible'. The point was driven home by Father Pinamonti's *Hell Opened to Christians*, a seventeenth-century work which was still being brought out in the 1840s by the Catholic Book Society. The damned souls were in total darkness, Pinamonti insisted, and were denied the comfort that light could bring, yet in the darkness all the horrors and torments of hell were fully visible. And the agent of torment, the element in which the damned would writhe for evermore, was fire – 'fire bed, fire food, fire drink', as one outraged critic of the doctrine put it. Nor did it need either theologians or geologists to point out that darkness and fire were not incompatible: miners had always known it and the appalling accidents that happened when fire took command below ground showed that the imagined subterranean world and the real one had something in common. It only remained to put actors on to the stage, to fill out Cumming's depopulated fiery gulf with tormentors and tormented.

This was done, at any rate as far as the real underground world

13

was concerned, early in June 1842. With the earthquake scare still fresh in the minds of Londoners the House of Commons debated a report on the employment of children in mines and factories. Members soon learned that the earth under them was indeed a place of suffering where children were chained and tortured. 'I went into the pit at seven years of age,' said one of them, 'when I drew by the girdle and chain, the skin was broken and the blood ran down. If we said anything they would beat us. I have seen many draw at six. They must do it, or be beat. They cannot straighten their backs during the day.' The passages along which he and other children had to draw cartloads of coal, in foul air and in total darkness, were deep underground and were sometimes less than two feet high. It was therefore essential, said those who understood the requirements of the job (and they included clergymen as well as doctors), that children should start work young so that they could become suitably deformed while the bones were still soft. Lord Ashley, presenting the report, gave details of the treatment received by Edmund Kershaw, whom the parish authorities of Castleton in Lancashire had apprenticed to a nearby collier:

His back and loins were beaten to a jelly; his head, which was almost cleared of hair on the scalp, had the marks of many old wounds ... One of the bones in one arm was broken below the elbow, and seemed to have been so for some time. The boy, on being brought before the magistrate, was unable to sit or stand and was placed on the floor in the office. It appeared that the boy's arm had been broken by a blow with an iron rail, and the fracture had never been set, and that he had been kept at work for several weeks with his arm in that condition. It was admitted – what an admission! – by the master that he had been in the habit of beating the boy with a flat piece of wood, in which a nail was driven and projected about half an inch ... The boy had been starved for want of food and his body presented all the marks of emaciation. This brutal master had kept him at work as a waggoner until he was no longer of any use, and then sent him home in a cart to his mother, who was a poor widow residing in Rochdale.

The world revealed by the report was strikingly similar to the one depicted in *Hell Opened to Christians*. The only difference was that in the latter the sufferers were being punished while in the former they were merely being employed. However, the one might well lead to the other. Ashley was especially eloquent about the ignorance of the children: they were benighted spiritually as well as physically. They had never known God, they were not taught their catechism, so how

14

could they avoid hellfire? The darkness they knew in life might be followed by an even deeper darkness after death.

Darkest of all was the view of God and of man which such a train of thought revealed. Indeed, the least justifiable thing in Ashley's outburst was the use of the word 'brutal', for the cruelties he described were uniquely human. No brute beast could have been capable of them. 'What are men better than sheep or goats,' Tennyson's King Arthur had asked, 'If, knowing God, they lift not hands of prayer?' By the same token what were men better than tigers or vipers if, knowing the cruelties sanctioned by God for the punishment of sinners, they did not emulate them? Christianity had long ago relegated the brute creation to an inferior place in God's scheme of things: only human beings had souls, only human beings would go to heaven or to hell. And only human beings practised cruelty for its own sake. Why? Had the human mind created images of evil or had it been created by them? Did the earthly torturers create the fiends of hell or were they inspired by them? Had human compassion given itself over to the underworld or was the underworld rising, in mental if not in geological terms, in order to engulf the senses of mankind?

The apocalyptic scenario, like the infernal one, required human participation. This was especially true of war, the third of the four horsemen. And the fear in the summer of 1842 was not just of foreign war but of something far worse. Even as Parliament debated the report strikes broke out in the Staffordshire pits and by the middle of August, when the Chartists met in Manchester, one of their leaders was convinced that 'the spread of the strike would and must be followed by a general outbreak'. '1842 was the year in which more energy was hurled against the authorities than in any other of the nineteenth century', one historian has written, 'It was the nearest thing to a general strike that the century saw.' God-fearing Christians echoed Marsh's words: 'What is Chartism but opposition to all human government? What is Socialism but opposition to all moral and religious control?' First reactions to Ashley's revelations were of shock and shame and horror but as the threat of revolution grew a reaction set in. He was arraigned for his sensationalism and for his indelicacy – it was intolerable, said his critics, that such disgusting things should be published in the newspapers to distress susceptible ladies – and clergymen who had at first thought that there might be something unchristian in the way the children were treated soon came to see that the really sinful thing was working-class insubordination.

15

Antichrist was where he always had been, down among the discontented in the infernal regions, only too ready to clamber out and distress the susceptible.

While the British contemplated the possibility of a man-made apocalypse, an Armageddon of working-class revolt, America was promised divine intervention. William Miller, a farmer from Low Hampton in New York State, gathered a large following around him when he announced that Jesus Christ would come to earth between 21 March 1843 and 21 March 1844. The righteous would be 'caught up to meet the Lord in the air', while the wicked would have their bodies destroyed by fire and their souls 'shut up in the pit of woe until their resurrection unto damnation'. Once the earth had been cleansed by fire Christ and his saints would take possession of it and rule it for ever. Camp meetings – ecstatic outdoor services which were a special feature of American Christianity – were held all across the United States and it was reckoned that more than half a million Americans were devoutly awaiting the coming of their Lord. The *New York Tribune* published a special extra number on 2 March 1843 explaining the prophecies of the Book of Daniel and the Book of Revelation and concluding that 'the Lord has most plainly showed us that we are living in the days of the voice of the seventh angel ... This sound of the last trump, at which the dead will rise and BE JUDGED we now expect to hear. Reader, slight not the Lord's warning. Improve the present moment. PREPARE TO MEET THY GOD!'

'The time, as I have calculated it, is now filled up,' said Miller on 25 March 1844, 'and I expect every moment to see the Saviour descend from heaven'. But the skies failed to open and the prophet had to tell his followers that 'he confessed his error and acknowledged his disappointment'. Then his friend Samuel Snow made a new calculation showing that Christ would come on the tenth day of the seventh month of the current Jewish year – Tuesday 22 October 1844 in Christian terms – and once more excitement mounted. Crops were left unharvested, shops and offices put up their shutters, people resigned from their jobs and gave their money away in order to prepare for the great day:

Many have become maniacs, wasting their property and leaving their families to suffer in indigence. The religious community seems, as it were, convulsed to its centre. Nor is it strange or wonderful if the credulous, from the signs of the times, should become alarmed or apprehensive of the approach of

some dread event or revolution. All is fanaticism, feigned or real ... If an intelligent stranger should now land in this country he might suppose that they were on the verge of a revolutionary outbreak.

What they were in fact on the verge of, what they had to face up to once the great day had come and gone, was less dramatic but ultimately more damaging. Every cosmic non-event, every doomsday that failed to arrive, was another nail in the coffin of a God who was apparently unable to give substance to the visions he had inspired or to the predictions he was supposed to have prompted. The prophets and those who believed them were caught in a descending spiral of despair. Their sense of loss at the absence of God convinced them that the end was nigh; the end's stubborn refusal to arrive intensified the sense of loss, even of betrayal. Nevertheless the spate of prophecies continued unabated and unabashed. They were now regarded by many as the only way to keep Christians in a proper state of readiness, to 'awaken the unbelieving and profane'. If they were not heeded by those few nations which had so far not committed 'national crimes', then what hope was there for mankind? In a twilight world of blasphemy and unbelief, with no prayers to make the heavens relent, the darkness would continue to deepen.

And it was Christianity, for so long the proudest of the world's religions, which had caused the gods to turn away. For many thousands of years, in all kinds of societies from the most primitive to the most advanced, religious observance had preserved the universe. Men had acted out the required rituals, offered up the necessary sacrifices and prayers, and in return the gods had lit up the heavens and replenished the earth. In ancient Mexico the priests had promised that the sun would continue to rise as long as sufficient human blood was poured out upon the altars. Their will had been done and the sun had not failed. Elsewhere, in remote and secret regions, prayer wheels had turned tirelessly in the knowledge that if they stopped the thread of existence would snap and nothingness would blot out the meaning of the world. Gods had been replaced by other gods – or perhaps had merely changed their names – as their followers had migrated or been conquered or converted. But always there had been worship, always there had been the sustaining breath of prayer to hold up the sky. Now, for the first time in human history, there were thousands upon thousands of men and women who denied the need for any gods at all. By spawning open unbelief Christianity had undermined

17

not just its own foundations but the whole world's delicate balance between fantasy and reality, faith and knowledge.

Sixty years later, in *Peter Pan*, J.M. Barrie produced the appropriate image. The fairy Tinkerbell lay dying and the children in the audience were told that they could only save her by affirming their belief in fairies. It is not recorded that any audience ever remained silent but it is interesting to wonder what would have happened if one had. Would Tinkerbell have died and if so why? Because Barrie was right, because supernatural beings only existed as long as they were believed in, or because the uncaring audience must be punished for its silence? As with fairies, so with gods: if silence on earth produced silence in heaven was it from necessity or from choice? Was God dead for lack of belief in him or had he merely turned away from an uncaring humanity? For God's audience in the 1840s, deeply divided as to whether it should shout its belief, this issue of choice or necessity was a painful one. If God was absent out of choice, because unbelief had offended him, then the surrounding darkness was the darkness of his anger and would lift only when enough people affirmed their belief; but if he was absent from necessity, because he had never been anything more than man's yearning for him, then the darkness of superstition would be dispelled only by enlightened unbelief. Either way the drama could not proceed, the shades of night could not give way to a new dawn, until the members of the audience agreed among themselves. In this situation Goya's recommended union of reason and imagination would be hard to bring about.

There were many for whom the prospect of empty untenanted skies was too appalling to contemplate. It was the worst of all possible cosmic tragedies, something which could only be conveyed by the metaphor of God's death. A German thinker called Jean Paul Richter – like Winwood Reade a great favourite of Sherlock Holmes – had already proclaimed that God was dead and mankind orphaned. In March 1844, just as God was failing to keep the first of the appointments made for him by William Miller, the same proclamation was heard again, this time from France. Gérard de Nerval's poem 'Le Christ aux Oliviers' described Christ on the eve of his crucifixion staring into the void and realizing that his father who had once been in heaven was now dead, with the result that the coming sacrifice on the cross would achieve nothing. The trumpet would not sound, the dead would not be raised, the promised apocalyptic drama would never take place. The whole world, the whole universe, could only

18

grow colder and darker.

Others detected not darkness but dawn. One of the most influential was George Jacob Holyoake, a London atheist who started a magazine called *The Reasoner or Herald of Progress* in June 1846. 'The last census informs us that Great Britain is afflicted by no fewer than 23,000 clergymen,' he complained in his first editorial, 'centres of 23,000 local associations which in effect, so think we, cripple the moral energies of men, humiliate their native spirit and divert them from independence and social amelioration, chaining the spirit of progress to musty records and drivelling dogmas – and not one Association rears its head against this vast organized error!' He was quick to publicize American atheism, telling how in Boston 'the disciples of Thomas Paine, Infidels by profession' had offered the free use of their hall to a Christian anti-slavery lecturer who had been ostracized by all the Christian communities there. 'Boston is professedly a Christian city,' the lecturer had commented, 'hence I blush while I am constrained to acknowledge the superior humanity of what is called Infidelity.'

As the exponents of atheism and rationalism came more and more into the open the beleaguered believers needed to find out what proportion of the audience they formed. Holyoake's interpretation of the 1841 census was fallible since neither that nor any previous census had taken a count of religious services and attendances. When one was taken in 1851 it only covered England and Wales and it showed that there were 34,467 places of worship, 14,077 belonging to the Church of England and 20,390 belonging to other denominations. Out of a population of nearly eighteen million there were some ten and three quarter million church attendances on the Sunday chosen for the count but these covered morning, afternoon and evening services and many people attended more than once, so that the number of individual worshippers was clearly much less. However, taking into account those who worked on Sundays or were for other reasons prevented from going to church – the census officials put them at four tenths of the total population – it was a respectable figure. And there were clearly many people who did not attend church but still believed in God and would shout out their belief if and when the moment came. The figures for Scotland, though less reliable and more belated, suggested that about sixty per cent of the population worshipped regularly. In Ireland the fierce dissension between Catholics and Protestants bore witness to the intensity of religious fervour on both sides.

19

The Almighty need not languish and die because of any uncaring silence on the part of his British audience.

America was another matter. The constitution of the United States expressly forbade any established church and many people in Britain imagined that American religion was a matter of frenzy and fanaticism, what one historian has called 'the swamp fire of religious conversion, the emotionalism of rural America'. On the other hand Charles Dickens, by no means an admirer of the United States, insisted that the Americans were no more fanatical than the British. 'I have beheld religious scenes in some of our populous towns which can hardly be surpassed by an American camp meeting,' he wrote, 'and I am not aware that any instance of superstitious imposture on the one hand and superstitious credulity on the other has had its origin in the United States which we cannot parallel.' Others sought more precise information and *Painter's Church of England Gazette* estimated shortly after Queen Victoria's accession that there were about one and three quarter million communicant members of recognized churches in the United States, ranging from the Episcopal Church, an American version of the Church of England, to Methodists, Baptists, Congregationalists and Presbyterians. The American census of 1840 showed the population to be just over seventeen million, so these communicants represented about a tenth of the total. So, whether Dickens was right or wrong, the shout for God from America would have to go up also from the unrecognized, from strange sects, from camp meetings, from the followings of itinerant preachers.

It seemed that the moment of truth could not be long delayed. Early in 1847 Holyoake published a letter from a correspondent in Paris who proclaimed that in Communism, 'the Religion of the Future', Europe was keeping all that was best in the old faith while abandoning the dark imaginings that still held sway in Britain and in America. 'Communism abroad rests mainly on the essential maxims of Christianity, which would hardly be safe with you, where there is danger of being dragged into all the absurdities tacked on to them.' At the beginning of September *The Times*, usually quick to dismiss talk of revolution, published a leading article on the Communist threat in France. There was real danger, it warned solemnly, of 'disasters to which no living man can assign a termination.'

In November 1847 the Congress of the Communist League, meeting in London, gave Karl Marx and Friedrich Engels the task of drawing up the *Communist Manifesto*, printed in England and then published

in Europe as successive revolutions broke out there during the spring and summer of 1848. Capitalist society, declared Marx and Engels, was like 'a sorcerer who is no longer able to control the powers of the nether world whom he has called up with his spells'. The potentates of Christianity had frightened ordinary men and women for centuries with talk of hellish torments; now it was time for them to be buried under the debris in which they had traded. 'What the bourgeoisie produces above all are its own gravediggers,' concluded the *Manifesto*. Whatever the God of the Christians had done in the past, however cleverly he had rolled back stones and slipped from sepulchres and appeared in visions to his disciples, his days were now numbered. The gravediggers of bourgeois society were also the gravediggers of God. The surrounding darkness was the darkness before the dawn of a bright new world purged of superstition and unreason.

Meanwhile another voice had spoken of deepening darkness, of shadows that would flee, of a morning that would soon break. On Sunday evening 5 September 1847, the day before *The Times* published its prediction of revolution and disaster, the Rev. Henry Frances Lyte preached what was to be his last sermon in his church at Brixham in Devon. It was not an especially distinguished sermon because he was mortally ill and speech was not easy. But in his pocket he had a sheet of paper on which he had written out a hymn which he showed to members of his congregation after the service. It was called 'Abide with me' and it was to prove one of the most enduring messages of comfort that the English-speaking world had ever known. While Holyoake and Marx and Engels gestured their sections of the audience into silence, stifling the shout of affirmation that might yet save a dying God, Lyte's hymn sang out in unquenchable praise and trust. With men like this to believe in him there was life in the old God yet.

2 ASPECTS OF ANTICHRIST

ON FRIDAY 3 SEPTEMBER 1847, AS LYTE PREPARED the final draft of his hymn, Londoners living in the streets around Euston station woke up to find that an immense quantity of human remains had been dumped outside their homes. The station was being extended and debris of all kinds was being tipped into the excavations. The gravediggers from some overcrowded burial ground – suspicion fell on those from St Pancras – had seized the opportunity to get rid of their unwanted dead in order to make more money. In many London burial grounds the corpses were piled upon one another to within a few inches of the surface to make the land yield more in fees. Coffins were often dug up once the mourners had left and sold, either as firewood or for re-use. Once the dead were out of their coffins they were horribly at the mercy of the living: Parliament was told of two St Pancras gravediggers who had been seen hacking a body apart and cramming the pieces into a shallow hole. There was often only a thin covering of earth between the dead and the living. August had seen an angry meeting of the Anti-Interment in Towns Association, as well as a gruesome lecture by a medical man describing the injurious effects of the metropolitan graveyards. Now *The Times* produced equally gruesome details of this latest exhumation:

Large numbers were drawn to the spot and not only were human bones found in large quantities but pieces of flesh were picked up. The children who were there amused themselves by raking over the soil for the purpose of finding teeth of which great numbers were picked up. The reporter who was present had a whole handful shown him, the urchin who had picked them up telling him that he should take them to a dentist's and sell them.

The Euston scandal provoked a spate of angry letters. 'Day by day, year by year,' wrote one outraged citizen, 'we go on displacing

22

one generation, only yet partially returned to the dust, to make room for another ... the narrow slip of earth is sold over and over again ere the bones of its rightful owner are unclothed of their flesh.' The London Cemetery Company saw its chance and ran a series of advertisements for its splendidly appointed establishments at Highgate, Kentish Town and Nunhead. 'A part of each cemetery remains unconsecrated,' it added, conscious that some potential patrons had little time for Christian hopes. While 'Abide with me' grew more popular, affirming that death would dispel earth's vain shadows and reveal the glories of heaven, sceptics saw such fantasies as cruel and childish delusions. 'One might as well take lodgings over a cooking establishment in the Cannibal Islands,' remarked Holyoake in *The Reasoner*, commenting on the idea that those in heaven would be able to watch the smoke of torment rising from hell. 'The quiet sense of submission to annihilation is infinitely preferable,' he concluded.

It had also to be admitted that the last verse of 'Abide with me', with its picture of heaven's morning breaking at the moment of death, was not entirely orthodox. Christianity taught that only the saints would be taken directly to heaven when they died, while ordinary mortals waited in the graveyards for their bodies to be resurrected at the Day of Judgement. Lyte's hymn seemed at odds with this doctrine on two counts: he hoped to go straight from his death-bed to eternal bliss and he hoped that his soul would be accorded this privilege irrespective of his body's decay. Longfellow's 'Psalm of Life', as popular in America as 'Abide with me' was to become in Britain, went further, implying that the body was itself part of those earthly appearances which eternity would reveal as being unreal:

> Life is real! Life is earnest!
>   And the grave is not its goal;
> Dust thou art, to dust returnest,
>   Was not spoken of the soul.

Nevertheless the Anglican creed spoke of the resurrection of the body and most Christians thought of heaven as being inhabited by real people and not by disembodied souls. Mrs Elizabeth Stone, in a popular book on the subject, pointed out that whereas devotees of other religions might burn their dead Christians had to ensure that burial was carried out 'consistently with the revealed doctrine of the resurrection of the body'. 'Yes, *this body*,' she continued, 'waiting, sleeping, changed – this human chrysalis shall waken.' Some took

23

the prospect even more literally. Sabine Baring-Gould, author of 'Onward, Christian soldiers', was shocked to find that his parishioners in Yorkshire insisted on putting a candle and a coin in every coffin, the former to light the corpse's way to heaven and the latter to pay its toll at the gate. The doctrine of the resurrection of the body found expression in customs of this kind, primitive though they might seem, just as it found expression in the horror with which the practices of the gravediggers were regarded. They were seen not just as unhygienic but as sacrilegious. Instead of merely containing putrefying flesh, dangerous to health and divorced from the person who had once inhabited it, the coffin housed a sleeping human being destined for some kind of physical resurrection and possibly already under the protection of the angels or demons associated with its eventual fate. That being or its protectors might take revenge on anyone who disturbed the body. Christianity might have blunted the fear of death but it had certainly not blunted the fear of the dead.

Fear and fascination were closely linked. It could well be argued that the horror story was a specifically Christian literary genre. Other religions had devils and monsters and ghosts but Christianity excelled in tales in which visitors from the next world were actual corpses rather than mere spirits. No other religion led men to write with such ghoulish glee about the walking dead, the opening vault, the cold cadaverous hands closing around the throat. The power of such images sprang, like the hopes of the devout, from the doctrine of the resurrection of the body. The stench of the charnel-house mingled, usually quite pleasurably, with the odour of sanctity. In America there were no urban burial grounds, no horrific juxtaposition of the living and the dead, but in spite of this – or perhaps because of it – Edgar Allan Poe's strange tales of the undead became increasingly popular while in Britain *Varney the Vampire* enjoyed an enormous success when it was published in monthly parts between 1845 and 1847. Dr Mayo, founder of the medical school at the Middlesex Hospital, wrote an article for *Blackwood's Magazine* in April 1847 in which he tried to scotch the vampire myth. The supposed vampires were simply people in comatose or cataleptic states who had been buried alive. He quoted one case of a youth who was thought to have become a vampire and was therefore exhumed. To their horror his relatives found him lying as if alive, colour in his cheeks and a ghastly smile on his lips. They prayed for him and hacked off his head, whereupon he writhed and screamed most horribly. It was not the curse of the vampire that

24

was departing from him, Mayo said grimly, it was life itself. And the same was true of all the other poor wretches who had been disinterred down the centuries in order to have stakes driven through their hearts while the fresh blood gushed and spurted.

It was a timely article which seemed to endorse Holyoake's prediction of the coming triumph of reason over superstition. Yet Mayo left some awkward questions unanswered. How had these supposed vampires been identified? If all the rigmarole of vampirism was imagined, the scratching at the window and the monstrous bat-like form and the punctures in the neck, why was it only the relatives and neighbours of the prematurely buried who imagined it? And how did they know which graves to go to? Did the prematurely buried have telepathic powers, seeking release or revenge by projecting a vampire image on to those who had entombed them? Or was there some strange force in the minds of the living which led them to fill the dark void of death with evil creatures? The idea of hell rising to engulf the human mind might be a superstition but the idea of the human mind immersing itself in hell was a fact. Nor were Christian fantasies the only ones to influence popular thinking. Alongside the advertisements for the hygienic and enlightened services of the London Cemetery Company were other and stranger announcements. 'TO CAPTAINS and others GOING TO SEA,' proclaimed one, 'A CHILD'S CAUL to be DISPOSED OF, in perfect condition.' Seamen had long believed that a caul, the membrane sometimes found on a baby's head at birth, was a sure safeguard against drowning. In the autumn of 1847, as Holyoake and Lyte put forward their differing visions of the morning that was about to break, this superstition was still powerful enough to ensure a steady sale for cauls at ten guineas or more. Even a newspaper as respectable as *The Times* advertised at least one a fortnight. Holyoake's belief in the reasonableness of mankind seemed as much a matter of faith as Lyte's confidence in the mercies of God.

Each awaited the dawn in his own way. Lyte did his best to live out what was left of his life in the spirit of his hymn. 'O for more of entire dependence on Him!' he wrote, 'Entire confidence in Him! Conformity to the will and image of the Lord is no easy attainment and it takes much hammering to bend us to it.' Two months later he died, searching passionately for the vision he had conjured up in his verses. It was to be hoped that it was granted. Holyoake on the other hand looked for an actual earthly daybreak, a tempestuous dawn which would dispel the shadow of human tyranny as well as

the imagined dominion of the divine. Revolution in one country would lead to universal change, just as *The Times* had predicted, and all the old hierarchies would crumble. But *The Times* had now regained its composure and was assuring its readers that there would be no revolution in France. On 24 February 1848 it published a leading article declaring that no insurrection could possibly succeed in Paris. 'We suspect, however,' it continued, 'that no serious popular insurrection is even probable ... If lives are lost in this miserable brawl the reckoning will lie heavily on those who inconsiderately commenced an agitation which they had no power to bring to a successful termination.'

The pronouncement was singularly ill-timed, for the French monarchy had already fallen after fighting in the streets of Paris had left insurrectionary forces in control. Revolutions followed in Hungary, Austria, Prussia and Italy. By the end of March it seemed that the old Europe of priests and kings and noblemen was on the point of collapse. In *The Reasoner* Holyoake mocked *The Times* for its failure to comprehend the new dawn of reason which was sweeping away old superstitions. He also took the opportunity to mock the Earl of Arundel, a Catholic who spoke in Parliament in defence of papal efforts to re-establish the Jesuit order in England. 'Were honourable members aware', Arundel asked, 'of the atheistical and infidel publications which were sold at a cheap rate among the lower classes?' He brandished a copy of the rationalist *Northern Star*, containing advertisements for such subversive tracts as *Discussions on the Bible* and *Socialism made easy*, and declared that the Church of England desperately needed Jesuit help in combating such horrors. Most Englishmen associated the Jesuits with Catholic bigotry and the torture chambers of the Inquisition, so that Holyoake was able to make considerable capital out of the confrontation, especially when Arundel declined to produce any arguments in support of his point of view. Even the *English Review*, a piously orthodox journal, referred scathingly to 'sophistries put forth by the Romanists under shelter of Lord Arundel's name' and predicted that the papacy would be overthrown altogether if it did not yield to revolutionary demands.

Arundel was not to be deflected. He continued to attack European revolutionaries and British radicals alike, proclaiming that they were 'rebels to their God'. He was not old enough to remember the way in which Antichrist had been manifested in the 1790s, but many who were shared his fears. Lord Brougham, once a trenchant critic of

26

Britain's wars against revolutionary France, now came forward to deplore the new uprisings: 'I everywhere observe all the elements of mischief; and turn which way we will the repose of the world seems in peril.' He went on to allege that Parisians had already put out reports of the overthrow of Queen Victoria and the setting up of a godless republic in Britain. Dr Cumming, preparing for publication his immensely popular lectures on the approaching end of the world, warned that the seventh and final vial of God's wrath was now being poured out and that the 'People's Charter', the cherished manifesto of British radicals, was the Devil's work, 'a war-cry of rebellion, a code of treason, a prescription for crime on a large scale'. The bright new dawn was in truth a deepening apocalyptic darkness.

It was true that Holyoake's sunrise was by now a little clouded. All across Europe revolutionary movements split into warring factions while the brave new world of rational conduct dissolved into unreasoning violence. In Britain the radicals marched not to triumph but to disaster. Rebels in Ireland failed dismally, making their last sad stand in a cabbage patch in County Tipperary, while the Chartist petition to Parliament was ridiculed and rejected. Pitched battles between police and Chartists followed, resulting in hundreds of arrests and the virtual extinction of the radical movement for more than a decade. 'Every species of folly and wickedness seems to have been let loose to riot on the earth,' wrote Charles Greville as the year 1848 came to an end. It was not just the god of the Christians who was absenting himself but the supposed goddess of reason as well. A lifetime ago, in the calm and confident world of the eighteenth-century philosophers, it had been possible to believe in her: man had seemed then to be a rational being who had only to remodel society and government along rational lines in order to be permanently and rationally happy. The French Revolution had changed all that: Goya had not been the only one to think that reason had slept while madness spawned monsters. 'There was a time when I believed in the persuadability of man,' the poet Robert Southey had written in 1797, 'and had the mania for man-mending. Experience has taught me better ... The ablest physician can do little in the great lazar-house of society, it is a pest house that infects all within its atmosphere.' Even if Holyoake's readers were rationally motivated they were almost certainly outnumbered by those who were at home in the dark world of the vampire or were ready to see shrivelled membranes as a charm against drowning.

The man whose predictions had been vindicated by the year's events was neither George Holyoake nor the editor of *The Times* but **Karl Marx**, who had always insisted that mankind was moving not to some rationalist utopia but to bloodshed and violence, to a world in which only conflict could bring progress. Few of god's defenders in 1848 had read the *Communist Manifesto* and fewer still understood the thinking which lay behind it, but most knew there was something called 'German metaphysics', an ominous iceberg of which Marx's dialectical materialism was but the ugly tip. It was this strange new philosophy, monstrous and shapeless and half-hidden, which was increasingly seen as the real danger. It was the darkness of German unreason, not the light of reason shining from France, which now threatened to engulf God. The clerics and thinkers who formed his first line of defence hastened to proclaim themselves rationalists in order to form a common front against the metaphysicians.

In October 1849 the *Edinburgh Review* published an article called 'Reason and Faith; their Claims and Conflicts' by Henry Rogers, who was a teacher of logic as well as a Christian apologist. 'We fear that many young minds in our day are exposed to the danger of falling into one or other of the prevailing forms of unbelief, and especially that of pantheistic mysticism, from rashly meditating in the cloudy regions of German philosophy,' Rogers warned. A young man would do well to shun German philosophers, he declared sternly, 'at least till he has matured and disciplined his mind'. Only then could he be sure of reconciling reason and faith in a properly Christian manner: 'God has created two great lights – the greater light to rule man's busy day – and that is Reason; and the lesser to rule his contemplative night – and that is Faith. But Faith itself shines only so long as she reflects some faint illumination from the brighter orb.' Some writers still had their doubts about following the dictates of reason – the Unitarian J.R. Beard thought that the 1848 revolutions sprang from 'the combined influence of Rationalism and Pantheistic Philosophy, which has gone far to blight and uproot the positive religious convictions of France as well as Germany' – but most were convinced that German metaphysics was the greater danger. The *English Review* launched two attacks on it, one attributing recent subversion of the faith in Britain to its influence and the other explaining how 'that character, literary, moral and social, which we may denominate the German mind' had done more to undermine true religion than even 'the audacity of Voltaire'.

28

Yet German philosophy was a good deal more religious than Voltaire had ever been. Just as Christians considered sinning or not sinning more important than abstract reasoning or scientific observation, so German thinkers from Kant to Hegel thought moral values more important than physical appearances. They insisted that life was about the imperative commands that came from the will, not about the abstract patterns that came from the intellect. Eighteenth-century rationalists who had traced such patterns had imagined that they were explaining everything, that the rational nature of man reflected the rational nature of the universe. This was the delusion that had bred disillusion and brought violence and suffering on an enormous scale instead of the ideal world of which the philosophers had dreamed. Man must learn to see life as something dynamic, something continually re-moulded by the will of God, rather than the two-dimensional backcloth painted by the rationalists. Just as a man's fate was shaped by the inner commandments of the individual will, so the fate of mankind would be shaped by the universal commandments of God.

Instead of revealing himself once and for all and then retiring to remote eternity God was now seen as unremittingly involved in human affairs. He was Antichrist's constant and cunning antagonist. History, said Hegel, was the march of God in the world. It was not a steady upward march, as the rationalists had imagined, but a series of conflicts. The Greeks had sought truth by a process called dialectic, the clash of thesis and antithesis in order to produce synthesis, and Hegel thought that history worked in the same way. So far from digging God's grave the German thinkers had given him a new and vital role. But was it the same god? Certainly Marx's materialist version of Hegel's dialectic saw history as moulded not by a personal god but by blind economic necessity and it could be argued that the god of the earlier German thinkers was a similarly uncaring juggernaut. And he was all the more dangerous because he was born of conviction rather than doubt. He existed on a moral plane rather than an intellectual one and so to the orthodox his adherents seemed not merely misguided but heretical. For the prophets of apocalypse the matter was even simpler: like all false gods this one was a manifestation of Antichrist. One of Dr Cumming's reasons for predicting the end of the world was the fact that 'Germany and America are over-run with fanaticism of the most hideous description.' German metaphysicians had succeeded where French revolutionaries had failed: they had

infiltrated the English-speaking world and corrupted a large part of it.

The most prominent American disciples of the German philosophers were the Transcendentalists, a group of Boston intellectuals led by Ralph Waldo Emerson. Emerson sought what he called 'the ideal' and set more store by consciousness than by appearance. 'The idealist takes his departure from his consciousness,' he wrote in 1843, 'and reckons the world as an appearance ... Mind is the only reality, of which men and all other natures are better or worse reflectors.' Since there was no established church in America it was left to the Roman Catholics to sniff out heresy: in a withering article called 'Protestantism ends in Transcendentalism' Orestes Brownson, a Roman Catholic journalist, predicted that the new religion would end by overthrowing Protestantism altogether. By claiming to put everyone in direct touch with the universal it did away with the need for ministers, for sacraments, for intermediaries of any kind.

Even less interested in intermediaries were the utopian communities which had been a feature of American life since the beginning of the century and were now proliferating at an astonishing rate. More than fifty such settlements were set up in the 1840s, far more than had appeared in any other decade, and most were concentrated in New York and neighbouring states. The latest was the Oneida community, established in New York State in February 1848 by John Noyes and his band of Bible Communists after they had been chased from Vermont by a hostile crowd. These sects looked forward – like Holyoake's correspondent in Paris they saw Communism as 'the Religion of the Future' – but they also looked back to the ideals of the early Christian church. 'The apostasy of the United States from their original principles in respect of slavery affords precisely the illustration that is needed,' wrote John Noyes, 'to set forth the backsliding of Christendom from the standard of original Christianity.' And like the early Christians the new sects had their martyrs. In 1844 the Mormon prophet Joseph Smith and his brother were shot dead by a mob which invaded the jail where they were being held. The murderers were acquitted and bands of rioters ranged through Illinois burning Mormon homes. *The Times*, always ready to castigate American lawlessness, was able to lick its lips over 'the threatened crusade for the extermination of the Mormonites'. It was worth remembering that when the Mormons had undertaken missions in England in 1837 and again in 1840 they had not been persecuted, even though their success had been sufficiently spectacular to make a body of Anglican clergy petition Parlia-

ment to act against them. It was difficult to know whether the hideous American fanaticism which Cumming detected came from the sects or from their persecutors.

At the beginning of 1848 the British sent a champion of orthodoxy to America. He was not a cleric but an astronomer, Professor John Pringle Nichol of Glasgow University, and he gave a series of lectures at the New York Mercantile Library Association premises in January and February. The *New York Tribune* sent Oliver Dyer, its expert phonographic writer, to take down every word the professor uttered. The poet Edward Young had once said that Christian devotion was 'the daughter of astronomy' and Nichol bore this out. Ignoring pantheism and metaphysics, ignoring the claims of the sects and the communities to have a direct and intimate relationship with infinity, he put God back on his throne and man back in his place as a humble and distant worshipper:

O what a world is this! Change rising above change, cycle growing out of cycle in majestic procession ... what must be the Creator, the Preserver, the Guide of all! He at whose bidding these phantasms come from nothingness and again disappear, whose Name – amid all things – alone is EXISTENCE – I AM THAT I AM! The All-Encompasser; the All-Sustainer! He enwraps, he upholds all those gorgeous Heavens! Reverentially before Him – humbly grateful that in the course of His beneficial arrangement He has permitted such intimation of His glory to reach us – let us conclude in the rapt language of the Psalmist: *How manifold, oh God, are thy works, by wisdom Thou hast made them all!*

A few blocks away, in the New York Society Library building, another lecturer was presenting a different picture of God's creation. During the previous summer and autumn, while Lyte had been walking the hills above Brixham composing 'Abide with me', Edgar Allan Poe had been pacing the heights above the Harlem river working out a view of the universe based on the doctrine of the inner consciousness. Now, on 3 February 1848, he made his ideas public in the form of a lecture on 'The Cosmogony of the Universe'. It was a cold night, the audience was sparse and Poe was profoundly disappointed, even though the *Tribune* said next morning that his lecture had been 'characterized by the strong analytical powers and intense capacity of imagination which distinguish him'. Some of his insights into the nature of the universe were startling – he declared, a lifetime before Einstein, that space and time were the same thing – while others were merely

31

idiosyncratic. But it was his unrepentant pantheism, his insistence that God was everywhere and that everything was God, which gave his lecture its driving force. He went further, proclaiming that every human being partook of divinity. 'This Heart Divine – what is it? *It is our own.* Each soul is, in part, its own God – its own creation.' Forty years earlier Wordsworth had suggested that there was life before birth: 'trailing clouds of glory do we come, From God, who is our home'. This idea had recently been incorporated into Christian belief by the Mormons and now Poe made it the keystone of his philosophy. 'We live out a youth peculiarly haunted by such dreams,' he said, referring to man's sense of the infinite, 'and yet never mistaking them for dreams. As Memories we know them. *During our youth* the distinction is too clear to deceive us even for a moment.' As the beginning, so the end: all would one day return to be part of the godhead. 'The sense of individual identity will be gradually merged in the general consciousness – Man, ceasing imperceptibly to feel himself Man, will at length attain that awfully triumphant epoch when he shall recognize his existence as that of Jehovah.'

So far it was only Cumming and the apocalyptic fanatics who saw the United States as the stamping-ground of Antichrist but they were soon to be joined by Samuel Wilberforce, Bishop of Oxford, who included American heresies among those which represented 'the first stealing over the sky of the lurid lights which shall be shed profusely around the great Antichrist.' He condemned pantheism roundly – 'the human soul cannot bear to be told that God is nowhere, but can be cajoled by the artful concealment of the same lie under the assertion that God is everywhere' – but he reserved his fiercest denunciations for American spiritualism, which he regarded as the final blasphemy. Spiritualism, even more than Poe's pantheism or the Bible Communism of the Oneida community, was the American version of the 1848 revolutions. It was in March 1848, as thrones tottered and Marx consigned the bourgeois God to the gravediggers, that the spirit of a dead man was said to have communicated with Katherine and Margaretta Fox in their cottage at Hydesville near New York. The Fox sisters later confessed that they had produced the so-called 'spirit rappings' themselves, but no amount of confessions or exposures could stop spiritualism's triumphant progress. One of its earliest historians, compiling her account 'at the command and under the supervision of the Wise and Mighty Beings through whose Instrumentality the Spiritual Telegraph of the Nineteenth Century has been con-

structed' was told that the house at Hydesville had been chosen 'as one peculiarly suited to their purpose from the fact of its being charged with the aura requisite to make it a battery for the working of the telegraph'.

Spiritualism brought to a climax the long reaction against the rationalism of the eighteenth century. The wise and mighty beings had apparently transformed the unreasonable into the reasonable, the supernatural into the natural. The greatest of all reasons for disbelieving in God, the conviction that there was nothing outside material existence, had now lost its power. Lyte's distinction between the glory of heaven and the vanity of earthly things, like Longfellow's insistence that the only reality lay beyond the grave, now stood vindicated. The spirit world might not be quite the heaven which the pious looked for but it was at least a life after death, a proof that the atheists had been wrong about the most important thing of all. If spiritualism could stand up to investigation the years of cold unbelief could perhaps be brought to an end. Whatever reservations orthodox Christians might have about earlier manifestations of unreason, about the metaphysics of the Germans or the enthusiasms of the Americans, they would surely now unite with spiritualists to confound the sceptics and demonstrate the immortality of the soul.

The orthodox did nothing of the sort. Long before Bishop Wilberforce launched his denunciations Christians feared that spiritualist manifestations were the work of Antichrist. Mrs Fox's first reaction, once she was convinced that the rappings were supernatural, was to worry in case her children had been possessed by an evil spirit. Just as Hamlet had concluded that his father's ghost came from hell or from purgatory so Christians throughout the ages had assumed that only the dead who were themselves troubled would have need to trouble the living. 'Do you think it's all a fraud and the spirits do not appear?' asked Hall Caine when Dante Gabriel Rossetti advised him not to go to a spiritualist séance. 'No,' Rossetti replied, 'but they're evil spirits – devils – and they're allowed to torment and deceive people.' As the son of a lifelong student of the occult and the nephew of the man who introduced the vampire into English literature, Rossetti very much wanted to get in touch with the dead, especially after his wife's suicide and her subsequent exhumation. Nevertheless he shunned spiritualism as a modern form of necromancy. *The Spirit World*, a spiritualist journal launched in London in May 1853, took such charges in its stride: 'If there are bad spirits there may

33

be good,' it observed, 'equally powerful for good as the others for evil.' The comparison with past sorcerers was a gently ironic weapon in the hands of sceptics – 'all our present degenerate mediums would have to hide their heads in the presence of Cagliostro,' said Senator Shields of Illinois when he asked Congress to investigate spiritualism – but it was a very real one in the hands of ecclesiastical authority. When the medium Daniel Home went to Rome he was arraigned before the Inquisition and expelled from the city as a necromancer.

Nor did spiritualists always want to unite with Christians. 'Spiritualism is the acknowledgement of a fact, not the enunciation of a creed,' declared the London *Spiritual Herald* in April 1856. The American spiritualist Eliab Capron also refused to talk in terms of religious experience or divine intervention, even though his wife had been cured of an illness by a medium exerting healing powers at a distance and without her knowledge. He found that no two spirits agreed about the nature of truth and he thought they were in no better position than mortals to know whether or not God existed. 'I see nothing in the new revelations that would of necessity lead an atheist to change his views,' he concluded. Many of the spirits were American Indians who knew little of Christianity and who tended to manifest themselves, perhaps not entirely coincidentally, after the publication of Longfellow's *Hiawatha* in 1855 had highlighted the Indian's mysterious affinity with elemental forces. Meanwhile in the summer of 1852 dead John Murray sought out John Spear, a medium who was also a clergyman, in order to deliver 'important instructions to the inhabitants of the earth'. Mortals must stop regarding Jesus as a god and they must also give up heaven and hell. 'All goes on in infinite progression,' Murray explained, 'that poor, foolish, unwise man – he goes into a lower state; and there are those ready to welcome him, to teach him; and, as rapidly as possible, to raise him from that estate to a higher and more perfect condition.'

This confounding of the virtuous and the wicked was particularly galling to the devout. 'A miserable debauchee like Poe, who lived without the thought of a Redeemer, dies and straightway through a "medium" announces himself to be in glory!' cried *Blackwood's Magazine* indignantly when Edgar Allan Poe manifested himself in a spiritualist séance shortly after his death in 1849. If there was indeed an 'infinite progression' then Poe had vaulted infinity with deplorable ease. Clearly there was no tedious delay in the grave, no waiting for

the Last Trumpet, no eventual emergence of an incorruptible body. Heaven's morning would break at the moment of death just as Lyte had hoped and it would break for saint and sinner alike, welcoming them as disembodied souls and freeing them from the physical frame and its supposedly sinful appetites. There would be no raging Antichrist, no apocalyptic horsemen, no bursting of bodies from graves, no coming of Christ in glory to judge both the quick and the dead, none of the spectacular cosmic happenings that Dr Cumming and Bishop Wilberforce predicted. It was hardly surprising that both men saw spiritualism as being itself a manifestation of Antichrist and a sign of his imminent arrival.

Nevertheless they were in the minority, not only because of their apocalyptic predictions but also because of their view of the afterlife. Tennyson's *In Memoriam*, published in London in May 1850 before spiritualism had made much impact in Britain, rested on a view of the next world which was even less orthodox than the hopes expressed in 'Abide with me'. Far from being mere suspended dust, trapped in cold earth until time should end, the dead were already in glory and could enter the hearts and minds of the living. Tennyson was convinced that his dead friend Arthur Hallam could see into his inmost soul, could 'look me through and through', and he decided – after some understandable hesitation – that this prospect must be welcomed. The poem quickly became a best seller and Tennyson was able to get married on the strength of it: his fiancée's father had opposed the match for ten years but now at last the success of *In Memoriam* made him give in. The Queen and her husband Prince Albert read the poem eagerly and before the end of the year Tennyson was made Poet Laureate. When the Queen opened the Great Exhibition in Hyde Park a few months later *The Times* remarked that the scene was like the coming Day of Judgement, 'that day when all ages and climes shall be gathered round the throne of their MAKER'. It did not, however, venture to rebuke the Poet Laureate for releasing the dead from their coffins in advance of that momentous occasion. Popular belief and enlightened opinion were anticipating the spiritualists and turning away from the darker aspects of Christian orthodoxy.

When the British and the French attacked Sebastopol at the beginning of the Crimean War Dr Cumming's friends pointed out excitedly that in Greek the word 'Sebastopol' meant what 'Armageddon' meant in Hebrew. Even *The Times* admitted that 'in the turmoil and excitement of the fight many fancied they beheld the preliminary skirmishes

35

which were to lead us to the grand battle of Armageddon'. According to the Book of Revelation this last great combat would take place when 'the spirits of devils, working miracles, go forth unto the kings of the earth and of the whole world to gather them to the battle of that great day of God Almighty'. In April 1855 one of Elizabeth Barrett Browning's friends wrote to ask whether she thought Cumming was right. 'That *you* should ask me about "Armageddon" is most assuredly a sign of the times,' she replied, 'I don't, for the rest, like Dr Cumming. His books seem to me very narrow ... The end of the world is probably the end of a dispensation. What I expect is a great development of Christianity in opposition to the churches'. England in particular, she thought, would need to be shaken out of its smugness: 'I begin to think that nothing will do for England but a good revolution and a "besom of destruction" used dauntlessly.' In August of that year, after attending a séance conducted by Daniel Home, she wrote to tell her sister that spiritualism would be at the heart of the new dispensation:

You may be quite sure that these things are developing themselves, even here in England, more and more, though the secret of them is being kept in order to avoid the derision of a sceptical public. Lord Stanley said to Sir Edward Lytton, a few days back, that the government should appoint a committee of investigation so as to get as far as possible at the facts ... A very little patience and we shall not speak such things in a whisper: *for it is but the beginning*.

There was no committee of investigation but an impressive number of influential people in London society were converted to spiritualism. In August 1860 Thackeray's *Cornhill Magazine* printed an article called 'Stranger than Fiction' describing a séance held by Daniel Home at the London house of the President of the Board of Trade, Thomas Milner-Gibson. It told how Home had been miraculously raised four or five feet above his chair and then placed in a horizontal position – 'he said he felt as if he had been turned in the gentlest manner as a child is turned in the arms of a nurse' – before floating backwards and forwards in the air for several minutes. All this had taken place in the presence of eight or nine distinguished ladies and gentlemen. It was hard to believe that the spirits were merely communicating with the living. They seemed much more concerned to overawe the living by showing off their supernatural powers. Cumming did not doubt that they were emissaries of Antichrist seeking to infiltrate the

ranks of the powerful: he had recently published yet another apocalyptic best seller saying that the growth of spiritualism in Boston and other American cities showed how close was the end of all things. Another of Antichrist's tentacles, the Roman Catholic Church, had made its latest bid for dominion by re-establishing the popish hierarchy in England in 1850 and by holding its first Plenary Council in the United States in 1852. And for good measure there had been 'a star of almost supernatural brilliancy' over the Holy Land in 1857. It was small wonder that another prophet, P.S. Desprez, published two triumphant editions of *Apocalypse Fulfilled* to prove that the Second Coming had already taken place.

In February 1861 the *Revue des Deux Mondes* in Paris published an article by Edmond Schérer proclaiming the death of God. 'I cannot think of these things,' he said, speaking of current varieties of unbelief, 'without remembering that voice which rang out long ago across the deep to tell man that the great God Pan was dead ... Now the voice sounds once more in the world, telling us of the end of another age, of the last moments of another God. The absolute is dead in the souls of men: who will bring it back to life?' *The Times* had recently recommended the *Revue des Deux Mondes* to its readers as being 'the only periodical publication in France pretending to anything like independence', but this was more like irresponsibility than independence. It was time for all men of weight and influence to unite in defence of orthodoxy, especially as a group of Anglican clerics had recently published *Essays and Reviews*, a collection of articles which propagated many of the dangerous German heresies. A formal denunciation of the book by the Archbishop of Canterbury was published on the day after Schérer's article appeared. Bishop Wilberforce arranged for the publication of a volume of replies and it was in the preface to this work, written in December 1861, that he provided a postscript to Schérer's epitaph on God by announcing the arrival of Antichrist. It could be no mere coincidence, he thundered, that so many insolent objections to Holy Writ were being put forward at the same time:

Much more true is the explanation which sees in it the first stealing over the sky of the lurid lights which shall be shed profusely around the great Antichrist. For these difficulties gather their strength from a spirit of lawless rejection of all authority, from a daring claim for the unassisted human intellect to be able to discover, measure and explain all things ... Thus the pride of man's heart is flattered to the utmost; thus the old whisper, 'Ye shall be as gods,' disguises itself in newest utterances. Such a state of the

human mind may be traced with more or less distinctiveness during this century everywhere in Christendom. It may be seen speculating in German metaphysics, fluttering in French literature, blaspheming in American spiritualism.

It was perhaps unfortunate that the bishop's indignation should culminate in a denunciation of spiritualism at this particular moment. Thirty miles away, in the Blue Room at Windsor Castle, Prince Albert lay dying. The end came at a quarter to eleven on the night of 14 December and for Queen Victoria it was the end of the world. 'My life as a happy one is ended,' she told her uncle Leopold, 'the world is gone for me!' She found consolation in a view of the afterlife that owed more to *In Memoriam* and to the spiritualists than to Christian orthodoxy. 'He is near me,' she cried desperately, 'his spirit will guide and inspire me!' Dr Cumming was quick to adjust his views and within a matter of days he had preached and published two sermons under the title *From Life to Life*. The spirit of the dead Prince Albert was indeed able to speak to the living, he declared, and all the Queen's subjects must 'let the voice that comes from a shroud be heard.' 'It is generally understood,' *The Spiritual Magazine* announced in October 1864, 'that Her Majesty holds constant communion with the spirit of Prince Albert. A statement to the same effect has been widely circulated by the Continental and American press.' The widowing of Queen Victoria, rather than her accession, was the real beginning of the Victorian age. It opened with talk of Antichrist's triumph and God's death but what was really in prospect was the painful dismembering of the image of Antichrist and the equally painful recasting of the image of God.

3 THE HARROWING OF HELL

On 30 March 1842, at Jefferson in the state of Georgia, Crawford W. Long gave sulphuric ether to James Venables before removing a tumour from his neck. The operation was a success and the patient felt no pain. Long used ether in several more operations during the next few months but did not communicate his discovery to the medical world. In 1844 at Hartford in Connecticut Horace Wells, a dentist, inhaled nitrous oxide before having a tooth extracted. He felt no pain and he suggested to his partner W. T. G. Morton that the technique could be used in major surgery; but Morton was more interested in ether, which he administered on 16 October 1846 at the Massachusetts General Hospital during an operation performed by John Collins Warren. The operation was successful and within a month an account of it was given to the American Academy of Sciences and published in the *Boston Medical and Surgical Journal*. Long and Wells contested Morton's claim to have pioneered the new painless surgery and Wells continued his experiments until he became addicted to chloroform. Early in 1848, while under its influence, he created a disturbance in New York and was locked up in the city prison, where he committed suicide.

Up to this time the only known form of painless surgery had been that undertaken under hypnosis or 'Mesmeric Sleep', which was by no means infallible. A strikingly successful operation was performed in March 1844 at Sedgley in Staffordshire. It was an amputation, the removal of a finger, and the room was thronged with 'medical and other gentlemen'. 'The cutting of the flaps and the dividing of the bone by the nippers was watched with breathless anxiety by all present,' reported the *Wolverhampton Chronicle*, 'but not a muscle quivered, nor did a sigh escape, nor any single thing occur to betray the slightest sensation. During the dressing the hand was suspended

39

over the table in a cataleptic state without any further support.' Even though such results could be achieved in cases where patients were susceptible to hypnotism, for most people surgery of any kind meant appalling suffering. But now at last, as medical men took in the good news from Boston, anaesthesia became a reality on both sides of the Atlantic. By January 1847 the distinguished obstetrician Professor James Simpson of Edinburgh was giving ether to relieve the pain of childbirth. Later in the year he and other doctors switched to chloroform as being safer and more effective. In 1853 it was administered to Queen Victoria when Prince Leopold was born. With startling suddenness there had taken place a revolution in medical practice, a revolution which the American physician Weir Mitchell summed up as 'the death of pain'.

The phrase was a good deal too sweeping. The agony of surgery was only a fraction, albeit a ghastly fraction, of man's inheritance of pain. The immemorial burden of human suffering could not be so easily lifted. But at least a start had been made. Doctors were quick to see that if surgery was less painful it would be more painstaking. Speed was no longer paramount, so that more care could be taken and the chances of success greatly improved. Short-term alleviation of pain meant long-term alleviation of suffering. Even more important was the new attitude to pain which anaesthetics brought. 'They altogether destroy,' proclaimed the *Westminster Review*, 'the old belief in physical suffering having an expiatory purpose.' Such suffering need no longer be regarded as a necessary and ultimately beneficial aspect of the human condition but as an enemy to be conquered. War had been declared and the first battle won.

On the face of things it would seem that Christians must be on the side of the doctors both in the battle and in the war. Christ had been concerned to relieve suffering, sometimes by means which seemed miraculous, and he had told his followers that by faith they would do the same. For centuries Christians had claimed that their religion was a caring and compassionate one which contrasted with the callous inhumanity of the heathen. 'Barbarian', which had once meant anybody outside the world of Greece and Rome, now meant anybody outside Christian civilization; and 'barbarity', savage and unmitigated cruelty, was the distinguishing mark of such people. It was also, in Protestant eyes, the distinguishing mark of Roman Catholicism. The British had had two Catholic monarchs since the Reformation, Mary Tudor and James ii. Mary was known as 'Bloody Mary' and James

was known for the 'Bloody Assizes', while Protestant cruelties in other reigns were unremembered.

Unfortunately there were those even in the Protestant English-speaking world who used Christianity as an excuse for the deliberate and savage infliction of pain. 'John McCue of Augusta county in Virginia, a Presbyterian preacher, frequently on the Lord's day tied up his slaves and whipped them,' reported *The Times* in February 1841, 'and left them bound while he went to the meeting house and preached, and after his return repeated the scourging.' Mrs Pence, also of Virginia, did the same except that she put a 'negro plaster' of salt, pepper and vinegar on the raw backs of her slave girls to make the pain fiercer while she went to church 'demure as a nun' between their first and their second floggings. When asked whether it was fitting to do this on a Sunday she pointed out that if she whipped them on any other day she would lose a day's work. It was important to make proper use of the sabbath. 'Their backs get well enough by Monday morning,' she concluded crisply. A few months later the United States census returns showed that there were about two and a half million slaves, well over a sixth of the nation's population, who were liable to be treated in this way. In May 1846 the negro abolitionist Frederick Douglass told a shocked London audience that slavery was 'identified with religion and exposes those who denounce it to the charge of infidelity'. 'The church and the slave prison stand next to each other,' he added, 'the groans and cries of the heartbroken slave are often drowned in the pious devotions of his religious master.'

The accusations were thrown back at the accusers. When a posse of Kentucky slavers crossed into Ohio in December 1844 and beat up several respectable citizens whom they suspected of sheltering runaway slaves, burning down their houses for good measure, the *New York Sun* insisted that the affair was prompted by the rabid anti-slavery propaganda put out by misguided Christians in London. *Punch* replied with a wry comment on President Polk's inauguration in 1845: 'It is not generally known – and the touching circumstance ought to be published to the whole world – that the Bible on which Mr Polk took the presidential oath was very handsomely bound for the purpose in the skin of a negro.' The revelation, macabre though it was, did at least suggest that there were skins sufficiently unscarred to be used for bookbinding. According to one historian visitors to the southern states seldom told of 'anything but the most inconsequential whipping, nothing like, indeed, what the traditional English

41

schoolboy expected and endured in many of the public schools in those days.' In 1842, as if anticipating this countercharge, Charles Dickens dealt both with the whipping of slaves and with the birching of schoolboys in *American Notes*, a book which gave great offence across the Atlantic. He attacked the 'foul growth and tangled root' of American life, giving as instances of it not only the horrifying treatment of negroes but also the appalling insolence and arrogance of white American youngsters, which he attributed to the fact that they were not properly birched.

British attitudes to corporal punishment had extremely tangled roots. The birch, as Phillipe Ariès has remarked, was 'above all an opportunity for the boy being flogged to exercise self-control, the first duty of an English gentleman.' Nor was stoicism under the rod a gentleman's monopoly. At all levels of society it was thought right to beat children frequently and severely, not only because the Bible advised it but also because it did them good by teaching them to endure pain. Dr Johnson's schoolmaster told him that he whipped him to save him from the gallows but he might equally well have said that he did it to steel him against the surgeon's knife. In a world in which pain was unavoidable fortitude was not merely a virtue but a necessity. Initiation rites, ceremonies in which boys were ritually tortured in order to prepare them to be warriors, were far older than Christianity. By advising the mortification of the flesh against the assaults of Satan, rather than the brave endurance of the wounds of combat, Christianity merely produced variations on a theme. It was perhaps strange that a religion which made a virtue out of relieving pain should also make a virtue out of its well-meaning infliction and its dutiful acceptance. While Mr McCue and Mrs Pence whipped their slaves in order to make sure that they remained their inferiors, British schoolmasters whipped their charges in order to make sure that they became their equals.

Both kinds of infliction could quote biblical authority, for the stark truth was that pain was approved and endorsed by God. 'I will greatly multiply thy sorrow and thy conception,' he had told Eve angrily after she had persuaded Adam to eat the forbidden fruit, 'in sorrow thou shalt bring forth children.' Could such sorrow be lightly dispelled? If Professor Simpson did away with it by the use of chloroform was he flying in the face of God? The pangs of childbirth were only a beginning: 'we know that the whole creation groaneth and travaileth in pain until now,' St Paul had written. Pain had been the key to

God's plan for the world ever since Adam and Eve had offended him. The agony his son had suffered upon the cross had brought the chance of redemption – hence St Paul's 'until now' – but it had not been universally accepted. There was still sin in the world and so there must still be pain. Indeed Christ taught that pain in this world might be the only way to avoid far greater pain in the next. 'If thy hand offend thee, cut it off,' he advised, 'it is better for thee to enter into life maimed than having two hands to go into hell, into the fire that never shall be quenched.' There was added point to the advice now that the hand could be amputated painlessly, especially since there was no evidence that chloroform would be available in hell. There pain still reigned supreme, just as it had reigned when Christ had redeemed the world. It was difficult to believe that the torture of God's son would have been efficacious had it been carried out under a general anaesthetic.

Yet it was equally difficult to believe that God revelled in human suffering or would resent the relief which anaesthetics had brought. The Greeks had thought of all life's afflictions as being wished on mankind by Zeus himself: the king of the gods had sent Pandora down to earth knowing full well that she would open her box and let loose every evil upon the world. The Christian myths which fleshed out the skeletal account given in Genesis were more respectful. Milton summed them up in *Paradise Lost* when he pictured Satan buying his way out of hell by promising sin and death that they would henceforth have dominion over mankind. It was not just sin but pain and suffering as well, 'death and all our woe', that had come into the world once Eve had eaten the apple. God had seen to it that all evil and all pain were confined securely in hell but Satan's rebellion had led first to their being released and then to their being let loose upon mankind as retribution for sin. Hell was the source of present and temporal pains as well as the home of future and eternal ones.

But there was also a belief, admittedly based on extremely slender scriptural evidence, that between his death and his resurrection Christ had gone down into hell in order to secure the release of all those who had had the misfortune to be born between Adam's original sin and the redemption of mankind. The harrowing of hell, as this divine gesture was called, was a concession wrung from Satan by the power of the cross as an instrument of torture. Christ had been able to defy the foul fiend not merely because he was God but because of the agony of his death. And for nearly two thousand years, in fact and

in fiction, Christians had held out the cross as a sure defence against the forces of hell. 'We wrestle,' St Paul had said, 'not against flesh and blood, but against principalities and powers, against the rulers of the darkness of this world.' Yet it was flesh and blood, the torn flesh and the spilt blood of an incarnate God, which could defeat those powers and dispel that darkness. Hell was the kingdom of pain, actual bodily pain, and its tribute could only be paid in its own currency. It must have been created by God, in order to be available as a place of punishment for the fallen angels, and so he must have decreed its laws. He had had a share in the birth of pain, but the harrowing of hell, like the crucifixion itself, suggested that it was a share he had cause to regret. Now that the death of pain was in prospect, now that man was moving in for the kill, God would surely wish to play his part.

As anaesthetics and spiritualism crossed the Atlantic the scene was set for this new harrowing of hell. It was not so much a matter of changing the nature of God as of seeing it clearly for the first time. Just as God had once saved man from being hell's victim so man would now rescue God from being hell's master. The responsibility for creating evil and ordaining pain, loaded upon God by superstitious Christians of the past, must be lifted by enlightened Christians of the present. Frances Power Cobbe, an eager though unorthodox Christian journalist, spelled out the challenge: 'the current teaching of our present divines shall grow unendurable and we shall insist that to the All Righteous All Merciful God shall be attributed no longer deeds and modes of government we should abhor as unjust and cruel from a despot of the earth.' The inspiration for the campaign against hell came from America: it was there that the frontiers of pain's domain had been rolled back and the notion of bodily resurrection dispelled. But the campaign itself could not be fought in America because there was nothing to fight, no established church whose dogmas could be challenged. Hell's destruction must be achieved in the old world or not at all.

Predictably enough the first shot was fired by George Holyoake. It was fired not against the Church of England but against Roman Catholicism, which he saw as 'the predominant religious influence of Europe and the great enemy of philosophy and freedom'. In the spring of 1850, just as Tennyson published his bland and sanitized vision of the hereafter in *In Memoriam*, Holyoake ran a series of articles in *The Reasoner* in which he summarized Pinamonti's *Hell Opened to*

Christians. There was nothing bland or sanitized here: Holyoake gave his readers all the horror of the original, with its emphasis not only on the fires of torment but also on the filth and the stench of the bottomless pit: 'as in dead bodies worms are engendered from putrefaction, so in the damned there arises a perpetual remorse from the corruption of sin.' 'Its effects on the imagination of children and sympathetic women are appalling to contemplate,' Holyoake commented, 'To these brimstonian tortures Roman Catholics consign all who do not believe in Popery; and Protestants all who do not believe in the Bible; so that, if both churches are right, a very small portion of the human race have any chance of going to heaven.'

Anglicans were genuinely worried by the attacks on hell and by the problem of God's apparent responsibility for sin and for its punishment. The anonymous author of *The Bible History of Satan* tried to solve it by denying that the Prince of Darkness was a fallen angel at all. 'It is infinitely more likely,' he declared, 'that the Devil has existed from eternity as an evil spirit.' In the end God would destroy him and there would be no more evil. 'Reason may cavil at the delay,' he concluded, 'but cannot deny the omnipotence of the act, and must admit that God's toleration of sin for a season is self-imposed, and not from external necessity.' Catholics made no concessions. In Dublin Father Furniss published *The Sight of Hell*, one of a series of tracts for children. It told of one little girl who was wearing a bonnet of fire for ever because she had been too fond of pretty clothes while she was alive. 'It is pressed down close over her head,' Furniss assured his young readers, 'it burns into the skin, it scorches the bone of the skull and makes it smoke.' In another fiery dungeon he found a boy whose eyeballs were alight, bursting out of his head with a noise like a kettle on the boil, while his blood was liquid fire which ate into the very marrow of his bones. When questioned the lad admitted that he deserved this punishment because he had frequented dance halls and theatres. More than four million of these tracts were printed and the publishers reported that *The Sight of Hell* sold particularly well because of 'attacks by enemies of the Church'. Furniss's biographer declared that the tracts would be found 'of incalculable utility for school and family use', especially now that the doctrine of hell was being questioned by 'whatever is unsound and vague in the Protestant mind'.

In the eyes of the orthodox, Catholic and Anglican alike, the unsoundness and vagueness of the Protestant mind came indubitably

45

from Germany. Progressive thinkers were equally sure that German philosophy and German biblical criticism constituted the best defence against papal tyranny. The Americans might well save themselves, as many German Catholics had done, by setting up their own Catholic church. The *New York Herald* proclaimed proudly that republicanism bred a spirit of freedom, in religious as in secular matters, and that there might soon be an independent Catholic church in the United States with its own American pope. But if Protestant Europe was to escape what one contributor to *Essays and Reviews* called 'those shadows of the twelfth century which with ominous recurrence are closing round us', it must look to Germany for its salvation.

At first *Essays and Reviews* was favourably received. 'We cannot but honour,' wrote the *Spectator* in April 1860, 'the men who have so courageously set the example of "open teaching" in the Church of England'. It was the atheist Frederic Harrison, writing in the September issue of the *Westminster Review*, who deliberately goaded the ecclesiastical authorities into taking action against the book. 'No fair mind can close this volume,' he claimed, 'without feeling it to be at bottom in direct antagonism to the whole system of popular belief.' It replaced the orthodox doctrine of hell with 'idealized damnation' and it showed that Anglican intellectual circles were 'honeycombed with disbelief'. Why then had it not been condemned? 'Nowhere,' he continued, 'has there been seen or heard a sign of official repudiation. These professors, tutors, principals and masters still hold their chairs and retain their influence. No authorized rebuke has been put forward.' Stung by Harrison's mockery, Bishop Wilberforce reviewed the book in the *Quarterly Review* for January 1861 and declared that its contributors were heretics. 'Holding their views, they cannot, consistently with moral honesty, maintain their posts as clergymen of the Established Church'. He then set to work to make sure that the Church condemned the book and punished its authors.

Once again it was Edmond Schérer in the *Revue des Deux Mondes* who saw the significance of what was going on. In May 1861, just three months after his announcement of the death of God, he published an article called 'The Crisis of Protestantism in England'. 'Do you know what pre-occupies and excites the English at this moment?' he wrote, 'It is not Armstrong guns or armour-plated warships or the affairs of China or the Lebanon; it is not the budget or the famine in India; it is not even Garibaldi or the crisis in the cotton industry. It is a book, a book whose innocuous title, *Essays and Reviews*, gives

no hint of the tempest it has unleashed.' In his view the storm was about the part which myth and fantasy should play in religion. Roman Catholicism accepted them because it knew that man could not live by reason alone. The Church of England, poised between Catholicism and Protestantism, had managed hitherto to combine the religion of myth and the religion of reason. Now it was being forced to choose and the choice was about the nature of religious myths as well as the nature of supposedly rational doctrines. It was the future of Christianity, not just the future of the Church of England, which was at stake.

Also at stake was the future of hell. At the outset it had played a minor part in the argument. All that had been said in *Essays and Reviews* was that 'we must entertain a hope that there shall be found, after the great adjudication, receptacles where the stunted may become strong and the perverted be restored'. It was a kindly and comparatively harmless suggestion, certainly not as destructive of Christian doctrine as many other things in the book, but it quickly became the thing upon which the whole volume was judged. Henry Bristow Wilson, the man who had written it, was one of the only two contributors who were parish priests and thus subject to the authority of the bishops. The other was Rowland Williams, who had denied that the Bible was literally true or divinely inspired. Both were found guilty by a church court and suspended from their benefices for a year. 'This apparently interminable case', as *The Times* called it, was then referred to the Judicial Committee of the Privy Council, headed by the Lord Chancellor, which mulled it over for eight months. Edward Pusey, Professor of Hebrew at Oxford and a doughty champion of Anglican dogma, kept hell in the public eye by telling how a man had plucked his sleeve in a crowded street and told him: 'Dr Pusey, I have been burning in hell the last hour for that lie I told you.' He had then gone to the man's house and discovered he had died an hour earlier. Nevertheless the Lord Chancellor's Committee finally reversed the sentences in February 1864. Little was heard about Williams but much about the Committee's ruling that Wilson must be acquitted because the doctrine of eternal punishment formed no part of the teaching of the Church of England. 'He dismissed hell with costs,' said the *Spectator* of the Lord Chancellor in words quickly taken up by other journals, 'and took away from orthodox members of the Church of England their last hope of everlasting damnation'.

Orthodox members of the Church of England determined to fight

to the last for their unforgiving God. *The Times* insisted that the two defendants had only escaped 'by the skin of their teeth' and that there was no parish in the country which would not throw them out if they dared to preach such heresies. Wilberforce persuaded Convocation to pronounce a 'synodical condemnation' of *Essays and Reviews*, while Pusey set up a committee which sent out to all Anglican clergy a declaration of belief in eternal punishment. Less than half of the clergy signed and some wrote in fury to the newspapers saying that they would resist this 'hateful tyranny' and throw the document into the waste-paper basket. John Keble wrote *A Litany of Our Lord's Warnings for the Present Distress*, addressed to 'all those whose hearts are aching at the recent decision of the Privy Council touching the eternal punishment of the wicked'. How many souls would be damned, he wondered, now that priests could lie to their flocks and tell them there was a chance of the wicked escaping the eternal flames? 'Only think what men and women risk as it is,' he shuddered, 'knowing as they do our Lord's awful words and as yet untaught how to explain them away; what will it be when the Evil One has met them and put this word into their mouths?' Keble followed up his tract with a letter to *The Times* demanding an inquiry into the powers of the Privy Council. 'Men are free to think they should have a Church without dogma,' he concluded, 'but they are also free to think they should have one *with* dogma.'

The final humiliation of hell's defenders took place in the House of Lords on Friday 15 July 1864 and was brought about by Lord Houghton, who combined outward piety with an encyclopaedic knowledge of pornography and had been nominated by Thomas Carlyle for the office of 'Perpetual President of the Heaven and Hell Amalgamation Society'. Houghton asked whether Convocation had any right to make its much-publicized 'synodical condemnation', whereupon the Lord Chancellor replied that Convocation was a futile body which had only recently been allowed to resume business after being suspended for more than a century. Its ridiculous pronouncements had no significance and if it continued to make them it would have to be suspended again 'to check its eccentricities'. The Church of England was by law established and so the law must have the last word. Pusey preached a final defiant sermon, declaring that the fires of hell burned for evermore, and there the matter rested until 1876, when the Privy Council once again quashed an ecclesiastical decision. The Rev. Flavel Smith Cook had been supported by the church courts when he refused

Communion to a certain Henry Jenkins because he did not believe in the Devil. The Privy Council ruled that belief in the Devil was no part of Anglican doctrine and ordered Cook to administer the sacrament. As the Prince of Darkness went the way of eternal torment hell's new harrowers could celebrate total victory.

But had they been fighting on the wrong field of battle? Harrison's initial challenge had not been about legal decisions but about 'the whole system of popular belief'. The Lord Chancellor for all his powers could not do much about popular belief. Tennyson had edged it along a little with his *In Memoriam*, but even he could not entirely shake off older and cruder visions of the hereafter. A few weeks after the poem's publication he and his bride found themselves in a house full of strange nocturnal noises. When they were told it was haunted by the spirit of a murdered child they left hurriedly. Their own first child was accidentally strangled at birth and died unbaptized. 'I thy father love thee and weep over thee,' said Tennyson sadly, 'though thou hast no place in the universe.' Popular belief – and Tennyson's belief too, it seemed – still feared that only sacramental technicalities could admit a human soul to the divine mercy. And the end of the story mirrored its beginning: when the Privy Council decided against Cook his parishioners presented him with a testimonial, paid his legal costs and made it clear to Jenkins that he must not insist on receiving Communion. A quarter of a century of controversy had done a lot at the legal level but very little at the level of popular belief.

Nor had spiritualism changed conventional attitudes as much as might have been expected. When the London *Spirit World* was set up in May 1853 its very first issue told how Mrs Hayden, the American medium who had recently arrived in England, had been put in touch with her dead child. 'The Good Shepherd has taken into his ever loving arms the sweet innocent lambkin,' she had been assured, 'that you may follow to the fold of heavenly love.' Although the orthodox clearly knew more about the parameters of paradise – Queen Victoria's chaplain published a useful little book called *The Recognition of Friends in Heaven*, while the Rev. Richard Shimeall of New York plotted heaven's exact astronomical position – the spiritualists were not far behind. They also received accounts which came close to traditional visions of posthumous punishment. When the Tsar of Russia died in 1855 the spirits told their mortal contacts that he had been shut up in an iron cage to curb his haughtiness.

In addition spiritualists showed a ghoulish interest in the corpses

49

whose total irrelevance they had originally proclaimed. In 1860 the *Spiritual Magazine* printed with some excitement a piece about 'singular displacement of coffins in a vault in a burying ground', even though the events described had taken place forty years earlier and thousands of miles away on the island of Barbados. It could have been the work of no human hand, the journal declared solemnly, pointing out that two of the bodies had been those of suicides. A later issue contained a report on a vault in Wiltshire where the coffin of the local squire had turned itself round and risen several feet in the air. In view of such revelations it was not surprising that the advent of spiritualism did little or nothing to check the growing popularity of tales of horror about vampires and other manifestations of the undead. Soon the National Association of Spiritualists in London was proudly exhibiting casts of spirit hands and spirit feet. These had remained intact even after the spirit limbs had dissolved and disappeared – 'a thing manifestly impossible had they encased any human limb'. 'This corruptible must put on incorruption,' St Paul had written in explanation of the resurrection of the body. Now it seemed that the supposedly disembodied spirits were doing just that. What had begun as a challenge to orthodoxy had now become suspiciously like an endorsement of it.

Meanwhile pain was an unconscionable time dying. The anaesthetists might be smothering it but there were many who had an interest in keeping it alive. Sarah Potter, keeper of a whipping brothel in Chelsea, was arrested in July 1863 while the future of hell was still unresolved. She fell foul of the authorities because she forced her girls to let her clients flog them, but in most of these places it was the client who suffered the pain. It had been said of Theresa Berkley, queen of the profession, that 'her instruments of torture were more numerous than those of any other governess... at her shop, whoever went with plenty of money could be tortured till he had a belly full.' By the time she died in 1836 there were at least ten such establishments in London and the number increased during the next quarter of a century. The 1860s and early 1870s also saw an impressive number of pornographic or semi-pornographic works portraying flagellation in schoolrooms and in bedrooms with equal and impartial gusto. It was Henry Salt, an old Etonian with considerable experience of the birch, who pointed out that 'Spare the rod and spoil the child' had been said not by King Solomon in the Bible but by a lascivious lady in an erotic seventeenth-century poem. 'Love is a boy, by poets styl'd,

Then spare the rod and spoil the child,' she had told her lover when he seemed reluctant to submit to aphrodisiac flagellation.

It was not only the grimly sadistic rulers of the great English public schools who needed Salt's reminder. The Wiltshire curate Francis Kilvert was the gentlest of men and yet he could commend a little girl's parents who 'very wisely have not spared her nor the rod' while remarking of another child whose bottom he glimpsed while she was on a swing that 'her flesh was plump and smooth and in excellent whipping condition'. Nor did he spare his own flesh: 'I sat down in my bath upon a sheet of thick ice which broke in the middle into large pieces,' he wrote one Christmas morning, 'whilst sharp points and jagged edges stuck all round the sides of the tub like chevaux de frise, not particularly comforting to the naked thighs and loins, for the keen ice cut like broken glass.' While disciplinarians and ascetics made sure that the pains of this world survived the advent of anaesthetics, theological subtleties did the same for the pains of hell. If bodily pain could be killed by deadening the mind, wrote Gerard Manley Hopkins, then it must exist in the mind irrespective of the body. God could therefore inflict bodily torture on souls in hell even though their actual bodies had been consumed by worms or by fire.

Even English law could not dispense with hell as easily as the Lord Chancellor might think. In 1860, just as the row over *Essays and Reviews* was getting under way, Mrs Maden of Rochdale in Lancashire sued her stepfather for damages because he had refused to let her take her piano with her when she left his house to marry an atheist of whom he disapproved. She had become an atheist herself and for this reason the judge in the county court would not let her take the oath or proceed with her case. It would be a mockery, he said, because she did not believe in hell. How could the court possibly accept the evidence of someone who did not know that she would be tortured for ever if she failed to tell the truth? The Rochdale Secular Society, encouraged by the publicity given to the case in *The Reasoner* and in Parliament, raised money for a re-trial and then for an appeal. At every level the original ruling was upheld: those who did not believe in hell could not give evidence and so could not have recourse to the law. Holyoake's friend Sir John Trelawny brought a Bill before Parliament to allow atheists to affirm instead of taking the oath, but he was told he was endangering the whole fabric of society and so consideration of his measure was adjourned indefinitely. The same thing happened in 1862 and 1863, after which he gave up the attempt.

51

On Sunday 1 July 1860, as Mrs Maden embarked on her attempt to recover her piano, Arthur Munby went to Oxford for the day. He was a Cambridge man, an unsuccessful barrister who worked at the London office of the Ecclesiastical Commissioners, but he had friends in Oxford who were quick to welcome him and tell him about the dramatic confrontation which had taken place there at the previous day's meeting of the British Association for the Advancement of Science. Bishop Wilberforce, seeking to ridicule Darwin's theory of evolution, had asked Professor Huxley whether he would rather have a man or an ape for an ancestor. Huxley had replied that an ape would be preferable to a man like Wilberforce who sought to obscure scientific truth with religious prejudice. Munby's friends assured him that this was the end as far as belief in the literal truth of the Bible was concerned – 'defence is no longer possible – the controversy has been pushed to the last point and that will soon be given up' – but Munby insisted that even if science excluded God from the natural world he personally would still regard him as supreme in the moral world. 'Even if Love be not Power, I will yet believe in Love: I must and will have a Father in Heaven, and a Christ too, if I have even to create them out of old memories and tottering beliefs. In religion, at least, let us be allowed to live through the Imagination if we can find no stronger aliment.' Three weeks later, when he came home one evening to discover that he had been robbed of some silver and a favourite coat, Munby found that he needed a God of retribution as well as a God of love. 'I feel a magnanimous pity for the miscreant,' he noted in his diary, 'I will enjoy my triumphs over him if he is caught: and if not I know – blessed thought! – that he will suffer for his doings in a future world.'

Munby was typical of the many thousands of devout Christians on both sides of the Atlantic who saw the publication of *The Origin of Species* in 1859 as a threat to their faith. The challenge to the Book of Genesis, the suggestion that man was the descendant of an ape rather than the image of God, was the most obviously alarming thing in the book but not necessarily the most fundamental. More important was Darwin's insistence on competition and conflict as the instruments of all evolution and progress. Karl Marx welcomed this as 'a basis in natural science for the class struggle in history' and Lord Houghton's young protégé Algernon Charles Swinburne went further, proclaiming that 'if we would be at one with nature let us continually do evil with all our might'. Herbert Spencer had already declared in 1852

that 'the survival of the fittest' was the determinant of human as well as animal evolution and even *In Memoriam* had lamented that God and nature were at strife, the one the image of perfect love and the other 'red in tooth and claw', indifferent to the fate either of individuals or of species. Darwin's book was not so much a sudden bombshell as part of a continuing cannonade.

It was perhaps surprising that the traditional view of pain as the offspring of hell should have stood up to this bombardment for so long. Christian myth, like the myth of Pandora and her box, envisaged a painless golden age in which men and women had basked before all the woes bottled up in hell had been released upon them. It was now becoming clear that such a golden age was a blank impossibility. Pain was not so much an added evil as a basic necessity, an essential warning system without which no species could have evolved or survived. Nature was red in tooth and claw because it could not be otherwise. 'What a book a devil's chaplain might write,' remarked Darwin in 1856, 'on the clumsy, wasteful, blundering, low and horribly cruel works of nature!' When *The Origin of Species* appeared some thought that it was indeed diabolically inspired, but in fact no devil would have had any reason to be proud of it. It did not describe the cruelty which had resulted from Satan's success in tempting mankind but the cruelty which must have existed before that event took place, the cruelty which had underpinned the allegedly idyllic world of God's original creation. And if pain had not come from hell why should it be thought that it would return there? Suffering and happiness were complementary and constituent parts of human life – of all life – rather than moral absolutes to be separated out like wheat and chaff in some great winnowing operation at the end of all things.

But the world of the imagination, the world in which Munby built a god out of old memories and took satisfaction from the thought of a petty thief writhing in hell, was almost totally unaffected by abstract reasoning or by scientific observation. It was also unaffected by decisions of the Privy Council or the House of Lords. On the afternoon of Friday 15 July 1864, as Lord Houghton confronted Bishop Wilberforce, Munby took a stroll in St James's Park with one of the park keepers who showed him the outcasts of London, the starving and the homeless, who lay motionless on the grass. Gustave Doré's illustrated edition of Dante's *Inferno* had recently been published in England and it was the sinners in hell who came into Munby's mind. 'I looked and looked,' he wrote in horror, 'it was Dante and Virgil

53

gazing on the damned; and still they did not move.' Charles Dodgson, who was soon to achieve fame under the name of Lewis Carroll, was also in London that afternoon playing croquet in George Macdonald's garden in the Kensington Road. In his mind was another croquet game in a dream world of unreason where, as Alice remarked, 'they're dreadfully fond of beheading people'. Nor were Houghton's own private imaginings free from the visions of torment which he condemned in public. He had recently introduced Swinburne to the writings of the Marquis de Sade, only to be told that de Sade's torture chambers with their 'loaded iron whips and elaborately ingenious racks and horses' were less exciting than 'the simple common birch rod and daily whipping block' which Swinburne had known at Eton.

An age enlightened enough to scout belief in eternal punishment and the Prince of Darkness should surely be able to banish such images. Frances Power Cobbe, one of those who had first pointed the way to the conquest of hell, certainly thought that the intellect had finally penetrated and dispelled the darkness which lay at the edges of thought. She wrote a glowing review of Albert Réville's disproof of the Devil's existence when it was translated into English in 1871, pointing out that belief in evil as a positive force, rather than as the absence of good, was as silly as belief in positive lightness as opposed to the absence of weight. And yet she knew, for all her brave words, that there were areas in the human mind where reason still slept and where monsters came forth and strode across the world as confidently as ever they had done in Goya's day. She therefore developed the idea of Unconscious Cerebration, one of the neglected masterpieces of Victorian ingenuity, which stood Freudian psycho-analysis on its head a generation before it was born.

Her theory was put forward in two articles in *Macmillan's Magazine* in November 1870 and April 1871. She first showed that a great deal of thinking was done unconsciously, particularly when the thinker was asleep. When he woke he could remember names or words or tunes which he had tried in vain to recall the night before. Some people found they had performed necessary tasks, often menial tasks, without being conscious of what they had done. 'But our Familiar is a great deal more than a walking dictionary, a housemaid, a *valet de place* or a barrel-organ man,' Miss Cobbe continued, 'He is a novelist who can spin more romances than Dumas.' The world of fantasy and dreams was unbelievably rich and yet it was outside the control of the conscious self. It was a world of violence, often of obscenity,

a world in which the Devil and hell might well seem more real than God and heaven. 'The small share occupied by the Moral Law in the dream world is a significant fact,' proclaimed Miss Cobbe, 'Our dream-selves, like the Undines of German folk-lore, have no Souls, no Responsibility and no Hereafter.'

The assumption that the lack of moral responsibility ruled out the possibility of personal immortality was the vital stage in the argument. Men and women might be 'such stuff as dreams are made on', but 'in that "stuff" there enters not the noblest element of our nature, that Moral Will which allies us, not to the world of passing shadows, but to the great Eternal Will in whose life it is our hope that we shall live for ever.' 'We are not centaurs, rider and steed in one,' Miss Cobbe concluded triumphantly, 'but horsemen'. Each conscious human being, able to reason and make moral decisions, sat astride an unconscious thinking machine which would eventually sink and die. And the separability of rider and steed was in itself the proof of immortality. The survival of the conscious reasoning mind would bear witness to the reality of the god it worshipped, just as the death of unconscious fantasies would demonstrate the emptiness of the demons they had conjured up. It was a comforting prospect, a fitting tailpiece for the uplifting story of hell's destruction. Heaven was of course intact and undamaged because it was the inspiration and destination of the rider, not the foul fantasy of the steed. Bad imaginings came from the unconscious and were mortal, good imaginings came from the conscious and would inherit eternity. To sceptics the distinction sounded like wishful thinking but for Miss Cobbe it had to be real because the mind that rode was itself more real than the instinctive mechanism that was ridden. It was as well she did not live to see Sigmund Freud turn her riders into steeds and her steeds into riders.

4 OTHER GODS BEFORE ME

THE WARNING THAT EDMOND SCHÉRER DELIVERED IN 1861 when he spoke of a mighty voice announcing 'the end of another age, the last moments of another God', referred to an incident during the reign of the Emperor Tiberius. The crew and passengers of a ship sailing near the isles of Paxi had heard a loud voice, seemingly supernatural, crying that the great god Pan was dead. Tiberius had ordered an inquiry but no satisfactory explanation had emerged and Christians had been quick to assume that the heavens had been announcing the passing of Christ's pagan predecessor. It seems rather more probable that the travellers had overheard a ritual lament intoned by worshippers on the islands. Schérer's experience was less dramatic, less authenticated, but it was not entirely self-induced. There were certainly laments to be heard, whether human or divine, and there were heralds eager to proclaim a new dispensation. If the opening of the Christian era had meant great Pan's death then its close might bring about his rebirth.

A few months earlier Thackeray's *Cornhill Magazine* had printed a full-page picture of Pan to accompany Elizabeth Barrett Browning's poem 'A Musical Instrument'. The legs were suitably hairy and hooved, a reminder that here was a being who defied Miss Cobbe's separation of rider from steed, but of Pan's lusty and archetypal genitals there was no sign. If this was the symbol of the lewd unconscious mind, the bringer of pagan ecstasy, then it seemed to lack the means of bringing either lewdness or ecstasy to a suitable consummation. In her poem Mrs Browning was concerned not with Pan's sexuality but with the changes he wrought in those who worshipped him. 'Half a beast is the great god Pan,' she declared, telling how the faun-like god tore a reed from the bed of the river in order to make music so piercing sweet that the sun forgot to set. A poet was like a reed,

56

she concluded: Pan blew through him and touched him with his magic but in order to do so he had to tear out his soul as surely as he drew the pith from the reed. The poet would never again live a conventional life, 'as a reed with the reeds of the river', and the true gods, the gods who put virtue above ecstasy, would have to 'sigh for the cost and pain'.

A rather different view of the magic and the pain of paganism was given in a novel which Nathaniel Hawthorne published in London and in Boston in the spring of 1860. He called it *The Marble Faun* and it was published under this title in America, though his London publishers thought it too fanciful and brought out their edition under the rather more solemn title *Transformation*. Hawthorne was not too fond of living respectably with the other reeds in the river: after four laborious years as American consul in Liverpool he gave in his resignation in 1857 and set off for Italy. There he found what he called 'a sort of poetic or fairy precinct where actualities would not be so terribly insisted upon as they are, and must needs be, in America'. He dismissed his native land as 'a country where there is no shadow, no antiquity, no mystery, no picturesque and gloomy wrong, nor anything but a commonplace prosperity'. He did not encounter the great god Pan in Italy but he did develop a great affection for a marble faun which he saw in Rome and which seemed to him to have 'a strain of honest wildness'. What if 'this race of fauns, the most delightful of all that antiquity imagined,' had somehow become 'intermingled with the human race'? What would happen when a wild creature, half man and half faun, was confronted with conventional Christian morality? The reverse, presumably, of what happened in Mrs Browning's parable: the reed would lose its magic but regain its pith so that it could be bedded down comfortably among the other reeds while the false gods who put ecstasy above virtue were suitably chagrined.

Hawthorne's answer was not so neat. There was nothing comfortable about the Christianity which bore down upon Count Donatello, the faun of his title, and upon the girl he loved. It came in the form of a threatening figure in monk's garb who spoke of heavy sins and harsh penances and continued to haunt the couple even after Donatello had seemingly killed him in an outburst of that 'honest wildness' which Hawthorne admired in his marble counterpart. Christian morality, aided by some sinister supernatural happenings, then managed to strip Donatello of his honest wildness and saddle him with an unaccus-

57

religious ideas outside the Bible were those enshrined in the mythology of Greece and Rome. They knew about Pan and his attendant fauns and satyrs but very few of them knew about Cernunnos, the Pan-like horned god who had once been worshipped in Britain. Some of them still danced round a pole on a May morning but they did not care to be reminded that it had once been a phallic symbol. Some scholars even suggested that Christ's cross had been such a symbol but they got short shrift from the devout. 'I have said that the phallic origin attributed to the cross is destitute of evidence,' wrote Sabine Baring-Gould angrily in 1868 in his *Curious Myths of the Middle Ages,* 'In a work like this, which will be in the hands of general readers, it is impossible to enter into the subject.' There was no disguising the pagan nature of celebrations such as the Horned Dance at Abbot's Bromley in Staffordshire or the Puck Fair at Killorglin in County Kerry, where a he-goat presided over a drunken saturnalia, but most of those who took part in them were folklore enthusiasts rather than lusty devotees of the old fertility cults. Any reversion to paganism which took place among the Victorians was likely to be an intellectual game rather than a physical reality.

Things might have been different in the United States, where horizons were wider and where the old gods were closer at hand. To the south was Mexico with its relics of the most bloodthirsty of all pagan religions, to the west a host of indigenous Indian cultures. After working closely with Emerson and other transcendentalists Henry David Thoreau spent more than two years living alone in a hut on the shores of Walden Pond in an attempt to reach to the heart of nature and find what gods reigned there. He hoped that from America's forests and wildernesses would come images more powerful and more universal than those of Greece and Rome. 'Mythology is the crop which the Old World bore before its soil was exhausted,' he wrote, 'The West is preparing to add its fables to those of the East.' But *Walden, or Life in the Woods,* which came out in 1854, was certainly no storehouse of fables. Thoreau reached out for the spirit of the woods but showed little interest in those who had populated them with gods and demi-gods before the coming of the white man. His own response to the natural world was ambivalent, poised between the instincts of the hunter and the aspirations of the transcendentalist intellectual. 'I found in myself, and still find,' he wrote, 'an instinct toward a higher, or, as it is named, spiritual life, as do most men, and another toward a primitive rank and savage one, and I reverence them both.

I love the wild not less than the good. The wildness and adventure that are in fishing still recommend it to me.' It was a somewhat cautious confession of bloodlust, milder than most Indian braves or most devotees of Pan would have produced, and it was hardly the stuff of a new mythology.

Three years earlier Henry Lewis Morgan, later to be known as the father of American anthropology, had published an account of Iroquois beliefs based partly on the researches of Ely Samuel Parker, son of a Tonawanda Seneca chief and later an Iroquois supreme chief in his own right; but this kind of collaboration was rare and the book long remained unique. In 1855 Longfellow's *Hiawatha* gave a sympathetic picture of Indian nature worship but ended by suggesting that its true destiny lay in conversion to the Christian faith. In the eyes of most white Americans Indian culture was not something to be studied but something to be destroyed: in 1866 General Patrick Connors declared that Indians must be 'hunted like wolves' and his soldiers had orders to kill all males over the age of twelve. Lands guaranteed to Indian tribes were invaded, usually in search of gold, and when the Indians fought back their bravery in battle was reviled as murderous savagery. Meanwhile the war against Mexico had also brought in land which was rich in gold, as well as its own crop of stories of heroism. It was left to an Englishman, Edward Burnett Taylor, to give the first scientific account of Mexico in *Anahuac, or Mexico and the Mexicans, Ancient and Modern*, published in 1861. The only fables the Americans contributed to the world's store concerned their own exploits rather than the cultures they had fought against. They did indeed seem to be more interested in what Hawthorne called 'commonplace prosperity' than in 'poetic or fairy precincts'.

They were therefore especially pleasing to Frances Power Cobbe, who had always hoped that the study of comparative religion would lead to the genteel gods of the riders and not to the hairy gods of the steeds. Her great hero was Theodore Parker, a Boston clergyman who rejected Christian orthodoxy and saw all the world's religions and all the world's myths as revelations of one universal truth. The *Massachusetts Quarterly Review*, which he and Emerson established in 1847, discussed religion and philosophy in an impressively wide context but said little about such indelicate gods as Pan. Emerson kept a close eye on what was going on in Europe and made sure that he was always supplied with Max Müller's latest work. His journals and notebooks were preoccupied with Greek mythology, which he

61

said was 'more catholic than any other' and therefore of central importance in the modern world. He related it to Greek thought, showing
how 'the Greeks wrote their metaphysics in names and attributes of
gods', but he left Pan and Dionysus, the gods of unreason, out of
his exposition. Miss Cobbe told how some disciples of Theodore Parker
had given their son Greek myths to read before they introduced him
to the Bible, thus making him 'without exception the most religious
boy I ever knew', but she was reluctant to probe the fertility cults
from which such myths sprang. In a review of James Fergusson's
Tree and Serpent Worship she remarked that 'the ever-recurring connection between the Tree and the Serpent, the beautiful and beneficent
vegetable and the noxious reptile, is well-nigh incomprehensible.' She
would not entertain the possibility that both were phallic symbols
and declared instead that the book demonstrated 'the moral unity
of our race'.

One American who did conjure up the great god Pan was Edmund
Clarence Stedman, a poet who was also a stockbroker. His poem 'Pan
in Wall Street' showed the god in an unusually playful mood, bringing
the New York financiers thoughts of 'ancient, sweet-do-nothing days'
and encouraging a newsboy and a peanut girl to dance together in
the streets. Shortly before publishing the poem Stedman received a
letter from his friend Bayard Taylor who was travelling in Europe
and had met Swinburne, an altogether more passionate devotee of
the horned god. 'What I admire in him – yet admire with a feeling
of pain,' wrote Taylor, 'is the mad, unrestrained preponderance of
the imagination. It is a god-like quality, but he sometimes uses it
like a devil. He told me some things unspeakably shocking... his
aberration of ideas is horrible.' When young Henry Adams was in
London in 1862 as secretary to his father, who was American minister,
he met Swinburne at one of Lord Houghton's house parties. 'The
idea that one has actually met a real genius dawns slowly on a Boston
mind,' he wrote, 'but it made entry at last.' Like Taylor, he was both
horrified and fascinated by what he heard: Swinburne's invocation
of the old gods was very different from the rarefied pantheism of the
American intellectuals. 'One felt the horror of Longfellow and Emerson,' Adams recorded, 'at the wild Walpurgis night of Swinburne's
talk.'

Swinburne's public reputation as a pagan was based on *Poems and
Ballads*, which he published in 1866. The most notorious poem in
the volume was 'Dolores', a hymn to a bloodthirsty pagan goddess

whom he addressed as 'Our Lady of Pain', begging her to 'come down and redeem us from virtue'. It was this prayer for redemption from virtue which stuck in the gullet of most reviewers. John Morley in the *Saturday Review* said that it revealed Swinburne as either 'the apostle of a crushing iron-shod despair' or 'the libidinous laureate of a pack of satyrs'. Most readers took the latter view and a gentleman in Dublin wrote threatening castration if the poems were not withdrawn. 'He would way-lay me,' Swinburne wrote in some amusement, 'slip my head in a bag, and remove the obnoxious organs; he had seen his gamekeeper do it with cats'. Later Swinburne was encouraged to hear that his young cousin had been so severely birched for reading 'Dolores' that the blood had 'soaked through his shirt and the seat of his breeches in patches and stripes, to the wild delight of the junior male members of the household'. It was an auspicious beginning for his new religion, he told Rossetti, for like any other faith it needed the blood of the martyrs to make it grow.

But this libidinous laureate, this red-blooded poet of revived paganism, was not all he seemed. There was more despair than libido in his make-up and he spoke darkly of 'the diabolic government of this worst of all possible worlds'. His Satanism was ostentatious – his friends received letters promising to meet them 'by the grace of Satan, Deo Nolente' – but it betrayed little of the ecstasy which might have been expected of a worshipper of the old gods. When Rossetti and Burton arranged for Adah Menken, his real-life Dolores, to knock on his door and say that she had come for the night he showed no desire to take her to his bed. When she died a few months later he said it was 'a great shock to me and a real grief', but by that time he was seeking consolation of another kind in a whipping brothel in St John's Wood. Even this was a second best: his private correspondence made it clear that his real longing was for the strictness of the schoolroom rather than the excitements of the bawdy-house. Morley came to the heart of the matter when he said that Swinburne's poems would have been more effective if they had 'vindicated passion, and the strong and large and rightful pleasures of sense, against the narrow and inhuman tyranny of shrivelled anchorites'. Instead they dwelt upon severities which the anchorites themselves could scarcely have bettered. Somewhere inside this defiant devotee of the ancient liberated gods there was a sadly unliberated Victorian schoolboy kneeling at the whipping block, his posture and his punishment both dictated by the Christian penitential requirements from which he had

entertained the Sultan of Turkey and the Khedive of Egypt, an unprecedented gesture, and the soldiers who had stood guard over these eastern potentates with flaming brands had been hailed by the newspapers as 'human torches'. Although Disraeli's peculiar ability to inject pagan fantasy into Britain's humdrum politics was not to come to full flower until 1874 he was already a master of invention, having bombarded the Queen throughout the autumn of 1867 with stories of conspirators who were renting empty houses throughout London in order to set fire to them. He also conjured a ship out of thin air, a Danish brigantine which he said had left New York with a crew of thirty men sworn to assassinate Victoria and her ministers. Neither the arsonists nor the brigantine ever materialized.

Probably the most symbolically significant of the pagan gods who arrived in London in 1867 came in a large crate to a house in Maitland Park Road two days before Christmas. It was a statue of Zeus, more than life-size, and it was a Christmas present for Karl Marx, to whom it bore a striking physical resemblance. In his youth Marx had published poems celebrating the horned gods in their Christianized form as devils and demons and he also had a lively interest in the things they had originally stood for: his letters to Engels were peppered with erotic references and with descriptions of his own genitals. But it was appropriate that he should now see himself as Zeus rather than as Pan because he had recently returned from delivering the first volume of *Das Kapital* to his publishers in Hamburg. He had overthrown Christianity and its capitalist advocates not with bawdy or with devilry but by the use of reason and calculation. Starting as a rebel against a particular god he had ended by laying down iron laws which held captive both gods and men. Like Zeus, he looked down from Olympian heights on the whole of the universe.

William Winwood Reade was going through a somewhat similar experience. He had spent the early 1860s in West Africa collecting material for an ambitious work to be called *The Origin of Mind*, which was to do for the history of the human mind what *The Origin of Species* had done for the history of the human frame. His avowed aim was to record Africa's share in the spiritual evolution of mankind: he knew a lot about the varieties of African religious experience, the rituals which Bishop Heber had dismissed as heathens bowing down to wood and stone, and he wanted to give them as honourable a place in the history of religion as the Greeks and the Egyptians already had. But when his book appeared in 1872 under the title *The Martyrdom of Man*

66

it contained surprisingly little about African beliefs and a great deal about Greece and Egypt. 'There is no problem in history as interesting as the unparalleled development of Greece,' he declared early in the book. Nearly three hundred pages later, as his argument moved towards its triumphant conclusion, he invoked Apollo, the Greek god of reason and enlightenment: 'Glorious Apollo is the parent of us all.' 'Where now is Isis the mother, with the child Horus on her lap?' he asked, 'They are dead; they have gone to the land of the shadows. Tomorrow, Jehovah, you and your son shall be with them. Men die, and the ideas which they call gods die too.'

But not apparently Apollo, who was the god of reason as well as the god of the sun. As science continued to explore and explain the universe, reason, which Apollo defended both against the old horned gods and against dark Christian superstitions, would be seen to be supreme in the moral sphere just as the sun was supreme in the physical sphere. 'Life is bottled sunshine,' Reade wrote, 'and Death the silent-footed butler who draws out the cork.' He had nothing but contempt for Marx and the Communists – 'every millionaire enriches the community,' he proclaimed defiantly – but his scientific determinism proved as dogmatic as Marx's economic determinism. Men must accept the conclusions of science and acknowledge 'the supreme and mysterious Power by whom the universe has been created, and by whom it has been appointed to run its course under fixed and invariable laws; that awful One to whom it is profanity to pray, of whom it is idle and irreverent to argue and debate.' Reade wore the mantle of Apollo as confidently as Marx wore the mantle of Zeus. Just as Miss Cobbe saw beliefs that did not fit into her universal religion as products of an unreal dream world, so Reade saw the Africans whose contributions to spiritual history he was supposed to have been celebrating as 'savages who have been led by indigestion and by dreams to believe in ghosts'. 'The savage lives in a strange world,' he explained a little condescendingly, 'He knows nothing about the laws of nature. Death itself is not a natural event. Sooner or later men make the gods angry and are killed.' Hence the reaction of one African chief who cried out furiously: 'If I could see God I would kill him at once, because he makes men die!'

Some indignant readers found Reade's own threats equally outrageous. As well as consigning God to the land of shadows along with Isis and Horus he dismissed the promise of personal immortality as 'a sweet and charming illusion'. If he killed the God who conquered

67

death then the future would indeed be the season of mental anguish which he predicted, a sad and dark world from which youth and beauty would have vanished for ever. When he passed into the land of shadows himself in 1875 at the sadly early age of thirty-six his uncle, Charles Reade the novelist, felt constrained to write to the press saying that if he had lived longer he would no doubt have 'cured himself, as many thinking men have done, of certain obnoxious opinions which laid him open to reasonable censure'. Nor was he censured only by the orthodox: even those who welcomed the merging of Christianity and other religions still felt a desperate need to believe in a hereafter. During the 1860s they formed the Radical Club and the Free Religious Association in America while in London they found an effective vehicle for their ideas in the *Theological Review*. And it was precisely because they were becoming respectable that they were determined not to be thought atheistic, especially where immortality was concerned. Now that more and more people were drawn to their attractively multi-coloured religious umbrella it was vital that it should not let in the rain. Miss Cobbe in particular felt that belief in an afterlife was essential for the future of civilized society. 'It would probably need only that five per cent of the population should publish their conviction that there is no Future State,' she warned, 'to make the greater part of the remainder so far lose reliance upon it as to become quite insensible to its moral influences.'

This did not stop her being extremely angered by the startling success of Guillaume Figuier's *Le Lendemain de la Mort*, which was published in English in 1872 as *The Day after Death; or, Our Future Life according to Science* and ran through five editions. 'Simple readers ask for bread,' she cried indignantly, 'and the Frenchman drops into their mouths a bonbon.' Figuier certainly had produced an enticing confection. 'Of course you do not believe that your soul will be extinguished with your life on the day of your decease,' he wrote comfortingly at the beginning of his book. He then went on to assure his readers that life after death was a scientific fact and was made possible by the sun. Reade had made Apollo the parent of all mortal things and now Figuier made him the parent of immortality as well: eternal life, like life on earth, was bottled sunshine: 'solar radiation is maintained by the continuous unbroken succession of souls in the sun.' Science proved that sunbeams were the souls of the virtuous floating for ever through the interplanetary ether. Imperfect souls remained below on earth and were reincarnated again and again until they achieved

perfection and were conveyed to the sun. The souls of animals might be reincarnated in human beings, which accounted for inborn talents and tendencies. 'A child who has a faculty for music may have received the soul of a nightingale, the sweet songster of our woods. A child who is an architect by vocation may have inherited the soul of a beaver.' Although Figuier claimed to be a scientist he was in fact a student of comparative religion, since most of what he said could be traced to Hindu and Buddhist beliefs. Miss Cobbe might find him infuriating but she had nevertheless played her part in creating the climate of opinion which helped to make him so astonishingly popular.

By the early 1870s this climate was coming to be taken for granted and the wrath of the orthodox was vented upon outright atheists rather than upon the Free Religious Association or the contributors to the *Theological Review*. Ten years of literary and intellectual excitement on both sides of the Atlantic had led not to the rebirth of the lascivious horned gods but merely to a polite accommodation between Christianity and the more rational of the pagan deities. There had been such accommodation before – after all it had been Virgil who had guided Dante on his journey through hell and purgatory and heaven – and theologians and philosophers had always known that Christian thought was based firmly on the Greek Socratic tradition. As long as Pan and Dionysus were kept out there was no harm in letting Apollo in, even though Reade and Figuier might make unwelcome use of him. And for every man or woman who read Reade or Figuier or any other of the innovators there were at least ten who read nothing on the subject but continued to believe what they had been brought up to believe. In spite of the ferocious things Jehovah had once said to Moses he could safely allow a few enthusiasts to play with some of his more respectable rivals.

One man who did vent his wrath upon innovators and intellectual games was Matthew Arnold, who said some extremely scathing things about Miss Cobbe and her like. For him the 1860s were desolate years. He saw anarchy ahead, both political and spiritual, and he despised those who prattled about new dawns and universal truths. Back in 1851 he had written 'Dover Beach' but had put it aside because its pessimism was out of tune with the times. Now he felt that the times were changed and in July 1867 he included it in his new volume of poems. Swinburne was delighted with it, saying that Arnold had finally abandoned 'the sad task of sweeping dead leaves fallen from the dying tree of belief'. It was a poem about the sea, the sea which

69

5 THE COMING OF THE LORD

WHAT WAS NEEDED WAS ACTION. GOD MUST COME down to earth in order to show once and for all that he was real and his rivals mere phantoms projecting and personifying the delusions of misguided men. In the Bible he had done this in differing ways. He had made Mount Sinai quake in order to appear to Moses in the midst of thunder and lightning but some time later, on Mount Horeb, he had produced storm and fire and earthquake only to pass them by and speak to Elijah in a still small voice. The change suggested progress: perhaps on Sinai other gods had been present and had had to be outdone, while on Horeb God had been in sole charge and had been able to use his stage effects as a prologue rather than as a demonstration. It remained to be seen which course he would follow halfway through the increasingly faithless nineteenth century.

Dr Cumming was still announcing that the Lord would be accompanied by meteorological disturbances which would make those on Sinai and on Horeb look like spring sunshine. Harcourt Bland, a comedian at the Theatre Royal in Glasgow, took issue with Cumming in 1855 and the prophet's replies were not particularly convincing. *The End: or, the Proximate Signs of the close of this Dispensation*, published in the same year, was less successful than *Apocalyptic Sketches* and seemed confused on some points. Whereas earlier prophecies had cited the growth of popery as proof that the world was about to end, this one made the decline of popery serve precisely the same purpose. And it seemed that the bottom of the barrel was being scraped in search of signs: even phylloxera, the blight which had recently struck French vines, was dragged in to prove approaching apocalypse. More predictions followed, fixing on 1867 as the year in which the existing dispensation would come to an end. *The Times* reviewed Cumming's work respectfully and when the *Saturday Review* dared to ridicule him his

supporters dismissed it as 'a notoriously irreligious paper'. 'It is not uncommon for great Revelations, Discoveries and Warnings to be treated with scornful indifference or mirthful contempt,' wrote a Sheffield clergyman when audiences in that city laughed at Cumming's lectures.

The change of heart over popery highlighted a puzzling question about God's coming. Would it happen when men were at their worst or at their best? 'An evil and adulterous generation seeketh after a sign,' Christ had told the pharisees, 'and there shall be no sign given to it.' Originally Cumming had seemed to be saying the same thing: times were wicked, popery strong, and so the sign would come from Antichrist and not from God. Now he seemed more hopeful. 'Should we be about to enter very soon upon a new and nobler era, let us lift up our heads: our redemption draweth nigh,' he wrote in 1855. Now that Christians were less popish and more worthy it was perhaps God himself who was coming and not the Great Beast of the apocalypse.

It was hard to believe that he was coming to the British, who showed few signs of preparing themselves for a new and nobler era. There were riots in London in 1855 when Lord Robert Grosvenor tried to get Parliament to limit Sunday trading and he had to yield to the violence and withdraw his measure. There was more trouble when the authorities wanted to stop bands playing in the parks on Sundays. By the spring of 1856 it became necessary to fortify the Archbishop of Canterbury's London residence against attack from an infuriated mob. Lord Palmerston, Prime Minister since February 1855, had a reputation for caring little about religion and even Queen Victoria accused Grosvenor and his like of 'incomprehensible blindness and mistaken piety'. In September 1857, when she was asked to sanction a Day of National Prayer and Humiliation because of the mutiny in India, she replied that such things did more harm than good. Meanwhile the Archbishop of Canterbury and nine other prelates were supporting a new divorce law which working people said would make the country 'too wicked to live in'. The efforts of religious enthusiasts served only to push Britain farther away both from godliness itself and also from any agreement between different social classes as to what it was.

America seemed to have achieved both. It was said of the great religious revivals in New York State in 1855 that 'they all commenced and made their first progress among the higher classes of society.

73

This was very favorable to the general spread of the work and to the overcoming of opposition'. Philip Schaff of Pennsylvania declared in the same year that 'Providence has evidently prepared this country and nation for the greatest work and no power on earth can arrest its progress and prosperity if we are true to our calling, if we fear God and love righteousness.' He was sure that the 'unbridled radicalism and fanaticism' of which Americans had once been accused had died out and that the pursuit of material success had had 'a most salutary influence on the moral life of the nation'. Roman Catholicism would also die out because its 'mediaeval traditions, centralized priestly government and extreme conservatism' were at odds with liberty and republicanism. The Protestant Reformation would culminate in the United States, which would become 'the phoenix grave not only of European nationalities but also of all European churches and sects'. 'All is yet in a chaotic state,' he concluded, 'but organizing energies are already present and the spirit of God broods over them, to speak in time the almighty word: "Let there be light!" and to call forth from chaos a beautiful creation.'

Organizing energy and the spirit of God provided themes for Robert Baird's *Religion in America*, the New York edition of which came out in 1856. Because the United States allowed no established religion, because church revenues were neither provided nor sanctioned by the secular government, everything sprang from 'the mere unconstrained goodwill of the people, especially those among them who love the Saviour and profess His name'. Nor was it just a matter of the things that could be seen and heard on Sundays, the packed churches built by those who worshipped in them and the well loved ministers paid by those to whom they preached. On the other six days as well, at work and in the home, the voluntary principle harnessed organizing energies to the service of God. Workshops and factories were 'proverbial for ignorance and vice' in Britain but in America they were virtuous and well-ordered. 'Those may tremble for the result,' Baird wrote, 'who do not know what the human heart is capable of doing when left to its own energies, moved and sustained by the grace and love of God.' Americans who did know these things knew also that they were ideally placed to greet God when he came.

It was generally agreed that he arrived in America during the late summer of 1857. 'It is recognized as among the most noteworthy phenomena of the day,' wrote the English author Mrs Bishop early in 1859, 'that the influence of the Holy Spirit has been felt during the

past eighteen months in the United States to an extent unprecedented in any other country or period.' As early as January 1857 Dwight Moody, going to revivalist meetings in Chicago every evening, became convinced that God was present in the city; but it was not until the Ohio Life Insurance Trust Company collapsed on 24 August of that year, starting a disastrous financial panic, that the divine presence was universally felt. 'It would seem that the mighty crash was just what was wanted,' one evangelist wrote, 'to startle men from their golden dreams.' God made his appearance 'in our chief commercial centres, precisely where the credit of religion had been most impaired and the tide against it was the strongest,' and he showed that he could use even the uncaring world of finance for his own purposes. Within a few months nearly five thousand firms went bankrupt and as confidence in man-made prosperity crumbled confidence in God soared. 'This winter of 1857–58 will be remembered as the time when a great revival prevailed throughout all the Northern states,' wrote the preacher Charles G. Finney, 'It swept over the land with such power that for a time it was estimated that not less than fifty thousand conversions occurred in a single week.' One man arriving in Boston from distant Omaha reported that his journey had been one continuous prayer meeting as men and women came together to share their sense of God's presence.

Finney went on to say that 'a divine influence seemed to pervade the whole land', bringing with it at least half a million conversions, but his definition of the whole land was still limited to the Northern states. 'Slavery seemed to shut it out from the South,' he concluded, 'the Spirit of God seemed to be grieved away from them.' Philip Schaff, who could claim credit for predicting the revival, saw slavery as less of a problem. He was sure it was dying out and indeed would have died out already had it not been for the reaction produced by the abolitionists. He seemed to regard the campaign for abolition as part of that 'unbridled radicalism and fanaticism' whose passing he was so anxious to see. He was writing shortly after Theodore Parker had incited an illegal attempt to rescue Anthony Burns, an escaped slave whom the authorities were about to hand over to his Virginian master. Parker's view of the matter was clear: if the law sent men back into slavery the law must be defied. He had already given up his life's work, a history of world religion, in order to concentrate on the campaign against slavery. He was chairman of a secret committee to help Captain John Brown, a fanatical abolitionist who was believed to be

planning a large-scale negro revolt throughout the Southern states. If such an uprising did take place Schaff would not be alone in condemning its instigators as unbridled radical fanatics. The social tensions which religious enthusiasm produced in Britain were mild compared with the holy war to which rival interpretations of the coming of the Lord might yet give rise in America.

Most of those who watched the American religious revival of 1857–58 from across the Atlantic thought of it as the prelude to the abolition of slavery. Mrs Bishop declared that America was 'rapidly assuming a prominence among empires to fulfil God's purposes towards the human race,' but she could not imagine this fulfilment taking place until the slaves were free. The British and Foreign Anti-Slavery Society had been campaigning against the slavers of the Southern states for many years and it had inspired the 1841 articles in *The Times* describing their cruelties. But in the wake of these articles an angry army officer had written to the paper saying that there was 'a conviction of immense superiority to the English deeply seated in the national mind and temper of the Americans' and that this would inevitably lead to war between Britain and the United States. In such a war Britain's strategy must be to turn them into the disunited states, to break up the Union by blockading the North and starving its industries, and it was therefore very unwise to alienate the South by inveighing against slavery and by hinting, as some sources in Britain did, that there might be British support for a slave revolt.

He had been by no means alone in his opinions even in the 1840s and now there were added reasons for the British – or at any rate for the English and the Scots – not to get involved in a crusade for the freeing of the slaves, however loudly people like Mrs Bishop might hail it as fulfilling God's purposes for the human race. In New York during the winter of 1857–58 John O'Mahony, an Irish rebel who had escaped arrest in 1848, formed the Fenian Brotherhood, a society dedicated to the overthrow of British rule in Ireland by violent means. 'Every Irishman in the United States is in favour of slavery,' Theodore Parker pointed out grimly. If the British backed the abolitionist crusade they might find its opponents seeking to free one of the many races they themselves held in subjection.

A British version of the threatened slave insurrection had already taken place in India during the summer of 1857. 'What a terrible time dear old England has in India,' wrote Theodore Parker to Miss Cobbe that December, 'but I suppose Father Bull will conquer, kill

ten men and violate twenty women where the Indians did but one or two, and then celebrate thanksgivings in all his churches.' 'Of course you know what a sad commercial panic we are passing through in America, as in England,' he continued, 'I hope both nations will come out of it wiser than before.' London had been hard hit by the financial crisis – Palmerston told Queen Victoria on 12 November that the Bank of England's reserve funds were running out – and it might seem that God was giving the two countries the same treatment, shaking their complacency by means of financial uncertainty and assailing their consciences with the cries of oppressed peoples. In December 1858, when he felt that the American revival had enough impetus to be able to do without him, Charles Finney went to England 'to see if the same influence would not pervade that country.' He found his friends at the Borough Road chapel in London demoralized and depressed, but after he had preached 'it was soon very perceptible that the Spirit of God was poured out'. He had similarly gratifying experiences in the northern and eastern counties and soon there was talk of an English as well as an American revival. Finney had little doubt that God had crossed the Atlantic with him.

Meanwhile in February 1858 the Virgin Mary had appeared to Bernadette Subirous in a cave near Lourdes in southern France. Catholics were somewhat more cautious in welcoming her, somewhat more scrupulous in seeking her credentials, than Protestants had been when they had felt God moving among them. For this reason if for no other her visit was to be remembered and celebrated long after the revivals had been forgotten. In July 1858 the American Catholic editor Orestes Brownson published a crushing condemnation of Protestant hysteria, saying sternly that 'in the Catholic Church this excitement is judiciously directed and moderated.' Gradually, reluctantly, the fashion for detecting God's presence in every gathering, his hand behind every event, began to wane. In New York a start was made on building St Patrick's Cathedral, a sign that Catholicism in America was far from sinking into the decline that Schaff had predicted. Its phenomenal growth was to be the most spectacular feature of American religious life during the next quarter of a century. 'Mediaeval traditions, centralized priestly government and extreme conservatism' were to prove more durable than the God-intoxicated fervour of 1857–58.

There were still those who saw the powers of darkness and the forces of good forming up for a great cosmic confrontation. 'I hold Louis Napoleon in loathing and count him Beelzebub,' wrote Theodore

Parker to Miss Cobbe from Switzerland in July 1859, 'but he is now casting out other devils'. To the south of him Louis Napoleon, Emperor Napoleon III of the French, was helping the King of Sardinia to throw the Austrians out of Italy, a struggle which Parker described to his congregation back in Boston as 'the great battle of mankind against institutions which once helped but now hinder the progress of mankind.' 'The actual war is local,' he explained, 'confined to a small part of Italy. It may become general before you read this note.' The Rev. Richard Shimeall of New York identified Napoleon III as the Beast of the Apocalypse and Catholic intellectuals in America were worried about the hold he had over their priests. 'France not Rome governs the Catholic mind in this country,' wrote Orestes Brownson, 'There is the great difficulty.' And was France now to swallow up Rome, as she had nearly done in the time of the first Napoleon? If the French Emperor's Italian allies wanted to unite their country they would be ranged against the papacy as well as against the Austrians. It would indeed be ironic if the Great Beast, the incarnate Beelzebub, should cast out the Scarlet Woman and robe himself in her garments. Events might not yet be fulfilling Dr Cumming's predictions but at least they helped to explain his uncertainty as to the Papacy's place in the apocalyptic scenario.

It had been hoped that Parker's trip to Europe might restore his shattered health. Instead he grew worse and he was near to death when he got to Florence in May 1860. Miss Cobbe was there waiting for him and at last the two met. He asked her what day it was and she said it was Sunday, 'a blessed day.' 'True, it *is* a blessed day,' he replied, 'when one has got over the superstition of it.' He died four days later. At the end of his life his thoughts turned from fears of Armageddon to more hopeful things. He was unable to read *The Origin of Species* but he was sure it was 'one of the most important works the British have lately contributed to science.' He also conceded, in spite of his recent remarks about India, that the British had done much to deliver mankind from superstition and tyranny. In Britain itself there was less confidence. Wilberforce's campaign against Darwin's book opened shortly after Parker's death and the heavens provided portents in the shape of a spectacular comet and a winter that lasted until July. As death rates rose *The Times* published a leader on the ominous weather, calling it 'a strange season of menace and gloom.' There was menace from other quarters as well. Irish papists were kidnapping Protestant children and Napoleon III, 'the disturber

of the world', was thought to be about to launch an attack. Two years earlier a pamphlet called *Invasion invited by the Defenceless State of England* had caused a great stir and now, as the report of a Royal Commission on Defence came out, fears were renewed. It was alleged in the press that the French could 'effect a landing in Sussex or the Isle of Wight and bombard Portsmouth and Spithead from a safe distance.'

During Parker's absence his friends looked after his congregation in Boston. Emerson preached there and in November 1859 Thoreau gave a lecture entitled 'A Plea for Captain Brown'. On 16 October John Brown with a force of five negroes and sixteen whites had seized the arsenal at Harper's Ferry in Virginia, an action reported in New York under such headlines as 'Negro Insurrection at Harper's Ferry' and 'Extensive Negro Conspiracy in Virginia and Maryland'. The insurrection had not materialized and Brown had had to surrender after he had been wounded and ten of his men killed. Thoreau told how even in prison, wounded and in the shadow of death, Brown was regarded as 'a supernatural being'. 'Sure enough, a hero in the midst of us cowards is always so dreaded,' he added. His plea was ignored and Brown was hanged. Thoreau gave two further lectures, 'The Martyrdom of John Brown' and 'The Last Days of John Brown', in which he completed his transformation of the man from abolitionist fanatic to Christian saint: 'What a transit was that of his horizontal body alone, but just cut down from the gallows-tree! Like a meteor it shot through the Union from the southern regions towards the north! It seemed to me that John Brown was the only man who *had not died*: he has earned immortality.' Emerson also described Brown as a saint and Longfellow in his diary marked the day of the execution as 'the date of a new revolution, quite as much needed as the old one.'

The revolution was not long delayed. In 1860 the Democratic party split and put up two opposing presidential candidates, one representing the party as a whole and the other the slave states, whose determination to stand firm against the abolitionists had been stiffened by the affair at Harper's Ferry. Between them they polled more of the popular vote than Abraham Lincoln, the Republican candidate, but their divisions and his strength in the electoral college secured his election. Since Lincoln had made his opposition to slavery clear in the strongest terms the slave states thought they had no choice but to secede from the Union. This they prepared to do. Queen Victoria's eldest son, the Prince of Wales, was touring Canada and the United

States in the autumn of 1860 and saw the crisis at first hand. In Philadelphia on 6 October he joined Republican crowds who were celebrating success in the Pennsylvania elections, the victory which finally made Lincoln's presidency certain. He then went to New York and was greeted with 'the enthusiasm of more than half a million people worked up almost to madness and yet self-restrained within the bounds of a most perfect courtesy'. The actress Fanny Kemble wrote that 'the whole land was alive with excitement and interest'. London newspapers were delighted to hear of the Prince's reception and could not believe that a people capable of restraining madness within the bounds of a most perfect courtesy could really be on the brink of civil war. 'For the safety of the Union itself we confess we have no fear,' said *The Times* when the news of Lincoln's election came through, 'Of course, it will take some time before men can cool down from the bluster which has been so profusely used.' Five months later the Confederacy of slave states ordered its forces to open fire on a Federal fort in Charleston harbour.

God's re-emergence was immediate and dramatic. Armies on both sides marched behind him and the Confederate commander Robert E. Lee habitually quoted him in his General Orders. In Boston a clergyman suggested that his congregation should think of the Stars and Stripes as nailed to the Cross, since Christ and the Union were inseparable, and a Cincinnati newspaper told its readers that Confederates killed in action were slain 'through the instrumentality of an avenging God' and sent straight to hell. Finally, in December 1861, Mrs Julia Ward Howe made the most famous of all declarations of the divine presence. She was attending a review of the troops encamped around Washington, the Federal capital, when news of enemy activity brought the review to a hasty end and the bugles sounded to call the men to action. As Mrs Howe and a clergyman called Mr Clarke tried to make their way back to the city their carriage was frequently held up by marching columns and to pass the time they joined in the soldiers' songs, the most popular of which was 'John Brown's body'. 'Mrs Howe,' said Mr Clarke, 'why do you not write some good words for that stirring tune?'

And so she did, telling how her eyes had seen the glory of the coming of the Lord, how she had seen him in the watchfires of a hundred circling camps, how she had heard him sound the trumpet that should never call retreat. At first it was just a poem, a poem which her friend James Fields published in the *Atlantic Monthly* under

the title 'The Battle Hymn of the American Republic', but as the struggle grew more ferocious and more embittered the idea that it was God himself who watched over their camps and sounded their bugle calls became more than a literary exercise for the Federalists. This new and more glorious coming of the Lord far outshone his earlier visits during the revival. But there was a price to be paid. 'As he died to make men holy, let us die to make men free,' cried Mrs Howe, reminding Federalists that they had gone to war not just to preserve the Union but to end slavery. As Lincoln seemed to evade the issue, declaring in his inaugural address that he would not interfere with slavery, he lost support not only at home but across the Atlantic. Whatever the dangers from their own subject races the British would back a war against slavery but they would not back coercion for merely constitutional reasons. 'No distinction can in my eyes be broader,' wrote Gladstone, 'than the distinction between the question whether the Southern ideas of slavery are right and the question whether they can justifiably be put down by war from the North.'

Lincoln proclaimed emancipation at the beginning of 1863. Although the proclamation was so hedged round as to have little practical effect it did turn the war into a crusade to free the slaves. In Britain it even secured the support of the Lancashire textile workers, who were unemployed because of the Federal blockade of Confederate cotton exports. In America it brought about such a change of heart that James Fields, in an *Atlantic Monthly* editorial looking back on 1863, could speak of God's presence and aid:

Such was the year of the Proclamation, and its history is marvellous in our eyes. It stands in striking contrast to the other years of the war ... We have been saved 'by the mighty hand of God.' Whether we had the right to expect Heaven's aid, we cannot undertake to say; but we know that we should not have deserved it, had we continued to link the nation's cause to that of oppression, and had we shed blood and expended gold in order to restore the system of slavery and the sway of slaveholders.

The words 'In God We Trust' started to appear on American coins in 1864 and when Lincoln was re-elected for a second term his inaugural address declared that if God willed it the war would continue 'until every drop of blood drawn by the lash shall be paid by another drawn by the sword'. 'The judgments of the Lord are true and righteous altogether,' he concluded. On 4 April 1865, just a month after delivering the address, he walked through Richmond, the captured

Confederate capital, and was greeted with cries of 'The kingdom is come and the Lord is with us!' 'I'd rather see him than Jesus!' cried one liberated slave. The Confederate commander surrendered five days later and on 14 April Lincoln was shot and mortally wounded. He died early the next morning. The struggle which had begun with one martyrdom ended with another. Thoreau had died in 1862 and there was nobody to speak of Lincoln as he had spoken of John Brown. Perhaps it was not needed: many felt that Lincoln had long walked with the immortals and waited upon his God. The years of conflict had brought President and nation immeasurably closer to the glory of the Lord.

A little of the glory spilled over into British life. The greatest of the American revival hymns, 'Stand up, stand up for Jesus, Ye soldiers of the cross!', crossed the Atlantic during the 1860s and the marching songs of the civil war took their place alongside equally bellicose British hymns written and published during the same period. *Hymns Ancient and Modern* appeared in 1861 and close on its heels came 'O happy band of pilgrims' and 'Christian, dost thou see them' in 1862, 'Fight the good fight' and 'Soldiers of the cross, arise' in 1863, 'For all the saints' and 'Onward, Christian soldiers' in 1864. Never in the history of hymnody had so much been written in so short a time on the military duties of Christians. Metaphorical soldiers of Christ marched steadfastly through the pages of the hymn books with their loins girded, urging on their counterparts in the real world to deeds of valour. There was no crusade against slavery to be undertaken in Britain but there was still a holy war to be waged. Its nature was made clear in the hymn with which Sabine Baring-Gould brought the Christian war cries to a climax in 1867: 'Through the night of doubt and sorrow'. It was 'the light of God's own presence,' wrote Baring-Gould, that would chase away the gloom and terror which the doubters had spread. The coming of the Lord would be at once the inspiration and the reward of those who made a stand against unbelief. If Christians in Britain wanted to share Mrs Howe's vision they must fight the sceptics and the materialists as manfully as the Americans had struggled against the slave owners.

The Times led the way in May 1864 with a leading article on the encroachment of science upon religious belief. Six months later Disraeli told Wilberforce's Society for Increasing Endowments of Small Livings in the Diocese of Oxford that he was 'on the side of the angels' against

Darwin and that man was 'a being born to believe'.* More than seven hundred scientists signed a formal declaration regretting that their investigations had cast doubt on the Bible, while a group of clergymen set up the Victoria Institute as a centre from which Christian thinkers could combat science and all its works. The Duke of Buccleuch brought the campaign to a triumphant conclusion by telling the British Association for the Advancement of Science that its activities must always be subordinated to religion: 'I cannot put discoverers of that which exists in a higher position than the Author of that which is discovered.' When James Bowling Mozley was invited to give the 1865 Bampton lectures in Oxford he chose to speak about miracles. There were two possible explanations of them: that of the scientists, that they were legends, and that of the Christians, that they did indeed happen. Of these it was the scientific account that was irrational because it failed to recognize 'the supremacy of a Personal Will in nature'. Christians on the other hand 'dare trust our reason and the evidence which it lays before us of a Personal Supreme Being'. The 1866 Bampton lecturer, Henry Parry Liddon, defended the miracle of the loaves and fishes and other supernatural happenings in the New Testament against those who wished to expunge them from allegedly 'scientific' lives of Christ. Such a life had just been published anonymously under the title *Ecce Homo* and Lord Ashley, now Earl of Shaftesbury and the most influential Christian layman in the country, called it 'the most pestilential book ever vomited from the jaws of hell'.

Meanwhile Dr Cumming was preparing for the ultimate miracle. *Behold, the Bridegroom Cometh, The Last Warning Cry* and *The Reasons for the Hope that is in me* appeared in 1865 and in the following year he settled down to his most urgent work, *The Sounding of the Last Trumpet, or, The Last Woe.* He quoted *The Times* as saying that 'public law in Europe, such as it is, is shaken to its foundations and the last seven years have brought about portentous changes'. He also pointed to a paralysis of transport, unprecedented shipwrecks, pestilence reminiscent of the plagues of Egypt, 'financial and monetary convulsions', extensive earthquakes. Finally there was a widespread desire for reunion with Rome which showed 'degeneracy in the hearts of many Anglicans'. As he wrote the night sky above him was lit up by showers of meteors which looked, said the newspapers, 'like sparks flying from an incandescent mass of iron under the blows of

* See above, p.65.

a Titanic hammer'. That was in the middle of November, a mere six weeks before the opening of the year which was to see the coming of the Lord. Torrential rains, terrible thunderstorms, disastrous floods, all bore witness to the cosmic drama which was about to unfold. The weather was one long succession of 'wonderful phenomena and antagonistic manifestations,' declared *The Times*. 'We are about to enter on the Last Woe,' Cumming told his readers, 'and to hear the nearly-spent reverberations of the Last Trumpet'.

To Arthur Munby, alone in his room in London as the bells rang in 1867, it seemed that the everyday world was unreal. 'Within the room there is warmth and light,' he wrote, 'and signs of comfort and culture; selfish comfort which may vanish, profitless culture which leads to nothing.' Twenty-four hours later the everyday world disappeared under deep snow, the beauty of which came as a revelation. 'Instead of the roar and rush of wheels, the selfish hurry, the dirt and cloudy fog,' marvelled Munby, 'we had the loveliness and utter purity of new-fallen snow.' Others fulminated against the halting of transport, the incompetence of the authorities, the idleness of labourers who failed to sweep away the snow. Matthew Arnold was horrified by London's 'state of helplessness' and even the *Annual Register*, usually a fairly level-headed publication, wrote ominously of approaching disaster. 'The signs, for those who can read, are present and can be plainly seen,' it said darkly, 'when the signs become clearly visible the catastrophe will perhaps have ceased to be avertible.' The root cause was 'unreasonable disagreement between class and class'.

Neither the Prime Minister Lord Derby nor his Chancellor of the Exchequer Benjamin Disraeli did much to dispel the gloom. There had been serious rioting in 1866 when a Reform Bill giving working men the vote had been thrown out by Parliament and now Disraeli, with much talk about dark horizons and impending storms, brought forward a second Bill. He foresaw anarchy if it was defeated and a spate of strikes running through the spring and into the summer gave point to his warning. Derby thought that reform was 'a leap in the dark' and others talked of 'Shooting Niagara'. The Bill became law in August but widespread anti-Catholic riots and Fenian outrages showed that the danger had not passed. Matthew Arnold wrote that the country was in 'a strange uneasy state, a loosening of all old prejudices, respects and habits'. The fears he had just made public in his poem 'Dover Beach', fears of a world robbed of stability and meaning, were now modulated from a religious into a secular key. And at this

point, as the gullible listened for the trumpet calls promised by Cumming and saner men wondered whether their secure world was indeed coming to an end, the Anglican bishops met in conference at Lambeth Palace. They concluded by issuing an address which seemed to give official approval to Cumming's apocalyptic imaginings. 'Beloved brethren,' they said solemnly, 'with one voice we warn you; the time is short; the Lord cometh; watch and be sober.'

It was not only the conventionally devout who felt a sense of unease. John Addington Symonds, a brilliant young man who was later to be a scourge of the orthodox, wrote that he was 'in a strange state in which the unreality of everything tortures me hourly and I long for God or what of Truth abides behind these phantoms to burn in on me. The great fact of my life is that the spiritual cannot emerge from the material.' He was not alone in his aspirations or in his frustrations. Lord Derby resigned in February 1868 and Disraeli became Prime Minister, determined to winkle the spiritual life of the nation out of its material shell. He had already insisted that he stood for 'a philosophic system of politics' and this, as he later explained, meant that 'the spiritual nature of man is stronger than codes or constitutions ... He who has a due sense of his relations to God is best qualified to fulfil his duties to man.' 'Society has a soul,' he declared, 'as well as a body'. Under his guidance the British would follow the example of Tancred, the nobly born hero of his most recent novel, who spurned 'the fatal drollery called a representative government' in order to go to the mysterious orient and listen to the voice of God.

Queen Victoria's initial doubts about having such a visionary as her Prime Minister were dispelled when he heaped praise on her *Leaves from the Journal of Our Life in the Highlands*, which was published at the beginning of 1868. It was above all a book about her beloved Albert and its success convinced her that he was still alive in her people's hearts as well as in her own. When her second son the Duke of Edinburgh survived a Fenian assassination attempt in March 1868 she thought she saw the hand of God, Mozley's 'supremacy of a Personal Will', and the Prince of Wales publicly called his brother's escape a miracle. Then the Queen's youngest son, Prince Leopold, fell ill and was restored to her 'from the brink of the grave', so that she became even more convinced of the divine presence. Longfellow visited England that summer, a reminder not of the embittered postwar politics of the United States but of the white heat in which Americans had seen the coming of the Lord. The only discordant note was struck

85

by Gladstone and the Liberal opposition, who set up a cry for the disestablishment of the Irish Church as a first step towards redressing Irish grievances. Disraeli accused them of wanting to 'dissolve for the first time the connection between government and religion' and when they forced disestablishment resolutions through Parliament he told the Queen that 'the time has gone by for ministries to be subverted by abstract resolutions'. He dismissed the Liberals as 'one of those bands of minstrels one encounters in the sauntering of a summer street'.

At the end of the year the band of minstrels defeated him in a General Election and formed a government which disestablished the Irish Church. In Dublin a Church Congress railed against 'a creedless and godless State' and for good measure it also condemned 'the influence of scientific investigations on the minds of those who conduct them'. John William Draper, a professor in the University of New York, had recently published *A History of the Intellectual Development of Europe*, a sustained attack on Christianity as the blinkered opponent of scientific progress, and the orthodox on both sides of the Atlantic saw all liberals and all scientists as enemies of religion. A further storm broke when Gladstone invited Frederick Temple to be Bishop of Exeter. As headmaster of Rugby school Temple had introduced science into the curriculum and he had also been a contributor to *Essays and Reviews*. Pusey said that the appointment 'surpassed in its frightful enormity anything which has been openly done by any Prime Minister' and suggested that if Gladstone was going to behave like this he might as well disestablish the Church of England as well. There were angry demonstrations when Temple's election was confirmed and there was also an attempt to condemn him formally in Convocation.

Gladstone described the anger of the orthodox as 'vehement but thin' and as his administration went from strength to strength, sweeping away abuses in almost every corner of the nation's life, the same seemed to be true of Disraeli's claim to be the guardian of society's soul. *The Times* published a remarkable leading article on the relation of religion to politics, saying that twenty or thirty years earlier 'men who leant towards Liberalism in secular politics were brought back to Conservatism by their religious sympathies. We now see just the reverse'. Gladstone had turned Liberalism from something godless and suspect into a philosophy in tune with the infinite, performing here on earth the things which all good men hoped to see performed in a better life to come. When set beside this progressive idealism

Disraeli's visions seemed like the gaudy illusions of a fairground conjuror. 'Conservatism is now felt to have in it a certain element of comedy or even of farce. The leaders of the party do not believe in it ... their accession to power would be but the accident of a day'. Party leaders held a secret meeting to consider replacing Disraeli with someone less given to exotic flights of religious fantasy. One of the whips told them that Disraeli's leadership could cost them forty or fifty seats at a General Election. The time had come to put aside heady talk of the coming of the Lord and fight the Liberals with their own less imaginative weapons.

But the outbreak of the Franco-Prussian War in July 1870 had already set in motion a chain of events that would totally change the political and religious climate, saving Disraeli and bringing the British into unexpected contact with their God. The defeat of the French Emperor turned France into a Republic and the King of Prussia into the Emperor of Germany. French troops withdrew from Rome and the Romans voted to become part of the new Kingdom of Italy, thus ending the temporal power of the papacy. Three weeks later there was an unparalleled display of the aurora borealis and terrified crowds knelt in the streets of Rome at this obvious sign of divine displeasure. Londoners also took to the streets, not to beg forgiveness but to watch 'what they imagined to be the progress of the largest fire that had ever occurred', and the engines of the city's Salvage Corps rushed hither and thither looking for the non-existent conflagration. Swinburne was so excited by the overthrow of Napoleon III and the discomfiture of the Pope that he wanted to kiss everybody he met and roll naked upon the ground. From her eldest daughter, who was married to the Crown Prince of Prussia, Queen Victoria learned that the Prussian victory meant the triumph of liberal principles over an unprincipled Napoleonic state which had constantly corrupted the morals of visiting Englishmen.

The Queen was not reassured. 'The bloody, sad, eventful year '70 has sunk in dark clouds,' she noted in her diary on New Year's Day, 'and '71 rises as sad and gloomy'. On the same day the *Fortnightly Review* proclaimed that the events of the past few months had 'shaken the monarchical principle itself among classes otherwise not easily accessible to theory and doctrine'. In Britain it was shaken further by fears of a German invasion and the consequent unpopularity of the Queen's German connections. 'From private sources I know that the military aristocratic caste in Prussia, the Junkers, already assert

"the turn of England will come next",' wrote an army officer in the *Contemporary Review. The Times* printed a solemn warning that no proper steps had been taken to fortify London and that 'the utter collapse of the Empire' would follow when the capital fell. 'The Battle of Dorking', a fictitious account of such an event, was published in *Blackwood's Magazine* in May and was enormously successful. A German newspaper, the *Allgemeine Zeitung*, made matters a good deal worse by announcing that England was 'in her decay and decrepitude' and should agree to be ruled by Germany.

Atheists and republicans took the opportunity to read funeral orations over Christianity and monarchy. 'Communism is a not impossible future. Positivism is a not impossible future. The *status quo* is impossible,' declared Frederic Harrison. Positivists, of whom Harrison was one, believed that the science of society was more sacred than revealed religion and had sacraments and prayers of their own based on sociology instead of on the supernatural. Communists were already in control of Paris and the Queen was horrified to learn that 'they go on quite as in the days of the old Revolution in the last century'. On Whit Sunday Gerard Manley Hopkins and his fellow Jesuits prayed for those of their order who were held hostage by the Paris Commune. The Introit for the day was grimly appropriate: 'Let God arise and let his enemies be scattered'. The next day they learned that the hostages had been shot. The Communists in their turn were massacred as government troops recaptured the city.

Yet even Hopkins, a conventional English gentleman converted to Roman Catholicism, could find it in him to admire the Communists. 'I must tell you I am always thinking about the Communist future,' he wrote to Robert Bridges, 'Horrible to say, in a manner I am a Communist ... The more I look the more black and deservedly black the future looks'. The press openly discussed the possibility of a British republic, to Swinburne's huge delight. 'Shall we live after all to see the Hanover rats smoked out,' he asked Rossetti in June, 'and the old mother of the royal rabbit-warren stifled in her burrow?' When a son born to the Princess of Wales died soon after birth a radical newspaper attacked 'the miserable mockery of interring with royal funeral ceremony a piece of skin and bone, grandiloquently called "Prince", not twenty-four hours old ... to augment the folly of the entire proceedings the Court goes into mourning for the loss of the wretched abortion'. A few weeks later the Queen was faced with public demonstrations against her favourite son and when she insisted on

leaving London for Balmoral Gladstone said that her conduct was 'the most sickening piece of experience which I have had during near forty years of public life'. 'Worse things may be easily imagined,' he continued, 'but smaller and meaner cause for the decay of Thrones cannot be conceived'. When the Queen's doctors hinted that her mental condition was such that she would probably retire more and more from public life they were told roundly by her secretary that this would mean abdication and 'an alteration in our form of government'.

On 6 November Sir Charles Dilke, MP for Chelsea and a close associate of French republicans, made an elaborate attack on the incompetence of the Prince of Wales during recent army manoeuvres. He then went on to advocate a British republic. His speech, in a crowded hall in Newcastle, was wildly cheered. 'The meeting was largely composed of the working classes,' *The Times* noted apprehensively, 'and there was great enthusiasm.' 'There is a widespread belief,' Dilke concluded amidst tremendous applause, 'that a Republic here is only a matter of education and time. I say, for my part – and I believe the middle classes in general will say – let it come!' Republicanism was now a political force and its champions, led by Dilke and George Odger, began a triumphant round of speech-making. The Queen tried to ignore the movement but when Gladstone failed to rebut it her anxieties came into the open and she told him coldly that she was dissatisfied with his lukewarm defence of monarchy. 'At present, and now for many days,' she added, 'these Revolutionary Theories are allowed to produce what effect they may in the minds of the Working Classes. Gross mis-statements and fabrications injurious to the credit of the Queen and injurious to the Monarchy remain unnoticed and uncontradicted.'

On 22 November, the tenth anniversary of the Prince Consort's fatal attack of typhoid, the Queen heard that the Prince of Wales was ill with the same disease. 'How all reminded me so vividly and sadly of my dearest Albert's illness,' she noted in her journal as the Prince's condition got rapidly worse. Sunday 10 December was a Day of National Prayer and Supplication, observed everywhere with extraordinary fervour, but the Prince continued to weaken and the next day the Queen was told he was beyond hope. Public entertainments were cancelled out of respect for his approaching death. But on 14 December, the day his father had died, he began to mend. 'Instead of this date dawning upon another deathbed, which I had felt almost certain of,' Victoria wrote, 'it brought the cheering news that dear

6 THE USES OF FANTASY

In the summer of 1871, replying to the accusations of the *Allgemeine Zeitung*, *The Times* admitted, not without a certain pride, that Britain had a tradition of 'saturnalia of a political character'. At the same time Parliament instituted Bank Holidays and one of these was the occasion for a political saturnalia in Manchester to launch Disraeli's assault on the prosaic statesmanship of the Liberals. Arriving on Easter Monday 1872 he was greeted by huge holiday crowds who removed the horses from his carriage and drew it through the streets in triumph. Two days later, assisted by two bottles of a liquid which his audience thought was water but was in fact a conveniently colourless brandy, he roused a mass meeting to frenzy with his vision of a country regenerated by the loyalty and piety of its people. 'England is a domestic country,' he cried amidst tremendous cheering, 'Here the home is revered and the hearth is sacred. The nation is represented by a family – the Royal Family.' He rounded on Gladstone for supporting republicans and he told his audience that Britain's future greatness would spring from the twin institutions of throne and altar. Geography had intended her to be part of some European state but if she was true to her spiritual inheritance she would find a more glorious rôle. A few weeks later, in the appropriate setting of the Crystal Palace, the Bank Holiday dream world in the London suburbs, he declared that Britain must be 'an Imperial country, a country where your sons, when they rise, rise to paramount positions and command the respect of the world.'

Tennyson embarked upon a similar imaginative journey from personal piety through national regeneration to imperial greatness. 'If I ceased to believe in any chance of another life, and of a Great Personality somewhere in the Universe, I should not care a pin for anything,' he told his friends in the summer of 1872. He remodelled his Arthurian

poems yet again, adding to them an epilogue addressed to the Queen in which he reminded her how 'London roll'd one tide of joy through all her trebled millions' at the time of the Thanksgiving Service. This moment of inspiration would lead 'the mightiest of all peoples under heaven' to be true to its 'ocean-empire'. The shameful demand to give away Canada, voiced recently by some Liberals, would be dropped and the dangers he had pinpointed in his Arthurian allegory – 'softness, breeding scorn of simple life', 'cowardice, the child of lust for gold', 'art with poisonous honey stol'n from France' – would be met and mastered.

Others still saw science as the real enemy and with the miracle of the Prince's recovery to reassure them they took up the struggle anew. 'Let science set herself to reform man's belief in his own immortality,' wrote Thomas Fowle angrily in the *Contemporary Review*, 'instead of engaging in the unnatural and hopeless task of destroying it.' *The Times* had already attacked Darwin for the 'disintegrating speculations' of his new book, *The Descent of Man*, and the *Family Herald* declared that 'society must fall to pieces if Darwinism be true'. When Charles Bastian published *The Beginnings of Life* in July 1872, claiming that organic life had evolved from the inorganic world without a divine creator, he was told sternly that 'when science, passing beyond its own limits, assumes to take the place of theology ... it is invading a province of thought to which it has no claim.' There was a warm welcome for the pious pseudo-science of St George Jackson Mivart's *Genesis of Species*, which seemed to show that natural selection was 'perfectly compatible with the creative and guiding power of God'. It was 'a most interesting and satisfactory book', noted Charles Dodgson.

Mrs Lynn Linton's novel *The True History of Joshua Davidson, Christian and Communist* hinted that God might have been involved in the events of the previous year in a very different way from that envisaged by the orthodox. Her hero Joshua Davidson, a Christ-like figure who championed the oppressed in England and in France, was denounced as an atheist on his return from the Paris Commune. The denunciation, made at a public meeting by a clergyman who should have been his friend, resulted in Joshua being beaten to death by an angry mob shouting 'You insulted God and religion'. The parallel with the crowds who had been incited to demand Christ's crucifixion was too obvious to be missed. Meanwhile in August 1872 Darwin's cousin Francis Galton, a distinguished scientist and explorer, had dealt the

miraculous interpretation of the Prince's recovery a shrewd blow. His article in the *Fortnightly Review*, 'A Statistical Inquiry into the Efficacy of Prayer', showed that among social groups having 'the advantages of affluence' the shortest lived were members of the Royal Family, even though they were prayed for regularly in every church in the land. 'The prayer has therefore no efficacy,' he concluded coldly, 'unless the very questionable hypothesis be raised, that the conditions of royal life may naturally be yet more fatal, and that their influence is partly, though incompletely, neutralized by the effect of public prayers.'

Floods in Cheshire that summer swept away four bridges, prompting the county surveyor to bring an action against the lady whose ornamental lakes had overflowed and caused the damage. He lost his case because the courts decided it had been an Act of God. The lawyers, like the Duke of Cambridge, could infer divine action even if they could not see it. A terrible storm later in the year convinced Francis Kilvert that 'the Almighty was making the clouds His chariot and walking upon the wings of the wind', but he did not claim to have seen God with his own eyes. Only foolish papists did that. For Bernadette Subirous in France to say she had seen the Virgin Mary was superstitious nonsense but for dukes and men of law in England to detect God's hand in the recovery of princes or in the overflowing of lakes was sound religion. In July 1872 the *Westminster Review* set out to explode this sort of humbug. Christians must make up their minds whether or not God could override natural law. If he could the so-called superstition of the Roman Catholics was simple recognition of truth. If he couldn't all forms of Christianity were suspect. There was no halfway house between superstition and open disbelief, even though Protestants might think they had built one. Their religion had provided 'a resting place which has sheltered man on his way from bondage to freedom,' rather than 'a permanent dwelling place for the mind'. 'We deem not only its eclipse but its disappearance to be merely a question of time: the ultimate contest must take place over the admission of the Supernatural, in any form, into the observed phenomena of the universe'.

Frederick George Lee, ritualist vicar of All Saints Lambeth, took up the challenge gleefully and cited the phrase about the ultimate contest in the introduction to *The Other World, or Glimpses of the Supernatural*, a two-volume work based on the proposition that Christianity was meaningless without belief in miracles and visions. His convictions were soon to lead him to accept consecration as an Anglican bishop

at the hands of some rather dubious Roman Catholics at a secret meeting in Italy, but for the time being he contented himself with recording all the instances of ghosts and witches and visitations he could find. *The Times* was furious. 'The worst enemies of the Church of England or of Religion,' it thundered, 'could hardly seek a better ally than a clergyman who drags into the light of day these relics or survivals of heathenism and who claims our belief in the name of religion for every lying legend'. It was a point of view with which most Anglicans agreed: in spite of the *Westminster's* strictures they jealously guarded their right to tread the tightrope which Protestantism had stretched between popish gullibility and scientific scepticism.

In the United States the rope was harder to tread because there was no established church, no divinely ordained monarchy, to keep it taut and to regulate the performance. There were certain parallels between Julia Ward Howe and Queen Victoria – they had been born within three days of each other and their respective visions, the coming of the Lord and the spiritual presence of Prince Albert, had both been vouchsafed in December 1861 – but 'The Battle Hymn of the Republic' could hardly be said to have the same standing as 'God Save the Queen' where divine aid was concerned. God was well used to being asked to save Victoria and his recent intervention on her behalf was more specific and more dramatic than anything he had done on the other side of the Atlantic. It had also been endorsed and promulgated by the Church of which she was Supreme Head, a process which could not be duplicated in the United States.

The forces which American religion could field in the fight against unbelief had plenty of enthusiasm but they had no figure-head to follow and no army to join. If the *Westminster Review* was right, if Protestantism was being crushed between Roman Catholic superstition and scientific scepticism, then the pressure was worse in America than in Britain. On the one hand Irish immigration was daily swelling Catholic ranks and on the other the influence of scientific and materialist thought was growing as never before. Whitelaw Reid, editor of the *New York Tribune*, declared in 1873 that American students no longer read English poetry and English novels in their spare time, as they had done in earlier years, but English science and English philosophy. 'Herbert Spencer, John Stuart Mill, Huxley, Darwin, Tyndall, have usurped the places of Tennyson and Browning and Matthew Arnold and Dickens,' he concluded. Henry Ward Beecher, one of the most influential preachers in America, told teachers and students at

Yale in 1872 that if Christianity resisted scientific progress it would shrivel and die. 'The providence of God is rolling forward in a spirit of investigation that Christian ministers must meet and join,' he warned.

But the common ground which devout scientists and progressive Christians sought to occupy was already being raked by atheist fire. Robert Green Ingersoll, Republican politican and former attorney general of Illinois, embarked in the early 1870s on a series of nationwide lecture tours. They were enormously successful – Ingersoll's manager said they brought in more money than any others in the history of lecturing – and their chosen target was the Christian religion. For more than twenty years 'the notorious infidel', as he came to be called, held huge audiences spellbound as he reduced conventional beliefs to an unsightly rubble of delusions. And there was no potent wizard, no charismatic politician of Disraeli's standing, to overcome Ingersoll's spells and lead pious processions into fantasy of the sort witnessed in Manchester.

The only active and self-confessed wizard in American politics was General Nathan Bedford Forrest, Grand Imperial Wizard of the Ku Klux Klan, and his message was not divine love but human hate. Originally founded for sport, so that its members could scare super-stitious negroes by riding at night through the Southern countryside dressed as the sheeted dead, the Klan soon developed into a sinister secret society. Klansmen's fantasies ran to imagined orders of chivalry – Knights of the Black Cross, Knights of the Rising Sun, Knights of the White Carnation – whose avowed purpose was to defend their vision of Christianity against decadent latter-day liberalism. Jefferson Davis, president of the Confederation during the Civil War, had de-clared that the emancipation of the slaves was an offence against God and would mean that 'several millions of human beings of an inferior race, peaceful and contented labourers in their sphere, are doomed to extermination, while at the same time they are encouraged to a general assassination of their masters'. Now, in the name of the God who had been offended, the Ku Klux Klan set about righting the wrong and asserting white supremacy by means of terror and intimida-tion. In North Carolina a teacher who dared to bring a crippled negro boy to church was expelled by his congregation and then taken to nearby woods at night to be ritually whipped and disfigured by a posse of Klansmen. The *Westminster Review* had seen the coming struggle as one between superstition and materialism but in the

Southern states the superstition had turned into a nightmarish fanaticism.

This was largely because materialism had turned into the worst kind of corruption. Enlightened liberals of the kind envisaged by Whitelaw Reid and Henry Ward Beecher, trying to combine Christian values with an awareness of intellectual and scientific progress, soon found their ideals used to cover squalid self-seeking. Unscrupulous Republican politicians from the North moved into the Southern states and used the Reconstruction Acts, passed by Congress to rebuild the areas devastated by war, as a means of establishing their own supremacy. They made the liberated slaves pawns in their political game and this helped to provoke the excesses of the Klan. Dishonest electoral practices became so common that in Louisiana, after a particularly notorious rigged election, there were two rival governors and two rival state legislatures.

In Texas bitterness was laced with hope because the war had left unscathed vast herds of cattle whose value increased tenfold when they were taken a thousand miles north to the railheads in Kansas. The cowboys who drove them rode a trail into fantasy as well as into Kansas. In 1872, only five years after Joseph McCoy set up the first Kansas cattleyard at Abilene, Buffalo Bill Cody starred in Edward Zane Judson's play *The Scouts of the Prairie* and then began to tour the country with a Wild West show which included Wild Bill Hickok, who had just completed a stint as marshal of Abilene. Hickok claimed to have killed over a hundred men and Cody had certainly killed over four thousand buffalo. Writing under the name of Ned Buntline, Judson went on to produce more than four hundred dime novels about the Wild West, most of them with Buffalo Bill as hero. Prentiss Ingraham, also a friend of Buffalo Bill, contributed a further six hundred. The legendary world of the Wild West, where lawless cowboys emptied their six-shooters into whisky bottles and into one another, was destined to play a vital part in the imaginative life of the English-speaking peoples.

Britain too had its images of lawlessness. After the serious rioting which accompanied the General Election of February 1874, there was once again talk of the danger of revolution. In the Birmingham area there were fears that 'the whole population would be up in arms' and *The Times* compared the sinister advance of the working classes to an encroaching ocean. 'The better class public watches the swelling tide and the rising breakers till they come to its very feet,' it said anxiously, 'and knows not the laws which will compel them to ebb

in due time, or at least prevent an inundation.' During the ensuing months William Rathbone Greg, once an industrialist and now a writer both on religion and on class conflict, published a series of articles in the *Contemporary Review* under the title 'Rocks Ahead, or the Warnings of Cassandra'. Like many other writers of the time he was worried about possible industrial decline and about what he called 'the political supremacy of the lower classes', but he was even more concerned with the gulf between conventional Christianity and contemporary thought. If politicians and other leading men were keeping up a mere pretence, trying to hold the lower classes off by brandishing spiritual and moral precepts in which they had themselves lost faith, then how could social breakdown and revolution be avoided? He concluded with an eloquent but despairing appeal for a change of heart before the country finally ran on the rocks:

Is there no other way of escape? Is it hopeless to avert and preclude the danger instead of meeting and mitigating it when it comes? Is it idle to dream that in the course of years the Religion of the nation may be modified in the direction and under the guidance of its best Intelligence, since that Intelligence can no longer accept the common Creed? The thing is possible, but not likely. I seem to see how it might be done, but I have no hope that it will be done. The divergence is too wide; the sources of the alienation lie too deep.

In the 1840s writing of this kind would have been the province of the prophets of apocalypse. Self-appointed seers like Marsh and Elliott and Cumming would have used the approach of anarchy and revolution on both sides of the Atlantic as proof that God had finally lost patience with the turbulence and infidelity of mankind. But now Marsh was dead, Elliott was dying and Cumming had fallen silent after publishing one last book to show that the events of 1870 had proved him right. It had made very little impact. In his day he had been enormously influential and the public had shown an insatiable appetite for his successive prognostications. But now his day was done and the business of prediction had passed into other hands. The disaster which Greg foresaw would not be divine retribution for loss of faith but quite the reverse: it would happen in spite of God rather than because of him and it would result from a failure to abandon conventional religion. The contrast between the two kinds of prophecy showed how much attitudes had changed in the space of thirty years. It was hard to imagine that thousands of ordinary people would ever again flock to hear men like Cumming tell them what God was up

98

to and how the threats and promises he had made in the Bible were being fulfilled.

But there was still an appetite for fantasy, a hunger for signs and portents. It was not gullibility that was dying but merely the readiness to clothe it in conventional biblical forms. The public wanted something more exciting, more occult, than pious expositions of the Book of Revelation. In 1862 Charles Hindley of Brighton had published a prophecy by Mother Shipton, a fifteenth-century witch from Yorkshire, which included the lines:

> The world to an end shall come
> In eighteen hundred and eighty one.

Hindley had subsequently admitted that he had written the prediction himself but this made little difference to its popularity. It was constantly re-issued, selling many thousands of copies, and it had a particular appeal to those who had recently been bereaved and did not want their loved ones to wait too long for their resurrection. Moses Hickman, an undertaker who had premises in the Commercial Road in London, was quick to see the value of such concern. He put a prominent advertisement in the 1872 edition of the pamphlet offering a lead-lined coffin, the ultimate in sepulchral security, for as little as £20 – a price which included a hearse and four horses, two mourning coaches, ostrich plumes, black velvets and a suitable number of funeral mutes. The publishers declared that the lines about 1881 had become 'the talk of the whole civilized globe' and offered to sell the page containing them separately, 'believing that many of our readers would prefer it in this shape for Albums, Scrap Books, etc.'

Mother Shipton received support from an unexpectedly authoritative quarter. Professor Charles Piazzi Smyth, Astronomer Royal for Scotland, had spent many years examining the Great Pyramid and was sure that it was a divinely inspired calendar in stone. Having noted that 985 years had elapsed between the building of the Tower of Babel and the Exodus of the Jews, followed by a further 1,542 between the Exodus and the birth of Christ, he had then found these figures were reproduced in inches as principal dimensions of the Grand Gallery of the pyramid. And the other main dimension, from the end to the great wall, was precisely 1,881.4 inches. This proved that the rule of Christ would last for 1,881.4 years, just as the 'Mosaic dispensation' had lasted for 1,542. Because of inaccuracies as to the accepted

date of Christ's birth the moment of destiny would arrive not in 1882 but in the spring of 1881. Smyth's book *Our Inheritance in the Great Pyramid* was illustrated with photographs taken during a royal tour of Egypt and when he gave the Royal Society a first report on his findings in 1864 he was assured that 'if they are facts they form the most remarkable discovery of the age.'

But when in 1874 he announced that his definitive account was now ready he found that the officials of the Society had changed their minds. They refused to give his paper a hearing and after a furious row he resigned from the Society – though not from his position as Astronomer Royal – and turned from his fellow scientists to the general public. He brought out three successive revised and enlarged editions of his book, lacing his calculations with predictions as lurid as any that Cumming had produced. 'Badly as the last 1250 years of the Christian dispensation have distinguished themselves by their numerous wars and over-abundant bloodshed,' he warned, 'the last few years still remaining to it threaten to be more terrible than ever.' And the event to which these remaining seven years would lead was no longer seen merely as the end of the Christian era but as Christ's Second Coming. 'And meanwhile the Great Pyramid will assist in witnessing to the supernatural preparations for the universal earthly kingdom of the returned Lord Christ.' Even though Smyth's starting point in the dark tombs of ancient pharaohs had all the fascination of the occult his conclusions were the same as those reached by conventional pedlars of biblical apocalypse.

It was by no means certain that the returned Lord Christ would be prepared to rule over all who claimed to be Christians, for the book made it clear that the inheritance was that of the English-speaking peoples only. They had been especially favoured with the divinely ordained measurements of yards and feet and inches, the language in which God spoke to mankind, and they must be sure to remain true to them if they wished to come into their inheritance. 'National apathy, if not apostasy, has brought some Englishmen so low that they have begun to talk about abolishing their own hereditary measures,' Smyth wrote angrily. The proposed alternative, 'the Communistic French metric system', was 'part of the general drifting of the European nations into infidelity.'

On the day Smyth resigned from the Royal Society, 7 February 1874, Gladstone decided to concede defeat in the General Election and make way for Disraeli. Smyth's career as a popular prophet and

100

Disraeli's period of office as Prime Minister had begun together and might well end together, either triumphantly or otherwise, for under the Septennial Act the new Parliament could not last longer than 1881. Disraeli's fantasy of Britain's imperial destiny, that spiritual inheritance of which he had spoken in his Crystal Palace speech, must unfold alongside the predictions of the Astronomer Royal for Scotland. Both men had staked their reputations on a conviction that visions would become realities within seven years. The two visions had much in common – both rejected all things European and both drew inspiration from the mysterious orient, especially from ancient Egypt – but more significant was the mere fact that both were dreams. There were precedents for allowing dreamers to decide the fate of peoples. The Book of Genesis told how it had happened in ancient Egypt after Joseph had interpreted Pharaoh's dream about the seven fat years and the seven lean. However, it would be strange if such things were allowed to mould national policies and popular culture in the last quarter of the nineteenth century.

In the realm of popular culture successive accretions of occult wisdom quickly built up around the prophecies of Mother Shipton and Professor Smyth. Vast crowds gathered at Ham Hill in Somerset on Good Friday 1879 to watch the local stone quarries disappear into the earth on the stroke of noon, an event which Mother Shipton was said to have foretold but which failed to take place. She was back in the news the following year when a Yorkshire village slid into the Leeds Corporation reservoir. It was widely claimed that she had predicted this disaster as one of the things which would herald the end of the world. Indeed it seemed that no natural phenomenon could escape being woven into her remarkable foresight. 'Should the spring be late, the summer cold, or snow fall earlier than usual,' one sceptic wrote angrily, 'we are at once told that Mother Shipton prophesied that we should not know winter from summer, except by the leaves on the trees, before the world was at an end.' In 1880 Houlton and Sons of Paternoster Square in London brought out *The End of the World in 1881–2, according to Mother Shipton, the Great Pyramid of Ghizeh and other Ancient Prophecies related to Russia and Turkey*, a curious compilation which hovered between simulated disapproval and unashamed sensationalism. It told how an eminent professor had declared that the 1881 census would show that England had 33,950,000 inhabitants, a figure pregnant with meaning for those who knew that Smyth had put the length of the Grand Gallery at precisely 339.5 inches. It pointed

101

out that the contract for carrying mail between London and Bombay ran out at the beginning of 1881, as did the Protectorate set up in Syria and the tenure of certain emoluments in Britain. Even the completion of the new Law Courts in the Strand, scheduled for New Year's Day 1881, was cited as evidence that this would inaugurate the year of destiny.

There were also suggestions that 1881 might not be an end but a beginning. It seemed that the height of a certain step in the Great Pyramid indicated that 'the period of tribulation' would last until 1887. Professor C.A. Grimmer, 'an American astrologer of some repute', was quoted as saying that the years from 1880 to 1887 would witness 'one universal carnival of death'. In fact Professor Grimmer had used a less frivolous word. His book *The Voice of the Stars, or the coming Perihelia of Jupiter, Uranus, Neptune and Saturn with attendant Plagues, Storms and Fires from 1880 to 1887 supported by Historical Facts* predicted 'one universal carnage of death'. Ships would rot upon the ocean, 'their dead human freight drifting where the winds and waves might take them', and the sun would be as red as blood. The poor would rise against the rich, bringing fanaticism and anarchy, and the face of the earth would be changed by volcanic action. It would be impossible to eat either fish or meat and God would show his rejection of the human race by producing 'remarkable displays of electricity, frightful to witness'.

While Smyth's dream gathered adherents Disraeli's ran into trouble. 'You were very right in saying that the only obvious difficulties might be religious ones,' he told his colleague Lord Salisbury shortly after forming his administration. Before he could propose any other measures Victoria made it clear that priority must be given to a law to stop 'all these Ritualistic practices, dressings, bowings, etc., and everything of that kind'. Salisbury, who had only agreed to join the government if no steps were taken against the High Church, began to talk not just of resignation but of 'civil war in the Church of England'. The Queen admitted that such a measure would cause 'inconvenience and difficulty' but insisted that it could not be put off. Disraeli gritted his teeth and prepared to trim his vision of Britain's destiny to fit the convictions of his sovereign.

The first step was to suggest that the proposed Public Worship Regulation Act would defend the Church of England against insidious pseudo-Catholicism, against what Disraeli called 'the Mass in masquerade'. 'I have never addressed any body of my countrymen for

102

the last three years,' he told the House of Commons, 'without having taken the opportunity of intimating to them that a great change was occurring in the politics of the world, that the great struggle between the temporal and the spiritual power, which had stamped such indelible features upon the history of the past, was reviving in our own time.' Having thus preserved the British from papal tyranny he would turn his attention to his avowed policy of lifting them from base materialism to true spirituality and imperial greatness. But in September 1874, when the Bill became law and he went to Balmoral as the honoured guest of a grateful sovereign, he fell seriously ill. 'I am a sort of prisoner of state in the tower of a castle,' he wrote to Lady Bradford, 'a royal physician comes two or three times a day to feel my pulse, etc., and see whether I can possibly endure the tortures that await me.' While he languished in his tower the religious strife predicted by Lord Salisbury became increasingly bitter. High Churchmen proclaimed that they would not obey the new courts set up by the Act and Gladstone said that the country now resembled 'the field on the eve of the Battle of Armageddon'.

Several London clergymen defied the Act and went on with their ritualistic practices. The most notorious was the Rev. Arthur Tooth of Hatcham near New Cross. By the beginning of 1877 special trains were arriving at New Cross station on Sundays, packed with men and boys who had allegedly been hired to break up Tooth's services. One of his outraged parishioners claimed that the men had been paid a pound each and the boys a shilling. Even *The Rock*, a periodical hostile to the High Church, reported that 'forty dockyard "lambs" or labourers received ten shillings each together with seats in the church and the whole body, police and lambs included, were fed at one shilling and sixpence a head by Mr Page of New Cross.' There were ugly brawls, involving up to eight thousand people, and the police had to send for reinforcements. Even when Tooth gave himself up and was gaoled the troubles did not end. Fighting in his church was worse than ever and further violence erupted in Folkestone, where another turbulent priest persisted in the dressings and bowings that had so angered the Queen. Worst of all, it seemed that the Act had increased rather than reduced the Catholic danger: 'It is to Rome that individuals are silently migrating,' wrote the Bishop of Gloucester anxiously.

Meanwhile another and very different threat to established belief was opening an even wider gulf between Anglican clergymen and

their flocks. Shortly before Disraeli became Prime Minister the *Contemporary Review* published an article by Sir Henry Thompson, an eminent surgeon, advocating cremation. Most of his arguments were practical ones – graveyards were getting crowded, pollution from cemeteries was a cause of disease – but his real target was belief in bodily resurrection and in the grave as a place of eternal rest. 'Could I paint in its true colours,' he wrote grimly, 'the ghastly picture of that which happens to the mortal remains of the dearest we have lost, the page would be too deeply stained for publication.' It was inconceivable that what the writhing maggots left behind could ever walk the walls of heaven.

There was worse to come. Bishop Fraser of Manchester, consecrating new burial land at Bolton in March 1874, took occasion to refer to the cremation controversy because 'he wished his hearers to dissociate the resurrection from physical conditions'. If God so wished he could raise up a body 'out of elementary particles which had been liberated by the burning' as easily as from 'the elements of bodies which had passed into the structure of worms'. But he might well do neither, for the words of the burial service did not constitute a guarantee. When the priest at the graveside said that Jesus Christ would 'change our vile body, that it may be like unto his glorious body' he was merely stating a personal belief, not making promises to the corpse at his feet. Some bodies might prove too vile to be changed and their owners might never inherit eternal life.

Some bodies might even be too vile to be buried. When Frederick Merrett of Cowley near Oxford died in January 1875 his vicar, the Rev. J. Coley, refused to bury him because of his 'notorious life'. Eight days later, with the corpse still above ground, Merrett's relatives tried to get Coley to let somebody else officiate. He refused to see them and locked himself in his church while several hundred of Merrett's supporters rioted outside. Three days later, when another clergyman finally arrived to bury the body, he found the church locked. The crowd of mourners and sympathizers, numbering well over a thousand even though it was a working day, forced its way into the church after a dozen men had climbed in through the belfry and ripped off the lock from the inside with crowbars. Merrett was given a proper funeral and a fortnight later an enormous crowd paraded Coley's effigy round Oxford with a placard on its chest proclaiming 'Cremation of Rev. J. Coley'. The figure was then publicly burned.

Perhaps the most significant feature of this extraordinary affair was

the placard on the effigy. In the thirteen months since Thompson's article cremation had come to be regarded with horror and revulsion. It was an insult to the dead, an obscenity, and so it was appropriate that it should be visited on one who had tried to obstruct the progress to eternal life which burial was thought to guarantee. Those who voluntarily burned their dead were viewed with disgust. When Sir Charles Dilke's wife died in September 1874 he had her cremated in Dresden, 'in a furnace recently invented by Herr Siemens, with large numbers of scientific men attending'. The English press gave a horrific timed account of the proceedings: the coffin burst after six minutes, the flesh began to melt after another five and the skeleton was laid bare after another ten. Later the *Annual Register* recorded the 'intense horror and amazement' of the people of Woking in Surrey when they discovered that a certain Professor Gorini was constructing 'a cremating apparatus right in their very midst'.

There were other attacks on traditional interment and on the hopes which went with it. Francis Seymour Haden, a surgeon and a noted artist, argued that while ordinary burial was certainly insanitary cremation had even greater dangers, being a positive incentive to poisoners. What was needed was a wicker or *papier-maché* coffin so that the worms could obtain easier entry and complete their work more quickly. Swift decomposition was the best guarantee of public hygiene. His proposed perforated and perishable coffins, looking like overgrown wastepaper baskets according to *The Times*, were put on public display in London in the summer of 1875. The exhibition was open daily 'on presentation of an ordinary visiting card' but few undertakers bothered to go. They knew that their customers wanted security, with lead linings if they could afford them, rather than swift decomposition. The resurrection of the body might be an unhygienic fantasy for Haden but it was a profitable one for undertakers.

The authorities were worried about the impact the American revivalists Dwight Moody and Ira Sankey might have on a Britain torn apart by ritualism and beset by doubts about the dead. After a successful mission in Scotland in 1873 and 1874 Moody and Sankey held their first London meeting in March 1875. At first it was noted with some relief that their congregations 'appeared for the most part to consist of the middle class', but later *The Times* had to admit that they had brought in 'not less than 335,000 of every class of society'. The Prince of Wales attended a meeting but the Queen declined on the grounds that this was sensationalism and not true religion. 'The

105

attraction is a love for religious excitement,' *The Times* explained loftily, 'apt at times to run riot in ordinarily sober races'. The Marquis of Bath brought the business of the House of Lords to a standstill in June by demanding parliamentary action to stop the Americans holding a meeting at Eton. *The Times* published a letter of protest against the meeting signed by seventy-four members of Parliament, all Etonians or parents of Etonians. Edward Hugessen Knatchbull-Hugessen, who orchestrated the campaign against Moody and Sankey, had written a book called *Whispers of Fairyland* and this led to a certain amount of mockery; but he stood his ground and insisted that as a writer of children's books he knew that 'spasmodic and sensationalist religion' did harm to boys of an impressionable age. In the end the battle on the playing fields of Eton between fairyland and the kingdom of God resulted in a draw: Moody and Sankey were prevented from using the marquee which had been prepared for them but they drew a crowd of 500 to an impromptu meeting which they held in the back garden of a draper's shop.

Meanwhile the Prime Minister who had proclaimed the importance of society's soul was having to concern himself with its body. A deepening trade depression led to wage reductions and strikes. The government put forward a programme of reform but this had little effect on the immediate situation. Disraeli spoke of 'much fright and confusion' but he still had faith in his own visionary powers. 'I see, as from a tower, the end of all,' he wrote calmly when things were at their worst. In the autumn of 1875, as the Prince of Wales set off on a tour of India, the vision began to unfold. *The Times* had already said, in connection with a ball at which the Prince's brother had appeared in a leopard skin with gold claws, that 'The pride of our people requires that there should be a well-ordered magnificence in the lives of their Princes'. Now the accounts of the oriental splendours with which the Prince was received in India ministered both to the nation's pride and to Disraeli's politics of fantasy.

In the midst of the splendours, just after he had shot his first tiger, the Prince learned that one of his companions, the loose-living Lord Aylesford, was being paid in his own coin: his wife was running off with Lord Blandford. And when the party reached Egypt on its way home the Prince heard that Blandford's brother, Lord Randolph Churchill, had shown the Princess of Wales some letters from the Prince which were allegedly so compromising that if they were to be published the Prince would never succeed to the throne. The Prince sent Lord

Charles Beresford off across Europe with a curt letter challenging Churchill to a duel. The royal procession out of India appeared to have little respect for conventional morality and the satirists began to talk of 'Prince Pagan'. Pagan or not the Prince certainly had that strange power over animals which Nietzsche had promised to the followers of Dionysus. Lord Lytton, who went aboard the royal yacht *Serapis* in the Suez Canal, was astounded by the vessel's barbaric splendours and by the tigers and other beasts who roamed its decks. 'The Prince really seems to have won the hearts not only of the Rajahs and Maharajahs but also of the wild beasts in India,' he told the Queen.

During the Prince's absence in India the British government had acquired the Khedive of Egypt's shares in the Suez Canal. Disraeli described his achievement in typically colourful terms: 'We have had all the gamblers, capitalists, financiers of the world, organized and platooned in bands of plunderers, arrayed against us, and secret emissaries in every corner, and have baffled them all'. The route to the riches of the east was secure and the land of the pharaohs was locked as firmly into the popular mind as even Professor Smyth could have wished. *Punch* published a cartoon showing Disraeli in the sands of Egypt brandishing his acquisition in the form of a key – 'The Key of India' – while the Great Pyramid looked on and the immemorial sphinx winked. At a ball given by the Lord Lieutenant of Ireland a lady came dressed as the Suez Canal:

A head-dress of Egyptian fashion, formed of pearl and turquoise beads, with a tiara of diamonds; and a long flowing robe of rich cloth of gold, to represent the Desert, traversed by wavy bands of azure satin, embroidered with pearls, to typify the blue waves of the Mediterranean passing through the sands of the Desert and bearing the wealth of the Indies; a red satin under-skirt embroidered with Egyptian designs, to represent the Red Sea; the corsage of blue satin, to represent the Mediterranean Sea, girdled with roses and lilies for England and France; the neck and arms covered with Egyptian jewels; and a long flowing veil, enveloping the whole figure, of tissue of gold, like a cloud of gold-dust. At her girdle was a golden key, with a label attached, 'Suez Canal, four millions'.

But the lady had not come alone. She was part of a quadrille entitled 'The Eastern Question' and her three companions represented the Mediterranean, the Neva and Constantinople – reminders that Russia and Turkey, now moving steadily towards war, were also interested

107

in Egypt. In 1876 the Turks put down with barbaric cruelty a revolt in Bulgaria and many people felt that Disraeli – now Earl of Beaconsfield – should join with Russia in a crusade against Turkish power in the Balkans. Instead the Queen and her ministers supported the Turks. The Queen was convinced that Russia had incited the revolt in order to push through the Balkans and cut Britain's route to India. 'It *ought* to be brought home to Russia,' she wrote angrily, 'and the world *ought* to know that on *their* shoulders and *not* on *ours* rests the *blood* of the murdered Bulgarians!' And in any case the Bulgarians were not true Christians at all but ritualists, idolaters, kissers of icons, 'far worse than the Mussulmans'. The Low Church journal *The Rock* told its readers that the Whore of Babylon, the Roman Catholic Church, was leading a conspiracy of all forms of superstition, Russian, Bulgarian and ritualist, against the British Empire, the only true citadel of the only true faith. When Beaconsfield said publicly that there was a network of secret societies trying to undermine Turkey and Britain the exasperated Russian ambassador in London told his government that British foreign policy was now 'a conspiracy of a half-mad woman with a minister who once had genius but has degenerated into a political clown'.

The Queen and her Prime Minister did not have a monopoly of fantasy. Gladstone told his colleagues in the Liberal party that Beaconsfield, as a Jew, was working deliberately against Christianity. W. T. Stead, editor of the *Northern Echo* and a violent critic of the government, proclaimed that God was behind Gladstone and Antichrist behind Beaconsfield. As both sides prepared for Armageddon, each totally convinced of its own rectitude, charges of madness and diabolic possession began to accompany the other insults. An article in the *Contemporary Review* on 'Working Men and the Eastern Question' declared that both leaders had taken leave of their senses, Beaconsfield because of his fantasies about secret societies and the hidden destiny of nations and Gladstone because he seriously thought that Britain could drive the Turks from Bulgaria. Nevertheless Gladstone's impassioned speeches, together with his pamphlet *The Bulgarian Horrors and the Questions of the East*, did much to mobilize public opinion against the government. Then in the autumn of 1877 the Turks caught the popular imagination by their defence of Plevna, a fortress in Bulgaria, against the Russians. By the time Plevna fell in December 1877 its defenders had become heroes in Britain and a popular music-hall song, based appropriately enough on the conjuror's cry of 'Hey

Jingo!',* served to project Beaconsfield's wizardry onto a wider stage than ever before:

> We don't want to fight, but by jingo if we do
> We've got the ships, we've got the men, we've got the money too.

By the end of January 1878 the song's impact was so overwhelming that Liberals in the House of Commons accused the government of encouraging its mindless belligerence. In February Gladstone's house was attacked by a Jingo mob and the opposition press began to speak of 'the Jingoes – the music hall patriots who sing the Jingo song' with an indignation that was tinged with apprehension. A few months earlier the Queen had been ready to abdicate rather than 'remain the sovereign of a country that is letting itself down to kiss the feet of the great barbarian', but now she took heart as Beaconsfield went from strength to strength, halting the Russians with naval threats and then wringing from them concessions of dubious significance at an international conference in Berlin. When he returned in July 1878, claiming that he had brought back 'Peace with Honour', the London streets were filled with rapturous crowds uplifted by his vision of Britain's imperial destiny. Even more remarkable was the reaction of Londoners a few weeks later when 'Cleopatra's Needle' was erected on the Thames Embankment. There had been many complaints about the expense of bringing this obelisk from Egypt and when it was put in place there were last-minute delays and the crowd was expected to be hostile. Instead there was a strange atmosphere of awe and excitement. 'So far from displaying any chagrin or disappointment,' reported *The Times* in some surprise, 'the enthusiasm of the crowd burst forth in ringing cheers'. The aura of Egypt had become so pervasive that even an inanimate object could cast its spell.

More familiar and more domestic visions seemed tame by comparison. To Francis Kilvert, walking in his Herefordshire churchyard and gazing at a host of tombstones facing the morning sun, 'it seemed as if the morning of the Resurrection had come and the sleepers had arisen from their graves and were standing upon their feet silent and solemn, all looking toward the East to meet the Rising of the Sun'. Such moments had comforted countless generations but now they paled before the great cosmic drama projected by Professor Smyth

* 'Hey Jingo' is the counterpart of 'Hey Presto': the first is used to make things appear and the second to make them disappear.

109

and Lord Beaconsfield. Country life itself, the rhythm of seed-time and harvest which had seemed changeless and divinely ordained, was being transformed by the vision of empire and by its economic results. There were terrible storms and floods throughout the summer of 1878 but in spite of the bad weather wheat prices fell, causing widespread rural distress, because of imports of cheap grain from the colonies. British agriculture was being sacrificed on the altar of imperial greatness and there was little that Beaconsfield could do about it. 'Starvation has no answer', he wrote grimly. Even his most admiring biographer admitted that his proposals for dealing with the agrarian depression were 'somewhat fanciful'.

The American stockbroker poet E.C. Stedman visited England in 1879 and was appalled by the contrast between the richness of her imaginative life and the poverty of her economy. She would soon be 'more of a Museum, Park, Picture Gallery, for the world at large to visit than anything else.' An Egyptian obelisk similar to the one in London was on its way to New York, where it was to be set up in Central Park, but there was to be no need for a miraculous change of public mood because the costs were borne by the railroad millionaire William Henry Vanderbilt. The rough edges of public controversy, spiritual as well as secular, were smoothed away by America's growing wealth just as they were sharpened by Britain's deepening recession. 'Everybody finds his income reduced,' reported the American consul in Birmingham, 'and everybody blames America for the reduction.'

Gladstone saw a dreadful consistency in everything that had happened since the Prince's illness. At every turn common sense and sound religion had been pushed aside by overblown imaginings. So far from defending God against the sceptics and the materialists these fantasies were playing into their hands. True Christians must assert the supremacy of reason before it was too late. 'Thought,' he exclaimed passionately, 'thought is the citadel'. The politics of fantasy had been tried and found wanting. 'The government have done and said many strange things,' remarked one critic, 'The public mind, which at first responded adequately to the surprises prepared for it, has latterly become jaded and insensitive. It has supped too full of marvels. Lord Beaconsfield and his colleagues have in fact debauched the national faculty of wonder.'

Nevertheless in March 1880, after a run of government by-election victories, Beaconsfield advised Victoria to dissolve Parliament early. She did so with a will: 'The Queen believes the time has been well

110

chosen,' she wrote, 'and that the Government will be more successful even than they would have been later.' She was outraged and horrified when the General Election gave the Liberals a majority. 'If the Opposition force themselves upon her it will make her quite ill,' she told her Private Secretary. She fought off Gladstone as long as she could but in the end she had to accept a ministry which even included the objectionable Sir Charles Dilke. All that had been achieved since her son's miraculous recovery seemed now in jeopardy. Gladstone for his part saw his return to office as the triumph of thought over fantasy. 'The downfall of Beaconsfieldism is like the vanishing of some magnificent castle in an Italian romance,' he wrote. The simile was appropriate but over-confident. The castle of fantasy might no longer be manned by politicians but it could still boast many thousands of defenders. Its battlements stretched halfway round the world and those who stood upon them were already proclaiming a new dawn.

7 WATCHERS UPON THE HIGH TOWERS

BEHIND THE TALK OF THOUGHT AND FANTASY, BEHIND the metaphorical citadel of the one and the insubstantial castle of the other, lay the oldest and most difficult question of all. Was the outward appearance of things a guide to their real nature? Could the universe be understood simply by observing and cataloguing the elements of which it was made up or was there a more reliable way of interpreting it? Plato had long ago suggested that outward appearances might be mere shadows cast by a reality men could not see, while eastern sages taught that existence was a veil which concealed rather than revealed creation's true glory. Christians had inherited these doubts about the physical world and some had seen it as nothing but a facade devised by the Devil for the deception and damnation of anyone foolish enough to take it at its face value. By the 1870s even the most pious were reluctant to dismiss scientists as mere dupes of Satan but the churches still taught that the 'scientific method', the drawing of conclusions and the framing of laws from the observation of physical phenomena, could never explain God's creation unless it was based on an understanding of God himself. The scientists were like men visiting a craftsman's workshop with the craftsman absent and the bits of his masterpiece spread out on the floor: they might learn something of the masterpiece by examining the bits but they would learn far more by looking for evidence of the craftsman's intentions.

God had provided such evidence in the Bible and also – if Roman Catholics were to be believed – in divinely authorized statements from St Peter's successors in Rome. Observation by itself could describe things but it could not define them. It was as if beings from outer space, aliens with no buttocks and no concept of sitting, were to imagine they had understood a chair once they had catalogued its

112

dimensions. They would know everything about it except the one thing that mattered – its purpose. The unaided scientific observer would know everything about what he observed except the one thing that mattered – its part in God's plan. So where was the line between thought and fantasy to be drawn? Those whom Gladstone saw as denizens of some imaginary castle in an Italian romance were at least working the right way round: they were putting divine revelation before the deceptions of outward appearance, even if the revelations in which they dealt were a little bizarre. They did not mistake mere observation for thought. They had behind them not just eighteen centuries of Christian teaching but many thousands of years of other creeds and other philosophies. The distrust of outward appearance, the search for deeper meaning, pervaded both eastern and western thought. It was science's battering ram, not fantasy's castle, that was new and unorthodox. Christians who heard its blows hurried to the ramparts without stopping to think which fortress they were defending. When the Evangelical Alliance met in New York in 1873 many Protestants expected it to come out against the recent declaration of Papal Infallibility. Instead it ranged itself alongside the Roman Catholic Church in the struggle against science.

Professor Draper of the University of New York, author of *A History of the Intellectual Development of Europe*,* determined to take over the citadel of thought in the name of science. His new book, *A History of the Conflict between Religion and Science*, published in 1873, insisted that Protestantism and science must be allies in the war against superstition. There was 'a great and rapidly increasing departure from public religious faith' on both sides of the Atlantic because established Christianity, especially Roman Catholicism, rested on 'fiction and fraud' and was 'steeped in blood'. Intelligent men and women must decide not just between scientific method and the search for God's intentions but between scientific laws and the acceptance of God's caprices: 'We are now in the midst of a controversy respecting the mode of government of the world, whether it be by incessant divine intervention or by the operation of primordial and unchangeable laws'. In Belfast, arguably the most religious city in the British Isles, Professor Tyndall told the British Association for the Advancement of Science that questions about the meaning of the universe or about the origin of life could no longer be left to theologians: 'We claim

* See above, p. 86.

113

the freedom to discuss them. The ground which they cover is scientific ground'. Creation's ultimate secrets must yield not to revelation but to observation. Outraged clergymen denounced Tyndall from their pulpits and the Belfast newspapers orchestrated a campaign of hate against him. Even after the initial fury had cooled the London *Annual Register* still felt that he had given 'serious alarm to the religious world, as seeming to betoken the atheistic leanings of modern science'.

While men like Draper and Tyndall stormed the citadels of Christian thought the defenders of the castles of Christian fantasy sallied forth to claim the whole field of battle for their own. In 1876 the Countess of Caithness brought out a book called *Old Truths in a new light, or, An Earnest Endeavour to Reconcile Material Science with Spiritual Science and with Scripture.* 'The further I read and the deeper I go into the spirit of this admirable address,' she wrote, 'the more I see that, so far from being opposed to each other, Professor Tyndall and I can shake hands over it ... To those who can read the signs of the times the present seems to presage a greater and more important change than any that has preceded it'. When this change came, when the new light dawned, the workings of God's universe would at last be clear. There would be no need to argue about measuring the pieces or reading the craftsman's notes because the craftsman himself would be once more in his workshop and would reveal all. In the following year, in a work on the Eastern Question entitled *England and Islam*, the Countess's admirer Edward Maitland suggested that Tyndall knew there were more things in heaven and earth than mere scientific observation: 'To this ingenious scientist are due the thanks of the intuitionalist for the recognition he has accorded to the imagination as an instrument of scientific research.' There was some indication of what an intuitionalist might be in Maitland's account of how the book had been written:

The first physical manifestation received by me consisted in my wrist being grasped by some invisible agency, while I was using my typewriter, and forcibly guided over the keys, the words being presented simultaneously to my mind, but only as they were being written ... The presence I had felt bending over me darted itself into me just below the cerebral bulb at the back of my neck, the sensation being that of a slight tap, as of a finger-touch; and then in a voice full, rich, firm, measured and so strong that it resounded through the room, exclaimed in a tone indicative of high satisfaction, 'At last I have found a man through whom I can speak!'

114

There were greater marvels to come. It seemed that intuition, as well as putting one in touch with would-be authors from other worlds, could also carry out summary executions in this one. In February 1878, sitting on the steps of the *Ecole de Médecine* in Paris, Maitland learned from his friend Anna Kingsford that her thought waves had just killed Claude Bernard, a French scientist notorious for his experiments on animals. 'If it prove that I really possess such a glorious power, woe be to the torturers!' she exulted, 'I will make it dangerous, nay deadly, to be a vivisectionist.' She had been in touch with the spirit world since childhood and she had long ago left her husband, a pious clergyman in Shropshire, in order to study the occult and develop supernatural powers. When she and Maitland returned to London they realized that if they were to cast other and more potent spells they would need a manual of magic arts. They asked Lady Caithness, who was still in Paris, to get them the works of the French sorcerer Eliphas Lévi. She did so willingly, remarking that the miraculous extermination of vivisectionists was a sign of the cosmic change which was coming. There would be, she assured them, 'a New Dispensation whose light is already dawning upon the humanity of the earth, at least upon the minds of those who are, as it were, the watchers upon the high towers'.

Once they had received their compendium of necromancy Edward Maitland and Anna Kingsford quickly built their own high tower. 'The revelations came in rapid succession,' Maitland recorded excitedly. In *England and Islam* he had inveighed against 'the materialistic rule in politics', by which he had meant Gladstone's rejection of the destiny prepared for the English-speaking peoples in ancient Egypt. Professor Smyth and Lord Beaconsfield had told of it and now Edward Maitland saw it with his own eyes. He found himself, 'between waking and sleeping', in a tomb hewn from the rock in the ancient Egyptian city of Thebes. He realized that this was the place of his initiation into the divine mysteries in a previous incarnation, since Thebes was the birthplace of the god Osiris who had been hacked to pieces and then restored to life by Isis. All was confirmed when Maitland visited a friend who painted Egyptian scenes. 'Several of his paintings of that country were then in the studio and in one of them, a view of Thebes, I instantly recognized the scene of my vision'.

Meanwhile Anna Kingsford left her physical body and visited the planets one by one, each with its own attendant angel. She had visions of a future in which France had become a battlefield for British and

115

German armies, with the Germans in occupation of Belgium, and this led her to seek out Joan of Arc, 'who hated women's clothes and loved fighting against oppression just as I do'. Having discussed transvestite pleasures with Joan of Arc she went on to speak with Winowa, a Red Indian girl acquainted with Osiris and Jesus Christ. The presence of Jesus was especially welcome since Anna knew that in an earlier life she had been Mary Magdalene. Clearly the change which the watchers upon the high towers could now glimpse would bring together both these gods who had died for their people and would thus reconcile science not only with Christianity but also with the older revelations from which both had sprung. When they went to the British Museum to check up on the prophetic measurements of the Great Pyramid they were referred to shelf number 1881 for books on the subject. 'The officials to whom we pointed out the coincidence were greatly amused thereat,' Edward wrote later, 'We refrained from telling them that the prophecy was actually in course of fulfilment and that the world was really coming to an end in that year in the sense intended'. From New Year's Day 1882 Lady Caithness dated her letters 'Anno Lucis 1' – Year One of the Enlightenment.

The three of them no longer watched from lonely towers. They had joined the Theosophical Society, a corps of international observers walking the battlements of fantasy from New York to Madras. It sprang from a meeting in New York in September 1875 at which George Felt lectured on 'The Lost Canon of Proportion of the Egyptians, Greeks and Romans'. As well as elucidating Professor Smyth's predictions he also suggested that the Dwellers of the Threshold might be persuaded to materialize. These mysterious beings, who controlled the destiny of mankind from another world, had been described in some detail in Edward Bulwer-Lytton's novel *Zanoni*, which had been enormously successful in America as well as in Britain. Helena Petrovna Blavatsky, a Russian lady who heard the lecture, maintained that under the guise of fiction Lytton had revealed the greatest of all truths, for she and her friend Colonel Olcott, a New York newspaper correspondent and author of *People from the Other World*, had been favoured with a supernatural message from a similarly elemental being called Tuiti Bey of the Brotherhood of Luxor in Egypt. It was decided to form a society to 'collect and diffuse a knowledge of the laws which govern the universe'. At first it was to be called the Egyptological Society but it soon became clear that its business was theosophy, the quest for divine wisdom. Edward Maitland and Anna Kingsford

joined the London lodge of the Society and Lady Caithness was soon presiding over a branch in Paris.

Madame Blavatsky set to work on *Isis Unveiled*, an enormous compilation of occult learning which linked the Dwellers of the Threshold with Serapis, a god who had combined the attributes of Osiris and Dionysus and had been popular in Greece when Alexander the Great had taken his armies to India and re-enacted the legendary Dionysiac procession. As Blavatsky delved into these matters the Prince of Wales brought his Dionysiac entourage back from India in the yacht *Serapis* and Lord Lytton, son of the man who had told of the Dwellers, marvelled at the tigers who caressed the Prince's feet. Coincidences like this, mere converging symbols, helped to prepare theosophists for the greater convergence which would come when Christianity rediscovered the wisdom of the ancients. By the time *Isis Unveiled* was published in September 1877 public opinion in the United States as well as in Britain was falling into line behind Beaconsfield's vision, just as Maitland had predicted in *England and Islam*. 'We have a sort of truce in our home politics while we watch politics abroad,' wrote the American correspondent of *The Times*. The hatred which Americans had felt towards Britain in the 1860s was turning to sympathy. The unenlightened attributed the change to Sir Edward Thornton, British ambassador in Washington since 1867, but the watchers knew that more profound forces were at work.

While politicians looked beyond the Balkans and the Suez Canal to the riches of India, the theosophists gazed over the heads of Greek and Egyptian gods to the Buddha and the Hindu Vedanta. In May 1878 the society was renamed 'The Theosophical Society of the Arya Samaj' after Blavatsky and Olcott met Swami Dayananda Saraswati, leader of a Hindu revivalist movement of that name. One of the Masters of Wisdom, Indian Dwellers of the Threshold, projected his astral body several thousand miles from his mountain fastness in the Himalayas in order to appear to Olcott, who set out for India with Blavatsky. After a brief visit to the London Theosophical Society they landed at Bombay in February 1879 and set up their headquarters at Adyar near Madras. They did not entirely please the Masters of Wisdom, who sent a magical message to Alfred Sinnett, a theosophist in Bombay, instructing him to write a book without telling Olcott or Blavatsky. He sailed for England forthwith and on the voyage he wrote *The Occult World*, which was published in London in June 1881.

It was not very well received. Reviews of *Isis Unveiled* had been

117

mixed – the *New York Herald* hailed it as 'one of the most remarkable productions of the century' while the *New York Sun* called it 'discarded rubbish' – but few critics had a good word to say for Sinnett. The *Saturday Review* treated him as a lone eccentric, describing him ironically as 'the torch-bearer of the new light from the East' and insisting that the ancient soothsayers he cited 'made a mystery of their knowledge because they knew very little'. But there were other and more reputable torch-bearers. 'The study of Indian wisdom, conducting by another path to conclusions entirely in harmony with the results of natural science, is destined to affect, and is affecting, the European mind in a degree not inferior to the modification accomplished by the renaissance of Hellenic philosophy,' wrote Helen Zimmern in a book on Arthur Schopenhauer which she published in February 1876. Schopenhauer had been a masterly interpreter of Indian thought, 'a European Buddhist', and when Lord Lytton first read him he found that it was 'like visiting the house of a stranger and finding it full of my oldest and most intimate acquaintances'. The Bishop of Madras published an article suggesting that the exorcising of evil spirits by Indian holy men might be a continuation of the same miraculous process which had been seen in Galilee eighteen centuries earlier. If Europeans dismissed such things as the delusions of unwashed fakirs were they not also dismissing that first fakir who had healed the sick and raised Lazarus from the tomb?

The American faith-healer Phineas Parkhurst Quimby had already bridged the gap between Christ and the fakirs. One of those he helped, Mary Baker Eddy, coined the term Spiritual Science to describe what he did. Whereas ordinary table-rapping spiritualism was of little importance, Spiritual Science was nothing less than a rediscovery of the principles of healing known in Christianity's early days. Her book *Science and Health and a Key to the Scriptures*, published in 1875 after Quimby's death, became the basis for a new religion, Christian Science, which had apparently been foretold in the Book of Revelation. The title echoed Lady Caithness's 'Earnest Endeavour to Reconcile Material Science with Spiritual Science and with Scripture' and anticipated Madame Blavatsky's book, the full title of which was *Isis Unveiled: a master key to the mysteries of ancient and modern science and theology*. All three ladies claimed that the coming dawn would unite the revelations of God and the observations of men instead of setting them against one another.

In London James Knowles, editor of the *Contemporary Review*,

decided that the time had come to debate the credibility of these two approaches in public and see if a convergence could be achieved. For some years past such matters had been the concern of the Metaphysical Society, which he ran from his house on Clapham Common. Protestants and Catholics, scientists and laymen, freethinkers and traditionalists, had all given papers to the Society, many of which had subsequently been published. Now he founded a new journal, *The Nineteenth Century*, to bring such things to the attention of a wider public. It began publication in March 1877 and its first number opened with a poem by Tennyson which indicated the aims, as well as the agonies, of its varied contributors:

> For some, descending from the sacred peak
> Of hoar high-templed Faith, have leagued again
> Their lot with ours to rove the world about;
> And some are wilder comrades, sworn to seek
> If any golden harbour be for men
> In seas of death and sunless gulf of Doubt.

Once Tennyson had been the most trusted of navigators on the waters of death and doubt. He was to regain his mastery of this most compelling of images with the publication of 'Crossing the Bar', but in 1877 things were different. Lewis Carroll had recently brought out *The Hunting of the Snark*, a strange and disturbing epic about a Bellman who took a shipload of assorted characters to hunt for a Snark. One of them, a Baker, had been warned by his uncle that if his Snark turned out to be a Boojum he would softly and suddenly vanish away and never be met with again. In the end this fate had overtaken him, leaving the Bellman discomfited and discredited. Henry Holiday, the poem's illustrator, made the Bellman into an unmistakeable likeness of Tennyson. Suddenly the Poet Laureate's solemnity seemed outlandish and a little portentous, closer to that of the controlled fanatic who led the Baker to his doom than to the needs of the real world. When John Bright met him at Gladstone's house he thought him 'a weird-looking tall old man', while Lord Houghton began to refer to him as 'His Poetic Majesty'. London society was more amused than over-awed when this monarch of the pen took a town house for three months in March 1877 and announced grandly that he would only accept dinner invitations if they were for his chosen time of seven o'clock.

The deep dark sea, the sunless gulf of doubt, dominated the first

few issues of *The Nineteenth Century*. The Bellman was able to keep the members of his crew from getting wet by 'supporting each man on the top of the tide, By a finger entwined in his hair', but Tennyson had no such power. Some contributors were confessedly engulfed by the tide of unbelief and saw Christianity only as wreckage floating on its surface. 'No drowning sailor ever clutched a hencoop more tenaciously than mankind will hold by such dogma, whatever it may be,' wrote Professor Huxley. William Mallock, an Anglican who lived in a state of recurring spiritual crisis and ended up a Roman Catholic, produced a piece called 'Is Life Worth Living?' He concluded that without God, without belief in life after death, it most certainly was not: 'For unless, let our Atheists remember, we can find such an end in life as that which we have been demanding, we shall be like dismasted ships, without sail and without rudder, left to welter on a sluggish sea of small and weary impulses, with no escape from the shoreless accursed surface, till at last, and one by one, we sink for ever under it.'

What Mallock feared and what Lewis Carroll portrayed had much in common, for there were few seas as shoreless as that sailed by the Bellman and his crew. The Bellman's chart of it was 'A perfect and absolute blank ... Without the least vestige of land'. The only relief from the empty unending ocean was a nightmare landscape of chasms and crags and when the Baker fell into a chasm he was sucked down into nothingness. It was a vision not merely of death but of total annihilation. For the Baker, as for all whose Snarks were Boojums, there was no future, perhaps no past, certainly no eternity. In his other incarnation as Charles Dodgson, Oxford mathematics don, Lewis Carroll told how the final line, 'For the Snark *was* a Boojum, you see', came into his head unbidden as he tramped alone over the Surrey hills. 'I knew not what it meant then,' he said, 'I know not what it means now; but I wrote it down: and sometime afterwards the rest of the stanza occurred to me, that being its last line: and so by degrees, at odd moments during the next year or two, the rest of the poem pieced itself together, that being the last stanza'. He would never admit that it might be prophetic, that at the end men and women might fall not into the everlasting arms but into the emptiness of a Snark that was a Boojum.

Even stranger things came into the head of another solitary walker in high places during the fateful year 1881. There were earthquakes and cyclones all across Europe that summer and the Alps themselves

120

seemed to be on the move. Across them strode Nietzsche, laughing and shouting with exultation in the mountain silence. 'On my horizon,' he cried, 'thoughts have arisen such as I have never seen before. I sang and talked nonsense, filled with a glimpse of things which put me in advance of all other men'. The previous year, in Marienbad, he had stumbled on the imagery in which his revelation was now to be clothed: there had been a mysterious crime in the hotel in which he had been staying, with strange agonized cries and digging in the forest at dead of night. The dark memories came flooding back as he put into words his vision of a world without meaning, a world which had seen the most terrible of all crimes:

Whither is God? I shall tell you. *We have killed him* – you and I. All of us are his murderers ... Whither are we moving now? Away from all suns? Are we not plunging continually? Backward, sideward, forward, in all directions? Is there any up or down left? Are we not straying as through an infinite nothing? Do we not feel the breath of empty space? Has it not become colder? Is not night and more night coming on all the while? Must not lanterns be lit in the morning? Do we not hear anything yet of the noise of the gravediggers who are burying God? Do we not smell anything yet of God's decomposition? Gods too decompose. God is dead. God remains dead. And we have killed him.

It was ironic that the year which was supposed to have seen God giving a new message to the world should see instead this image of the world killing God. This was, wrote Maitland, 'The year announced in so many prophecies as the pivot upon which the world's destinies hinged, the turning point between that old and that new dispensation, the former of which had been divinely condemned as "evil and adulterous" and the latter indicated as introducing the kingdom of heaven on earth.' Nietzsche stood such hopes on their heads. Instead of a future in which religion became as certain as science he saw one in which the scientists were as impotent as the pious. And the ultimate irony was that this vision came just as the world's existing scientific framework was indeed crumbling. The first to feel the breath of empty space was the American physicist Albert Abraham Michelson who was carrying out experiments in 1881 to find the speed of the earth's movement through space. He devised an instrument which split a beam of light in two, sending one half in the direction of the earth's movement and the other in the opposite direction. The halves were then brought together again so that the fringe of interference where

121

they met could show the difference between the speed of the one which had ridden with the earth and the speed of the one which had gone against it. He found no interference at all, suggesting that whatever the light was travelling through – the framework of the universe, God's firmament on high – was not itself still.

Perhaps there was no framework, no firmament. Perhaps there was no up and no down, only a purely relative difference between one direction and another, one movement and another, one dimension and another. Michelson's conclusions, confirmed and extended as a result of more experiments undertaken with Edward Morley in 1887, were to provide the basis for Albert Einstein's revelation of a universe in which traditional scientific absolutes had no more place than the spiritual absolutes of the Christian religion. Edmond Schérer's prediction had come true: the absolute was dead in men's souls. For centuries they had thought they were slowly discovering and deciphering the meaning of the universe. Now they found that they had conjured that meaning from their own heads and imposed it upon a universe which knew nothing of absolutes, which was in the final analysis a question and not a statement.

There were still those who waited for the world's destinies to hinge on the 1881 pivot. As the year began Gerard Manley Hopkins greeted the return of the age of miracles when a boy dying of typhus recovered after being anointed. 'It was no doubt due to the sacrament,' he noted. Certainly there were portents for those who sought them. There was ominously cold weather early in the year, with harbours icebound along the Atlantic coast of America and enormous ice floes in the Thames which halted shipping and carried away piers. All over Europe the cold brought wolves out of the forests and into towns and villages. Snow blocked railways on both sides of the Atlantic and when it thawed floods rendered thousands homeless. In Lancashire hussars were called out to break up riots and at Windsor men were heard plotting to blow up the Queen. Gladstone cut his head open, causing great public concern, and his colleague John Bright, 'wearied with the disorder which it seemed impossible to suppress', felt that 'we must be approaching some crisis or catastrophe.' But when Beaconsfield died in April, the supposed month of destiny, the climax of his visions had still not arrived. Then came the death of Dr Cumming, who had also 'debauched the national faculty of wonder', but his predictions remained equally unfulfilled.

As Fenian and Nihilist atrocities became commonplace, as the assas-

122

sination of the Tsar of Russia was followed by that of the President of the United States, Maitland's hopes of heaven on earth seemed increasingly inappropriate. Some thought hell more likely and Bright wrote that the crimes and cruelties were 'rather the doings of fiends than men'. But the year had one last surprise in store for optimists and pessimists alike. It came, like Christianity, from an empty tomb. In early December, as devotees of Mother Shipton noted the unseasonable fruiting of the strawberry plants, the dead Earl of Crawford was found to be missing. Nobody knew the size of the stone which had been taken from Christ's sepulchre but the granite slabs covering the Crawford family vault at Dunecht in Scotland were six feet square and several inches thick. They might have been moved by an angel but certainly not by an unaided human being. Crawford had died in Florence a year earlier and after elaborate embalming he had been brought home in a wooden coffin sealed inside a soldered lead shell. This had then been placed in another coffin of carved oak ornamented with silver. Now all three stood empty in the vault and the body was gone.

Queen Victoria was appalled. The Home Secretary was instructed to drop everything else and give Dunecht his undivided attention. The affair aroused great interest in America, where a millionaire's body had recently been held to ransom. Scores of policemen came up to Dunecht, bringing the sleuth-hound Morgan, 'the same sagacious animal that was the means of discovering the fragments of the body of the child killed at Blackburn'. When the sagacious animal found nothing spiritualists were called in. They had a vision of three men taking the body to a field which sloped down to a little copse. The press pointed out that a man whose dream had been published a short time before had seen the same thing. The police dug in the spot indicated but found nothing. Then they took up Charles Soutar, a poacher who told them he had disturbed four masked men burying a body at night several months before. They had terrified him into silence but now he led police to the spot and they dug up the body. The Queen sent a congratulatory telegram to Lady Crawford and everyone waited for the body snatchers to be apprehended.

But the finding of the body had contradicted rather than confirmed the assumptions on which the police had been working. Hypotheses crumbled, reputations were put in jeopardy. And so the police turned on the only culprit they had: they committed Soutar for trial, not for concealing evidence but for stealing the body. This raised awkward

123

questions. If he was guilty, why did he not denounce his accomplices and claim the reward and free pardon which had been offered to anyone who turned Queen's evidence? And if there were no accomplices what had happened to police insistence that no man could have committed the crime alone? These considerations were worrying but the press said a conviction was unlikely and in any case the penalty would be light. *The Times* assured its readers that body snatching had never been punished with more than two years in prison. At Soutar's trial there were no witnesses for the defence and nobody cross-examined witnesses for the prosecution. There was amazement in court when he was found guilty in spite of the flaws in the police case and there was even greater amazement when the judge brushed aside the precedents of the past: 'What was adequate punishment in those offences is not, in my opinion, adequate punishment on this occasion. The sentence of this Court is that you be subjected to penal servitude for a period of five years.'

For the watchers upon the high towers prospects were good. The Dunecht affair made the occult popular and in the summer of 1882 a group of men who had been members of a Ghost Society as Cambridge undergraduates formed the Society for Psychical Research. Edward Maitland was an associate member and his books were to be found in the Society's library along with those of Lady Caithness and other theosophists. Arthur Balfour, future Prime Minister and author of *A Defence of Philosophic Doubt*, was a vice-president of the Society and with a splendid sense of timing went straight from its inaugural meeting to the House of Commons in order to prevent an atheist member, Charles Bradlaugh, from taking his seat. Bradlaugh had Gladstone's support but it, availed him nothing; the castles of fantasy were more respectable than the citadels of thought. And hopes that Year One of the Enlightenment would bring Christianity closer to ancient Egypt were certainly not disappointed. Progressive Victorian society, the society that had condemned the excesses of Frederick Merrett's friends at Cowley, the society that had been told by its church leaders to dissociate hopes of resurrection from physical conditions, had defended the hallowed dead as fiercely as any curse inscribed on a pharaoh's sarcophagus. Charles Soutar's fate, the mockery of his trial and the savagery of his sentence, showed that the funeral chambers of the pyramids had indeed cast a shadow over the English-speaking world, even if not quite the one forecast by Professor Smyth.

A few weeks after Soutar's conviction Gladstone chose Bishop

Benson of Truro as Archbishop of Canterbury. Benson had founded the Cambridge Ghost Society and was still deeply interested in psychic phenomena. 'Our illustrious premier,' wrote Swinburne to Edward Burne-Jones, 'has been mercifully guided in the election of a substitute who will (I cannot doubt) fill the highest seat in our Church more worthily than myself.' In more serious vein Dr Hort, Professor of Divinity at Cambridge, wrote to warn Benson that the Church must put fact before fantasy if it was to win back ordinary people: 'The convulsions of our English Church itself, grievous as they are, seem to be as nothing beside the danger of its calm and unobtrusive alienation in thought and spirit from the great silent multitude of Englishmen, and again of alienation from fact and love of fact: mutual alienations both.' He described the country's religious state as 'self-glorifying chaos'. The alienation of ordinary people from established religion was shown some months later when the authorities prosecuted G.W. Foote, editor of *The Freethinker*, for blasphemy. The judge told him that he had 'prostituted his talents to the work of the Devil' – even though the Privy Council had already relegated the Devil to the realm of fantasy – and gave him twelve months hard labour. 'The sentence was followed by a scene such as has seldom been witnessed within the walls of the Court,' reported *The Times* in horror, 'a perfect storm of hissing'.

Meanwhile Edward Maitland was hard at work on his book *How the World came to an End in 1881*. It might seem odd to be writing an epilogue to apocalypse but he did not doubt that the prophecies had been fulfilled 'in the sense intended'. Like Nietzsche he was 'filled with a glimpse of things which put me in advance of all other men'. He could not see the death of God but he could see the passing away of the dogmas and rituals and half-truths by which God had so far been sought. The old dispensation had gone and old intimations of the divine were dying. They would be replaced by something brighter, more direct, more potent. Josiah Strong, Ohio representative of the American Home Missionary Society, had similar hopes. His nation-wide lectures, delivered in the early 1880s and published in 1885 under the title *Our Country*, looked forward to the transformation of the world within a decade as a result of the efforts of Americans. 'It is fully in the hands of the Christians of the United States, during the next ten or fifteen years,' he cried, 'to hasten or retard the coming of Christ's kingdom in the world by hundreds, and perhaps thousands of years.' But first they must stop letting members of inferior races into America,

since only the Anglo-Saxons were 'exponents of a pure *spiritual* Christianity'. Then they must steer clear of idleness, atheism, popery, alcohol and above all socialism, 'which attempts to solve the problem of suffering without eliminating the factor of sin'. Labouring men could be heard quoting 'the infidel ribaldry of Robert Ingersoll, the socialistic theories of Karl Marx' and many were idlers who had no right to live: 'If loafers had any appreciation of the eternal fitness of things they would die.' The Librarian of Congress later said the book had an impact second only to *Uncle Tom's Cabin*.

Predictions about the destinies of nations came from men of science as well as from men of God. 'Looking to the world at no very distant date,' wrote Charles Darwin in July 1881, 'what an endless number of the lower races will have been eliminated by the higher civilized races throughout the world!' He did not say how the elimination would be achieved. Would there have to be genocide or would the lower races, like the American loafers, appreciate the eternal fitness of things and die? Six weeks after this forecast Lord Hartington, Secretary for India, answering routine questions in the House of Commons, revealed that in one gaol in Bengal the death rate had risen from 282 per thousand in 1879 to 612 per thousand in the first quarter of 1881. He could not be sure whether prisoners had been starved to death or whipped to death: there had been more than thirteen thousand floggings during this period and in most cases men had been flogged for non-performance of hard labour when their diet was already below starvation level. In their modest way the Indian authorities were helping to hasten the day to which Darwin looked forward.

Hartington's calm revelations, like the sentencing of Soutar and Foote, left doubts as to which aspects of God had died with the old dispensation and which were the glory of the new. The watchers upon the high towers had seen a great light, a fiery dawn in which the true God had arisen phoenix-like from the ashes of ancient error. It had been hoped that this revelation would shame the mere observers, the weighers and measurers of the world's constituent parts, into admitting that there were more things in heaven and earth than their scientific method could fathom. Instead it had made them more contumacious than ever and it had alienated ordinary men and women from spiritual and secular leaders whose values seemed to have little in common with those of Jesus Christ. Being a fabulous creature the phoenix was in any case more likely to appeal to lovers of fantasy than to lovers of fact; now it looked as though its appeal was even

126

more limited. It seemed to be an Anglo-Saxon bird, or at any rate a bird of 'the higher civilized races', and it hovered more happily over thrones and dominions and powers than over the humble and the oppressed. It was a poor substitute for the dove, the earlier and gentler Christian symbol of God's love. Now that the year of destiny had come and gone it was easier to believe in the death of the old dispensation than in the birth of a new one.

8 THE TRIUMPH OF FICTION

ONE OF THE BENEFICIARIES OF THE DUNECHT AFFAIR was Robert Louis Stevenson. He was staying at Pitlochry, some sixty miles from Dunecht, and writing stories about the dead. One, 'Thrawn Janet', concerned a woman whose soul belonged to the Devil and whose body, neck awry because of hanging, walked the earth long after death until it was finally exorcised by a godly minister. The other, 'The Body Snatcher', was about a dismembered corpse which found a grisly way of terrifying those who had handed it over to the anatomist's knife. It was so gruesome that it shocked even its author, who said it had been 'laid aside in a justifiable disgust, the tale being horrid'. The disgust was not to last long. 'Thrawn Janet' was published shortly after the theft of Crawford's body had generated renewed interest in the vengeful dead. Stevenson was then able to take 'The Body Snatcher' from its shelf and offer it to the editor of the *Pall Mall Gazette*, who greeted it with enthusiasm and advertised it all over London with placards so horrific that they were seized by the police, thus ensuring the story's notoriety. Meanwhile the enormous success of *Treasure Island*, which its author described as 'quite silly and horrid fun', led the *Saturday Review* to hail Stevenson as a writer who would lift fiction above 'the mere annals of the boudoir and the tennis lawn'.

Stevenson was more ambitious than the *Saturday Review* realized. For most of his adult life he had agonized over the conflict between his literary aspirations and the conventional piety of his parents. 'I have a pistol at my throat,' he told his friend Charles Baxter, 'If all that I hold true and most desire to spread is to be such death, and worse than death, in the eyes of my father and mother, what the *devil* am I to do?' He knew that there was more to life than outward appearances and animal appetites yet he could not bring himself to mumble conventional prayers and seek a conventional heaven. 'I feel

every day as if religion had a greater interest for me,' he told his father, 'but that interest is still centred on the little rough-and-tumble world in which our fortunes are cast for the moment. I cannot transfer my interests, not even my religious interest, to any different sphere'. Now that he was an authority and an oracle he would reconcile art and religion. By transforming fiction he would transfigure everyday life. He would bring God into the rough-and-tumble world. 'A stately music. Enter God!' he wrote to W.E. Henley in 1883, 'Ay, but you know, until a man can write that "Enter God" he has made no art!' In November 1884 he asserted publicly the right of the creative artist to hold back the curtain, to thrust aside the veil of existence, to herald God's entry upon the world's stage. As a means of interpreting reality fiction was just as respectable, just as reliable, as the sciences:

Man's one method, whether he reasons or creates, is to half-shut his eyes against the dazzle and confusion of reality. The arts, like arithmetic and geometry, turn away their eyes from the gross, coloured and mobile nature at our feet and regard instead a certain figmentary abstraction. Geometry will tell us of a circle, a thing never seen in nature; asked about a green circle or an iron circle, it lays its hand upon its mouth. So with the arts ... Life is monstrous, infinite, illogical, abrupt and poignant; a work of art, in comparison, is neat, finite, self-contained, rational, flowing and emasculated.

The scientists and the philosophers were indeed laying hands upon their mouths. Ernst Mach's *Science of Mechanics*, published in 1883, declared that it was no longer possible to believe in absolute space, in absolute time or even in the concept of cause and effect. The Oxford philosopher Thomas Hill Green had long argued that observation and scientific method were fallible because when human beings tried to perceive the external world they only achieved an understanding of their own thought processes. By the time he died in 1882 he had gathered around him a school of thought dedicated to the proposition that any order or coherence observable in the universe could only have been put there by the observers themselves. Mankind hung like a spider, suspended by a thread spun from its own guts. Must it spin God in the same way? Stevenson shared with Nietzsche the ability to sniff and savour prevailing winds of thought without clogging his lungs with their every particle. His vision of man bringing God on stage was the counterpart of Nietzsche's image of man doing God to death. Dead or alive, skeleton or marionette, the deity danced to

man's tune. The respectful perspectives of conventional religion were gone.

Where Stevenson led others were quick to follow. Herbert George Wells, who was soon to make his name by putting science to the service of fiction, did a piece for the *Fortnightly Review* called 'The Rediscovery of the Unique'. 'When we teach a child to count,' he proclaimed, 'we poison its mind almost irrevocably.' How could men think that number had meaning, that ten score separate entities could lose their unique qualities simply by being paraded as two hundred allegedly identical objects? Just as geometry was about imagined and unreal circles, so arithmetic and the statistical sciences based upon it were about imagined and unreal quantities. Individuality would triumph, no two peas in a pod would ever be alike, science would find its generalizations bouncing helplessly back from the surrounding darkness:

Science is a match that man has just got alight. He thought he was in a room – in moments of devotion a temple – and that his light would be reflected in pillars carved with philosophical systems and wrought into harmony. It is a curious sensation, now that the preliminary sputter is over and the flame burns up clear, to see his hands lit and just a glimpse of himself and the patch he stands on visible, and around him, in place of all that human comfort and beauty he anticipated – darkness still.

Man must stand resolute on his own patch and know the flame for what it was – his own imagination. Fantasy and fiction kindled it, fantasy and fiction kept it alight, fantasy and fiction reached out into the dark and brought back such comfort and beauty as could be found. And that was all. If you wanted pillars carved with philosophical systems you must carve them for yourself. Even members of the government seemed to prefer imagining to calculating. George Goschen, Chancellor of the Exchequer, told students at Edinburgh University that the human imagination was the source of all knowledge as well as 'your most faithful guide on all the problems which a governing people such as ours has to solve.' A week later Arthur Balfour, First Lord of the Treasury, reminded Glasgow students of the limitations of mathematical and scientific thought: 'The future of the race is encompassed with darkness; no faculty of calculation that we possess, no instrument that we are likely to invent, will enable us to map out its course, or penetrate the secret of its destiny'.

Meanwhile the worshippers of fiction grew more devout. George

Saintsbury in the *Fortnightly* declared that mankind was sick, dulled and enfeebled by intellectualism and solemn analysis. Things would not improve until 'the aspect of society is quite changed and we have bathed once more long and well in the romance of adventure and passion'. The *Westminster Review* burst out in praise of Hall Caine, a young novelist who would 'transmute the ordinary into the marvellous'. Caine said he was proud to believe in fiction as 'a beautiful lie, a lie that is at once false and true – false to fact, true to faith'. 'It satisfies our inborn sense of right;' proclaimed Amelia Edwards, 'it transports us into a purer atmosphere; it vindicates the ways of God to Man.' 'If the battle between the crocodile of Realism and the cata-wampus of Romance is to be fought out to the bitter end,' wrote Andrew Lang, 'I am on the side of the catawampus.' When Lord Randolph Churchill visited Eton in the summer of 1883 he found every-one there reading Stevenson's *Treasure Island* and he drew Arthur Balfour aside in the House of Commons to urge him to get a copy. Gladstone glanced through it at Lord Rosebery's house and then scoured London for a copy of his own. *King Solomon's Mines* had an equally overwhelm-ing success in 1885 and its author, Rider Haggard, was hailed in his turn as a high priest of the new cult. 'More and more, as what we call culture spreads,' he wrote, 'do men and women crave to be taken out of themselves. More and more do they long to be brought face to face with Beauty and stretch out their arms towards that vision of the Perfect, which we only see in books and dreams.'

The new religion had its shrines as well as its scriptures. The rich could afford to buy novels but most people who wanted to stretch out their arms towards a fictional vision of the perfect had first to visit their local public library. The early nineteenth century had been a great age of church building but now, on both sides of the Atlantic, new churches were outnumbered by new public libraries. The Ameri-can Library Association was formed in 1876 and public funding was supplemented by private benefaction. Andrew Carnegie, the steel mil-lionaire, endowed nearly three thousand libraries in the United States as well as many in Britain. And it was works of fiction, not religious or educational books, which were in demand at these multiplying centres of mass culture. Even the *Westminster Review*, a friend to public libraries, had to confess that three out of every four books borrowed was a novel. It hoped that 'the time is not far distant when we shall have a good free library in every town in the kingdom', but it feared that 'these libraries are chiefly frequented by idlers, and such as seek

131

amusement in novel reading'. Mr J. Taylor Kay of the Manchester Free Library declared that 'schoolboys or students who took to novel reading never made much progress in after life. They neglected real practical life for a sensually imaginative one'. William James, America's leading philosopher and psychologist, proclaimed that there was no more contemptible human character than the 'nerveless sentimentalist and dreamer' produced by excessive novel reading. The fact that his younger brother Henry was a successful novelist did little to reconcile him to fiction's onward march.

Diatribes against the effect of fiction on the young were not new. In 1867 *The Bookseller* had launched a bitter attack on penny dreadfuls such as *Tyburn Dick, the Boy King of the Highwaymen* and *Admiral Tom, the King of the Boy Buccaneers*, which sold a quarter of a million copies a year in London alone while more wholesome publications, tales about God-fearing lads who fought and tamed natives in the outposts of the British Empire, had to be discontinued for lack of support. Ten years later the anonymous author of *Five Years Penal Servitude by One who has Endured it* told how he had shared a cell with a boy of thirteen who had battered in an old woman's head with a hammer and stolen £70 from her. 'I found from a few questions I asked that his head had been stuffed with the rubbish he had read of gentlemen pirates, highwaymen and bandit captains.' Opponents of public libraries said they were full of 'loafing office boys or clerks, who were using their masters' time for devouring all the most trivial literary trash they could get', while supporters insisted that on the contrary libraries converted youth from penny dreadfuls to better things.

By the 1880s the rearguard action against fiction was losing heart. It was no longer possible, argued Professor Jevons in the *Contemporary Review*, to prevent the masses from reading fiction and being influenced by it. All that the educated classes could do was to ensure that as far as possible it was good fiction. George Alfred Henty, editor of a boys' magazine called *The Union Jack*, set to work to undo the damage which *The Bookseller* had earlier lamented. Sales of his books about boys who helped to win the British Empire mounted steadily from 1884, when *With Clive in India* came out, until his death in 1902. The Religious Tract Society started *The Boy's Own Paper* in 1879, concentrating at first on tales of overseas adventure. R. M. Ballantyne's 'The Red Man's Revenge' was followed by Ascott Hope's 'Adventures of a Boston Boy Amongst Savages', both set in America and both showing white lads winning the respect of natives. They were followed by a

school story, *The Fifth Form at St Dominic's*, by Talbot Baines Reed. It was in some ways more adult than its famous predecessor *Tom Brown's Schooldays*: there was comparatively little beating and bullying and the plot hinged upon cheating in an examination rather than upon rivalry on the games field. Yet there was an extraordinary obsession with fighting: it seemed that if Reed's young heroes did not have a fight a day they were not getting full value from public-school life. In this way they proved their superiority over the lower classes. The only villains in the story were working-class idlers, great gangs of whom were easily vanquished by 'a pair of well-trained athletic schoolboys'.

The Boy's Own Paper was only one of the Religious Tract Society's many ventures into fiction. By the end of the century its publication of religious tracts had been far outstripped by the twenty million books and magazines which it put out from its home depot alone. The Society for Promoting Christian Knowledge, a more venerable institution, was issuing three times as many works of fiction as tracts, while similar changes were taking place in nonconformist and Roman Catholic publishing houses. With remarkable docility the devout and the orthodox were heeding Stevenson's stage direction. God was entering upon the stage – or at any rate entering into the consciousness of the young – through fiction rather than through conventional homilies and scriptural readings.

God's stage appearance posed problems. The Christian religion was firmly anchored in history and the curtain had come down on its earthly adventure more than eighteen centuries ago. It had been spectacular while it lasted, with vast crowd scenes and supernatural happenings and an impressive climax, but it had not been intended as drama and there was no room for a repeat performance. God had suffered an agonizing death not for man's entertainment but for his salvation: the sequel would take place in heaven and it would be a spiritual transformation scene, not another display of divine derring-do. It was not easy to turn the God of the Christians into the God of the adventure story. Thomas Hughes, the author of *Tom Brown's Schooldays*, did his best in a series of lectures published under the title *The Manliness of Christ*. He stressed not so much the humility and the purity of Christianity's founder as his physical courage and his ability to endure pain bravely – qualities that had already endeared the fictitious Tom Brown to admiring schoolboys. Stevenson talked about 'a theory of living in the Gospels which is curiously indefinable

133

and leans towards asceticism on the one side, although it leans away from it on the other'. 'I have never been in a revolution yet,' he told his cousin Katharine, 'I pray God I may be in one at the end, if I am to make a mucker. The best way to make a mucker is to have your back set against a wall and a few lead pellets whiffed into you in a moment.' The heroism of the Christian martyr still had its links with that of the contemporary idealist.

Stevenson soon found his latter-day hero and martyr. Although 1881 did not see the Second Coming predicted by Professor Smyth it did see the rise of a self-styled Messiah, the Mahdi, who led a revolt in Upper Egypt and the Sudan. The British government decided to evacuate the garrisons in the area and put General Gordon in charge of the operation. Brave and chaste, deeply religious and a natural leader of men, Gordon was a living story-book hero. He was also a great believer in Smyth's impending apocalypse. When he got to the Sudan he determined on defence rather than evacuation and before long he was besieged in Khartoum by rebel forces. As he had disobeyed orders Gladstone's government was reluctant to send a relief expedition. When a British force did arrive, on 28 January 1885, it found that Gordon had already been killed. The outcry against Gladstone was immediate and impassioned. Stevenson was appalled by the disaster but he knew in his heart that he and his fellow writers must share responsibility for it. They had raised men's sights but they had given them nothing to aim at. Why sing of the glory and the beauty and the nobility of life, he asked John Addington Symonds, if you had no idea what it was for?

My own conscience is badly seared. What a picture this is of a nation! No man that I can see, on any side or party, seems to have the least sense of our ineffable shame: the desertion of the garrisons. Millais (I hear) was painting Gladstone when the news came of Gordon's death; Millais was much affected and Gladstone said 'Why? It is the man's own temerity!' *Voilà le Bourgeois! le voilà nu!* But why should I blame Gladstone when I too am a Bourgeois? When I have held my peace? Why did I hold my peace? Because I am a sceptic: i.e., a Bourgeois. We believe in nothing, Symonds: you don't and I don't; and these are two reasons, out of a handful of millions, why England stands before the world dripping with blood and daubed with dishonour.

So there was more to be done. It was not enough to make fiction the equal and even the master of scientific thought. It was not enough

to bring God into the world and trace the magnificent shadow he cast upon the human mind. Mankind must be given a purpose, an aim in life, sufficiently noble to justify the visions which fiction had conjured up. In 1886 Stevenson read Dostoevsky's *Crime and Punishment*, an experience which he found totally overwhelming, more like having an illness than reading a novel. It was the greatest book he had read for many years and it made him see that 'fundamental errors in human nature stand on the skyline of all this modern world'. Men and women should not pursue mere happiness in the real world any more than in the world of the adventure story. They would only find their true selves if they lived for 'rivalry, effort, success – the elements our friends wish to eliminate ... As for those crockery chimney-piece ornaments the bourgeois and their cowardly dislike of dying and killing, it is merely one symptom of a thousand how utterly they have got out of touch of life'.

In the spring of 1887, Queen Victoria's Golden Jubilee Year, when most journals were full of smug articles about the wonderful things achieved during her reign, Stevenson struck a discordant note with a piece in the *Contemporary Review* called 'The Day After Tomorrow'. 'Liberty has served us a long while,' he wrote, 'and it may be time to seek new altars.' Democracy was dying and Parliament in London was as decadent as Congress in Washington. On both sides of the Atlantic man had been deceived into pursuing false aims and dreaming false dreams. 'He is supposed to love comfort; it is not a love, at least, that he is faithful to. He is supposed to love happiness; it is my contention that he rather loves excitement.' Danger and adversity, not comfort and happiness, were 'the true elixir for all vital spirits'. Stevenson's own sharpest experience of such things had been in America a few years earlier, when he had journeyed in extreme discomfort from Scotland to California to seek out and wed Fanny Osbourne. From San Francisco he had written to Edmund Gosse confessing that for six weeks he had been unable to decide whether to live or to die: 'I felt unable to go on farther with that rough horseplay of human life'. Now, in the summer of 1887, he crossed the Atlantic again, this time as the advocate of the horseplay, of mankind's delight in danger and adversity.

He had certainly come to a land where the horseplay of human life was achieving a kind of glory. In December 1881, shortly after the famous gunfight at the O.K. Corral in Tombstone Arizona, President Arthur told Congress that armed desperadoes menaced the peace

135

of the western territories. A few months later, as the President threatened to put Arizona under martial law, the young English writer Oscar Wilde arrived in St Joseph, Missouri to find the whole town mourning the notorious train-robber Jesse James, who had just been murdered. 'Two speculators absolutely came to pistol-shots as to who was to have his hearth-brush, the unsuccessful one being, however, consoled by being allowed to purchase the water-butt for the income of an English bishop ... The Americans, if not hero-worshippers, are villain-worshippers.' The immense popularity of the dime novels meant that the Wild West, though never as wild in reality as in fiction, was rapidly becoming the most significant single source of the elixir which Stevenson wished to dispense to vital spirits.

Rider Haggard, writing angrily about American fiction in February 1887, refused to take Wild West stories into account. He reckoned there were forty million novel readers in the United States, all of them subsisting on a diet of stories pirated from England. 'Most of the books patronized by this enormous population are stolen from English authors ... The Americans are destroying their own literature, that cannot live in the face of the unfair competition to which it is subjected'. Instead of red-blooded tales of adventure American writers produced effete romances which had about them 'an atmosphere like that of the boudoir of a luxurious woman'. It sounded like a description of the kind of fiction the *Saturday Review* had said Stevenson would transcend. It might almost have been a description of the work of Henry James, whom Stevenson had already dismissed as a man incapable of appreciating Dostoevsky. The American novel which did suit the new cult was Mark Twain's *Huckleberry Finn*, which came out in 1884. Stevenson said it was 'incredibly well done' and its reputation continued to grow. T.S. Eliot was to compare Huck Finn to Ulysses, Faust, Don Quixote, Don Juan, Hamlet 'and other great discoveries that man has made about himself ... His is not the independence of the typical or symbolic American but the independence of the vagabond'. And the vagabond, like the vital spirits beloved of Robert Louis Stevenson, despised mere comfort and happiness. 'I reckon I got to light out for the Territory ahead of the rest,' said Huck at the end of the book, 'because Aunt Sally she's going to adopt me and sivilize me and I can't stand it. I been there before.'

British authors could only produce part-time boy vagabonds. When Richard Jefferies put his pagan vision of the natural world into *Wood Magic* in 1881 it met with considerable hostility but in the following

year, when he laced it with boyhood adventure in *Bevis, the Story of a Boy*, it proved far more popular. Bevis and his friend Mark left civilization behind and lived for a time close to nature. 'In those days of running, racing, leaping, exploring, swimming,' wrote Jefferies, 'the skin nude to the sun and wind and water, they built themselves up of steel, steel that would bear the hardest wear of the world. Had they been put in an open boat and thrust forth to sea like the Vikings of old, it would not have hurt them.' Two years later the survivors from the shipwrecked yacht *Mignonette* were landed at Falmouth and admitted that after three weeks in an open boat they had killed and eaten their companion, a boy of seventeen named Richard Parker. He too had been in good physical condition when he was first 'thrust forth to sea like the Vikings of old', but it had not saved him. He did not have Jefferies or Stevenson to write a happy ending for him. Nor were the imagined benefits of a harsh life confined to boys. Maurice Hewlett, whose romantic tales were set in a shadowy mediaeval world, had a heroine who dressed as a boy and fell in with some charcoal-burners who starved her and thrashed her and over-worked her. Mediaeval graveyards had been well stocked with children who had succumbed to such treatment but in the case of Hewlett's Lady Isoult it proved therapeutic: 'Her hair curled and wove about her neck, her eyes shone and were limpid, her roses bloomed unawares; she grew sinewy and healthy in the kind forest air. She worked very hard, ate very little, was as often beaten as not. All this made for health.'

In real life cruelty killed and the cruel survived. Actual conflicts and excitements, unlike adventure stories, tended to result in the triumph of the 'crockery chimney-piece ornaments' and the salvation of their world. In America the years that saw the cowboy trails blazed from Texas to Kansas in the West also saw the rise of rich and powerful industrialists in the East who were determined to bring down the cost of labour. Dominant in the money markets, buttressed by widespread political corruption, they enforced wage reductions and when workers protested the militia fired point-blank into crowds, killing and wounding hundreds of men in Baltimore, Pittsburgh, Chicago and other cities. Churchmen urged the authorities to continue the slaughter. 'If the club of the policeman, knocking out the brains of the rioters, will answer, well and good,' wrote one, 'but if it does not promptly meet the exigency, then bullet and bayonet, canister and grape, constitute the one remedy and the one duty of the hour.' 'There are times when mercy is a mistake,'

added the periodical *Christian Union.*

The climax came in May 1886 in Chicago, where police fired indiscriminately into an anarchist demonstration after a bomb had been thrown. Eight anarchist leaders were arrested and seven were condemned to death though there was no evidence to connect them with the bomb. In November 1887, as Stevenson told the Americans of the importance of danger and excitement, the President of Cornell University told the British of the importance of these convictions. In a piece for the *Contemporary Review* on 'Contemporary Life and Thought in the United States' he remarked that 'the decision of the Supreme Court of Illinois, that the condemned anarchists of Chicago have no legal cause for complaint over their sentences, has exerted a wholesome influence ... some of our best political thinkers are firm in the belief that the wage-worker has no real grievance'.

In Britain too the violence of the real world vied with fiction. A man shot at Queen Victoria in March 1882 and a few weeks later another was given ten years penal servitude for threatening to murder her. Meanwhile the Secretary and Under-Secretary for Ireland had been set upon and hacked to death with surgical knives in Phoenix Park in Dublin. 'The Queen must call on her Government to protect her subjects from murder and outrage,' Victoria wrote furiously to Gladstone. 'The mischief Mr Gladstone does is *incalculable*,' she told the Prince of Wales, 'instead of *stemming* the current and downward course of Radicalism, which he could do *perfectly*, he *heads and encourages it*'. Her anxieties had an American dimension, for many in Britain thought that it was the cult of violence in the United States that lay behind the terrorism in Ireland. The *New York Tribune* strenuously denied that Americans would 'support inflammatory orators or arm malcontents', but this did not deter a gang of dynamiters in New York from announcing publicly that they would kill the Prince of Wales if he set foot in Ireland.

The Queen sought reassurance from the man whose magical island-valley of Avilion had brought comfort to her subjects. She summoned Tennyson to her own island-valley on the Isle of Wight and together they agreed to reject 'unbelievers and philosophers, who would try to make one believe there was no other world, no immortality, who tried to explain everything away in a miserable manner.' Tennyson was hopeful about eternity but not about things temporal. 'I am afraid I think the world is darkened,' he told the Queen. In London strange things happened in the darkness. Early in February 1886, in thick

fog, a terrible panic gripped the city. There were said to be armies of revolutionaries pouring in from every side. To the south of the Thames, *The Times* reported, 'all shops closed and the people stood at their doors straining their eyes through the fog for the sounds of ten thousand men who were said to be marching'. A telegram was received at the paper's offices saying: 'Fearful state all round here in South London. Thirty thousand men at Spa Road moving to Trafalgar Square. Roughs in thousands trooping to West. Send special messenger to Home Office to have police in fullest force, with fullest military force also, to save London'. Detachments of mounted police galloped down the Old Kent Road to scatter the legions of revolt. Not until the fog began to clear was it apparent that the marching men had never existed. They were as insubstantial as the fog which had engendered them. The human imagination, the faculty which was supposed to bring God into the world and solve a governing people's problems, had given other and stranger proof of its power.

The gathering darkness which weighed upon Tennyson was the counterpart of the dazzling exhilaration of the adventure story. Each in its different way bore witness to the gap between man's aspirations and his understanding, between the vivid reality of the God within and the apparent indifference of the God who presided over the workings of history. In the year of the Queen's accession Tennyson had written 'Locksley Hall', a poem in which he had looked forward to a better and happier society brought about by technical achievement and religious zeal, by science harnessed to the service of democracy and Christianity. 'Forward, forward let us range,' he had cried, moving into the confident metallic metaphors of the railway age, 'Let the great world spin for ever down the ringing grooves of change'. As Jubilee Year approached he determined to take stock and see whether his earlier hopes had been fulfilled.

It seemed they had not. 'Locksley Hall Sixty Years After', published at the end of 1886, was among the bleakest of his poems. It was about darkness, the darkness of man's deeds, the darkness of his imaginings, the darkness of his despair now that high hopes of progress had withered. The cry of 'Forward, forward' was now 'lost within a growing gloom'. Democracy, instead of working for the good of all, had 'slaked the light with blood' and mankind was slipping into a new Dark Age without faith and without hope. Writers were concerned only to 'Rip your brother's vices open, strip your foul passions bare', while politicians bowed either to the bombs of the terrorist or

to the feckless votes of the uneducated. Many reviewers thought the poem 'unnecessarily melancholy' and Gladstone was furious. It should never have been published, he declared roundly in an angry article in *The Nineteenth Century* in January 1887: 'Justice does not require, nay rather she forbids, that the Jubilee of the Queen be marred by tragic tones.' In view of all the reforms that had been achieved during the Queen's reign pessimism such as Tennyson's was quite inadmissible. Gladstone came close to suggesting that those who did not believe in the inevitability of progress and in the efficacy of liberal reforms were as dangerous, as heretical, as religious unbelievers had been in an earlier age.

Across the Atlantic reactions were less indignant but equally dismissive. 'I think I should like to write a bit about Tennyson and the new Locksley Hall,' Walt Whitman told the editor of the *Critic*, 'intended for your first page if you wish.' The piece duly appeared on the front page of the journal on 1 January 1887. 'The course of progressive politics (democracy) is so certain and resistless, not only in America but in Europe,' Whitman wrote, 'that we can well afford the warning calls of such deep-sounding and high-soaring voices as Carlyle's and Tennyson's'. His article made reference not to the poem itself but to 'an apparently authentic summary' which said that 'a cynical vein of denunciation of democratic opinions and aspirations runs throughout the poem'. 'I should call it a signal instance of democratic humanity's luck that it has such enemies to contend with – so candid, so fervid, so heroic,' Whitman continued. 'We have a beautiful singer in Tennyson,' commented Robert Buchanan in London, 'and some day it will be among Tennyson's highest honours that he was once named kindly and appreciated by Whitman'.

Both Gladstone's indignation and Whitman's condescension overlooked the most important lines in the poem:

> Ay, for doubtless I am old, and think gray thoughts, for I am gray:
> After all the stormy changes shall we find a changeless May?
>
> After madness, after massacre, Jacobinism and Jacquerie,
> Some diviner force to guide us through the days I shall not see? ...
>
> All the full-brain, half-brain races, led by Justice, Love, and Truth;
> All the millions one at length with all the visions of my youth? ...
>
> Ere she gain her Heavenly-best, a God must mingle with the game:

Nay, there may be those about us whom we neither see nor name,

Felt within us as ourselves, the Powers of Good, the Powers of Ill,
Strowing balm, or shedding poison in the Fountains of the Will.

Clearly Tennyson did not rule out the possibility of progress towards higher things. What he doubted was man's ability to make that progress without 'some diviner force to guide us'. The summary that Walt Whitman had seen, with its talk of cynical denunciation, was a travesty of the poem's true intentions. There was nothing cynical about Tennyson's desperate concern for the future of mankind. The darkness of his despair about unaided human beings was relieved by the brightness of his hopes for them if they had a God to guide them. But the God whom theologians called 'God transcendent', the God out there, the all-powerful being who was supposed to hold the universe in the palm of his hand, seemed to grow more shadowy with every passing year. 'Locksley Hall Sixty Years After' was about his demise, about his desertion of mankind, just as much as it was about human fallibility. But there was still the God imminent, the God who was 'felt within us as ourselves'. This was the God for whom Robert Louis Stevenson had sounded his fanfare, the God who had been saved from extinction as the pundits of the 1880s hailed the new-found power of fiction. Men of science and men of orthodoxy shared the same darkness, straining their eyes as the match flared up and the pillars carved with philosophy failed to appear. Only vital spirits fortified by the elixir of adventure and unreality could still dream dreams and see visions. The rise and recognition of fiction had not changed the nature of God but it had changed man's perception of him.

As darkness closed in on him the God transcendent suffered the ultimate ignominy: he was snubbed by *The Times*. Early on 23 February 1887 an earthquake shook the French Riviera coast. It was Ash Wednesday, the first day of the lenten season of fasting and penitence, and exhausted Shrove Tuesday revellers were rudely awakened. One was the Prince of Wales, in Cannes for the festivities. 'If everybody had behaved like the Prince,' remarked *The Times*, 'the panic would not have been so great. Apprised by his suite of the fright caused by the earthquake, he declined to go down into the garden and, having tranquillized everybody, remained in bed.' Another was Nietzsche, who had long said the absurdities of the age could only end in a carnival of chaos. Now, as masked merry-makers fled in terror through streets littered with debris, he saw himself justified. 'We are living,

141

in fact, in the interesting expectation *that we shall perish*,' he wrote, 'thanks to a well-intentioned earthquake'.

But the days had gone when earthquakes could be thought to have intentions. *The Times* pointed out that the disaster had missed what surely should have been its prime target, 'the reprobate but fascinating Monte Carlo', 'We can imagine the sensation that would have been caused throughout the world,' it continued, 'had the Casino fallen a victim to the shock. What so appropriate as that on the first morning of Lent that home of wickedness should have been suddenly destroyed by the forces of outraged nature! Piety would have regarded the ruin as a judgment on a place that had so long tempted Providence and scepticism would have remarked that it was a singular coincidence'. The tone of the article was bantering, flippant, even contemptuous. It implied not just that God had missed his aim but that it was a delusion to think of him aiming at all. In its own inimitable way *The Times* was bidding farewell to the universe which had once been thought to be 'governed by incessant divine intervention'. But even *The Times* had no power over that other universe which Stevenson had had in mind when he wrote his 'Enter God!' There, on the spacious stage of fiction, there were still some spectacular results to be achieved.

9 ALL TRUTH IS CHANGE

IN JUBILEE YEAR BRITISH READERS WERE BOMBARDED with prophecies of a new and nobler kind of religion. The *Fortnightly Review* was particularly insistent. 'The narrow thoughts, the petty sympathies, the anthropocentric creeds, the anthropomorphic gods that once sufficed us will no longer satisfy the yearnings of our enlarged natures. New beliefs and new impulses gather strength and head within us', declared the anonymous author of a piece called 'Our Noble Selves'. He was sure that for all its scientific scepticism the human race was still profoundly religious and would 'pour forth its full heart in profuse strains of unpremeditated cosmical music'. John Addington Symonds spoke of 'the restoration of spirituality to our thoughts about the universe' and of 'the destiny of the scientific spirit to bring God, Law, Christian morals, into a new and vital combination which will contribute to the growth of rational religion'. Richard Jefferies pictured mankind fortified by science and standing on 'huge mounds of facts' to glimpse the starry horizon of infinity. Professor Huxley said that although science was a drudge, a Cinderella who did all the hard work while religion and philosophy behaved like the ugly sisters, she had the clearest insight into the ultimate mystery: 'She lights the fire, sweeps the house and provides the dinner; and is rewarded by being told that she is a base creature devoted to low and material interests. But in her garret she has fairy visions out of the ken of the pair of shrews who are quarrelling downstairs. She sees the order which pervades the seeming disorder of the world'.

As long as this glimpse of underlying order was a genuine insight, not just a airy vision, Nietzsche's image of chaos following upon God's death could be discounted together with Tennyson's dark forebodings. Instead of leaving man 'straying through an infinite nothing' and 'lost within a growing gloom' the demise of the old God would allow him

143

at last to see the creator as he or she or it really was, not just as a projection of man. The years of error would be over and the age of true religion, natural religion, could begin. The atheist poet James Thomson pointed out that there was a sense in which those who had talked of the death of Christ and the rebirth of Pan had been proved right: 'Now it is full time to proclaim the death of the great god Christ. Fate, in the form of Science, has decreed the extinction of the gods ... Pan lives, not as a God, but as the All, Nature, now that the oppression of the Supernatural is removed.' If Huxley was right the oppression of the irrational would also be removed. Instead of a sleep of reason bringing forth monsters there would just be rational human beings understanding and accepting the rational universe which had begotten them.

It was a pleasantly reassuring prospect but not one that all could share. Thomson himself in his darker moments felt the terrible oppression of the supernatural, of a universe ruled by cruel and monstrous and irrational forces, and his poems contained some of the ugliest nightmares brought forth by this age of dying gods and doubting humans. Huxley said that even Christianity at its worst, belief in the supremacy of evil and in man's innate depravity, chimed better with scientific truth than did 'the "liberal" popular illusions and other optimistic figments'. Whatever he might say in public his private convictions were closer to Tennyson's fears than to Gladstone's hopes. He told Tyndall in 1892 that Tennyson was 'the first poet since Lucretius who has understood the drift of science'; and this drift was clearly not towards a neat picture of a fixed and stable universe. Tennyson had foreseen this nearly sixty years ago. 'All truth is change' he had proclaimed in an early poem on the Greek philosopher Heraclitus. Whereas Socrates and Plato had taught that there were unchanging realities behind the shifting world of appearances, Heraclitus had argued that change was the reality and fixity the passing illusion. Just as Nietzsche rejected 'Socratic man' in favour of the older and fiercer dispensation represented by Dionysus, so Tennyson saw that if Heraclitus was right mankind would have to jettison moral absolutes along with scientific certainties: 'All thoughts, all creeds, all dreams are true.'

In the 1830s Tennyson had been alone but now he was part of a chorus. 'Men are beginning to look to Heraclitus not Socrates as the exponent of the true Greek spirit,' wrote Havelock Ellis in 1890. In 1889 Professor Patrick of the State University of Iowa published a new edition of Heraclitus and used Tennyson's poem to introduce

144

it. The rediscovery of Heraclitus was a recent thing, Professor Patrick explained: it had taken place within the past few decades, largely in Germany, and it was linked with Schopenhauer's rejection of the Socratic tradition. The link with Nietzsche was equally apparent and a few years later Patrick and his wife were to translate a history of contemporary German philosophy in which more space was given to Nietzsche than to any other thinker. Although only fragments of Heraclitus's works survived they were enough to show the vast gap between his dynamic vision of creation and the tidy world of Socrates. 'All things are exchanged for fire and fire for all things,' proclaimed Heraclitus, 'Good and evil are the same'. There was no such thing as a state of being, calm and complete and defined: there was only a state of becoming, mercurial and restless and unresolved. Violence and conflict were the only creators: 'War is the father and king of all and has produced some as gods and some as men, and has made some slaves and some free'.

'The world will be standing on its head for the next few years,' wrote Nietzsche in December 1888 as the new edition of Heraclitus went to press, 'since the old God has abdicated I shall rule the world from now on.' His title to the succession came not from Heraclitus but from Dionysus, in whose name he now began to sign his letters. Within a month he was declared insane. He had parted company not just with Socratic thinking but with reason itself. Others found reason and even faith compatible with a world standing on its head. Gerard Manley Hopkins wrote a sonnet called 'That Nature is a Heraclitean Fire and of the comfort of the Resurrection', the only poem he completed in 1888. It spoke of a universe without rest and without apparent meaning, an unfathomable dark in which the dead dross of matter and the brief fire of life were both overwhelmed. Yet they had met, the fire that was God had entered into the dross that was man. Christ's resurrection had made possible man's immortality just as surely as the meeting of fire and carbon inside the earth had made possible the dazzling and indestructible beauty of the diamond.

Hopkins was able to reconcile Christian and Heraclitean thinking, giving new intensity to both, because of his own sense of the God within him, the God imminent. The God transcendent, pavilioned for more than two hundred years in Sir Isaac Newton's stable universe, could not be so sure of surviving the baptism of Heraclitean fire. Nor for that matter could science, which in the hands of Newton's successors had turned from revealing God's glory to usurping it. Newton

145

had shown the lovers of system and order that the God of the Bible was the right god for them. Other scientists, equally tidy-minded, had laid down universal laws in order to contrast them with the vagaries of biblical revelation. But pious and impious alike wanted universal laws. They all needed to be sure there was a heavenly throne even though some knelt on its steps while others sat in it. How else could thought be objective? How could either God or man make sense of the whirling infinities without observing them from some fixed point where motion and direction were absolute and not relative?

Heraclitus could offer no such refuge and it was to be nearly twenty years before Einstein taught physicists to turn relativity itself into an observation platform. In the meantime it was the literary men rather than the scientists who made confident generalizations. The same Jubilee issue of the *Fortnightly Review* in which Symonds insisted that the scientific spirit would foster rational religion also contained a complacent account of Victorian scientific progress by Grant Allen, a Canadian-born philosopher who was making a name for himself in London literary circles. 'In marvellous contrast to the fragmentary and disjunctive science of fifty years ago,' he wrote, 'modern science offers us the spectacle of a simple, unified and comprehensible cosmos.' Like Symonds he saw this as the key not just to the physical world but to spiritual life as well. It was a sublime cosmic synthesis, 'one and the same throughout, in sun and star and world and atom, in light and heat and life and mechanism, in body, soul and spirit, mind and matter.' But he too sensed the shift from Socrates to Heraclitus and a few months later he substituted a dynamic Heraclitean theory of the universe for the comfortably comprehensible cosmos which he had praised so extravagantly. When he published his new ideas in 1888 he felt constrained to apologize for being a heretic and rejecting current scientific orthodoxy.

It seemed that only scientific heresies, not religious ones, needed apologies. In an article in the *Fortnightly Review* in January 1890 Grant Allen dismissed God as a lump of rock: 'Jahveh, the God of the Hebrews, the God of Abraham and of Isaac and of Jacob, the God who later became sublimated and etherealized into the God of Christianity, was in his origin nothing more nor less than the ancestral fetish stone of the people of the Israel'. He then went on to publish *The Evolution of the Idea of God*, saying that all religions had originated in the worship of the deified dead. Winwood Reade had put forward a similar theory a quarter of a century earlier and had contrasted

146

the imagined gods of the gullible with the real god of the scientists, 'the supreme and mysterious Power by whom the universe has been created and by whom it has been appointed to run its course under fixed and invariable laws; that awful One of whom we should never presume to think save with humility and awe'. Allen observed Reade's commandments as well as using his ideas. Pulling the old God to pieces, ferreting out the fetishes and detailing the stages of deification, was a legitimate activity of which nobody need feel ashamed; doubting the fixed and invariable laws of the awful One was matter for contrition.

In August 1894 the British Association for the Advancement of Science met in Oxford for the first time since the notorious 1860 meeting which had seen the confrontation between Huxley and Wilberforce over the rival claims of Darwin and God. Lord Salisbury, a past and future Conservative Prime Minister, was both Chancellor of Oxford University and President of the Association. His opening address ended by quoting the eminent scientist Lord Kelvin: 'Overpoweringly strong proofs of intelligent and benevolent design lie around us, teaching us that all things depend on one everlasting Creator and Ruler'. It sounded like a defence of the old God against the scientific doubters but it could also have been a vindication of Reade's awful One. Huxley, thanking Salisbury for his address, passed over the remarks about the Creator and Ruler and contented himself with pointing out that the orthodox biblical account of the immutability of species was now totally discredited. *The Times*, predicting confidently that Salisbury's address would have 'a beneficial influence on all serious-minded scientific workers', noted with approval the contrast between these civilized exchanges and the dreadful events of 1860. The passage of time might have softened the grim watchdogs of the God of the Book of Genesis but it remained to be seen whether it would do the same for those who defended the awful One and his invariable laws.

Some of the old watchdogs still had teeth. *Lux Mundi*, a collection of essays which appeared in 1889, contained a piece which suggested that some biblical stories might be dramatic narratives, 'true myths', rather than reliable history. Liddon, preaching in St Paul's, attacked this notion as fiercely as he had denounced the heresies of the 1860s. There was no half-way house, he told his congregation uncompromisingly: unless they believed everything in the Bible they would finish up believing nothing. Two years later Dr Alfred Williams Momerie, Professor of Logic and Mental Philosophy at King's College London,

147

was ousted after accusations of unorthodox teaching. Things might have changed at the British Association since the slanging match of 1860 but they had not changed much at King's College since the enforced resignation of F.D. Maurice in 1853. Many Anglicans still felt that they were ringed round with atheism. In 1888 a bishop declared indignantly that you found unbelief everywhere, lurking in newspapers and novels, airing its views in your club or your drawing-room. You might even hear it from the lady who sat next to you at dinner.

Nevertheless the orthodox were reasonably cheerful, certainly more cheerful than agonized intellectuals trying to fit new trends in science and philosophy into a coherent whole. In 1886 churchmen were claiming that their influence had grown spectacularly during the past twenty years. It suffered something of a set-back in 1888 and 1889 in Wales, where there was a ferocious and determined campaign against the payment of tithes. Farmers threatened to shoot anyone who tried to collect them and vicars who demanded payment were burned in effigy. Hundreds of policemen were involved in hand-to-hand fighting with angry labourers. Finally Mr Stevens, the agent of the Ecclesiastical Commissioners, refused to make any further attempts at collection after large crowds armed with heavy sticks had forced him and his bodyguard to retreat. However, Archbishop Benson remained confident that he was healing the rift of which Dr Hort had warned him. He was sure that the masses were coming back to God in spite of tithe riots and in spite of the fashionable scepticism of the club and the dinner table. 'It is well known,' he said in 1891, 'that throughout the country the number of those who attend church has largely increased and is still increasing'. It looks now as though he was quite wrong: 1886 seems to have been the year in which the churches first fell behind and failed to keep pace with population increase. Attendances began to fall, especially in towns where the population was still rising. But such trends were not apparent at the time and so the optimism of the devout was undented.

There was optimism of another kind in America. In 1890 Congress decided to hold a World's Columbian Exposition to mark the four hundredth anniversary of the discovery of America. Charles Carroll Bonney, President of the Exposition's Congress Auxiliary, determined to make this the occasion for a World's Parliament of Religions, where representatives from every religion on earth would meet to proclaim the one over-riding divine truth. After many delays the Exposition finally opened in Chicago in May 1893, four hundred and one years

148

after Columbus's voyage, and the Parliament of Religions opened on 11 September. Cardinal Gibbons of Baltimore led the delegates in the Lord's Prayer while Hindus and Muslims and Buddhists beamed approvingly at his side. Archbishop Benson had refused to have anything to do with the enterprise and so the Church of England was represented on the platform by Dr Momerie. At home he was now in deep disgrace, unable to preach without special permission from his bishop, but in Chicago he gave a confident address on 'The Philosophic and Moral Evidence for the Existence of God'. It was a strange piece of work which combined out-dated Newtonian arguments about the universe with some remarkably harsh remarks about the need for children to suffer for the sins of their fathers in accordance with the wishes of the God of the Old Testament. Nor was Momerie alone in rooting for his own God. The Chairman of the Parliament quoted with approval a bishop who said that 'civilization, which is making the whole world one, is preparing the way for the reunion of all the world's religions in their true centre, Jesus Christ'. It would be a difficult convergence if each religion saw itself as the only true centre.

Zenshiro Noguchi, a Buddhist from Japan, was not dismayed. 'Is there a hope of decreasing the number of religions?' he asked, 'Yes. How far? To one. Why? Because the truth is only one.' Laura Ormiston Chant of London was welcomed 'with more than the usual demonstrations of interest and applause' when she said that God himself was about to reveal the nature of this ultimate truth: 'Today, for the first time in the world's history, we are certain that God's duty to us will be performed'. She had just listened to a paper on comparative theology and she was not impressed. 'What marvellous intellectual jugglers these theologians are!' she observed tartly. She had had hopes of a new Day of Pentecost when the Holy Spirit would descend in tongues of Heraclitean fire not just on Christians but on the whole of mankind. Instead she found that many delegates regarded the whole affair as just another academic conference. Julia Ward Howe was even more contemptuous of theological subtleties, dismissing them as the tricks and charms of mischievous priests. Contributions like those of Mrs Chant and Mrs Howe, visions of a new heaven and a new earth, contrasted sharply with the cautious and scholarly papers of the intellectuals. Nevertheless the Parliament closed in an atmosphere of excitement and satisfaction and hope. 'What men deemed impossible, God has finally wrought,' said the chairman. Momerie, thanking his American hosts on behalf of all the foreign delegates, declared that 'It is

149

the greatest event so far in the history of the world and it has been held on American soil.'

Perhaps it was the event that Tennyson had been waiting for, the moment at which God 'mingled with the game' and led mankind away from the horrors into which it had been straying. Tennyson had welcomed the World Parliament and had agreed to serve on its Advisory Council for Great Britain, though by the time it opened he was dead. While Archbishop Benson raged at the very idea of the Parliament because it put Christianity on a par with other religions Tennyson and other eminent laymen gave it their support. As well as being the possible realization of their hopes it could also be seen as fulfilling the predictions of the watchers on the high towers, who had always said that divine truth would soon reconcile conventional thinking and occult inspiration, science and scriptural revelation, eastern mysteries and western observances. But the obstinate fact remained that the traditional God of the English-speaking peoples, the robed and bearded figure presiding over a stable Newtonian universe, was in no position to make such a breakthrough. He was in full retreat, pursued by the whirling furies of relativist and Heraclitean thought. When many of the buildings put up for the Columbian Exposition were destroyed by fire in January 1894 it did not occur to *The Times* to make play with the disaster as it had made play with the earthquake of 1887. It was no longer even amusing, let alone instructive, to consider whether the power that ruled the galaxies could indicate approval or disapproval of what had been going on in Chicago. It might seem a sad irony of the late Victorian age that an upsurge of questing spirituality should have coincided with the undermining of the foundations upon which spirituality was popularly supposed to rest.

In fact there was no irony and no coincidence. The search for God was as old as mankind and the desire for his presence had usually been in direct proportion to the fear of his absence. The deepest spiritual yearnings had always sprung from a sense of loss. What was new was that the yearnings and the loss had become separated. Instead of the same saints and mystics passing from the dark night of God's absence to the ecstatic knowledge of his presence, instead of the same congregations being led from a sense of sin through worship and contrition to a sacramental union, there was a number of people agonizing and theorizing in public as to whether or not God was in charge of the universe while another and far larger number agonized in private

over the gap between their aspiring fantasies and their circumscribed lives. In previous ages the very existence of this gap had been proof of God's presence. Browning had set it in a religious context only thirty years ago: 'A man's reach should exceed his grasp, Or what's a heaven for?' But now, as Rider Haggard had already pointed out, 'men and women stretch out their arms towards that vision of the Perfect which we only see in books and dreams'. The manuals of devotion had been replaced by novels, the collective fantasies of the pious had given way to the individual fantasies of the impressionable. Mystics had spoken of self-transcendence while Haggard spoke of men and women 'craving to be taken out of themselves'. The language differed but the yearning was the same. Could God rebuild his shattered image, could he pass through fiction as well as fire in order to bring his imminence and his transcendence together again?

This was perhaps the only way in which the hopes of 'Locksley Hall Sixty Years After' could be fulfilled. Characters from fiction might be better than real people at 'strowing balm or shedding poison in the Fountains of the Will'. Anna Kingsford was one of the few in the real world who attempted such things: her imperious will sought to bring balm to animals in laboratories and poison to those who tortured them. On 11 November 1886, as Tennyson's lines were going to press, she learned that she had 'smitten another vivisectionist', the scientist Paul Bert. But it was not a very convincing smiting: it had taken her several years to do it and the likelihood of it being a coincidence was even greater than in the case of Claude Bernard. The drugs which had helped to heighten her ecstasies had taken their toll and she had only fifteen months to live. The fountains of the will were not hers to command. As she celebrated her triumph over Paul Bert a struggling doctor in Southsea called Arthur Conan Doyle was celebrating the sale of his book *A Study in Scarlet*, a story about a private detective named Sherlock Holmes. The watchers upon the high towers had sought strange powers by moving from reality into a world of fantasy: Sherlock Holmes was to do precisely the opposite. No other character in fiction has been so successful in convincing readers of his reality. As men combed Baker Street to find the exact location of his lodgings, as they argued passionately about which university he had attended, he was able to mingle with the game of human life in a way which exceeded even Tennyson's expectations.

A Study in Scarlet was ruthlessly pirated in the United States, where it proved so popular that the Philadelphia publisher Joseph Marshall

151

Stoddart came to London to commission a second Holmes story. The result, *The Sign of Four*, was serialized in an American magazine in 1890. The story opened in the summer of Jubilee Year, when 22b Baker Street – unlike the non-fictional world – was swathed in a thick yellow fog. It was this unseasonable pea-souper, swirling down the street and drifting across dun-coloured houses, that drew from Holmes his cry of despair about the unprofitable world and its commonplace values.* It soon became clear that he was a devotee of Jean-Paul Richter, who had long proclaimed God dead, as well as a convert to Winwood Reade's impersonal supreme being. If men and women stretched out their arms to Holmes for 'a vision of the Perfect which we only see in books and dreams' they would find themselves clutching at something far from orthodox.

Sherlock Holmes began to cast his extraordinary spell over British readers in July 1891, when short stories about him started to appear in *The Strand Magazine*. Circulation soared and the public clamoured for more stories. Conan Doyle obliged, though with an increasingly bad grace because he felt that Holmes was keeping him from more worthwhile writing. At last in December 1893, after twenty-two stories, he decided the time had come to get rid of him. And so in the twenty-third story, 'The Final Problem', the great detective fell to his death over the Reichenbach Falls, locked in mortal combat with his arch-enemy Moriarty. It was supposed to be the end but it was not. Readers saw Holmes as a character too real to be a mere figment subject to the whims of an author and they also saw him, consciously or unconsciously, as a mythical figure who could never die. Conan Doyle was like a conjuror who tires of his tricks only to find them hailed as miracles. He found himself cast as a heretic against the divinity he had created, a doubting Thomas who refused to countenance the resurrection in which others so desperately wanted to believe. In the end he gave in and decided that Holmes had survived and had deliberately allowed himself to be presumed dead. The great detective had then plunged into a typically Holmesian mixture of scientific research and occult investigation, travelling for two years in Tibet and spending several days with the Dalai Lama – something which no non-fictional character could have done and which was closer to Colonel Olcott's dealings with the Dwellers of the Threshold than to the doings of ordinary mortals.

* See above, p.4.

The resurrection of Sherlock Holmes anticipated the scene in *Peter Pan* in which Tinkerbell was restored to life by the concerted acclaim of the audience. Like her he conquered death because those who believed in him were united in their determination that he should do so. He took on God's mantle, coming back to life by dint of the faith of his worshippers, but he was far from being a god himself. On the contrary, he seemed concerned to teach people to do without gods. In spite of his occasional perfunctory expressions of piety it was clear that he had little time for established religion or conventional morality. He made no apologies for his addiction to cocaine and he expected Watson to join him unhesitatingly in breaking the law when he thought it necessary. He said that his life was 'spent in one long effort to escape from the commonplaces of existence,' yet the end product of that life was the defence of the commonplace, the familiar and reassuring world of hansom cabs and Mrs Hudson's cooking, against all manner of strange and outlandish evils. His astonishing powers of deduction seemed like witchcraft – 'You would certainly have been burned had you lived a few centuries ago,' Watson told him – but he was always careful to show how they were based purely on observation and reason. He might be superhuman but he was not supernatural.

Nor was there anything supernatural about the threats he faced. The first of them, in *A Study in Scarlet*, originated in America, in Mormon fanaticism, and it was no accident that President Arthur was engaged in a campaign against the Mormons at the time the book was being written. Later Conan Doyle widened his net, calling forth horrors from Asia and Africa and Australia, but he still seemed fascinated by the United States as a breeding ground of hatred and violence. In the fifth short story, 'The Five Orange Pips', it was emissaries of the Ku Klux Klan who infuriated Holmes by killing his client. 'That hurts my pride, Watson,' he remarked when he saw the body, 'It is a petty feeling, no doubt, but it hurts my pride.' It was a typically Holmesian reaction, nicely poised between arrogance and apology. Rather similar had been his response in the first short story of all, 'A Scandal in Bohemia'. Then, when he had been outwitted by Irene Adler, he had asked his client for her photograph as the only reward for his services. He had no affection for her, no time for thoughts of love – 'for the trained reasoner to admit such intrusions was to introduce a distracting factor' – but he treasured her photograph and always spoke of her as *the* woman,

153

one who rivalled his own superhuman powers.

To be superhuman without being supernatural was an enviable state and one to which many in the real world were beginning to aspire. George Saintsbury had said in Jubilee Year that society could be regenerated if it 'bathed long and well in the romance of adventure and passion'. Now Sherlock Holmes had added deduction and observation to the bathwater and the resulting heady mixture must surely refresh those souls whom religion could not reach. 'A wave of unrest is passing over the world,' wrote Hugh Stutfield in *Blackwood's Magazine* in 1895, 'Humanity is beginning to sicken at the daily round, the common task, of ordinary humdrum existence and is eagerly seeking for new forms of excitement. Revolt is the order of the day'. 'A new renaissance lies ahead of us,' cried Alfred Hake a few months later, 'and we are all struggling to reach it'. The philosophers of an earlier renaissance had proclaimed that man could make of himself whatever he wished. Now at last he would do so. The drive towards self-transcendence must be shifted not just from religious into secular terms, not just from Christian mystics to ordinary men and women seeking inspiration in fiction, but also from the one to the many, from the individual to the group. 'Christ made no attempt to reconstruct society and consequently the individualism that he preached to man could be realized only through pain or in solitude,' wrote Oscar Wilde. Once society was regenerated and the Christian ideals of pain and solitude rejected 'a larger, fuller, lovelier individualism' would spring from the realities of social co-operation.

One of the most uncompromising prophets of social regeneration was Edward Carpenter, an English disciple of Walt Whitman who had relinquished holy orders at the age of thirty. After visiting Whitman in New Jersey and finding in him 'a certain radiant power' he had made his home among labouring people and had tried to share their life. He was appalled by the blindness with which respectable guardians of society – clergymen, politicians, financiers, men of property – destroyed themselves as well as others. Unquiet, unresting, uncomprehending, they spun cobwebs over 'the calm miraculous beauty of the world' and fed their children on 'the refuse of dinner parties and the insides of committee rooms'. If there was a god at all it was not the one set up by these cardboard figures; it was 'the goat-legged God peering over the tops of clouds, shameless, lusty, unpresentable'. Havelock Ellis's *The New Spirit*, which began by proclaiming the return to Heraclitean thought, went on to hail Carpenter

as one who had found 'the perennial fountain which springs up within and which the measuring rod of science has never meted'. Ellis himself in his student days had been likened both to Jesus Christ and to Pan. His mistress found his naked body essentially Christlike but his wife insisted that he was 'a mixture of satyr and Christ'. She even took him to the National Gallery to show him, in a picture by Rubens, which satyr he was.

Ellis took such comparisons in his stride. He had already decided, during three lonely years of meditation in the Australian outback, that his mission in life was to bring together knowledge and belief by demonstrating the supremacy of sex in human affairs. Born into an age in which the collective fantasies of religion jarred against the seemingly unfantastic discoveries of science and materialism, he would restore unity to human thought by showing how all these things converged in the individual fantasies which governed the reproductive urge. For him 'the perennial fountain which springs up within' was a description of physical desire as well as a metaphor for true wisdom. Hence the picture by Rubens was of more interest than the scores of religious pictures in which he might have identified the Christlike part of his nature. Man's regeneration would come from within himself, by understanding and harnessing his urges instead of denying them, and if a god presided over the process it would be Pan and not Christ. Christianity turned away from the physical realities of human life while paganism accepted them and gloried in them. 'The free Greek was not ashamed of sex,' wrote Grant Allen, 'not ashamed of his own body and its component members. He despised the barbarian who shamed to show himself in the palaestra as the gods had fashioned him.' Having revised his ideas about Greek thought, having rejected Apollo in favour of Dionysus, Socrates in favour of Heraclitus, modern man must now come to terms with Greek life as well. Like all real life it was centred not on asceticism and the search for heaven but on sexuality.

The neo-paganism of the 1890s was more thoroughgoing than earlier dalliances with Pan. In the first place the phenomenal rise of fiction had given new life to the ancient concept of the hero, the archetypal figure who saved society not because he was supernatural but because he was superhuman. Already thinkers in Germany were hailing Nietzsche as prophet of the age of the superman: man had reached a dead end and could only survive by transcending himself. Philosophies of this kind were seen as blasphemies by many people in Britain

155

and America. How could men seek to become supermen without seeking to becomes gods? One possible answer was given in the first volume of Sir James Frazer's *The Golden Bough*, the publication of which in 1890 gave fresh impetus to the neo-pagan movement. It took its title from a priest who gained his office by plucking a golden bough in the sacred grove of Nemi. To do so he had to kill the priest who was there already, so that every priest was a murderer and would in due course become a victim. It was, as *The Times* pointed out, a ritual of life: the divine man in the grove never grew old, his strength and his virility were constantly renewed as they passed from one priest to the next.

Needless to say it was also a ritual of death. 'They shall grow not old, as we that are left grow old', words soon to be inscribed on countless war memorials, could equally well have been written of the priests of the sacred grove. It was to become clear in 1914, when the young heroes set off on their high adventure, that the demand for the ultimate sacrifice was as implicit in paganism as it was in Christianity. But in the 1890s 'the new paganism' seemed to be a life-enhancing force which would sweep away old inhibitions and prohibitions. In August 1892, when William Sharp brought out *The Pagan Review*, he put on its title page the motto *Sic Transit Gloria Grundi*: the long rule of Mrs Grundy, of Victorian prudery, was at last over. In a controversial article on 'The New Hedonism' in 1894 Grant Allen proclaimed that 'everything high and ennobling in our nature springs directly out of the sexual instinct'. Society would only be regenerated when it substituted this truth, the truth which lay at the root of the ancient Greek ideal of self-development, for the deluded Christian ideals of asceticism and penitence and self-sacrifice. Clearly the new hedonism was the new paganism under another name.

Grant Allen's piece was exceptional in that it presented a case rather than telling a tale. For the most part the neo-pagan movement of the early 1890s found expression in fiction rather than in disputation. Kenneth Grahame's *Pagan Papers* told of an approaching cataclysm which would sweep away the grey cohorts of respectability and leave the pagan hunter to 'string his bow once more and once more loose the whistling shaft'; but the prophecy was contained not in a philosophical or theological argument but in a series of stories. The new paganism, like Sherlock Holmes, sought to change the real world by invading it from the realms of fantasy. But where were the red-blooded pagans of fiction? There had been many influential fictitious characters

in the years since Saintsbury had recommended the bath of adventure and passion, but how many of them acted as though everything high and ennobling in their natures sprang directly out of the sexual instinct? There had been plenty of adventure but precious little passion. There was certainly none in Sherlock Holmes, cold and aloof with his photograph of Irene Adler filed away. 'They seem happier in their dealings with men than with women, and with war than with love,' remarked Andrew Lang of Rider Haggard and Robert Louis Stevenson, 'Mr Haggard's savage ladies are better than his civilized fair ones, while there is not a petticoat in *Kidnapped* or *Treasure Island*.' Contemporary fiction did not seem to be a very good medium for demonstrating the supremacy of sex in human affairs.

Rider Haggard was unrepentant. 'Sexual passion is the most powerful lever with which to stir the mind of man,' he wrote in 1887, 'for it lies at the root of all things human; and it is impossible to overestimate the damage that could be worked by a single English or American writer of genius if he grasped it with a will.' Then, in one revealing question, he betrayed the reason for his reluctance to seize the sexual lever. 'Why do *men* hardly ever read a novel?' he asked plaintively. The young lions of neo-paganism might discuss sex as men of the world but novelists could not mention it as long as most of their readers were women and children. With Stevenson and Haggard and Conan Doyle pulling in the adult male readers it might be thought things were changing. But in 1891, when the Bristol public librarians divided their readers into categories, they found that 'females of no occupation' had taken out over ten thousand books, four times as many as clerks and nearly ten times the number taken out by professional men. The number of books read by schoolboys, errand boys and apprentices, either at home or in the library, was over fifteen thousand.

Boys in the upper classes were also at risk even though they might not frequent public libraries. In 1885 Dr Clement Dukes published a treatise on masturbation, which he said was practised by 'ninety to ninety-five per cent of all boys at boarding schools.' With a somewhat injudicious choice of idiom he declared that this terrible situation must be remedied 'if we, as a nation, are to hold our own'. The cure lay in what he called 'the elevation of women', though he admitted this was difficult when 'the demand for them for base purposes is so great.' It was entirely appropriate that boys should have fantasies about killing and fighting and torments and injuries but it was quite

157

undesirable that they should know how men and women made love or even that they felt the need to do so. Books given to schoolboys must encourage them to think of themselves as brave knights performing deeds of valour for chaste and elevated ladies. Companionship in arms and pure love between man and man had been ideals both of the ancient Greek world and of the knightly tradition – had not Tennyson's King Arthur spoken of the knights of the Round Table as 'the men I loved'? – and 'the new chivalry' became another name for 'the new paganism'. 'For one pleasure of life and physical delight in each other's presence, touch and voice which man and woman ordinarily share, it is not too much to say that the new chivalry has ten,' declared *The Artist and Journal of Home Culture*, after rhapsodizing about men sharing 'the evening tent-pitching of campers out and the exhilaration of the early morning swim'.

In 1891 a sensationally successful novel of schoolboy love was published. It was called *Tim* and it was by Howard Overing Sturgis, an American who had been at Eton under William Johnson Cory, a master who had to leave the school because of his affairs with boys. The book was very well received, having to be reprinted within a month of publication, and in some ways it was very conventional: its young hero died in the last chapter and in death he brought about harmony, persuading his father at last to accept his young lover. He also took care to have his ecstasies in the chapel at Eton and not in some pagan grove:

It happened that morning that the first lesson was the beautiful lament of David over his dead friend Jonathan; and Tim, listening to the history of those two friends long ago, felt his love for his friend almost a religion to him. 'Thy love to me was wonderful,' said the voice of the reader, 'passing the love of woman.' 'What woman could ever love him as I do?' thought Tim, as he looked naturally to the seat where Carol sat. At that moment a sunbeam from some hole high in the roof fell on the golden curly head which seemed transfigured; and as Tim's hungry eyes rested on the face of his friend, he turned towards him and smiled upon him in his place.

It was becoming clear that in going back to ancient Greece the new paganism might be going back to the Greek ideal of homosexual love. 1891 also saw the publication of *A Problem of Modern Ethics*, a treatise on homosexuality by John Addington Symonds which was later reprinted as an appendix to Havelock Ellis's study of sexual inversion. In 1892 Symonds told of 'men whose bodies you have

158

touched and handled' in *Our Life in the Swiss Highlands*, a book whose title was an obvious mockery of the Queen's literary efforts. From America came Oscar Wilde's *The Picture of Dorian Gray*, commissioned by Stoddart at the same time as *The Sign of Four* and published in *Lippincott's Magazine* in 1890. By the time it appeared as a book in April 1891 most reviewers had decided it was immoral. One said it was a thinly disguised account of the Cleveland Street scandal of 1889, when revelations made by good-looking telegraph boys had led to the uncovering of a male brothel frequented by the nobility and even, it was alleged, by members of the Royal Family. Accused of peddling 'moral putrescence', Wilde infuriated his critics by replying loftily that 'there is no such thing as a moral or an immoral book. Books are well written or badly written. That is all.'

Could there perhaps be worse things than the promiscuity of telegraph boys? In 1886 Baron Richard von Krafft-Ebing's *Psychopathia Sexualis* had given clinical details of sadism and masochism and other sexual idiosyncrasies. *The Artist and Journal of Home Culture* provided an unwitting footnote to these findings when it suggested that painters should choose as a subject the whipping of Spartan boys at the altar of Artemis Orthia. 'The expression of steady and determined endurance under pain in a young face' would be a joy to behold. And William Sharp's most notable defiance of Mrs Grundy in *The Pagan Review* was not a description of the sexual act but an account of a pagan sacrifice of five youths and five maidens 'in a wide spirt of blood'. Just as the inability to be explicit about copulation had helped to push the new paganism into a hothouse of half-admitted homosexuality, so the restraints of the hothouse itself led to a darker eroticism that was seldom admitted or understood.

One man who understood it very well was Max Nordau, a doctor from Budapest who had studied Krafft-Ebing and now lived in Paris. In 1893 his book *Degeneration* claimed that much of the fashionable art and music and literature of the time was the work of men who should have been Krafft-Ebing's patients. It was sick and degenerate, produced by neurotics and fit only for neurotics. It betokened 'a Dusk of the Nations in which all suns and all stars are gradually waning and mankind with all its institutions and creations is perishing in the midst of a dying world'. The rhetoric was reminiscent of Nietzsche's threnody on the death of God and indeed Nordau had spurned God a decade earlier in *The Conventional Lies of our Civilization*, a book in which he had declared that 'Every separate act of a religious ceremony

becomes a fraud and a criminal satire when performed by a cultivated man of the nineteenth century'. But to echo a writer was not to approve of him: Nietzsche was dismissed as 'a sufferer from sadism in its most pronounced form' and his works were consigned to the waste-paper basket of degeneration along with those of Wagner, Ibsen, Tolstoi, Zola, Baudelaire and many others. And the man who had infected Britain and America with these pernicious ideas, the man cast by Nordau as the high priest of decadence in the English-speaking world, was Oscar Wilde.

By now the enemies of the new movement were beginning to accuse it openly of homosexual tendencies. 'The New Morality might have gone elsewhere for its ideal than to Sodom and Gomorrah,' wrote *The Review of Reviews* grimly. Everyone knew what God had done to Sodom and Gomorrah: what would he do to this hydra-headed thing that called itself new paganism, new chivalry, new morality, new hedonism? The London *Christian Leader* said that *The Picture of Dorian Gray* 'portrays the gilded paganism which has been staining these latter years of the Victorian epoch with horrors'. By the time the English version of *Degeneration* came out at the beginning of 1895 Oscar Wilde's name stood for fashionable comedy rather than pagan horrors. *An Ideal Husband* was running in London at the Haymarket Theatre and *The Importance of Being Earnest* opened at the St James's Theatre on 14 February. The Marquis of Queensberry, who thought Wilde was corrupting his son Lord Alfred Douglas, attempted unsuccessfully to interrupt the performance. He then left a card at Wilde's club accusing him of 'posing as a sodomite'. Wilde brought an action for criminal libel and when it failed he was himself arrested and charged with acts of gross indecency with male persons. After a first trial at which the jury failed to agree a second ended on 25 May 1895 with a verdict of guilty. Wilde was sentenced to two years' imprisonment with hard labour and the pious rejoiced that God had cut off all the heads of the hydra at one stroke. In a sense they were right, for the downfall of Oscar Wilde was a turning point in moral attitudes as well as in literary fashions. However, the direction in which things turned was not to be quite what the orthodox had anticipated.

10 THE POWER OF EVIL

IT WAS CLEAR FROM THE OUTSET THAT THE SINS OF the world of literature were on trial along with those of real life. During the libel case Queensberry's lawyers read out passages from *The Picture of Dorian Gray* in an attempt to make Wilde reveal his sexual proclivities by identifying with his characters. On 6 April 1895, the day he was arrested, solicitors representing the publishers of the magazine *Chameleon* wrote to the newspapers saying its sale had been stopped because it was thought to have homosexual leanings. The trickle of such disclaimers became a flood and Edward Carpenter's *Homogenic Love*, which had been published in January, was killed stone dead. Other books, most of them far less overt, were abandoned or withdrawn. Within a week of Wilde's conviction the London *Christian World* was celebrating the defeat of paganism and decadence in a leading article entitled 'Culture and Gomorrah'. Sane and healthy-minded people must make a stand, declared *Blackwood's Magazine*, against 'the gilded and perfumed putrescence which is creeping over every branch of art'. The *National Observer* commented that *Degeneration* 'has made its appearance in its English dress at a very appropriate time. Herr Nordau is most indubitably right'.

But there was a difficulty. If all this was God's doing, if he had really arisen to scatter his enemies and cut off the heads of the hydra as the devout liked to think, he would hardly have chosen an atheist scientist like Nordau as his instrument. Alfred Hake's *Regeneration: a reply to Max Nordau* showed that many of the works Nordau dismissed under the heading of 'mysticism, a cardinal mark of degeneration' were in reality products of a religious revival which had offended him because it rejected clinical scientific thought. The publisher William Heinemann drove the point home when he followed up the success of *Degeneration* by bringing out *The Conventional Lies of our Civilization*,

161

which had made little impression when it had first been published in English in Chicago in 1884. Nordau's attacks on 'The Lie of Religion' were not calculated to make the orthodox feel happy in his company. They would have been even more worried if they had known that Wilde himself was to invoke Nordau. In July 1896, petitioning to have his sentence reviewed on grounds of mental illness, he stressed that *Degeneration* had singled him out as 'a specially typical example of the intimate connection between madness and the literary and artistic temperament'. In the eyes of the conventionally pious the things that Wilde had done, both in his life and in his work, were not merely unbalanced but evil. His proper place was in hell, not in a lunatic asylum. Nordau was of little avail if he could be used to advance excuses instead of condemnation.

As far as Oscar Wilde himself was concerned there were limits even to the vindictiveness of the British public. Where his works were concerned the limits were less discernible and years after his trial, when he had become an object of pity or indifference rather than horror, *The Picture of Dorian Gray* was still being shunned as an immoral book. In 1908 *The Sunday Times* called it 'a *tour de force* of morbidity, interesting mainly because it gave a forecast of Oscar Wilde's own eclipse'. Critics compared it to Stevenson's *Dr Jekyll and Mr Hyde*, since both books were about incarnations of evil. In Dr Jekyll's case the evil in him became a second self, Mr Hyde, who grew steadily more monstrous until he took over Jekyll altogether. Dorian Gray was able to transfer the evil within him – or at any rate its physical manifestations – not to a second self but to his own portrait, which became foul and loathsome while he remained young and unmarked by his unspeakable sins. When he could bear the sight of the painting no longer he put a knife through it. The picture of Dorian Gray was then restored to its original beauty while the body of Dorian Gray, stabbed with his own knife, was invaded by all the foulness which had been on the canvas. Evil already possessed his soul and now it took over his body as well, just as it had in the end taken over the whole personality of Dr Jekyll.

At the time, in the eyes of ordinary outraged citizens, the portrayal of evil did not seem to be terribly relevant. They had been shocked by what they regarded as sins, offences against the law of God, and they had been repelled by what they regarded as indecencies, departures from normal wholesome behaviour. Such things must be punished if they took place in real life and condemned if they took

place in fiction. And that was all there was to it as far as the conventionally respectable were concerned. They thought of sin and indecency as realities while dismissing evil as an outdated absurdity, a relic of primitive imaginings. But already the ground was being cut from under them as God's law slid into a vortex of Heraclitean fire carrying man-made morals with it. In this uncertain and relativist universe evil was to prove remarkably resilient, far more so than concepts like sin and immorality and indecency which were its outward accoutrements. The Wilde affair, which seemed a signal for society to nestle back into its reassuring cocoon of respectability, was to prove part of a process which would tear the cocoon to shreds. And one of the aspects of the process was an increasing awareness of the power of evil.

Something of that power was suggested in Arthur Machen's *The Great God Pan*, published at the end of 1894 and greeted with howls of disapproval which soon made it notorious. It was said to be 'a most gruesome and *unmanly* book' and 'the most acutely and intentionally disagreeable we have yet seen in English'. Mudie's circulating library refused to catalogue it or put it on display. It portrayed Pan as ultimate and unbearable evil, 'before which the souls of men wither and die and blacken, as their bodies blacken under the electric current'. Other visions of evil were more conventional. *Studies of Death*, a book of stories by Count Stenbock which also came out in 1894, included 'The true story of a Vampire', about a vampire who drained the blood from a young boy and then vanished after kissing him on the lips. There were obvious homosexual connotations and the censorious might note that Stenbock had recently written an erotic story about a werewolf for *Spirit Lamp*, Lord Alfred Douglas's undergraduate magazine to which Oscar Wilde had contributed. Julian Osgood Field's 'A Kiss of Judas', published at the end of 1894 in a collection of tales entitled *Aut Diabolus aut Nihil*, featured a sinister blend of vampire and werewolf, a corpse-like figure with the face of an animal. A decent and wholesome Englishman who offended this creature ended up nailed to a tree through the hands with his own knife. Another vampire, appearing in the form of an unbelievably beautiful woman, then killed him with a kiss.

It was ironic that these unpleasant images should be appearing just when Wilde himself, their supposed originator and eventual scapegoat, had turned from the portrayal of evil to the portrayal of society's foibles. Where had the visions of corruption and malevolence come

163

from? Dr Mayo had suggested half a century ago that they were linked with fears of being buried alive and now such fears were again being voiced. 'A concurrence of peculiar circumstances, beginning in May 1895, has directed public attention to the subject of premature burial,' declared William Tebb. In 1896 he published an authoritative work on the subject, written in collaboration with Colonel Edward Vollum, formerly Medical Inspector to the United States army. 'Ask any ten men and women at random what is the worst nightmare which oppresses the ordinary sane person,' commented the *Spectator*, 'and they will say the fear of being buried alive.' A disturbing number of funerals had been interrupted by knocking from within the coffin and the House of Commons had set up a Select Committee to inquire into the abuses associated with the issue of death certificates. A woman in Sheffield habitually carried hers around with her: it was signed by a doctor who had assumed she would die and had not bothered to find out whether she had actually done so.

It would have been comforting to think that evil was nothing but a shadow thrown by premature burial, a nightmare which would vanish if greater care was taken over death certificates. Unfortunately the nightmares themselves suggested otherwise. 'From the evidence of dreams we are more or less at liberty to believe that the dead and the living may exist together in a world of spirit in which the so-called living are less living than very many of the so-called dead,' declared Frederick Greenwood's *Imagination in Dreams and their study* in 1894. For centuries Christianity had denied the reality of this 'world of spirit': apart from the saints, who got special treatment, the dead would remain dead until all were raised at the Last Trumpet. But the notion of instant resurrection had always had its appeal and the advent of spiritualism had made it respectable. For most people eternity was no longer the sea into which the river of time would empty but the country through which it flowed. In dreams and in other unconscious imaginings the dead – especially dead parents – stood along the banks watching and judging. In Vienna Sigmund Freud was coming to appreciate their appalling power as he struggled to break their iron grip on the living. His work on the interpretation of dreams, which he was to publish in 1900, would make that power seem less malevolent, less calculated, but it would do little to reduce it.

As yet the English-speaking world knew nothing of Freud. Krafft-Ebing's work on sexual deviation attracted little attention when it

came out in English in 1892 and the first of Havelock Ellis's *Studies in the Psychology of Sex* was widely condemned when it appeared in 1897. The only kind of sex which was acceptable, as Edward Carpenter pointed out bitterly in his doomed book on homogenic love, was 'matrimonial sex-intercourse and child-breeding'. Anything else was either a sin or an illness. Yet in the world of fantasy, in dreams and in tales of horror, things happened which were the work either of evil spirits or of perverted sexuality. Could it be that the lonely fantasies of masturbation, the images that had so alarmed Dr Dukes, were taking over from the collective fantasies of religion? Were they perhaps the same thing, were the demons and the avenging angels simply parental prohibitions and guilty desires in fancy dress? The horror story stood at the meeting of the ways, its ambiguous fascination explicable either in sexual terms as fear of parents or in religious terms as fear of the wrath of God and the works of the Devil. The proudly rational men and women of the 1890s were reluctant either to go back to belief in the wiles of Satan or to go forward to belief in the supremacy of sex.

This ambivalence was shown very clearly in the work of Ambrose Bierce, the most gifted American writer of horror stories in the 1890s. His portrayal of the vengeful things that rose from the tomb was remarkably and overtly Freudian: one of his characters 'found himself staring into the sharply drawn face and blank, dead eyes of his own mother ... he felt the cold fingers close upon his throat'. It seemed a signal for all the ghosts and vampires and werewolves to doff their grisly disguises and take their places in Freud's gallery of complexes. Yet Bierce also confessed to a profoundly religious dream which had haunted him since childhood and which lay behind all his best work. In it he found himself on an endless plain swept by some final and consuming fire. On it there stood a vast castle, its battlements and towers silhouetted against a dead sky, and deep inside this castle the black and shrivelled body of a man lay on a bed. Slowly it opened its eyes and he knew that he was himself the corpse. The horror of the dream lay not in this recognition but in the realization that the universe was empty and meaningless because God was dead: 'that hateful and abhorrent scrap of mortality, still sentient after the death of God and the angels, was I!' To the psycho-analyst such an outstandingly egocentric dream might suggest nothing worse than fear of a dead parent, but to the devout Christian it could presage cosmic disaster.

165

There was more reassurance in Bram Stoker's *Dracula*, one of the most popular of all horror stories, which was published in 1897. Here God was still very much alive and able to provide mankind with an impressive armoury of weapons against the power of vampires. The hero Jonathan Harker began by proclaiming his rationalist and Protestant contempt for the crucifix – 'as an English Churchman I have been taught to regard such things as in some measure idolatrous' – but he found his crucifix saved him when Count Dracula made his first attack. Professor van Helsing, called in because he was 'one of the most advanced scientists of his day', soon gave up relying on such clinical devices as blood transfusion and went to the British Museum to search out 'witch and demon cures'. The most potent of these was the body of God, the consecrated host. 'To superstition,' van Helsing declared in his shaky English, 'must we trust at the first; it was man's faith in the early, and it have its root in faith still'. He made Harker and his American friend Quincey Morris abandon Protestant scepticism and give credence to the beliefs of the Roman Catholic Church. Only thus were they able to rid the world of the menace of Dracula.

Algernon Blackwood was determined to bring the horror story out of these mediaeval shadows into the twentieth century. He created a character called John Silence, a 'Psychic Doctor' conversant with recent work on psychopathology and the paranormal. The John Silence stories, published in 1908, contained vivid accounts of spiritual possession laced with impressive jargon culled from the proceedings of the Society for Psychical Research. Yet their popularity was short-lived and Blackwood soon found that traditional tales of terror sold better. Montagu Rhodes James, who produced his first batch of *Ghost Stories of an Antiquary* in 1904 and the second in 1911, returned to the shadows and put the phenomenon of evil firmly back into its religious context. 'The technical terms of "occultism", if they are not very carefully handled, tend to put the mere ghost story upon a quasi-scientific plane and call into play faculties quite other than the imagination,' he wrote. His ghosts rose from the dark world of popish superstition and they obeyed no laws that either Freud or the Society for Psychical Research could propound. They came from the grave and they brought its putrefaction with them. 'I can tell you one thing,' ran a schoolboy's shuddering description of one of them, 'he was beastly thin: and he looked as if he was wet all over: and I'm not at all sure that he was alive.' These were not insubstantial spirits but things of horrifying power:

166

one, a dead child in its shroud, was able to tear a man's heart out.

In the real world the struggle between the Roman Catholic Church and the powers of darkness began in the spring of 1895, a fortnight before the Queensberry libel trial. A Parisian journalist calling himself Léo Taxil launched a periodical entitled *Le Palladium régénéré et libre – Directrice Miss Diana Vaughan*. Miss Vaughan was apparently descended from a seventeenth-century emigrant to America who had fornicated with a demon after signing a pact with Satan. In 1889, by order of Lucifer, she had been presented to her fiancé Asmodeus, another demon, in a Masonic lodge in Charleston, Virginia. Taxil then revealed that after meetings with Beelzebub and Moloch she had renounced Satanism. The Roman Catholic authorities were glad to hear this and convoked a congress at Trent in northern Italy to declare war on the devilish practices of the Freemasons. It opened in September 1896 with a procession of nearly two thousand people. Thirty-six bishops attended, another fifty were represented by delegates and the Pope sent a telegram of approval. Diana Vaughan promised to address the congress and describe the various demons she had seen enthroned in American Masonic lodges. When she failed to appear doubts began to be voiced as to whether she really existed, but the Pope still believed in her and told his chaplain to write to her. Eventually, at a meeting in Paris on Easter Monday 1897, Taxil admitted it had all been a hoax.

Not everyone accepted his explanation. The papacy refused to believe it had been duped and the *Contemporary Review* ran an article on 'The Devil in Modern Occultism' suggesting that the real Satanists were not respectable Freemasons but practitioners of black magic who operated on the fringes both of Roman Catholicism and of the Church of England. Diana Vaughan had alleged that evil spirits were raised by the Order of the Golden Dawn, an occultist circle meeting in rooms near Euston Station in London, and when Arthur Edward Waite replied to these charges in his book *Devil Worship in France* he chose to dwell on the Satanic activities of the French occultists instead of questioning Miss Vaughan's existence. There were unpleasant stories coming out of Paris at this time, stories of secret cults where devils and werewolves were called up and where children were sacrificed at the Black Mass. Some of those recruited to the Golden Dawn were certainly meditating similar excesses. Aleister Crowley, who joined at the end of 1898, was convinced that he possessed magical powers and that he should use them in the service of evil. He regarded the

strange sexual appetites revealed by Krafft-Ebing not as perversions but as magical acts which put men in touch with the powers of darkness.

Before Oscar Wilde's downfall his wife had joined the Golden Dawn but had been persuaded to break with it in case she brought discredit on her husband. Arthur Machen was a member and was making experiments which he described as 'halfway between psychology and magic'. The practice of strange rituals, the sense of belonging to an esoteric circle, gave an edge to the writing of fiction and sometimes fact and fantasy became interwoven. Machen wrote a novel in which a boy aspiring to mystic powers slept naked on thorns; Crowley made an aspirant sleep naked on a litter of gorse for ten nights after receiving thirty-two strokes with a gorse switch. Later Crowley and his aspirant dedicated acts of homosexual love to Pan on an altar on a desolate mountain top. Machen meanwhile became convinced that Crowley was hiring ruffians all over London to beat him up. Lord Alfred Douglas, who was editor of *Academy*, asked Machen to write for it on religious matters and soon there were accusations that the magazine had fallen into Roman Catholic hands. Douglas sued for libel and lost his case after Machen admitted writing that the Protestant Reformation was 'the most hideous blasphemy, the greatest woe, the most monstrous horror that has fallen on the hapless race of mortals since the foundation of the world'.

In Protestant eyes there was an obvious connection between popery and Satanism. Anyone superstitious enough to believe in the power of rituals and sacraments to ward off evil would be tempted to dabble with evil himself in the way doctors experimented with disease in order to test the efficacy of their remedies. How could you distinguish the experiment from the real thing, how could you tell whether papists were girding themselves against Satan or preparing to serve him, since both activities involved the same mumbo-jumbo? Worse still, how could you be sure that your Protestant brethren were not papists or Satanists in disguise? In 1894 Walter Walsh lectured to the Protestant Truth Society on 'The Secret Work of the Ritualists'. He claimed that the Church of England was 'literally honeycombed with secret societies', whose object was 'nothing less than that of bringing not only the Ritualists themselves but the whole Church of England into Popish bondage'.

Walsh's campaign against Anglo-Catholicism was greatly assisted by the revelations of Miss Povey, who had been an Anglican nun

for seventeen years in convents founded by Father Ignatius Lyne. Her book *Nunnery Life in the Church of England*, telling of whippings and other harsh penances, was used to great effect by the Protestant Truth Society. John Kensit, the Society's secretary, mounted a display of penitential scourges, 'of well hardened and polished steel, each end of five chains neatly finished with a steel rowel', in his shop window in Paternoster Row. The proprietor of a neighbouring establishment selling such things confirmed that 'for every one he sold to a Catholic he sold three to Church of England people'. Satanists using gorse to induce mystic experiences were gentle compared with this. Father Ignatius was touring America when Miss Povey's book came out and it had an adverse effect on his reception there. At the beginning of his tour he had drawn enthusiastic crowds in New York and also in Boston, even though the Episcopalian Bishop of Boston had banned him from preaching in any Massachusetts church; but when he came back to New York his second mission there was 'a hard and trying ordeal ... those who had flocked to the first now held aloof because of public opinion'.

Public opinion was to harden still further. In a series of official pronouncements beginning in January 1895 the Pope rebuked the Catholic hierarchy in America for its liberal tendencies and in particular for taking part in 'promiscuous assemblies' such as the Parliament of Religions. The papacy, gulled by Taxil's lies, prepared to confront the devil-worshipping Freemasons of the United States. Progressive American Catholics were squeezed out of key positions and reconciliation with Protestants was discouraged. Catholic confidence was soaring – the number of Catholics in America went up from six million in 1880 to twelve million in 1900 – and Protestant fears were growing. In Britain there were similar fears. Figures published in 1897 suggested that Protestants were losing ground while Catholics, helped as in America by Irish immigration, were becoming more influential and more numerous. Walter Walsh's warnings about popish bondage found ready listeners when he returned to the attack in 1897 with *The Secret History of the Oxford Movement*. John Kensit became notorious for breaking up ritualist services in London churches and by 1898 even *The Times* was insisting that a stand must be made against Catholicism within the Church of England. 'If the Bishops cannot or will not make it,' it declared grimly, 'the people have Parliament to appeal to'.

There were those who felt that the time had come for a crusade

to defend Protestant enlightenment and Protestant liberty against Catholic superstition and Catholic tyranny. Josiah Strong had already sounded the clarion call for such a crusade and his book was now at the height of its popularity. And while Strong talked of the Americans and the British standing together because of their shared religious convictions and their Anglo-Saxon racial superiority, others put forward a less crude by equally persuasive view of the matter. Having described the British writer Rudyard Kipling as 'the laureate of the larger England, the great England whose far-strewn empire feels its mystical unity in every latitude and longitude of the globe', the New York critic William Dean Howells went on to claim that Americans were inspired by equally lofty ideals, by 'a patriotism not less large than humanity ... we have made a home here for all mankind. Upon this hypothesis we may claim Mr Kipling, whether he likes it or not, as in some sort American.'

When the Cubans rose in revolt against Spanish rule at the beginning of 1895 there was a chance to move from rhetoric to action. A concerted press campaign throughout the United States demanded intervention on behalf of the rebels. Here surely was a chance to show 'patriotism not less large than humanity' by helping the oppressed to defy Catholic tyranny. But the Cuban revolt came at a time when Anglo-American relations were strained, so that President Cleveland faced what he called 'a tide of jingoism' against Britain as well as against Spain. 'This folly puts an end to my good wholesome life here,' wrote Rudyard Kipling, who had been living in Vermont for the past three years. Fearing war between his native country and his adopted one he took his family back to England in August 1896, by which time the larger England whose laureate he had been called was moving towards war with the Boers in South Africa. However, the British were still capable of being inspired by American imaginings. Stephen Crane, born in New Jersey five years after the end of the Civil War and brought up by a devout father who laid down 'a rigid iron rule for the guidance of all – total abstinence from novel-reading henceforth and forever', nevertheless managed to produce the greatest of all Civil War novels, *The Red Badge of Courage*. It attracted little attention when it appeared in New York and Philadelphia magazines at the end of 1894 but in London a year later it was hailed as a work of genius for its picture of a raw recruit turning into a soldier. 'It is glorious,' said George Wyndham in the *New Review*, 'to see his youth discover courage in the bed-rock of primeval antagonism after

170

the collapse of his tinsel bravado'. Crane had shown how men in battle, like women in love, were 'of the few to whom God whispers in the ear'.

Other critics made clear what it was God was whispering in British ears. News was coming in of an armed raid into Boer territory by Dr Jameson and Sir John Willoughby which ended in disaster but enraptured jingoists in Britain. The *Saturday Review* ran a piece entitled 'In the School of Battle: the Making of a Soldier', rejoicing that Crane's book had come 'at a time like the present, when England is showing that the heart of the nation is as sound after the long Victorian peace as it was in the days of the Armada, that the desperate if lawless enterprise of Jameson and Willoughby is as near to the general heart of the people as were the not very dissimilar enterprises of the old Elizabethan captains'. Major Martin Hume produced a piece called 'The Defeat of the Armada: an Anniversary Object-Lesson' in which he claimed that memories of this great victory were encouraging the British to hold their heads higher. 'For once we have cast aside our habitual reserve and self-depreciation and frankly glory in the qualities which have enabled our race to form the stately brotherhood of free and prosperous nations we call the British Empire.'

In April 1898 war broke out between the United States and Spain over Cuba. A few days later the British Colonial Secretary made a speech stressing the need for Anglo-American friendship. 'What is our next duty?' he asked amid loud cheers, 'It is to establish and to maintain bonds of permanent unity with our kinsmen across the Atlantic. They are a powerful and generous nation. They speak our language, they are bred of our race.' No formal alliance was signed but the two nations shared the same confident imperialism, the same religious fervour. 'I went down on my knees and prayed Almighty God for light and guidance,' President McKinley told his friends, 'and one night late it came to me.' He received divine instructions to annex the Philippines. The Treaty of Paris which ended the war with Spain in December 1898 accordingly ceded the islands to the United States, along with Puerto Rico and Guam, while Cuba was granted its independence. Voices were raised in Congress against the Treaty, claiming that annexation and subjugation were against everything America stood for, but the imperialists won the day. 'We will not renounce our part in the mission of the race, trustee under God of the civilization of the world,' cried Senator Beveridge of Indiana, 'He has marked the American people as his chosen nation to finally

171

lead in the regeneration of the world. This is the divine mission of America.'

Alfred Austin, who had succeeded Tennyson as Poet Laureate, published verses in *The Times* in praise of Jameson. They were jejune and jingoistic, closer to a juvenile adventure story than to poetry, and they failed to convey the full arrogance of British imperialism. It came across better in Kipling's 'Recessional', a poem in honour of the Queen's Diamond Jubilee in 1897. Here Kipling spoke directly to God, 'beneath whose awful hand we hold dominion over palm and pine', and made it clear that he was expected to be the God of war, 'Lord of our far-flung battle-line'. Early in 1898 Kipling went to South Africa to see things for himself and on his return he was hailed by Rider Haggard as one who had 'communed with the very spirit of our race'. Haggard, like Senator Beveridge, claimed 'the divine right of a great civilizing people'. When war with the Boers came in the autumn of 1899 Kipling went back to Africa and stood on the sidelines of battle as a privileged spectator. He was there for the relief of Ladysmith and when he got back to England there was the even greater excitement of the relief of Mafeking. Patriotism took strange forms: on 6 January 1900, at a remote spot in Wales, the mystic weapon known as the sword of Gorsedd was solemnly unsheathed, not to be returned to its scabbard until 'the triumph of the forces of righteousness over the hordes of evil'.

The dawn of a new century seemed to bring this triumph nearer. In 1895, after complaining that Wilde and other decadent writers were 'sapping manliness and making people flabby', Hugh Stutfield had concluded that 'the world seems growing weary after the mighty work it has accomplished during this most marvellous of centuries'. Now these *fin de siècle* literary languors could be dispelled. 'In 1900,' wrote W.B.Yeats, 'everybody got down off his stilts; henceforth nobody drank absinthe with his black coffee; nobody went mad; nobody committed suicide; nobody joined the Catholic church'. On the continent of Europe, it was true, the arts continued along the path which Nordau saw as leading to degeneration. Painting without representational intent, music without melody, writing without plot or moral values, all reflected the futility of human life in a universe stripped of meaning. But then in Europe even the new century was born into uncertainty, for the German Emperor officially decreed that it started in January 1900 while French scientists insisted that it must wait until January 1901. For the British an epoch ended on 22 January

1901 when Queen Victoria died. President McKinley ordered the flag on the White House to be flown at half-mast and when he was assassinated eight months later business was suspended in London on the day of his funeral. Fortified by these mutual courtesies the two nations moved into the twentieth century more convinced than ever of their divine mission. It was summed up in the ode that Archbishop Benson's son wrote for the coronation of the new king:

> Land of Hope and Glory, Mother of the Free,
> How shall we extol thee, who are born of thee?
> Wider still and wider shall thy bounds be set;
> God who made thee mighty make thee mightier yet.

Having mothered the free in Cuba – and less convincingly in the Philippines, where the Filipinos resisted fiercely – the United States did the same thing in Panama in 1903. The Colombians, who ruled Panama, refused to ratify a treaty whereby America leased land to build a canal linking the Atlantic and the Pacific. The American government incited a revolution in Panama, secured the Panamanians their independence and then got them to sign a treaty giving the United States the canal zone in perpetuity. 'I took Panama,' was the terse comment of Theodore Roosevelt, who had become President on the death of McKinley. Famous for his gospel of 'the strenuous life', Roosevelt had been an advocate of America's divine mission since 1895, when he had campaigned for intervention in Cuba. He had been a friend of Rudyard Kipling, who found his muscular Christianity a refreshing contrast after the 'colossal agglomeration of reeking bounders' he said President Cleveland had gathered around him. In later years, when Roosevelt visited England, he made a point of meeting leading writers and telling them how important it was to keep romance alive. 'The most priceless possession of the human race is the wonder of the world,' he declared, 'Yet latterly the utmost endeavours of mankind have been directed towards the dissipation of that wonder'.

There were those who had their doubts. George Bernard Shaw held the triumph of fiction directly responsible for the prevailing mood of belligerent jingoism. 'Ten years of cheap reading have changed the English from the most solid nation in Europe to the most theatrical and hysterical,' he wrote in 1901. Most of the cheap reading consisted of full-blooded adventure stories glorifying the strenuous life and the martial virtues. A.E.W. Mason's immensely successful novel *The Four*

173

Feathers, which came out in the same year as 'Land of Hope and Glory', was the story of a man redeeming himself not from sin but from a charge of cowardice. 'Dost never dream of adventures, Morice?' cried a character in one of Mason's later books, 'A life brimful of them and a quick death at the end?' Even *Dracula* joined in the chorus. 'A brave man's blood is the best thing on this earth when a woman is in trouble,' Van Helsing told a blood donor solemnly. And in the end Jonathan Harker's American friend Quincey Morris, 'a gallant gentleman', sacrificed his life in order to destroy Dracula.

Gallant gentlemen who had no vampires to impale or wars to fight turned to sport. One of the oddest results of the Wilde affair was the success of the Daily Telegraph National Shilling Testimonial to the cricketer W. G. Grace. 'Panic-stricken citizens hastened to contribute lest their sexual normality should be doubted – the connection was subtle but felt at the time to be real'. Already *Harper's Magazine* had asked 'Is American Stamina Declining?' and had insisted that sport was the remedy. 'Especially impress it on the weak, the poorly built and the over-studious, who are not good at any sport, that they are going to make very one-sided men and women, if they live that long, and get them out of doors in all weathers'. It was some consolation that when the Olympic Games were revived in Athens in 1896 the United States won nine of the twelve events. Henry Newbolt's poem 'Vitae Lampada', first published in Queen Victoria's Diamond Jubilee Year and constantly reprinted throughout the Edwardian era, told of a school cricket match and a battle in the desert, the two of them linked by a single cry: 'Play up! play up! and play the game!' It rallied the cricket team and it rallied the soldiers in the sand. And it was the cry which dying heroes 'flung to the host behind', so that those still left alive would be ready to follow their example. The same theme ran through H. A. Vachell's *The Hill*, which was hailed as 'a fine, wholesome and thoroughly manly novel' when it came out in 1905. It culminated in a lyrical celebration of the heroism of Henry Desmond, whom the book followed from his schooldays at Harrow to his death in battle:

To die young, clean, ardent, to die swiftly, in perfect health; to die saving others from death – or worse, disgrace – to die scaling heights; to die and to carry with you into the fuller, ampler life beyond untainted hopes and aspirations, unembittered memories, all the freshness and gladness of May – is not that cause for joy rather than sorrow?

174

There were some questionable assumptions underlying this rhapsody. The first and most obvious was that God approved of war and made the ampler life available to those killed by it. The second was that clean and ardent young men inspired by high sporting ideals would rather die in battle than have their high hopes tainted. They were 'magnificently unprepared,' as Frances Cornford later said of Rupert Brooke, 'for the long littleness of life'. This was all very well in Britain and America, where military service was still voluntary, but it was by no means certain it would survive the introduction of conscription. Another assumption seemed to be that any war in which Britain or America might become involved would be a just one, a genuine struggle against the hordes of evil. But if this was the case, if this struggle had an existence outside the hysteria and theatricality of those drunk with adventure stories, it was not likely to be won by playing the game. Evil had little respect for the courtesies of the games field. Even human enemies could sometimes be bad sports, as the British found when the Boers turned to guerrilla warfare. Kipling brought out a savage poem called 'The Islanders', attacking the comfortable delusion that sport was a breeding ground for heroes. The British were being humiliated by the Boers – 'a little people, few but apt in the field' – because they cared more for games and mock combat than for military preparedness. They must take war seriously, Kipling urged with bitter irony, 'as if it were almost cricket, as it were even your play'.

Sport was not the only route leading from fears of physical degeneracy to the excitements of war. In 1895, as anxiously heterosexual men rushed to give their shillings to the W.G. Grace fund, H.G. Wells gave expression to these same fears in *The Time Machine*. He saw the remote future as 'The Sunset of Mankind', a world without challenge and therefore without response. With nothing to fight for and nothing to fight against, men and women had become effete and enfeebled. 'We are kept keen on the grindstone of pain and necessity, and it seemed to me that here was that hateful grindstone broken at last!' When the Martians invaded the earth in *The War of the Worlds*, published in 1898, the pious preached repentance but an unnamed artilleryman preached defiance – defiance of God's wrath and also of man's conventions. What was the point of people living at all if they hadn't the guts to lay proper hold on life?

They haven't any spirit in them – no proud dreams and no proud lusts;

175

and a man who hasn't one or the other – Lord! what is he but funk and precautions? They just used to skedaddle off to work ... Lives insured and a bit invested for fear of accidents. And on Sundays – fear of the hereafter. As if Hell was built for rabbits!

There was certainly nothing rabbit-like about Bert Smallways, a suburban greengrocer's son who survived the breakdown of society in *The War in the Air*. Having shot his rival 'very accurately through the chest' he shot the man's friend 'much less tidily through the head' and then went to the nearest public house to establish his control of the neighbourhood at gun point. In 1903 Jack London's *The Call of the Wild* produced a canine counterpart to Bert Smallways in the shape of Buck, a family pet stolen from his California home and taken as a sledge dog to the wastes of Alaska. There he reverted to the wild. 'His development (or retrogression) was rapid. His muscles became as hard as iron, and he grew callous to all ordinary pain ... He could eat anything, no matter how loathsome or indigestible.' In the end he lived for the joy of the chase, 'running the wild thing down, the living meat, to kill with his own teeth and wash his muzzle to the eyes in warm blood.' 'There is an ecstasy that marks the summit of life, and beyond which life cannot rise,' the author commented, 'This ecstasy comes to the soldier, war-mad on a stricken field and refusing quarter; and it came to Buck, leading the pack, sounding the old wolf-cry.'

Heraclitus had said that war was father and king of all, producing some as gods and some as men. Did it make men into gods by means of this ecstasy beyond which life could not rise or by means of a hero's death carrying untainted hopes into an ampler life? Was hell built for rabbits and heaven for manly lovers of fair play or was there a pagan Valhalla for those who had reverted to the wild and put themselves beyond conventional ideas of good and evil? As long as the peace was kept, or broken only by minor wars which could be fought by a few brave volunteers, these questions could remain unasked. But if war should indeed become father and king of all, a fight to the finish which required unflinching sacrifice from every household in the land, they would have to be answered. And the answers could only come from God or from someone with unimpeachable authority to speak for him. God would need to whisper in everyone's ear, not just in the ears of a privileged ecstatic few.

176

THE WASTE
LAND

THE TURN OF THE CENTURY BROUGHT MORE TALK OF
cosmic change. 'Like most people of my generation,' wrote H.G. Wells
in 1906 in the introduction to *The Future in America*, 'I was launched
into life with millenial expectations ... it might be in my lifetime
or a little after it, there would be trumpets and shoutings and celestial
phenomena, a battle of Armageddon and the Judgment'. Once he
had had high hopes of the Americans – 'these people can do anything,'
he had cried – but now he saw only 'a dark disorder of growth' fouled
by cruelty and indifference: 'little naked boys, free Americans, work
for Mr Borden, the New York millionaire, packing cloths into bleach-
ing vats, in a bath of chemicals that bleaches their little bodies like the
bodies of lepers'. Before the final trumpeting there would have to
be 'yet another Decline and Fall', that of the callous, careless, jangling
civilization of America. In the same year he published *In the Days
of the Comet*, in which a celestial phenomenon fulfilled his own millenial
expectations. As the earth passed through the tail of a comet it
was enveloped in a strange green vapour which sent all creatures
great and small to sleep. 'The whole world of living things had
been overtaken by the same tide of insensibility; in an hour, at
the touch of this new gas in the comet, the shiver of catalytic change
had passed about the globe.' The gas proved highly subversive,
breathing socialism into men and women as they slept, so that on
waking they overturned all existing authority. Many suspected
that Wells was also looking forward to the collapse of existing sexual
morality. No doubt the comet's undisclosed afflatus would lead men
to share their women as well as their goods, commented one outraged
reviewer.

Astronomers contributed to the book's success by predicting that
in May 1910 the earth would pass through the tail of Halley's comet,

an event awaited with some trepidation on both sides of the Atlantic. A charging rhinoceros might as well worry about colliding with a cobweb, wrote one scientist crisply. Nevertheless panic grew. There was talk of the wrath of God, of universal conflagration, of the human condition being transformed. In Pittsburgh a clergyman announced that the comet's arrival would herald Armageddon and the Second Coming. King Edward VII died on 6 May 1910, just as the tail was about to engulf the earth, and in the skies over Bermuda, as the official salute to the new king George V was being fired, 'the comet's tail flared a decided red end. The head, now distinctly visible, became a ball of fire'. Local people fell to their knees, convinced that this meant the new reign would bring the bloodiest of wars. Some sensed a growing power of evil, a cosmic force which demanded desperate forms of propitiation. In California a prospector named Paul Hammerton made a large wooden cross and crucified himself on it. As he was alone he was only able to nail his feet and one of his hands. When his rescuers came he implored them not to take him down but to complete the work.

The comet came and went without changing very much, though the newspapers followed the celestial happenings with banner headlines and farmers all across the United States retreated to their cyclone cellars. Nevertheless there were those who detected a mysterious transformation. 'In or about December 1910,' wrote Virginia Woolf, 'human character changed'. In her analysis, as in Wells's fiction, the result was the undermining of hierarchy: relations between master and man, between superior and inferior, became more relaxed. Domestic servants no longer lived for ever below stairs in a separate world but instead were 'in and out of the drawing-room, now to borrow the *Daily Herald*, now to ask advice about a hat'. From San Francisco a warning was sounded by Homer Curtiss, Secretary of the Order of Christian Mystics, and his wife Harriette. They revealed that astronomers at Harvard had found that 'the earth and this whole solar system has gone astray and is trailing off away from its path around the great sun Alcyone in the Pleiades towards the constellation Andromeda in the Milky Way . . . there is a terrible commotion in the mental and astral worlds'. It was all very well to be told not to fear cobwebs, but what if the rhinoceros was out of control? The inevitable outcome would be 'a terrible mental revolt against all forms of restraint, both in government and religion'.

While some proclaimed that God was using comets or solar mig-

178

rations to transform the human race others suggested that he was acting directly on the hearts and minds of men and women. 'We stand now on the threshold of one of those mysterious Thought Waves which often arise suddenly in the world's spiritual development and are the very breath of the Living God,' declared the Rev. F.W. Orde Ward in 1908. Mankind was learning that God's creation was Heraclitean and that God himself was not fixity but movement, the sum of the dimensions of an expanding universe: 'The universal acceptance of Christ as the kinetic centre of modern thought, even apart from theology, seems far and away the most characteristic feature of our age.' And since Orde Ward's grasp of modern thought extended to the geometry of curved surfaces, the mathematics of five dimensions and the interdependence of space and time, he could not be written off as a mere religious fanatic. Albert Einstein was only part of the way along the road from his Special to his General Theory of Relativity but Orde Ward had already glimpsed the sort of universe he was revealing and was determined to stake God's claim to it.

Philosophers too were beginning to take note of Heraclitus. Henri Bergson's *Evolution Créatrice* had appeared in 1907, two years after Einstein's Special Theory, and in 1911 William James's Harvard colleague Arthur Mitchell brought out an English translation. While Einstein considered time in relation to space Bergson considered it in relation to thought. Time was continuous and yet when human beings thought about it they split it into separate moments like a cinema film. In the cinema the separate frames were the reality and movement the illusion but in the real world it was the other way about. This meant that what Bergson called 'conceptual thought' was bound to distort reality. 'In vain we force the living into this or that one of our moulds. All the moulds crack.' Philosophy was both too proud and too humble, too ready to squeeze all reality into its moulds but also too ready to acknowledge something called the Unknowable, the Divine Mystery, when the moulds cracked. What was needed was a new kind of thought, a mould which would make everything knowable and so do for philosophy what Einstein was doing for physics.

Those who sought this new way of thinking felt they were embarking on a high adventure, a quest that would unlock the ultimate secrets of the universe. Orde Ward called his book *The World's Quest* and in London in the spring of 1909, at a meeting in Kensington Town Hall, the Quest Society was formed. Its motto was 'Seek and ye shall find' and its declared aims were 'to promote investigation and

comparative study of religion, philosophy and science on the basis of experience and to encourage the expression of the ideal in beautiful forms.' Another objective, not mentioned in the manifesto but soon made apparent in the pages of the Society's journal *Quest*, was to establish spiritualism as a scientific fact. G.R.S. Mead, first President of the Society and editor of the journal, wrote confidently of 'the rising psychic tide' which was engulfing traditional theologians and sceptical materialists alike: 'organized bodies, societies, associations and groups have sprung up like mushrooms in well-nigh every country ... as to the members of such bodies, they must be estimated in millions'. James H. Hyslop, Secretary of the Psychical Research Society of America, was one of Mead's staunchest supporters and one of the first to have his work published in book form under the Society's imprint.

The Quest Society's aspirations meant that serious scholarship was liable to be laced with eccentricity but they also gave the society an affinity with a wider public. 'The impulse which drives men to penetrate into the unexplored region of the Arctic and Antarctic zones finds its counterpart in the minds of those who feel the call to explore undiscovered fields in the region of Psychical Research,' declared *Quest*. A.E.W. Mason expressed much the same sentiment when he said that the best way for a man to know beyond a shadow of a doubt that he would go on living after death was to climb alone in the high Alps. Raymond Blathwayt, writing in the *Fortnightly Review* on 'England's Taste in Literature,' reported that 'Any writer who deals brightly and sincerely with anything that tends towards the rending of the veil hiding the invisible from the visible is certain of a respectful, I may say an enthusiastic, welcome ... upper-class women all over the country are coming under the spell of the mystic'. 'The novelist who succeeds,' wrote another critic, 'is he or she who gives expression and currency to the ideas and aspirations which are floating about the various classes of society'.

The ideas and aspirations in question were theosophy and spiritualism and other fashionable forays into the divine mystery. The new trends in science and philosophy which had discredited the theologians had consoled and encouraged ordinary men and women: 'with Lodge and other leading men of science a belief in the supernatural is not necessarily an indication of feeble intellect or an evidence of incapacity for advanced science.' Sir Oliver Lodge, a highly respected physicist and Principal of Birmingham University, was the author of *The Survival of Man*, in which he proclaimed personal immortality as a scientific

180

fact. He was even able to say what would be carried over into the world to come and what would be left behind: 'Essential belongings, such as memory, culture, education, habits, character and affections – all these, and to a certain extent tastes and interests, – for better for worse, are retained. Terrestrial accretions, such as worldly possessions, bodily pain and disabilities, these for the most part naturally drop away.' 'In consequence of the new evidence,' wrote Frederick Myers confidently, 'all reasonable men, a century hence, will believe in the Resurrection of Christ, whereas in default of the new evidence no reasonable men a century hence would have believed it.' So far from merely corroborating Christianity the new certainties transcended it: 'In the age of Christ Europe felt the first high authentic message from a world beyond our own. In our own age we reach the perception that such messages may become continuous and progressive'.

Blathwayt's article was a progress report. It came out in 1912, a quarter of a century after the *Fortnightly* had asked George Saintsbury to review the state of literature in Britian and America. Saintsbury had suggested then that society could only be saved from its dessicated scepticism and materialism by bathing long and well in the romance of adventure and passion: now it was time to see if the prolonged immersion had had the desired effect. It seemed it had. Blathwayt concluded that 'there is in this country a pretty general arrival at a belief in the after life' and he attributed it to the immense influence wielded by novelists. Saintsbury had made his plea for fiction to an England with relatively few public libraries; now there were hundreds of them, each lending out hundreds of thousands of novels a year. 'Those who decry the work of our Public Municipal Libraries on the ground that works of imagination are extensively read have a poor case to present,' one librarian was reported as saying. Sales were also up: 'novels which formerly sold less than 3,000 copies at six shillings a copy now sell 300,000 copies at sixpence a copy.' All this had stimulated 'a hankering after the unknown' which had completely replaced the old interest in devotional works. 'Theology is now a drug on the market,' Blathwayt added. Fiction had succeeded where faith had failed. Scepticism and materialism had been washed away.

Already the sceptics and the materialists had been confounded in open court. The Rev. Thomas Colley, rector of Stockton in Warwickshire, claimed to have frequent encounters with persons from beyond the grave and in 1907, after being called a fraud by a professional

181

conjuror, he sued for libel. The climax of the case came when Colley described from the witness box how he had been levitated some twenty feet in an attempt to 'grasp a white-attired Egyptian and try to keep him from getting back to invisibility' and how he had then been left clutching the 'psychic clothing' which the dead visitor had been wearing. The jury found in his favour and awarded him damages of £75 with costs. The figure was low – he had claimed £1,000 – but not so low as to be derisory. Although the verdict took into account other libels as well as the fraud charge there was no escaping the fact that the materialization of the dead had been accepted as evidence in a court of law. It seemed that the veil hiding the invisible from the visible was being rent in fact as well as in fiction.

All this made the frontier between reality and fantasy hard to define and even harder to defend. What Bergson and Einstein and other revolutionary thinkers were saying was so odd that most educated men and women regarded it as flying in the face of common sense. Common sense itself was soon to be a casualty, revealed as being neither common nor sense, but in the meantime it was easy to dismiss all aspects of the new thinking as manifestations of eccentricity. Just as the members of the Quest Society saw the Heraclitean view of the universe and the Bergsonian view of thought and the spiritualist view of eternity as converging on the same exciting truth, so their critics saw them all as aspects of the same crack-brained delusion. Neither the inspired minority nor the sceptical majority was very good at separating the pure metal from the dross. And this in its turn meant that the novelists and the story-tellers moved in a very uncertain world when they gave 'expression and currency to the ideas and aspirations floating about the various classes of society'.

Nevertheless Mead's Society was well named. The ancient image of the quest, challenging and mysterious and divinely ordained, promised the highest kind of adventure as well as the loftiest kind of reward. It could accommodate the intellectual and spiritual adventurers as well as the fictitious ones, people with millenial expectations and immortal longings as well as people who simply wanted a good yarn. And the most famous of all Christian quest legends, that of the Holy Grail, had recently become remarkably fashionable in the academic world. From Chicago to Cologne, from the Modern Language Association of America to the Imperial Academy in Vienna, scholars were showing an unprecedented interest in it and many significant contributions to its study had appeared during the past two

decades. In 1908 Robert Eisler gave an important lecture to the Oxford International Congress for the History of Religions, tracing the connections between the Grail and ancient Orphic mysteries, and one of the first papers given to the Quest Society was 'The Romance of the Holy Graal' by A.E. Waite, Arthur Machen's associate in the Order of the Golden Dawn. Machen took little interest at first, telling Waite that all the highest things could be found in Holy Church 'without reference to the Quest of the Sangraal', but he later wrote *The Secret Glory*, a story about a schoolboy entrusted with the Grail, and also *The Great Return*, in which a town was redeemed by its power. He was taken to task by the *Times Literary Supplement* for having the bad taste to allow the Holy Grail to appear to 'common farmers, village grocers and the like'.

Waite's paper led him into lengthy controversy with Miss Jessie Weston, who took exception not only to his pretentious spelling but also to his suggestion that the story of the Grail was mere romance. She pointed out that in mediaeval times, when the legend was first written down, 'more was believed, more was known, than the official guardians of faith and morals cared to admit ... this undercurrent of yearning and investigation was concerned with the search for the source of Life – Life physical, Life Immortal'. She went on to argue that the Grail was an ancient symbol of female sexuality while the lance which figured so prominently in the legend was patently phallic. Neither had anything to do with Christ's blood. They were memories of a pagan ritual in which men overcame death without the help of the crucified Christ. She later published in *Quest* a story called 'The Ruined Temple' in which a traveller came upon the remains of a Phoenician altar sacred to Adonis. He fell asleep and found himself facing a slab on which lay a corpse: 'this was not a dead man; it was *Death Itself*'. Then, after a mystical re-enactment of the ancient Grail ritual with a chalice filled with blood and a spear which became 'a quivering shaft of flame', he found that he had conquered death and was 'drawing closer, closer, to the very Fount of Life itself'.

Miss Weston was to publish two authoritative accounts of the Grail ritual, *The Quest of the Holy Grail* in 1913 and *From Ritual to Romance* in 1921. In 1922 her second book was to be acknowledged by the expatriate American poet T.S. Eliot as the principal inspiration for his poem 'The Waste Land'. Eliot appreciated the significance of the Grail story as a convergence of fantasy and reality. He understood the pagan roots from which it sprang as well as the Christian

aspirations which had been grafted onto it. Others were less percipient. As the shadow cast by fiction upon the real world lengthened, as the Edwardian cult of heroic adventure darkened into the First World War cult of heroic self-sacrifice, devotees turned increasingly to the Grail legend. It was after all not just about the personal redemption of a hero but about restoring a whole society to health. The Grail was guarded by a wounded or sick King in a castle in the midst of a Waste Land. The King's mysterious weakness could only be cured and the Waste Land brought back to life if a brave knight could be found to undertake the quest. In August 1914 the relevance of the legend seemed clear, at least in the world of fantasy, as Watson talked of God's curse on a degenerate world and as Sherlock Holmes looked forward to men dying in order that England might be cleaner and better and stronger.

In reality the Grail legend was not primarily about fighting or about dying. The knight's business was not to lay down his life but to ask a certain question, the nature of which was not revealed. It was a ritual of testing, of initiation, but not of sacrifice. If it was a fertility rite it was not the sort in which a god or a hero had to die before the earth would bring forth its bounty. There was no propitiation of the forces of evil. In one early German version the Grail was said to have been the talisman of those angels who had refused to take sides in the conflict between God and Satan. The two great adversaries who had waged war in heaven must both take blame for the desolation of the Waste Land. Even the iconoclastic Nietzsche was closer than conventional Christians to the Grail story: it looked back to a world before good and evil just as he looked forward to one beyond good and evil. His ideas were at last beginning to be taken seriously in Britain and America. In 1909 the *Westminster Gazette*, a Christian journal, said that whatever his faults he was at least 'at war with frivolity and the mere craving for pleasure and ease which infects the modern world'. *Quest* suggested that his evolutionary theory of morals was the necessary counterpart to Bergson's thinking. An unchanging view of good and evil was as outdated as a fixed concept of the universe: 'The virtues of yesterday are no use today save as stepping-stones towards higher ideals.' When the quest reached its goal, when all the strands of the new thinking came together, the resulting transformation of human character would be far more fundamental than the whimsical fancies of Virginia Woolf.

Most readers on both sides of the Atlantic were more interested

in present adventuring than in future transformation. Hilaire Belloc scored a success with *Hills and the Sea*, a collection of short pieces about two men who pitted themselves against the elements. When their leaky boat was hit by a gale 'there were no men on earth save these two who would not have got her under a try-sail and a rag of storm-jib with fifteen reefs and another; not so the heroes. Not a stitch would they take in.' Their valiant stupidity was duly rewarded: 'when they slept the Sea Lady, the silver-footed one, came up through the waves and kissed them in their sleep; for she had seen no such men since Achilles ... The high gods, which are only names to the multitude, visited these men.' Even the most eccentric member of the Quest Society would have hesitated to write such stuff, yet Belloc's readers loved it. And they loved it partly because of its hint of auto-biography, because these fantastic things might just have happened in real life to Belloc and his trusty companion.

It seemed that fortune not only favoured the brave but touched them with some kind of divinity. In some strange way they would redeem society simply by being brave. The *Fortnightly* followed up Blathwayt's account of literary tastes with a poem in which Laurence Binyon called upon the young and valiant to bring about this unspeci-fied and miraculous transformation:

> High-beating hearts, to your deep vows be true!
> Live out your dreams, for England lives in you.

Although Binyon did not yet know it five high-beating hearts had just lived out a dream which was to have an immense impact in Britain and America. Captain Scott and his four companions died of exposure and frostbite in the Antarctic early in 1912 and a year later, when news came of the discovery of their bodies, they became instant heroes. Of Scott it was said that 'his dominant thought was the placing of his country in the van of heroism. The dream in his far-away blue eyes was scarcely so much success as sacrifice.' Lieutenant Oates, one of his companions, was said to have 'embraced Death, the bride whom he had gone out to seek in the wilderness, with all the purpose of his strong heart.' In life the two men had been very different. Scott had been a harsh and incompetent leader and towards the end, when Oates was in agony from gangrene, he told him he was 'a terrible hindrance'. At last, almost delirious with pain, Oates left the tent and disappeared into the blizzard. It was an act of desperation, a form of suicide committed by a man driven beyond endurance by

Scott's hectoring, and when the details emerged from the diaries his mother made it clear that she regarded Scott as her son's murderer.

Nobody was interested in the recriminations of Mrs Oates. 'Greater love hath no man than this,' Christ had said, 'that a man lay down his life for his friends.' Everyone was sure this was what Oates had done. As for Scott, he was a man inspired, a prophet who had foreseen what wonders his heroism would work. 'Had we lived,' he wrote in his 'message to the public' from the tent in which he died, 'I should have had a tale to tell of the hardihood, endurance and courage of my companions which would have stirred the heart of every Englishman.' His Scottish friend J.M. Barrie hastened to correct the narrow word 'Englishman'. 'Almost every Briton alive,' he wrote to *The Times*, 'has been prouder these last days because a message from a tent has shown how the breed lives on'. Members of the search party who had found the bodies said it was 'a ghastly sight' but Barrie revamped their accounts to suit his own imaginings. 'Scott and his comrades emerge out of the white immensities, always young,' he told an audience at St Andrew's University. King George v set aside precedent and paid his tribute in person at the memorial service at St Paul's Cathedral in London. What Queen Victoria had been unable to do even for the greatest of her subjects her grandson was prepared to do for the members of an unsuccessful polar expedition, one of whom had helped to drive another to suicide.

Barrie's vision of immortal explorers emerging from white immensities was a new and more powerful version of Mead's doctrine that the quest for adventure and the quest for eternal truth were two sides of the same coin. But there had been an ominous change in the coin's superscription. It was not now about quest but about sacrifice. 'We are showing that Englishmen can still die with a bold spirit fighting it out to the end,' Scott had written. His expedition had become not a quest but a combat, a battle which must be fought out to the end. Against whom was he fighting with such a bold spirit? Not against his rival Amundsen, for he and his expedition had already reached the Pole and returned from it. Not against the elements, unless desolation and icy winds could be personified or regarded as demonic. Yet the image was one of conflict rather than search. Scott was not like the Grail hero, facing mysterious dangers in order to resolve an enigma which transcended good and evil. He was like a soldier on the field of battle, ready to lay down his life because there were still good and evil in the world and the one must triumph over the other.

186

The road that led from the fictitious self-sacrife of Henry Desmond to the presumed self-sacrifice of Scott and Oates was already well marked out. In 1908, when the archaeologists dug up the temple of Artemis Orthia where Spartan youths had been ritually flogged, *The Times* pointed out that this gruesome practice had been a relic of earlier human sacrifices – the goddess had had to be content with the blood of the living instead of the blood of the dead – but it also reminded its readers that such 'rigorous discipline' was necessary in societies dedicated to war. If the ordeal was a substitute for one kind of sacrifice it was also a preparation for another. 'You can bear a spot of pain, Pete old lad, can't you?' said bluff Dr Wadd to Peter Ackerley as he prepared to lance his poisoned hand with a pair of borrowed scissors, 'Or do you want an anaesthetic?' The boy told him to go ahead and when his palm was slit he turned pale but did not cry out. 'It was what my father would have called "a jolly good show",' commented his brother later after Peter had been killed in battle. In 1909 Charles Doughty's verse drama *The Cliffs* showed a ceremony in which those about to die for their country kissed a basket of earth and then had some sprinkled on their heads to show that they looked forward to the hero's grave for which they were destined. Like Christ in the garden of Gethsemane they must come willingly to the sacrifice and contemplate their approaching agony without flinching.

Strictly speaking such comparisons were blasphemous. Christianity taught that the crucifixion was 'a full perfect and sufficient sacrifice, oblation and satisfaction for the sins of the whole world'. There was no need for a repeat performance and when Paul Hammerton tried to give one he was pronounced insane. And if the re-enactment of Christ's suffering was madness and impiety in the eyes of traditional theologians it was even more of an absurdity in the eyes of those who trod the converging paths of the new thinking. *Quest* had called yesterday's virtues, 'stepping-stones towards higher ideals' and the supposed virtue of self-immolation was surely one of them. If Myers was right and messages from the world beyond were becoming continuous and progressive, if there was an easier route to immortality than the one carved out on Calvary, what point was there in the idea that he who would save his life must lose it? If the ferment of the past few years meant anything at all, if mankind really was experiencing a thought wave breathed out by the living God, then the signposts of the new thinking might possibly point

187

to a hero's quest but not to a hero's death.

Towards the end of the Boer War, as H.A.Vachell was meditating Henry Desmond's death in battle, Thomas Hardy had produced a poem announcing the demise of the god of war, Kipling's 'Lord of our far-flung battle-line'. 'The Battle-god is god no more,' he had proclaimed triumphantly. Now, a decade later, he published in the *Fortnightly Review* in March 1912 a more ambitious poem entitled 'God's Funeral: an allegorical conception of the present state of Theology'. In suitably ponderous stanzas he described how he had seen, at twilight on a darkling plain, a line of mourners who bore the now defunct ruler of the universe to his last resting place. They blamed themselves for his birth as well as for his death – 'Whence came it we were tempted to create One whom we can no longer keep alive?' – and they wept bitterly for the happy assured days that were gone, the days when life had been lapped and cradled in the certainty of the divine presence. The language and imagery were predictable enough – the darkling plain was very like those Matthew Arnold and Ambrose Bierce had glimpsed, while the penitence of the mourners echoed Nietzsche's insistence that man was the murderer of God – but there were also some topical touches. *Peter Pan*, first produced in 1904, was fast becoming an annual favourite and as Hardy's mourners lamented that they could no longer keep God alive his readers might perhaps have recollected the call for children in the audience to clap out their belief in order to save the dying Tinkerbell. Now God had fallen victim to an insufficiently enthusiastic audience. His shrivelled form lay like a deflated child's balloon, lacking the breath of faith which alone could give it substance and reality.

The parallel could be pushed further, for it seemed that the young and trusting were as ready to save God from the theologians as the excited and adventurous had been to save Sherlock Holmes from Conan Doyle. Hardy noted that all the mourners were aged – 'lined on the brows, scoop-eyed and bent and hoar' – while in the background youths and maidens protested that this premature interment of the deity was a hideous mistake. 'Still he lives for us!' they cried, pointing to a gleam of light on an otherwise dark horizon. But their elders refused to see it and continued on their funereal way. Thirty years ago Nietzsche had greeted the image of God's death as 'a glimpse of things which put me in advance of all other men' but now the position was reversed. Orthodoxy itself, 'the present state of theology', was unable to keep God alive and only the young, the unconventional,

188

the advanced, were sure of his existence.

Those who had followed the new developments in science and philosophy found it easy to interpret Hardy's metaphor. The god of the old men was dead, the god who had been thought to preside over a fixed and unchanging universe, and a dynamic god of Heraclitean fire now lived in the hearts and minds of the young. Grail enthusiasts could go further. For them the god who had died was the one who had set good against evil by waging war in heaven. The ancient vision of a world not polarized into good and evil could therefore be recaptured: perhaps the Waste Land could be restored. More practical men and women concentrated on the reality of peace rather than on its spiritual or intellectual foundations. In America a World Peace Foundation was established, endowed with a million dollars by the industrialist Edwin Ginn. It was followed by the Church Peace Union, which included Catholics, Protestants and Jews. The steel magnate Andrew Carnegie was so sure of its success that when he funded it he stipulated what further use should be made of his money once war had been abolished.

On the other hand Marxist Socialists, for whom religion was the opium of the people, wished to slay the God of war not with capitalist millions but with international working-class solidarity. In October 1912, while Hardy's readers were still considering the rights and wrongs of God's funeral, the Church of England Congress considered the rights and wrongs of Socialism. Did British Socialism follow Karl Marx or Jesus Christ? While one lay speaker regretted that 'members of religious bodies, including the Established Church, were coquetting with Socialism', the Bishop of Hull insisted that not all Socialists were 'predatory, revolutionary, materialistic and anti-Christian'. When the Second Socialist International met three weeks later to inveigh against the escalating war in the Balkans only thirteen out of more than four hundred delegates were British and none was American.

In the Balkans the god of battles was by no means dead. On 18 October 1912 the Archbishop of Sofia held high a crucifix bearing the ancient promise 'In this sign shalt thou conquer' and the King of Bulgaria called on 'all those who love justice and progress' to support a crusade against the Ottoman Turks. The British and Foreign Bible Society distributed copies of the New Testament to Bulgarian troops, earning shouts of 'Three cheers for England!', but *The Times* remarked sourly that 'neither Europe nor the Christians in the Ottoman Empire

189

need thank King Ferdinand for introducing sectarian issues into what is mainly a political and racial struggle'. The Archbishop of Canterbury was ready to back his own country's war preparations – his wife had recently launched one of Britain's most powerful battleships – but he did not care for King Ferdinand's god of war. He instructed his clergy instead to pray to the God of peace, 'that the course of this world may be so peaceably ordered by thy governance that thy Church may joyfully serve thee in all godly quietness'. In the United States the World Peace Foundation and the Church Peace Union began to make preparations for a World Peace Congress in Switzerland on 2 August 1914. The Socialist International planned to meet in Belgium at the end of July and the orgy of peacemaking would be completed by an international peace congress in Vienna and by a Catholic Peace Conference at Liège in Belgium on 4 August.

August 1914 brought not peace but the sword. German armies entered Belgium and attacked Liège on the day the Catholic Peace Conference was to have met. European nations mobilized their forces, trains were commandeered, delegates to the congresses were unable to reach their destinations. The bureau of the Second International met in Brussels to hear French delegates announce that their German comrades had failed to hold their government in check and so it was the duty of all Frenchmen to fight for their country and for civilization. British Socialists followed suit and *The Times* was soon able to proclaim that 'the International Socialist League has been crushed out of existence'. The god of war was proving more than a match for the Marxists, even if he was only a figment of bourgeois imagining.

Some of his other opponents put up a more determined fight. Mead wrote a *Quest* editorial declaring that governments would now put the welfare of the world above their own petty interests. 'Humanity as a whole would have at long last acted morally for the first time in its history,' he concluded. As late as April 1915 he could still convince himself that 'the devotion of the nation in its public prayers is taking a higher form of petition than ever before. There is much to show that the majority have become ashamed of the old "god of battle" order of procedure.' When the Archbishop of Canterbury preached on 2 August 1914, as Britain stood on the brink of war, he praised the international peace movements and studiously avoided any talk of a divine call to arms. Nevertheless he proclaimed that 'the thing which is now active in Europe is not the work of God but of the Devil'; and it was this insistence on the diabolical nature of

190

the enemy that was to prove the divine warlord's greatest strength.

As soon as the British entered the war they took charge of all transmission of news across the Atlantic. Most American newspapers gave the impression that God was on Britain's side and the British press assured its readers that they had the unbounded sympathy of their transatlantic cousins. 'The American citizen who in the crowd before Buckingham Palace cried out to King George "New York is with you" did not misrepresent the feelings of this country,' wrote the American correspondent of *The Times*. Carnegie issued a public apology, eagerly copied in the British press, because his attempts to avert war had been unduly friendly towards the German Kaiser. 'We advocates of heavenly peace and foes of hellish war must not fail to expose and denounce the guilty originators thereof,' he wrote, 'I feel that Britain was in honour bound to protect Belgium'. The World Peace Foundation was stopped in its tracks and its director David Starr Jordan held a breakaway congress in Chicago and enlisted the aid of the motor millionaire Henry Ford. 'We're going to get the boys out of the trenches before Christmas,' Ford declared, 'I've chartered a ship and some of us are going to Europe'. Cardinal Gibbons gave his support to the venture but withdrew it after he had been mauled by the press. When Ford and his peace delegates finally crossed the Atlantic in December 1915 the British navy made sure that they were unable to influence British opinion or get anywhere near the boys in the trenches.

The lord of the far-flung battle-line seemed to be giving the British powerful support. On 23 August 1914, according to an account written by a British officer, an angel on a white horse with a flaming sword stopped the German advance at Mons. Other stories told of skies filled with angels on outstretched wings and of a figure in golden armour recognized as St George by the British and as St Michael by the French. 'The radiant forms of the spiritual hierarchies can only be made manifest to mortal eye in a form which the beholder can interpret,' declared the *Occult Review* by way of explaining these differences of interpretation. The *Evening News* pointed out that the tales of supernatural assistance seemed to spring from 'The Bowmen', a story by Arthur Machen which it had published at the end of September 1914. One critic said that a typed copy of 'The Bowmen' had been sent to him with a statement that it had been taken down 'from the lips of a wounded soldier in a London hospital'. When Machen insisted that he had made the whole thing up he was accused

of irreverence and disloyalty. 'To have entered upon a scene of such awful havoc and desolation for a story of mystery is in itself, I think, an act very near to sacrilege,' wrote Harold Begbie in his book *On the side of the angels: a reply to Arthur Machen.*

If God and his angels were on the side of the British it followed that Satan and his legions were on the side of the Germans. Shortly before the war a group of British theologians had published a symposium entitled *Is there a Hell?*, pointing out that 'mankind has abandoned the conception of hell as a real pit full of fire and brimstone'. The Devil was a myth and the only punishment in store for sinners was the absence of God. But now it was necessary to re-invent the Devil and all his works. Ironically enough it was an admirer of Germany who was one of the first to do so, in a letter to *The Times* four days after war broke out. It was tragic, he wrote, that the British should find themselves at war with a people so much like themselves. 'It makes one despair of human intelligence unless it is believed that this calamity may be ascribed to an anti-human, devilish influence which has found its instrument in the extraordinary arrogance of the Emperor William.' 'The idea that a monarch of modern Europe could fulfil in his person an ancient prophecy of the coming of Antichrist is astounding to twentieth century thought,' wrote the *Occult Review*, 'yet this conception is coming home to us today'. *The Faith and the War*, a collection of essays by church leaders in Britain, asserted among other things that Germany had abandoned Christianity and reverted to paganism. *The Times* claimed to have known for some time that the Germans had re-established the worship of Odin and the Chancellor of the Exchequer proclaimed that their aim was the destruction of Christianity.

It was to be expected that churchmen would back the secular authorities and portray the conflict as a holy war against the forces of evil. What was more surprising was the alacrity with which unconventional thinkers came round to the same view. The very people who had been least conformist in peace were most fervent in war. By November 1914 Bergson was alleging that the values for which the Allies stood were in line with the creative evolutionary processes of the universe whereas those of the Germans were opposed to them. Miss Weston turned away from the Grail that stood beyond good and evil and wrote instead of a chalice which sacrilegious Germans had filled with swine's flesh in a church near Verdun. From this and other incidents she deduced that a failure to defeat and punish Germany would be

'an act of treason against humanity'. Orde Ward used his religious and scientific insights to develop a theory that conflict was as central to the moral universe as energy was to the physical one. 'Without conflict there would be no rest, without evil no good ... We can no more stop war than we can stop the tides or the stars in their courses ... We should recognize in the Spirit of War the Spirit of Love ... We have no choice but to fight and fight for ever'. The resurrected god of battle and the newly revealed dynamic Heraclitean god had become one and the same. Algernon Blackwood joined Orde Ward in the pages of *Quest* to greet the war as a miracle, a triumph of spiritual values over the material world. The Dean of St Paul's hoped that it had come in time to save the British from 'godless civilization, a disease of which nations die by inches'.

Angelic helpers and questing heroes and novelists' miracles were not enough for the warring nations. They needed something more sublime and they found it in Christianity's ultimate fantasy, the re-enactment of Christ's passion. *The Treasury*, a journal run by a clergyman later made chaplain to King George v, carried an article called 'The Precursor': 'before God permitted this passion of the human race in which, reverently be it said, the Lord Christ is once more crucified in all Christianity and the forces of evil are let loose in hideous conflict against the powers of good, He sent his precursor'. The precursor was Captain Scott, whose voice in the great white wilderness of Antarctica had repeated the Baptist's cry in the wilderness of Judaea. Even before the outbreak of war Scott's deeds had been described as 'equally as great as any committed on a battlefield' and now it seemed that his death had pointed the way ahead to the sacrificial slaughter just as the death of John the Baptist had pointed the way to Calvary. *The Last Crusade*, Orde Ward's collection of patriotic verses, was hailed as 'profoundly religious'. It opened with 'The Eternal Passion', a vision of Christ sharing the agonies of British soldiers: 'He suffers and delights to die, In awful pangs and seeks his Calvary.' Other poems described the Germans as the murderers of God, casting down his cross and dancing on the broken body.

Orde Ward's recurring phrase, 'Our Lord is crucified again in France', was soon taken up by other writers who had the English Channel between them and the battlefield. But in the horror and desolation of Flanders Wilfred Owen had a more ironic version of the fantasy:

For 14 hours yesterday I was at work – teaching Christ to lift his cross by numbers, and how to adjust his crown; and not to imagine he thirst till after the last halt; I attended his Supper to see that there were no complaints; and inspected his feet that they should be worthy of the nails. I see to it that he is dumb and stands to attention before his accusers. With a piece of silver I buy him every day and with maps I make him familiar with the topography of Golgotha.

There were other bridges from fantasy to reality. British soldiers were subject to Field Punishment Number One: they could be tied to a post for several hours a day, sometimes within range of enemy fire. Although this was popularly known as 'crucifixion' an artist illustrating it in a War Office manual was told peremptorily to change his drawing and make the post look 'entirely unlike the Cross'. Those at home might perhaps draw comfort from the notion that their loved ones had played the part of the Son of God but in the field the metaphor had its dangers, especially if it suggested that Christ's tormentors were not the Germans at all but his superior officers.

The real value of the fantasy lay not in comforting the bereaved but in influencing public opinion in neutral countries, above all in America. Owen Wister, an able publicist of the Allied cause, produced *The Pentecost of Calamity*, saying that an American declaration of war would be 'a great stride in national and spiritual maturity' and painting the familiar picture of Germans exulting in fiendish cruelties while martyred Belgians and Frenchmen were transfigured and brought to glory. At the beginning of 1917 Winston Churchill and sixty-four other public figures signed an appeal to Christians in America not to support moves for a negotiated peace because 'the just God who withheld not His son from the cross would not look with favour upon a people who put their fear of pain and death above the holy claims of righteousness and justice'. But the British did not have it all their own way. A group of pro-German intellectuals led by Professor Yandell Henderson of Yale sponsored C. L. Droste's *Germany's Golgotha*, yet another image of Christ re-crucified: 'As during the last days of July 1914 Germany prayed in its Gethsemane and there was kissed by its Iscariot in the shape of England, so it now finds itself on its Golgotha, with the prayer of supreme beauty on its lips: "Father, forgive them, for they know not what they do".'

Nevertheless most Americans accepted that it was the Allies who were imitating Christ. As early as January 1915 a Massachusetts preacher told his flock that they should 'catch the spirit of battle'

because they had been anointed by God as champions of Christian civilization. A few weeks later a British clergyman said that the war had halted what he called 'the German conspiracy' in the United States and in May, after the sinking of the *Lusitania* by a German submarine had resulted in the loss of 128 American lives, a Baptist minister in Pennsylvania proclaimed that the German government was in league with hell. But he also prayed that America should not be drawn into the fighting and when the *New York Times* conducted a survey of opinion on the issue most of the ministers of religion who were polled said that the Germans were guilty of murder but few called for war. Nevertheless well over a hundred clergymen took part in New York's Preparedness Parade of May 1916. 'I advocate it because of its moral and spiritual value,' wrote one of those pressing for compulsory military training, 'It will make our young men better Americans, better citizens and better Christians.' After the United States declared war on Germany in April 1917 American religious leaders took part eagerly in the great game of reading God's mind. 'He is the most powerful, the most active and the most important of all who are influencing the war,' wrote one, 'He is delaying victory to either side in the deadlock until men shall comprehend that the war is being waged between spiritual principles and vital philosophies rather than between mere armed forces.'

Spiritualists did not need to be so presumptuous. Instead of asking God why the war had happened they could ask the dead. Mrs Elsa Barker, whose *Letters from a Living Dead Man* had caused a stir in America in 1913, got in touch with her deceased friend Judge Hatch again and was told that 'it is because man has not made moral progress corresponding to his material progress that evil elemental beings who fear for their rule in the elemental kingdom have come so near to succeeding in their attacks on the human race'. At a spiritualist séance in March 1916 Sir Oliver Lodge was told by his dead friend Frederick Myers that 'man has made the earth plane into such a hotbed of materialism and selfishness that man again has to atone by sacrifice of mankind in the prime of their physical life'. Through Myers he was able to speak to his son Raymond, who had been killed in action, and an account of these conversations was later published under the title *Raymond, or Life and Death*. As the killing grew more monstrous the need to believe in personal survival became more desperate. Hereward Carrington, a psychic investigator who had once been extremely sceptical, now seemed totally convinced. His book *Psychical Phenomena*

and the War listed cases in which relatives had received messages from the fallen and insisted that 'These experiences can be repeated in the lives of every mourner if they will only put aside prejudice'. The *Occult Review*, now enjoying unprecedented popularity, poured scorn on 'the orthodox who believe that those who have passed over are dead and asleep and unable to communicate with us'. On the contrary, it declared confidently, most of those killed were 'probably helping to form a Britain or Empire beyond the grave, a better Britain or Empire than exists now on the material plane'.

The idea of posthumous patriotic empire-building might seem grotesque but it was less damaging than the fantasies which centred on Christ. 'I've been a Christian all my life,' one recruit remarked in 1914, 'but this war is a bit too serious.' Here in a single sentence was the cold truth of the matter. The war required men to disobey Christ's greatest commandment and if they were to do so as free human beings, rather than as beasts driven to the slaughter, then they must decide what it was that was too serious, what it was that forced them to set Christian morality aside. Nor was it only Christian morality that must go. They must also defy the God of the Old Testament, as Wilfred Owen saw very clearly in 'The Parable of the Old Man and the Young'. He looked back beyond the crucifixion to the earlier sacrifice Jehovah had demanded of Abraham, the sacrifice of his son Isaac. Abraham had been told at the last minute to sacrifice a ram instead but now, as the hideous ritual was played out again in the trenches, the old man refused to obey the divine command because the ram represented his pride. And so he slew his son 'and half the seed of Europe, one by one'. Abraham had been shown that it was not necessary to sacrifice man to the supposed needs of God but nobody was going to stop the world's rulers from sacrificing God to the supposed needs of man.

In the summer of 1916, in a cottage in New Hampshire, Aleister Crowley crucified a frog which he had baptized as Jesus of Nazareth. 'Give thou place to me, O Jesus,' he cried, 'thine aeon is passed; the Age of Horus is arisen by the Magick of the Master, the Beast that is Man'. He now regarded himself as the Great Beast, the Antichrist who would take over the dominion of the world. His gesture in the name of the supposed powers of evil was puny beside those being made in the name of the alleged powers of good. 'The state, the nation, national honour, became the idols and both sides voluntarily sacrificed their children to these idols,' wrote the psychologist Erich

Fromm many years later. 'The ubiquity of human sacrifice,' said Arthur Koestler, 'is one of the earliest manifestations of the paranoid trend in the human psyche.' But human sacrifice, as anthropologists have shown, has always required that the victim be sinner as well as saviour. He must himself be in some sense guilty of the sin he is expiating. And it was unthinkable that the war dead should be seen in this way. They must be idealized, apotheosized, even deified, in order that the carnage should be raised to a level higher than mere human sacrifice. The reversal of roles was complete: just as it was man rather than God who demanded the sacrifice so it must be God rather than man who was the victim. Christ must be re-crucified in the human imagination whether or not he liked it, whether or not he survived it.

When the killing at last came to an end the full power of the re-crucifixion myth was revealed. From being an offensive and rather silly idea in the minds of people like Orde Ward it had become a national necessity. On 11 November 1920, the second anniversary of the armistice, a soldier who had been so badly mangled that his identity was unknown was buried in Westminster Abbey while King George v stood in mute respect before his coffin. 'Oh, 'tis Christ that passes,' declared a versifier in *The Times*, 'In thee, poor soldier, who didst die for me.' A year later a similar ceremony took place at Arlington National Cemetery in the presence of President Harding. Honoured above all men the two unidentified corpses took on a glory that was more than human.

Such were the fantasies of war. Sir Philip Gibbs, who covered the London ceremony for the *Illustrated London News*, had just published a book called *The Realities of War*. He had described unknown warriors as they actually were – 'bodies, and bits of bodies, and clots of blood, and green, metallic-looking slime . . . Scraps of flesh, booted legs, blackened hands, eyeless heads'. Now he had to feel respectful and uplifted as putrefied remains were honoured by those who had commanded the carnage. He did his best, speaking of 'remembrances, ghosts, pities, subconscious and unuttered thoughts,' but his piece lacked the pious assurance which was expected of him. Nor was he alone. All over the country the two aspects of the dead, the disembodied memories held sacred by the bereaved and the appalling realities which haunted the survivors, had to live cheek by jowl. In the same house there might be those who woke from nightmares with the smell of dead men in their nostrils and those who knew only a face in a fading

197

photograph and saw it transfigured and sanctified.

Slowly the pious and the orthodox realized what it was they had done. Already an angry clergyman had complained about men in battle thinking of death as 'a hideous foe'. 'The war has brought back again much that underlay the old pagan conception of death,' he thundered, 'It has not brought the idea of death as a friend.' He was displeased to learn that men who had seen rats eat their dead comrades – 'they go into a man at one place, they come out at another' – found it difficult to think of death as a blessed reunion with God. Those who peddled the fantasy of Christ re-crucified implied that the imitation of Christ gave a Christ-like ability to rise again from the dead, or at least to inherit the eternity he had promised. Those who had survived the slaughter had their doubts. They insisted that the dead be honoured – anyone who failed to observe the Armistice Day silence was liable to be roughly handled – but they did not do so out of respect for Christian doctrine. 'The leaders of the Church seem to have no idea of the extent to which the great mass of the people are hostile to, and not merely out of contact with, organized religion,' wrote Canon Green of Manchester in November 1919. The faithful continued to sing that 'a thousand ages in thy sight are like an evening gone' but in truth it had taken little more than five years for the shadows to lengthen in the quiet places which God inhabited. Whatever name they went by – the human soul, the human spirit, the human imagination – these places would never be the same again after the assaults that had been made upon them. The gun carriages that rolled to Westminster and to Arlington were part of God's funeral procession.

POSTSCRIPT

On the day after the Arlington ceremony T.S. Eliot left England for Lausanne to be treated for what he called 'an emotional derangement'. 'It is a commonplace,' he later remarked, 'that some forms of illness are extremely favourable, not only to religious illumination, but to artistic and literary composition'. In Lausanne he wrote the first draft of 'The Waste Land'. Readers familiar with Miss Weston's book and with *The Golden Bough* would find, he explained, 'certain references to vegetation ceremonies'. In the first section, originally called 'The death of Saint Narcissus' but later changed to 'The Burial of the Dead', he found himself discussing horticulture with a man called Stetson who had been with him in an ancient battle long ago. 'That corpse you planted last year in your garden,' he inquired, 'Has it begun to sprout? Will it bloom this year?'

Ezra Pound thought it was 'a damned good poem, about enough to make the rest of us shut up shop.' Eliot said it was 'a personal and wholly insignificant grouse against life, a piece of rhythmical grumbling' and he shrugged off attempts by critics to interpret it as 'criticism of the contemporary world'. The contemporary world had other and more exciting fantasies to explore. *The Strand Magazine*, Sherlock Holmes's happy home, had published an article by Arthur Conan Doyle claiming that fairies had been photographed by two little girls at Cottingley in Yorkshire. That story was hardly cold before Doyle was in the news again, this time commenting on the fact that Lord Carnarvon had died in Cairo shortly after he had opened up the tomb of the Pharaoh Tutankhamun. 'An evil elemental may have caused Lord Carnarvon's illness,' Doyle told reporters, 'One does not know what elementals existed in those days, nor what their power might be. The Egyptians knew a great deal more about those things than we do.' At the precise moment of Carnarvon's death all the lights

199

in Cairo went out and no satisfactory explanation of the power failure was forthcoming, even though Lord Allenby as High Commissioner took the matter up with the English engineer in charge of the electricity supply. At home in England, also at the precise moment of death, Carnarvon's favourite dog howled a terrible howl and expired.

There were others as well as outraged pharaohs who might have been expected to call up an evil elemental. Carnarvon had infuriated the press on both sides of the Atlantic by giving exclusive coverage of his expedition to *The Times*. 'The tomb is not his private property,' raged the *Daily Express*, 'By making an exclusive secret of the contents of the inner tomb he has ranged against him the majority of the world's most influential newspapers.' But it did not occur to anyone that the anger of an excluded reporter might have been more deadly than that of an exhumed monarch. The craving was not just for supernatural powers but for supernatural beings to wield them. And so was born the fantasy of pharaoh's curse, even though most of the other members of the expedition lived out their lives happily enough. Soon the fantasies which fed the popular press were dwarfed by those which ruled the destinies of nations. Italian fascism made myth the basis of political action and in the beer-halls of Munich the Nazis nursed the obscene nonsense of racialism. Russia was governed by the Marxist conviction that capitalism was an agent of fantasy, 'a sorcerer who is no longer able to control the powers of the nether world he had called up by his spells', while the capitalist world in its turn dismissed as fantasy the supposedly inexorable historical forces which the Marxists recognized.

In this counterpoint of thinking and imagining the constant, the universal, seemed to be respect for the heroic dead. There was a war memorial at the heart of most communities, whatever might have happened to their churches and their centres of social and political cohesion. And so Eliot's image of a corpse sprouting and blooming in the garden was hardly welcome. Yet it was the one sane thing in a world gone mad, the one reality in a welter of fantasy. Early in the war Arnold Bennett had seen 'wheat absolutely growing out of a German' and by the summer of 1919 the Imperial War Graves Commission found that 'vegetation is fast covering up all traces of the dead.' 'It is a tremendous fact to bear in mind,' observed *The Times*, 'that there are more dead soldiers lying in isolated areas than constituted the whole of the Expeditionary Force of 1914... The French peasant is not going to allow these vast areas to remain unculti-

vated'. The armies had completed the planting of corpses and now the owners of the gardens and the fields and the woodlands were returning to plant other things and reap a richer harvest. The war memorials announced piously that the heroes had died in order that others might live; the ancient fertility cults had proclaimed the same truth in a way which was, quite literally, more down to earth. It was not an accident that the early twentieth century had seen a revival of interest in these rituals and that Eliot had now woven them into one of the most important poems of the post-war years. The waste land of which he wrote was a place of desolation but it was not without hope. It was the land in which the human imagination had once been nurtured and in which it might yet become whole again.

'Patterns of Worship in 1851', *Journal of Ecclesiastical History*, December 1960, pp. 74–86 and W.S.Pickering, 'The Religious Census of 1851 – a useless experiment?', *British Journal of Sociology*, September 1967, pp. 382–407.

p.20　'... *of itinerant preachers.*' F.Thistlethwayte, *The Great Experiment*, Cambridge 1961, p. 17; C.Dickens, *American Notes*, J.S.Whitley and A. Goldman (eds), 1972, p. 290; *T*, 13 April 1838, p. 3.

p.20　'... *assign a termination.*' *R*, Vol. II, No. 39, p. 93; *T*, 6 September 1847, p. 4.

p.21　'... *superstition and unreason.*' Karl Marx and F.Engels, *The Manifesto of the Communist Party*, authorized English translation 1933, pp. 14, 20.

p.21　'... *old God yet.*' *T*, 11 November 1947, p. 5.

CHAPTER 2

p.22　'... *this latest exhumation:*' *H*, cxi, 1076; *T*, 13 August 1847, p. 1; 27 August 1847, p. 1.

p.22　'... *and sell them.*' *T*, 6 September 1847, p. 3.

p.23　'... *he concluded.*' *T*, 4 September 1847, p. 6; 6 September 1847, p. 1; *R*, Vol. IX, No. 8, p. 87; No. 7, p. 74.

p.24　'... *of the dead.*' E.Stone, *God's Acre*, 1858, p. 9; John Morley, *Death, Heaven and the Victorians*, 1971, p. 33; S.Baring-Gould, *Further Reminiscences*, 1925, p. 21.

p.25　'... *gushed and spurted.*' *Blackwood's Magazine*, April 1847, pp. 432–40.

p.25　'... *mercies of God.*' *T*, 16 September 1847, p. 1; 5 October 1847, p. 1; 21 October 1847, p. 1; 11 November 1847, p. 1.

p.26　'... *a successful termination.*' *T*, 11 November 1947, p. 5; 24 February 1848, pp. 4–5.

p.26　'... *to revolutionary demands.*' *R*, Vol. II, p. 196; IV, pp. 182, 267, 303; *H*, xcvi, 754–55; *English Review*, March 1848, pp. 90–96.

p.27　'... *deepening apocalyptic darkness.*' *H*, xcviii, 287, 1330; J.Cumming, *The True Charter*, 1850, p. 120.

p.27　'... *charm against drowning.*' Thompson, *Chartists*, p. 329; Charles Greville, *A Journal of the Reign of Queen Victoria from 1837 to 1852*, 3 vols, 1885, iii, 256; Alfred Cobban, *The Debate on the French Revolution*, 2nd edn 1960, p. 376.

p.28　'... *audacity of Voltaire.*' *Edinburgh Review*, October 1849, pp. 338–39, 356; A.Saintes, *History of Rationalism in Germany*, tr. J.R.Beard 1849, pp. v–vi; *English Review*, December 1848, pp. 357–58. See also M.A. Crowther, *Church Embattled: Religious Controversy in Mid-Victorian England*, Newton Abbot 1970.

p.30　'... *part of it.*' J.Cumming, *Apocalyptic Sketches*, 1849, p. 494.

p.30　'... *of any kind.*' Gaustad, *Doc. Hist.*, pp. 342, 440–42.

p.31　'... *from their persecutors.*' Arthur E.Bestor, *Backwoods Utopias*, Philadelphia 1950, pp. 238–42; *Bible Communism: a compilation from the Annual*

Reports and other publications of the Oneida Association, New York 1953, p. 65; *T*, 23 October 1844, p. 5; 15 October 1845, p. 6; Robert Mullen, *The Mormons*, 1967, p. 57.

p.31   '... *made them all!'* J.P.Nichol, *View of Astronomy*, 1848, p. 41.

p.32   '... *that of Jehovah.*' Harold Beaver (ed.), *The Science Fiction of Edgar Allan Poe*, 1976, pp. 395–96; 307; 308–9.

p.33   '... *of the telegraph.*' E.M.Goulburn (ed.), *Replies to 'Essays and Reviews'*... *with a preface by the Lord Bishop of Oxford*, 1862, preface pp. xii–xiii; Emma Hardinge, *Modern American Spiritualism*, New York 1869, ii, 29.

p.34   '... *as a necromancer.*' Ruth Brandon, *The Spiritualists: The Passion for the Occult in the Nineteenth and Twentieth Centuries*, 1983, p. 3; Hall Caine, *My Story*, 1908, p. 231; *The Spirit World*, May 1853, p. 3; *The Congressional Globe*, Washington 1854, vol. xxviii, pt 2, p. 923; *Spiritual Magazine*, June 1864, pp. 255–60.

p.34   '... *more perfect condition.*' *The Spiritual Herald*, April 1856, p. 65; Eliab Capron, *Modern Spiritualism*, Boston and New York 1855, pp. 378–79; S.C.Hewitt (ed.), *Messages from the Superior State; communicated by John Murray through John M.Spear in the summer of 1852, containing important instructions to the inhabitants of the earth*, Boston 1852, p. 119.

p.35   '... *his imminent arrival.*' Brandon, *Spiritualists*, p. 32.

p.35   '... *of Christian orthodoxy.*' *Poems of Tennyson*, p. 907; Charles Tennyson, *Alfred Tennyson*, 1949, pp. 243, 253–56; *T*, 2 May 1851, p. 4.

p.36   '... *the new dispensation:*' J.Cumming, *The Seventh Vial*, 1870, pp. xiv–xv; F.G.Kenyon (ed.), *The Letters of Elizabeth Barrett Browning*, 2 vols, 1897, ii, 193–94.

p.36   '... *but the beginning.*' Elizabeth Barrett Browning, *Letters to her sister 1846–59*, 1929, p. 221.

p.37   '... *already taken place.*' *Cornhill Magazine*, August 1860, pp. 222–23; J.Cumming, *The Great Tribulation*, 1860; P.S.Desprez, *Apocalypse Fulfilled*, 1854.

p.37   '... *the same time:*' *Revue des Deux Mondes*, Paris 15 February 1861, pp. 812–56; *T*, 10 November 1860, p. 8; 16 February 1861, p. 10.

p.38   '... *in American spiritualism.*' *Replies to 'Essays and Reviews'*, pp. xi–xiii.

p.38   '... *image of God.*' *LQV(1)*, ii, 602–3; J.Cumming, *From Life to Life*, 1861, p. 9; *Spiritual Magazine*, October 1864, p. 470.

CHAPTER 3

p.39   '... *he committed suicide.*' Arturo Castiglioni, *A History of Medicine*, tr. E.B.Krumbhaar 2nd edn New York 1947, pp. 723–24.

p.40   '... *death of pain.*' *T*, 30 March 1844, p. 8.

p.40   '... *first battle won.*' *WR*, July 1871, p. 203.

p.41   '... *his religious master.*' *T*, 18 February 1841, p. 3; Gaustad, *Doc. Hist.*, p. 474.

p.42   '... *not properly birched.*' *T*, 10 January 1845, p. 5; 7 April 1845,

p. 6; E.Channing, *History of the United States,* 7 vols, New York 1905–32, vi, 18; Dickens, *American Notes,* pp. 282, 287.

p.42 '*... became their equals.*' Philippe Ariès, *Centuries of Childhood,* Penguin Books 1986, p. 254; G.B.Hill (ed.), *Boswell's Life of Johnson,* rev'd edn L.F.Powell, 6 vols, Oxford 1934–50, i, 46.

p.44 '*... not at all.*' Frances Power Cobbe, *Broken Lights,* 1864, p. 152.

p.45 '*... going to heaven.*' *R,* 29 May 1850, p. 86.

p.45 '*... the Protestant mind.*' (Anon), *The Bible History of Satan,* 1858, pp. 25, 32; Rev. J.Furniss, *Books for children and young persons: Book X The Sight of Hell,* Dublin 1861, pp. 17–18, 20; Rev. T. Livius, *Father Furniss and his work for children,* 1896, pp. 116, 114.

p.46 '*... for its salvation.*' *T,* 20 November 1845, p. 2; *Essays and Reviews,* 1860, p. 93.

p.46 '*... punished its authors.*' *S,* 7 April 1860, pp. 331–33; *WR,* October 1860, pp. 293–332; *QR,* January 1861, p. 302.

p.47 '*... was at stake.*' *Revue des Deux Mondes,* Paris 15 May 1861, pp. 403–24.

p.47 '*... of everlasting damnation.*' *Essays and Reviews,* p. 206; *T,* 9 June 1863, p. 14; Margaret Goodman, *Sisterhoods in the Church of England,* 1863, p. 25; *S,* 27 February 1864, p. 229.

p.48 '*... one with dogma.*' *T,* 1 July 1861, p. 8; 14 March 1864, p. 12; 17 March 1864, p. 7; John Keble, *A Litany of Our Lord's Warnings,* 1864, p. 8; *T,* 22 September 1864, p. 7.

p.49 '*... celebrate total victory.*' *H,* clxxvi, 1544; *Everlasting Punishment: a sermon preached ... by the Rev. E.B.Pusey,* Oxford 1864; *T,* 17 July 1875, p. 13; 20 January 1876, p. 10; 21 January 1876, p. 10; 22 July 1876, p. 10; 17 February 1876, p. 10.

p.49 '*... of popular belief.*' *Alfred Tennyson,* pp. 259–60, 262; *T,* 21 February 1876, p. 5; 23 February 1876, p. 5; 28 February 1876, p. 10.

p.49 '*... curb his haughtiness.*' *Spirit World,* May 1853, p. 7; Rev. Norman Macleod, *The Recognition of Friends in Heaven,* 1863; Rev. Richard Cunningham Shimeall, *The Unseen World,* New York 1870, pp. 37, 214; *Spiritual Herald,* July 1856, p. 197.

p.50 '*... endorsement of it.*' *Spiritual Magazine,* December 1860, pp. 549–50; November 1861, p. 500; S.E.Gay, *Spiritual Sanity,* 1879, p. 16.

p.51 '*... to aphrodisiac flagellation.*' Peter Fryer (ed.), *Forbidden Books of the Victorians,* 1970, pp. 130–31, 23–24; Donald Thomas, *Swinburne: the Poet in his World,* 1979, pp. 18–19. See also Iain McCalman, 'Unrespectable Radicalism: Infidels and Pornography in early Nineteenth-Century London', *Past and Present,* August 1984, pp. 74–110.

p.51 '*... or by fire.*' Kilvert, *Diary,* pp. 253, 293, 97–98; Christopher Devlin (ed.), *Sermons and Devotional Writings of Gerard Manley Hopkins,* Oxford 1959, p. 241.

p.51 '*... up the attempt.*' Edward Royle, *Victorian Infidels: the Origins of the British Secularist Movement 1791–1866,* Manchester 1974, pp. 270–71;

H, clxi, 697, 1936–40; clxiii, 953–75; clxvii, 1024–26; clxix, 223, 1285–1302.

p.52 '... *a future world.*' Derek Hudson (ed.), *Munby: Man of Two Worlds*, 1974, pp. 64, 67.

p.53 '... *a continuing cannonade.*' Gertrude Himmelfarb, *Darwin and the Darwinian Revolution*, 1959, pp. 347, 332, 185; *Poems of Tennyson*, p. 912.

p.53 '... *of all things.*' The *Oxford Dictionary of Quotations*, 3rd edn Oxford 1979, p. 172.

p.54 '... *known at Eton.*' Hudson, *Munby*, pp. 198–99; R.L.Green (ed.), *The Diaries of Lewis Carroll*, 2 vols, 1953, i, 220; Cecil Y.Lang (ed.), *The Swinburne Letters*, 6 vols, New Haven and London 1959–62, i, 55.

p.54 '... *it was born.*' Frances Power Cobbe, *Darwinism in Morals and other essays*, 1872, pp. 173–74.

p.55 '... *and no Hereafter.*' *Ibid.*, pp. 312, 314.

p.55 '... *steeds into riders.*' *Ibid.*, pp. 333–34.

CHAPTER 4

p.57 '... *cost and pain.*' *Cornhill Magazine*, July 1860, p. 84.

p.57 '... *were suitably chagrined.*' J.D.Crowley (ed.), *Hawthorne: The Critical Heritage*, 1970, p. 315; *Centenary Edition of the Works of Nathaniel Hawthorne, Volume IV*, Ohio State University 1968, p. xxi.

p.58 '... *from a reed.*' *Ibid.*, p. xxxiii.

p.59 '... *those of Christianity.*' Chadwick, *Victorian Church*, ii, 36.

p.60 '... *a physical reality.*' S.Baring-Gould, *Curious Myths of the Middle Ages, Second Series*, 1868, p. 371.

p.61 '... *a new mythology.*' B.Torrey and F.H.Allen (eds), *The Journals of Thoreau*, 14 vols, New York 1906, ii, 145; H.D.Thoreau, *Walden*, Everyman's Library 1908, p. 185.

p.62 '... *of our race.*' S.S.Smith and H.Hayford (eds), *Journals and Notebooks of R.W.Emerson, Volume XIV*, Cambridge Mass. 1978, p. 194; L.A.Allardt, D.W.Hill, R.H.Bennett (eds), *Journals and Notebooks of R.W.Emerson, Volume XV*, Cambridge Mass. 1982, pp. 155, 222; Cobbe, *Darwinism in Morals*, p. 201.

p.62 '... *of Swinburne's talk.*' E.C.Stedman (ed.), *An American Anthology*, Boston, New York, Chicago, San Francisco 1900, pp. 334–35; Swinburne, *Correspondence*, i, 233–34; H.Cabot Lodge (ed.), *The education of Henry Adams*, Boston and New York 1918, p. 141.

p.63 '... *make it grow.*' *SR*, 4 August 1866, p. 147; Swinburne, *Correspondence*, i, 173–74; ii, 72–76.

p.64 '... *the schoolmaster's tune.*' *Ibid.*, i, 103–4, 288, 276n.; Bernard Falk, *The Naked Lady*, 1934, p. 227; *SR*, 4 August 1866, p. 145.

p.64 '... *as a wolf.*' S.Baring-Gould, *The Book of Werewolves*, 1865, pp. 107–8.

p.65 '... *throughout the world.*' Cobbe, *Darwinism in Morals*, pp. 269–70, 271; *AR*, 1890, p. 8.

p.65 '... *almost supernatural being:*' T.E.Kebbel (ed.), *Selected Speeches of*

Lord Beaconsfield, 3 vols, 1882, iii, 606, 612; *Punch*, 23 February 1867, p. 77; 15 June 1867, pp. 246–47.

p.65 '... *gets the chance.*' *M&B*, ii, 292–93.

p.66 '... *brigantine ever materialized.*' *AR*, 1867, pp. 107–8; *M&B*, ii, 307–8.

p.66 '... *of the universe.*' R. Payne, *Karl Marx*, 1968, pp. 398, 62–64, 349–50.

p.67 '... *gods die too.*' Reade, *Martyrdom of Man*, pp. 51, 328.

p.67 '... *makes men die!*' *Ibid.*, pp. 328, 417, 446, 137–40.

p.68 '... *its moral influences.*' *Ibid.*, p. 447; *Daily Telegraph*, 27 April 1875; Frances Power Cobbe, *Hopes of the Human Race, Hereafter and Here*, 1874, pp. ix–x.

p.69 '... *so astonishingly popular.*' *Ibid.*, 11n.; Guillaume Figuier, *The Day after Death; or, Our Future Life according to Science*, 1872, pp. 1, 113, 217.

p.70 '... *clash by night.*' *FR*, October 1867, p. 417; K. Allott (ed.), *The Poems of Matthew Arnold*, 2nd edn rev'd M. Allott 1979, pp. 253–57.

p.70 '... *had yet seen.*' Christopher Middleton (ed.), *Selected Letters of Friedrich Nietzsche*, Chicago and London 1969, pp. 67, 68.

p.70 '... *India into Greece.*' *Ibid.*, p. 22; Friedrich Nietzsche, *The Birth of Tragedy*, Section 20, cited in John Cruickshank, *Aspects of the Modern European Mind*, 1969, p. 76.

CHAPTER 5

p.73 '... *at Cumming's lectures.*' Harcourt Bland, *A Reply to Dr Cumming's Lectures*, Glasgow 1855; '*The End of the World*', *Correspondence between Rev. Dr Cumming and H. Bland, Comedian*, Glasgow 1855; J. Cumming, *The End; or, the Proximate Signs of the close of this Dispensation*, 1855; 'Investigator', *The Rev. Dr Cumming and his Critics*, 1860; Rev. J. F. Witty, *What have we, and what has Dr Cumming, to do with 1867?*, Sheffield 1862, p. 3.

p.73 '... *of the apocalypse.*' Cumming, *The End*, pp. 137, 251.

p.73 '... *what it was.*' Chadwick, *Victorian Church*, i, 467–70, 482; *LQV(1)*, iii, 314.

p.74 '... *a beautiful creation.*' Rev. C. G. Finney, *Memoirs*, New York 1876, p. 437; Philip Schaff, *America: a Sketch of its Political, Social and Religious Character*, ed. Perry Miller, Cambridge Mass. 1961, pp. 29, 36, 39–40, 181, 80–81.

p.74 '... *when he came.*' Robert Baird, *Religion in America*, New York 1856, pp. 264, 365–66.

p.75 '... *of God's presence.*' Isabel Bishop, *Aspects of Religion in the United States*, 1859, p. 1; J. C. Pollock, *Moody without Sankey*, 1963, p. 29; Perry Miller, *Life of the Mind in America*, New York 1965, pp. 90, 89; Finney, *Memoirs*, pp. 442–44.

p.76 '... *rise in America.*' Finney, *Memoirs*, p. 444; Schaff, *America*, p. 43; John Weiss, *Life and Correspondence of Theodore Parker*, 2 vols, New York 1864, ii, 125–54, 161.

p.76 '... *a slave revolt.*' Bishop, *Aspects of Religion*, p. 188; *T*, 12 October 1841, p. 4.

p.76 '... *held in subjection.*' Weiss, *Parker*, i, 463.

p.77 '... *Atlantic with him.*' *Ibid.*, i, 463; *LQV(1)*, iii, 323–24; Finney, *Memoirs*, pp. 449ff.

p.77 '... *fervour of 1857–58.*' Gaustad, *Doc. Hist.*, pp. 393–95.

p.78 '... *the apocalyptic scenario.*' Weiss, *Parker*, ii, 315, 301; Rev. Richard Cunningham Shimeall, *The Political Economy of Prophecy*, New York 1866, pp. 157–62. (For an account of the Emperor's being invited to a lecture proving he was Antichrist see Augustin Filon, *Souvenirs sur l'Impératrice Eugènie*, 1920, p. 259. I am indebted to Dr W.H.C.Smith for this reference); Gaustad, *Doc. Hist.*, p. 448.

p.79 '... *a safe distance.*' Weiss, *Parker*, ii. 438, 423, 405; *T*, 4 October 1860, p. 6; 9 November 1860, p. 6; 4 August 1860, p. 9.

p.79 '... *the old one.*' Wendell Glick (ed.), *Henry D. Thoreau: Reform Papers*, Princeton 1973, pp. 135, 152; P.M.Angle and E.S.Miers, *Tragic Years 1860–1865: A Documentary History of the American Civil War*, 2 vols, New York 1960, i, 33.

p.80 '... *in Charleston harbour.*' Sir Sidney Lee, *King Edward VII*, 2 vols, 1925–27, i, 98, 101–4; *T*, 20 November 1860, p. 6.

p.80 '... *that stirring tune?*' Angle and Miers, *Tragic Years*, i, 160, 189; *Reminiscences of Julia Ward Howe 1819–1899*, Boston 1899, pp. 274–75.

p.81 '... *from the North.*' Morley, *Gladstone*, i, 705.

p.81 '... *sway of slaveholders.*' Angle and Miers, *Tragic Years*, ii, 721.

p.82 '... *of the Lord.*' *Ibid.*, ii, 1007, 1022–23.

p.83 '... *jaws of hell.*' *T*, 25 May 1864, p. 8; Kebbel, *Speeches of Disraeli*, iii, 606, 617; Chadwick, *Victorian Church*, ii, 7, 25; *AR*, 1867, p. 347; J.B.Mozley, *Eight Lectures on Miracles*, 1865, p. 165; H.P.Liddon, *The Divinity of Our Lord and Saviour Jesus Christ*, 1867, p. 231; Chadwick, *Victorian Church*, ii, 65.

p.84 '... *the Last Trumpet.*' J. Cumming, *The Sounding of the Last Trumpet*, 1867, pp. 224, 233, 228; *AR*, 1866, pp. 172–75; *T*, 2 January 1867, p. 11; Cumming, *Last Trumpet*, p. 413.

p.84 '... *class and class.*' Hudson, *Munby*, p. 235; *T*, 3 January 1867, p. 7; 4 January 1867, p. 10; G.W.E.Russell (ed.), *Letters of Matthew Arnold*, 2 vols, 1895, i, 346; *AR*, 1867, p. 307.

p.85 '... *and be sober.*' *M&B*, i, 260, 262; E.L.Woodward, *The Age of Reform*, Oxford 1958, p. 181; Russell, *Letters of Arnold*, i, 378–79; *AR*, 1867, p. 139.

p.85 '... *voice of God.*' H.M.Schueller and R.L.Peters (eds), *The Letters of John Addington Symonds*, 3 vols, Detroit 1967–69, i, 687–88; *M&B*, ii, 291, 605, 606; Benjamin Disraeli, *Tancred or the New Crusade* (Bradenshaw edition of the novels of Benjamin Disraeli, Volume X), 1927, p. 141.

p.86   '... *a summer street.' T*, 4 May 1868, p. 10; *M&B*, ii, 317; *LQV(2)*, i, 512, 529.

p.86   '... *formally in Convocation.' AR*, 1868, p. 124; J.W.Draper, *History of the Intellectual Development of Europe*, 2 vols, New York 1864; Chadwick, *Victorian Church*, ii, 86–87, 89.

p.87   '... *less imaginative weapons.'* Morley, *Gladstone*, ii, 40; *T*, 20 November 1871, p. 9; *M&B*, ii, 511, 513.

p.87   '... *of visiting Englishmen.'* H.House and G.Storey (eds), *Journals and Papers of Gerard Manley Hopkins*, Oxford 1959, pp. 200–1; *AR*, 1870, p. 127; Swinburne, *Correspondence*, ii, 124–26; *LQV(2)*, ii, 61, 104.

p.88   '... *ruled by Germany.' Ibid.*, ii, 101; *FR*, January 1871, p. 66; *CR*, January 1871, p. 224; *T*, 9 February 1871, p. 6; *Blackwood's Magazine*, May 1871, pp. 539–72; *T*, 19 June 1871, p. 9.

p.88   '... *recaptured the city.' FR*, August 1871, p. 155; *LQV(2)*, ii, 126; House and Storey, *Journals of Hopkins*, pp. 210–11.

p.89   '... *form of government.'* C.C.Abbott (ed.), *Letters of Gerard Manley Hopkins to Robert Bridges*, Oxford 1935, pp. 27–28; Swinburne, *Correspondence*, ii, 151; *Newspaper Warfare! The Grand Ink Battle between Figaro and Reynold's Newspaper*, 1872; Philip Guedalla (ed.), *The Queen and Mr Gladstone*, 2 vols, 1933, i, 304; Elizabeth Longford, *Victoria R.I.*, 1964, p. 384.

p.89   '... *unnoticed and uncontradicted.' T*, 9 November 1871, p. 6; *LQV(2)*, ii, 164–65.

p.90   '... *to save us.' LQV(2)*, ii, 171; *T*, 11 December 1871, p. 9; *LQV(2)*, ii, 179; *T*, 30 December 1871, p. 7; Lee, *Edward VII*, i, 329.

p.90   '... *offered them up.' T*, 11 December 1871, p. 5; Kilvert, *Diary*, p. 158; *T*, 24 November 1871, p. 5.

p.91   '... *grasp of reality.' Ibid.*, 13 February 1872; Guedalla, *Queen and Gladstone*, i, 321; *M&B*, ii, 523.

CHAPTER 6

p.92   '... *of the world.' T*, 19 June 1871, p. 9; 4 April 1872, p. 5; 25 June 1872, pp. 7–8.

p.93   '... *met and mastered.'* H.Grisewood (ed.), *Ideas and Beliefs of the Victorians*, 1949, p. 76; *Poems of Tennyson*, pp. 1755–56.

p.93   '... *noted Charles Dodgson., CR*, May 1872, p. 738; *T*, 8 April 1871, p. 5; Chadwick, *Victorian Church*, ii, 25; *AR*, 1872, p. 370; Green, *Diaries of Lewis Carroll*, ii, 334.

p.94   '... *of public prayers.'* Eliza Lynn Linton, *Joshua Davidson*, 1872, pp. 267–74; *FR*, August 1872, pp. 125–35.

p.94   '... *of the universe.'* John Burke (ed.), *Jowitt's Dictionary of English Law*, 2 vols, 2nd edn 1977, i, 33; Kilvert, *Diary*, p. 204; *WR*, July 1872, pp. 97–98.

p.95   '... *and scientific scepticism.'* Rev. F.G.Lee, *The Other World; or Glimpses of the Supernatural*, 2 vols, 1875; *T*, 19 April 1876, p. 4.

p.96　'... *he warned.*' Winthrop S.Hudson, *Religion in America*, 3rd edn New York 1981, pp. 249, 265–66, 268–69.

p.96　'... *witnessed in Manchester.*' *Ibid.*, p. 267.

p.97　'... *a nightmarish fanaticism.*' Allen W.Trelease, *White Terror: the Ku Klux Klan Conspiracy and Southern Reconstruction*, Westport Conn. 1979, pp. 19, 51, 88, 202; Angle and Miers, *Tragic Years*, i, 462.

p.97　'... *English-speaking peoples.*' Robin May and Joseph G.Rosa, *Cowboy: the Man and the Myth*, 1980.

p.98　'... *on the rocks:*' *T*, 5 February 1874, p. 9; 16 February 1874, p. 9.

p.98　'... *lie too deep.*' *CR*, August 1874, p. 358.

p.99　'... *were being fulfilled.*' J.Cumming, *The Seventh Vial, or the Time of Troubles Begun*, 1870.

p.99　'... *Scrap Books, etc.*' *Notes and Queries*, 4th series vol. xi (26 April 1873), p. 355; *The end of the world and other remarkable prophecies*, 1872, pp. 4, 5.

p.100　'... *of the age.*' Charles Piazzi Smyth, *Our Inheritance in the Great Pyramid*, 1864, unnumbered page following title page.

p.100　'... *of biblical apocalypse.*' Smyth, *The Great Pyramid and the Royal Society*, 1874 (for his account of his differences with the Royal Society); *Great Pyramid*, 3rd edn 1877, pp. 569, 582.

p.100　'... *nations into infidelity.*' Smyth, *Great Pyramid*, 2nd edn 1874, p. 485.

p.102　'... *year of destiny.*' *"The End of the World" in 1881–2, according to Mother Shipton, the Great Pyramid of Ghizeh and other Ancient Prophecies related to Russia and Turkey*, 1880, pp. 5–6; *Palatine Note-Book*, Manchester April 1881, pp. 64–66; *"The End of the World" in 1881–2*, pp. 42–44.

p.102　'... *frightful to witness.*' *Ibid.*, pp. 50, 58; C.A.Grimmer, *The Voice of the Stars*, London and Manchester 1880, pp. 7, 9, 11.

p.102　'... *of his sovereign.*' *M&B*, ii, 633, 657; *LQV(2)*, ii, 290.

p.103　'... *Battle of Armageddon.*' *M&B*, ii, 665, 670, 685; *CR*, June 1876, p. 26.

p.103　'... *of Gloucester anxiously.*' Joyce Coombs, *Judgment on Hatcham: the History of a Religious Struggle 1877–1886*, 1969, pp. 63–64; *AR*, 1877, p. 50; *NC*, July 1877, pp. 753–73.

p.104　'... *walls of heaven.*' *CR*, January 1874, p. 326.

p.104　'... *inherit eternal life.*' *T*, 25 March 1874, p. 12.

p.104　'... *then publicly burned.*' *Ibid.*, 1 February 1875, p. 5; 4 February 1875, p. 12; 20 February 1875, p. 9.

p.105　'... *their very midst.*' *Ibid.*, 14 October 1874, p. 5; *AR*, 1878, pp. 127–28.

p.105　'... *one for undertakers.*' *T*, 20 May 1875, p. 10; 14 June 1875, p. 12; 17 June 1875, p. 12; 18 June 1875, p. 13.

p.106　'... *a draper's shop.*' *Ibid.*, 22 March 1875, p. 11; *LQV(2)*, ii, 385–86; *T*, 19 March 1875, p. 8; 21 June 1875, p. 9; 22 June 1875, pp. 6, 8; 23 June 1875, p. 12.

p.106　'... *politics of fantasy.*' *M&B*, ii, 731; *T*, 23 July 1874, p. 10.

p.107 '... *told the Queen.*' Kinley Roby, *The King, the Press and the People,* 1975, pp. 197–98; Allen Andrews, *The Follies of King Edward VII,* 1975, pp. 126–35; Anon (S.O.Beeton, A.A.Dowty, E.Jerrold), *Edward the Seventh,* 1876; Lady Betty Balfour (ed.), *Personal and Literary Letters of Robert, first Earl of Lytton,* 2 vols, 1906, ii, 3–6.

p.107 '... *Canal, four millions.*' *M&B,* ii, 789; *Punch,* vol. lxix, p. 245 (11 December 1875); *AR,* 1876, pp. 27–28.

p.108 '... *a political clown.*' *LQV(2),* ii, 480, 567–68; R.T.Shannon, *Gladstone and the Bulgarian Agitation 1876,* 1963, p. 64; R.W.Seton-Watson, *Disraeli, Gladstone and the Eastern Question,* reprint 1971, p. 203.

p.109 '... *than ever before:*' Shannon, *Bulgarian Agitation,* pp. 200, 14; *CR,* October 1876, pp. 855–65.

p.109 '... *cast its spell.*' *H,* ccxxxvii, 769; *Daily News,* 13 March 1878, pp. 3–4; Longford, *Victoria,* p. 412; *T,* 13 September 1878, p. 9.

p.110 '... *were 'somewhat fanciful'.*' Kilvert, *Diary,* p. 327; *M&B,* ii, 1276, 1371.

p.110 '... *for the reduction.*' Herman Ausubel, *In Hard Times: Reformers among the late Victorians,* Westport Conn. 1960, p. 22; *T,* 7 February 1881, p. 5; Ausubel, *Hard Times,* p. 29.

p.110 '... *faculty of wonder.*' Morley, *Gladstone,* ii, 198; *NC,* August 1878, p. 910.

p.111 '... *a new dawn.*' *LQV(2),* iii, 73; Morley, *Gladstone,* ii, 223.

CHAPTER 7

p.113 '... *struggle against science.*' J.W.Draper, *History of the Conflict between Religion and Science,* New York 1873, pp. 352.

p.114 '... *of modern science.*' *Ibid.,* pp. v, xi, xv, 327, 367; *T,* 20 August 1874, pp. 4–5; *AR,* 1874, pp. 375–77.

p.114 '... *had been written:*' Countess of Caithness, *Old Truths in a new light,* 1876, pp. 9, 12; Edward Maitland, *England and Islam,* 1877, pp. 198–99.

p.114 '... *I can speak!*' Edward Maitland, *Anna Kingsford: her life, letters, diary and work,* 2 vols, 1896, i, 107.

p.115 '... *the high towers.*' *Ibid.,* i, 250–52, 1–11, 279.

p.115 '... *of my vision.*' *Ibid.,* i, 282; Maitland, *England and Islam,* p. 98; Maitland, *Kingsford,* i, 415, 427.

p.116 '... *of the Enlightenment.*' *Ibid.,* i, 229, 236–38, 215, 15; ii, 3–4, 50.

p.117 '... *branch in Paris.*' John Symonds, *Madame Blavatsky,* 1959, p. 76; S.B.Liljegren *Bulwer-Lytton's novels and Isis Unveiled,* Cambridge Mass. 1957, pp. 11–13; Symonds, *Blavatsky,* p. 66; Josephine Ransom, *The Direction of the Theosophical Society by the Masters of Wisdom,* 1942, p. 15; Maitland, *Kingsford,* ii, 119; James Webb, *The Flight from Reason,* 1971, p. 181.

p.117 '... *were at work.*' *T,* 18 April 1878, p. 4.

p.117 '... *in June 1881.*' Symonds, *Blavatsky,* pp. 103, 108–10, 150.

p.118 '... *from the tomb?*' *Ibid.,* p. 90; *SR,* 25 June 1881, p. 823; Helen

Zimmern, *Schopenhauer*, 1876, p. x; Lady Betty Balfour, *Letters of Lytton*, ii, 275–76; *CR*, February 1876, pp. 369–76.

p.119 '... *its varied contributors:*' *Metaphysical Society Papers*, n.d. (1880?), contains 44 papers given between 1869 and 1879.

p.119 '... *gulf of Doubt.*' *NC*, March 1877, p. 1; *Tennyson's Poems*, p. 1239.

p.119 '... *of seven o'clock.*' Martin Gardner (ed.), *The Annotated Snark*, rev'd edn 1974, p. 45; R.A.J,Walling (ed.), *The Diaries of John Bright*, 1930, pp. 456–57; Sir T.Wemyss Reid, *Life, Letters and Friendships of Richard Monckton Milnes, first Lord Houghton*, 2 vols, 1890, ii, 359.

p.120 '... *ever under it.*' *NC*, May 1877, p. 539; September 1877, p. 273.

p.120 '... *was a Boojum.*' Gardner, *Annotated Snark*, pp. 55–56, 93–96, 16.

p.121 '... *of all crimes:*' Middleton, *Nietzsche Letters*, pp. 178, 173.

p.121 '... *have killed him.*' Nietzsche, *The Gay Science*, cited in Cruickshank, *Modern European Mind*, pp. 80–81.

p.122 '... *not itself still.*' Maitland, *Kingsford*, i, 416; *Dictionary of American Biography*, new edn 1957–64, vi, 593–96.

p.122 '... *remained equally unfulfilled.*' Hopkins, *Letters to Bridges*, pp. lxxi, 116; *AR*, 1881, pp. 5, 6, 9, 11, 14–15; *Diaries of Bright*, pp. 456–57.

p.123 '... *body was gone.*' *Ibid.*, p. 460; *T*, 3 December 1881, p. 6.

p.123 '... *to be apprehended.*' *T*, 10 December 1881, p. 6; 9 December 1881, p. 8; *AR*, 1882, pp. 11–12; *T*, 20 July 1882, p. 6.

p.124 '... *of five years.*' *T*, 26 September 1882, p. 10; 25 October 1882, p. 5.

p.124 '... *by Professor Smyth.*' *Proceedings of the Society for Psychical Research, 1883*, pp. v–xvii; *H*, cclxvi, 1234–65.

p.125 '... *storm of hissing.*' Swinburne, *Correspondence*, v, 13; A.F.Hort (ed.), *Life and Letters of F.J.A.Hort*, 2 vols, 1896, ii, 290, 291; *T*, 6 March 1883, p. 12.

p.126 '... *Uncle Tom's Cabin.*' Josiah Strong, *Our Country*, ed. Jurgen Herbst, Cambridge Mass. 1963, pp. 218, 133, 225–26, ix.

p.126 '... *Darwin looked forward.*' Himmelfarb, *Darwinism*, pp. 343, 407; *H*, cclxv, 216–19.

CHAPTER 8

p.128 '... *the tennis lawn.*' S.Colvin (ed.), *The Letters of Robert Louis Stevenson*, 4 vols, 5th edn 1919, ii, 39, 213n., 49–51; *SR*, 11 November 1882, pp. 633–34.

p.129 '... *as the sciences:*' Colvin, *Letters of Stevenson*, i, 53–54, 224; ii, 123.

p.129 '... *flowing and emasculated.*' *Longman's Magazine*, November 1884, p. 142.

p.130 '... *the surrounding darkness:*' *FR*, July 1891, p. 109.

p.130 '... *anticipated – darkness still.*' *Ibid.*, p. 111.

p.130 '... *of its destiny.*' *T*, 20 November 1891, p. 6; 27 November 1891, p. 10.

p.131 '... *books and dreams.*' *FR*, March 1887, p. 417; *WR*, December 1887,

pp. 840–49; *CR,* April 1890, p. 485; April 1894, pp. 225–26; November 1887, pp. 683–93; Amy Cruse, *The Victorians and their Books,* 1935, pp. 308–9; *CR,* li, February 1887, p. 173.

p.132 '... *fiction's onward march.*' *WR,* October 1872, pp. 333–77; *CR,* March 1881, p. 398; William James, *Principles of Psychology,* 2 vols, 1890, i, 125.

p.132 '... *to better things.*' *The Bookseller,* 28 February 1867, pp. 121–23; *Five Years Penal Servitude by One who has Endured it,* 1877, p. 67.

p.133 '... *well-trained athletic schoolboys.*' *CR,* March 1881, pp. 385–402; *Boy's Own Paper,* vols i–iv, 1879–82.

p.133 '... *and scriptural readings.*' Altick, *Common Reader,* pp. 361–62.

p.134 '... *the contemporary idealist.*' Thomas Hughes, *The Manliness of Christ,* 1879; Colvin, *Letters of Stevenson,* i, 224, 209.

p.134 '... *daubed with dishonour.*' *Ibid.,* ii, 228–29.

p.135 '... *touch of life.*' *Ibid.,* ii, 274–76.

p.135 '... *danger and adversity.*' *CR,* April 1887, pp. 473, 477; Colvin, *Letters of Stevenson,* i, 285–86.

p.136 '... *to vital spirits.*' *Congressional Record,* Vol. xiii, pt 1, Washington 1882, pp. 834, 856; Rupert Hart-Davis (ed.), *The Letters of Oscar Wilde,* 1962, pp. 112–15.

p.136 '... *been there before,*' *CR,* February 1887, p. 175; Colvin, *Letters of Stevenson,* ii, 274–76, 228; Kenneth S. Lynn (ed.), *Huckleberry Finn: Texts, Sources and Criticism,* New York 1961, pp. 199, 202, 141.

p.137 '... *made for health.*' Richard Jefferies, *Bevis: the Story of a Boy,* illustrated edn 1932, pp. 478–79; *T,* 7 November 1884, p. 11; Maurice Hewlett, *The Forest Lovers,* 1898, p. 240.

p.138 '... *periodical Christian Union.*' Hudson, *Religion in America,* p. 311.

p.138 '... *no real grievance.*' *CR,* November 1887, pp. 731–32.

p.138 '... *foot in Ireland.*' *AR,* 1882, pp. 10, 21; *LQV(2),* ii, 293, 298–9; *T,* 13 January 1880, p. 6.

p.139 '... *of its power.*' *LQV(2),* iii, 438; *T,* 11 February 1886, p. 6.

p.139 '... *had been fulfilled.*' *Poems of Tennyson,* p. 699.

p.140 '... *an earlier age.*' *Ibid.,* pp. 1362, 1365; *S,* 18 December 1886, pp. 1706–7; *NC,* January 1887, p. 18. For an illuminating discussion of the confrontation between Tennyson and Gladstone see Charles Morgan, *Liberties of the Mind,* 1951, pp. 18–34.

p.140 '... *appreciated by Whitman.*' *The Collected Writings of Walt Whitman: The Correspondence, Volume IV 1886–89,* New York 1969, p. 58; J.D. Jump (ed.), *Tennyson: the Critical Heritage,* 1967, pp. 348–49; Robert Buchanan, *A Look Round Literature,* 1887, p. 345.

p.141 '... *of the Will.*' *Poems of Tennyson,* pp. 1365, 1369.

p.142 '... *a well-intentioned earthquake.*' *T,* 26 February 1887, p. 7; Middleton, *Letters of Nietzsche,* pp. 262–63.

p.142 '... *to be achieved.*' *T,* 24 February 1887, p. 9.

CHAPTER 9

p.143 '... *of the world.*' *FR*, February 1887, p. 224; June 1887, pp. 885–92; May 1887, p. 656; December 1886, p. 802.

p.144 '... *had begotten them.*' James Thomson, *Satires and Profanities*, 1884, p. 108.

p.144 '... *dreams are true.*' Himmelfarb, *Darwinian Revolution*, pp. 336–37, 190; *Poems of Tennyson*, pp. 257–58.

p.145 '... *and some free.*' G.T.W.Patrick (ed.), *Heraclitus of Ephesus: The Fragments on Nature*, Baltimore 1889, p. 1; O.Kulpe, *The Philosophy of the Present in Germany*, tr. G.T.W.Patrick and M.L.Patrick, 1913; *Heraclitus: Fragments*, p. 95.

p.145 '... *of the diamond.*' Middleton, *Letters of Nietzsche*, p. 335; W.H.Gardner and N.H.Mackenzie (eds), *The Poems of Gerard Manley Hopkins*, 4th edn 1967, pp. 105–6.

p.146 '... *current scientific orthodoxy.*' *FR*, June 1887, p. 884; *AR*, 1888, p. 79.

p.147 '... *matter for contrition.*' *FR*, January 1890, p. 116; Grant Allen, *The Evolution of the Idea of God*, 1897, pp. 433, 438; Reade, *Martyrdom*, pp. 446–47.

p.147 '... *his invariable laws.*' *T*, 9 August 1894, p. 6; 10 August 1894, p. 12; 11 August 1894, p. 11; 18 August 1894, p. 12.

p.148 '... *you at dinner.*' Chadwick, *Victorian Church*, i, 102, 112.

p.148 '... *devout was undented.*' *Ibid.*, ii, 224; *T*, 27 December 1888, p. 10; 31 December 1888, p. 12; 9 January 1889, p. 9; 22 March 1889, p. 10; 29 March 1889, p. 12; 30 March 1889, p. 12; 2 April 1889, p. 4; Chadwick, *Victorian Church*, ii, 224, 232.

p.149 '... *only true centre.*' Rev. J.H.Barrows (ed.), *The World's Parliament of Religions*, 2 vols, Chicago 1893, i, 14, 21–22, 62, 112, 25.

p.150 '... *on American soil.*' *Ibid.*, i, 442, 592; ii, 1250–51; i, 185, 160.

p.150 '... *supposed to rest.*' *Ibid.*, i, 45; *T*, 9 January 1894, p. 8.

p.151 '... *even Tennyson's expectations.*' Maitland, *Kingsford*, ii, 291.

p.152 '... *far from orthodox.*' Hart-Davis, *Letters of Oscar Wilde*, p. 291n.; Doyle, *Complete Long Stories*, pp. 131, 178, 137.

p.152 '... *of ordinary mortals.*' Doyle, *Complete Short Stories*, pp. 556, 569.

p.153 '... *was not supernatural.*' *Ibid.*, p. 55.

p.154 '... *own superhuman powers.*' *Ibid.*, pp. 121, 3.

p.154 '... *of social co-operation.*' *Blackwood's Magazine*, June 1895, p. 833; A.E. Hake, *Regeneration: a reply to Max Nordau*, 1895, p. 235; *FR*, February 1891, pp. 317, 319.

p.155 '... *satyr he was.*' Edward Carpenter, *Days with Walt Whitman*, 1906, p. 6; *Towards Democracy*, Manchester and London 1883, pp. 97, 98, 23; Henry Havelock Ellis, *The New Spirit*, 1890, p. 28; *My Life*, 1940, p. 82.

p.155 '... *but on sexuality.*' *FR*, March 1894, p. 390.

p.156 '... *to the next.*' *T*, 30 August 1890, p. 4.

p.156 '... *under another name.' The Pagan Review*, No. 1, Rudgwick Sussex 15 August 1892; *FR*, March 1894, p. 384.

p.157 '... *in human affairs.'* Peter Green, *Kenneth Grahame*, 1959, p. 123; *CR*, November 1887, p. 690.

p.157 '... *over fifteen thousand.' Ibid.*, February 1887, p. 177; Altick, *Common Reader*, p. 237.

p.158 '... *early morning swim.'* C.Dukes, *The Preservation of Health as it is affected by Personal Habits such as Cleanliness, Temperance etc.*, 1885, pp. 150, 155, 161; Timothy d'Arch Smith, *Love in Earnest*, 1970, p. 87.

p.158 '... *in his place.'* Howard O.Sturgis, *Tim*, 1891, p. 159.

p.159 '... *That is all.'* Smith, *Love in Earnest*, pp. 13, 27; H.Montgomery Hyde, *The Cleveland Street Scandal*, 1976; Colin Simpson, Lewis Chester, David Leitch, *The Cleveland Street Affair*, Boston 1976; *FR*, March 1891, p. 480.

p.159 '... *admitted or understood.'* Smith, *Love in Earnest*, p. 182; *Pagan Review*, August 1892, pp. 5–18.

p.160 '... *was Oscar Wilde.'* Max Nordau, *Degeneration: translated from the second German edition*, 1895, p. 2; *The Conventional Lies of our Civilization*, Chicago 1884, p. 63; *Degeneration*, pp. 450, 317.

p.160 '... *orthodox had anticipated.'* Smith, *Love in Earnest*, pp. 110, 155; 'Stuart Mason' (Christopher Millard), *Oscar Wilde: Art and Morality*, 2nd edn 1912, pp. 137–38; Hart-Davis, *Letters of Wilde*, 1962, pp. 380, 382, 383, 384, 389.

CHAPTER 10

p.161 '... *most indubitably right.'* Mason, *Oscar Wilde*, pp. 203–19; Smith, *Love in Earnest*, p. 59; Mason, *Oscar Wilde*, p. 139; *Blackwood's Magazine*, June 1895, p. 843–44. The *National Observer* review of *Degeneration* is quoted, together with others, at the end of Heinemann's 1895 edition of *Conventional Lies*.

p.162 '... *instead of condemnation.'* Hake, *Regeneration*, p. 78; Nordau, *Conventional Lies*, pp. 55ff.; Hart-Davis, *Letters of Wilde*, p. 402.

p.162 '... *of Dr Jekyll.'* Mason, *Oscar Wilde*, p. 201.

p.163 '... *with a kiss.'* S.Aidan Reynolds and William Charlton, *Arthur Machen*, 1963, pp. 43–46; Arthur Machen, *The Great God Pan*, 1894, p. 93; Eric, Count Stenbock, *Studies of Death*, 1894, pp. 120–47; *The Spirit Lamp*, Oxford June 1893, pp. 52–68; Julian Osgood Field, *Aut Diabolus aut Nihil*, 1894, pp. 145–226.

p.164 '... *actually done so.' S*, 14 September 1895, p. 232; William Tebb and Edward Perry Vollum, *Premature Burial*, 1896, pp. 242–43.

p.164 '... *to reduce it.'* Frederick Greenwood, *Imagination in Dreams and their study*, 1894, p. 113.

p.165 '... *supremacy of sex.'* Edward Carpenter, *Homogenic Love*, Manchester 1895, p. 45.

p.165 '... *presage cosmic disaster.*' *The Collected Works of Ambrose Bierce*, 12 vols, New York 1966, iii, 20, 29–30; x, 127–31.

p.166 '... *menace of Dracula.*' Bram Stoker, *Dracula*, 1897, pp. 5, 26, 280–81, 337.

p.167 '... *man's heart out.*' M.R.James, *More Ghost Stories of an Antiquary*, 1911, pp. v, 15.

p.167 '... *been a hoax.*' Henry Charles Lea, *Léo Taxil, Diana Vaughan et l'Église Romaine: histoire d'une mystification*, Paris 1901, pp. 18–24.

p.168 '... *powers of darkness.*' *CR*, May 1897, pp. 694–710; A.E.Waite, *Devil-Worship in France*, 1896; Robert Baldick, *The Life of J.-K.Huysmans*, Oxford 1955, pp. 140, 154; John Symonds, *The Great Beast: the Life and Magick of Aleister Crowley*, 1971, p. 16.

p.168 '... *of the world.*' Ellic Howe, *The Magicians of the Golden Dawn 1887–1923*, 1972, p. 50, 52; Reynolds and Charlton, *Arthur Machen*, pp. 70–79; Arthur Machen, *The Hill of Dreams*, 1907, pp. 113–15; Jean Overton Fuller, *The Magical Dilemma of Victor Neuburg*, 1965, pp. 148–50; Reynolds and Charlton, *Arthur Machen*, pp. 73, 106–7.

p.168 '... *into Popish bondage.*' Walter Walsh, *The Secret Work of the Ritualists*, 1894, pp. 43, 11.

p.169 '... *of public opinion.*' Sister Mary Agnes (Miss J.M.Povey), *Nunnery Life in the Church of England*, 1890, p. 99; Walter Walsh, *Secret History of the Oxford Movement*, 1897, pp. 38–39; Father Michael, O.S.B., *Father Ignatius in America*, 1893, pp. 101–3, 237.

p.169 '... *to appeal to.*' Hudson, *Religion in America*, pp. 257–61, 249; *CR*, February 1897, pp. 276–79; *Dictionary of National Biography Supplement 1901–1911 Volume II*, 1912, pp. 389–90; *T*, 17 September 1898, p. 9.

p.170 '... *some sort American.*' R.L.Green (ed.), *Kipling: the Critical Heritage*, 1971, pp. 192–93.

p.171 '... *in the ear.*' Allan Nevins, *The Letters of Grover Cleveland*, Boston and New York 1933, p. 419; Charles Carrington, *Kipling*, 3rd rev'd edn 1978, pp. 283, 297; R.W.Sallman and L.Gilkes (eds), *Letters of Stephen Crane*, 1960, pp. 5, 43n.; S.Bradley, R.C.Beatty and E.H.Long (eds), *The Red Badge of Courage; an annotated text*, New York 1962, p. 196.

p.171 '... *the British Empire.*' *SR*, 11 January 1896, p. 44; *FR*, August 1897, pp. 286–96.

p.172 '... *mission of America.*' *T*, 14 May 1898, p. 12; Charles S.Olcott, *Life of McKinley*, Boston 1916, ii, 110–11; *Congressional Record*, Vol. XXXIII, pt 1, Washington 1900, pp. 704–12.

p.172 '... *hordes of evil.*' *T*, 11 January 1896, p. 9; 17 July 1897, p. 13; M.Cohen (ed.), *Rudyard Kipling to Rider Haggard: the record of a Friendship*, 1965, pp. 34–37; *AR*, 1900, p. 2.

p.173 '... *the new king:*' *Blackwood's Magazine*, June 1895, p. 842; Bernard Bergonzi, *The Turn of the Century*, 1973, p. 39; *AR*, 1899, p. 76; 1901, pp. 9, 25.

p.173 '... *of that wonder.*' Carrington, *Kipling*, pp. 277–78; Green, *Grahame*, pp. 301–2.

p.174 '... *to destroy Dracula.*' *The Works of Bernard Shaw*, Vol. IX, 1930, p. xxii; R.L.Green, *A.E.W.Mason*, 1952, p. 60; Stoker, *Dracula*, pp. 152, 389.

p.174 '... *death in battle:*' Evelyn Sharp, *Unfinished Adventure*, 1933, p. 57; *Harper's Magazine*, July 1889, pp. 241–44.

p.174 '... *rather than sorrow?*' H.A.Vachell, *The Hill*, 1905, p. 313.

p.175 '... *even your play.*' *T*, 4 January 1902, p. 9.

p.175 '... *hold on life?*' H.G.Wells, *The Time Machine*, 1895, p. 27.

p.176 '... *built for rabbits!*' H.G.Wells, *The War of the Worlds*, 1898, p. 195.

p.176 '... *the old wolf-cry.*' H.G.Wells, *The War in the Air and particularly how Mr Bert Smallways fared while it lasted*, 1908, pp. 336–67; Jack London, *The Call of the Wild*, 1903, pp. 61, 90, 91.

CHAPTER 11

p.177 '... *one outraged reviewer.*' H.G.Wells, *The Future in America*, 1906, pp. 9, 354, 78, 154, 355; *The Days of the Comet*, 1906, p. 189; *Experiment in Autobiography*, 2 vols, 1934, ii, 480.

p.178 '... *complete the work.*' *T*, 10 February 1910, p. 11; Brian Harpur, *The Official Halley's Comet Book*, 1985, pp. 44, 51, 44.

p.178 '... *government and religion.*' *Ibid.*, p. 40; *Collected Essays by Virginia Woolf*, 2 vols, 1966, i, 320; Harriette and Homer Curtiss, *The Philosophy of War*, Los Angeles and San Francisco 1914, pp. 33, 38 (passage written May 1909, revised September 1914).

p.179 '... *claim to it.*' Rev. F.W.Orde Ward, *The World's Quest*, 1908, pp. 1, 223; *'Falling Upwards': Christ the Key to the Riddle of the Cosmos*, 1911, p. 5; *Quest*, p. 1.

p.179 '... *doing for physics.*' Henri Bergson, *Creative Evolution*, tr. A.Mitchell, 1911, pp. x, 322–23.

p.180 '... *the Society's imprint.*' *Quest*, October 1909, pp. 29–43; April 1912, p. 401; James H.Hyslop, *Psychical Research and Survival*, 1913.

p.180 '... *classes of society.*' *Quest*, January 1916, p. 320; R.L.Green, *A.E.W. Mason*, 1952, p. 59; *FR*, January 1912, p. 161; *AR*, 1904, p. 36.

p.181 '... *continuous and progressive.*' *FR*, January 1912, p. 166; Sir Oliver Lodge, *The Survival of Man*, 1909, p. 339; F.W.H.Myers, *Human Personality and its Survival of Bodily Death*, 2 vols, 1903, ii, 288, 281.

p.181 '... *been washed away.*' *FR*, January 1912, pp. 166, 170, 167, 161.

p.182 '... *as in fiction.*' *T*, 27 April 1907, p. 14; 1 May 1907, p. 4.

p.183 '... *and the like.*' Emma Jung and Marie-Louise von Franz, *The Grail Legend*, tr. Andrea Dykes, 1971, pp. 401–7; *Quest*, October 1909, pp. 125–39, 91–107; Reynolds and Charlton, *Arthur Machen*, pp. 101, 103–4, 116.

p.183 '... *of Life itself.*' *Quest*, October 1909, pp. 170–74; April 1910,

p. 524; Jessie L.Weston, *The Quest of the Holy Grail*, 1913, p. 138; *Quest*, October 1916, pp. 127–39.

p.184 '... *of Virginia Woolf.*' Jung and von Franz, *Grail Legend*, pp. 150–51; D.S.Thatcher, *Nietzsche in England 1890–1914*, Toronto 1970, p. 41; *Quest*, April 1911, pp. 417–37.

p.185 '... *his trusty companion.*' Hilaire Belloc, *Hills and the Sea*, 1906, pp. x, xii–xiii.

p.186 '... *her son's murderer.*' *FR*, June 1912, p. 116; *The Treasury*, January 1916, pp. 323–29; Roland Huntford, *Scott and Amundsen*, 1979, p. 559.

p.186 '... *another to suicide.*' Huntford, *Scott and Amundsen*, pp. 554–55; Andrew Birkin, *J.M.Barrie and the Lost Boys*, 1979, p. 209.

p.186 '... *over the other.*' Huntford, *Scott and Amundsen*, p. 543.

p.187 '... *agony without flinching.*' *T*, 10 June 1908, p. 10; J.R.Ackerley, *My Father and myself*, 1968, p. 53; Charles M.Doughty, *The Cliffs*, 1909, pp. 223–24.

p.188 '... *substance and reality.*' James J.Gibson (ed.), *The Variorum Edition of the Complete Poems of Thomas Hardy*, 1979, pp. 97–99; *FR*, March 1912, pp. 397–99.

p.189 '... *of his existence.*' *Ibid.*

p.189 '... *had been abolished.*' Ray Abrams, *Preachers Present Arms: a study of the war-time attitudes and activities of the churches and clergy in the United States 1914–1918*, Philadelphia 1933, p. 9.

p.189 '... *none was American.*' *T*, 5 October 1912, p. 3; Georges Haupt, *La Deuxième Internationale 1889–1914*, Paris and the Hague 1964.

p.190 '... *on 4 August.*' *T*, 19 October 1912, p. 6; 19 November 1912, p. 4; 22 October 1912, p. 5; *AR*, 1911, p. 4; *T*, 15 October 1912, p. 6; Abrams, *Preachers Present Arms*, p. 9.

p.190 '... *of bourgeois imagining.*' *T*, 29 July 1914, p. 7; 26 September 1914, p. 6.

p.191 '... *warlord's greatest strength.*' *Quest*, October 1914, pp. 160–63; April 1915, p. 519; *T*, 3 August 1914, p. 8.

p.191 '... *in the trenches.*' *T*, 6 August 1914, p. 5; 29 August 1914, p. 5; Louis P.Lochner, *America's Don Quixote*, 1924, pp. 4–19.

p.192 '... *to Arthur Machen.*' John Terraine, 'A Comfortless Mythology', *T*, 11 November 1978, p. 8; Ralph Shirley, *The Angel Warriors of Mons*, 1915, p. 15; Arthur Machen, *The Bowmen and other Legends of the War*, 1915; *The Treasury*, October 1915, p. 46; Harold Begbie, *On the side of the angels: a reply to Arthur Machen*, 1915, p. 12.

p.192 '... *destruction of Christianity.*' *Is there a Hell? A Symposium by Leaders of Religious Thought*, 1913, p. 4; *T*, 8 August 1914, p. 9; *Occult Review*, September 1914, p. 355; F.J.Foakes-Jackson (ed.), *The Faith and the War*, 1915, p. 234; Cate Haste, *Keep the Home Fires Burning: propaganda in the First World War*, 1977, pp. 79–83.

p.193 '... *die by inches.*' Henri Bergson, *The Meaning of the War*, 1915, pp. 37–38; Jessie L.Weston, *Germany's Crime against France*, 1915, pp. 17,

27; *Quest,* January 1917, pp. 256, 259, 262; January 1915, pp. 244–49, 203–6.

p.193 '... *the broken body.*' *The Treasury,* January 1916, pp. 323–29; *Quest,* April 1917, pp. 452–53; F.W.Orde Ward, *The Last Crusade: Patriotic Poems,* 1917, pp. 7, 19.

p.194 '... *topography of Golgotha.*' Harold Owen and John Bell (eds), *Wilfred Owen: Collected Letters,* 1967, p. 562.

p.194 '... *his superior officers.*' John Hughes, 'The evidence for war objectors' "crucifixion"', *Sunday Times,* 19 October 1975, p. 11.

p.194 '... *what they do.*' *Ibid.*; Owen Wister, *The Pentecost of Calamity,* 1915, pp. 98, 121; Abrams, *Preachers Present Arms,* p. 41; C.L.Droste, *Germany's Golgotha,* New York 1917, p. 22.

p.195 '... *mere armed forces.*' Abrams, *Preachers Present Arms,* pp. 27; *CR,* March 1915, pp. 339–45; Abrams, *Preachers Present Arms,* pp. 28, 37–38, 59.

p.196 '... *the material plane.*' *Occult Review,* January 1916; Sir Oliver Lodge, *Raymond,* 1916, p. 249; Hereward Carrington, *Psychical Phenomena and the War,* 1918, p. 251; *Occult Review,* January 1916, p. 39.

p.196 '... *needs of man.*' C.E.Montague, *Disenchantment,* 1922, p. 71; Edmund Blunden (ed.), *The Poems of Wilfred Owen,* 1931, p. 57.

p.197 '... *he survived it.*' Symonds, *Great Beast,* pp. 203–4; Erich Fromm, *The Anatomy of Human Destructiveness,* 1977, pp. 243–44; Arthur Koestler, 'What's Wrong With Us?', *Observer Review,* 28 April 1968, p. 25; Nigel Davies, *Human Sacrifice in history and today,* 1981.

p.197 '... *more than human.*' *T,* 26 October 1920, p. 10.

p.198 '... *transfigured and sanctified.*' Sir Philip Gibbs, *The Realities of War,* 1920, p. 84; *Illustrated London News,* 20 November 1920, p. 806.

p.198 '... *God's funeral procession.*' *The Treasury,* May 1917, p. 100; Laurence Housman (ed.), *War Letters of fallen Englishmen,* 1930, p. 214; *T,* 18 November 1919, p. 9.

POSTSCRIPT

p.199 '... *bloom this year?*' Valerie Eliot (ed.), *The Waste Land: facsimile and transcript,* 1971, pp. xxii, 95.

p.200 '... *howl and expired.*' *Ibid.,* pp. xxii, 1; Edward L.Gardner, *Fairies: the Cottingley Photographs and their sequel,* 2nd edn 1951, p. 9; Leonard Cottrell, *The Lost Pharaohs,* 1976, pp. 180–81.

p.201 '... *become whole again.*' *T,* 4 June 1919, p. 11.

INDEX

A Study in Scarlet 151, 153, 155
'Abide with me' 21, 23, 35
abolitionists 75; *see also* slavery
absolute space 129
absolute time 129
acts of God 94; *see also* earthquakes; natural disasters
Adam and Eve 43; *see also* creation myth
adventure 141, 186
adversity 135
afterlife, belief in 68
age of miracles 122
Age of Reason 1
Albert, Prince Consort 35, 38, 85, 95
Allen, Grant 146, 147, 156
Allies, First World War 194
  death of 38
America 16
anaesthesia 39, 40, 44; *see also* pain, death of
anarchists, American 138
anarchy 69, 84
ancient Egypt 64, 101
angels 5–6, 9, 11
Angels of Mons 5, 6, 191
Anglican creed 23
Anglo-American friendship 171
Anglo-Catholicism 168
anti-Catholic riots 84
Antichrist 9, 11, 12, 16, 26, 29, 32, 33, 36, 37, 73, 192

Anti-Interment in Towns Association 22
apocalypse 13, 72
Apollo 67, 69, 70, 155
appearance 2, 30, 112
architecture 9
Ariès, Phillipe 42
Aristotle 70
Armageddon 16, 36, 177
Armistice Day 198
Arthur, President 135
Artist and Journal of Home Culture 159
Arundel, Earl of 26
asceticism 134, 153, 155
Ashley, Lord 14, 15; *see also* Shaftesbury, Earl of
aspiration, Christian 183–4
astral body 117
atheism 2, 9, 12, 96, 148
  American 19
aurora borealis 87
Austin, Alfred 172

Baird, Robert 74
Balfour, Arthur 124, 130, 131
Balkan Question 108
Balkan War 189
Ballantyne, R.M. 132
Bank Holidays 92
barbarity 40
Baring-Gould, Sabine 24, 60, 64, 82
Barrie, J.M. 18, 186
Bath, Marquis of 106

'Battle Hymn of the Republic' 81, 95
Beaconsfield, Lord 109, 110, 115
   death of 122
   see also Disraeli, Benjamin
Beard, J.R. 28
Beecher, Henry Ward 95–6, 97
Belloc, Hilaire 185
Bennett, Arnold 200
Benson, Bishop (later Archbishop)
   124–5, 148, 149, 150
Bergsonian view of universe 182
Berkley, Theresa 50
Bible Communism 30, 32
biblical authority 10, 42, 147
biblical criticism 46
biblical revelation 146
Bierce, Ambrose 165, 188
bigotry 26
birching 42
Birth of Tragedy, The 70, 71; *see also*
   Nietzsche, Friedrich
Bishop, Mrs 74, 76
black Americans 41–2
black magic 167
Black Mass 167
Blackwood, Algernon 166, 193
Blackwood's Magazine 24, 34
blasphemy 12, 17, 32, 125
Blathwayt, Raymond 180, 181, 185
Blavatsky, Helena 116, 117, 118
blood 34
bodily resurrection 44
Boer War 170, 171, 188
Book of Werewolves 64
bourgeois society 21
boy vagabonds 136–7
Boy's Own Paper 132, 133
Bradlaugh, Charles 124
bravery 185
Bright, John 119, 122, 123
British and Foreign Anti-Slavery
   Society 76
British and Foreign Bible Society
   189

British Association for the Advance-
   ment of Science 52, 83, 113, 147
Brooke, Rupert 175
Brotherhood of Luxor 116
Brougham, Lord 26–7
Brown, John 75, 79
Browning, Elizabeth Barrett 36, 56,
   71, 95
Brownson, Orestes 30, 77, 78
Buccleuch, Duke of 83
Buchanan, Robert 140
Buddha 117
Buffalo Bill 97
Bulwer-Lytton, Edward 116
Buren, Martin van 8
burial grounds 22
Burne-Jones, Edward 125
Burns, Anthony 75

Caine, Hall 33, 131
Caithness, Countess of 114, 115, 117
Call of the Wild, The 176
Cambridge, Duke of 90
Cambridge Ghost Society 125
capitalism 21
Capron, Eliab 34
Carlyle, Thomas 48
Carnegie, Andrew 131, 189, 191
Carpenter, Edward 154, 161, 165
Carrington, Hereward 195
Carroll, Lewis 119, 120; *see also*
   Dodgson, Charles
catalepsy 24
catastrophes 12
Catholic Book Society 12
Catholic tyranny 170
Catholicism, American 169; *see also*
   Irish immigration
cause and effect 129
chaos 143
Chartism 12, 15, 27
child sacrifice 167
childbirth 40
children, employment of 14, 15
chivalry 10, 158

chloroform 40, 42
Christ 155
   agony of 43, 187
   death of 144
   passion of 193
   resurrection of 145
   suffering of 40
'Christ aux Oliviers, Le' 18
Christian military duties 82
Christian morality 57
Christian orthodoxy 61
Christian Science 119
Christian World 161
Christianity 2, 5, 20
   American 16
church attendance 19, 148
Church of England 9, 10, 11, 26,
   44
Church of England Union 189, 190
Church Peace Union 189, 190
civilization, Christian 40
class conflict 52, 98
Cleopatra's Needle 109
Cleveland, President 170
Cleveland Street scandal 159
Cobbe, Frances Power 44, 55, 56, 61,
   64, 68, 69, 71, 76, 78
Coleridge, Samuel Taylor 2, 4
Coley, Rev. J. 104
collective unconsciousness 3
Colley, Rev. Thomas 181–2
common sense 182
Communism 20, 30, 88
Communist Manifesto 20, 21, 28
companionship in arms 158
comparative religion 47, 64, 69
compassion 15
competition 52
conceptual thought 179
conflict 52, 193
Congress of the Communist League
   20
consciousness 30
   general 32
Conservatism 86, 87

*Conventional Lies of our Civilization,
   The* 161
Cook, Rev. Flavel Smith 48–9
Cornford, Frances 175
Cornhill Magazine 36, 56
corporal punishment 42
Cory, William 158
cosmic change 177
cosmic disaster 165
cosmic synthesis 146
cowardice 174
creation 2, 4, 10, 53, 114
creation myth, Jewish 59
creative evolutionary process 192
creative intelligence 10
creativity 4
Crane, Stephen 170
Crawford, Lord 123–4
Crime and Punishment 135
Crimean War 35
'Crossing the Bar' 119
Crowley, Aleister 167
   as Antichrist 196
crucifix 43–4
cruelty 15, 137
Cuban revolt 170
Cumming, Dr John 13, 27, 29, 32,
   35, 36, 72, 73, 78, 83, 84, 95, 122

danger 135, 138
Daniel, Book of 16
Dante 53, 69
darkness 8, 13, 18, 21, 139, 141, 167
Darwin, Charles 52, 53, 58, 93, 126
dawn of reason 26
Day of Judgement 23
Day of National Prayer and
   Humiliation 73
Day of National Prayer and
   Supplication 89–90
Day of Pentecost 149
de Nerval, Gerard 18
de Sade, Marquis 54
death 2, 23
   fear of 24

death (*contd.*)
pagan conception of 198
degeneracy 7
democracy 135, 139
Derby, Lord 84, 85
Descent of Man, The 93
desire, guilty 165
desire, physical 155
despair 17
Desprez, P.S. 37
Devil 13, 45
belief in 49
disproof of 54
as myth 192
devils 24
dialectical materialism 28, 29
dialectics 29
Diamond Jubilee 172, 174
Dickens, Charles 20, 42, 95
Dilke, Sir Charles 20, 89, 90, 105, 111
Dionysus 62, 69, 144, 145, 155
disasters 101
disbelief 94
discipline 187
disembodied souls 35
disestablishment 86
Disraeli, Benjamin 65–6, 82, 84, 85, 91, 100, 102–3, 106, 107
Divine Mystery 179
divine retribution 12
divine right of civilized nations 172
divine truth 148
divine wisdom 116
divinity 185
Dodgson, Charles 54, 93, 120; *see also* Carroll, Lewis
Doré, Gustave 53
Dostoevsky, Fëdor 135, 136
Douglas, Lord Alfred 160, 163, 168
Douglass, Frederick 41
dove, symbolism of 127
'Dover Beach' 69, 84
Doyle, Sir Arthur Conan 4, 6, 151, 199

Dr Jekyll and Mr Hyde 162
Dracula 166, 174
Draper, Professor John William 86, 113, 114
dreams 1, 4, 32, 54, 165
interpretation of 198
Dwellers of the Threshold 116, 117, 152
Dyer, Oliver 31

earthquakes 12, 13, 14, 120
Cannes 141–2
Eastern mythology 64
Eastern Question 114
eccentricity 182
Ecclesiastical Commissioners 148
economic necessity 29
ecstasy 176
Edinburgh, Duke of 85
Edinburgh Review 28
Edward VII 178; *see also* Wales, Prince of
Edwards, Amelia 131
Einstein, Albert 31, 122, 146, 179, 182
Eisler, Robert 183
elementals 200
Elijah 72
Eliot, T.S. 136, 183, 199, 200, 201
Elliott, Rev. Edward Bishop 11, 98
Ellis, Havelock 144, 154–5, 158, 165
emancipation of slaves 81
Emerson, Ralph Waldo 30, 60, 79
emotionalism 20
end of the world 99
Engels, Friedrich 20, 21, 66
England and Islam 114, 115, 117
English Review 26, 28
Ensor, Sir Charles 1, 2, 4
eroticism 159
Essays and Reviews 46, 51, 86
eternal punishment 47, 48
ether 39
Euston scandal 22
Evangelical Alliance 113

evil 15, 43, 162, 184, 186
  belief in 54
  power of 178
  supremacy of 144
expanding universe 122, 179; *see also*
    relativity, theory of
evolution 52

fact 1
faith 28
  decay of 9
faith healing 118
fallen angels 44
fallibility 141
fanaticism 9, 29, 31, 75
fancy 4
fantasy 1, 2, 3, 4, 6, 8, 47, 54, 71,
    99, 130, 165, 193
  politics of 110
  religious 87
  and thought 111
fear
  of the dead 24
  of death 24
Fenian Brotherhood 76
Fenian outrages 84, 85, 122
Fergusson, James 62
fertility cults 60, 62, 65, 184, 201
fiction 129, 130, 181
  popular 6
Fields, James 80, 81
Figuier, Guillaume 68–9
fin de siècle 172
financial crisis, 1857 77
Finney, Charles 75, 77
fire 13
  as cleansing agent 16
First World War 6, 190–4
flagellation 169
  erotic 50–1
Foote, G.W. 125
Ford, Henry 191
Forrest, General Nathan 96
fortitude 42
Four Feathers, The 173–4

Four Horsemen of the Apocalypse
    10, 35
Fowle, Thomas 93
Fox, Katherine and Margaretta 32
Franco-Prussian War 87
Frazer, Sir James 156
Free Religious Association 68, 69
Freemasonry 167, 169
Freethinker 125
French Revolution 8, 9, 11, 27, 29
Freud, Sigmund 3, 65, 164
Fromm, Erich 196

gallantry 5, 174
Galton, Francis 93–4
Genesis, Book of 10, 13, 43, 52, 101
geologists 13
George v 178, 186, 197
German metaphysics 28, 29, 59
German philosophy 46
ghosts 24, 165
Gladstone, William Ewart 9, 11, 81,
    86, 89, 90, 91, 100, 108, 110,
    111, 122, 134, 138, 140
God 2
  absence of 13, 17, 18, 192
  anger of 18, 165, 175, 178
  of battle 6, 188, 190, 193
  commandments of 29
  death of 18, 37, 121, 143, 159,
    165
  image of 7, 38
  imminent 141, 145
  knowledge of 9–10
  as movement 179
  of peace 190
  plan of 113
  transcendental 141, 145
  will of 29
godhead 32
'God's Funeral' 188
golden age 53
Golden Bough, The 156, 199
Golden Jubilee 135, 139, 143
goodness 145, 184, 186

Gordon, General 134; *see also* heroism; self-sacrifice
Goschen, George 130
Gosse, Edmund 135
Goya, Francisco 1, 2, 5, 11, 18, 27
Grace, W.G.; as heterosexual hero 174
Grahame, Kenneth 156
Great Exhibition 35
Great God Pan, The 163
Great Pyramid 99–100, 101, 102
Greece 67
Greek mythology 60
Green, Thomas Hill 129
Greenwood, Frederick 164
Greville, Charles 27
Grosvenor, Lord Robert 73
guardian angels 5

Haden, Francis Seymour 105
Haggard, Rider 131, 136, 151, 159, 172
Hake, Alfred 161
Hallam, Arthur 9, 35; *see also* 'Morte d'Arthur'; Tennyson, Alfred Lord
Harrison, Frederic 46, 49, 88
hatred 153
Hawthorne, Nathaniel 57–8
heaven 1, 2, 4, 13, 55
    glories of 23, 33
Hegel, Georg 29
hell 1, 2, 4, 13, 25, 55
    destruction of 44
    harrowing of 43
    as kingdom of pain 44
    torments of 13
Hell Opened to Christians 13, 14, 44–5
hellfire 12
Heraclitean creation 179
Heraclitean fire 145, 149, 163, 189
Heraclitean theory of the universe 146, 182
Heraclitean thought 150, 154

Heraclitus 144, 145, 146, 155, 176, 179
heresy 30
    German 37
heroism 6, 134, 155, 174, 175, 185, 187
Hewlett, Maurice 137
Hiawatha 34, 61
hierarchy, undermined 178
Hindley, Charles 99
Hindu revivalism 117
Hindu Vedanta 117
Holmes, Parson 10,11
Holmes, Sherlock 4, 5, 18, 151–3, 184, 188
Holy Grail 183, 184
holy war 192
Holyoake, George Jacob 19, 20, 21, 23, 25, 26, 27, 28, 44, 45
Homogenic Love 161
homosexuality 158, 160, 168
Hopkins, Gerard Manley 51, 88, 122, 145
horror stories 24, 165
Hort, Professor F.J.A. 125
Houghton, Lord 48, 52, 53, 54, 119
Howe, Julia Ward 80, 81, 95, 149
Howells, William Dean 170
Huckleberry Finn, 136; *see also* boy vagabonds
Hughes, Thomas 133
human sacrifice 187, 197
Hume, Daniel 34, 36
Hunting of the Snark, The 119–20
hymnody 82
Hymns Ancient and Modern 82

ideas, history of 3
illusion 5, 7
'Imaginatio' 4
imagination 1, 2, 3, 4, 52, 53, 130, 139
    and knowledge 130, 145
    and reason 5

immortality 2, 5, 55, 64, 163, 187
 personal 180
immutability of species 147
imperial destiny 101, 109
imperialism 92, 172
impiety 187
indecency 163
Indian culture 61
individuality 130
industrial decline 98
Inferno 53
infidelity 9
Ingersoll, Robert Green 96, 126
initiation 184
initiation rites 42
inner consciousness 31
Inquisition 26
insubordination 15
intellectualism 131
International Socialist League 190
Ireland 19
Irish immigration to US 95, 169
irrationality 8, 144
Isis Unveiled 117, 118

James, Henry 132, 136
James, Jesse 136
James, William 132, 179
Jesuits 26
Jevons, Professor 132
jingoism 109, 171
 belligerent 173
Joan of Arc 116

Kant, Immanuel 29
Keble, John 10, 48
Kelvin, Lord 147
Kensit, John 169
Kilvert, Francis 51, 90, 94, 109
King Solomon's Mines 131
Kingsford, Anna 115, 151
Kipling, Rudyard 170, 172, 188
Knights of the Round Table 158
Knowles, James 118
Koestler, Arthur 197

Krafft-Ebing, Baron Richard von
 159, 164, 168
Ku Klux Klan 96, 97, 153

'Land of Hope and Glory' 174
Last Judgement 1, 2, 4, 6
lawlessness 97
Lee, Frederick George 94
Leopold, Prince 85
Lévi, Eliphas 115
lewdness 56
Liberal Party 86
liberty 135
life after death 5, 33, 120
life before birth 32
Lincoln, Abraham 79, 80, 81
 assassination 82
Linton, Mrs Lynn 93
'Locksley Hall' 139
'Locksley Hall Sixty Years After'
 139, 141, 151
Lodge, Sir Oliver 180, 195
London 12
London Cemetery Company 23, 25
London, Jack 176
Long, Crawford 39
Longfellow, Henry Wadsworth 2,
 23, 33, 34, 61, 79, 85
love 52, 53
Lusitania, sinking of 195
lycanthropy 64
Lyell, Charles 10
Lyne, Father Ignatius 169
Lyte, Rev. Henry Francis 2, 21, 31,
 33, 35
Lytton, Lord 107, 117, 118

Mach, Ernst 129
Machen, Arthur 163, 168, 183, 191
Maden, Mrs 51, 52
Mafeking 172
magic 57
Maitland, Edward 114, 115, 116,
 121, 123, 124, 125
male brothels 159

Mallock, William 120
man as God's image 58, 59
Manliness of Christ, The 133
Marble Faun, The 57–8
Marsh, Rev. William 11, 12, 15, 98
martyrdom 134
Marx, Karl 20, 21, 28, 52, 126
Marxism 200
Marxist Socialists 189
masochism 159
Mason, A.E.W. 173, 180
Massachusetts Quarterly Review 61
masturbation 157, 165
materialism 4, 33, 96, 155, 181
materialization of the dead 182
Mayo, Dr 24, 25, 164
McKinley, President 171, 173
Mead, G.R.S. 180
Merrett, Frederick 104
Metaphysical Society 119
Mexico 17, 60, 62
Michelson, Albert Abraham 121–2
Mill, John Stuart 95
millenial expectations 177
Miller, William 16, 18
Milton, John 13, 43, 58
mining 14
miracles 83, 85
Momerie, Dr Alfred Williams 147–8,
    149–50
monarchists 90
money markets 137
monsters 1, 11, 24, 54
Moody, Dwight 75, 105, 106
moral law 55
moral progress 195
moral responsibility 55
moral universe 193
moral values 29
moral will 55
morality 107
Morgan, Henry Lewis 61
Morley, Edward 122
Morley, John 63
Mormon Church 30, 32

Mormon fanaticism 144
'Morte d'Arthur' 9, 10
mortification of the flesh 42
Morton, W.T.G. 39
Moses 72
Müller, Friedrich Max 59, 61
Munby, Arthur 52, 53, 84
muscular Christianity 173
Murray, John 34
Myers, Frederick 181
mysticism 25, 161
myths 2
    and religion 47
myth-making 6

Napoleon III 77, 78–9
    as Beelzebub 77
    as beast of the Apocalypse 78
    overthrow of 87
National Association of Spiritualism
    50
national crimes 17
natural disasters 120–1
natural law 94
natural selection 93
nature 53, 70
necromancy 33, 115
neo-paganism 155, 156
neuroticism 159
new hedonism 156
new paganism 155, 156
Nichol, John Pringle 31
Nietzsche, Friedrich 70, 71, 121, 129,
    141, 144, 145, 155, 159, 160,
    184, 188
nihilism 122
Nineteenth Century 119
nitrous oxide 39
Nordau, Max 159, 161, 162, 172
novel reading 132; *see also* fiction;
    public libraries
Noyes, John 30

Oates, Lieutenant 185, 186, 187; *see
    also* self-sacrifice, heroic

oath-taking 51
observation 153
occult 124, 166
Occult Review 196
occultism 166
Odger, George 89, 90
O.K. Corral 135; *see also* Wild West
old dispensation 126, 127
Olympic Games 174
O'Mahoney, John 76
Oneida Community 30, 32; *see also*
    utopian communities
'Onward, Christian soldiers' 24
order 146
Order of Christian Mystics 178
Order of the Golden Dawn 167, 168
Origin of Mind, The 66
Origin of Species, The 52, 53, 66, 78
orthodoxy 23, 188
Our Lady of Lourdes 77
Owen, Wilfred 193, 196

pagan conception of death 198
pagan ecstasy 56
pagan fantasy 66
pagan gods 58
Pagan Papers 156
Pagan Review 156, 159
pagan rituals 59
pagan sacrifice 159
paganism 155
    nostalgia for 58
pain 42, 43, 50
    death of 40, 44; *see also* anaesthesia
    infliction of 41; *see also* whipping
    necessity for 53
    and paganism 57
Painter's Church of England Gazette 20
Palmerston, Lord 73
Pan 62, 69, 155
    death of 37, 56
    rebirth of 144
'Pan in Wall Street' 62
Pandora 43, 53

pantheism 28, 31, 32, 62
papal infallibility 113
papal tyranny 46
paradise 8, 10
Paradise Lost 13, 43, 58
Paradise Regained 58
paranoia 197
paranormal 166
parental prohibition 165
Paris Commune 88, 93
Parker, Ely Samuel 61
Parker, Theodore 61, 62, 71, 75, 76,
    77–8
patriotism 172
peace 189
penitence 156
penny dreadfuls 132
People's Charter 27
pestilence 11
Peter Pan 18, 153, 158
phallic symbolism 60, 62
'Phantasia' 4
pharaoh's curse 200
phoenix 126–7
Phoenix Park murders 138
physical degeneracy 175
physical desire 135
Picture of Dorian Gray, The 159, 160,
    161, 162
piety 48
Pinamonti, Father 13, 44
Plato 2, 70, 112, 144
Plevna, fall of 108
Poe, Edgar Allen 24, 31–2, 34
Poems and Ballads 62
poetic genius 2
political corruption 137
politics
    and religion 86
Polk, President 41
Pope, Alexander 65
popery, and satanism 168
popular culture 101
portents 99
positivism 88

Pound, Ezra 199
Povey, Miss 168–9
prayer 17, 94
premature burial 164; *see also* Dr
    Mayo; vampire myths
Prince of Darkness 54
Principles of Geology 10
progress 52
  inevitability of 140
progressive idealism 86
prophecy 17, 72
  of apocalypse 29
Protestant Enlightenment 170
Protestant hysteria 77
Protestant Reformation 74
Protestant scepticism 166
Protestant Truth Society 168
Protestantism 11, 30
    and fanaticism 11
    and science 113
pseudo-Catholicism 102
psycho-analysis 3, 54
public libraries 131
Public Worship Regulation Act 102
punishment 13
pure love 158
Pusey, Professor Edward 47, 48, 59,
    86

Quimby, Phineas 118
Queensberry libel trial 167; *see also*
    Douglas, Lord Alfred; Wilde,
    Oscar
Queensberry, Marquis of 160
Quest 187, 190
Quest Society 179, 180, 182

racialism 200
Radical Club 68
radicalism 75, 138
rational religion 143, 146
rationalism 1, 12, 19, 28, 29, 33
Reade, Winwood 4–5, 6, 18, 66, 67,
    69, 146, 147, 152
realism 131

reality 1, 2, 3, 7
reason 1, 2, 28, 153
  god of, *see* Apollo
  goddess of 27
Reasoner, The 19, 23, 26, 44, 51
recrucifixion fantasy 197, 198
redemption 43
Regeneration 161, 162
reincarnation 68–9
relative universe 163
relativity, theory of 146
religion, history of 3
religious conversion 19
religious fantasy 87
religious fervour 19
religious observance 17
religious prejudice 52
religious revival 73, 75, 76
  hymns 82
Religious Tract Society 132, 133
reproductive urge 155
republicanism 89
resurrection of the body 23, 24, 104
  instant 164
Resurrection of Christ 181
retribution 52
revealed religion 10
Revelation, Book of 10, 12, 16, 36,
    99, 118
revolution 8
  of 1848 21
  threat of 15
Revue des Deux Mondes 37, 46
Richter, Jean Paul 18, 152
riots 73, 122
ritual of death 156
Rochdale Secular Society 51
Rogers, Henry 28
Roman Catholicism 37, 40, 44, 74,
    167
  and superstition 11, 95
Roman mythology 60
romance 131
Roosevelt, President 173
Rossetti, Dante Gabriel 33, 63, 88

Rubáiyát of Omar Khayyám 59
rural distress 110
Russia 108

sacrifice 17, 176, 186, 196
sacrilege 24
sadism 159, 160
St Paul 42, 44, 50, 64
Saintsbury, George 130–1, 154, 181
Salisbury, Lord 101, 147
Salt, Henry 50
sanctity 24
Sankey, Ira 105, 106
Satan 43, 53
satanism 63, 166, 168
scepticism 181
Schaff, Philip 74, 75, 77
Schiller, Friedrich 58
schoolboy love 158
Schopenhauer, Arthur 18, 145
science 67, 155
    and democracy 139
    as enemy 93
    and religion 82–3
scientific determinism 67
scientific heresy 146
scientific laws 113
scientific method 112
scientific progress 86, 96
scientific research 10
scientific scepticism 95, 143
scientific truth 52
séances 33, 36, 145
Second Coming 16, 37, 72, 100, 134
Second International 189
Second Reform Bill 84
self-control 42
self-immolation 187
self-sacrifice 6, 156, 157
    heroic 184
self-transcendence 151, 154
sexual deviation 164, 165
sexual instinct 156, 157
sexual inversion 158
sexual morality 177
sexuality 56, 155

Shaftesbury, Earl of 83; *see also*
    Ashley, Lord
Shaw, George Bernard 173
Shimeall, Rev. Richard 78
Shipton, Mother 99, 101, 123
Sight of Hell, The 45
Silence, John, 166
Simpson, Professor James 40, 42
sin 11, 29, 43, 163
sinners, punishment of 15
Skelton, Sir John 65, 91
slavery 41, 75
    and religion 41
'Sleep of Reason, The' 1, 2, 11, 54,
    144; *see also* Goya, Francisco
Smith, Joseph 30
Smith, Sydney 9
Smyth, Professor Charles Piazzi 99–
    100, 101, 102, 109, 115, 134
social breakdown 98
social co-operation 154
social regeneration 154
socialism 12, 15
Society for Psychical Research 24,
    166
Socrates 70, 144, 146, 155
Socratic tradition 69, 98
soldiers of Christ 82
soul 15
    in hell 51
    sacrifice of 5
    sleep of 2
Southey, Robert 27
space 31
Sparta 187
Spencer, Herbert 52, 95
Spirit Lamp 163
spirit rapping 32, 118
Spirit World 33–4, 49
spirits, evil 33
spiritual evolution 66
Spiritual Magazine 38, 50
spiritual science 118
spiritualism 32–4, 36, 44, 49–50, 164,
    180

spirituality 150
sport 174
starvation 11
Stead, W.T. 108
Stedman, Edmund Clarence 62, 110
Stevenson, Robert Louis 128–9, 134, 135, 136, 141, 143, 157
stoicism 42
Stoker, Bram 166
Stone, Elizabeth 23
strikes 15, 84, 106
Strong, Josiah 170
Sturgis, Howard Overing 158
Stutfield, Hugh 172
Subirous, Bernadette 77, 94
suffering 40
superhuman 153, 154, 155
superman 155
supernatural 38, 153, 154, 180
superstition 1, 11, 12, 18, 59, 94
surgery 39–40; see also anaesthesia, pain
survival 195
    of the fittest 53
sword of Gorsedd 172
Symonds, John Addington 85, 134, 143, 146, 158

Taylor, Bayard 62
Temple, Frederick, Bishop of Exeter 86
Tennyson, Alfred 9, 10, 15, 35, 44, 49, 92, 119, 138, 141, 144, 150
terrorism, Irish 138
Theosophical Society 116
theosophy 180
Thompson, Sir Henry 104, 105
Thomson, James 144
Thoreau, Henry David 60, 71, 79, 82
thought 111
Tiberius 56
time 31
Time Machine, The 175
Tinkerbell 18, 153, 188

tithe payments 148
Tom Brown's Schooldays 133
tomb of the unknown soldier 197
Tooth, Rev. Arthur 103
trade depression 106
transcendentalism 30, 60
Treasure Island 128, 131
Trelawny, Sir John 51
Turkey 108
Tutankhamun 199
Twain, Mark 136
Tyndall, Professor John 95, 113, 114, 144
tyranny 11

ultimate reality 2
ultimate sacrifice 156
ultimate truth 61, 149
unbelief 10, 11, 17
Unconscious Cerebration 54
unconscious mind 56
underworld 15
Union Jack 132
union of man and beast 64
universal archetypes 3
universal law 146
universe, nature of 31
Unknowable 179
unreality 141
USA 19, 74
    Catholicism 169
    divine mission of 173
utopian communities 30

valour 185
vampire myths 24–5, 50, 163, 165, 166
Vanity 33
Varney the Vampire 24
Victoria, Queen 11, 35, 38, 40, 85, 95, 101, 110
    assassination attempt 138
    death of 173
Virgil 69
violence 138, 153
    as creative force 145

virtue 34, 57, 184
  redemption from 63

Waite, A.E. 183
Walden 60
Wales, Prince of 80, 85, 89, 105, 106, 117, 141
  as pagan prince 107
walking dead 24
Walsh, Walter 169
war 15, 145, 175
War of the Worlds, The 175
Ward, Rev. F.W.Orde 179, 193
'Waste Land, The' 183, 189, 199; *see also* Eliot, T.S.
Wells, H.G. 130, 175, 177
Wells, Horace 39
werewolves 163, 165
Weston, Jessie 183, 192
whipping 41–2
whipping brothels 50, 63
white supremacy 96
Whitman, Walt 140, 141, 154

wickedness 34
Wilberforce, Samuel 32, 35, 37, 46, 48, 52, 53, 59, 65, 78
Wild Bill Hickok 97
Wild West 97, 136
Wilde, Oscar 136, 154, 159, 160, 162, 163, 168
William IV 9
Williams, Rowland 47
Wilson, Henry Bristow 47
Woolf, Virginia 178, 184
Wordsworth, William 9, 32, 58
working-class revolt 16
World Peace Foundation 189, 190
World's Parliament of Religions 148–9
worship 17

Yeats, W.B. 172
Young, Edward 31

Zeus 43, 66
Zimmern, Helen 118